ON HINDUISM

OXFORD
UNIVERSITY PRESS

ON
HINDUISM

~

Wendy Doniger

OXFORD
UNIVERSITY PRESS

OXFORD
UNIVERSITY PRESS

Oxford University Press is a department of the University of Oxford. It furthers the University's objective of excellence in research, scholarship, and education by publishing worldwide.

Oxford New York
Auckland   Cape Town   Dar es Salaam   Hong Kong   Karachi
Kuala Lumpur   Madrid   Melbourne   Mexico City   Nairobi
New Delhi   Shanghai   Taipei   Toronto

With offices in
Argentina   Austria   Brazil   Chile   Czech Republic   France   Greece
Guatemala   Hungary   Italy   Japan   Poland   Portugal   Singapore
South Korea   Switzerland   Thailand   Turkey   Ukraine   Vietnam

Oxford is a registered trade mark of Oxford University Press in the UK and certain other countries.

Published in the United States of America by
Oxford University Press
198 Madison Avenue, New York, NY 10016

Library of Congress Cataloging-in-Publication Data

Doniger, Wendy.
 [Essays. Selections]
 On Hinduism / Wendy Doniger.
    pages cm
 ISBN 978-0-19-936007-9 (hardback : alk. paper) 1. Hinduism. I. Title.
 BL1210.D66 2014
 294.5--dc23
                          2013038952

9 8 7 6 5 4 3
Printed in the United States of America on acid-free paper

CONTENTS

INTRODUCTION

FOREWORD INTO THE PAST

'How can I tell what I think till I see what I say?'
—*E.M. Forster,* Aspects of the Novel *(1927), chapter 5.*

'If I had to live my life again, I'd make all the same mistakes, only sooner.'
—*Tallulah Bankhead*

HOW I CAME TO STUDY HINDUISM

My heart always sinks when a stranger at a dinner party or a conference asks me, brightly, 'How did you [ever] get interested in the study of India?' as if this were some weird perversion that required an elaborate explanation. But perhaps the moment has finally come to answer this question properly, in the foreword to a book about India, and one of the world's great religions, that spans my entire academic life.

It all began when I was about twelve years old, and my mother gave me a copy of E.M. Forster's *A Passage to India*. It changed my life. At a time when I was consumed by religious questions, Forster persuaded me (wrongly, I now know) that everyone in India was constantly thinking and talking about nothing but religion, and that they had the answers. I found a copy of Robert Hume's translation of the Upanishads, and was stunned by their beauty and wisdom.

My mother also gave me Rumer Godden's *The River* and *Mooltiki*, and Aubrey Menen's wicked satire on the *Ramayana*, and Kipling's *Just So Stories* and *Jungle Book* and, later, *Kim*. She was an amateur Orientalist in her own way, and was crazy about Angkor Wat (which she pronounced, in the Viennese manner, Angkor Vat); she cherished her copy of the great four-volume work on the temples of Angkor published in 1930 by the École Française de l'Extrême Orient. All her life she wanted to visit those temples, and she finally did. When I went to live in India for a year, she came to visit me and went on by herself to see Angkor despite the rumbles of war (it was 1964), and when she was dying, thirty years later, she told me that that had been the high point of her whole life. That old French book remained a kind of icon to me throughout my youth; when my mother died, it came to me, and it still holds for me the mystery and glamour that it had then. I passed it on (together with my mother's politics) to my son, Michael Lester O'Flaherty (born in 1971), who began his graduate study of the history of Southeast Asia at Cornell in 1995. And I finally visited Angkor Wat, too, just this past January of 2012. But I'm getting ahead of my story.

Barely into my teens, I discovered that I loved the glorious excess of things Indian: I preferred Indian painting, with its infinite detail, to Renaissance paintings; I preferred Indian temples, with their rococo carvings, to the great cathedrals of Europe, let alone the sleek Bauhaus that was admired in my day. I rebelled against the moderation and restraint of what was called 'good taste'—clothing of beige, mauve and basic black— and delighted in the reds and purples and oranges and yellows of Rajasthani silks and cottons. I liked Indian music, particularly the sarod, which moaned like a human voice as it slid from note to note, far better than Western music where every note had to fit into a rigid slot. My favourite food was Indian food, which I liked eating with my hand(s); I had always hated knives and forks. I watched Satyajit Ray's *Pather Panchali* (1955) more times than I can now remember; it was the most beautiful film I had ever seen.

But most of all, I loved Hindu mythology, the stories of the gods; I particularly loved the way that the stories were told and retold, over and over, each time differently. I had been, from very early childhood, enchanted by stories about other worlds, fairies and gods, a fact that is corroborated by a large portrait of me that my uncle, Harvey Haines, painted (badly) when I was just five years old: I'm holding a fairy tale castle, Disney-turreted and covered with swirls of oil paint patterned like Florentine endpapers, and I'm reading a book that begins, 'Once upon a time . . .' In high school I continued to flee from what I had come to regard as the excessive reality of the real world by studying Latin and, in unofficial sessions with my devoted Latin teacher, Anita Lilenfeld (now Seligson), ancient Greek. She casually mentioned to me that Sanskrit, closely related to Greek and Latin, was the language of ancient India, which meant to me the language of *A Passage to India* (and, by extension, Angkor Wat). By then I was thoroughly hooked, and I chose to go to Radcliffe, rather than Swarthmore, largely because I could learn Sanskrit at Harvard.

And so I began the study of Sanskrit as a seventeen-year-old freshman in 1958. Surely the long shadow of Angkor fell over me as I sat in the dusty little room at the top of Widener library, studying Sanskrit with Daniel H.H. Ingalls. He taught me not only Sanskrit but Indian literature, Indian history, Indian religion, and something else, harder to define, something about the pleasure of scholarship, the elegance of the written word, the luxury of the world of the mind.

So I was trained as a Sanskritist. But I was not a real Sanskritist; real Sanskritists (Ingalls was not at all typical) are cold-blooded pedants interested only in verbs and nouns, and I was a hot-blooded ex-ballet dancer still interested in stories. *Real* Sanskritists, on two continents, have been known to turn and leave a room when I entered it. I looked elsewhere for my intellectual nourishment. I roomed with an anthropologist, Alice Kasakoff, whom the Radcliffe authorities had assigned to me on the very first day; in those times of unspoken quotas, Jewish girls somehow just seemed to end up with Jewish roommates. Alice introduced me to her colleagues (Vogt, Kluckholn, the Whitings, Beidelman, Mayberry-Lewis) and instilled in me an enduring admiration for anthropologists. I also, in the manner of old-fashioned Sanskritists and 'Orientalists', studied Greek with Zeph Stewart, Sterling Dow, John Finley and Adam Parry; English literature with Reuben Brower, William Alfred and Harry Levin; and folklore with Albert Lord.

And when I moved to England, in 1965, it was again the anthropologists who supplied much of my intellectual nourishment—Evans-Pritchard and Rodney Needham in Oxford, Edmund Leach, Mary Douglas and Claude Levi-Strauss in Cambridge, London and Paris. But I was also sustained by the old Raj crowd (Penelope Chetwode Betjeman, Bill and Tim Archer, Stuart Piggott), even while I worked on a second dissertation with Robin Zaehner (who did know Sanskrit, but not as well as he knew Persian). In 1968, when Christoph von Fürer-Haimendorf (an anthropologist) wanted to hire me to teach in the School of Oriental and African Studies, where he was acting as Director, he found it impossible to sell me to the Sanskritists, and instead winkled me into the History Department, where Bernard Lewis welcomed me and protected me until I left England in 1975, for Berkeley.

In Berkeley (my lean years), again an anthropologist, Alan Dundes, was my best, almost my only, friend. Only when I reached my final home, the University of Chicago, in 1978, did I find Indologists broadminded enough to welcome me in—Hans van Buitenen, Milton Singer, A.K. Ramanujan, the Rudolphs, Ed Dimock—though even there, the historians of religions Mircea Eliade and Frank Reynolds, and the classicist David Grene were in many ways my closest colleagues. The nourishment I drew from friends in such a wide range of academic disciplines is reflected in the rather eclectic nature of what I wrote.

Which brings me to the present volume.

WHAT THIS BOOK IS NOT

This is not a collection of all the essays I've written on Hinduism since I finished my Harvard dissertation in 1968, or even a selection of such essays. It started out to be that. Of the 324 essays I've published (as of autumn 2012), 140 are on Hinduism. From those 140, as I reread them, I selected 63 that I thought have something substantial or interesting to say about Hinduism for both the general reader and the scholar. (Of these 63 essays, seven were written under the name of Wendy Doniger O'Flaherty, from 1968 to 1988, and 56 as Wendy Doniger, from 1989 to 2012.) The basic criterion of selection was to include only essays that never, in their entirety, became parts of books (though passing references to related books are sprinkled throughout, as the topic of an essay often spun off from a larger, broader discussion in a book). I also excluded essays that were either deadly boring or dead wrong. (None were both, but in some cases I did cut out the boring or wrong parts of an otherwise salvageable essay.)

Some essays that I included were unknown in the sense that they had been published in obscure places where I think only three or four people ever saw them. But I also added material never published before: a few limericks (I could not resist) and five new essays—a couple written for Festschrifts, paved with good intentions, that will probably never appear; others that had fallen into other sorts of unpublished limbos. I then condensed those 63 essays into the 43 chapters of this volume. This is a traditionally Indian way of producing a text: boiling down a large text into its essence in a smaller text, and then boiling down that smaller text into a still smaller essence, and so forth.[i]

I had planned to arrange the final selection chronologically, write a brief

---

i See 'The Mythology of the *Kamasutra*'. The *Mahabharata* also claims that it was condensed in this way.

introduction, and send it off. But it didn't turn out that way. As a publisher's daughter, I was born with a red pencil in my hand, which compels me, obsessively, to edit everything I read, no matter what: my students' papers, of course, but also (mentally) the *New York Times*, subtitles on Hindi films, recipes on cracker boxes, programme notes, everything. (For years I would shout at the opening credits of my favourite television programme, *Star Trek*, 'Boldly to go! Boldly to go!') So, naturally, I could not resist editing every other sentence as I worked through these essays. At first, the corrections were trivial, as I updated the essays and tidied them up in the obvious, superficial ways: made the footnotes and endnotes consistent in style, revised the sexist language, removed the italics from dharma and karma (now regarded as English words). I reworded the translations[ii] in a few places, such as (in Manu) changing 'priest' back to 'Brahmin' where I should have left it in the first place. I simplified the Sanskrit transliteration and made it consistent, changed Ceylon to Sri Lanka, AD to CE, Untouchable to Dalit, Sepoy Mutiny to Great Rebellion. I cut out the references to 'today' and 'nowadays' and 'recently' in articles written a quarter century ago. All quite straightforward.

But then I began to do a bit more. I had written all my other books for an American audience, primarily for my students. That was one reason why I was totally blindsided by the passionate Hindu response to my book *The Hindus: An Alternative History*: it hadn't occurred to me that Hindus would read it. I had figured, the Hindus already knew all about their own religion, or at least knew as much as they wanted to know, or in any case didn't want to learn anything more from an American woman (I was right about that last point, but in ways I had not foreseen). I was therefore pleasantly surprised, at first, that Hindus read *The Hindus*, but then appalled that some of them read it so confrontationally, or did not read it at all but just parroted what others were saying about it.

But now, for the first time, I designed a book specifically for an Indian audience. And so I took out allusions to things that might distract or puzzle an Indian reader, references to American trivia, TV programmes, Hollywood films, New York jokes. At first, I was sorry to see them go, particularly the jokes; but then I had to admit that the arguments really did read better without them.

---

ii All the translations from Sanskrit are my own except where otherwise noted; generally, though not always, they are taken from my published translations of the *Rig Veda*, the *Kamasutra*, the Puranas, the *Mahabharata*, *The Laws of Manu* and other texts. Some long texts are summarized, rather than translated in full.

HOW THIS BOOK DIFFERS FROM THE ESSAYS FROM WHICH IT WAS CONSTRUCTED

At the same time, that invisible red pencil in my hand kept making me clarify the language in more significant ways, cutting some of the asides that now seemed irrelevant, revising myself the way I would revise my own students, changing passive constructions to active, clarifying referents, cutting adjectives, finding ways to say things better, trying to avoid long sentences with strings of clauses like this one. Gradually I started updating not only the language but the content. I started adding new things I had learned on each topic since first writing about it, new ideas, new facts, new sources I had discovered. I cut out statements that I no longer believe to be true. I revised some of the basic assumptions that had changed in my thinking over the years. I changed a lot. But I generally did *not* update the essays with references to new articles by other people on the subject; that really would have meant writing another, entirely different book. I contented myself with an attempt to clarify my own thinking in this book.

As I rewrote and rearranged the essays, I found myself generating cross-references[iii] and moving pieces from one file to another, beginning with the first occurrence of essential definitions but then going on to texts, insights, generalizations, changing every single essay with reference to other essays. I cut out of many essays things that were explained better in other essays and citations of texts that were more fully translated in other essays. And gradually it dawned on me that they were no longer essays but chapters, that I was developing an integrated argument in which the reader needed to have read certain chapters in order to understand other chapters. The separate essays had come together like the broken pot in those films that they run backwards, so that all the broken pieces jump up and form an unbroken pot. I had accidentally written a new book, about what I think about Hinduism now, not what I thought about Hinduism when I wrote the original essays. It had 'just growed', like Topsy.[iv]

And so I arranged the essays not chronologically but logically, like chapters; the chapters within each of the seven units are connected not nose to tail like elephants in a line but like rays of light shining from different angles upon a single object. Since the book 'just growed' like a banyan tree, the 'original' roots of many pivotal chapters lie in other

---

[iii] I put the cross-references in footnotes.

[iv] Actually, the 'just' is a common mistake made in this oft-quoted metaphor for spontaneous generation. Topsy was the slave girl in *Uncle Tom's Cabin* (an anti-slavery novel by Harriet Beecher Stowe, written in 1862). When asked if she knows who made her, she says, 'Nobody, as I knows on. I s'pect I growed. Don't think nobody never made me.'

chapters, one chapter sprouting from roots in another. Some chapters are palimpsests; the chapter on intolerance, for instance, underwent major changes every few years. For readers interested in chronology, I have provided, in Appendix II, a list of the original 140 essays on Hinduism, showing when each began, though not when it was finished.

There are discernible differences between the early and later essays. There were, to begin with, superficial differences of style and format. The old essays used the more technical transliteration (Śiva, Kālī), which I shed in the new ones (Shiva, Kali) and in this book. Some, mostly the older articles, are bristling with endnotes;[v] some, mostly the later ones, are based on newspaper or journal articles or public lectures that were written for a general audience, and these do not have as much documentation as an academic essay would have. But there were also more significant changes.

As I read through the older essays, the dial on my ego ricocheted wildly back and forth between 'How much I knew then that I've forgotten now' and 'How badly I wrote'. Looking back at the early essays, I am amazed at the density of the data, text after text after text, but generally I find them rather tedious, a bit light on analysis or ideas about the texts; still, some of them are impressive in a mindless, brutal sort of way, flashy with scholastic pyrotechnics. Were I to write some of the older articles from scratch today, I probably would not have the patience to pore over quite so many arcane Vedic and Puranic texts, nor would I quote quite so many late nineteenth-century British and German Indologists. In revising, I changed the data-rich articles less than the others, as the data remained pretty much the same for most articles, but even there the framing opinions changed; some softened, others hardened.

Nowadays I would also pay far more attention to the historical context of each version of each myth, and to the social significance of the ideas embedded in them. The early essays are more interested in texts, the later ones in people. The older essays are content to delve into the past; the newer ones are on topics more explicitly relevant to contemporary issues such as gender and race. The early essays on Manu focus on what he said about women, not about caste; only later did I find the question of caste central to my work. So, too, I used the *purusha sukta* at first just as a myth of cosmic creation; only later did I value it as a myth of the origin of the class system.

---

[v] In essays about a single source, I left the bibliographic citations of verse and number of that source in the text; if there were several basic sources, I used standard abbreviations (given in the bibliography) in the text. I cited other sources in endnotes.

WHAT THIS BOOK IS ABOUT

Despite these differences among essays written at different times, there are strong continuities throughout the book, as I kept coming back to certain themes and texts that remained central to my thinking. Not surprisingly, there is a lot about women and about animals; more surprisingly, there is also a lot about heresy and dharma and karma. In general, I chose to write about what other scholars were not writing about and to write about texts that were not saying what other texts of their time were saying, about authors who were out of step with their times as I am often out of step with mine, who shared my desire to go against the grain (*pratiloma*, 'against the hair', as the Sanskrit term so nicely puts it) of current opinion. I kept trying to point out things that contradict what most people believe about Hinduism. This concern for people who bucked the system, who swam upstream against the current, is there from the start, in the 1971 essay on heresy. Antinomianism calls the shots—theologically, in the early essays, and politically and socially, in the later ones.

Even my choice of texts to work on was, in its time, Bolshy. As an undergraduate at Radcliffe, 1958-62, I discovered the Puranas, anonymous texts on traditional themes more narrative than philosophical, written in a simple, often pretty bad Sanskrit. Now, at that time, serious Sanskritists disdained the Puranas as the pulp fiction of ancient India. The only people who paid any attention to the Puranas were the few wrongheaded historians who tried (in vain) to use them to construct ancient Indian political history. For my undergraduate dissertation, I compared the story of the conflict between Shiva and Kama as it appeared in the poet Kalidasa's *Kumarasambhava* and in the *Shiva Purana*. My preference for the Puranic versions of the myth of Shiva and Kama over the 'courtly' literary version horrified my Sanskrit professor, Ingalls, an old-style Virginia gentleman who had exquisitely refined tastes; it was as if I had expressed a preference for Elvis Presley over Mozart. But I knew I had found my métier, a literary goldmine, a world of rich and neglected texts that would continue to be my primary sources, increasingly supplemented, as time went by, by the *Mahabharata* and the *Ramayana*.[vi]

Each of the seven sections in this book treats of a single theme. The first is about the nature of Hinduism. It begins by defining what Hinduism is

---

[vi] On the other hand, I was surprised to see, as I read through my early essays, how much material from the Vedas and Brahmanas and Upanishads I had used from the very start; it wasn't all Puranas.

('Hinduism by Any Other Name'), particularly its pluralism ('Are Hindus Monotheists or Polytheists?', 'Three (or More) Forms of the Three (or More)-Fold Path in Hinduism', 'The Concept of Heresy in Hinduism'). Then it explores several of the enduring central themes of Hinduism, all of which involve karma ('Eating Karma'), birth ('Medical and Mythical Constructions of the Body in Sanskrit Texts'), death ('Death and Rebirth in Hinduism') and rebirth ('Forgetting and Re-awakening to Incarnation'). It ends with threats to Hindu pluralism ('Assume the Position: The Fight over the Body of Yoga', 'The Toleration of Intolerance in Hinduism', 'The Politics of Hinduism Tomorrow').

The second section explores concepts of divinity: the material and immaterial aspects of god ('*Saguna* and *Nirguna* Images of the Deity'); the changing role of the gods in creation ('You Can't Get Here From There: The Logical Paradox of Hindu Creation Myths', 'Together Apart: Changing Ethical Implications of Hindu Cosmologies') and in sacrifice ('Sacrifice and Substitution: Ritual Mystification and Mythical Demystification in Hinduism'); disputes over the sexual nature of god ('God's Body, or, the *Lingam* Made Flesh: Conflicts over the Representation of Shiva') and the grace of god ('The Scrapbook of Undeserved Salvation: The *Kedara Khanda* of the *Skanda Purana*').

Section three considers Hindu attitudes to gender, beginning with Manu's attitude to women in general ('Why Should a Brahmin Tell You Whom to Marry?: A Deconstruction of *The Laws of Manu*') and then looking at stories about several individual females: a goddess who flees from her husband ('Saranyu-Samjna: The Sun and the Shadow'), a Brahmin woman rejected by her husband ('The Clever Wife in Indian Mythology') and a forest-girl seduced and abandoned by a king ('Rings of Rejection and Recognition in Ancient India'). The question of gender is then addressed by essays on several transgressive forms of sexuality: homosexuality and gender-bending ('The Third Nature: Gender Inversions in the *Kamasutra*'), bisexuality and transsexuality ('Bisexuality and Transsexuality Among the Hindu Gods', 'Transsexual Transformations of Memory and Subjectivity in Hinduism').

The fourth section deals with desire and the control of desire in Hinduism, beginning with the problem ('The Control of Addiction in Ancient India') and going on to consider the social context of desire ('Reading the *Kamasutra*: It Isn't All About Sex'), its mythologization ('The Mythology of the *Kamasutra*') and finally its transformation in history ('From Kama to Karma: The Resurgence of Puritanism in Contemporary India').

Animals, in section five, are taken not as subjects in their own right but as metaphors and keys to the understanding of philosophical and sociological concepts central to Hinduism: the attempt to come to terms with violence ('The Ambivalence of Ahimsa'), the bestial aspects of human nature ('Zoomorphism in Ancient India: Humans More Bestial than the Beasts'), the transformation of political and economic subjugation into theological power ('The Mythology of Horses in India'), the fear of women overlapping with the fear of cosmic destruction ('The Submarine Mare in the Mythology of Shiva'), the tension between miscegenation and incest ('Indra as the Stallion's Wife'), the persecution of Dalits ('Dogs as Dalits in Indian Literature'), and the rise of Hindu supremacy in India ('Sacred Cows and Beefeaters').

Section six considers the question of reality and illusion, the impermanent and the eternal, in the two great Sanskrit Epics. The general consideration of these themes in the *Mahabharata* and in the visual arts and performance ('Impermanence and Eternity in Hindu Epic, Art and Performance') leads to a more specific analysis of doubles and shadows ('Shadows of the *Ramayana*'), of women who challenge Hindu patriarchy ('Women in the *Mahabharata*') and the gradual emergence of a submerged expression of conscience about the treatment of the lower castes ('The History of Ekalavya').

Finally, four short pieces of autobiography discuss the author's debt to Orientalism ('"I Have Scinde": Orientalism and Guilt'), her agreement with her imagined academic critics ('Doniger O'Flaherty on Doniger'), her clash with her Hindu critics ('You Can't Make an Omelette') and her coming to terms with her life and work ('The Forest-dweller').

ACKNOWLEDGEMENT TO FRIENDS LIVING AND DEAD

Looking back over what I wrote over forty-four years was like drowning and watching my life pass before my eyes. The ghosts rose up before me, the colleagues I learned so much from, friends whose ideas became a part of my life. Even the bibliographic citations stirred up, like Proust's *madeleines* of Combray, the ghosts of the books I had read in the old, old days; their titles transported me back to the Bodleian Library, the old India Office, the Indian Institute in Oxford, the stacks of Widener, the godown of Firma K.L. Mukhopadhyay in Calcutta. I could smell the sweet, dusty odour of the old books, with the brown pages that threatened to crumble into powder, each page breaking off the minute I turned it, or the wide, unbound sheets of the Sanskrit texts.

I've always written easily and joyously, because I've always assumed that the people who read what I wrote would be on my side, would go the extra mile to meet me when my writing was inadequate, would get the jokes, groan at the puns, be struck with wonder at the amazing stories I had found. The reader I have always carried around in my head, even now long after his death in 1971, is my father, who was, as I have said, a publisher. He read every word I wrote, carefully and wisely and generously, and gave me detailed, constructive feedback. He was my ideal reader: someone highly intelligent and erudite but without special knowledge about India, and who wanted to understand and to like what I wrote. After him came other publishers and editors who became friends and mentors, first the great Betty Radice at Penguin Classics, then Phil Lilienthal in California and Morris Philipson in Chicago. I've never understood the feelings of so many of my writer friends who regard authors and publishers as natural enemies, like snakes and mongooses. All my life I've depended on the kindness of publishers.

After the attacks on me on the Internet, particularly after the publication of *The Hindus*,[vii] I almost lost my old sense of trust in my readers, and for a while I actually thought I would stop writing about India altogether; I had other books planned, on other subjects—a novel, a memoir of my mother, and so forth. But I began to waver when I read emails of appreciation from a number of Indian readers and when I saw the sales of *The Hindus* continue so vigorously in India. And then along came Ravi Singh, whom I had gotten to know and to admire when he had edited *The Hindus* for the edition of Penguin India.

Ravi came up with the idea for this book, talked me into doing it, and worked closely with me on it from the very start. He was always on my side; he read my work carefully and appreciatively, got the jokes, encouraged me. But he also had a sharp eye for what might be offensive, called me to attention when I got careless, asked for examples and expansions when I was vague, caught repetitions and overlaps that I had not noticed, saw opportunities for connections that I had not seen. I could never have written *On Hinduism* without him. I dedicate this book, which is in a way the book of my books, to him, and to all my other publishers, beginning with my dad.

[vii] See 'You Can't Make an Omelette'.

A CHRONOLOGY OF HINDUISM

ca. 1500–1000 BCE	*Rig Veda*
ca. 1200–900 BCE	*Yajur Veda, Sama Veda* and *Atharva Veda*
ca. 800–600 BCE	Brahmanas
ca. 600–500 BCE	Aranyakas
ca. 500 BCE	Shrauta Sutras
ca. 500 BCE	Yaska's *Nirukta*
ca. 500–400 BCE	Early Upanishads
ca. 483/486 BCE	Siddhartha Gautama, the Buddha, dies
ca. 468 BCE	Vardhamana Mahavira, the Jina, founder of Jainism, dies
ca. 450 BCE	Shaunaka's *Brihaddevata*
ca. 400–100 BCE	Later Upanishads
ca. 400 BCE	Jaimini's *Purva Mimamsa Sutras*
ca. 400 BCE	Badarayana's *Vedanta Sutras* (*Brahma Sutras*)
ca. 300 BCE	Grihya Sutras
ca. 300 BCE	Panini's *Ashtadhyayi*
ca. 300–100 BCE	Dharma Sutras
ca. 300–200 BCE	Kanada founds the Vaisheshika school
ca. 300–200 BCE	Bharata's *Natyashastra*
ca. 300 BCE–300 CE	*Mahabharata*
ca. 200 BCE–100 CE	*Tolkappiyam*
ca. 200–100 BCE	Gautama founds the Nyaya school
ca. 200 BCE–200 CE	Valmiki's *Ramayana*
ca. 150 BCE	Patanjali's Yoga Sutras
ca. 100–300 CE	Cankam poetry composed in Tamil Nadu
ca. 100 CE	*Bhagavad Gita*
ca. 100 CE	Manu's *Manava Dharmashastra*
ca. 150 CE	Monuments of Bharhut and Sanchi built
ca. 200 CE	Kautilya's *Arthashastra*
ca. 250–550 CE	*Markandeya Purana* (the *Devimahatmya* portion is added later)
ca. 250–500 CE	*Matsya Purana*
ca. 300 CE	Vatsyayana Mallanaga's *Kamasutra*
ca. 300 CE	*Panchatantra*
ca. 350–950 CE	*Brahmanda Purana*
ca. 400–477 CE	Kalidasa
ca. 400 CE	Hinduism spreads to Southeast Asia
ca. 400–500 CE	Ilanko Atikal's Tamil epic *Cilappatikaram*

ca. 450 CE	*Harivamsha*
ca. 450 CE	*Vishnu Purana*
ca. 450–900 CE	*Vamana Purana*
ca. 500–800 CE	Nayanmar Shaiva Tamil poets, authors of the *Tevaram*
ca. 550–850 CE	*Kurma Purana*
ca. 600–750 CE	*Padma Purana*
ca. 600–1000 CE	*Linga Purana*
ca. 600–930 CE	Alvar Vaishnava Tamil poets
ca. 650–800 CE	Early Tantras
ca. 700–1100 CE	*Skanda Purana*
ca. 750–1350 CE	*Shiva Purana*
ca. 788–820 CE	Shankara
ca. 800 CE	Manikkavacar's *Tiruvacakam*
880–930 CE	Nammalvar, author of *Tiruvaymoli*
ca. 900–1000 CE	*Brahmayamala Tantra*
ca. 900–1300 CE	*Yogavasishtha*
ca. 950 CE	*Bhagavata Purana*
ca. 1056–1137 CE	Ramanuja
1106–1167/8 CE	Basava, founder of Lingayatas/Virashaivas
1148 CE	Kalhana's *Rajatarangani* in Kashmir
ca. 1100–1200 CE	Mahadeviyakka
ca. 1178 CE	Kamban's *Iramavataram* (Tamil version of *Ramayana*)
ca. 1200 CE	Jayadeva's *Gitagovinda*
ca. 1200 CE	*Ramacharitam* (Malayalam version of *Ramayana*)
ca. 1200 CE	Early Sufis in North India
ca. 1250 CE	Palkuriki Somanatha's *Basava Purana*
ca. 1238–1317 CE	Madhava, dualist philosopher, in Karnataka
ca. 1300 CE	Shri Vaishnavas split into Cats and Monkeys
ca. 1350 CE	Sayana's commentary on the *Rig Veda*
ca. 1352–1448 CE	Vidyapati of Mithila
ca. 1375–1450 CE	Chandidas
ca. 1398–1518 CE	Kabir
ca. 1400 CE	Villiputtur Alvar's Tamil version of the *Mahabharata*
ca. 1400 CE	Krittibas Ojha's Bangla *Ramayana*
1408–1503 CE	Annamayya (Telegu poet)
1469–1539 CE	Guru Nanak, founder of Sikhism
1479–1531 CE	Vallabha (founder of sect devoted to Krishna)
1483–1563 CE	Surdas
1486–1533 CE	Chaitanya
ca. 1489–1565 CE	Rupa Goswami
ca. 1498–1547 CE	Mirabai
1532/43–1623 CE	Tulsidas
ca. 1574–1577 CE	Tulsidas's *Ramcharitmanas*
ca. 1600 CE	Kashirama Das's *Mahabharata*
1608–1649 CE	Tukaram
1622–1673 CE	Kshetrayya
ca. 1700 CE	*Mahanirvana Tantra*

ca. 1700 CE	*Kalki Purana*, last of the major Puranas
ca. 1700–1800 CE	*Parthayana*, Balinese Kakavin text
ca. 1720–1781 CE	Ramprasad Sen
1772/4–1833 CE	Rammohun Roy
1824–1883 CE	Dayananda Sarasvati
1828 CE	Rammohun Roy founds the Brahmo Samaj
1829 CE	Burning of widows banned
1834/6–1886 CE	Ramakrishna Paramahamsa
1843 CE	Debendranath Tagore revives Brahmo Samaj
1861 CE	Michael Madhusudan Datta's *Epic of Meghananda*
1863–1902 CE	Vivekananda (founder of the Ramakrishna movement)
1869–1948 CE	Mohandas Karamchand Gandhi
1872–1948 CE	Aurobindo Ghose
1873–1924 CE	Mahakavi Kumaran Asan
1875 CE	Dayananda Sarasvati founds the Arya Samaj
1875 CE	Helena Blavatsky founds the Theosophical Society
1891–1956 CE	B.R. Ambedkar
1893 CE	Vivekananda attends World's Parliament of Religions in Chicago
1893 CE	Cow Protection issue ignites Hindu-Muslim hostility
1896–1977 CE	A.C. Bhaktivedanta, Swami Prabhupada (founder of ISKCON)
1897 CE	Vivekananda founds Ramakrishna Mission
1918–2008 CE	Maharishi Mahesh Yogi
1919 CE	Gandhi's Rowlatt *satyagraha*
1920–22 CE	Gandhi's non-cooperation campaign
1923 CE	Vinayak Damodar Savarkar's *Hindutva: Who is a Hindu?*
1927 CE	Ambedkar leads Dalit protest at Chavadar Lake
1931–1990 CE	Bhagwan Shree Rajneesh (Osho)
1930 CE	Gandhi leads Salt *satyagraha*
1932 CE	Gandhi-Ambedkar pact reserves seats for Untouchables
1948 CE	(January 30) Gandhi assassinated
1956 CE	Ambedkar and many Dalit followers convert to Buddhism
1960's CE	Hinduism and Yoga popularized in the West
1961 CE	Dowry Prohibition Act
1970 CE –	Diaspora Hindus come to the US and Europe
1971 CE	Tamil Nadu government decrees Sanskrit not sole language of liturgy
1992 CE (Dec. 6)	Destruction of the Babri Masjid in Ayodhya
1996 CE	Kancha Ilaiah's *Why I am Not a Hindu*
2002 CE	Hindu-Muslim riots in Gujarat
2007 CE	Hindutva groups challenge construction of Sethusamudram shipping canal
2010 CE	Allahabad Court rules that the Ayodhya site should be divided in three
2011 CE	Indian Supreme court stays the Allahabad Court's ruling on Ayodhya

ON BEING HINDU

HINDUISM BY ANY OTHER NAME[1]

'But it isn't a Hedgehog, and it isn't a Tortoise' [said the young Painted Jaguar].
'It's a little bit of both, and I don't know its proper name.'
'Nonsense!' said Mother Jaguar. 'Everything has its proper name. I should call it
"Armadillo" till I found out the real one. And I should leave it alone.'
—*Rudyard Kipling, 'The Beginning of the Armadillos',*
in *Just So Stories (1902)*

For the past few decades, scholars have raised several and strong objections to the use of any single term to denote one of the world's major and most ancient faiths. The name 'Hinduism' that we now use is of recent and European construction. But it is Eurocentric to assume that when Europeans made the name they made the game. 'Hinduism' (dare I use the 'H' word, and may I stop holding up my hands for mercy with quotation marks?) is, like the armadillo, part hedgehog, part tortoise. Yet there *are* armadillos, and they were there before they had names. I would like to suggest some ways in which the disparate parts of what we call Hinduism have in fact existed for centuries, cheek by jowl, in a kind of fluid suspension.

It is true that before the British began to categorize communities strictly by religion, few people in India defined themselves exclusively through their religious beliefs; their identities were segmented on the basis of locality, language, caste, occupation and sect. Even today, despite attempts by extreme right-wing groups like the Rashtriya Swayamsewak Sangh (RSS) and Vishwa Hindu Parishad (VHP) and the more mainstream Bharatiya Janata Party (BJP) to 'Hinduize' India, most people in the country would define themselves by allegiances other than their religion. There is, after all, no Hindu canon; ideas about all the major issues of faith and lifestyle—vegetarianism, nonviolence, belief in rebirth, even caste— are subjects of debate, not dogma. And yet, if we look carefully, there are shared ideas, practices and rituals that not only connect the diverse people

3

generally called 'Hindus' today, but also link the people who composed and lived by the Vedas in northwest India around 1500 BCE with the Hare Krishna converts dancing in the streets of twenty-first-century New York.

It is not, however, a simple matter of listing things that 'all Hindus' believe or, even, that 'all Hindus' do: there are no such things. Although there are a number of things that have been characteristic of many Hindus over the ages (the worship of many gods, belief in karma and rebirth and in the caste system), none have been true of *all* Hindus. What we need instead of a definite list of shared factors, therefore, is something rather more like a Venn diagram,[2] a set of intersecting circles of concepts and beliefs and practices, some of which are held and done by some Hindus, others by other Hindus, and still others shared not only by Hindus but also by members of other South Asian religions, such as Buddhism or Jainism.[i] Scholars differ as to the number and nature of the elements of this cluster, but they should combine aspects of both the literary tradition and popular Hinduism: belief in the Vedas (which excludes Buddhism and Jainism); karma, the doctrine of actions that determine one's reincarnation (which does not exclude Buddhism and Jainism); dharma, the Hindu concept that combines religion, law and justice (different from Buddhist *dhamma*); a cosmology centred around Mount Meru; devotion (bhakti) to one or more members of an extensive pantheon; the ritual offering (puja) of fruit and flowers to a deity; sacrificial offerings of butter into a fire; vegetarianism as an ideal, if not necessarily a practice; nonviolence and blood sacrifice (which may or may not be mutually exclusive); pilgrimage; offerings to snakes; worship of local gods and goddesses; worship at shrines of Muslim saints; and so forth.

This polythetic Venn diagram might be further grouped into sectors of different colours—one for beliefs or practices that some Hindus share with Buddhists and Jains, another largely confined to Hindu texts in Sanskrit (the ancient literary language of India), a third more characteristic of popular worship and practice, and so forth. But since there is no single central quality that all Hindus must have, the emptiness in the centre suggests that the figure might better be named a Zen diagram, a Venn diagram that has no central ring. Among the many advantages of the cluster approach is the fact that it does not endorse any single authoritative view of what Hinduism is; it allows them all.

---

[i] We would need a similar Venn diagram to do justice to Christianity or Judaism; religions are messy.

In addition to this cluster of beliefs and concepts that may help us define Hinduism, however loosely, there are other markers of Hindu identity that can be useful, such as sacred and classical texts shared among different linguistic groups, class and caste, and geography. Let us begin with language.

The majority of people in India (approximately seventy-six per cent) speak an Indo-European language derived from the language believed to have been brought into the subcontinent by the Indo-European people.[ii] Dravidian-language speakers account for twenty-two per cent, and the remaining two per cent are taken up by Austro-Asiatic, Tibeto-Burman and tribal languages. However, while these linguistic groups have different origins, all of the linguistic traditions in India—Sanskrit[iii] and vernacular, liturgical and secular, as well as the Sanskrit-based languages of north India and the Tamil-based languages of the south—have culturally influenced one another. We use the concept of 'intertextuality' to describe the ways in which these different groups refer to, or implicitly assume knowledge of, a corpus of shared oral and written texts. The *Ramayana*, for instance, and the *Mahabharata* were first recorded in Sanskrit but have been retold— both written down and orally performed—in Tamil, Bangla and most of the other languages of India.

And the people who share these texts did have ways of referring to themselves long before they called themselves 'Hindu'. The term 'Hindu' was coined in opposition to other religions, but this self-definition through otherness began centuries before there was contact with Europeans (or, indeed, with Muslims). All of us identify who we are in contrast with who we are not, and the 'who we are not' changes all the time.

[ii] Technically, there are no Indo-Europeans, merely Indo-European-speakers; there is no Indo-European race. But since, wherever the languages went, there had to be people to carry them, Indo-European-speakers are often called Indo-Europeans. (They used to be called Indo-Aryans or Aryans, but since the Nazis usurped the latter term it is seldom used in scholarly writings.) We are able to construct some of Indo-European culture, not merely from isolated words and parallel grammar structures but from more substantial historical and archaeological evidence. But the debate about the place where Indo-European civilization began is still lively; some say the Caucasus (hence the term 'Caucasian' is wrongly applied to a non-existent race of people who speak Indo-European languages), others the Arctic, others India, but there is no conclusive evidence one way or another.

[iii] Nineteenth-century German and British linguists demonstrated that Vedic Sanskrit was one of the oldest recorded forms of a language family that included ancient Greek and Latin, Hittite (in ancient Anatolia), the Celtic and Norse-Germanic languages and, ultimately, French, German, Italian, Spanish, English, and all their friends and relations. All these languages are alleged to have run away from the home of a single parent language sometime in the fourth millennium BCE, a language that linguists call Indo-European.

In the earliest preserved text of Hinduism, the *Rig Veda*, the people who referred to themselves as 'we' defined themselves in contrast with the 'aliens' or 'slaves', who spoke non-Indo-European languages, had dark skin and blunt features, and had been in possession of the Indian subcontinent before the Indo-Europeans (the 'Aryans') entered it from, most probably, Central Asia.

But Hindu identity is complicated by the intricate, fluid interplay of caste and class by which Hindu society came to define and hierarchize itself. Caste (*jati*), of which there are many thousands, is the actual social group into which one is born and with whose other members one eats, works and marries.[iv] Class (*varna*) is more a theoretical construct within which each caste situates itself.[v] A whole caste may occasionally change its class, though traditionally an individual cannot. If the caste prospered, it could adopt the ritual and diet of the Brahmin—the highest—class, change its trade, begin to associate with Brahmins, and perhaps even become a Brahmin caste.[3]

Society was already divided into four classes in the *Rig Veda*: the priests (Brahmins) who ruled the roost of the first class, the warrior-kings of the second class, the merchants and landowners who made up the third class, and a fourth class of servants, the defining 'others' who were disenfranchised, not Aryan, but still marginally Hindu.[vi] Later, other groups below even the servants formed the ranks of the 'not-us' who were only questionably Hindu or not Hindu at all. The largest 'not-us' group comprised the castes of people once called Untouchables, now called Dalits, whose deep-rooted pariah status was reinforced by their performing jobs, such as scavenging and sweeping cremation grounds, that higher-caste Hindus, 'the twice-born', did not do. Others in the 'not-us' category included Buddhists, Jains, various sorts of heretics[vii] and most foreigners (*mlechas*).

But there were also ways in which the 'us' group attempted to define who they *were* (as against who they were not). Our word 'Hindu' originates in the geographical feature of the Indus River. It comes from a word for 'river' (Sindhu) that Herodotus (in the fifth century BCE[4]), the

---

[iv] While some of this is changing, and interactions among castes are much more frequent, caste remains a defining aspect of Hinduism and appears in matrimonial advertisements, in news reports when young couples are killed by their families for marrying into the same or the wrong *gotra*, or lineage, (in states like Haryana), and in many aspects of politics, for instance, when political parties cultivate caste vote banks.

[v] A complication: English-speakers often translate *varna* as 'caste'.

[vi] See 'You Can't Get Here'.

[vii] See 'The Concept of Heresy'.

Persians (in the fourth century BCE), and the Arabs (after the eighth century CE[5]) used to refer to everyone who lived beyond the great river of the northwest of the subcontinent, still known locally as the Sindhu and in Europe as the Indus.[viii] It was an outsider's name for the people who inhabited the territory around the Indus River. The Persians called the region 'Hindustan',[6] as did the Mughal emperor Babur in his memoirs in the sixteenth century CE: 'Most of the people in Hindustan are infidels whom the people of India call Hindu. Most Hindus believe in reincarnation.'[7] (It is noteworthy that Babur does not ascribe the belief in reincarnation to all Hindus, implicitly acknowledging their diversity.) 'Hindu' has, however, been an insider's word too for centuries, and it is the word that most Hindus do use now to refer to themselves. It is not uncommon for one culture to take from another a word to designate a concept for which the original culture had a concept but not a word.

Most Hindus still define themselves by geography. But it is not just the word but the very concept of Hindus and Hinduism that is geographically rooted in history. The textbook of legal code (dharma) attributed to Manu[ix] (first century CE) does not use the word 'Hindu', for instance, but does offer a geographical definition of the people to whom his dharma applies:

> From the eastern sea to the western sea [the Bay of Bengal and the Arabian Sea], the area in between the two mountains [the Himalayas and the Vindhyas] is what wise men call the Land of the Nobles ['Aryas']. Where the black antelope ranges by nature, that should be known as the country fit for sacrifices; and beyond it is the country of the barbarians. The twice-born [the upper classes, and particularly Brahmins] should make every effort to settle in these countries; but a servant [Shudra] may live in any country at all if he is starving to death. [2.23-24]

Much has happened since the time when one could define India as the land where the (deer and the) antelope roam from sea to shining sea. The belief that all Hindus (should) live in India may have been strong once, with strictures against crossing the 'dark waters' (though these seem to

---

[viii] James Joyce, in his novel *Finnegans Wake* (p. 10), in 1939, punned on the word 'Hindoo' (as the British used to spell it), joking that it came from the names of two Irishmen, Hinnessy and Doo-ley: 'This is the hindoo Shimar Shin between the dooley boy and the hinnessy.' Even Joyce knew that the word was not native to India.

[ix] See 'Medical and Mythical Constructions' and 'Why Should a Brahmin?'

have been more honoured in the breach than in the observance). But, in fact, not everyone in that geographical area is (or was) Hindu.[x] Nor, for that matter, have all Hindus lived there for many centuries now. (The Hindus, a great merchant civilization from very ancient times, spread first throughout Southeast Asia and later through the British Empire, and they can now be found scattered from Trinidad to Africa to Fiji.) But this geographical definition of Hinduism is still where Hindus generally begin.[xi]

Sometimes the Hindus defined themselves not by geography but by texts: 'We are the people whose canon is the Veda.' This textual definition was often given a social corollary: 'We are the people who revere the Brahmins, the custodians of the Veda.' And this social corollary, in turn, was also expanded: 'We are the people who follow the dharma of the four social classes and the four stages of life: student (*brahmacharya*), householder (*grihastha*), forest-dweller (*vannaprastha*) and renouncer (*sannyasa*).'[xii] This definition in terms of social praxis prevailed for such a long time that Europeans often argued that Hinduism was not a religion but a social system (just as they argued that Buddhism was not a religion but a philosophy).

In general, though, Hindus have defined themselves not by beliefs, or even by geography, but by practices. The Hinduism of the Vedas was pluralistic.[xiii] It advocated the worship (often through animal sacrifice) of a pantheon of many gods, most of whom by around 200 CE had been assimilated to Shiva, Vishnu in his many incarnations (including both Krishna and Rama), or the goddess in her many forms (which range from the bloodthirsty Kali to Parvati, the mild-mannered wife of Shiva). Pluralistic Hinduism was further characterized by its dharmas that differed not only for every caste but for different individuals at different stages of life and for different social groups.

The complex system of interlocking, sometimes contradictory ideas and ideals about caste, karma, renunciation[xiv] and the worship of various gods

---

[x] Today, an estimated 80 per cent of Indians are Hindu, which still leaves enough Muslims—14 per cent—to make India, after Indonesia, the most populous Muslim nation in the world. And then there are the Christians, Buddhists, Sikhs, Parsis and Jews. Even the 80 per cent figure is disputed: many Dalits (appproximately 16 per cent) and Adivasis (8 per cent) do not consider themselves Hindu.

[xi] For the Hindus of Nepal, for instance, till recently the world's only officially Hindu nation, India is the land of their holiest sites.

[xii] See 'Three (or More)'.

[xiii] See 'Are Hindus Monotheists?'

[xiv] See 'Three (or More)'.

has formed the religious scuttlebutt, the common wisdom, of all Hindus for many centuries. Different Hindus may accept or deny different elements of this conceptual world, and while all Hindus pay lip service to certain ideals, relatively few truly embody them. But all Hindus have been part of the same conversation: All Hindus know about these things, as Jews and Christians know about Adam and Eve. Their kids pick them up in what Americans refer to as 'the street'. Hindus are programmed with many of the same unconscious, unexamined assumptions, whether or not they believe them or like them.

So the fact that the people whom we call Hindus have defined themselves in many different ways—and that these definitions do not always delineate the same sets of people—does not invalidate the category of Hinduism. It has proved convenient for us to call this corpus of concepts Hinduism; naming is always a matter of the convenience of the namers, and all categories are constructed.

Scientists nowadays make a similar sort of assumption when they define light as both a wave and a particle. Categories have to be recycled, like newspapers or tin cans; they are ladders that we climb up and then kick out from under us. The Venn diagram of Hinduism is constantly in motion, because it is made of people, also constantly in motion. But it is there, no matter what the Hindus themselves, or the non-Hindus, choose to call it.

ARE HINDUS MONOTHEISTS OR POLYTHEISTS?[1]

The wise speak of what is One in many ways.
—Rig Veda 1.164.46

Right from the beginning, Hindu texts and practices tell of the simultaneous existence of polytheism and a broader belief in the ultimate oneness of the divine—not exactly monotheism, but a unitary substratum supporting a vigorous polytheism. And yet there has been from time to time an angry debate, in which some Hindus find it insulting to be called polytheists. The answer to this paradox lies in the history of Hinduism.

To the question, 'Is Hinduism monotheistic or polytheistic?' the best answer is, 'Yes' (which is actually the answer to most either/or questions about Hinduism). Not only have elements of both theologies been woven through Hindu texts for thousands of years, but different factions have argued passionately for one view and against the other during this entire period, and the issue still raises Hindu hackles today. The force of the passion comes from the political issues that have often driven this question, particularly since the time of the British Raj and now again in the Age of the Internet.

KATHENOTHEISM IN THE *RIG VEDA*

Hindu texts began with the *Rig Veda* ('Knowledge of Verses'), composed in northwest India around 1500 BCE; the first of the three Vedas, it is the earliest extant text composed in Sanskrit, the language of ancient India. At first glance, it would seem to be unequivocally polytheistic: there are certainly many gods. Indra is the king of the gods and the god of rain (much like his Greek and Roman cousins Zeus and Jupiter); Varuna the god of the heavenly vault and moral law (related to the Greek Ouranos); Agni the god of fire (cf. the Latin *ignis*, and the English 'ignite'); and so forth. Vividly anthropomorphized, these gods are like us, in fact, more so, and understand our appetites and desires since they want what we do— things like physical love, wealth, fame and praise. Each individual worshipper would know, and might use, several different poems to different gods. Always, there was an awareness of the multiplicity of the gods. At time of war or drought, for instance, one prayed to Indra; and in a sacrifice, one invoked Agni (the sacrificial fire). We can detect in the Veda both what might be called internal polytheism (one person worshipping several gods) and communal polytheism (several people worshipping several gods and respecting, or at the very least acknowledging the existence of, one another's gods).

But the polytheism of Vedic religion sometimes functioned as a kind of serial monotheism that the Vedic scholar Friedrich Max Müller (1823- 1900) named 'henotheism' or 'kathenotheism', the worship of a number of gods, one at a time, regarding each as the supreme, or even the only, god while one is talking to him. Thus, one Rig Vedic poem will praise a god and chalk up to his account the credit for separating heaven and earth, propping them apart with a pillar,[i] but another Vedic poem will use the same words to praise another god:

> To the unknown creator: 'He by whom the awesome sky and the earth were made firm, by whom the dome of the sky was propped up . . .' [10.121.5]
>
> To Soma: 'He who is the pillar of the sky . . .' [9.74.2]
>
> To Tvastri: 'He measured apart the two realms of space . . . and fixed them in place with undecaying pillars.' [1.160.4]
>
> To Varuna: 'He stretched out the middle realm of space . . . placed the sun in the sky.' [5.85.2]
>
> To Vishnu: 'Vishnu, who has measured apart the realms of the earth, who propped up the upper dwell-place.' [1.154.1]

In addition, each god would have characteristics and deeds that were his alone: no one but Indra kills the demonic serpent of drought (Vritra), for instance.

Bearing in mind the way in which the metaphor of adultery has traditionally been used by monotheistic religions to stigmatize polytheism ('whoring after other gods'), and used by later Hinduism to characterize

---

[i] See 'Together Apart'.

the love of god (as in the Bengali tradition of Krishna and Radha), we might regard this attitude as a kind of theological parallel to serial monogamy, or, if you prefer, open hierogamos: 'You, Indra, are the only god I've ever worshipped; you are the only one.' 'You, Varuna, are the only god I've ever worshipped; you are the only one.' 'You, Draupadi, are the only woman I've ever loved; you are the only one.' 'You, Subhadra [or Chitrangada, or Ulupi], are the only woman I've ever loved; you are the only one.' This made possible a kind of non-hierarchical pantheon; the attitude to each god was hierarchical ('You are the best'), but the various competing claims of supremacy cancelled one another out, so that the total picture was one of equality: each of several was the best.

The idea of 'the [only] one' as applied to several different members of a polytheistic pantheon also appears in some of the later verses of the *Rig Veda*: 'They call it Indra, Mitra, Varuna, Agni, and it is the heavenly bird that flies. The wise speak of what is One in many ways; they call it Agni, Yama, Matarishvan.' [1.164.46]² And 'The One' is neuter, not male nor female: *ekam sad vipra bahu vadanti*. Neuter, like *brahman* (the impersonal Absolute). Not masculine, like Vishnu.

VEDANTIC MONISM

The *Atharva Veda* too, a fourth Veda composed around 900 BCE, asked how many gods there might be: 'Who and how many were those gods who fastened together the chest and neck of the Primeval Male?ii How many fixed his breasts? Who formed his elbows? How many joined together his ribs and shoulders?' [10.2.4]

To this polytheism question ('How many?') of the *Atharva Veda*, the Upanishads, philosophical texts composed from around the fifth century BCE, suggested a different answer. The gods were often called 'The Thirty-Three'. But one of the earliest Upanishads mocked this number with a dialogue in which, in response to the pupil's repeated question, 'But how many gods are there, really?' the increasingly impatient teacher replies, first, 'Three hundred and three, and three thousand and three,' then, 'Thirty-three,' then, 'Six,' then, 'Three,' then, 'Two,' then, 'One and a half,' and finally, 'One.'³ This 'One' is the emblem not of monotheism but of Upanishadic monism, which assumes that all living things are elements of a single, universal being (often called *brahman*), reached by individual meditation, a philosophy often contrasted with the polytheistic

ii See 'You Can't Get Here'.

world of group sacrifice to multiple gods. An image often used to characterize the relationship between the individual soul and *brahman* is that of salt dissolved in water. 'Thou art that [*tat tvam asi*]', the Upanishads insist.

The doctrine of the Upanishads is also sometimes characterized as pantheism (in which God is everything and everything is God) or, at times, panentheism (in which God encompasses and interpenetrates the universe but at the same time is greater than and independent of it). And as the Upanishads are 'the end of the Vedas' (Vedanta), Upanishadic philosophy is also called Vedanta. These Vedantic doctrines view the very substance of the universe as divine, and view that substance and that divinity as unitary.

The vague monism of the Vedas was, thus, sharpened by the more systematized Vedantic monism of the Upanishads. The term 'Vedanta' later came to be applied to the philosophy of Non-Dualism (that is, the doctrine that there is no distinction between the soul and *brahman*), particularly with respect to the Shaiva philosopher Shankara (788-820 CE), whose teachings may have been buoyed by a need to respond to the monotheist philosophies of the great proselytizing religion, Islam, which arrived in India around the middle of the seventh century CE. (Shankara's competitors argued that he championed monism because he was so stupid that he could only count to one.[4])

Vedantic monism stands in contrast both with Vedic polytheism and with the sort of monotheism that posits a single deity with consciousness and/or a physical form, like some of the deities of the medieval bhakti (devotional) movement. That sort of monotheism, unlike most other forms of Hinduism, did (and does) actively proselytize, and could be doctrinaire, even violently persuasive, at times. The South Indian bhakti authors even mocked their own proselytizing:

> A Shaiva saint was a great proselytizer. He converted those of this world by any means whatever—love, money, brute force. One day Shiva came down in disguise to test him, but the devotee did not recognize Shiva and proceeded to convert him, forcing holy ash on the reluctant-seeming god. When his zeal became too oppressive, Shiva tried to tell him who he was, but the baptism of ash was still forced on him. Even Shiva had to become a Shaiva.[5]

PURANIC POLYTHEISM

But monism and polytheism, growing up side by side as they did in ancient India, learned to live together, to grant one another's existence. Monists acknowledged the reality of the gods of the pantheon but accorded them a secondary, illusory status in comparison with the enduring, real status of the underlying monistic being. Thus the many gods of the Hindu pantheon were often grouped under a monistic umbrella, so that all gods are said to be aspects of one particular god (sometimes Vishnu, sometimes Shiva) or, more often, aspects of the universal, ineffable *brahman*. At other times, individual, effable gods are said to be the manifestations of the true god that is 'without qualities' (*nir-guna*), but the manifestations are 'with qualities' (*sa-guna*)—with names, adventures, distinct appearances.[iii]

All of these theological variations, and many more, appear in the Puranas, the encyclopaedic medieval Sanskrit (and later vernacular) texts that expound the myths, rituals and philosophies of sectarian Hinduism. Here we encounter the several avatars (incarnations) of Vishnu, which make Vishnu a kind of walking one-god polytheism; he appears as a fish, as a boar, as half-lion-half-man, as various human beings (Rama, Krishna, even the Buddha), most of which were originally individual deities who later became absorbed into the over-arching figure of Vishnu. His incarnations are often said to be 'partial': while Vishnu appears on earth as Krishna, for instance, he also remains in his heaven, entire in his original form.

In contrast with the complete lives that Vishnu takes on in his avatars, the god Shiva becomes multiple by manifesting himself in various forms, usually during relatively brief masquerades: we have seen him disguised as a proselytizing saint (Shankara); on occasion, he may take the form of the mother of a woman alone in childbirth,[6] or of a guest who demands that his hosts kill and cook their only son for him.[7] And although the goddesses of India are as various as the gods, people—both scholars and the texts—often speak of the Goddess Devi, and tend to treat all goddesses, from Kali to Durga, as nothing more than aspects of Devi.[iv]

Even when Hindus acknowledge, or insist upon, the ultimate oneness of *brahman*, or say that all paths lead to *brahman*, the spirit in which they actually worship the god they pray to, the god they tell stories about, the god they make their art for and about—the god of their religion, as opposed to their philosophy—is seldom if ever *brahman*, but Shiva or

[iii] See '*Saguna* and *Nirguna*'.
[iv] One gets the impression that, in the dark, all goddesses are grey. (So, too, while gods, ogres and anti-gods often have multiple heads—Brahma has four, Shiva five, Skanda six, Ravana ten—Hindu goddesses not only seldom have more than one—they have lots of arms, but not heads—but often less than one: several of them are beheaded. This gendered pattern makes one stop and think.)

Vishnu or the goddess, or, more precisely, a local form of Shiva or Vishnu or the goddess. And Bengalis and Tamils will berate their god if he fails to answer their pleas, and often they will say; 'If you don't come through for me, I will worship another god.' They're joking, but even to be able to say it reveals a profoundly polytheistic turn of mind.

MONISM AND UNIVERSALISM UNDER THE MUSLIMS AND THE BRITISH

Eventually, the monistic view of the universal *brahman* turned itself inside out to generate another sort of universalism: it argued not only that all physical and immaterial things were one, but that all *religions* were essentially the same, or, as it were, one—that Muslims and Christians really worshipped the same god that Hindus worshipped, but just called him Allah or Christ. (An early seed of this belief may be seen in Krishna's much-quoted line from the *Bhagavad Gita* [9.13]: 'Even those who are devotees of other gods and sacrifice to them with faith, they too worship me,' though those who quote this line often fail to cite the final clause: '—but in the wrong way.') This idea took on new meaning and power in twelfth-century India, when Sufism (a mystical form of Islam) proclaimed that Muslims, Christians, Jews, Zoroastrians (called Parsis in India) and Hindus were all striving towards the same goal and that the outward observances that kept them apart were false. Such a move had obvious political motives, of course, in a country where interreligious tensions were already in evidence, but it also expressed a genuine mystic view of universalism.

The Mughal emperor Akbar (1542-1605) sponsored religious debates between different Muslim groups (Sunni, Shia and Ismaili, as well as Sufis), Parsis, Hindus (devotees of Shiva and of Vishnu), Sikhs, Jains, Jews, Jesuits and Materialists, but he was particularly partial to Sufism. He proclaimed that 'the wisdom of Vedanta is the wisdom of Sufism',[8] thus further universalizing the two great universalizing religions by equating (which is to say universalizing) them. The Jesuits misunderstood his pluralism and thought they had converted him; they sent joyous messages back to Rome: the emperor of India has become a Christian! But then, alas, they saw him going into a mosque. Horrified, they asked him, was he not a Christian? Of course, he said; but I'm also a Muslim. He could encompass them, but they could not encompass him.

When the British took over India from the Mughals, they too entered the arena where polytheism, monism and universalism were duking it out. The officers and missionaries under the British Raj—who were, by and large, not just Protestants but Victorian Protestants—regarded polytheism as just one more form of Oriental excess: all those arms, all those heads—all those *gods!* Moreover, Hindu polytheism reminded them of Catholicism (which Hinduism resembles uncannily in many ways)—all those saints, all those relics. European translations of Indian religious texts in the eighteenth century had included a fraudulent document: the so-called 'Ezourvedam' (presumably a corruption of *Yajur Veda*, the second Veda), a French text in the form of a dialogue between two Vedic sages, one monotheist and one polytheist, who find that the monotheism of 'pristine Hinduism' points to Christian truth. Voltaire was deeply impressed by it and cited it often.[9] Its authorship remains unknown, but it is now certain that it was an original French composition that claimed to be a copy of a lost Sanskrit text— monotheism masquerading as polytheism concealing monotheism.

The fraction of Hinduism that appealed to Protestant, Evangelical tastes at all was firmly grounded in philosophical monism. The Evangelists in India assumed that God had prepared for their arrival by inspiring the Hindus with a rough form of monotheism—the monism of the Upanishads; but pukka monotheism, in their view, was available to Brahmins and not to the lower castes, who were fit only for polytheism.[10] The British tended to prefer the company of Muslims to Hindus for a number of reasons, including the simple fact that Islam was a monotheism that revered the Hebrew Bible and the Christian New Testament. Some Protestants within the British Raj tried to recast Hinduism as a monotheism, with a Bible: the *Bhagavad Gita*. By positioning the *Gita* as the Hindu Bible, the British also validated the worship of Krishna/Vishnu as a form of monotheism. But focusing on this single text ignored not only the many other texts in which other gods, such as Shiva, were similarly represented as the one and only god, but other parts of the very text in which the *Gita* occurs, the *Mahabharata*, in which Shiva and other gods reveal their powers. Moreover, the *Gita* had never had anything remotely approaching canonical status before this, though it had always been an important text. Other texts— Sanskrit texts like the Upanishads and vernacular texts such as the Hindi and Tamil version of the *Ramayana*, and, most of all, oral traditions—were what most Hindus actually used in their worship. The British exclusionary focus on the *Gita*, and on Krishna/Vishnu, amounted to mistaking kathenotheistic polytheism for monistic monotheism.

Scholars have noted a pattern in which colonized people take on the mask that the colonizer creates in the image of the colonized, thus mimicking their colonizer's perception of themselves.[11] Many highly-placed Hindus so admired their British rulers that, in a kind of colonial and religious Stockholm syndrome, they swallowed the Protestant line themselves, and not only gained a new appreciation of those aspects of Hinduism that the British approved of (the *Gita*, the Upanishads, monism), but became ashamed of those aspects that the British scorned (polytheism, erotic sculptures on temples, devadasi temple dancers). Following the British lead, lifting up this monolithic form of Hinduism, they trampled down and largely wrote off the dominant strain of Hinduism that celebrated the multiplicity of the divine, the plurality of forms of worship. But they could not kill it; indeed, most of the rank-and-file Hindus remained as pluralistic and polytheistic as ever.

The highly Anglicized Indian elite, however, developed new forms of Hinduism heavily influenced by British Protestantism. The key figure in this movement was Rammohan Roy (1772-1833), who cast aside the polytheistic Hinduism of his family and turned to monotheism instead. His intense belief in strict monotheism and his aversion to Puranic Hinduism (small shrines in the house, temple worship, pilgrimage) began early. It was derived from a combination of monistic elements of Hinduism and Islam (he had studied the Qu'ran as well as the Vedas and the Upanishads) and, later, eighteenth-century Deism (belief in a transcendent Creator god reached through reason), Unitarianism (belief in god's essential oneness), and the ideas of the Freemasons (a secret fraternity that espoused some Deistic concepts). In 1804, he published a tract in Persian, *A Gift to Monotheists*. Influenced by the Islamic idea of the absolute unity of god, he began issuing critiques of the polytheism of the Hindus and searching Hindu texts for traces of monotheism, trying to prove that textual references to polytheism ('idolatry') were purely allegorical whereas references to an overarching Supreme Deity were the essential nexus of Hinduism. His beliefs were further fuelled by his realization that the colonial government viewed Hindu customs alternately with abhorrence (Vedic polytheism) and fascination (Vedantic monism), and by his desire to rebut the scathing critiques of the missionaries. Rammohan Roy formulated a new Hinduism, called the Brahmo Samaj ('Assembly of God'), which extracted the Sufism from Islam, the Vedanta from Hinduism and Unitarianism from Christianity. Much of his thought influenced Hindus far beyond the bounds of the Brahmo Samaj, inspiring the form of Hinduism called Sanatana Dharma (Eternal or Universal Dharma), or Neo-Vedanta, embraced by many Hindus to this day.

NEO–VEDANTA IN AMERICA

A related form of Neo-Vedanta was carried to Europe and America in 1893, at the World's Parliament of Religions in Chicago. The great sensation at the Parliament was Swami Vivekananda (1863-1902), a disciple of Ramakrishna Paramahamsa (1836-86). Ramakrishna, a devotee of Kali at the temple of Dakshineshvar, north of Kolkata (Calcutta), was not a member of the Brahmo Samaj but attracted a different sort of educated lay follower. His studies and visions had led him to conclude that 'all religions are true' but that the religion of each person's own time and place was the best expression of the truth for that person. He gave educated Hindus a basis on which they could justify their religion to an Indian consciousness increasingly influenced by Western values.

Vivekananda, Ramakrishna's disciple, was the first in a long line of proselytizing gurus who exported the ideals of reformed Hinduism to America and, in turn, brought back American ideas that became infused into Indian Vedanta. Influenced by progressive Western political ideas, Vivekananda set himself firmly against all forms of caste distinction and advised people to eat beef.[12] In 1897, he brought a small band of Western disciples from Chicago to India. There he founded the Ramakrishna Mission, whose branches proclaimed its version of Hinduism in many parts of the world.

Vivekananda took up the famous Vedic line about the multiplicity of the gods ('The wise speak of what is One in many ways'), which clearly presupposes a polytheistic pantheon, cited it out of context, made it refer not to a divine force but to an enlightenment force ('Truth is one; sages speak of it variously'), and invoked it in defence of the argument that the *Rig Veda* was monotheistic.[13][v] Vivekananda's Hinduism jettisoned the particulars of Hindu polytheism (doctrines, dogmas, rituals, oral traditions and temples) in order to extract a universal essence of 'spirituality.'

A second wave of Hindu imports began in the second half of the twentieth century. This was in part a response to changes in American immigration policy from 1965 on, allowing far more Hindus to come to America, and to bring their families with them. It was also the age of the Hindu Hippie Heaven. In 1965, in Los Angeles, A.C. Bhaktivedanta (Prabhupada) founded the Hare Krishna movement, officially known as the International Society for Krishna Consciousness (ISKCON). In 1974,

---

[v] Vivekananda's version was the one quoted by Lisa Miller in her 15 August 2009 *Newsweek* article, 'We Are All Hindus Now': 'Truth is One, but the sages speak of it by many names'.

followers of Swami Muktananda established the Siddha Yoga Dharma Associates (SYDA) Foundation. In 1981, Bhagwan Shree Rajneesh (later Osho) moved his headquarters from Pune (Poona) to Oregon. At this time, the overwhelmingly male, self-conscious form of Hinduism, from Vivekananda through the middle of the twentieth century, began to be supplemented by a more female, uninhibited form of Hinduism, as Hindu men brought their wives with them. The women imported a diverse and ritual-oriented Hinduism, a private, individual Hinduism, a counterweight to the largely philosophical content of American Hinduism until then. And female gurus began to appear, too. Mother Meera, Shri Karunamayi Ma, Shri Ma—all these (and many more) have routinely visited the USA, many of them since the 1980s. Mata Amritanandamayi, known to her followers as Amma ('Mother'), came from Kerala to the United States in 1987; she specialized in Vedanta and hugs; from 1,500 to 9,000 people attend her programmes in the United States (closer to 30,000 or 40,000 in India).[14] Amma was one of the speakers at the 1993 World's Parliament of Religions in Chicago, a century after Vivekananda had brought his very different form of Hinduism to a very different sort of Chicago.

FUNDAMENTALISM AND DIVERSITY IN INDIA

In our day, as fundamentalism raised its ugly head among the major monotheisms (Judaism, Christianity and Islam), Hinduism in India caught it too. The movement known as Hindutva ('Hindu-ness'), while protesting that it is a reaction against European pressures, actually apes Protestant evangelical strategies, including fundamentalist agendas. Its hatred is directed not only against Hindus of the more diverse traditions—the ones that the British, and Rammohan Roy, taught the Hindus to despise—but also, ironically, against the very monotheisms (Islam and Christianity) that nurtured the Hindu insistence that Hinduism is monotheistic.

Some critics of this sort of contemporary Hindu revisionism have noted that, 'By spelling God with a capital letter they are trying to position Hinduism as monotheistic, making it look more "modern".'[15] But the argument about Hindu monotheism is anything but modern; it is as old as Hinduism itself. Nor has Hindutva had the last word. Nowadays Hindus in India and throughout the diaspora who regard Vishnu as the supreme god not only acknowledge other gods such as the elephant-headed Ganesha (or, for that matter, Jesus) but offer them worship on special occasions, just as they will occasionally use penicillin to supplement, rather than replace, one of the native homeopathic systems. They worship the goddess Durga on the days of Durga Puja, Shiva on the nights of Shivaratri and Ganesha when they begin any new enterprise. Quite a few go to church on Christmas Eve and worship at the shrines of Sufi pirs from time to time. Many of them, as a 1911 Gazetteer remarked of the relationship to Hinduism and Islam of one particular group, 'keep the feasts of both religions and the fasts of neither'.[16] The wording of the still operative legal definition of a Hindu is powerfully polytheistic: 'Acceptance of the Vedas with reverence; recognition of the fact that the means or ways to salvation are diverse; and realization of the truth that the number of gods to be worshipped is large, that indeed is the distinguishing feature of Hindu religion.'[17]

And so it appears that I asked the wrong question at the start, the either/or question. Monotheism and polytheism are not mutually incompatible. Hindus are both monotheists and polytheists. No argument.

THREE (OR MORE) FORMS OF THE THREE (OR MORE)-FOLD PATH IN HINDUISM[1]

THE HISTORY OF TRIADS IN INDIA

When King Pururavas went from earth to heaven to see Indra, the king of the gods, he saw Dharma (religion/duty) and the other human goals, Kama (pleasure) and Artha (power), embodied. As he approached them, he ignored the other two but paid homage to Dharma, walking around him in a circle to the right. The other two, unable to put up with this slight, cursed him. Because Kama had cursed him, he was separated from his wife, Urvashi, and longed for her in her absence. When he had managed to put that right, then, because Artha had cursed him, he became so excessively greedy that he stole from all four social classes. The Brahmins, who were upset because they could no longer perform the sacrifice or other rituals without the money he had stolen from them, took blades of sharp sacrificial grass in their hands and killed him.

This story was told by the commentator Yashodhara in the thirteenth century, to explain the very first line of the third-century *Kamasutra*:[i] 'We bow to dharma, artha and kama'. This means, Yashodhara says: 'The three goals of human life are the three divinities in charge of this work; if they were not divinities it would not be right to bow to them. And there is textual evidence that they are in fact divinities.' This text shows us how very important this triad—and, as we shall see, triads in general—are in Hindu intellectual history.

'Three' was a kind of shorthand for 'lots and lots'; the number three, in Sanskrit, signifies both 'plural' and 'complete'. These triads represented the multivalent, multifaceted, multiform, multi-whatever-you-like nature of the real phenomenal world. Other religions, too, of course, had their

---

[i] See 'Reading the *Kamasutra*'.

21

trinities, but Hinduism used the concept of the triad in a particularly pervasive way, to produce a consistent, popularly recognized scaffolding on which to organize the otherwise unimaginably chaotic richness of Hindu conceptual thought.

Perhaps the most basic triad, attested in brief references as early as the *Atharva Veda* (c. 900 BCE) and the *Chandogya Upanishad* (c. 500 BCE), is that of the three qualities of matter (the *gunas*), woven like the three strands of a braid: lucidity or goodness (*sattva*), energy (*rajas*) and darkness or entropy (*tamas*); or intelligibility, activity and inertia.[2] Classical Sankhya philosophy,[ii] which provides us with the earliest detailed discussion of the three strands,[3] expands the initial triad into several others: intellect, egoism (*ahamkara*, the sense of 'I') and the subtle elements; the classes of gods, humans and animals-plants; satisfaction, frustration and confusion; and perception, inference and authority.[4] A related triad is constituted by the humours of the body, the *doshas*: phlegm (*kapha*), bile (*pitta*) and wind (*vata*). It is probably significant that *guna* and *dosha* in combination mean 'virtues and faults', a dichotomy of moralization that was to prove useful for the formation of hierarchical judgements within the triads, for hierarchy was, as we will see, an essential organizing principle of Hindu thought.

Another major triad in Hinduism, which was later to prove unstable in ways that we will consider at some length, is that of the three human goals or *purusharthas* (also called the triple path or *trivarga*) that the *Kamasutra* invokes: dharma, artha and kama. For assonance, one might call them piety, profit and pleasure, or society, success and sex, or duty, domination and desire. (Dharma, in a sense the most central goal, is famously difficult to translate; it includes duty, religion, religious merit, morality, social obligations, the law, justice and so forth.) Every human being was said to have a right to all three of these goals, to have a full life; in addition, each individual was also supposed to follow a unique path laid out for him at birth, a path determined primarily by his caste—the social class into which he was born. (I use the male pronoun advisedly; these rules were not meant to apply to women.) Each person had his own particular dharma, his *svadharma*.

Sanskrit texts were devoted to each of the three human goals. There are many texts devoted to dharma, but only one to artha—the *Arthashastra*, or textbook on politics—and one to kama—Vatsyayana's *Kamasutra*—survive from the earliest period. Clearly, dharma was both more important and more complex than artha or kama.

[ii] One of the six classical Indian philosophies, Sankhya is dualistic and atheistic.

The *Arthashastra* is generally attributed to Kautilya ('Crooked'), the minister of the Mauryan emperor Chandragupta in the fourth century BCE, but it was completed in the early centuries of the Common Era, perhaps by 200 CE. The *Arthashastra* is a compendium of advice for a king, and though it is often said to be Machiavellian, Kautilya makes Machiavelli look like Mother Teresa. In addition to much technical information on the running of a kingdom, the *Arthashastra* contains a good deal of thought on the subject of human psychology. The *Kamasutra* was probably composed around 300 CE and is attributed to a man named Mallanaga Vatsyayana, about whom we know virtually nothing. *The Laws of Manu* (in Sanskrit, the *Manava Dharmashastra* or *Manu-smriti*, and informally known as Manu, probably composed around 100 CE) is by far the best known of the many dharma texts.[iii] It is attributed to Manu, but that is almost certainly a pseudonym.

There are other enduring triads basic to Hindu thinking, such as the three debts that every man traditionally owed—study to the sages, funeral offerings to the ancestors and sacrifice to the gods; the trinity of the gods Brahma, Vishnu and Shiva (a false construction, since Brahma was never worshipped like the other two); mind, body and speech; the three 'times'—past, present and future; and many others. And each of these triadic systems of classification may be applied on three major levels: the cosmos (which may be, as we shall see, further divided into three worlds), the chain of being on earth (which was divided into three or more classes) and the human body (divided into various members). Like the *gunas* and the *doshas*, these triads remained stable for ever; that is, they were never squared, as were the human goals and other paradigmatic triads that we will soon encounter. Indeed, their resistance to quadripartition is one of the props of the argument that triads, rather than quartets, are the basis of Hindu thinking.

But this argument doesn't always hold. The triad of the *gunas*, for instance, is often contrasted or combined with that of the three elements—water, fire and wind. But this latter does not prove a stable triad; a fourth element, earth or ether, is often added, or *both* earth and ether, making five. Though the triad did remain the numerical unit of choice in ancient India, at least for a while, even then the Hindu drive toward hierarchization[5] invariably ranked the elements of these triads, emphasizing their relative subordination rather than their mutual interaction (although the same elements are not always subordinated in the same way throughout the culture).[6]

[iii] See 'Medical and Mythical Constructions' and 'Why Should a Brahmin?'

THE TRIADS OF MATTER IN MANU

It has been argued that all the other Hindu triads are constituted by implicit reference to the three basic qualities of matter itself, the strands or *gunas*. The *Bhagavad Gita*, the metaphysical dialogue between Arjuna and Krishna composed after the Sankhya texts and dependent upon them for its typology, presents the version by which the theory of the strands is best known today. It speaks of the triad of knowledge (*jnana*), action (karma) and actor (*kartri*), and within each of them it further differentiates three levels: three kinds of knowledge, three kinds of karma and three kinds of actors. It then goes on to distinguish three kinds of intelligence (*buddhi*), fortitude (*dhriti*) and happiness (*sukha*).[7]

This is complex enough, but not as complex as the schema in the last book of *The Laws of Manu*. Manu draws, like the *Gita*, upon the basic Sankhya typology, and correlates the three qualities of matter with the three human goals as well as with three kinds of bodily action (good, bad and neutral), three bases of action (the mind-and-heart, speech and the body), the three times (past, present and future) and the three species of rebirth (gods, humans and animals):

> The action that arises in the mind-and-heart, speech and the body bears good and bad fruits; the highest, lowest and middle levels of men's existences come from their actions. Know that the mind-and-heart sets in motion the body's (action) here on earth, which is of three kinds and has three bases and ten distinctive marks.[iv] The three kinds of mental action are: thinking too much about things that belong to others, meditating in one's mind-and-heart about what is undesirable and adhering to falsehoods.[v] The four kinds of speech (acts) are verbal abuse, lies, slander of all sorts and unbridled chatter. The three kinds of bodily (action) are traditionally said to be taking things that have not been given, committing violence against the law and having sex with another man's wife. A man experiences in his mind-and-heart the good or bad effects of past actions committed in his mind-and-heart, he experiences in his speech what he has committed in his speech, and

---

[iv] The three kinds are good, bad and neutral; the three bases are the mind-and-heart, speech and the body; and the ten distinctive marks, distributed among the three bases, are about to be defined in the next three verses, which give only the negative version of each mark that distinguishes good actions from bad or neutral actions.

[v] The commentators offer examples of what is undesirable (killing a Brahmin and other things that are forbidden) and a falsehood (saying, 'There is no world beyond' or 'The body is the soul'). See 'The Concept of Heresy'.

in his body what he has committed with his body.[vi] A man becomes a stationary object as a result of the faults that are the effects of past actions of the body, a bird or wild animal from those of speech, and a member of one of the lowest castes from those of the mind-and-heart. [12.3-11]

This passage, which demonstrates the truly baroque quality of the Hindu obsession with triads, also tells us a great deal about the right and wrong ways to lead the religious life and usefully correlates the qualities of matter with the possibilities and consequences of human action. But it does not really tell us *three ways* to lead the religious life.

Manu, however, goes on immediately to make another, more surprising correlation. He has already introduced us, at the very beginning of his work [1.15-20], to the three strands as attributes of the physical world. But now Manu asserts that the self or soul, the *atman*, which one might regard as transcendent in the most basic sort of way, also partakes of the three hierarchical qualities, which account for the fact that it continues to be trapped in matter through its various incarnations:

> Know that lucidity, energy and darkness are the three qualities of the self, through which the Great One pervades and endures in all these existences, without exception. Whenever one of these qualities entirely prevails in a body, it makes that particular quality predominant in the embodied (soul). Lucidity is traditionally regarded as knowledge, darkness as ignorance, and energy as passion and hate; this is their form, that enters and pervades all living beings. Among these (three), a person should recognize as lucidity whatever he perceives in his self as full of joy, something of pure light which seems to be entirely at peace. But he should recognize as energy whatever is full of unhappiness and gives his self no joy, something which is hard to oppose and constantly seduces embodied creatures. And he should recognize as darkness whatever is full of confusion, undifferentiated, whatever is sensual and cannot be understood through reason or intelligence.
>
> Now I will also explain, leaving nothing out, the highest, middle and hindmost fruits that result from these three qualities. The recitation of the Veda, inner heat, knowledge, purification, suppression of the sensory powers, the rites of duty and meditation on the soul are the mark of the quality of lucidity. Delight in enterprises, instability, persistence in doing what should not be done and continual indulgence

---

[vi] He experiences sorrow, verbal abuse by others and diseases, respectively.

in the sensory objects are the mark of the quality of energy. Greed, sleep, incontinence, cruelty, atheism, losing jobs, habitually asking for hand-outs and carelessness are the mark of the quality of darkness.

The following should be regarded as the marks of the qualities in a nutshell, in order, as each of these three qualities occurs in the three (time periods). When someone who has done, or is doing, or is going to do an act feels ashamed, a learned man should realize that that whole act has the mark of the quality of darkness. When someone hopes to achieve great fame in this world by a certain act, but does not feel sorry if it fails, that should be known as (an act with the quality of) energy. But when he longs with his all to know something and is not ashamed when he does it, and his self is satisfied by it, that (act) has the mark of the quality of lucidity. Pleasure (kama) is the mark of darkness, profit (artha) is said to be the mark of energy, and dharma the mark of lucidity, and each is better than the one before it. [12.24-38]

It behoves us to be as lucid as possible, both in body and in soul, and certain religious acts, and religious thoughts, are more lucid than others. Manu tells us how to recognize the signs of the triad in ourselves. His discussions of the triad are placed like bookends to frame his entire text, a text which provides obsessively detailed laws for human behaviour. But Manu provides no bridge between the bookends and the legal substance. He never tells us what to do in order to foster the good and fight the evil in terms of his framing triadic paradigm. But his stark, idealistic hierarchy provides the cosmological scaffolding for his rich discussion of the specific forms of the religious life.

THE TRANSCENDENT FOURTH

The Hindu triads, therefore, are not sufficient paradigms for the religious life. Moreover, most of them did not even remain triadic at all in Indian history. Many, though not all, of the Vedic triads became quartets when later Hinduism added a fourth term, usually a transcendent Vedantic term.

Here I should make it clear that, throughout this book, I am using the word 'Vedic' not in its narrower sense, designating the *Rig Veda* and the texts dependent on it (which include the Brahmanas and the Upanishads and constitute what the Hindus call *shruti*), but in its broader sense, designating the subsequent Hindu tradition called *smriti* that defines itself by its allegiance to the Vedas.[8] The term thus includes not merely the Vedas but the entire strain of Hinduism that endorses Vedic sacrifice and the worship of a pantheon of gods, as it is carried on to this day in Hindu temples and households. 'Vedic' Hinduism developed into 'Puranic' Hinduism when the encyclopaedic texts called the Puranas were composed in the medieval period. In this broader sense, 'Vedic' Hinduism may be contrasted with 'Vedantic' Hinduism, which defines itself primarily by reference to the Upanishads (which are technically part of *shruti*, but are called 'Vedanta', literally, 'the end of the Veda'). Though Vedantic Hinduism has its seeds in the Upanishads, it is fully developed in the great commentaries on the Upanishads, particularly those of the Vedantic philosophers Shankara and Ramanuja, at the end of the first millennium of the common era.

The Vedantic shift away from sacrifice and worldliness is at the heart of all the fourths added to the original triads of Hinduism. The world of the triads is the India of fabled elephants encrusted with jewels and temples covered with copulating couples, the world of sensuality from which the omphalosceptic yogis fled—but which continues to thrive in India to this day.[vii] It is also the world of many gods, each with many arms (often many heads), who replace one another, compete with one another and help one another—and one another's worshippers.[viii] This classical paradigm prevailed in India for many, many centuries, and still prevails in certain traditional sectors of Hindu society. But it came to exist alongside another paradigm that might have subverted or destroyed it altogether, but which, instead, simply came to supplement it as an alternative view of human life. For many of the Hindu triads, as we have already noted, became quartets when later Hinduism added a fourth term, usually a transcendent fourth, to accommodate the shift to a paradigm of renunciation and asceticism.

This religious revolution took place some time around the sixth century BCE, a time of great religious ferment that saw the rise of Buddhism, Jainism and many other ascetic and renunciant sects. There are many reasons for these changes. One was a reaction against the worldliness and sense of overcrowding caused by the move down from the nomadic culture of the mountains of the Punjab to the newly-founded great cities of the Ganges Valley. Another was the growth of a merchant class and the impact of many traders from abroad.[ix] The development of the idea of merit or karma as something to be earned, accumulated, and transferred owes much to the post-Vedic moneyed economy. Where there's trade,

[vii] See 'From Kama to Karma'.
[viii] See 'Are Hindus Monotheists?'
[ix] Parallel movements in ancient Greece and China have led some people to call this the Axial Age.

people leave home; new commercial classes emerge; and, above all, new ideas spread quickly and circulate freely. There was little to stop them when this happened in ancient India: the Vedas did not constitute a closed canon and there was no central temporal or religious authority to enforce a canon even had there been one. Many small kingdoms arose, whose rulers gathered around them philosophers debating the new doctrines. As always, Hinduism adapted, co-opted and carried on, changed, yet unchanged.

At first, there were three ways of life (*ashramas*): that of the student (*brahmacharya*), the householder (*grihastha*, the locus for acts, of all kinds) and the forest-dweller[x] (*vanaprastha*).[9] To these, later, was added a fourth way of life of the renouncer (*sannyasin*). These stages were at first simultaneous options that could be taken up at any time (though the third stage in the quartet, the forest-dweller, became highly problematic, especially when attempts were made to distinguish it from the new, fourth stage[10]), but they soon became regarded as serial.

At the same time, to the three human goals of dharma, kama and artha was added moksha, or release, the goal for the renouncer. Release meant freedom from the circle of rebirth (called *samsara*) and the trap of karma— the actions, good and bad, which accumulate and determine one's rebirth. In Hinduism, from the very start, the idea that transmigration occurred was immediately followed by two other ideas: that it was possible for some people to get free of it and that it was desirable for some people to get free of it.[xi] Now the triad of goals (*trivarga*) became a quartet, known as the *chaturvarga* (the quadruple path). But that quartet could also be regarded as a dualism, with release (moksha or *mukti*) contrasted with the rest of the group, the original immanent triad of dharma, artha and kama, now called 'enjoyment' (*bhoksha* or *bhukti*[xii])—just as physical and spiritual discipline is contrasted with enjoyment: yoga vs. *bhoga*. (These dichotomies also play upon the assonance betweeen moksha/*bhoksha* and yoga/*bhoga*.) People also spoke of the tension between moksha and dharma. Indeed, philosophical Vedanta reduced the human goals to another sort of a dualism: what one likes—*preyas*—consisting of kama and artha; and what is good for one— *shreyas*—consisting of dharma and moksha.[11] Moreover, the fourth goal was often, implicitly or explicitly, exalted above the other three, just as the triad as a whole, as a balanced set, had once constituted an implicit fourth term greater than any of its constituent parts.[12]

---

[x] See 'The Forest-dweller'.
[xi] See 'Death and Rebirth'.
[xii] See 'Eating Karma'.

THE FOURTH SOCIAL CLASS

The tendency to square the circle first enters India, however, not as a transcendent category at all, but, on the contrary, as a most worldly and politically-driven category. The Indo-Europeans—the civilization that preceded that of the Vedic Indians, a linguistic family that included Latin, ancient Greek, Avestan, and Sanskrit[xiii]—divided the world into three social classes (*varnas*): first, kings who were also priests; then, warriors; and finally, producers of fertility.[13] But this triad soon became a quartet within the text of the *Rig Veda*, composed in northwest India around 1500 BCE. For the *Rig Veda* gives evidence of one of the first recorded political coups: the kings appear here no longer in the first class, as priest-kings, but in the second class of warriors-kings (Kshatriyas), leaving the priests (Brahmins) alone to rule the roost of the first class. The commoners/workers (Vaishyas) remain below both the Brahmins and the warrior-kings. At the same time, these three classes came to be flanked by a fourth class, servants (Shudras),[xiv] who would have been the inhabitants of the Indian subcontinent before the Indo-Europeans arrived, or others with non–Indo-European origins. And so the Indo-European triad (priest-kings, warriors and workers) became a Hindu quartet (Brahmins, Kshatriyas, Vaishyas and Shudras). The Shudras were the outside class within society that defines the others (just as, later, Dalits, entirely outside society, define Brahmins). The Shudra roughly corresponds to the renouncer (*sannyasin*) in being both inside and outside the system. As was the case with the quartet of the human goals, Hindus often viewed the final combination not as a quartet but as a duet: all of Us (who are given several names, such as Aryans or twice-born, the three upper classes) vs. all of Them (the non-Us, the Others, the people who are excluded from privileged society). The hierarchical division of social classes (*varnas*) in some ways provides an intellectual structure for caste (*jati*), though castes arose much later than the four classes, are far more numerous, had different origins and have real social effects.[xv]

THREE AGAINST FOUR

Against the ancient triads, or against the whole pluralistic vision regarded as a single system and assigned one pole of the new dichotomy, monism

[xiii] See 'Hinduism by Any Other Name'.
[xiv] See 'You Can't Get Here'.
[xv] See 'Hinduism by Any Other Name'.

raised its ugly head. The renunciatory philosophies of the Upanishads (as well as of Buddhism and Jainism) were both sociologically and intellectually monistic.[xvi] Sociologically, the renunciatory movements proposed, in contrast to the particular dharma (svadharma) that differed for each individual, a single, universal dharma (sanatana dharma), involving general moral precepts such as honesty, generosity and nonviolence.[14] This was an overarching, unitary, non-hierarchical category of the religion for everyone, a universal goal. (Later, this final goal was sometimes compared with that other universal goal, moksha.) And intellectually, the renunciatory movements envisioned a single godhead—alongside and underneath the apparent polytheistic pantheon.[xvii]

These revolutionary ideas, as we've observed, did not finally replace the old Vedic concepts; Hinduism, as it has often done through the ages, simply co-opted them. It validated the plurality (and the hierarchy) of dharma by calling itself 'the religion of the four classes and the four stages of life' (varnashrama dharma); but at the same time, it validated the unity of dharma by endorsing sanatana dharma. The two basic approaches to human life, the worldly and the pluralistic, on the one hand, and the renunciatory and the monistic, on the other, interact throughout Indian religious thinking. After about the sixth century BCE, this interaction became a far more apparent aspect of Hinduism as the ancient triads were squared. Other triads followed the example of the basic triads of social classes (varnas) and human goals (purusharthas) in becoming quartets.[15] Where, for instance, once the Hindus formulated a group of three emotions—desire, anger and fear (or, in the Buddhist formulation, desire, anger and greed)— now a fourth, metaphysical, epistemological emotion was added: delusion (moha).

To the triad of the three Vedas, the canonical scriptures, was added a fourth Veda, the Atharva Veda, the book of magic (around 900 BCE). The Vedas continue to be regarded as a triad, and many Hindus to this day are named Trivedi, '(Knower) of the Three Vedas'. But the Vedas are also regarded as a quartet, and there are also many Hindus named Chaturvedi, '(Knower) of the Four Vedas'. In one sense, the Vedas as a class are intrinsically and definitively transcendent, and so the additional fourth Veda, the inversion of the inversion, the Atharva Veda, is not transcendent (it gives useful information on ways to make your wife's lover impotent,

---

[xvi] See 'Are Hindus Monotheists?'
[xvii] See 'Are Hindus Monotheists?'

and so forth). But, on the other hand, when we realize that the Vedas are the authority for the sacrificial tradition, the basis of the later worldly Hindu tradition of dharma texts and temple worship, we can see that as a group, including the *Atharva Veda*, they form one part of a new dualism, of which the second half, the non-worldly, Vedantic half, is supplied by the Upanishads.[xviii]

The new fourth also often involved the concept of silence, or absence: to the three priests of the sacrifice was added a fourth priest who was merely the silent witness; to the three Vedic modes of experience (waking, dreaming and deep, dreamless sleep), was added the 'fourth' (*turiya*) state— the deepest, transcendent stage of consciousness that is the merging into ultimate reality.[16] The fourth is always extra in India. When keeping time in music, Indians count three 'heavy' beats and a fourth 'empty' beat.[17] Sanskrit has two words for the fourth term, *chaturtha* for the fourth in any series (which may contain more than four terms), and *turiya* for the special fourth term of a quartet.

Similarly, the three worlds at first consisted of heaven, earth and the intervening ether; later, when hell was introduced, the ether vanished— became an absence—in order to preserve the triad, now heaven, earth and hell; and, finally, the renunciatory model stipulated the three worlds plus the non-world. Even that most basic triad, the triad of the *gunas*, came to be contrasted, as a group (called Prakriti—'nature', female, material, manifest), with their transcendent fourth (Purusha—'spirit', male, pure, unmanifest), especially in the Sankhya texts.[xix]

HIERARCHY

The triad, or the quartet, also tended to be hierarchized, though differently hierarchized by different people. The pervasive force of Hindu *svadharma*, particular dharma, different for each person, ran across the current of the four human goals, ranking them differently according to the point of view of each individual, depending upon the person's gender, social group and so forth. Various unsatisfactory, overlapping correlations between the four goals and the three (upper) classes were attempted: moksha and dharma for

---

[xviii] Later texts, like the *Mahabharata* and even the Tantras, attempted to legitimize themselves by referring to themselves as 'the fifth Veda', but that is truly another story.
[xix] The term *purusha*, however, was used, in the *purusha sukta* hymn from the *Rig Veda*, for the Primeval Male who is divided into the four classes. Hindu bricolage produces appropriations that are confusing to a non-Hindu mind used to words that usually stand up long enough to be counted.

Brahmins; dharma for Brahmins and kings; artha for kings and merchants (Vaishyas); and kama for kings. There was a slightly better fit with the four stages of life (*ashramas*): moksha for renouncers and, with modifications, for forest-dwellers; dharma for forest-dwellers, students and householders; artha and kama for householders. But the hierarchies were not uniformly accepted: different disciplines and philosophical schools ranked the goals differently, and each of the Sanskrit words had several secondary meanings which allowed people to rank them differently from their precribed rankings according to their primary meanings.

This same not-so-hidden agenda also operates in another passage in the *Bhagavad Gita*. We have noted, earlier, the triadization of *jnana* (knowledge), karma (works, rituals) and the actor (*kartri*). At first glance, these seem to form a stable triad. But when we look more closely at it, we see that the group was originally constituted as a dualism (of karma and *jnana*) mediated by a third term (*kartri*). The first term, karma, contains within it the worldly Vedic triad, equivalent to the three human goals and the three stages of life. But karma took on a negative meaning in renunciant Hinduism, where the goal is to get free of all karma, even the merit of good acts (including Vedic rituals, also designated by the term 'karma'). And this bias against *any* karma reinforced the dualistic contrast between karma (Vedic action) and *jnana* (the transcendent Vedantic fourth), roughly parallel to the tension between what Martin Luther, the founder of Protestantism, would have called works (karma) and faith (*jnana*).

Thus, in order to resolve the conflicting claims of the original binary opposition, a new term, bhakti, was introduced (by the *Bhagavad Gita* and other texts). This new concept became one *marga*, or path, in the paradigm of the three paths to salvation, also called the three yogas: karma (works, rituals), *jnana* (knowledge, meditation) and bhakti (worship, love, devotion).[18] In this way, a brand new triad was created, on the archaic model of the old triads, to solve, dialectically, the problem posed by a set of polar oppositions. But that very dualism (of karma vs. *jnana*, action vs. meditation) was originally composed of another triad (the three goals or stages of life) plus a fourth (the goal of moksha and the stage of renunciation, *sannyasa*). And now, each member of the triad of *jnana*, karma and bhakti was regarded by its adherents as the best, if not the only, path to salvation.

THE FOUR AGES

In the Puranas, composed after about the fourth century CE, there are also some new quartets that never seem to have been triads, such as the four

Ages of time, or Yugas, that formed a quartet in ancient Greece, too.[xx] The Yugas, which combine to make an aeon, are four ages in which human beings become increasingly wicked and live shorter and shorter lifespans. The ages are characterized by throws of the dice: the first age is the winning throw and the last age is the losing throw.[xxi] But the fourth age was always, from the start, entirely different from the first three: unlike the other ages, it is now, it is real, it is *always* our age. Historical time starts only when people have children and death enters the world. The first three groups form one group (Eden, the Golden Age, the way it was *in illo tempore*) and the last item (the Kali Yuga) forms the other group (now, reality). And so, as usual, the quartet can be reduced to a dualism.

The quartet of the four Ages was apparently invented in Hinduism when four had already become the number of choice and had provided many quartets, to which paradigm the four Ages were easily assimilated. Thus the four throws of the dice that name the four Ages, or Yugas, are visualized as the legs of dharma: dharma (imagined as a cow) begins on four legs in the first age (the age of the Krita, or throw of four), then has three legs in the second age (the Treta, the trey), two in the third (the Dvapara, the deuce) and totters on one leg in the Kali Age (snake eyes).

But in many texts, linear time (four-fold, square) becomes a circle. Instead of remaining linear, as in Greece, time in India becomes both linear *and* cyclical, a Möbius strip: it declines and is reborn over and over again, as each successive doomsday undergoes its sea change into each successive cosmogony. The four Ages (from the Golden Age to the Kali Yuga) become three cosmogonic stages (creation, maintenance and doomsday); the linear and worldly ages are combined into one whole polar element (an aeon, or *kalpa*) that is then set in opposition to another polar element: cyclical time, which is transcendent.

TENSION AND INTERACTION

Indian tradition came up with various solutions to these conflicts between the one and the many, between the unitary dharma of Vedantic Hinduism and the pluralistic dharma of Vedic Hinduism, between renunciation and the other three stages of life. Hindu tradition presents five ways of dealing with these tensions:

[xx] The four Ages in ancient Greece were characterized by metals, beginning with gold. Actually, Hesiod (in both the *Theogony* and *Works and Days*) really has five ages, but that, too, is another story.

[xxi] Where Einstein remarked that God does not play dice with the universe, Hindu texts state that god—Shiva—does indeed play dice, and cheats, at that.

First, it was said that the stages (or goals) were to be followed not simultaneously, but seriatim, one at a time. Release—moksha—was made a fourth stage, often indefinitely postponed while theoretically extolled. But this trivialized the original claims of the renunciant philosophy, which were opposed to the other three stages altogether.

Second was the argument from symbiosis, or plentitude: the two groups—worldly and transcendent, pure and impure—need one another to compose society as a whole. There are two forms of immortality, for instance, one through one's own children and one achieved through renunciation.[19] Thus the renouncer's holiness and knowledge are fed back into the society that supports him,[20] and the Brahmin must remain outside society in order to be useful inside.[21] This is a self-contradictory situation, another Möbius strip that folds back in on itself, a metaphysical martini with a twist.

The third solution was compromise, which proved unsatisfactory for a number of reasons, but basically because compromise is not a Hindu way of solving problems.[22] Hindu thinking prefers to proceed as a pendulum of extremes that are never resolved and that are also constantly in motion; it refuses to modify its component elements in order to force them into a synthesis. In this way, Hinduism celebrates the idea that all possibilities may exist without excluding each other, that variety and contradiction are ethically and metaphysically necessary.[23]

The fourth solution was identification, which came to replace hierarchy as Vedanta largely superseded Vedic thinking. Thus it was said that the householder was a renouncer if he played his role correctly, that dharma *was* moksha (as Krishna tells Arjuna in the *Bhagavad Gita*: do your work as a warrior well and you win the merit of renunciation). And now it was also said that one must have sons—usually regarded as the goal of the householder stage—to achieve moksha. Tantrism (and Zen) took this line of argument to the extreme: thus, just as release = enjoyment (moksha = *bhoksha*), so, in the formulation of the Buddhist philosopher Nagarjuna, the world of rebirth (*samsara*) = the place or condition of release from rebirth (nirvana). Four was thus reduced not only to two but, ultimately, to one. Monism has triumphed—but only in this particular paradigm.

The fifth, and ultimate, Hindu solution was hierarchy, which we have examined at some length. The drive to hierarchize—to rank classes of people in the order of the worth of their social roles, to rank human goals in the order of their sanctity, to rank qualities of matter according to their purity—here, as throughout classical Hindu thought, rides roughshod over the drive to present equal alternatives or even a serial plan for a well-rounded human life. Yet, though monism remained alive and well and living in India, in other parts of the forest, Hindu pluralism—the belief that numberless options are all valuable (if not necessarily equally valuable)—continues to obey the command to be fruitful and multiply.[xxii]

Chart of Hindu Triads

(A) Stable Triads

Elements	Humours	Debts	Locus	Times	Species	Actions
water	phlegm	study	mind	past	gods	good
fire	bile	funeral	speech	present	humans	neutral
wind	wind	sacrifice	body	future	animals	bad

(B) Squared Triads

Matter	Goals	Stages	Classes	Vedas	Emotions	Worlds	In the *Gita*
lucidity	dharma	student	Brahmin	Rig	desire	heaven	knowledge
energy	profit	house-holder	king	Sama	anger	earth	action
darkness	pleasure	forest-dweller	producer	Yajur	fear/greed	hell/ether	devotion
Spirit	release	renouncer	servant	Atharva	delusion	nonworld	release

[xxii] See 'Are Hindus Monotheists?'

THE CONCEPT OF HERESY IN HINDUISM[1]

Heresy is the lifeblood of religions. There are no heresies in a dead religion.
—André Suarès

Heresy is not really a Hindu idea at all. People have been killed in India because they did or did not sacrifice animals, or had sex with the wrong women, or disregarded the Vedas, or even made use of the wrong sacred texts, but no one was impaled (the Hindu equivalent of burning at the stake) for saying that god was like this rather than like that. Yet, the Hindus did have strong opinions about the difference between good and bad religious ideas, right and wrong doctrines, and their attitude to the people who held such ideas resulted in both dramatic confrontations and subtle accommodations throughout the history of Hinduism.

The Hindu concept of heresy did not develop in a sealed Hindu world. It evolved in response to invasions, the presence of foreign merchants, new intellectual movements and shifting balances of power among the many sects native to India. And the myths changed as historical circumstances changed. On the one hand, heresies became fragmented, developing hierarchies within hierarchies and competing allegiances—Hindu heresies versus non-Hindu and, within Hinduism, Shaiva heresies versus Vaishnava, and so on. On the other hand, the Brahmin authors of many Hindu texts devised various, often theologically convoluted, doctrines in order to include many heretics in the Hindu fold.

Hinduism has always been noted for its ability to absorb potentially schismatic developments; indeed, one of the prime functions of the caste system has been to assimilate various tribes and sects by giving them a place within the social hierarchy. And although many people regard the *Rig Veda* as a closed canonical collection, in actual fact this canon is not read by the vast majority of Hindus, few of whom know the many archaic passages that have baffled scholars. This general inaccessibility of the canon has facilitated an almost endless reinterpretation of doctrine. A particularly striking manifestation of this flexibility of Hindu tradition may be seen in the manner by which it has assimilated various heresies, to a degree so wide-ranging that, as Louis Renou remarked, 'It is quite difficult in India to be completely heretical.'[2] This flexibility has not even necessitated the element of masquerade, the ability to change without appearing to change that usually characterizes adaptations within a tradition; the myths of heresy make explicit note of the changes in doctrine. In part, this is made possible by the open-ended quality of the religion itself; in part, it is due to the vagueness of the Hindu definition of heresy.

THE HINDU DEFINITION OF HERESY

In order to understand the development of the Hindu attitude to heretics, it is necessary to understand precisely who these heretics were—and the texts are exasperating in their imprecision on this point. Our own use of the word 'heresy' is equally imprecise, though in a different way; this further obstructs the attempts of Anglophone readers to come to terms with the Indian issue. The Oxford English Dictionary defines heresy (from the Greek '*haireomai*', 'to choose') as

> theological or religious opinion or doctrine maintained in opposition, or held to be contrary, to the 'catholic' or orthodox doctrine of the Christian Church, or, by extension, to that of any church, creed or religious system, considered as orthodox. 2. By extension, opinion or doctrine in philosophy, politics, science, art, etc. in variance with those generally accepted as authoritative. 3. Opinion or doctrine characterizing particular individuals or parties; a school of thought; a sect.

Already the dangers of cross-cultural terminologies become apparent. The fit between two such different metaphysical systems as those encoded in English and Sanskrit is never exact; the word 'orthodox' is an inappropriate term to apply to mainstream Hinduism, which has often been described as more orthoprax than orthodox, i.e. insisting on authority more in adherence to matters of praxis, such as ritual, than in correct belief.[i]

---

[i] See 'Are Hindus Monotheists?'

The primary difficulty that arises when the Greek-derived term[ii] is applied to Indian religion is that the element of choice that is basic to the Greek concept is inapplicable to the Hindu concept of heresy. The Hindu heretic does not choose his false doctrine; it is thrust upon him by his own ignorance, or by a curse. A heretic is often called *vedabahya*, 'outside the Vedas', a condition that results from the action of the Hindu community: he is excommunicated, quite literally, the victim rather than the conscious agent of heresy.[iii]

Moreover, Hindus (like Buddhists) regard heresy as a failure of understanding rather than as a deliberate choice of the wrong idea; ignorance rather than sin is the root of all evil, 'an act of intellectual misapprehension and not . . . an act of volition and rebellion'.[3] In this respect, at least, the Hindu concept of heresy resonates with the Greek concept of sin, *amartia*—a mistake, a 'going-off-the-track', which is literally approximated by the Sanskrit concept of the 'wrong path' (*vimarga*) or 'error' (literally, 'wandering'—*bhranti*). The element of choice implicit in the English term 'heretic' but absent from the Hindu concept similarly distinguishes 'sin' from some of the more passive Sanskrit equivalents (*papa*, *moha*, *tamas*, etc.), though not, perhaps, from *adharma*, which often implies a failure of will or judgment.

The element of choice, however, re-enters the concept of heresy in some of the later bhakti cults in which individuals have a choice of action and consciously change their lives. But here, again, the choice is not entirely free—for it is conditioned by past karma, and a god must choose the worshipper (offer his love to the worshipper) as well as be chosen (worshipped). Moreover, in the mythology recorded in some bhakti Puranas, salvation, too, is sometimes thrust upon individuals, equally without their conscious agency or choice. Thus a sinner may commit all manner of sins, including robbing a temple, but be saved from the tortures

---

[ii] The Greek term was actually applied, by a Greek of the third century CE, to one form of Indian religion. In 234 CE, St Hippolytus wrote the *Refutation of All Heresies*. Portions 1.24.1-3 and 1.24.7 of this work refer to certain Brahmins who said that they had rejected 'foreign doctrine', a term that the author applies elsewhere to certain heretic sects who were influenced by Indian doctrines (see Filliozat, *Les relations extérieures de l'Inde*). As the people he described were ascetics living without women or children, it is conceivable that they might have been considered heretics by their Indian communities, but as they were called Brahmins it is more likely that they were heretics from the standpoint of the Christian author.

[iii] The association of the concept of choice with heresy is preserved in the middle Persian *varan*, related to the Sanskrit root *vr*, 'to choose', which is defined as heresy or concupiscence.

of hell because he made a new wick for the temple lamp so that he could see better to steal the offerings. In this view, salvation appears to be as accidental as heresy[iv]—though it should be noted that this view was vehemently challenged by later bhakti texts.[4] And some bhakti texts display a more dogmatic attitude towards the doctrines of heretics,[5] whom they regard as *bhavis* (worldly people), the polar opposite of *bhaktas*. But, overall, devotional sects seldom displayed the vehement disapproval of heretics that caste-oriented texts such as *The Laws of Manu* or the early Puranas manifest.

The Sanskrit term most closely corresponding in negative tone as well as in denotation to the English 'heresy' as well as 'heretic' is *pashanda* (also spelt *pakhanda* or *pashandin*), which Monier-Williams defines as '[m.] a heretic, hypocrite, impostor, anyone who falsely assumes the characteristics of an orthodox Hindu, Jaina, Buddhist, etc.; [n.] false doctrine, heresy.' The etymology of *pashanda* is obscure. A Sanskrit dictionary, the *Shabda-kalpa-druma* ('Wishing-tree of Words'), gives two etymologies that are traditional (though not supported by linguistic history): (a) 'He gains evil', from *pa(pam) san(oti)*; (b) 'They shatter [*khanda(yanti)*] the dharma of the Vedas [taking *pa* ('protection') to mean 'protection (of the dharma of the Vedas)].' This lexicographer adds that these people perform various rites opposed to the Vedas, wear several types of clothing, and bear the marks of all castes; they are Buddhists, Jains, etc. Manfred Mayrhofer suggests that *pashanda* may be derived from *parishada*, designating one around whom a group of disciples sat in a gathering.[6] If this etymology is valid,[7] the term might indicate a contrast with the Upanishads, for which a similar verbal base has been suggested—the *parishada* being the teacher around whom non-Brahmin students sat; the Upanishadic teacher being the one beside whom Brahmin students sat, or at least students who remained within the Hindu fold.

In spite of these differences of connotation, *pashanda* remains the Sanskrit term that most closely corresponds to the English 'heretic'. And, like the English term, it includes both the non-pejorative force of a 'sect' (in some early texts) and (later) the pejorative force of opinion or doctrine maintained in opposition not to any canonical authority, but to the core beliefs of ordinary pious Hindus (belief in the Vedas, the caste system).

The shift in the connotation of this term throughout its period of application supports the hypothesis of a gradual increase in intolerance. Its earliest occurrence, in the edicts of Ashoka (third century BCE), is not

---

[iv] See 'The Scrapbook'.

pejorative;[v] it merely denotes a sect or religious doctrine of any kind: 'I have arranged that some [Dhamma Mahamatas] will be occupied with the affairs of the [Buddhist] Sangha . . . some with the Brahmins and Ajivikas [another non-Vedic movement in this period] . . . some with the Nirgranthas ['Free from all Ties'; wandering ascetics, particularly Jains] . . . with other religious sects [*pasandesu*].'[8] The context does indicate that heterodox sects in particular may be denoted, and Ashoka's apparent religious toleration is challenged by a later Buddhist legend that he at first attempted to destroy all the Nirgranthas and was unwittingly responsible for the decapitation of his own brother, who was staying in the home of a Nirgrantha. But texts of the time tell us that when Ashoka learned of his error, he was profoundly saddened and issued an edict forbidding the execution of any monks, Buddhist or heretic.[9] Despite some bias and prejudice, therefore, the use of the term *pashanda* does not imply intolerance. This remained true even after Ashoka: his successor, Dasharatha, also patronized the Ajivikas.[10] But things changed over time, and in later texts the term *pashanda* is usually a pejorative term for heterodox sects.

THE TWO LEVELS OF HERESY

From a very early period, the question of heresy turned upon the acceptance of the Vedas,[11] a matter not of dogma but of ritual. The ritualistic approach to the Vedas as a touchstone of orthopraxy/heresy is clearly apparent from the writings of Kumarila Bhatta (c. 700 CE):

> Like milk that has been kept in the skin of a dog, the few statements appearing in these [heretical] texts which agree with the Vedas, such as the doctrine of non-injury, etc., are not to be believed until they are found in the *dharmashastras*; and when the meaning is clear from the *shastras*, the heretical texts have no use.[12]

Kumarila backhandedly acknowledges the earlier contribution which heretics made to a more receptive Hinduism when he refers grudgingly to 'the doctrine of non-injury, etc.'; but now the taint of heresy corrupts even the true doctrine, just as a dog pollutes a Hindu (or a cow) by his touch—indeed, sometimes by his mere shadow.[vi]

---

[v] In the *Arthashastra* too, which may draw upon texts from this period, *pashanda* sometimes has this non-pejorative force.

[vi] Kumarila rejects these 'true' bits of heretic doctrine on the same principle as that embraced by the Muslims who burnt the library at Alexandria, arguing that those texts which disagreed with the Qur'an were heretical, while those that agreed with it were redundant.

The contradiction of the Vedas remains the first criterion of heresy in the Hindu viewpoint, but this criterion may apply either to Hindus who disregard the Vedas or to people who belong to entirely separate religious traditions, such as Jains and Buddhists (who use scriptures other than the Vedas). This, coupled with the second criterion, the importance of caste (the need to obey one's own dharma, one's *svadharma*), has led to a basic distinction within the general ranks of heretics. The Hindu heretics are the members of those sects, such as the Kapalika, Kaula and Pashupata sects of Shaivism and the Pancharatra and Sahajiya sects of Vaishnavism, which pay lip service, at least, to the Vedas and thus remain technically within the Hindu fold, though they are deemed heretical on other grounds, such as the performance of rituals that involve impure substances or actions. The Jains, Sikhs and Buddhists, however, deny the Vedas and are complete outcastes. Some texts include both groups in their definition of heretics: those who carry skulls, are smeared with ashes, and wear matted locks (i.e., the Shaiva sects), as well as those who act against the Vedas (i.e., Jains and Buddhists).[13]

The division between the two sorts of heretics appears in the *Shankara-vijaya* ('Decisive Victory of Shankara') of Anandagiri (thirteenth century CE),[14] in which the Shaiva philosopher Shankara confutes heresy on both levels— the Hindu heretics (Vamacharas ['Left-hand Worshippers'] and Kapalikas) as well as Jains, Buddhists and Charvakas (Materialists, who mocked and rejected the Vedas, sacrifice and other religious rituals).[15] The Brahmin Kapalikas are heretics but can be enlightened. To the Shudra Kapalika, however, who says that there are only two castes (men and women), Shankara merely replies, 'Go where you wish. We have come to chastise Brahmins who adhere to evil doctrines, but what are your standards, you who have fallen from caste?'[16]

Various commentators on the dharma texts offer various definitions of heresy. Medhatithi, the most famous and one of the earliest of the commentators on Manu, who probably lived in the eighth or ninth century CE, glosses *pashandin* as an outcaste (perhaps Shaiva) ascetic (*bahyalingin*), one who wears a red robe, goes naked, or wanders about, etc.[17] Kulluka[vii] specifies that heretics bear marks (or the *lingam*) of vows outside the Vedas (*veda-bahya-vrata-linga-dharinah*), like Buddhist monks, Jains, etc., while Raghava merely says that they do not believe in the Vedas.[18] Vijnaneshvara defines heretics as those who have taken to an

---

[vii] Kulluka, Raghava, Vijnaneshvara and Narada all wrote commentaries on Manu, after Medhatithi.

order of life opposed to the dictates of the three Vedas,[19] or as those people known as Nagnas ('naked' [Jains]), Saugatas (Buddhists), etc., who deny the authority of the Vedas.[20] The *Tantradhikaranirnaya* (seventeenth century CE) refers to heretics born of evil wombs, who proclaim doctrines transgressing the Vedas.[21] According to the *Padma Purana* (c. 600-750 CE) heretics are those who perform non-Vedic rites as well as those who do not perform the actions enjoined by the Vedas.[22] A commentary on the *Vishnu Purana* (c. 450 CE) describes the heretic as a man who has fallen from his own dharma (his *svadharma*) and performs unlawful, prohibited acts (*vikarmastha, nishiddhakrit*).[23] The *Kurma Purana* (c. 550-800 CE) offers this list of heretics: Buddhists, Nirgranthas, Pancharatras, Kapalikas and Pashupatas.[24] When Manu mentions heretics,[25] Medhatithi interprets this as a reference to Kapalikas and those wearing red garments (probably Buddhists). Narada glosses heretics as 'Buddhists, and so forth.'[26]

Most texts, however, make a clear distinction between the two levels of heresy. The sectarian Hindu heresies are sometimes said to propound doctrines which emanate 'more or less directly from the doctrines of the original creed',[27] in spite of the fact that certain aspects of their rituals are clearly antagonistic to Vedic religion. The acceptance of these heresies is rationalized by some Hindus who consider that, although the Kapalikas, for instance, live contrary to the Vedas, they were formerly Brahmins.[28] The Hindu heresies are eager to maintain this dichotomy; a Kapalika in a Sanskrit play refers to the Jains' useless and false philosophies and evil shrines, and he wishes to cleanse his mouth (with wine, anathema to a pious Hindu) for having mentioned them.[29]

Sometimes the term 'heretic' is used in the course of vehement conflict between Vaishnava and Shaiva sectarians. One myth of this type shows with great clarity the imposition of specifically anti-Shaiva sentiments upon a typical myth of indeterminate heresy. In the first of two versions of this myth, no Shaiva is involved:

> There was a Dravidian king named Chitra, who was lustful and greedy and quick-tempered. He reviled Vishnu and hated the Vaishnavas, and he would go about saying, 'Who has ever seen this Vishnu?' He oppressed the Vaishnavas, refused to perform any Vedic ritual, and sided with the heretics. When he died, he went to hell and was tortured. Then he was reborn as a ghoul [*pishacha*], until a sage enlightened him and he found salvation.[30]

This Vaishnava text calls the king a heretic both for denying Vishnu and for failing to perform Vedic sacrifices. Another version of the same text, however, introduces a Shaiva heretic as the instrument of the king's corruption:

> There was a Dravidian king named Chitrasena, who was famous for performing Vedic rituals. One day he met some non-Vedic [*vedabahya*] heretic Shaivas who had matted hair and who smeared ashes on their bodies [i.e., Pashupatas or Kapalikas]. These Shaivas denounced the Vedas and the caste system and caused Chitrasena to abandon Vishnu and to join their sect. At their instigation, Chitrasena prohibited the worship of Vishnu in his kingdom and threw the images of Vishnu into the sea.'[31]

Although nothing is said here of the king's fate, the cause of his anti-Vaishnava behaviour is described at great length. His heresy becomes specific and more intense: he not only fails to perform rituals, but forbids them and speaks against the Vedas and caste.

The more pious sects refer to the Kapalikas and Pashupatas as heretics pure and simple,[32] but some—like Shankara, as we've seen—draw a line between Brahmin and non-Brahmin Kapalikas.[33] A similar distinction is sometimes made between 'Tantric' and 'Vedic' Pashupatas.[34] The 'Vedic' Pashupatas consider the presence of the 'Tantric' at funeral ceremonies polluting and hate even to mention them.[35] 'Vedic' Pashupatas are forbidden to talk to Shudras.[36] The *Kurma Purana*, a text of the 'Vedic' Pashupatas, describes at great length the merits of the Pashupata vow, while stating elsewhere that Pashupatas (by which one must understand Tantric Pashupatas) are wicked heretics. The text quotes Shiva himself to this effect:

> Formerly I created the Pashupata vow, auspicious, subtle, and containing the essence of the Vedas, for the sake of enlightenment. The adept should remain chaste, study the Vedas, smear his body with ashes, go naked or wear a loincloth, control his mind perfectly, and practice the Pashupata yoga . . . But there are other texts which, though narrated by me, cause delusion in this world and are contrary to the statements of the Vedas, such as the Vama [left-hand or perverse] Pashupata, the Soma, the Lakula [another Pashupata sect], and the Bhairava [Kapalika]. These doctrines are not to be practised, for they are outside the Vedas.[37]

Shiva emphasizes that his Pashupata sect is based upon the Vedas, just as he remarks, in the *Mahabharata* (c. 300 BCE to 300 CE), that the Pashupata vow that he revealed occasionally agrees with traditional *varnashrama* religion (the religion of the four *varnas*, social classes, and *ashramas*, stages of life),[viii] though it is basically contrary to that religion.[38] But Apararka,[ix] in rebutting this *Mahabharata* passage, cites a verse instructing the pious Hindu to gaze at the sun after seeing a Kapalika, Pashupata or Shaiva and to bathe after touching such a person.[39]

The dichotomy between the two groups of Pashupatas may be explained in the light of the possibility that the 'Vedic' sect, as represented by the *Pashupata Sutra* (perhaps as early as the first century CE) and its commentary by Kaundinya (in the sixth century CE), is the work of a reformer who attempted to cleanse the sect of its heterodox element,[40] the element represented by the older description of Shiva that appears in the *Mahabharata*.[41] The bowdlerized nature of the *Pashupata Sutra* is obvious: The devotee is instructed to 'pretend' to be drunk, to make indecent gestures toward women, etc., but not actually to violate any caste strictures. By this means he obtains the unjust censure of passers-by, and thereby his bad karma is transferred to them and their good karma to him.[42] Daniel H.H. Ingalls remarks, 'One suspects that the sutras concerning lechery, improper action and improper speech once referred to actions less innocent than those specified by the commentator Kaundinya.'[43] Since the whole logic of the expressed purpose of the Pashupata rites turns on this point— that the actions should seem to be more immoral than they actually are— this seems most likely. It may even be that the expected remarks of the bystanders ('This is no man of chastity, this is a lecher')[44] have reference to the original sect from which the Pashupatas were descended, a sect that conscientiously offended pious Hindus. The *Pashupata Sutra* then substituted mere symbolic gestures for the original rituals, and rationalized these as well.

The caste dichotomy within the heretic sects serves to explain certain apparently contradictory statements that may be understood in the light of the particular status and affiliation of the author of the text. Heresy, in ancient India, was in the eye of the beholder. To the Hindus as a whole, Buddhists and Jains (and Charvakas or Materialists, with whom the former two are often confused) were heretics. To many Vaishnavas, Shaivas were heretics, and to many Shaivas, Vaishnavas were heretics. Many North Indians regarded South Indians as heretics.[45] And just to round things out, some Jains regarded Hindus as heretics.[46] In short: 'I am a true believer;

[viii] See 'Three (or More)'.

[ix] Apararka, a king in the twelfth century CE, wrote a massive commentary on the dharma text of Yajnavalkya.

you are a heretic.' Hindus came to use the term 'heretic' as a useful swear word to indicate anyone who disagreed with them.

Sir Richard Burton satirized this attitude[x] in his 'translation' of the story of King Vikramaditya and the vampire.[xi] When asked to define the term 'atheist', the vampire replies:

> Of a truth, it is most difficult to explain. The sages assign to it three or four several meanings: first, one who denies that the gods exist; secondly, one who owns that the gods exist but denies that they busy themselves with human affairs; and thirdly, one who believes in the gods and in their providence, but also believes that they are easily to be set aside . . . Thus the Vishnu Swamis of the world have invested the subject with some confusion. The simple, that is to say, the mass of mortality, have confounded that confusion by reproachfully applying the word atheist to those whose opinions differ materially from their own.[47]

MATERIALISTS AND ATHEISTS

Next to the criterion of faith in the Vedas is the criterion of faith in the gods, and those who fail this test are often called 'Materialists' or 'Sceptics' or 'Atheists'—in Sanskrit, 'Lokayatas' ('worldly people') or 'Charvakas' (followers of the teachings of the philosopher Charvaka) or 'Nastikas' ('nay sayers') or 'Barhaspatyas' (from the lost text called the *Brihaspati Sutra*, attributed to Brihaspati, the mythical Machiavellian chief minister of the king of the gods). These groups, sometimes collectively described as *nastikas*, a term synonymous with heresy in India, do not really comprise a sect at all, nor are they guilty of any offensive behaviour, for they are simply products of a philosophical movement; but their philosophy condemns the Vedas as 'a pious fraud'.[48] The philosopher Madhava, in the fourteenth century, summed up the Charvaka doctrine thus: 'The Veda is tainted by the three faults of untruth, self-contradiction and tautology; the impostors who call themselves Vedic scholars are mutually destructive; and the three Vedas themselves are simply the means of livelihood for those devoid of wit and virility.'[49] Madhava accused Brihaspati of having mocked

---

[x] Burton's account may have been influenced by his reading of Plato, who (in the *Laws*, 10.885) distinguishes three impious views held by the corrupt: that the gods do not exist; that they exist but do not care for men; that they are easily bribed by offerings and prayers.
[xi] Burton produced a very loose translation of a popular Hindi text, the *Baital Pachisi* (the 'twenty-five tales of the vampire'), which was based on a Sanskrit text (the *Vetala Panchavimshati*) that is part of the eleventh-century *Kathasaritsagara*.

the Vedic ritual in which 'the sacrificed wife takes the phallus of the horse'.[50][xii]

The term *nastika* is traditionally (and probably historically) derived from the phrase '*nasti*'; a *nastika* is thus one who says 'It/he is not,' while an *astika* says 'It/he is.'[51] A *nastika* is, literally, a 'nay sayer', but that to which he says 'Nay' was regarded quite differently at different times. The subject of the copula is omitted, which has left the more precise meaning of the term open to dispute. 'It/he' may refer to a god, as in a phrase in the *Rig Veda*: 'They say of him [Indra], "He is not".'[52] In a passage in the *Katha Upanishad*, however, the unexpressed subject could refer to the *brahman/atman*: 'How can [it] be comprehended except by one saying, "[It] is"?'[53]

Indian commentators generally defined the primary meaning of *nastika* as 'atheist'—i.e., one who denies the existence of the gods. But a secondary qualification is also often included: a *nastika* believes that there is no other world nor any lord (*nasti paraloka ishvaro veti matir yasya*).[54] Finally, this definition is almost always linked with a third criterion that brings the *nastika* much closer to the heretic: the *nastika* denies the validity of the Vedas. Thus Manu refers to *nastikas* and revilers of the Vedas together,[55] and Hemacandra, a twelfth-century Jain scholar and poet, defines an *astika* as one who says, 'The lord exists,' and one who accepts the authority of the Vedas.[56] Surendranath Dasgupta suggests that the term *astikyam* originally referred to belief in the existence of another world but then came to denote 'faith in the ultimate truth being attainable only through the Vedas'.[57] Thus a *nastika* is equated with a *pashanda*;[58] a *nastika* is 'an atheist, unbeliever, one who denies the authority of the Vedas and a future life or the existence of a supreme ruler or creator of the universe', and *nastikyam* is thus 'atheism, infidelity, heresy'.[59] The great St Petersburg Sanskrit-German dictionary defines *nastika* as an 'unbeliever' (a definition which, like the Sanskrit word, leaves unspecified the actual doctrine which is not believed), but it defines an *astika* as one who believes in the truth of the tradition (*überlieferung*)—i.e., the Vedas.[60]

By these criteria, then, it is difficult, if not impossible, to distinguish the heretic from the atheist. Louis Renou remarks upon the early connection between 'the question of the *astitva* [existence or identity] of the gods—and, therefore, indirectly that of the Veda';[61] clearly, if one does not believe in the gods, one does not believe in a canon purported to have been inspired by them. Moreover, the contrast between the *nastika* and the *astika* was soon refined into a distinction between specific doctrines far more complex than simple atheism versus simple faith.

[xii] See 'Sacrifice and Substitution'.

There is disagreement upon the constituents of the *nastika* school. Traditionally, the *nastikas* are Buddhists, Jains and Charvakas, who deny both the Vedas and the *atman* of the Upanishads. According to Hemacandra, however, the *nastika* religion consists of the Barhaspatyas, Charvakas and Laukayatikas,[62] who are usually regarded as a single school, that of the Materialists. Other authorities observe yet finer distinctions: *nastikas* are of six[xiii] kinds: Charvakas, Digambaras (i.e., Jains), Madhyamikas, Yogacharas, Sautrantikas and Vaibhashikas (four great Buddhist schools).[63] In spite of these differences, it is apparent that the broad distinction between *astikas* and *nastikas* corresponds in application, if not always in theory, to that which came to distinguish the pious Hindu from the heretic (*pashanda*).

According to Jan C. Heesterman, the *nastika* or atheist was originally an integral part of the agonistic structure of the Vedic sacrifice, in which poets competed with one another, using riddles, poems and philosophical arguments—while patrons competed in chariot races—and parts of the ritual took the form of arguments in which the atheist or *nastika* might state one view, only to be rebutted by a theist or *astika*.[64] Many of the doubts expressed in the *Rig Veda*[65] are merely part of the verbal contest with the official 'reviler',[66] who does not reject sacrifice as a matter of abstract doctrine but merely rejects his *opponent*'s sacrifice. Later, however, these complementary ritual roles gave way to mutually exclusive doctrines, one of which denied the abstract institution of sacrifice.[67] As precise terms denoting opposition within the structure give way to imprecise pejoratives directed toward outsiders, we see the handiwork of the Brahmins closing ranks, drawing a sharper boundary between people within the Vedic fold and those who posed a challenge to it.

Thereafter, the *nastika* remained on the fringes of Hinduism. In the *Mahabharata*, Yudhishthira, whose ideas of nonviolence owe much to Buddhism, is accused by the warrior Bhima of having *nastika* tendencies.[68] An early mockery of *nastika* views appears in the *Ramayana* (c. 200 BCE to 200 CE) when the sage Jabali urges Rama to ignore family obligations and live for pleasure alone, and offers this argument:

> People here busy themselves because 'It is the Eighth Day, the rite for the ancestors'. But just look at the waste of food—what really is a dead man going to eat? And if something one person eats here could fill the belly of someone else, one could simply offer *shraddha* [the offering to

the ancestors] for a traveller, and he would need no provisions for the road. It was only as a charm to secure themselves donations that cunning men composed those books that tell us, 'Sacrifice, give alms, sanctify yourself, practise asceticism, renounce.' Accept the idea once and for all, high-minded prince, that there exists no world to come.'[69]

Jabali may merely be acting as the devil's advocate, to stir Rama into righteous indignation (which is precisely what happens), or he may mean it. In either case, his argument is what the 'Materialists' in non-Materialist Sanskrit texts (there are very few surviving Materialist texts) are always said to say.

HERESY BASED UPON THE VEDAS

In most cases, the subtle distinction between the two levels of heresy hinges upon a sect's actual or professed relationship to the Vedas. But there is danger of contradiction and confusion when the touchstone of the Vedas is applied to potential heresies. Certain Tantric sects that say that they agree with the Vedas, though actually propounding anti-Vedic, or at least non-Vedic, doctrines, may be accepted on the basis of their own statements of conformity. On the other hand, doctrines that, like Buddhism, maintain that they are not derived from Vedas, though they agree in fact with many essentials of mainstream Hinduism, are rejected. This situation is made possible by Hindu orthopraxy; one might commit almost any act or believe almost any doctrine, as long as one professes allegiance to the Vedas.

The complications arising from this point of view are apparent in Kumarila's discussion of certain heretics' claims to follow doctrines based upon the Vedas or upon a 'lost' branch of the Vedas:

> The Sankhyayoga, Pancharatra, Pashupata, Buddhist and Jain teachings have a very little bit in common with the Vedas and lawbooks [shruti and smriti], such as the doctrines of non-injury, speaking truth, control of the senses, charity and pity; [but these doctrines occur only occasionally and incidentally], just as herbs and mantras occasionally succeed in curing and expelling poison; and [they occur in small proportion] like [much] water fragrant with [a little] perfume. Their major portion consists in other teachings, outcaste texts mixed with barbarian practices; and since they contradict the Vedas and are sceptical [haituka], they are not to be accepted. Even if these sects were based upon a lost branch of the Vedas, they are to be rejected, for they do not

themselves accept the fact that the Vedas are the basis [of their teachings], just as an evil son who hates his parents is ashamed to admit his descent from them.

With the exception of a few doctrines like self-control and charity, the teachings of the Buddhists, etc., are altogether contradictory to the teachings of the Vedas and were composed by the Buddha and others like him whose behaviour is contradictory to the Vedas; they were then taught to people beyond the pale of the Vedas, people who do not follow the rules of the four *varnas*, and it is thus inconceivable that they could be based upon the Vedas. These are heretics who perform unlawful acts and produce sceptical arguments.[70]

Here Kumarila rejects, among other arguments, the 'lost Vedas' theory of the origin of heterodoxy. And he includes in his list not only the usual suspects but Sankhya-yoga, a philosophical school rather than a sect.

The *Matta-vilasa-prahasana* of Mahendra Varman, a seventh-century play, similarly satirizes the 'lost Vedas' theory as it appears in the mouth of a corrupt Buddhist monk:

Why did [the Buddha] not think of sanctioning the possession of women and the drinking of *sura* [liquor]? Since he knew everything, it must be that the small-minded and spiteful Elders, envying us young men, erased the sanction of women and *sura* in the books of the *pitaka* [the Buddhist canon]. Where now can I find an uncorrupted original text?[71]

Thus, the mainline view, which was well established by the time of Kumarila, rejects both levels of heresy in spite of their partial affinity with Vedic doctrine.

THE HYPOCRITICAL ASCETIC

Popular Hinduism, as it appears in the Puranic texts, does not maintain a strict or even a consistent attitude toward the various Indian heresies. Confusions of doctrine are further complicated by a tendency to equate the heretic with another religious figure well known to the lawbooks and myths: the hypocritical ascetic. The Sanskrit dictionaries themselves maintain this confusion. V.S. Apte gives 'hypocrite' as a secondary meaning of *pashanda*,[72] and Monier-Williams includes in his definition of this term 'any one who falsely assumes the characteristics of an orthodox Hindu, a Jaina, Buddhist, ib &c.[sic].'[73] The *Maitrayaniya Upanishad* juxtaposes the hypocrite and the heretic: 'There are those who falsely wear the red robe, earrings and skulls. And moreover, there are others who wish to erect themselves as judges concerning Vedic matters by weaving illusions with logic, illustrations and sophisms.'[74]

The term *nagna* ('naked') was originally applied to the Buddhists and Jains, who were 'clothed in the sky'(*digambara*), that is, nude. But certain Hindu sects went naked as well, while most Buddhists did not, and the term was later interpreted metaphorically as the rejection of what Horace Hayman Wilson called 'the raiment of holy writ'.[75] Thus, the *Vayu Purana* extends the word to naked Brahmins who 'practise austerities fruitlessly, that is, heretically or hypocritically', and adds: 'The Brahmin who falsely bears a staff, shaves his head, goes naked, undertakes a vow, or mutters prayers—all such persons are called 'Nagnas', etc.'[76]

No particular sect is mentioned in most of the examples of this genre, which is based not so much upon doctrinal offences as upon the deep-seated anti-ascetic as well as anti-Brahmin tradition in mainstream Hinduism.[77] Even the *Rig Veda* satirizes Brahmins who croak like frogs[78] and priests greedy for gold.[79] The ascetic's position was further weakened by the practice of kings, from the time of the Mauryan Empire at least, who employed as their spies both[xiv] heretics and men who masqueraded as ascetics.[80] That this tradition has persisted for more than two thousand years is apparent from suspicions of similar practices in recent times, for example the accusation made in 1968 by a member of the Indian Parliament who charged that the United States Pentagon and the CIA were infiltrating into the Himalayas with spies disguised as yogis.[81]

Shaiva ascetics are particularly liable to this kind of satire. The charlatan Kapalika in the *Shankaravijaya* has adopted the character of an ascetic as an excuse for throwing off all social and moral restraint.[82] The Kapalika in the *Mattavilasa* consorts with a female member of the sect in a *sura* bar that he likens to a sacrificial temple: The *sura* is the mythical elixir, the drunks are the priests, the drunken cries the hymns and the bartender the sacrificial sponsor.[83] But the folk motif of the hypocritical ascetic should not be taken as a literal index of the existence of such figures, for the motif is a naturally attractive and humorous one, throughout India and far beyond. Mockery, and even self-mockery, rather than fanatical disapproval is the motivating spirit of many Indian discussions of the religious hypocrite:

[xiv] The commentator on this particular verse interprets *munda* as a reference to Shakyas, Ajivakas, etc., and *jatila* as a reference to Pashupatas etc.; he thus includes both types of heretics

'So, friar [*bhiksho*], I see you have a taste for meat.'
'Not that it's any good without some wine.'
'You like wine too, then?' 'Better when I dine
With pretty harlots.' 'Surely such girls eat
No end of money.' 'Well, I steal, you see,
Or win at dice.' 'A thief and gambler, too?'
'Why, certainly. What else is there to do?
Aren't you aware I'm vowed to poverty?'[84]

The extensive anti-ascetic folklore of India is probably the source of animal nicknames given to religious hypocrites.[85] The *Vishnu Purana* excoriates 'heretics . . . by whom the three Vedas have been abandoned, evil ones who dispute the doctrine of the Vedas, . . . those who perform evil rituals, hypocritical 'cat' ascetics, sceptical 'heron' ascetics. These are the evil heretics, men who falsely wear matted locks or shave their heads.'[86] The commentator notes that the 'cat' ascetic seems pleasant at first but then acts very unpleasantly; the 'heron' is a rogue who is falsely polite. Manu similarly defines the 'cat' as one who is covetous, deceitful, injurious and hypocritical; the 'heron' is cruel, dishonest and falsely gentle. Manu does not refer to these two types as heretics, however, but merely as Brahmins, and he groups them with those who have sinned and hide their sins under a pretext of asceticism.[87] Yajnavalkya states that one should avoid hypocrites, sceptics, heretics and those who act like herons.[88] The heron appears in a Sanskrit court poem:

The ugly vulture eats the dead,
Guiltless of murder's taint.
The heron swallows living fish
And looks like an ascetic saint.[89]

The cat ascetic appears on the famous seventh-century bas-relief of the Descent of the Ganga at Mamallapuram; the cat stands on one leg with his paws above his head in imitation of the human ascetic who appears nearby, and he is surrounded by mice.[90] The *Markandeya Purana* omits any explicit reference to heresy but groups the 'cat' ascetics with those who retire to the woods like ascetics but continue to enjoy 'country pleasures' [*gramya-bhujan*] and those who have fallen from the rituals appropriate to their *varna*—one of the usual criteria of heresy.[91] The *Kurma Purana* lists 'cat' ascetics with heretics who perform evil rites, and the left-hand Pancharatras and Pashupatas. An alternative reading substitutes for 'cat' ascetics (*vaidala-vratinah*) Dalit ascetics (*chandala-vratinah*)—the polar opposites of Brahmin hypocrites.[92] The cat also appears in the *Tantropakhyana*:

A certain cat lived like an ascetic at the entrance to a mouse-hole, eating fallen fruits and leaves as if he had refrained from all sins. The mice made pious circumambulations around him and the cat grabbed and ate the last of the mice returning to the hole each day. The mice, noticing that their number was diminishing, decided to test the cat by sending a mouse named Romasha ('Hairy') to the cat, who ate him. When the rest of the mice saw the bones and hair of Romasha in the faeces of the cat they went to him and said: 'This is not virtue or proper behaviour, to make a living by performing *tapas*. Hairy faeces do not come from one who eats roots and fruits.' And so, after calling the cat a hypocrite and a heretic, the mice went away.[93]

It may be noted here that even in the folk literature the confusion between hypocrisy and heresy persists.

THE ASSIMILATION OF HERESY AND THE MYTH OF THE FALL

The fact that doctrines so widely divergent as those of the Charvakas, Buddhists, Shaiva Pashupatas, Dalit ascetics and Brahmin hypocrites are all subsumed under the term 'heretic' indicates the extent to which this term was used simply as a catchall to condemn anyone who challenged the religious and social status quo, that is, the authority of the Vedas and the Brahmins. But the vagueness of the term for heresy served not only to exclude various groups of heterodox thinkers but also to *include* many of them under the equally vague aegis of Hinduism itself. The general moral relativity of caste ethics—the notion that different moral codes apply to different social groups—also facilitated an infinitely elastic toleration of religious doctrinal deviation. If the bounds of heterodoxy ballooned over into the mainstream of religion, so, too, the bounds of orthopraxy proved extremely malleable.

Various non-Vedic rites practiced by the indigenous population of India were absorbed by Vedic religion and practised 'without incongruity or contradiction being felt by the participant'.[94] Sir Charles Eliot was surprised to find, almost a century ago, that although certain Shaiva rites were 'if not antagonistic, at least alternative to the ancient sacrifices, yet far from being forbidden they are performed by Brahmans, and modern Indian writers describe Shiva as peculiarly the Brahman's god'.[95] As the heretical sects were willing to make compromises in order to be accepted in traditional circles, so too these circles willingly stretched a point in order to accept the prodigal movements back into the fold. One of the texts cited in justification for this viewpoint is the *Bhagavad Gita*, in which Krishna says that those who worship other gods[xv] are actually worshipping him.[96] Eventually, even Parsis and Muslims were allowed to qualify as Hindus under certain circumstances.[97] This tradition continued well into the twentieth century, for, according to a 1966 ruling, a Hindu might even become a baptized Christian 'without ceasing to be a Hindu in both social and spiritual terms'.[98]

By this process of assimilation, many non-Brahmin ministers of non-Vedic cults, such as the Vratyas, came to claim Brahmin status and were finally admitted to that status but with the stigma that 'they had committed sins'. Kapalikas are said to have been Brahmins in former times.[99] The *Mahabharata* tells us that all castes were once Brahmins, but those who abandoned their own dharma and fell prey to passion and anger became Kshatriyas, those who took to agriculture and cattle-rearing became Vaishyas, and those who indulged in falsehood and injury became Shudras.[100] (On the other hand, according to Jain theory all castes once professed Jainism, but certain groups fell into false ways and became Brahmins who formulated a cult sanctioning the slaughter of animals.[101]) According to one myth, certain 'Brahmin giants' were Brahmins who had been turned into giants as a punishment for former crimes: 'Occasionally they adopted a hermit's life, without thereby changing their character, or becoming better disposed.'[102] In this myth, the 'fallen Brahmin' plays the role of the hypocritical ascetic.

The belief that impure status is the result of former crimes is widespread in India. Certain scriptures were said to have been revealed for the benefit of Brahmins whose sins had rendered them incapable of performing Vedic rites.[103] Even Manu considered the Yavanas [Greeks], Pahlavas [Persians], Kiratas [Indian tribal people], and other foreigners to be Shudras who had sunk from their former status as Kshatriyas when they disregarded Brahmins.[104] Similar reasoning allowed certain eighteenth-century Hindus to speak of the English as 'fallen Kshatriyas'. This theory completely mirrors the historical process; sects that had in fact risen to their position on the borders of Hinduism were said to have fallen from a yet more respectable position to their ambivalent status.

Yet, there is probably some truth in the legends as well. Brahmins who were excommunicated may have become the ministers of non-Vedic cults.[105] Certainly this is the Hindu viewpoint. Many castes consider themselves fallen Brahmins and justify their change of occupation when

---

[xv] See 'Are Hindus Monotheists?' and 'The Toleration of Intolerance'.

they move up the scale by stating that they are merely resuming their former status, often a part of the process that M.N. Srinivas called 'Sanskritization'.[106] Ambedkar revived the traditional myth when he argued that the Dalits, and many Shudras, were Buddhists who had suffered from the hatred of Brahmins in the nineteenth century when the reform movements of the so-called Hindu renaissance occurred.[107] Many Dalits claim in their myths that, when fighting the Muslims, their Kshatriya ancestors pretended to be Dalits and were cursed to remain in that state as punishment for their cowardice.[108] This 'pretence' neatly mirrors the Pashupata mime which may be a censored version of an actual sin, in contrast with the Dalit legend in which the pretence leads to the sin.

EXPLICIT HERESY WITHIN HINDUISM

In spite of, or perhaps because of, the conservative strength of the Brahmins, heretical doubts are raised in the mainstream of traditional Hinduism from the earliest records. Atheistic sentiments are expressed within the *Rig Veda* itself[xvi]: 'Whence this creation developed is known only by him who witnesses this world in the highest heaven—or perhaps even he does not know.'[109] In the *Rig Veda*, again, Vasishtha defends himself against charges of being a heretic or a sceptic: 'If I were a follower of false gods, or if I regarded the gods wrongly . . .'[110] Anti-Vedic ideas appear frequently in the Upanishads and Aranyakas, composed between about 600 and 400 BCE. In the *Aitareya Aranyaka*, certain sages remark: 'Why should we study the Vedas? Why should we sacrifice?'[111] The *Bhagavad Gita* considers the Vedas as much use to a wise Brahmin as a water tank in a flood.[112] And we have already encountered the 'Materialist' sage Jabali in the *Ramayana*.

A famous controversy over the sanctity of the Vedas appears in the *Nirukta* of Yaska, in the fifth century BCE: '"The Vedic stanzas have no meaning [*anarthaka*]," says Kautsa . . . "Moreover, their meaning is contradictory [*vipratishiddhartha*]."'[113] A later commentator, Durga, regarded Kautsa as a convenient invention used by Yaska in order to express Vedic scepticism.[114] But Kautsa appears in an ancient list of Brahmin teachers and may have been a historical rationalist.[115] Lakshman Sarup argues in support of the latter view: 'It is inconceivable that the learned theologians would reproduce, in their orthodox books, a controversy which challenges the most fundamental beliefs of their religion.'[116] Yet this is precisely what

---

[xvi] See 'You Can't Get Here'.

theologians in India have always done; the 'false' view is given first and is then rebutted by the favoured doctrine. Moreover, many originally controversial views have eventually been reproduced in authoritative books as accepted doctrine.

From Vedic times to the present day, heresy has been present within Hinduism. Politically, heresy has played a significant role; heretical creeds appealed to kings for assistance, and Brahmins called upon royal support for the status quo.[117] Various law books state that the king must support the customs of heretics.[118] As K.V.R. Aiyangar remarks: 'The heretic might be a nuisance, but an administrator could not ignore his existence in society, especially when he had a powerful following . . . Heterodoxy was often believed to possess a mystic power which was the source of its confidence. The rule is thus merely one of prudence.'[119] Baudhayana cites the view that non-Vedic local practices may be allowed in their own territory, but he immediately counters with his own opinion that one must never follow practices opposed to the tradition of learned authorities.[120]

From the Ashokan use of the term *pashanda* to designate any sect, the situation changed so that by the time of the *Mahabharata* the term had acquired definitely pejorative overtones.[121] Most of the law books remained unbendingly opposed to all forms of heresy. This bias is clear from many of the definitions of heresy and from such statements as Manu's 'Let not the householder honour . . . heretics'[122] and Yajnavalkya's 'One should avoid . . . heretics.'[123] Yajnavalkya[124] and Narada[125] disqualify heretics and atheists as witnesses. Kautilya, in his *Arthashastra*, allows the king to confiscate the property of heretics in an emergency[126] and advises him to fine people who entertain Shakyas, Ajivikas or fake ascetics [*vrishala-pravrajita*] at feasts of the gods or the ancestors.[127] This attitude grew more and more strict in later Hinduism. The *Saura Purana* says that Charvakas, Buddhists, Jains, Yavanas [Greeks], Kapalikas and Kaulas should not be allowed to enter a kingdom,[128] and the late text of the *Shukra-niti-sara* exhorts the king to punish atheists and those who have fallen from caste.[129]

By the tenth century CE, heresy was so widespread and so threatening to Brahmins that Shiva himself—whom (as we have seen) some texts credited with the creation of Shaiva heretics—was said to have become incarnate as the philosopher Shankara in order to explain the Vedas, destroy the temples and books of the Jains, and massacre all who opposed him,[130] particularly the followers of the Jain sect that, as we shall soon see, he himself had invented in his previous incarnation.[131]

In the *Prabodhachandrodaya* ('The Rise of Wisdom Moon'), a remarkable allegorical play written in the eleventh century by Krishna Mishra, the heresies themselves, personified, attempt the corruption of Hinduism in order to preserve their own race:

> Hypocrisy [*Dambha*] enters and says, 'Great Delusion [*Mahamoha*] has commanded me thus: Discrimination [*Viveka*] and his ministers have sent Tranquillity, Self-control and the others to various holy shrines in order to encourage Enlightenment (*Prabodha*). The destruction of our race is imminent and you must take pains to prevent it. Go to the city of Benares, the place on earth where moksha is obtained, and obstruct the welfare of those who follow the four stages of life.'[132]

And for a while, they succeed. But then there is a great battle between good and evil, proper Hinduism and heresy: 'The Pashandas placed the Lokayatas in front, because they conflicted with the other traditions, and they perished in the fight. After this defeat, the Pashanda texts were uprooted by the sea of correct teachings [*sad-agama*]; the Digambara [Jain] Pashandas, Kapalikas and others concealed themselves among the most abject men in the countries of Panchala, Malava, etc.'[133] The very vehemence of such texts hints at the strength of the threat, the degree to which heresy had penetrated Hinduism by this time. Much of the assimilation took place in an earlier, more tolerant period, and more continued to take place on a popular level—as expressed in the mythology of the Puranas—in spite of the exhortations of the Brahmins.

HERESY CREATED BY THE GODS

We have noted texts that argue that Shiva created the Shaiva heresies; and there are important myths that argue that Vishnu, too, created heresies. Why would the gods do such a thing? Sometimes, through sheer inadequacy. In the *Parashara Purana*, heresy arises through the mistaken ideas of the sectarian gods Vishnu and Brahma:

> Brahma and Vishnu were arguing, each shouting that he was supreme. In anger, Brahma cursed Vishnu: 'You will be deluded and your devotees will have the appearance of Brahmins, but they will be against the Vedas and the true path to release. They will be Tantric Brahmins, initiated into the Pancharatra, ever averse to the Vedas, law-books and the proper rituals that give release.'[134]

Other texts blame heresy not on the inadvertent fallout of flawed gods, but on divine intention. The *Linga Purana* attributes to a god the explicit wish to make the universe ambivalent by means of heresy as well as evil fortune (Alakshmi):

> Narayana made the universe twofold for the sake of delusion. He made the Brahmins, Vedas and the goddess Shri, and this was the best portion. Then he made Alakshmi and the lowest men, outside the Vedas, and he made *adharma*. When the goddess Jyeshtha ('the Eldest', goddess of misfortune) appeared from the ocean, the sage Markandeya said, 'Jyeshtha is Alakshmi. She must dwell far from where men follow the path of the Vedas and worship Narayana and Rudra. But she may enter wherever husband and wife quarrel, wherever there are people who delight in heretical practices and are beyond the pale of the Vedas, wherever there are atheists and hypocrites, Buddhists or Jains.'[135]

A similar explanation is given for the origin of the 'left-hand' Visaraga sect: 'Formerly Prajapati, in order to conceal [the true] teaching, created the branch of the Visaragas, which deluded even the Munis [silent sages], let alone ordinary men.'[136]

The statement that Prajapati acted 'in order to conceal' the true doctrine does not satisfactorily explain his motivation; but this may be implicit in the context of Hindu texts that argue for the necessity of evil and/or the hostility of the gods toward human virtue.[137] There are many early texts dealing with the basic disinclination of the gods to allow crowds in heaven. The *Shatapatha Brahmana* states that the gods, having conquered heaven, tried to make it unattainable by men; they drained the sacrificial sap and concealed themselves.[138]

In the Puranas, Vishnu uses books of heresy to thin out the ranks of heaven:

> Formerly, the inhabitants of the earth all worshipped Vishnu and reached heaven, filling the place of moksha. The gods complained, 'How will creation take place, and who will dwell in hell?' Vishnu assured them that in the Kali Age[xvii] he would create a great delusion, causing Shiva to teach the Nyaya Siddhanta and Pashupata shastras in order to delude those outside the path of the Vedas.[139]

The Pancharatras, in keeping with the usual sectarian biases of this motif, have their own version:

> The original religion (*adhyadharma*, to wit the Pancharatra) was first in the Krita age proclaimed by god Brahma to the sages of sharpened vows, who taught it to their disciples. All people followed the Pancharatra and were liberated or went to heaven; hell became naught

xvii See 'Three (or More)'.

and a great decrease of creation took place [*srishti-kshayo mahan asit*]. [Brahma complained to Vishnu,] 'All men, being full of faith and masters of their senses, sacrifice as prescribed in the Great Secret; and so they go to the Place of Vishnu from which there is no return. There is (now) no heaven and no hell, neither birth nor death.' This, however, was against the plan of the Lord, and so He started, with the help of Brahma, Kapila and Shiva, five more systems (Yoga, Sankhya, Bauddha, Jaina and Shaiva), conflicting with each other and the Pancharatra, for the bewilderment of men.[140]

In spite of their obvious axes to grind, these myths demonstrate an underlying assumption that it is not good for everyone to go to heaven. A peculiar example of this line of thought may be seen in the episode in which the mountain Himalaya, personified as a king, becomes so devoted to Shiva that he is about to leave earth and go to heaven. This would deprive the earth of all the valuable gems and magic herbs of which Himalaya is the prime source, and to prevent this Shiva himself comes to Himalaya, disguised as a Vaishnava Brahmin, and reviles himself just enough to make Himalaya lose his pure devotion and remain on earth.[141]

A similar episode occurs in the *Mahabharata*:

> Formerly, all creatures were virtuous, and by themselves they obtained divinity. Therefore the gods became worried, and so Brahma created women in order to delude men. Now women, formerly virtuous, became wicked witches by the will of Brahma, who filled them with wanton desires that they in turn inspired in men. He created anger, and henceforth all creatures were born in the power of desire and anger.[142]

Here, as so often in Hindu mythology, women are the root of evil, though in this case, not through their own fault.

TANTRIC HERESIES IN THE KALI AGE

A very different explanation is offered by the many myths that present heresy as the first step to salvation for those who are not yet capable of proceeding on the higher paths. This is the philosophy underlying certain rationalizations of Tantric religion: it is the path for those incapable of higher (Vedic) religion. Exponents of Vedic religion acknowledge the difficulty of understanding the Vedas: Vishnu, knowing that the Vedas were difficult to grasp, became incarnate as Vyasa Vitapasha and divided the Vedas into branches.[143]

So, too, the Tantras are said to be useful even for those who are excessively evil. Those who abandon the Vedas will be initiated into the Pancharatra, Kapala and other heresies.[144] For men of the Kali Age, ostracized from Vedic rituals, the late Puranas recommend the use of Tantric texts: people fallen from Vedic rites and afraid of Vedic penances should resort to the Tantras;[145] the Pancharatras, Vaikhanasas and Bhagavatas use Tantric texts written for people who have fallen from the Vedas.[146] The *Kurma Purana* tells of a King Sattvata, a Vaishnava, whom Narada prompted to teach a doctrine suitable for bastard sons of married women and widows, for their welfare.[147]

What may thus appear as a doctrine that allows immorality to members of a religion is presented in these texts more as a doctrine that allows religion even to those who are, in the eyes of other members of their religion, immoral. Thus, the *Kurma Purana* remarks that each man worships a divinity who appeals to him.[148] Blood-drinking anti-gods excuse themselves on the grounds that evil acts and sexual faults in their past have given them a nature unfit for higher action,[149] thus justifying immorality by immorality.[150] In many Sanskrit texts, Shudras and the victims of curses are forbidden to study the Vedas; certain others are incapable. Out of pity for all of them, Shiva teaches heresy, raising them up 'step by step'. A similar concept of 'weaning' was expounded by a British apologist for the Tantras: 'Shiva knowing the animal propensity of their common life must lead them to take flesh and wine, prescribed these [Tantric] rites with a view to lessen the evil and to gradually wean them from enjoyment by promulgating conditions under which alone such enjoyment could be had, and in associating it with religion. "It is better to bow to Narayana with one's shoes on than never to bow at all."'[151]

The Tantras are particularly suited for people of the Kali Age, the age of darkness, who are so stupid that they can neither understand nor appreciate the Vedas. People fallen from Vedic rites and afraid of Vedic penances should resort to the Tantras.[152] Such texts should not be used, however, by good men; the steps go down as well as up, and the gods often use them to bring good men down, just as they use them to bring heretics back to the Vedic fold.[153]

This argument—that only lowly men should follow heretical texts—is somewhat undercut by another argument which states that in the Kali Age, the present age, all men have fallen below the spiritual level necessary for Vedic religion and must proceed by the 'stairs' of heresy. This doctrine, which is foreshadowed in the Brahmanas (800 to 600 BCE),[154] is fully developed only in much later texts. It is significant that Shiva is said to be the god of the Kali Age,[155] as this is the age in which the Shaiva heresies flourish. In the Kali Age, Brahmins and Kshatriyas become Vamas, Pashupatas and Pancharatras;[156] Shudras become heretic ascetics,[157] shaving their heads, wearing ochre robes and propounding false doctrines;[158] Kapalikas are omnipresent;[159] and all kinds of heresy are rampant.[160] Shudra kings support heretics, who teach evil rituals and sell the Vedas;[161] men become heretics, thinking themselves wise.[162] Under the influence of the Kali Age, humans by their nature become wicked and inclined to all sins.[163] In fact, the degree to which the Kali Age is upon us may be measured precisely by the degree to which heresy thrives.[164] Two interesting arguments develop from the premise of the natural wickedness of humans in the Kali Age. One is the doctrine of the Kalivarjya, or the actions, such as widow remarriage, which, though previously acceptable, are only to be considered immoral in the present Kali Age, when people are not strong enough to indulge in them without ill effect. By this reasoning, a higher level of morality is to be striven for, since humans themselves are lower. Another inversion of values appears in the *Vishnu Purana* statement that the Kali Age is the best because by a small effort one will win the merit that would require great *tapas* in the Krita Age.[165] Wilson considers that this is not said in irony, but is taken literally by the commentator, who interprets it as an allusion to the worship of Krishna; here the 'easiest' path is equated with the best.

A third argument exalts the Kali Age because it is the last stage before the return to the Krita Age, the first Age, the Golden Age. At the end of the Kali Age, Vishnu will come as Kalki, riding on a white horse, and he will uproot the barbarians and heretics and usher in the golden age again.[166] Here the cyclic nature of evil becomes apparent.[167] Individuals prone to evil may be cursed to become so evil that they must eventually reform. Humankind may be delivered from the sins of the Kali Age only by being corrupted so completely by heresy that true enlightenment is the only possible consequence. This cyclic effect may be seen in a Buddhist myth of evil in the *Digha Nikaya*:

> When virtue is at its lowest ebb, there will not even be a word for good, let alone good deeds. Then for Seven Days of the Sword, men will look on each other as wild beasts and kill each other. But a few will think: 'We do not want anyone to kill us, and we do not want to kill anyone. Let us hide and live on the fruits of the forest.' Thus they will survive. And after the Seven Days of the Sword they will come out

and embrace one another and say, 'My friend, how good it is to see you still alive. We have lost so many of our kinsfolk because we took to evil ways; now we must do good. We must stop taking life.' Then they will increase in age and beauty and virtue. India will be as crowded then as purgatory is now.[168]

And so the next cycle begins with overcrowding on earth or in heaven.

Optimistic reformers might think it possible to hasten this inevitable turning point in the cycle of evil, and indeed Manu states that the king, by his good or bad behaviour, produces the character of the Kali or Krita Age, not vice versa.[169] Similarly, the *Arthashastra* suggests that the king, by maintaining the code of the Vedas, may cause the world to progress and not to perish.[170] But there is a Hindu myth, in which Kali,[xviii] the spirit of the Kali Age, is personified, that warns against the dangers inherent in this challenge to cosmic order:

> The anti-god Bali, ruling in the Kali Age, protected the universe with great virtue. When Kali saw this he sought refuge with Brahma, for his own nature was being obstructed. Brahma said, 'Bali has destroyed the nature of the whole universe, not merely your nature.' Then Kali went to a forest, and the Krita Age took place; asceticism, non-injury, truth and sacrifice pervaded the world. Indra complained that his kingdom had been taken; Vishnu conquered Bali and made him rule in hell.[171]

Underlying the doctrine of individual karma (for Indra must expiate his own former sins and transfer them to a savage tribe before Bali can be overcome)[172] is the deeper need for the karma of the universe, for evil to come when it is ripe. The myth then continues with a version of the well-known avatar of Vishnu as the Dwarf who tricks the anti-god Bali.[xix]

The corrupting and heretical nature of the Kali Age is expressed in the *Mahabharata* tale of Nala, in which Kali is again personified:

> The virtuous king Nala married Damayanti, whom Kali had wanted to marry, and Kali determined to break Nala and take Damayanti from him. For twelve years, Kali waited in Nala's presence, and finally he found an opportunity: Nala urinated at twilight and did not wash his feet. Then Kali entered Nala and caused him to lose his kingdom at gambling and to desert Damayanti. After many years, Nala mastered

---

[xviii] Not to be confused with the goddess Kali (whose name has, in Sanskrit, a long 'a' and 'i', where the Kali of the Kali Age has two short vowels).
[xix] See 'You Can't Get Here' and 'The Scrapbook'.

the science of numbers and dice, and Kali came out of his body and resumed his own form. When Kali was destroyed, Nala was free of fever.[173]

Here Kali is the incarnation of loss in gambling, for the *kali* throw is 'snake-eyes', the lowest throw of the dice. But Kali is also the incarnation of the heretic, who stands ready to invade the soul of a good man in a careless moment.

Later texts elaborate upon this myth. The *Kathasaritsagara* (from eleventh-century Kashmir) describes Nala's moral degradation at greater length, making him a drunkard and an adulterer as well as a gambler.[174] The twelfth-century *Naisadhacarita* of Shri Harsha attributes to Kali specific heresies:

> On the way to the wedding of Nala and Damayanti, the gods encountered the army of Kali. His generals were Desire, Anger, Greed, Delusion and others. A Charvaka in the ranks mocked the gods, citing various Buddhist doctrines. Indra became angry and called Kali's troops atheists; Yama called them materialists [Lokayatas], while Varuna called them heretics and atheists. Kali stood there surrounded by evils. When Kali determined to take Damayanti from Nala, he was at first unable to enter the city, because of Nala's virtues. He looked in vain for heretics, Jains or Buddhists in the city. At last he found an opportunity, and he entered Nala . . .[175]

The *Mahabharata* tale of a hero's moral dilemma is thus embroidered with traditional Puranic descriptions of the heresies of the Kali Age.

THE BUDDHA AVATAR OF VISHNU IN THE GUPTA AGE

It is inevitable that the universe should be destroyed at the end of the Kali Age, and for god to destroy us he must first weaken us with sin, just as he must corrupt the anti-gods with heresy before he can destroy them. It must be done, and only god can do it. Only god is great enough to undertake the responsibility for the creation of heresy.

This concept underlies the myth of the Buddha avatar of Vishnu. In this myth,[176] the enemies of the gods—the anti-gods, *asuras*—have become so powerful that they take over the three worlds, and the gods are helpless against them because the *asuras* are protected by the armour of the Vedic religion which they practice religiously. In order to conquer them, the gods must corrupt them, and they do this by persuading Vishnu to descend to earth in the form of the Buddha and convert the anti-gods away from

Vedic religion. In some of the many versions of this myth, the Great Delusion (*Mahamoha*) that Vishnu preaches is Jainism, or a casual mixture of Buddhism and Jainism, or a form of Tantrism. The deluded *asuras*, demonic heretics, then become, or convert, human Buddhists, Jains and Tantrics.

The myth of the Buddha avatar, the most important of the anti-Buddhist myths of this period, first appears in the *Vishnu Purana*, composed between 400 and 500 CE[177] under the Gupta Dynasty. The Guptas ruled all of North India and much of South India, from 320 to 550 CE, ending a long interregnum (after the fall of the Mauryan dynasty in 185 BCE) in which foreign dynasties from Central Asia, such as the Shakas (Scythians) and Kushanas, had ruled in India. The Guptas, though Hindus, also patronized the Buddhists, manipulating them with their patronage; in the Puranic texts composed by Brahmins in this period, the gods corrupt and destroy Buddhists. The religious enemies in these myths, the anti-god heretics of the Kali Age, are often disguised as 'foreigners' (*mlechas*); in this way, a myth of political extermination was crudely superimposed upon a myth of theological conflict.

As the net of heresy was cast more and more vehemently, to catch an ever-growing school of dissenters, the myth of the Buddha avatar of Vishnu became so well established that it served as the model for pseudo-historical writings. The *Skanda Purana* relates that, at the beginning of the Kali Age, and under the influence of monks known as *kshapanas* (i.e., Jains), the people of King Ama's kingdom renounced their Vaishnava faith and became followers of the Buddhist dharma. The king's daughter was influenced by the Jivika (*sic*; Ajivika?) named Indrasuri (the name of a famous Jain author), and the people followed the Jain teaching and disregarded the Brahmins. King Ama was surrounded by heretics and refused to shelter Brahmins who were deprived of their villages, for he considered them guilty of injury (*himsa*) in their animal sacrifices.[178]

The outline of this story, and many of its details, follow the classical myth of the Buddha avatar, but it superimposes this myth upon a historical personage: for according to Rajashekhara's Jain *Prabandhakosha* (fourteenth century), a Jain monk (some texts identify him as Indrasuri) converted King Ama, son of Yashovarman of Kanauj (728-753 CE), to Jainism.[179] History is now viewed through the screen of the dogmatic myth of the heretic. Similar stories of kings corrupted by Jains appear in other Indian texts.[180] It is significant that the myth of King Ama, a historical king, is set at the beginning of the Kali Age, the age in which true history begins.[181]

A Puranic myth of the Kali Age heresies in the *Linga Purana* includes strong Gupta evidence, not beyond any question of post-Gupta tampering but at least as suggestive of Gupta authorship as a trout is of water in the milk:

> When Time had reached its turning point, and the end of the Kali Age had come, a chastiser of the wicked (*asadhu*) creatures arose out of destruction. He was born in the lineage of Chandramas, the dynasty of the moon, and he was called Pramiti. In a former age, in the era of Manu Svayambhuva, he was born of a portion [of Vishnu]. For twenty years he wandered on the earth, commanding an army with many horses, chariots and elephants, surrounded by Brahmins wielding weapons, by the hundreds and thousands. He destroyed the barbarians by the thousands and killed all the kings who were born of Shudras, and cut down all the heretics. Those who were not excessively righteous—he killed them all, and those born of mixed classes (*varnas*), and their dependents. Turning the wheel of conquest, the powerful one made an end of the barbarians . . . At the age of thirty-two he set out, and for twenty years he killed all creatures by the hundreds and thousands, until this cruel act reduced the earth to nothing but seeds because of a causeless anger from one against another. He caused the lowly and the unrighteous to be generally exterminated. He and his followers established themselves between the Ganga and the Yamuna, together with his ministers and his army, after destroying all the barbarian princes. When the period of the turning point set in at the end of the Kali Age, there were very few subjects left over, here and there.[182]

Another text of this myth, in the *Matsya Purana*, differs on a few minor details and adds a significant list of political territories:

> When Time had reached its turning point, and the end of the Kali Age had come, a chastiser of the unrighteous [*adharmin*] arose in the family of the Bhrigus . . . He was called Pramati. For full thirty years he wandered on the earth . . . Those who were unrighteous—he killed them all: those in the north, and in the central country, and the mountain people, the inhabitants of the east and the west, those in the area of the highlands of the Vindhyas, and those in the Deccan, and the Dravidians and Simhalas, the Gandharans and Paradas, the Pahlavas and Yavanas and Shakas, Tusharas, Barbaras, Shvetas, Halikas, Daradas, Khasas, Lampakas, Andhras and the races of the Cholas. Turning the wheel of conquest, the powerful one put an end to the Shudras, putting all creatures to flight.[183]

These are the basic scriptures of Gupta paranoia and xenophobia: the barbarian kings kill women and children, indulge in the evil behaviour of the age, and kill off one another; all are devoid of dharma, or kama, or artha, and they mix indiscriminately with the Aryans.[184] The basis of this myth is the old theme, the story of the barbarian dynasties of the Kali Age, which each text develops with its own permutations. This particular list was compiled in the early part of the Gupta era (during the reign of Chandra Gupta I but before that of Samudra Gupta); it occurs (without the name of Pramiti/Pramati) in the *Matsya Purana, Vayu Purana, Brahmanda Purana* (all stemming from the *Bhavishya Purana*) and then in the *Vishnu Purana* and the *Bhagavata Purana*.[185]

F.E. Pargiter suggests that the standard lists were composed in the early part of the fourth century CE: 'The first portion of the description appears to depict the unsettled condition of the country in the early part of the fourth century,' though it builds upon 'gloomy Brahmanic forecasts, which were no doubt based on actual calamities, but which have no historical value'.[186] So we have the general 'gloomy' myth of the Kali Age first embroidered with more specific descriptions in the beginning of the fourth century; shortly thereafter, early Puranas like the *Vishnu Purana* insert passages describing the incarnation of Vishnu as Kalki to exterminate the barbarians.[187]

The next step transfers the role of Kalki to an actual king, Pramati—still said to be born of a portion of Vishnu, as Kalki is—who first achieves a general conquest and then, in the *Matsya Purana*, overcomes a specific list of political units in the subcontinent. Who is this king? Vasudeva S. Agrawala makes a strong case for the identification of Pramati with Chandra Gupta Vikramaditya (380-412 CE):[188] the reign of thirty-two years, the twenty-year military campaign, the lands of his conquest, the extermination of Shudra kings (a possible reference to the Shaka or Scythian dynasty that the Guptas uprooted)[xx], his birth as the son of Chandramas (this being a name of Samudra Gupta)[189]—all of these could indicate Vikramaditya. This development would give us a firm basis in time: right in the middle of the Gupta era.

A more explicit reference to Vikramaditya occurs in the *Bhavishya Purana*, in a text parts of which were certainly composed long after the Gupta period (for parts of the work demonstrate familiarity with British rule in Calcutta)[190]. But this text nevertheless extends the pseudo-historical tradition

---

[xx] Agrawala also suggests that the 'Brahmanas wielding arms' may be the Licchavi contingent in the Gupta army.

(parading the names of the dynasties that preceded the Guptas—Nandas and Mauryas and Shakas—and the historical birth of Gautama the Buddha) that links Vikramaditya with the extermination of heretics at the end of the Kali Age. Even if we cannot prove that all of the texts in this genre were actually composed in the Gupta age (as we can in fact prove for the earliest layer), we can at least demonstrate the persistence of the hope of the authors of the Puranas, the Pauranikas, that the Gupta kings would exterminate heretics:

> When King Kshemaka had performed a great sacrifice and destroyed all the barbarians, Kali incarnate begged Vishnu to produce more barbarians as is appropriate to the Kali Age, and Vishnu created Adam and Eve [Adama and Havyavati, in Sanskrit] and their descendants. These barbarians did not penetrate into Brahmavarta [the heart of North India], which was protected by the goddess Sarasvati, but they conquered many areas of India [these are enumerated at great length], and they were lamentably unable to pronounce Sanskrit words. As the generations passed, at the time of the Mauryas and Nandas, Kali reminded Vishnu of his duty, and so Vishnu was born as Gautama, son of Kashyapa, and he preached the Buddhist dharma. All men became Buddhists, and still the generations passed—Chandragupta, Bindusara and Ashoka. Then a Brahmin performed a Vedic ceremony, and by the power of the Vedic mantras four Kshatriyas were born: Pramara, Chapahani, Shukla and Pariharaka. They put Ashoka in their power and murdered all the Buddhists. Pramara had many descendants, and finally, when the full and terrifying Kali Age had arrived, Vikramaditya was born in order to destroy the Shakas and to promote Aryan dharma. At the age of twenty he went to the forest and practiced asceticism for twelve years, and then, at the age of thirty-two, he established his throne, by the grace of Shiva.[191]

This text does not give the details of Vikramaditya's conquest, but the conquest of the heretics has already been accomplished thrice: first, the barbarians (who murdered Kshemaka's father) are wiped out by the mythical King Kshemaka; then, the heretics created by Vishnu and descended from Adam (Jews and Christians?) are fended off by the goddess; and, finally, the Buddhists (also created by Vishnu) are exterminated by Pramara (perhaps yet another form of Pramati/Pramiti, standing in place of the usual Vaishnava avatar, Kalki). All that remains now for Pramara's descendant, Vikramaditya, to do is to destroy the Shakas (Scythians)—the one thing that we are fairly certain that he did actually do.

The destruction of the Shakas therefore stands for the 'extermination of heretics'. For despite the fact that the Shakas had been in India since the beginning of the second century CE and were thoroughly Indianized, Puranic dogmatism and jingoism still regarded them as foreigners, and conflated foreigners and heretics. The Purana embroiders the myth of Chandra Gupta Vikramaditya with the full pomp of the ancient images of righteous conquest. Perhaps by overreacting too long after the actual event—the Shaka invasion centuries before the Guptas climbed onto the throne—in a kind of historiographic *esprit de l'escalier*, the authors of the Gupta Puranas cast the Shakas as the heavies in the drama of the simultaneous political and religious catharsis of the land of the Aryans.

CONCLUSION: HERESY BEFORE, DURING AND AFTER THE GUPTA AGE

It is difficult indeed to tell where politics ends and religion begins in these myths, or even to tell precisely what axes are being ground in a given context. Further complications arise when one realizes that Buddhists and Jains, so often lumped together by the Hindu polemicist, each tended to regard the other as heretics, even as each of two castes may regard the other as lower and polluting; many of the myths of heresy may be expressing inter-caste tensions as well as political tensions on a higher scale.

The precise dates of the relevant texts are extremely difficult to fix, but the relative chronology is reasonably clear. Ashoka had promulgated his tactfully vague *dhamma* in an ultimately vain attempt to indoctrinate his subjects into an early form of reductionist comparative religion. Heresy and diversity had nevertheless flourished during the period of the Upanishads and the redaction of the *Mahabharata* and under the more loosely structured era of the Shakas and Kushanas, whose eclectic patronage stimulated the luxuriant growth of sectarian Hinduism and the emergence of highly original forms of Buddhism, from which Hinduism freely borrowed.

But the rapprochement with Buddhism and other heterodoxies waned by the time of the early Gupta Puranas. The need to maintain superficial political unity drove the Gupta rulers to play an uneasy game of impartial patronage. And since Buddhists and Hindus were competing, sometimes violently, for political patronage and popular support, the myths of this period depict the Buddha as deluded and destructive, the Buddhists as anti-gods. The heretical creeds that had been first tolerated, then assimilated or absorbed, were then excoriated, with the fanaticism that often characterizes the newly converted (in this case, Hindus who had at first borrowed from and then turned against the Buddhists). The Puranic texts of the Gupta period were weapons in a battle between the instigators of the Hindu revival and the still thriving establishments of Jainism and Buddhism. It has been said that the Puranas 'bear the scars of the battle to this day, in the form of numerous sharp and contemptuous denunciations of the Mohasastras ('scriptures of delusion') and their non-Vedic adherents.'[192]

The evidence of the Puranas and Dharmashastras suggests that attitudes to heretics and atheists became embittered in this period, losing ground that had been gained during earlier periods, ground that was, in part, regained after the Gupta period, under the influence of Tantrism. Still later, when Buddhism was waning in India, and the Hindus—many of them strongly influenced by Buddhist and Jain ideas of compassion and non-injury—held the field, the Hindus could afford to be generous; the tone of the myths underwent a complete transformation, and the Buddha was seen as a genuine and positive religious reformer in the thirteenth century works of Jayadeva and his contemporaries.[193] This general process, from tolerance to intolerance and back again to a kind of modified tolerance, may be seen in the development of the Puranic and Dharmashatra attitudes to heretics. The heretics who had been simply excluded during the Gupta age were received back into the fold in the post-Gupta, Tantric age by the same class of Brahmin authors of the Puranas who had originally written them off.

The Gupta age may or may not have been the Golden Age for some— for several poets, a lot of architects, and for the privileged in that elitist society—but it may well have been the Kali Age for those outside the inner sanctum, and its much-vaunted gold may have been little more than a thin plate over a tarnished Establishment made of baser stuff. Can we pinpoint the onset of intolerance in the Gupta era? The texts make this a difficult prospect. We have reasonably clear guidelines at either end of the spectrum: tolerance in the period of the Upanishads and the Ashokan reign, intolerance by the time of the *Vishnu Purana* in the Gupta age and until the flowering of the bhakti movement in subsequent Puranas after the sixth century CE. In discussing the myths of the heresies of the Kali Age and the Buddha avatar, H.H. Wilson interpreted the Kali Age heresies as Buddhist or Shaiva and remarked:

> The complaints of the prevalence of heterodox doctrines . . . indicate a period of change in the condition of the Hindu religion, which it would be important to verify. If reference is made to Buddhism, to which in some respects the allusions especially apply, it would probably

denote a period not long subsequent to the Christian era; but it is more likely to be of a later date, or in the eighth or ninth centuries, when Shankara is said to have reformed a variety of corrupt practices, and given rise to others.[194]

The first period, 'not long subsequent to the Christian era', would be the immediate pre-Gupta period, the period of invasions, when a 'period of change in the condition of the Hindu religion' most certainly took place, but probably without any organized counteraction by the Brahmins. The second period, in the 'eighth or ninth centuries', is indeed a period of reaction against heterodoxy, but is it the beginning of that period or the aftermath of it? My guess is the latter; and this places the heresies of the Kali Age right in the Gupta era.

But the later, positive transformation of the Buddha avatar went on to have a life of its own. J. Duncan Derrett applauded the message of such texts, that 'any genuine religious reformer may be treated as an abode of divinity'.[195] Arthur Berriedale Keith described the Buddha avatar as 'a curious example of the desire to absorb whatever is good in another faith.'[196] The Muslim sect of the Imam Shahis believed that the Imam himself was the tenth avatar of Vishnu and that the Qur'an was a part of the *Atharva Veda*.[197] (This view was supported by the traditional argument that only fragments of the Vedas still exist.) Christ is sometimes included among the avatars of Vishnu,[198] a practice that was once 'a cause of great alarm among Christian missionaries'.[199] Even Queen Victoria found a place in the Hindu pantheon; when a plague broke out in Bombay just after her statue had been insulted, certain pious Hindus believed that the disease was 'the revenge inflicted by her as insulted divinity'.[200]

And, on the other hand, those who identify themselves as Hindus even to the point of violent chauvinism may espouse heretical doctrines. Vinayak Damodar Savarkar (1883–1966), the founder and champion of Hindutva,[xxi] publicly announced and advertised 'lectures on atheism', on why there is no god and why all religions are false. That is why, when defining Hindutva, he said that Hindutva is not defined by religion, and tried to define it in a non-religious term: *Punyabhoomi* [the auspicious land].[201] A religion that can accommodate Queen Victoria, the orgiastic goddess of Tantric worship, and V.D. Savarkar is indeed a spacious abode.

[xxi] See 'You Can't Make an Omelette'.

EATING KARMA[1]

Food and eating function in South Asia to define the person more than anything else, even sex. Yet the precise nature of that definition has been debated, often to the death, for over two millennia. 'You are what you eat' is a cliché among non-Hindus, and the idea is basic to ancient India as well, though it has different meanings there. It represents the traditional view set forth by the classical texts on the caste system, which define the person by what he (rarely she) does (and does not) eat. *The Laws of Manu*, composed in the early centuries of the Common Era, goes into obsessive detail on the subject of food taboos, always emphasizing the negative, the foods not to be eaten. The class of prohibited food follows the general rule that good people have a narrower window of opportunity, of possibilities, than bad people; the higher you are, the less you can eat. A typical list of forbidden fruits goes like this:

> Garlic, scallions, onions, and mushrooms, and the things that grow from what is impure, are not to be eaten by twice-born men. The red sap of trees, and any exudations from a cut (in a tree), the 'phlegmatic' fruit, and the first milk of a newly-calved cow—you should try not to eat these. (And do not eat) a dish of rice with sesame seeds, or a spice cake made of flour, butter and sugar, or a cake made of rice, milk and sugar, if these are prepared for no (religious) purpose; or meat that has not been consecrated; or food for the gods, or offerings; or the milk of a cow within ten days of calving, or the milk of a camel or of any animal with a whole, solid hoof, or of an ewe, or of a cow in heat or a cow whose calf has been taken from her; and avoid the milk of women, the milk of all wild animals of the wilderness except the buffalo, and all foods that have gone sour or fermented. But among foods that have gone sour or fermented, yogurt can be eaten, and all foods made with yogurt, as well as whatever is extracted from auspicious flowers, roots and fruits.[2]

This text also supplies loopholes for times when one is *in extremis* (the Sanskrit term is *apad*, designating a disaster or emergency),[i] a time when you can eat any food whatsoever—even meat from a cow or a dog, or food bought by killing your son:

> Ajigarta, famished, stepped forward to kill his own son but was not smeared with evil, for he was acting to remedy his hunger. When Bharadvaja, who had amassed great inner heat, was distressed by hunger with his sons in a deserted forest, he accepted many cows from the carpenter Vridhu. When the sage Vamadeva, who knew the difference between right and wrong, was in distress and wanted to eat the flesh of a dog in order to save his life's breath, he was not smeared (with evil). When Vishvamitra, who knew the difference between right and wrong, was distressed by hunger, he set out to eat the hindquarters of a dog, which he received from the hands of a Dalit.[3]

Killing a cow is worse than killing a dog, and eating the meat of either pollutes you, though for opposite reasons: because the dog is impure, and because the cow is pure. The myth of the sage who eats dog meat (or the meat of a cow or a human boy) during a famine is a paradigmatic moral dilemma that begins in the *Rig Veda*, where the god Indra claims, 'Because I was in desperate straits, I cooked the entrails of a dog, and I found no one among the gods to help me.'[4] But eating dog-flesh has evil consequences in the texts that tell the stories at length.[5] Eating a dog or a cow, on the one hand, or eating your son (or eating food gained by having your son killed), on the other, raise entirely different moral questions.

The story of the dog-eating sage is often connected with the story of Ajigarta and his son Shunahshepha (whose name means 'Dog-penis'). Ajigarta's attempt to sacrifice his son, Shunahshepha, was reported first in a text composed in the eighth century BCE[6] and retold many times in ancient India. Though it is true that Ajigarta is not punished as a criminal, the text certainly depicts him as a most unsavoury character, and his son brutally rejects him when he attempts to 're-adopt' Shunahshepha after Shunahshepha has become a king. These moral dilemmas are posed in very different terms in devotional literature a millennium or so later, in texts in which a god may test the faith of a devotee by asking him to kill, cook, serve to the divine guest, and, finally, eat his own son.[7]

---

[i] See 'Sacrifice and Substitution' and 'Why Should a Brahmin?'

YOU ARE FROM WHOM YOU DO NOT EAT

But among Hindus, far more important than what you eat is *from whom* you eat, the people from whom you take food—or, most important of all, the people from whom you do *not* take food. The passage in Manu about eating dogs and cows begins with this verse: 'A man who eats the food of anyone, no matter who, when he is on the brink of losing his life is not smeared with evil, just as the sky is not smeared with mud.'[8] But 'no matter who' is normally a matter of fairly grave concern:

> A Brahmin should never eat (the food) of those who are drunk, angry or ill, nor (food) in which hair or bugs have fallen, or which has been intentionally touched by the foot; nor (food) which has been looked at by an abortionist, or touched by a menstruating woman, or pecked at by a bird, or touched by a dog; nor food sniffed by a cow, nor, most especially, food publicly advertised, nor the food of the hordes or of whores, or food that is disgusting to a learned man, nor the food of a thief, a singer, a carpenter, a usurer, a man who has been initiated for a Soma sacrifice, a miser, or a man bound in chains; nor of a man indicted, an impotent man, a woman who runs after men, or a deceiver, nor (food) that has been left out too long and soured, nor the leftovers of a servant; nor (the food) of a doctor, a hunter, a cruel man, one who eats leftovers, the food of a woman who has just given birth, the food left by someone who has gotten up to rinse his mouth, nor that of one still within the ten days (of pollution due to birth); nor food which is given disrespectfully or by a woman who has no man, meat without a sacrificial purpose, the food of an enemy, or of the mayor of a town, the food of a man who has fallen, nor (food) which someone has sneezed on; nor the food of a slanderer, a liar, or the seller of rituals, nor the food of a tumbler or a weaver, nor the food of an ingrate; nor that of a blacksmith, a member of the Hunter caste, a strolling actor, a goldsmith, a basket-weaver, or an arms-dealer; nor that of a man who raises dogs, a bootlegger, a washerman, a dyer, a cruel man, or a man whose wife's lover lives in his house; nor that of those who put up with such lovers, or who are dominated by their wives in all things, nor the food of those within the ten days (of pollution) due to death, nor unsatisfying food.[9]

This list strikes a contemporary reader as a mixture of what we would call rational concerns (food that is sneezed on, or has bugs or hair in it) and irrational concerns (the food of a strolling player). Yet, there are people with whom many people nowadays in all cultures would not, as the saying goes, break bread . . .

So much for being from whom you (do not) eat.

YOU ARE WHOM YOU EAT

The law for emergencies (*apad*) suspends the rules of civilization and returns human beings, temporarily, to the condition regarded as natural to them in a pre-civilized state: anarchy. 'Fish eat fish' is the dominant political metaphor of ancient India, and functions as a synonym for anarchy. There is a chain of food and eaters (dog eat dog, or, in the Indian metaphor, fish eat fish) which both justifies itself and demands that we break out of it. The Hindu view, underlying Manu, is that all animal nature is, as Tennyson put it, red in tooth and claw, that it happens, but it must not happen. Kingship was invented to put an end to anarchy.[10] But the more cynical texts of ancient Indian political theory acknowledge that the king eats the people:

> They say, 'When the deer eats the barley, (the farmer) does not hope to nourish the animal; when the low-born woman becomes the mistress of a noble man, (her husband) does not hope to get rich on that nourishment.' Now, the barley is the people, and the deer is the royal power; thus he makes the people food for the royal power, and so the one who has royal power eats the people. And so the king does not raise animals; and so one does not anoint as king the son of a woman born of the people.[11]

Thus the people either ate one another (anarchy) or were eaten by the king (kingship); either way, ancient India was literally a consumed, rather than consumer, society. In this view, you are whom you eat: you are bigger in political status than your prey.

YOU WILL BE WHOM YOU EAT

The idea of reincarnation, which enters Indian literature in the Upanishads, after the Brahmanas, in about the eighth century BCE, inspires the belief that you will be who you eat: you will become it in the next life.[ii]

YOU EAT WHAT YOU HAVE DONE

One of the most common Sanskrit words for 'eat' is the verb *bhuj*, which means a whole group of delicious things: the enjoyment or consumption of food, sex, experience, karma, fuel (by fire); it means to enjoy, eat, consume [as fuel], enjoy [as one enjoys sex or music], and burn up [fuel, or

---

[ii] See 'The Ambivalence of Ahimsa' and 'Death and Rebirth'.

karma]. To 'consume' karma is to destroy, through good actions, the residue of your bad actions—or to destroy, through bad actions, the residue of your good actions. In this view, you eat yourself.

The full range of meanings of 'eat' (*bhuj*) is enacted in the story of the ogress and the Brahmin's wife, narrated in a Sanskrit text composed in about 700 CE:

> A certain Brahmin came and with an aching heart said to the king, 'Great king, I am very unhappy; listen while I tell you about it, for the cure for the sufferings of men comes from nowhere but the king. While I was asleep, during the night, someone stole my wife, without even breaking open the door of the house. You must bring her back.' The king said, 'Don't you know who stole her? or where she was brought? With whom am I to fight? From where am I to bring her back?' The Brahmin said, 'While I was sleeping in my house, with the door shut just as tight as could be, someone stole my wife—I've already told you that.'
>
> The king said, 'I've never seen your wife. What sort of looks does she have, what sort of body? How old is she, and how patient? Tell me, what sort of character does your Brahmin lady have?' The Brahmin said, 'She has piercing eyes and is very tall; she has short arms, and a bony face. Her belly hangs down, and she has flat buttocks and small breasts. She is very ugly, your majesty; I am not blaming her, that's just the way she is. Her speech is coarse, too, your majesty, and her nature is not at all gentle. That is how I would describe my wife; she is hideous to look at. And she has ever so slightly passed her prime. That is what my wife looks like; I am telling you the truth.'
>
> The king said, 'You've had enough of her, Brahmin; I will give you another wife. Lack of beauty may sometimes be a cause of a very good character; but a woman who lacks both beauty and character should be abandoned. Your wife was carried off by someone else.' The Brahmin said, 'Every day that I live without a wife, I fail in dharma, because I have ceased to perform the obligatory rituals, and that, too, will cause me to fall. My future line of descendants is in her, your majesty; my lord, bring her back.'
>
> The king wandered this way and that way over the earth; he learned that an ogre named Balaka had taken the Brahmin's wife. And there the king saw the Brahmin's wife, who looked just as her husband had described her. She said, 'I was stolen by a bad ogre named Balaka. He brought me into this very deep forest, but then he abandoned me; I don't know why it is that he enjoys me neither carnally nor

carnivorously, neither for the pleasures of the flesh nor for the pleasure of flesh.'

The king saw the ogre, who was surrounded by his troops. The king asked him, 'For what purpose did you bring the Brahmin's wife here, night-wanderer? She is not good-looking; there are other wives, if you stole her for that. And if you brought her here to eat her, why haven't you eaten her? Tell me that.'

The ogre said, 'We don't eat people; those are other ogres, your majesty. But we eat the fruit of a good deed. And I will tell you about the fruit of a good deed: that is how I came to be reborn in the cruel and terrifying womb of an ogre. When we are dishonoured, we eat the very nature of men and women. But we do not eat flesh; we do not eat living creatures. When we eat the patience of men, they become angry; when we have eaten their evil nature, they become virtuous. We have gorgeous female ogres who are the equal of the celestial nymphs when it comes to beauty. While they are here, how could we take sexual pleasure in human females?'

The king said, 'If you want her neither for your bed nor for your table, night-wanderer, then why did you enter the Brahmin's house and steal her?' The ogre said, 'That Brahmin is outstanding when it comes to knowing mantras; as I went to sacrifice after sacrifice, he would recite the mantra that destroys ogres and prevent me from doing my job. We're starving because of the ritual of mantras that he uses to keep us from making our living. Where can we go? That Brahmin is the officiating priest in all the sacrifices. Therefore we brought this deficiency upon him: without a wife, a man is not fit to perform the rituals of sacrifice.'

The king said, 'Night-wanderer, since you did say, "We eat the very nature . . .," listen to what I would like you to do. Eat the evil nature of this Brahmin lady, right now. When you have eaten her evil nature, she may become nice. Then take her to the house of the man whose wife she is. When this is done, you will have done all that can be done for me as one who has come to your house.' Thereupon, by the king's command, the ogre used his own power of illusion to enter inside the woman and eat her evil nature. And when he had stripped the Brahmin's wife of her extremely fierce evil nature, she said to the king, 'By the ripening of the fruits of my own karma, I was separated from my noble husband; this night-wanderer was merely the proximate cause of that. The fault was not his, nor that of my noble husband; the fault is mine, no one else's; one eats the fruit of what one has done oneself. In another life, I separated myself from some man; and that separation has now fallen upon me; what fault could there be in my noble husband?'[12]

The ogre refuses to 'eat' (*bhuj*) the Brahmin's wife either as food or as sex; but then he consents to 'eat' her evil karma, even as he eats the good and evil natures of other creatures. He captures her because he and his colleagues are unable to eat food as long as her presence allows her husband to keep the ogres away from the sacrifice that is their food. Her husband, the sage, wanted her only in order to do the rituals, and the ogre wanted her only to stop him from doing those same rituals; she has no worth in herself. She is not food, but merely the obstacle to food. And her abduction is the result of her own previous actions; she is eating her own karma by experiencing the double rejection by her husband and by the ogre. As she herself admits, 'One eats the fruit of what one has done oneself.'

So much for eating karma, eating yourself.

YOU ARE WHAT YOU DO NOT EAT

Just as Manu cared more about the people you did *not* take food from, so too the ultimate definition of the good person was a matter of what, or how much, you did not eat. Hungrier than thou, holier than thou, was the rule, and remained the rule into the twentieth century. The anthropologist M.N. Srinivas coined the term 'Sanskritization' to designate the process by which a caste rises in large part by refusing to eat things they used to eat, and saying that they never ate them.[13]

Thus South Asia saw the connection between anorexia and religious chic at a very early period, and never let it go: starvation became and remained a religious goal, even while eating extremely well remained a worldly goal, and fat Brahmins were an object of mockery in Sanskrit literature. Rich and fat was one sort of ideal (the Hindus wrote poems about women with breasts like ripe melons and thighs like the trunks of plantain trees), while poor and thin was another. The sect called Aghoris ('those for whom nothing is disgusting') made a practice of eating human excrement, just to prove that they were above it all, above what Hindus call the 'dyads' (pleasure and pain, hot and cold, etc.), even while other sorts of Hindus became notorious for their subtle use of spices and for their gourmandise.[iii]

[iii] See 'Three (or More)'.

These various, apparently mutually opposed, agendas live cheek by jowl in India, but, wide-ranging though they are, they do not include any consistent consideration for nutrition or food distribution.[iv] Concerns of a very different nature in these mythologies of food provide the basis by which people make their decisions about both their own bodies and the bodies of those whom they kill either by consuming them or by dooming them to starvation. Manu damned in the same breath food that was sneezed on and food offered by a strolling actor, mixing practical concerns with dharmic ideals. You are what you think.

[iv] This statement applies to the religious texts under consideration here; another entire body of literature, the texts of Ayurveda, or 'The Science of Long Life', do indeed pay meticulous attention to nutrition, though still not to distribution. And parts of Manu also reflect Ayurvedic concepts of a healthy diet.

MEDICAL AND MYTHICAL CONSTRUCTIONS OF
THE BODY IN SANSKRIT TEXTS[1]

Scholars engaged in the wild goose chase of the search for universals once hoped to find support for their quest in the universal human problems posed by the universal structure of the human body. They hoped to ground even religious history in the study of the body. But, just as history is inevitably mediated by historiography, so the body is always mediated by symbolic expression of the culture. The deconstructionists argue that the body is not given, but constructed, and that each culture constructs it differently.

One could make a study of the Hindu approach to the body through an analysis of every major text, starting with the *Rig Veda* (which celebrates the body exuberantly) and the Upanishads (which warn of its treachery), through Sanskrit love poetry (predictably pro-body and libertine) and the Yogic texts (also pro-body, though in a rather different key, and certainly not libertine). I have confined this chapter to examples from three Hindu disciplines that have made relatively explicit the assumptions that most Hindus share about the construction of the human body—medical texts, Manu and the Puranas—while at the same time noting the significant differences between the approaches taken by different texts in different periods and different disciplines.

The Hindu boundaries of identity are fluid; acts of eating and sex further blur those boundaries by transgressing the limits of the human body. This is surely one of the factors contributing to the great danger that is thought, in India, to accompany the sexual act (and, indeed, eating): if you are not sure where your body ends, you will be very uneasy about exposing it to intimate contact with someone else's body. This anxiety hedges the openings of the body (Manu tells us to clean them obsessively), the things that fall off the body (nails, hair, mucous and, of course, semen), and, ultimately, sexual intercourse. This bias is revealed not just in myths that depict sadistic sexual acts or lethal love; it is regarded as a part of natural, everyday sex. Yet, throughout this discourse, ascetic and renunciant arguments interact with the passages that praise the sexual act as inherently sacred. The ascetic strain, often misogynist, often expressing a deep anxiety about the human body, challenges the other sort of Hinduism, the one that glories in the body both for its fertility and for its eroticism. The two traditions remain in tension to this day.[i]

THE MEDICAL TEXTS

A basic assumption of Hindu medical texts like the *Charaka Samhita* (composed sometime between 100 BCE and 100 CE) is the doctrine of the three humours, closely related to the Hindu belief that all matter, including the human body, is composed of the three elements of lucidity (*sattva*), energy (*rajas*) and torpor (*tamas*)[ii]:

> Wind, bile and phlegm are said to be the group of humours, the sources of disease, in the body; and energy and darkness are said to be the source of disease in the mind. Pathological changes that are regarded as curable are counteracted by medicines possessing qualities opposite [to the humours of the changes], applied with proper regard for place, dose and time. But no cure is prescribed for diseases that are incurable.[2]

This remains the prevailing view of Ayurvedic practitioners today.

The medical texts themselves acknowledge the existence of multiple theories about the body even within their own system:

> Once, a group of sages were summoned by the king to debate this question: The person is a mass of soul, senses, mind and sense objects. But is the origin of the person also thought to be the origin of diseases, or not? The sages offered various answers. One said, 'The individual person is born from the Soul, and so the diseases are also born from the Soul.' Another: 'No. When the mind that is conscious of lucidity is overwhelmed by energy and torpor, then it causes the origin both of the body itself and of pathological changes in the body.' Another: 'No. All creatures are born from *rasa* [the fluid essence of digested food], and so the various diseases are also born from *rasa*.' Another: 'No. The individual person is born of the six elements of matter [earth, water, fire, wind, space and mind, or soul], and so diseases are also born from the six elements.'

---

[i] See 'Three (or More)' and 'From Kama to Karma'.
[ii] See 'Three (or More)'.

Then another sage replied: 'No. How could someone be born out of the six elements, without a mother and a father? A person is born from a person; a cow from a cow, and a horse from a horse. Diseases such as urinary disorders are known to be hereditary. So the two parents are the cause.' 'No,' said another, 'for a blind person is not born from a blind person. But a creature is known to be born of his karma, and so diseases are also born from karma.' 'No,' said another. 'An agent must always precede an action [karma]. And no person can be the result of an action that has not been done; this is clear enough. No, nature is the cause, one's own nature, the cause of both diseases and the person, just as it is the nature of earth to be rough, water to be fluid, wind to move and fire to be hot.' 'No,' said another. 'The Creator had an unlimited imagination, and it was he who created the happiness and unhappiness of this universe, sentient and insentient.' 'No,' said another. 'The individual person is born of time, and diseases are born of time.'

Now, as the sages were arguing in this way, Punarvasu said: 'Don't talk like this. It is hard to get to the truth when people take sides. People who utter arguments and counter-arguments as if they were established facts never get to the end of their own side, as if they were going round and round on an oil press. Not until you shake off the torpor of factionalism from what you want to know will true knowledge emerge. The use of good food is one cause of the growth of a person, and the use of bad food is a cause of diseases.' To which one of the sages replied: 'Physicians have an abundance of different opinions. Not all of them will understand this sort of teaching.'[3]

Despite the acknowledgement of the complex metaphysical factors that influence the birth and development of the body, the final view stated, which Hindu texts always present as the favoured view, did in fact prevail in Hindu medical science: food is presented as the primary cause of the body; bad food as the primary cause of disease, and good food as the primary cause of healing. This is one reason for the great emphasis on the right and wrong food[iii] in the legal texts, to which we will now turn.

THE BODY IN *THE LAWS OF MANU*

The Laws of Manu, the paradigmatic text of Hindu religious law, composed in the early centuries of the present era, is a work of encyclopaedic scope.

[iii] See 'Eating Karma'.

It consists of 2,685 verses on topics as apparently varied—but actually intimately interrelated in Hindu thought—as the social obligations and religious duties of the various castes and of individuals in different stages of life; the proper way for a righteous king to rule and to punish transgressors in his kingdom; the appropriate social relations between men and women of different castes and between husbands and wives in the privacy of the home; birth, death and taxes; cosmogony, karma and rebirth; ritual practices; sin, expiation and salvation; and such details of everyday life as the procedure for settling traffic accidents and adjudicating disputes with boatmen. The text is an encompassing representation of life in the world—how it is and how it should be lived. It is about dharma.

Though it is certain that *The Laws of Manu* is the culmination of the work of several authors, informed by popular wisdom, it is attributed to someone named Manu, a mythological or legendary figure. Manu means 'the wise one', and Manu is the name of a king (an interesting attribution, given the Brahmin bias of Manu's text) who is the mythological ancestor of the human race, the Indian Adam. Thus *manava* ('descended from Manu') is a common word for 'human'; in terms of the lexical meaning of *manu* as 'wise', *manava* might also be the Sanskrit equivalent of 'Homo sapiens.'

Manu expresses several different attitudes to the body. First, in keeping with the general, rather grudging lip-service that he pays to the philosophy of renunciation, he offers a chilling image of the body: '[A man] should abandon this foul-smelling, tormented, impermanent dwelling-place of living beings, filled with urine and excrement, pervaded by old age and sorrow, infested by illness, and polluted by passion, with bones for beams, sinews for cords, flesh and blood for plaster and skin for the roof.'[4]

Manu also expresses a basic uneasiness about the body, especially about the openings through which fluids and pollutants may escape or enter. Thus the obsessional concern for the control of what enters the body (food) is balanced by an equally obsessional concern for the regulating of excretions (including sexual excretions) and the cleansing of the openings of the body. This physical model, of danger flowing in and out of the body at all times, is echoed in the social model of karmic transactions, where social dangers flow in and out of the body through contact with other people—primarily through the exchange of food or sex. The extreme degree of Manu's fear of pollution through such contact, very much like the traditional attitude to lepers, characterizes his attitude to all people with social diseases—which is to say any diseases at all, since diseases are punishments for sins against society—or with social disabilities—such as birth into a low caste or even, in many ways, birth as a woman.

But women and the body also have their uses for Manu: as vessels for the procreation of male heirs. There are two different, conflicting models of paternity in Manu, expressed through two agricultural metaphors, one about plants and the other about animals. The more basic argument is taken from plants: The sower of the seed is the biological father, who may or may not be the legal husband; the woman is the field, and the owner of the field is the legal husband. The son born in the field (the wife) by a man other than her legal husband is known as the *kshetraja*, literally 'born in the (husband's) field'.[5] The man who owns the field (the wife) owns whatever crop is sown in the field. Manu assumes that the field is entirely neutral, and that the crop (son) sown in it will always resemble the seed (the father). Therefore you should never waste your seed by shedding it in another man's 'field' or wife, but you are not harmed if another man sheds his seed in your wife (in that you own the son resulting from that act). Manu thus forbids a man to commit adultery in another man's wife, but encourages him to let a brother produce a Levirate heir in his own wife, through the Indian practice of *niyoga*, in which the widow of a man who has produced no male heirs is appointed to have a son by that man's younger brother.[iv] This argument—that the man owns the woman, 'the field'—prevails in India:

> They say that a son belongs to the husband, but the revealed canon is divided in two about who the 'husband' is: some say that he is the begetter, others that he is the one who owns the field. The woman is traditionally said to be the field, and the man is traditionally said to be the seed; all creatures with bodies are born from the union of the field and the seed. Sometimes the seed prevails, and sometimes the woman's womb; but the offspring are regarded as best when both are equal. Of the seed and the womb, the seed is said to be more important, for the offspring of all living beings [have] the mark of the seed. Whatever sort of seed is sown in a field prepared at the right season, precisely that sort of seed grows in it, manifesting its own particular qualities. For this earth is said to be the eternal womb of creatures, but the seed develops none of the qualities of the womb in the things it grows. For here on earth when farmers at the right season sow seeds of various forms in the earth, even in one single field, they grow up each according to its own nature. Rice, red rice, mung beans, sesame, pulse beans and barley

[iv] See 'Why Should a Brahmin?'

grow up according to their seed, and so do leeks and sugar-cane. It never happens that 'One seed is sown and another grown'; for whatever seed is sown, that is precisely the one that grows.[6]

The basic argument seems sensible enough; Manu acknowledges that the quality of the field does influence the quality of the crop (crops grow better in a well ploughed or 'good' field), but argues that the basic characteristics of the field do not influence the basic characteristics of the crop (barley, rather than mung beans, grows in any field in which barely is planted).

Manu also discusses the question of the ownership of the crop (the son) in terms of a livestock image, the point of which is not quite so obvious:

> Just as the stud is not the one who owns the progeny born in cows, mares, female camels and slave girls, buffalo-cows, she-goats and ewes, so it is too (with progeny born) in other men's wives. If [one man's] bull were to beget a hundred calves in other men's cows, those calves would belong to the owners of the cows, and the bull's seed would be shed in vain. This is the law for the offspring of cows and mares, slave girls, female camels and she-goats, and birds and female buffalo.[7]

These verses about livestock appear in Manu interspersed with the plant metaphor of seed and field, and are used in support of the prevailing argument that the one who owns the female, rather than the one who owns the seed, owns the offspring. But Manu himself elsewhere acknowledges the equal contribution of the mother and the father to the nature of the child when he discusses mixed marriages, again in terms of the mixed agricultural-pastoral metaphor. And he concludes: 'Some wise men value the seed, others the field, and still others both the seed and the field; but this is the final decision on this subject: seed sown in the wrong field perishes right inside it; and a field by itself with no seed also remains barren. And since sages have been born in [female] animals by the power of the seed, and were honoured and valued, therefore the seed is valued.'[8] Thus Manu moves into increasingly complex areas of speculation. Even the relatively simple seed-and-field image proves ambiguous; the livestock image introduces further complications, especially when, as Manu admits in the last line of the passage cited, humans mate with animals. And, when it comes to human beings, a third factor is introduced: the behaviour of the child, which must be regarded as a factor separate from the genetic contribution of either of his parents.[v]

It may well be that it is because men have given most of our texts their final form that those texts speak primarily of a man as the active knower of

---

[v] See 'Death and Rebirth'.

the passive woman-as-field (of knowledge, and of progeneration), just as they speak of the soul as 'the knower of the body-as-field'—*kshetrajna* (which forms a natural pun with *kshetraja*, 'born in the [husband's] field'; but which is the source and which the echo?). However, in chapter nine of his law book, Manu acknowledges the creative role of the woman as body/field, when he assumes that a Brahmin with wives of various classes produces children whose status is in part determined by their mothers' status.[9] And, finally, the human genetic pool is entirely transformed by culture, by the ritual transformations of the *samskaras*, so that a child obtains what McKim Marriott calls his 'coded substance'[10]—his somatic as well as social essence—not only from his parents, but from his teachers and priests, as Manu also argues.[11]

Classical Hindu medical traditions assumed that the woman's seed, physically incarnate in her menstrual blood, contributed the soft and red parts of a child (the flesh and blood), while the man's white semen contributed the hard and white parts (bone and sinew).[12] A commentator on the *Kamasutra* cites such a view:

> A woman can be impregnated by making love with another woman
> just as she can by making love with a man.
> 'When a woman and a woman
> make love together,
> and emit semen into one another,
> a child is born without bones.'
> For blood is formed out of the basic liquid of the body and becomes,
> under certain circumstances, menstrual blood, while semen is formed
> out of the marrow of the bones. [2.1.18]

This model gives women a much smaller role in the child, since it also assumed that semen was a much refined and concentrated form of blood: it takes ten drops of blood to make a drop of semen, so the woman's contribution is only one tenth of the man's.

The story of the two women who make love and produce a bone-less child is well known: A king died without an heir, and one of his two wives ate a special bowl of rice consecrated to make her pregnant, and the other 'acted the part of a man' with her, and she became pregnant; but the child had no bones, because that is the father's contribution to the embryo.[13] There is also an example of the opposite case, in which the child (Shiva's son Bhringi) is cursed to be without flesh because he denies his mother.[vi]

[vi] See 'The Scrapbook'.

The agricultural model remains a referent to this day in India, but it is not always accepted. Lina Fruzzetti and Ákos Ostör have demonstrated the variants that Bengali villagers ring on the basic theme,[14] and E. Valentine Daniel has recorded a wonderful conversation in which Tamil villagers cynically reject the whole concept of the seed and the field in favour of the concept of female seed.[15]

THE PURANAS

The Puranas (the popular medieval Sanskrit compendiums of myth and ritual) offer several explanations of conception and birth, which differ both from one another and from the ones that we have seen in Manu and the medical texts. The *Markandeya Purana* assumes that the menstrual blood (*rajas*, also the term for the quality of energy) is the woman's seed; hence the seed of which the child is born is regarded as two-fold, male and female:

The impregnation of human women is the emitting of the seed in the menstrual blood. As soon as [the soul] is released from hell, or from heaven, it arrives (in the womb). Overpowered by that [soul], the two-fold seed becomes solid. It becomes a speck of life, and then a bubble, and then flesh. And just as a shoot of a plant is born from a seed, so from the flesh the five limbs (two arms, two legs and the head) are born, with all their parts. The subsidiary limbs, too—fingers, eyes, nose, mouth and ears—grow out of the (five) limbs; and out of the subsidiary limbs, in the same way, grow the nails and so forth. The hair on the body grows in the skin, and the hair of the head grows after that.

The birth-sheath grows larger as it takes on flesh. Just as a coconut grows big along with its shell, so the sheath of the embryo, that opens out on the bottom, grows bigger. The embryo grows up in the bottom of the womb, placing its two hands beside its knees, with its two thumbs on top of its knees, the fingers in front; behind the two knees are the two eyes, and in between the knees is the nose; the buttocks rest on the two heels, and the arms and shanks are outside. In this way, the living (human) creature gradually grows up inside the woman's womb; other living creatures position themselves in the stomach according to their shapes.

The fire inside the stomach makes the embryo hard, and it lives on what is eaten and drunk [by the mother]. The sojourn of the living creature inside the stomach is meritorious and is made of retained merit. A channel called the 'Strengthener and Nourisher' is attached to the inside of the embryo's navel and to the channel from the woman's entrails, and the embryo stays alive by that means. For what the woman eats and drinks goes into the embryo's womb, and the living creature's body is strengthened and nourished by that so that it grows.

Then, as time goes by, the embryo turns around, head down, and in the ninth or tenth month it is born.[16]

The predominance of the father in the making of the body, that Manu insists upon, is here undercut by the role of the mother in contributing to the physical substance of the body.

There is, however, a third player here too: the embryo, who brings his own karma—carried on his transmigrating soul—to the construction of his body. For many Hindu philosophical texts view the body primarily as an obstacle to the freedom of the soul, a view that challenges some of the ideas, held by less philosophically-inclined Hindus, that we have considered in this chapter. But that is another story, for another chapter.[vii]

[vii] See 'Forgetting and Re-awakening' and 'Death and Rebirth'. And for changes in Hindu attitudes to the body in reaction to the presence of the British Raj in India, see 'God's Body' and 'From Kama to Karma'.

DEATH AND REBIRTH IN HINDUISM[1]

When people depart from this world, they go to the moon. Those who do not answer
the moon's questions become rain, and rain down here on earth, where they are
reborn according to their actions [karma] and knowledge—as a worm, an insect, a
fish, a bird, a lion, a boar, a rhinoceros, a tiger, a human, or some other creature.
Those who answer the moon's questions correctly pass to the heavenly world: They go
on the path to the gods, to fire, and finally to brahman.

—Kaushitaki Upanishad 1.1-4

There are many different approaches to death and rebirth in the Hindu tradition, offering many different non-solutions to the insoluble problem, many different ways that the square peg of the fact of death cannot be fitted into the round hole of human rationality. These approaches are often aware of one another; they react against one another and incorporate one another, through the process of intertextuality.

DEATH IN THE *RIG VEDA*

Surprisingly for a document so devoted to war and sacrifice, both of which involve killing, the *Rig Veda* says relatively little about death. It says a lot about the victory of life, and its central myth is the story of the triumph of Indra, the god of rain, of fertility, of war, of the phallus, of expansion in all senses of the word, over the serpent Vritra, the symbol of drought and restriction. What the *Rig Veda* does say about death, however, is not easy to reduce to a single idea. Death is an inevitable part of chaos, something to be avoided as long as possible. The poet says, speaking of the Creator, 'His shadow is immortality—and death,' and he prays, 'Deliver me from death, not from immortality.'[2] By 'immortality' the ancient sages meant not a literal eternity of life but rather a full lifespan, reckoned as a hundred years. And when it comes to the inevitable end of that brief span, the *Rig Veda* offers varied but not necessarily contradictory images of a vague but pleasant afterlife, a rather muted version of life on earth—shade (remember how hot India is), lots of good-looking women (this heaven is imagined by men) and good things to eat and drink.

One funeral hymn addresses the dead man: 'Go forth, go forth on those ancient paths on which our ancient fathers passed beyond . . . Unite with the fathers, with Yama [king of the dead], with the rewards of your sacrifices and good deeds, in the highest heaven. Leaving behind all imperfections, go back home again; merge with a glorious body.'[3] But, despite this 'glorious body' with which the dead person unites, another hymn expresses concern that the old body be preserved, and confidence that this will be so. That hymn begins by addressing the funeral fire, Agni: 'Do not burn him entirely, Agni, or engulf him in your flames. Do not consume his skin or his flesh. When you have cooked him perfectly,[i] only then send him forth to the fathers.'[4] Not only is the fire not to destroy the body, but it is to preserve it. Speaking to the dead man, the hymn says: 'Whatever the black bird has pecked out of you, or the ant, the snake, or even a beast of prey, may Agni who eats all things make it whole.'[5] But it also speaks, again to the dead man, of the ultimate dispersal of the old body: 'May your eye go to the sun, your life's breath to the wind. Go to the sky or to earth, as is your nature; or go to the waters, if that is your fate. Take root in the plants with your limbs.'[6] Another hymn says to the dead man: 'Creep away to this broad, vast earth, the mother that is kind and gentle. [And to the earth:] Open up, earth; do not crush him. Be easy for him to enter and to burrow in. Earth, wrap him up as a mother wraps a son in the edge of her skirt.'[7]

The *Rig Veda* is more concerned, however, with the living than with the dead, and the same hymn that addresses the earth is primarily addressed to the mourners:

> Go away, death, by another path that is your own . . . When you [mourners] have gone, wiping away the footprint of death, stretching farther your own lengthening span of life, become . . . swollen with offspring and wealth. Those who are alive have now parted from those who are dead . . . We have gone forward to dance and laugh, stretching farther our own lengthening span of life. Order [our] lifespans so that the young do not abandon the old . . . Rise up, woman [the wife of the dead man], into the world of the living. Come here; you are lying beside a man whose life's breath has gone . . . On a day that will come, they will lay me in the earth, like the feather of an arrow.[8]

[i] The great French Indologist, Louis Renou, translated the word for 'perfectly' as '*au point*'.

Thus, even at this early stage, we have several rather different, but all relatively mild, views of the fate of the dead, views that seem to represent several degrees of rebirth. We might rank these options on a continuum from the most vivid to the least vivid: the dead man may somehow merge with a glorious body, presumably (but not necessarily) in heaven; his mortal body may be somehow purified and restored by the fire and united with his ancestors (again, presumably in heaven); the parts of his body may be dispersed to the elements of the cosmos; or he may return to the kindly womb of mother earth. 'Take root in the plants with your limbs'[9] might be a hint of the sort of rebirth in plants that the Upanishads are going to describe in detail, especially when that verse is coupled, later in that same poem, with a rather suggestive, if cryptic, allusion to rebirth: 'Let him reach his own descendants, dressing himself in a lifespan.'[10] This verse could mean that Agni should let the dead person come back to his former home and to his offspring, or back to the earth in the form of rain (as the dead do in the Upanishads). But these are, at best, but the early, murky stirrings of a doctrine of rebirth that will become clear only in the Brahmanas and Upanishads.

RE-DEATH AND REBIRTH IN THE BRAHMANAS

In the texts that follow the *Rig Veda* and gloss it, the Brahmanas (c. 700 BE), death is far more explicitly feared, but also more explicitly transcended. 'Evil Death' is a cliché, an automatic equation throughout this corpus: death is evil, and the essence of evil is death. The fear of death, and the obsessive search for rituals that can overcome it, is the central concern of the Brahmanas.

The phrase 'recurring death' or 're-death' (*punar mrityu*) is an essential key to our understanding of the Hindu attitude to reincarnation.[ii] Most Hindus continued to believe that death was something to be feared, avoided. Many myths began with the natural premise of someone grieving, for the death of a loved one or for their own impending death, and being assured, in the course of the myth, that death was inevitable (for otherwise there could be no birth) or even desirable (for otherwise the world would be overcrowded: one myth about a time when death took a holiday says that, in heaven, everyone had to stand with their arms above their heads), or that if people lived forever they would be without ambition or a moral law.

[ii] See 'Three (or More)'.

The Brahmanas' fear of death, single or repeated, led to an entirely different approach to death in the texts that follow, and gloss, the Brahmanas: the Upanishads, composed from about 600 BCE. Like the Brahmanas, the Upanishads speak of re-death (*punar mrityu*) long before they begin speaking of rebirth (*punar janma*). The Buddha, preaching at roughly the same time, taught that misery (*dukkha*) is not so much suffering as the inevitable loss of happiness, a chaos from which nirvana (the Buddhist equivalent of moksha) offered deliverance. This recurrent loss of happiness is the problem faced by the Upanishads, the problem of re-death. The Upanishads reverse the Rig Vedic equation of death with chaos, life with order, and state, instead, that life (sex, birth, one damn thing after another) is chaos, a dream, or rather a nightmare, while death (or final release from life, moksha) is order, a dreamless sleep, or an awakening.

Though there are tantalizing precursors of a doctrine of rebirth in the Brahmanas and even in the *Rig Veda*, the first explicit discussion of the doctrine of rebirth in Indian literature occurs in the Upanishads. A king asks a young man named Gautama (no relation to the Buddha) if he knows the answer to the following questions:

'Do you know where created beings go from here?'
'No, sir.'
'Do you know how they come back again?'
'No, sir.'
'Do you know about the separation between the two paths, the path of the gods and the path of the fathers?'
'No, sir.'
'Do you know how the world (of heaven) over there does not get filled up?'
'No, sir.'
'Do you know how, in the fifth oblation, water comes to have a human voice?'
'No, sir.'

This Socratic routine goes on for some time until, eventually, the king tells the boy the answers:

When the embryo has lain inside the womb for ten months or nine months, or however long, covered with the membrane, then he is born. When he is born, he lives as long as his allotted lifespan. When he has died, they carry him to the appointed place and put him in the fire, for that is where he came from, what he was born from. Those who know this, and those who worship in the forest, concentrating on faith and asceticism, they are born into the flame, and from the flame into the day, and from the day into the fortnight of the waxing moon, and from the fortnight of the waxing moon into the six months during which the sun moves north; from these months, into the year; from the year into the sun; from the sun into the moon, from the moon into lightning. There a Person who is not human leads them to the ultimate reality. This is the path that the gods go on.

But those who worship in the village, concentrating on sacrifices and good works and charity, they are born into the smoke, and from the smoke into the night, and from the night into the other fortnight, and from the other fortnight into the six months when the sun moves south. They do not reach the year. From these months they go to the world of the fathers, and from the world of the fathers to space, and from space to the moon. That is king Soma. That is the food of the gods. The gods eat that.

When they have dwelt there for as long as there is a remnant (of their merit), then they return along that very same road that they came along, back into space; but from space they go to wind, and when one has become wind he becomes smoke, and when he has become smoke he becomes mist; when he has become mist, he becomes a cloud, and when he has become a cloud, he rains. These are then born here as rice, barley, plants, trees, sesame plants and beans. It is difficult to move forth out of this condition; for whoever eats him as food and then emits him as semen, he becomes that creature's semen and is born. And so those who behave nicely here will, in general, find a nice womb, the womb of a Brahmin or the womb of a Kshatriya or the womb of a Vaishya. But those whose behaviour here is stinking will, in general, find a stinking womb, the womb of a dog or the womb of a pig or the womb of an Untouchable.

Then they become those tiny creatures who go by neither one of these two paths but are constantly returning. 'Be born and die'—that is the third condition. And because of that, the world (of heaven) over there is not filled up. And one should try to protect oneself from that . . . Whoever knows this becomes pure, purified, and wins a world of merit, if he really knows this.[11]

This text explains, for the first time,[iii] the theory of karma (action), the theory that the actions that a person commits in life, for better or worse,

---

iii The idea of karma may have been foreshadowed by the Rig Vedic verse (10.14.7) that hints at the importance of the record of good deeds—which is to say, good karma: 'Unite with the fathers, with Yama, with the rewards of your sacrifices and good deeds, in the highest heaven.'

leave traces on the soul, and the nature of these traces will determine the nature of that person's rebirth. It would seem from this famous text that one would want to 'know this' and to 'protect oneself from that'—that is, to avoid rebirth altogether, or at least to avoid the possibility of 'a stinking womb' as the result of bad karma. But in fact, a lesser known early Upanishad also clearly envisions the possibility that some people will not want to get out: when the soul of the dead man reaches the moon, he may be given a choice of continuing with the process of rebirth or getting out altogether (moksha), and the text states that some people will choose to be reborn, presumably in a good womb as a result of good karma.[12] For many people, the ideal of freedom from rebirth was reabsorbed into the worldlier traditions of Hinduism, and inverted into the desire to be reborn, but reborn better in worldly terms: richer, with more sons, and so forth.

To many non-Hindu students of Hinduism, reincarnation seems to pose a possible solution to the problem of death: if what you fear is the cessation of life (we will set aside for the moment considerations of heaven and hell), then the belief that you will, in fact, live again after you die may be of comfort: how nice to go around again and again, never to be blotted out altogether, to have more and more of life, different lives all the time. This being so, the fact that major schools of Hindu (and Buddhist) philosophy strive not to be reborn, strive to attain release (moksha) from ever being born again, has struck many non-Hindu thinkers as a pessimistic or nihilistic attitude: such Hindus (the non-Hindu critic reasons) are throwing away not merely the present life but all those potential future lives as well, committing a kind of multiple proleptic suicide, a preventative euthanasia.

But this line of reasoning entirely misses the point of the Hindu doctrine. In the Hindu view, the cycle begins with death, not birth; texts explaining it always begin: 'When a man dies . . .' and go on to describe various adventures that the soul endures before finally alighting in some womb or other, and then progressing to death. What the authors of these early texts feared was not life but death—more precisely, 'old age and death' (jaramrityu). And what they feared most of all was what they called punar mrityu, recurrent death: how terrible to go on getting old and dying, over and over again. Re-death may have meant merely a series of ritual deaths within a natural lifespan, but it may have foreshadowed an actual series of rebirths and re-deaths. As one text states: 'When they die they come to life again, but they become the food of this (Death) again and again.'[13] And if it is a terrible thing to grow old and die, once and for all, how much more terrible to do it over and over again? This is what the fourth goal of life, moksha (which was added to the original Hindu triad of dharma, artha and kama)[iv], was designed to prevent.

These two tracks—one for people who want to get off the wheel, and one for those who don't—continue to this day as options for most South Asians.

KARMA AND REBIRTH

The first and most basic meaning of karma is action. The noun karma comes from the verb *kri*, cognate with the Latin *creo*, 'to make or do'—to make a baby or a table or to perform a ritual. It is often contrasted with mind and speech: one can think, say, or do [*kri*] something, with steadily escalating consequences. The second meaning of karma is ritual action, particularly Vedic ritual action; this is its primary connotation in the *Rig Veda*. Its third meaning, which begins to be operative in the Upanishads, is morally charged action, good or bad, a meter that is always running, that is constantly charging something to one's account. And its fourth meaning, which follows closely on the heels of the third, is morally charged action that has consequences for the soul in the future, that is retributive both within one's life and across the barrier of re-death: you become a sheep that people eat if you have eaten a sheep. (We see the germ of this theory in the Brahmana descriptions of people soundlessly screaming in the Other World[v] and in statements that sacrifice generates merit which guarantees an afterlife in the other world.) In this sense, karma determines the nature of your future rebirths. Consequences have consequences, and first thing you know, you're born as a sheep.

Turned on its head, this link led to a fifth meaning of karma, not as the cause of future lives but as the result of past lives and the agenda for this life, the inescapable role in life that one was born to play; one's work, or innate activity. The Hindu view extends the operative past and future beyond the boundaries of this lifespan. F. Scott Fitzgerald captured the spirit of karma in the final sentence of *The Great Gatsby*: 'So we beat on, boats against the current, borne back ceaselessly into the past.' In Hinduism, we are also borne back ceaselessly into the future.

The sixth, and last, meaning of karma is the implication that good and bad karma may also be transferred from one person to another under certain circumstances, not merely between parents and children and

---

[iv] See 'Three (or More)'.
[v] See 'The Ambivalence of Ahimsa'.

between sacrificial priest and patron, but between any people who meet. This transfer may take place either intentionally or unintentionally: the dharma texts say that if someone lets a guest depart unfed, the guest will take away the host's good karma and leave behind his own bad karma.[14] In a variant of the story of the boy in the other world, the boy remains in the house of Death for three nights without eating, and then tells Death that, in effect, on the three nights of fasting he ate 'your offspring, your sacrificial beasts (*pashus*), and your good deeds (*sadhu-krityam*)'.[15] This final item is an example of the transfer of good karma; unfed, the boy, Nachiketas, 'eats' (which is to say consumes) Death's good deeds (which is to say that he siphons off Death's good karma) as well as his children and cattle. (This blackmail is what forces Death to tell Nachiketas his secrets.)

It is not always clear which of these meanings of karma is intended in any particular passage in the Upanishads (or in other texts). The idea of the cyclicity of time leads to the circle of karma and rebirth in each individual life, which carries with it from the start the idea of escaping from that very circularity. The assumption is that we are all on the wheel of re-death, transmigration (*samsara*), but all Hindus do not at all agree as to whether it is good or bad to be on the wheel, or how best to go about getting off it if one does want to get off.[vi]

HEAVEN AND HELL IN THE *MAHABHARATA*

As we have seen, the *Rig Veda* already has a vague idea of heaven; it also has a rather vague idea of hell. But later texts rushed into this vacuum, with a vengeance. One might think that the cyclic concept of reincarnation would obviate any need, or indeed any use, for a heaven or hell in which one would be rewarded or punished for all eternity, but this is not the case. The older Vedic idea of heaven and hell was simply folded into the newer Upanishadic idea of rebirth.

This was how the combination worked: We have already seen, in the Upanishads, a bifurcation or dichotomy in the cycle of reincarnation: reincarnating souls go either to the flame, the sun, and finally to freedom or ultimate reality; or to the smoke, the moon, and the cycle of rebirth. In the case of heaven/hell and rebirth, it was simply said that after death, the reincarnating soul takes one of two paths: if good karma predominates over bad karma, the soul goes first to hell for a relatively brief period, where it works out or consumes its bad karma by being tormented, and

---

[vi] See 'Three (or More)'.

then to heaven for a long period, where it enjoys the fruits of its good karma. If bad karma predominates, the soul goes first briefly to heaven and then for a longer sojourn in hell. In either case, after the two sorts of karma are consumed, the soul is reborn in a station in life determined by the original balance of good and evil karma.

The final book of the *Mahabharata*, Book 18, the *Svargarohana Parvan* ('The Book of Climbing to Heaven') is devoted to a description of the final journey of King Yudhishthira, the son of Dharma. First he asks to see his brothers, and is taken on what appears to be a descent into hell:

> In front went the messenger of the gods, and behind him the king, on a path that was inauspicious, dangerous and frequented by evil-doers, covered with darkness, horrible, reeking with the smells of evil-doers, with hair for its moss and grass, flesh and blood for its mud, filled with flies and mosquitoes with their stings fixed sticking up, and crickets, surrounded on all sides with corpses, on this side and that, strewn with bones and hair, full of worms and maggots, surrounded on all sides by a blazing fire, overrun by crows and owls and vultures with iron beaks, and covered with ghosts the size of the Vindhya mountains but with mouths like needles, with severed arms, thighs, and hands covered in fat and blood, and amputated entrails and legs scattered here and there.
>
> In the midst of that inauspicious, hair-raising path that stank with the stench of corpses, the king who was the soul of Dharma walked, pondering a great deal. He saw a river full of hot water, hard to go through, and the forest whose leaves were swords, the ground covered with sharp razors. Heated mud and sand, free-standing iron rocks, and iron pots of simmering sesame oil were all around. Yudhishthira also saw spikey *salmalika* trees with sharp thorns, painful to touch, and the tortures of the evil-doers.
>
> When he saw that bad-smelling path, he said to the messenger of the gods, 'How far must we go on such a road? And where are my brothers? You should tell me that. To whom of the gods does this place belong? I want to know that.' Having heard the words of the Dharma king, the messenger of the gods stopped and said to him, 'This is as far as you go. For I must turn back; this is what I was told by those-who-dwell-in-heaven. If you are tired, lord of kings, you should come along.' And Yudhishthira, disgusted and fainting from that smell, set his mind on turning back and turned around.
>
> But when he turned around, suffering from unhappiness and sorrow, he heard there the wretched words of people speaking on all sides:

'Royal sage!' 'Son of Dharma!' 'Noble Pandava!' 'Stop as a favour to us, just for a little moment. When you come near, an auspicious breeze blows, carrying your smell, which brings us comfort. We here will obtain relief for a long time, as long as you are here, by looking at you. Stay here, even for a moment. While you stay here, torture does not hurt us.'

He heard in this place many sorts of words like that, pitiful words of those who were suffering, crying out on all sides. And he said, 'Alas, how painful,' and stayed. He had heard those voices before again and again, long ago, but he did not recognize them as they came from those wasted, suffering people. Then they told him that they were his brothers, and his wife. Then King Yudhishthira, the son of Dharma, spoke his sharp anger; he reviled the gods and even Dharma. Heated by the sharp smell, he said to the messenger of the gods: 'Go, good sir, to the presence of those whose messenger you are. For I will not go there; I am staying. Announce this, messenger. For taking refuge with me brings comfort to my brothers.'[16]

The gods then come to try to persuade him to leave, and as soon as they arrive, hell vanishes:

That darkness disappeared. The tortures of evil-doers were not seen there, nor the river of hell, with its spikey trees. The frightful iron pots and the rocks were not seen, and the distorted bodies which the king had seen there all around, became invisible. Then a good wind, pleasant to touch, carrying a good smell, very cool, blew from the presence of the gods. Then Indra, the lord of the gods, said to Yudhishthira this speech, which began with words of conciliation:

'My son, inevitably all kings must see hell. There are two piles of good and evil. Whoever enjoys the good deed first (in heaven) goes afterwards to hell. And whoever experiences hell first, goes afterwards to heaven. A person who has a record of mostly bad deeds experiences heaven first; therefore I made you come here this way because I wished to do what was best for you. Since you once deceived an enemy, you were shown hell in the form of a deception. And just like you, so too your brothers went to hell just in the form of a deception. Now they have been freed from guilt, and all the people on your side, princes killed in battle for you, have reached heaven. You will dive into this auspicious river of the gods, the Ganges in the sky, which purifies the triple worlds, and depart. And when you have bathed in it your human nature will go away. You will have no more grief, no exhaustion, no enmity. Inevitably all kings must see hell. But you have experienced this supreme misery just for a moment; none of you deserve hell for a long time.'

The story does not quite end there, however. Someone hearing the story asks: 'How long did they remain in heaven? Tell me that, too. Or did they perhaps have a place there that would last forever? At the end of their karma, what level of existence did they attain?' And the narrator replies, 'Everyone must go [from heaven] at the end of his karmas. The heroes all assumed the forms of gods and by degrees, your majesty, they all reached all the worlds, beyond which there is nothing.'[17]

Thus the *Mahabharata* weaves the concept of karma into a vivid depiction of hell, and a not so vivid description of heaven, and still there remains an unanswered question to which there is only a sketchily formulated answer: 'The worlds beyond which there is nothing.'

But people continued to worry about these questions. Yudhishthira's dilemma in hell was occasioned by a kind of transfer of merit: Yudhishthira sent a cool breeze to ease the torment of his friends and relatives. That concept, merely sketched there, is more fully developed a few centuries later in the *Markandeya Purana*:

> Once, when his wife named Fatso (Pivari) had been in her fertile season, King Vipashchit did not sleep with her, as it was his duty to do, but slept instead with his other, beautiful wife Kaikeyi. He went to hell briefly to expiate this one sin, but when he was about to leave for heaven, the people in hell begged him to stay, since the wind that touched his body dispelled their pain. 'People cannot obtain in heaven or in the world of Brahma,' said Vipashchit, 'such happiness as arises from giving release (nirvana) to suffering creatures.' And he refused to leave until Indra agreed to let the king's good deeds (karma) be used to release those people of evil karma from their torments in hell—though they all went from there immediately to another womb that was determined by the fruits of their own karma.[18]

The episode is clearly based on the *Mahabharata*, and uses some of the same phrases.[vii] But, significantly, the people in hell now are not related to the king in any way; the king's compassion extends beyond his family, to all creatures. And now the text begins to speak of Buddhist/Hindu concepts like nirvana and the transfer of karma, making it possible for the real, heaven-bound king to release real sinners from a real hell. Karma and

---

[vii] It also gives the sexually preferred second wife in this story the name of the sexually preferred second wife in the *Ramayana*, Kaikeyi. See 'Shadows of the *Ramayana*'.

samsara have the last word, though: in the end, having passed through heaven and hell, the sinners are reborn according to their just deserts—a theory that the final chapter of the *Mahabharata* had chosen not to invoke, preferring to send them all to a world beyond which there is nothing.

REBIRTH IN THE PURANAS

The early Sanskrit Puranas, c. 500–1000 CE, fleshed out, as it were, the philosophical concept of reincarnation developed in the Upanishads, in narratives about reincarnation. These texts, with their inevitable tendency to the rococo, posited many heavens and many hells, a complex mandala of retribution. The Puranas add psychological details to the basic *Mahabharata* concept of the time-sharing aspects of heaven and hell:

> Sometimes a man goes to heaven; sometimes he goes to hell. Sometimes a dead man experiences both hell and heaven. Sometimes he is born here again and consumes his own karma; sometimes a man who has consumed his karma dies and goes forth with just a very little bit of karma remaining. Sometimes he is reborn here with a small amount of good and bad karma, having consumed most of his karma in heaven or in hell. A great source of the suffering in hell is the fact that the people there can see the people who dwell in heaven; but the people in hell rejoice when the people in heaven fall down into hell. Likewise, there is great misery even in heaven, beginning from the very moment when people ascend there, for this thought enters their minds: 'I am going to fall from here.' And when they see the hells they become quite miserable, worrying, day and night, 'This is where I am going to go.'[19]

The misery of hell is thus somewhat alleviated by the pleasure that people take in the misfortunes of others, and the pleasures of heaven are somewhat undercut by the contemplation of what is to follow.

HINDU GODS AS DRAMATIS PERSONAE IN THE DRAMAS OF DEATH

Each of the great Hindu gods plays god—which is to say, plays death—but each plays it in a different way. And even though a Hindu generally gives his or her devotion primarily to one particular god, all of the gods are available at all times to all Hindus, and many Hindus draw upon several different mythological traditions.[viii] With this in mind, let me provide a

---

[viii] See 'Are Hindus Monotheists?'

kind of overview of the major myths of death that characterize each of the great Hindu gods and goddesses.

Although the Hindus, and Indologists, often describe a trinity of gods (Brahma the creator, Vishnu the preserver and Shiva the destroyer),[ix] in fact Brahma is hardly worshipped at all, and the other two great gods, Vishnu and Shiva, are each both creators and destroyers, as is the other great deity who forms the real quasi-trinity, Devi, the goddess. Each deity, therefore, is death, though they are different sorts of death.

Vishnu

Vishnu appears as death on many occasions. On the narrative level, he kills demons (*asuras*, anti-gods). He takes the form of the Man-lion, Narasimha, to kill a demon named Hiranyakashipu ('Golden Cushion'), who had been given a promise that he could not be killed by man or animal, by day or by night, on earth or in the sky, and so forth. Vishnu, therefore, took a thoroughly composite form: as the man-lion he was neither man nor animal; he attacked at sunset, neither day nor night; and he held the demon across his knees, neither in the sky nor on earth. Thus the god became a living category error, matter out of place—which is, as Mary Douglas has taught us, our unconscious definition of both dirt and sin.[20]

But Vishnu is also another, more abstract sort of death: he is Time, that destroys everything. When he sleeps, the universe dies; when he reawakens, the universe is reborn. Vishnu sleeps his cosmic sleep on a couch made of the serpent of Infinity (Ananta), also known as the Leftover (Shesha, what is left over when the world is destroyed, or left over from the sacrifice). Now the serpent that was a negative symbol of drought in the Vedas becomes a positive symbol of rebirth—and water—in Vedantic thought.

A third form of death that Vishnu assumes is doomsday, Time not in its passive, drowsy aspect but in its aggressive, devouring aspect. Vishnu's epiphany as Doomsday is best known from the *Bhagavad Gita*, where he appears at first in his charming human avatar of Krishna, but then in a terrifying form: as people are being sucked into his thousands of mouths that bristle with fangs, their heads are crushed, and some of them get stuck between his teeth.[21]

But Vishnu as Krishna plays both sides of the street, as it were: he also subdues Death, death in the form of a serpent. The serpent, named Kaliya, lived in a swimming hole where the child Krishna used to play with the

---

[ix] See 'Three (or More)'.

little boys who were his friends. As the serpent's poison polluted the water, Krishna resolved to subdue him. He plunged into the pool and danced on the cobra's many heads until he surrendered. But Krishna did not kill the serpent; after all, you can't kill death, you can't kill evil. He merely banished him to another part of the forest, where he would not harm us.[22]

Shiva

One set of myths pits death against withdrawal from life, in the form of renunciation (*sannyasa*). This network of myths begins with the premise that the Creator asks the god Shiva—the great god of ascetics, yogis and renouncers—to create living creatures. In the first set of stories, so great is Shiva's pity for creatures who would ultimately be subject to re-death that he refuses to create any creatures at all, engaging in a kind of prophylactic euthanasia, and the Creator gets another god to make the flawed creatures who are our ancestors. In a second set of variations, Shiva engages in yoga in order to create immortals, but either (subvariant a) he takes too long, and the Creator in his impatience creates us; or (subvariant b), when Shiva produces a kind of trial run of twelve immortals identical with himself, they prove to be so arrogant and destructive that the Creator refuses to let Shiva continue the line, and has someone else create us, as mortals with greatly limited powers.[23]

Shiva is known as the Destroyer, and indeed he is more closely associated with the deadly aspects of creation than Vishnu is; where Vishnu, like any good general practitioner, treats death as part of the whole, death is Shiva's specialty. Shiva is the author of the death of the entire universe in the myth of the destruction of the Triple City: three demons are given three magic cities, of gold, silver and black iron, one in heaven, one in the air and one on earth (i.e. the triple worlds of the universe—heaven, the ether and earth).[24] Brahma promises them that they can only be destroyed when the three cities come together and Shiva shoots them with a single arrow. At the appointed moment, the gods create a chariot for Shiva to ride in when he destroys the triple cities; this chariot is made by reassembling all the elements, animate and inanimate, abstract and concrete, that were so carefully dispersed and labelled at the time of primeval creation. The bow that Shiva uses is made of the Year, and his own shadow, the Night of Doomsday, is the bowstring, for Shiva himself is Time and Death. This is a myth of cosmic destruction by means of combining disparate elements, the mirror image of the myth of cosmic creation by means of dismemberment. To separate and put in order is to create, in this context;

to cause oppositional pairs to unite, and thus to lose their separate identities, is to produce chaos and annihilation.

Sometimes it is said that Shiva destroys the universe at doomsday not by shooting it with an arrow but by dancing it into smithereens, dancing his dance of doomsday, the *tandava*. Shiva as the yogi, however, is also the enemy of dancers, the death of dancers.[25] Thus when a sage dances in joy after he has cut his hand and seen plant sap flow from the wound, Shiva comes to him and cuts his own hand open; the sage sees ashes white as death, the ashes of corpses, flow from the wound, and he stops dancing.[26]

And Shiva is also the Death of Death (Yamantaka), the End of the Ender. When Yama, the king of the Dead, comes to lead away one of Shiva's devotees, Shiva fights him, kicks him in the chest, and forces him to promise immunity to all who worship Shiva. In the early mythology, this amazing grace leads to problems of a union nature: Yama complains that he is out of work, since everyone worships Shiva and goes to Heaven instead of Hell.[x] Ultimately, however, the mythology resorts to the open-ended, 'break-through-the-roof' system in which it is, in fact, possible to cheat not only evil but death forever.[xi] The world to which the devotees of Shiva are translated now is an infinity of something, of the love of god, perhaps, in place of the infinity of nirvana or moksha, the Vedantic/Buddhist infinity of emptiness.

The mythology of death seems to take a slightly different form in Buddhism, where the enemy of the Buddha, Mara, is a combination of erotic love and death. But in fact we may see this same synthesizing process at work in Hinduism. For Shiva also expresses his deadly power in the form of the doomsday mare, who ranges at the bottom of the ocean, consuming the excess waters with her flames even as the waters subdue the excess heat from her mouth. This hair-trigger tension between anger and lust will remain in uneasy balance until doomsday, when the mare will emerge from the ocean, and the repressed forces of anger and lust, death and sex, will burn the universe to ashes and flood it with the cosmic waters.[xii]

The forces of death and lust combine, again, in the mythology of the beautiful goddess Durga, whose name means "Difficult to Reach." Her great myth is the tale of the *Liebestod* of the Buffalo Demon, Mahisha, who lusted after her and asked her to marry him. She replied by challenging him to battle, in which she killed him, simultaneously releasing him from

---

[x] See 'The Scrapbook'.
[xi] See 'Together Apart'.
[xii] See 'The Submarine Mare'.

his demonic and buffalo form and uniting with him in a quasi-sexual embrace, '*la morte douce*'.[27] But death in Hinduism is, as we have seen, sweet even when it is meted out by a male god with whom we have no direct erotic contact. There are many deaths, and each has its sorrow, but each, in India, also has its meaning.

REINCARNATION FOR NON-HINDUS

Although ideas about reincarnation have occurred in many cultures, South Asian civilization has developed the most elaborate, subtle and varied forms of this belief, and is often regarded as its fountainhead. Belief in reincarnation has long appealed to non-Hindu consciousness. Karmic thinking continues to surface in New Age circles, in Hollywood (both in films and in the personal beliefs of stars like Shirley MacLaine), and in what might be called American folk belief.

Most scholars of Hinduism and Buddhism tread lightly upon the karma theory for reasons of inter-cultural tact (or raging relativism, depending on your point of view); some (including myself) go farther, and grant the theory some degree of useful wisdom, at the very least as a powerful metaphor. But a more critical stance is taken by scholars such as Robert P. Goldman, who has characterized the karma theory as 'nonsense'. He asks, 'What is going on here? What could possibly induce intelligent and well-educated people to take this nonsense seriously?' Then he exhorts us to ask down-to-earth questions about it:

> How do events in our real, as opposed to imaginary, pasts affect our later lives? What is our responsibility for events to which we were unwilling or even unwitting parties? What are the constraints upon our ability to recover clear memories of our early years? Central to these concerns are the issues of memory, its distortion, loss and recovery and guilt, its assignment and displacement.[28]

His answer begins with a perceptive discussion of the connection between repressed childhood memories and the alleged memories of former lives:

> [T]he feelings, and the terrible anxieties they generate are nonetheless real. What better way to partially confess to the former while at the same time fractionally discharging the latter than to ascribe the aggression to someone who both is and is not oneself? If these dark feelings are the result of real events in one's past life then by all means let us push the boundaries of our past back beyond our childhood into the shadowy realm of 'past lives'.[29]

'Someone who both is and is not oneself' is a fine statement of the ambivalence of the many people who do believe in the karma theory.

Another tenet of the karma theory also explains a kind of psychological projection: karma can be transferred from one person to another.[30] Goldman finds it preposterous to assert, as the theory does, that 'we live in a strange and morally blind universe in which our own actions may see their rewards in the lives of other people while we must content ourselves with the fruits of the actions of still others'.[31] Yet it needs no South Asian come from the grave to point out the relevance of this truth to our own lives, from the most tragic level to the most trivial: caught up in the great Rube Goldberg machine of human causation, we enjoy the shade of trees planted by other people generations ago, and we miss our plane because some idiot rear-ends another idiot on the freeway. The karma theory exaggerates and dramatizes a situation that is entirely banal; it expresses the intuition that the things that happen to us now, and that make us who we are, consist, in large part, of forces from the past over which we have no control and of which we have little or no knowledge.

The karma theory, however, goes on to add the less obvious assertion that the other people who take the guilt or credit for our deeds, or for whose deeds we take the guilt or credit, are forms of ourselves; these are people 'who—we must take it on faith—were somehow identical with us. We cannot even expect to know exactly what it is "we" have done.'[32] And the prime candidates for this role are, of course, our parents. The theory asserts both an identification and our ignorance of that identification. The identification sits well in a traditional society like Hinduism, which regards a son as his father reborn, but it goes against the grain of American individualism. Even an American, however, will acknowledge that a parent's crime may ruin the life of his or her child precisely because they are, in some significant sense, the same person. The ignorance (of the identification) also sticks in the American craw; and yet, even within one life, never mind the karma theory, we are, more often than not, ignorant of the precise deeds committed by the people (usually our parents) who have made us what we are—people who are part of the very substance of our minds and (in the case of parents) our bodies. We are ignorant of them either because we have forgotten (or repressed) them or because they took place before we were born. After all, we all forget many of our former selves—the infant altogether, much of the child, some of the adolescent, or the former marriage, the pain of childbirth, and so forth; one door opens and another shuts; we awaken from one dream not to full wakefulness but only to fall into another. The Hindu mythology of reincarnation analogizes the forgotten past life not to the lost or suppressed memories of childhood but to our lost memories of our dreams.

Hindu thinking does not regard the parents as the only, or even the primary, source of karma; the transmigrating soul is said to mix its own inherited karma with the karma of each of the new parents to form the cumulative karma of the new child.[33] But parents are, I think, the best way to translate the Hindu theory of karma into something that makes sense for people who do not believe in the rebirth of the soul after death. From unknown episodes in the lives of our parents, and grandparents, and more distant ancestors, we get not only the shape of our nose but our susceptibility to certain diseases and, perhaps, to certain sorts of people. There is a long continuum of parental influence: closest are the things we remember that our parents did for/to us relatively recently, and then the things that they did when we were so little that we cannot remember them clearly or at all, then the things (like smoking or contracting AIDS) that our mothers did to us while we were in the womb, then the things that our parents did before we were born, and finally both the genetic stock and the cultural memories transmitted from earlier generations: the things that happened during the pogroms in Russia, the traumas suffered during the Depression in America or Partition in India. The weight of these influences, the realization that we cannot simply invent ourselves as we would wish to be, is one of the insights that drive the karma theory.

My emphasis on the role of parents in the karma theory differs from Goldman's in several ways, but most significantly in his assumption that the parental influence will be negative and produce anxiety and guilt. My assumption is that it may indeed be and do all of that (Philip Larkin said it best: 'They fuck you up, your mum and dad; they do not mean to, but they do'), but that it also accounts for the transmission of talents, positive memories such as those stirred by music and art, and, above all, irrational love, or the capacity to fall in love at first sight, generally with a highly inappropriate person who either is or most definitely is not just like our father or mother.[34]

Many non-Hindus grant the karma theory some degree of useful wisdom, at the very least as a powerful metaphor and at the most as an expression, *mutatis mutandis*, of ideas that they, too, hold about the compelling force of the past. The karma theory *tells* us that we have lived other lives, that our souls have had other bodies. But how can we *feel*, as well as accept intellectually, the reality of those other lives if we cannot remember them? It is easier for Hindus to *feel* the theory of rebirth, as they feel themselves to be a part of a larger human group in a way that other people do not; they believe that they are joined in nature as well as in culture not only with the people in the past and future to whom they are related (people whom non-Hindus, too, regard as part of their physical substance) but also with the other people with whom they have present contact (people whom non-Hindus do not generally regard as physically connected with them). The Hindu texts tell us that we are karmically linked to all the other people in the world; 'they' are 'us'. For those of us who lack the imagination to perceive the infinity of our lives in time, it might be possible to perceive the infinity of our lives in human space.

My relationship with the karma theory changed in major ways over the half century since I first encountered India. In my book *The Origins of Evil in Hindu Mythology*, published in 1975, I argued that the theory of karma was not regarded as an adequate explanation of evil even in its own country, as evidenced by the fact that the Hindus developed many other approaches to evil, including the myths that I wrote about in that book. In the preface to the second edition of *The Origins of Evil*, I remarked that I had changed my evaluation of the karma theory, had come to respect it more, in part by editing a 350-page book about it, *Karma and Rebirth in Classical Indian Traditions* (1980). And in 1986, in *Other Peoples' Myths*, I took it very seriously indeed. I had gradually come first to think with and then to feel with the karma theory.

But my realization of this understanding happened at one particular moment. It was at a time when I was feeling rather sorry for myself for having only one child; I wished that I had had lots of children, and now it was too late. I felt that having six children would have meant having an entirely different life, not merely six times the life of a woman with one child, and I wanted that life as well as the life that I had. This thought was in my mind as I wandered on a beach in Ireland, and saw a woman with lots and lots of children, very nice children, too, and at their best, as young children often are on a beach. Normally, I would have envied her; but this time, I enjoyed her children. I was happy to watch them. And suddenly I felt that they were mine, that the woman on the beach had had them for me, so that they would be there for me to watch them as they played in the water. Her life was my life too; I felt it then, and I remember it now. What had been an idea to me until then, the idea of my karmic identity with other people, became an experience. I was able to live her life in my imagination.

One way of interpreting my epiphany of the woman on the beach was this realization that my connection to her—and, through her, to every other woman who had ever had or ever would have children—meant that my brief lifespan was expanded into the lifespans of all the other people in the world. This is a very Hindu way of looking at one's relationship with all other people. Woven through the series of individual lives, each consisting of a cluster of experiences, was the thread of the experience itself—in this case, motherhood. That experience would survive when her children and mine were long dead.

I felt then that all the things that one wanted to do and to be existed in eternity; they stood there forever, as long as there was human life on the planet Earth. They were like beautiful rooms that anyone could walk into; and when I could no longer walk into them, they would still be there. They were part of time, and though they could not go on being part of me for much longer, part of me would always be there in them. Something of me would still linger in those things that I had loved, like the perfume or pipe smoke that tells you that someone else has been in a room before you. This is the same 'perfume', the same karmic trace of memory (*vasana*) that adheres to the transmigrating soul.[xiii] And through my connection with the woman on the beach, I would be the people in the future who sensed in that room the perfume that I had left behind, though (unless I was a gifted sage) I would not recognize it as my perfume. Perhaps, since I am not a Hindu, that is as close as I can come to believing that I can remember my other lives: remembering other peoples' lives as my life. And perhaps it is close enough.[35]

[xiii] See 'Forgetting and Re-awakening'.

FORGETTING AND RE–AWAKENING
TO INCARNATION[1]

In the Hindu view, as we have seen,[i] reincarnation happens whether we know it or not; it is therefore an unfalsifiable proposition. But this did not stop Hindus from imagining, in glorious technicolour, people who did know about their past lives. The mythology of reincarnation jumps the barrier of rebirth, imagining the survival of consciousness on the other side. In this mythology, the new self is literally a part of the past not merely of the present life but of other, previous lives. At any moment, any of us may be awakened to the memory of another, lost life. We are constantly reinventing ourselves out of the scraps of the past; we are always imitating our past selves. The signals we send to ourselves from our former lives are wake-up calls, like the message the Chippendale Mupp, one of the creatures in *Dr. Seuss's Sleep Book*, sends to himself: at bedtime, he bites the end tuft on his *very* long tail, so that the ouch will work its way up the whole tail and, finally, wake him up in the morning.

THE LINGERING SCENTS OF MEMORY

In Hinduism, the myths of karma ask: Where is memory, in the mind or in the body? How can our bodies remember things that our minds have forgotten? Hinduism assumes that when the body dies, the soul transmigrates, taking with it the dead person's karma, the moral record of good and bad actions committed in all former lives. Indian philosophy locates memory in the *manas*, a combination of mind and heart: like the heart, it is a physical organ in the body, and like the mind, it is where you learn calculus; and like both mind and heart, it is where you fall in love—thus doubly blurring the Cartesian distinction between mind and body. But

---

[i] See 'Death and Rebirth'.

some branches of Indian philosophy locate memory in the soul, without, however, totally divorcing it from the body. For, although the transmigrating soul in Hinduism usually loses its memory as it crosses the boundary of rebirth and sheds its body, some particularly gifted and/or lucky people can remember their previous births. Some branches of Indian philosophy, therefore, locate memory along with karma in (or, more precisely, on) the soul, without, however, totally divorcing it from the body. The karma theory tells us that we have lived lives that we cannot remember and hence cannot feel. We can remember some things in life in our minds, and perhaps, therefore, in our souls, but other things can only be remembered with our bodies, which do not survive the trip across the barrier of death. According to the karma theory, however, memory is not all there is; there is also a reality of unrecalled experience that gives a kind of validity to our connection with lives that we do not recall. The karma theory recognizes the parallelism between events forgotten within a single life—the events of early childhood, or the things that we repress or that (in Hindu mythology) we forget as the result of a curse—and the events forgotten from a previous life.[2] It also recognizes a similarity in the ways in which we sometimes half-recall these various sorts of events, often with a sense of *déjà vu*, the feeling that one sometimes has, on seeing someone or someplace for the first time, that one has seen it before. We remember something that we cannot remember, from a lost past, through the power of the invisible tracks or traces left behind on our souls by those events; these traces the Hindus call *vasanas*, 'perfumes', scents that are the impressions of anything remaining unconsciously in the mind—the present consciousness of past perceptions.[3] These *vasanas* are what a king in a Sanskrit play (a man who has been cursed to forget his wife[ii]) has in mind when he says:

> Even a happy man may be overcome by passionate longing
> when he sees beautiful things or hears sweet sounds.
> Perhaps he is remembering something he was not conscious of before that
> moment,
> the loves of a former life, firmly rooted in the impressions of lingering
> emotions.[4]

The bits of experience that Hindus call the karmic memory traces cling to our transmigrating souls even in new bodies, loose threads trailing not merely from a former life within this lifespan but from a previous life, a

[ii] See 'The Clever Wife'.

previous incarnation. (One commentator remarks that it is impossible to shake off these impressions even after thousands of lives.[5])

Such 'perfumes' also correspond in many ways to the social chemosignals that Martha McClintock has studied, olfactory clues to social behaviour that are handed down genetically (which is, in a sense, through rebirths)— generally unconscious clues that influence our emotions. Parents, or, more generally, genetic inheritance, are what led McClintock to apply the term *vasanas* to the 'social chemosignals' that are handed down in the DNA 'referring to the effect of a previous life on one's current life'.[6] Appropriately, McClintock named one group of these chemosignals, closely related to what she has called pheromones, after the *vasanas* of Hindu philosophy:

> [S]ocial chemosignals are remarkably similar to the medieval Sanskrit term *vasanas*. *Vasana*, the singular noun, is derived from the Sanskrit term *vas*, meaning 'to perfume' . . . The term is used to explain why a person has a tendency to react to a situation in a particular way. We find it useful to adopt this philosophical term in our classification of human social chemosignals because both its etymology and its functional definition are so close to the findings from our empirical psychological data . . . *Vasanas* are those unconscious chemosignals whose functional effects are related to or predicted by their odour qualities when they are experienced consciously . . . The power of subconscious odours to evoke emotional memory-derived experience in humans is widely recognized . . . Because they are not necessarily conscious, the term *vasana* may be more appropriate than 'unconscious odours', which is an oxymoron.[7]

THE CYCLE

The unconscious memories of past lives, the *vasanas*, predispose the transmigrating soul to act in one way or another in its new life. It retains some sort of magnetic attachment to its old body and, with it, to its old personality. Even if we cannot remember who we were, we are reborn in the shadow of our previous personality. The soul gets typecast.

Hindu texts imagine the reincarnating soul meditating on its next life in the womb of the soul's future mother, where it (not yet he or she) not only remains fully conscious but remembers its previous lives in agonizing detail:

> Then it begins to remember its many previous existences in the wheel of rebirth, and that depresses it, and it tosses from side to side, thinking,

'I won't ever do *that* again, as soon as I get out of this womb. I will do everything I can, so that I won't become an embryo again.' It thinks in this way as it remembers the hundreds of miseries of birth that it experienced before, in the power of fate. Then, as time goes by, the embryo turns around, head down, and in the ninth or tenth month it is born. As it comes out, it is hurt by the wind of procreation; it comes out crying, because it is pained by the misery in its heart. When it has come out of the womb, it falls into an unbearable swoon, but it regains consciousness when the air touches it. Then Vishnu's deluding power of illusion assails him, and when his soul has been deluded by it, he loses his knowledge. As soon as the living creature has lost his knowledge, he becomes a baby. After that he becomes a young boy, then an adolescent, and then an old man. And then he dies and is born again as a human. Thus he wanders on the wheel of rebirth like the bucket on the wheel of a well.[8]

Chagrin at the memory of previous mistakes and despair at the realization that one will make them all again in this life, too, is what makes the baby cry as he enters the world. *The Laws of Manu* promises many upwardly mobile transmigrations, but not for everyone: 'Through the repetition of their evil actions, men of little intelligence experience miseries in womb after womb in this world.'[9]

Reincarnation is generally regarded as a fresh start, but the tabula is not always quite so rasa as more simplistic treatments of the doctrine assume. The goal of liberation theology, Hindu style, is to untangle the knots of karma, to achieve moksha, freedom from the same old same old in life after life. For a Hindu, this means to break out altogether from *samsara* (the cycle of transmigration), but it could also mean to be free to go forward without the compulsion for self-imitation. For people find it difficult to kick the Lethe habit. In many ways the *vasanas* that return to the reborn soul correspond not just to the unconscious as we have come to understand it but more particularly to the repressed unconscious that *returns*, in Freud's formulation.[10] Freud also referred to a 'memory trace' (*Erinnerungsspur*) that was not yet a part of conscious memory.[11]

THE MAN WHO FORGOT HE WAS GOD: THE MONK'S DREAM

Hindus continued to tell stories and to develop theories about reincarnation, many of them expressed in a kind of mixed genre of philosophical narrative whose masterpiece is the *Yogavasishtha*, a Sanskrit text composed in Kashmir between the tenth and the twelfth centuries CE, a time when

Hindus and Buddhists were in close contact.[12] There are many stories about reincarnation in this text, and one of the best (a very long text of which I can only sketch the outlines here) includes many detailed suggestions about the mechanisms that might determine the precise ways in which we are reborn. It presents a complex pattern of self-impersonation through reincarnation, and a circular model of the survival of consciousness. This is the tale of a man who dreams he is the god Rudra, a form of the god Shiva who is, in this text, the Supreme God:

> Once upon a time there was a monk who was inclined to imagine things rather a lot. One day, he happened to imagine a man named Jivata, who drank too much and fell into a heavy sleep. As Jivata dreamt, he saw a Brahmin who read all day long. One day, that Brahmin fell asleep, and as his daily activities were still alive within him, like a tree inside a seed, he dreamt that he was a prince. One day that prince fell asleep after a heavy meal, and dreamt that he was a great king. One day that king fell asleep, having gorged himself on his every desire, and in his dream he saw himself as a celestial woman. The woman fell into a deep sleep in the languor that followed making love, and she saw herself as a doe with darting eyes. That doe one day fell asleep and dreamed that she was a clinging vine, because she had been accustomed to eating vines; for animals dream, too, and they always remember what they have seen and heard.
>
> The vine saw herself as a bee that used to buzz among the vines; the bee fell in love with a lotus and was so intoxicated by the lotus sap he drank that his wits became numb; just then an elephant came to that pond and trampled the lotus, and the bee, still attached to the lotus, was crushed with it on the elephant's tusk. As the bee looked at the elephant, he saw himself as an elephant in rut. That elephant in rut fell into a deep pit and became the favourite elephant of a king. One day the elephant was cut to pieces by a sword in battle, and as he went to his final resting place he saw a swarm of bees hovering over the sweet ichor that oozed from his temples, and so the elephant became a bee again. The bee returned to the lotus pond and was trampled under the feet of another elephant, and just then he noticed a goose beside him in the pond, and so he became a goose. That goose moved through other births, other wombs, for a long time, until one day, when he was a goose in a flock of other geese, he realized that, being a goose, he was the same as the swan of the Creator. Just as he had this thought, he was shot by a hunter and he died, and then he was born as the swan of the Creator.

One day the swan saw Rudra, and thought, with sudden certainty, 'I am Rudra.' Immediately that idea was reflected like an image in a mirror, and he took on the form of Rudra. Then he could see all of his former experiences, and he understood them: 'Because Jivata admired Brahmins, he saw himself as a Brahmin; and since the Brahmin had thought about princes all the time, he became a prince. And that fickle woman was so jealous of the beautiful eyes of a doe that she became a doe . . . These creatures are my own rebirths.' And, after a while, the monk and Jivata and all the others will wear out their bodies and will unite in the world of Rudra.[13]

The swan, or wild goose, a natural and cross-cultural symbol of periodic return, is the emblem of both the individual soul and the mind of god, in this case Rudra. In this metaphysical world, we remember both our dreams and our rebirths—much the same thing—when we awaken from our primary amnesia, which makes us forget that we are god.

The story goes on to raise other metaphysical issues, but these passages make several important points for the topic at hand. The transition to a new life can take place either by thinking of something or by suffering a violent death, for dreaming and dying are conflated. Both dreaming and dying are brought on by over-indulgence in the pleasures of the senses, and those same pleasures of the senses determine the content of the dream or the new life. Indeed, sensual appeal is what attracts the soul to the next life: love, admiration (even, sometimes, in its negative aspect of jealousy), obsession, fascination. Rudra himself (the supreme deity, who is regarded here, as often in Hindu mythology, as existing on a level that encompasses the tasks and powers of the Creator) is caught up in this round of attraction, but he is also the source of our own attractions, the source to which we return when the cycle has played itself out.

The story does not reveal to us the entire rebirth of each of the characters; none of them is born, and most of them do not die within the story. Significantly, the first person the monk dreams of is named Jivata, a word derived from the word for a life or a soul, *jiva*. Some of the subjects are women (and female animals), with whom the male actors have no lasting attachments, merely brief physical encounters. These people dream and become what they have habitually dreamed about and are thinking about as they die. We awaken from ignorance, or from sleep, or from life; the same verb (*budh*) covers all three.

The creatures in the monk's dream form a pattern that is a masterful combination of order and chance. Though anything *can* happen, certain things are more *likely* to happen; this is how karma skews and orders the chaos of the universe. The text tells us: 'Again and again these lives revolve in creation like the waves in water, and some [rebirths] are strikingly similar [to what they were before], and others are about half the same; some are a little bit the same, some are not very much alike at all, and sometimes they are once again just the same.' This flexibility, together with the elements of pure chance and the gravity of karmic tendencies, makes certain coincidences not only possible but probable. For the text tells us that after the bee had become an elephant and was then reborn again as a bee, he went back to the same lotus pond where he had previously met with his unfortunate accident, 'because people who are not aware of their karmic traces find it hard to give up their bad habits.' So, too, the beautiful woman becomes a doe because she envies the beauty of the doe's eyes, and the text remarks, 'Alas, the delusion that results from the karmic traces causes such misery among creatures.'[14] Each of the people in the dream chain is reborn in a particular form *because they all want something*. There is a hunger, unsated in their present lives, that propels them across the barrier of death into a new birth where this still unfulfilled longing leads them to do what they do. By extension and implication, all of us, too, helplessly spin out of our desires the lives we have inherited from our former selves. And so in each new life, we pretend, once again, to be who we are, repeating lines from an earlier script even when we think that we are improvising or that we are not performing at all. We cannot escape from our own previous character, our desire, which sticks like tar to the transmigrating soul. Our memory of those ancient desires is also partly accidental, partly not so accidental; Hinduism offers several different praxes designed to help us remember our former lives, just as psychoanalysis claims to help us remember our dreams. For most of us, however, such memories remain largely unconscious and inaccessible.

THE GOD WHO FORGOT HE WAS GOD

All of us tend to forget that we are (a) god, according to the doctrine of Hindu idealism in the *Yogavasishtha*. But divinity is a continuum; some creatures are more divine than others, and some gods are more divine in certain texts than in others. The philosophical and mythological assertion that all humans are (conscious or unconscious) incarnations of a deity is enacted in the many rituals in which the worshipper masquerades as the god (through the use of masks, for instance). The *Yogavasishtha* depicts humans who forget that the god Shiva, as Rudra, is the very substance of consciousness, but in other texts, Shiva himself forgets who he is and engages in unconscious self-imitation when his wife Parvati tricks him by masquerading as another woman.[15] The chain continues when Shiva and Parvati become incarnate not merely in all human beings but in particular human beings (called partial incarnations) who slip in and out of consciousness of their incarnational status.

A Sanskrit text composed in Assam in the tenth or eleventh century CE explores the human complications that can arise out of such a partial (re)incarnation.[16] In this text, Shiva and Parvati impersonate a human king and queen on three, increasingly specific levels: First is the general philosophical doctrine that all creatures are made of *brahman* (the divine substance of which the universe is composed), and hence the king and queen are part of the godhead embodied in Shiva and Parvati. Second is the implicit metaphysical incarnation based on the belief that all men and women are forms of Shiva and Parvati, rather than of other deities, for human beings are all marked with the signs of the god Shiva and his consort, the male and female sexual organs, *lingam* and *yoni*.[17] And third, the proximate cause, is the explicit impersonation of the king by Shiva, necessitated by a sage's curse, a common cause of the incarnation of Hindu gods as humans.

The incarnations (or avatars) of the god Vishnu, particularly Rama and Krishna, have a more particular awareness of their own divinity, yet even they often forget their divine natures. In the *Mahabharata*, Krishna often forgets he is god until someone else remembers—a mortal or, occasionally, another god—or, occasionally, Krishna himself remembers. In later texts such as the tenth-century *Bhagavata Purana*, however, Krishna never forgets. Indeed, when Krishna is still a little child, he sometimes remembers not only that he is god but that he was previously incarnate as Rama, recalling, when he is drifting between sleeping and waking, this earlier birth.[18] He is also firmly in control of his knowledge of his own divinity when he deals with other people (including his mother) whom he allows to forget who he is because they cannot sustain the intensity of their brief visions of his true nature.[19]

Rama, too, often forgets his divinity. When Rama publicly doubts that his wife Sita remained faithful to him, the gods ask how he can do this, adding: 'Can you not know that you are the best of all the gods?' Rama, uncomprehending, says, 'I think of myself as a man, as Rama the son of king Dasharatha. Tell me who I really am, and who my father is, and where I come from.'[20] Sheldon Pollock cites commentators who have argued convincingly that in order to achieve his purpose of killing the demon Ravana, Rama must become truly human, for Ravana has secured a boon that no one but a human being can kill him. And to be truly human is to forget that you are god, which Rama must do—at least until after Ravana's death. Moreover, taking on a human body is the consequence of wrong knowledge,[21] for true knowledge would have brought enlightenment and freedom from the wheel of rebirth. The very act of incarnation would destroy the incarnation's true knowledge of his divinity, but, in addition (as we have seen), in the process of being born, the newborn child must also lose his knowledge. Therefore, an embodied avatar cannot possibly remember who he has been; the very fact of human birth robs him of the capacity to remember his past existences. Other commentators argued that Rama had intentionally become ignorant or that he merely pretended to forget who he was.[22] In other retellings of the narrative, too, Rama insists that he merely pretended to subject Sita to an ordeal and, presumably, pretended to forget that he was god.[23] If the gods themselves are subject to this constant forgetfulness of their true nature and equally constant reawakening to it, how could we mere mortals hope to do any better?

ASSUME THE POSITION:
THE FIGHT OVER THE BODY OF YOGA[1]

In India and abroad, particularly in America, yoga is big business, a cash sacred cow: about 15 million people in America practice (and generally pay for) something that they call yoga, making it a multi-billion dollar industry. The high stakes have led some American Hindus to express (in phrases dripping with heavy capitalist overtones) concern that Hinduism has 'lost control of the brand' of yoga and has been the victim of 'overt intellectual property theft' by people who have 'offered up a religion's spiritual wealth at the altar of crass commercialism'. But a deeper *casus belli* lies in an old fight over the lineage of yoga: such Hindus insist 'that the philosophy of yoga was first described in Hinduism's seminal texts and remains at the core of Hindu teaching', that yoga is the legacy of a timeless, spiritual 'Indian wisdom'.[2] This last argument is now almost a cliché among middle-class Indians, especially Hindus, who crowd the maidans and stadia where market-friendly yoga gurus like Baba Ramdev—the most popular and perhaps the richest of them all—teach people how the right technique of breathing can cure them of every physical and psychological illness.

Why do so many Hindus care so much whether yoga is Hindu? And is it?

Activists of Hindu-American identity politics[i] have made a two-fold historical claim: that yoga (a) was already described in the ancient Vedic texts of Hinduism and (b) has always been the core of Hinduism. Hindu Americans' deep investment (to continue the capitalist metaphor) in these claims about history has its own history. For, given the human obsession with roots, those claims generally take the form of arguments about the *origins* of yoga, a quest for purity of lineage, for undefiled racial descent, here as always a mad quest, since the history of yoga is, like most histories, a palimpsest.

[i] See 'You Can't Make an Omelette'.

116

The Hindu arguments, and the evidence for or against them, can be sorted into a chronology of four claims:

Claim 1: Yoga began before 2500 BCE, in the Indus Valley Civilization, in what is now Pakistan and northwest India (a civilization that left substantial archeological remains but no deciphered script). Evidence: There are a few tiny soapstone seals bearing the image of a man seated in what might be either just the way many people sit—knees apart, feet together or legs crossed—or a basic yogic posture, like the 'lotus' [*padma*] or 'perfect' [*siddha*] postures attested in much later yoga texts. Aside from its unverifiability, this claim assumes the position that the essence of yoga is in its 'positions' or 'postures' (asanas, literally 'sittings'), rather than, for instance, in its philosophical or religious concepts, or its breathing techniques. This assumption is contradicted by the next claim:

Claim 2: Yoga began in around 1500 BCE, in the oldest Sanskrit text, the *Rig Veda*. Evidence: The word 'yoga' occurs in this text, though only in the primary sense of 'yoking' horses to chariots or draft animals to ploughs or wagons (the Sanskrit and English words are cognate, as is the English 'junction'); and then, secondarily, designating the effort of 'yoking' oneself to do physical labour. Here we have neither philosophical nor postural yoga. Let's try again:

Claim 3: Yoga began sometime in the middle of the first millennium BCE in the Sanskrit philosophical texts known as the Upanishads. Evidence: The word 'yoga' occurs in a few (just a few) passages in the early Upanishads,[3] designating a spiritual praxis of meditation conjoined with breath-control, 'yoking' the senses in order to control the spirit, and then 'yoking' the mind, 'yoking' the body to the spirit, and the soul to the mind of god, in order to obtain an immortal body 'made by the fire of yoga'. This is the yoga that Mircea Eliade's *Yoga: Immortality and Freedom* (1958) illuminated for a generation of Americans.

Buddhist sources in this same period also speak of techniques of disciplining the mind and the body, and the word 'yoga', owing as much to Buddhism as to Hinduism, soon came to mean any mental and physical praxis of this sort.[ii] This is the general sense in which the word 'yoga' is used in the *Bhagavad Gita*, a few centuries later, to denote each of three

---

[ii] Similar disciplines arose in ancient Greece and, later, in Christianity, a subject on which Pierre Hadot and Michel Foucault had a great deal to say.

different religious paths (the yoga of action, the yoga of meditation and the yoga of devotion). But these texts say nothing about the physical 'positions' or 'postures' that distinguish contemporary yoga.

Claim 4: Yoga began in India in Patanjali's *Yoga Sutra*, probably in the third century CE. (Some would put it earlier, and it does draw on earlier sources.) Many contemporary yoga practitioners cite this text as the basis of their praxis. But Patanjali says nothing about the 'postures' other than remarking that the adept should sit in a manner that is relaxed and conducive to meditation and breath-control [2.49-53]. On the contrary, he speaks of cultivating 'aversion to one's own body' [2.40]. But he describes magical powers (*siddhis*, literally 'perfections') that result from the mastery of the mind, which include flying, becoming invisible, walking on water, foreknowledge of death, knowledge of past and future, entering the minds of others and understanding the languages of animals [3.16-34]— claims that were later made by Hindu ascetics who called themselves 'yogis' (or 'yogins').

A degree of confusion arises from the fact that Patanjali's text is foundational for one of the six classical philosophies of ancient India, the meditational school known as Yoga. This philosophy is often called 'Raja Yoga' ('royal yoga') or the Eight-fold (*ashtanga*) Yoga, to distinguish it from common or jungle varieties of yoga in the sense of any spiritual discipline, as well as from the later 'Hatha Yoga' ('the yoga of force'). The word '*yoga*/yoga/Yoga' thus became a triple homonym, referring sometimes to a physical praxis, sometimes to a mental praxis and sometimes to a particular philosophical school.

The confusion is compounded by the existence of various ascetics often called 'yogis' and connected to yoga in many different degrees. Scattered evidence for these traditions begins in the *Rig Veda*'s reference to naked ascetics who use (consciousness-altering) drugs and 'mount the wind' (i.e., both fly and control their breath); they are associated with Rudra,[4] the antecedent of the god Shiva who is closely associated with yogis, himself a great yogi and the Lord of Yogis (Yogeshvara). Some later yogic traditions cultivated 'the aversion to one's own body' in more extreme ways. Texts from the early centuries of the Common Era deconstruct the body (particularly, but not only, the female body) into its disgusting components of shit, piss, pus, and so forth, while others tell of men and women who, going after a kind of god one could find only by breaking away into madness and horror, subject themselves to extremes of heat and cold, fasting and other forms of physical mortification, going naked, sometimes eating out of human skulls, or eating carrion or faeces, generally demonstrating their indifference to both physical pain and social conventions, thumbing their nose at the body.

These disciplines often included difficult postures, such as standing on one leg for days at a time. By the seventh century CE, such postures became so notorious as to be subject to satire; the great frieze at Mamallapuram (Mahabalipuram) depicts a cat (a symbol of ascetic hypocrisy in Hinduism)[iii] standing on one leg in mimicry of a human ascetic in this posture. Many texts reflect the uneasiness and suspicion with which conventional householder Hindus regarded fringe groups of yogis, depicting them as lunatics or magicians with paranormal powers. Hindus were well aware that power corrupts, and divine power corrupts divinely. There was always a conflict between yogis as idealized superheroes and yogis as reviled super-villains. Yogis were often regarded as ritually polluting or downright dangerous, sinister in both senses of the word.[5]

Yogis also posed sexual threats, through an ancient Hindu belief in the erotic powers of yogis, along a spectrum from genuine ascetics, who were said to be able to use their unspent sexual powers to bless infertile women and thus make them fertile, to false ascetics,[iv] who were said to use their status as yogis as a mask through which to gain illicit access to women.[6] In the medieval period, the bad sexual reputation of yogis was exacerbated by the overlap between yoga and Tantra, an antinomian and often sexual ritual praxis. One yogic text composed sometime between the thirteenth and eighteenth centuries, the *Hatha-yoga-pradipika* ('Illumination of the Yoga of Force'), describes fifteen yogic postures. It also describes the Tantric technique of raising the coiled serpent power (the Kundalini) up the spine, through the series of chakras (centres of force), to the brain, and a related technique whereby the adept draws fluids (such as the secretions of his female partner in the Tantric sexual ritual) up through his penis (the *vajroli* process).

The followers of the Vedantic philosopher Shankara (c. 788–820 CE) rejected the physical discipline and engaged only the philosophy and the meditational praxis. By that time, most educated Hindus had nothing but scorn for postural yoga, though there was still respect for yoga as a spiritual discipline. Later, the *Hatha-yoga-pradipika* became an embarrassment for Hindus, who invented an apocryphal story about Dayanand Sarasvati

---

[iii] See 'The Concept of Heresy' and 'Zoomorphism'.
[iv] See 'The Concept of Heresy'.

(1824-83), the founder of the Bengal reform movement called the Arya Samaj, who allegedly pulled a corpse from a river, dissected it to see if the chakras were there, didn't find them, and threw his copy of the *Hatha-yoga-pradikipa* into the water. Well-born Bengalis considered exercise in general lower class.

When the British arrived in India in the eighteenth century, they came to share many of the Hindu anti-yogic biases, compounded by the European horror of the nakedness and self-torture of the extreme yogis. The yogi on a bed of nails became the stock European symbol of India's moral and spiritual backwardness. In addition to the individual yogis, bands of yogis often posed military threats, using yoga to strengthen their bodies for martial purposes. Warrior ascetics are a very old Indian tradition, going back to the menacing troops of Vratyas mentioned in the Veda. Under the Raj, militant yogis engaged in exercise regimes to make them tough, in order to oppose the British; they were generally indistinguishable from violent militants whose training centres for resistance masqueraded as centres of yogic instruction. In this period, to be a yogi often meant to train as a guerilla. The British rounded up many of the ascetic mercenaries and broke up their organizations; some yogis became beggars or itinerant carnival performers who displayed as circus tricks the more extreme postures, such as a handstand from the lotus posture.

But at this point, something transformative happened, which is the basis of a new claim, *not* made by Hindus, about the origins of yoga:

Claim 5: Contemporary postural yoga was invented in India in the nineteenth century. This is the provocative assertion made by Mark Singleton, who sets out (in his book, *Yoga Body: The Origins of Modern Posture Practice*) to demolish the assertion that the roots of modern yoga lie in ancient India. He argues that a transnational, Anglophone yoga arose at this time, compounded of the unlikely mix of British body-building and physical culture, American transcendentalism and Christian science, naturopathy, Swedish gymnastics and the YMCA, grafted onto a rehabilitated form of postural yoga adapted specifically for a Western audience. The Swedish gymnastics came from Pehr Henrik Ling, the physical culture from a number of people including Eugen Sandow, Bernard MacFadden, Harry Crowe Buck and Charles Atlas. Most influential was the YMCA, in whose hands physical culture was eventually elevated to a position of social and moral respectability.

The British had always considered Indians weaklings, and Indians shamefacedly agreed; Indian children in Gandhi's day used to chant a popular poem: 'Behold the mighty Englishman/ He rules the Indian small,/Because being a meat-eater/ He is five cubits tall.' The playing fields of Eton had made the English frightfully brave, as Noel Coward pointed out,[v] but so had a regimen of exercise that they now imported into India. Body-building became a religion that re-sacralized the body, and the British proselytized for this muscular Christianity in India just as the missionaries proselytized for their evangelical Christianity. In Indian schools, the gymnastics instructor was usually a brutal and ignorant retired low-ranking (subaltern) British officer, or, even more often, a sepoy, an Indian who served in the British army. In an ironic twist, Indian nationalists were able to use this colonial technique, designed to build soldiers to master the inferior races in the empire, to train their own people to combat and resist the Europeans. Even when they took poses from Hatha Yoga, they renamed them and interpreted them in the language of modern gymnastics. In 1915, the scholar S.C. Vasu, who wanted to make yoga medical and scientific, made an English translation of the *Hatha-yoga-pradipika* for the *Sacred Books of the Hindus* but omitted the passage about the *vajroli* technique.

The British then tried to suppress the Indian physical culture clubs in India because they wanted to do it their way and to control it, to inscribe English physical culture on the Indian body. YMCA leaders in India had made the postures part of the physical programme in service of Christian goals (leading some people to regard yoga as a variant of Christian Science), but the European postures then became reabsorbed back into Hindu culture. The British passion for physical culture, spilling over into the Hindu world, rescued physical yoga from the opprobrium into which it had fallen and made it once again respectable. Hindu leaders such as Swami Kuvalayananda developed more rigorous posture work to refute the YMCA types who had insisted that the postures were not an adequate physical regimen. Now the new yoga took the European techniques and couched them in the discourse of the Bengal Hindu Renaissance,[vi] which is to say the Vedantic language of the Upanishads. Many practitioners combined the more extreme postures, generally associated with the marginalized itinerant yogis, with the more central ancient meditative praxis, and regarded this yoga (now no longer limited to breath control but incorporating the postures) as a path to immortality.

[v] In his song 'The Stately Homes of England'.
[vi] See 'From Kama to Karma'.

The extreme postures then travelled back to England. Yogis in England, where contortionists had performed in London for hundreds of years, demonstrated exercises such as the Hatha Yoga technique of abdominal isolation (*nauli*), in which the muscles of the stomach are made to undulate in a separate column. K. Ramamurthy had a three-tonne elephant and a motor car driven over his body; he also included in the Indian physical culture system a number of sports that he insisted originated in India, including hockey, cricket, tennis, billiards and boxing.

The emphasis on the physical postures of yoga may have been bolstered by the sensational publication, in 1883, of Sir Richard Burton's English translation of the *Kamasutra*, a text that became notorious for its 'positions'.[vii] The tendency to confuse the teachings of yoga and the *Kamasutra* may have led to the overemphasis on the 'positions' in both, since yoga was often associated with sex in India and came to be eroticized in England, and the general English and Indian ignorance of the cultural content of the *Kamasutra* was matched by their ignorance of the philosophical content of (classical) yoga. Both yoga and the *Kamasutra* served the schizophrenic Victorian combination of public condemnation of sex and private obsession with it.[viii]

The advent of mass photography at the end of the nineteenth century greatly enhanced the erotic appeal of yoga. In 1902, Thomas Edison made a documentary about a 'Hindu Fakir' that was circulated along with other early forms of the peepshow. Undeniably erotic photographs of naked women and naked men performing yogic postures were published in journals like *Health and Science*, anthropologizing and Orientalizing yoga.

The pendulum of mutual influence continued to swing, as Hindus reacted against these new European versions of yoga and brought yet another form of yoga to America. In 1896, repulsed by the physical contortions and twisted bodies of the yogic postures, Swami Vivekananda said that he rejected Hatha Yoga because it was very difficult, could not be quickly learned and did not lead to much spiritual growth, and because the goal of making men live long and in perfect health was not as important as the spiritual goal represented by Raja Yoga, which Vivekananda claimed

---

[vii] See 'From Kama to Karma'.

[viii] The erotic view of yoga continues. In March 2003 a spoof, entitled 'Yoga: A Religion for Sex Addicts', imagined a Christian pastor defining the ultimate goal of yoga practitioners as contorting their bodies into demonic positions so as to be able to place their sexual organs in their mouths. Until now, available at http://www.landoverbaptist.org/news0303/yoga.html

to be reviving. Yet he believed that physical culture, of the European variety, was essential for Indian youth, and he is said to have held the view that one can get closer to god through football than through the *Bhagavad Gita*.[7]

But the Vedantic yoga of Vivekananda was not the antecedent of the yoga practiced in America today. That came from many sources, but particularly from the invention, by T. Krishnamacharya, between 1930 and 1950, of a novel sequence of movements, partially derived from a royal gymnastics tradition in Mysore; and from B.K.S. Iyengar's *Light on Yoga*, published in 1966.[8] Other techniques that we now recognize as yoga were, by the 1930s, already a well-established part of Western physical culture, particularly that intended for women, but were not yet associated in any way with yoga. At the same time, some women promoted 'spiritual stretching and deep breathing' which they called 'yoga for women'. For now yoga became gendered: postural yoga developed out of a male, muscular, Christian, nationalist and martial context (still practiced by the RSS and other Hindu nationalist organizations); while 'harmonial' yoga, of the 'stretch and relax' variety, was a synthesis of women's gymnastics and para-Christian mysticism.[ix]

After Vivekananda had expelled Hatha Yoga, the modern Hindu yogis brought it back by rewriting the Hatha Yoga tradition, leaving out the positions that they found repellent, repulsive, or simply impossible, and fleshing out the tradition with diet, relaxation, cleanliness and breathing, all attested in some of the many other forms of ancient Indian yoga. They replaced the unpalatable ancient Indian material with more attractive ancient material, as well as much new material, and claimed that that was what yogis had always used. Ultimately, new combinations of Western and Eastern physical culture methods were naturalized as ancient Hindu knowledge.

Yoga came into its own as a national pastime in America during the Happy Hippy Heaven of the 1950s and 60s. But it had attracted celebrities in Europe and America from Henry Thoreau (1817-62), the first American yogi, to Aleister Crowley, who published, in 1939, eight lectures about yoga under the megalomaniac pseudonym 'Mahatma Guru Sri Paramahansa Shivaji', using a bit of Patanjali but mostly pseudo-Tantric materials that further damaged yoga's reputation. In 1921, Fritz Lang made a film about crazy yogis. Lawrence Peter Berra picked up his famous nickname—

[ix] To this day, women greatly outnumber men as yoga practitioners.

'Yogi'—from a friend who said that whenever Berra sat around with his arms and legs crossed, waiting to bat, or looking sad after a losing game, he resembled a Hindu holy man they had seen in a movie.

Contemporary yoga practices are a far cry both from the Upanishads and from Hatha Yoga. Most of the new yogis want to relax after a hard day at the office, tighten up their abs and reduce their cholesterol and their blood pressure; their yoga of relaxation and stretching may also involve regular enemas, a cure for back pain, a beauty regime, a vegetarian diet with a lot of yogurt (which is not etymologically related to 'yoga')—oh yes, and a route to god. Siddha Yoga has become 'City Yoga'. Never the twain shall meet.

But they can, in fact, meet. For some people, yoga is a religious meditation, for some an exercise routine, and for some, both. A few years ago I met Gwyneth Paltrow, a yoga practitioner who delighted me by reciting a long passage from Patanjali in flawless and melodious Sanskrit. The union of physical and spiritual praxis was possible for ancient Indians and remains a real goal for many contemporary yogis. This sort of combination is affirmed by an old joke about a Jesuit priest who, when his Bishop forbade priests to smoke while meditating, dutifully agreed but argued that surely there would be no objection if he occasionally meditated while he was smoking. That one can, however, choose merely to smoke or merely to meditate is denied by some Christian ministers who forbid their parishioners to practice yoga, arguing that yoga is *only and always* a religious system.

On the other hand, some Hindus, concerned about their image, fear (not without cause[9]) that their religion has been stereotyped in the West as a polytheistic faith of 'castes, cows and curry'. They counteract these charges by swinging to the other extreme and arguing that everything in India is, and always has been, spiritual. They want to cash in the popularity of yoga in order to use it as the poster-child of a more spiritual 'Indian wisdom'. They argue that yoga—more than temple rituals, the worship of images of the gods, or other, more passionate, communal and widespread forms of Hinduism—is the essence of Hinduism, that yoga has always been entirely spiritual and entirely Hindu.

But this claim ignores the complex history of yoga. Yes, there is an ancient Indian yoga, but it is not the source of most of what people do in yoga classes today. That same history, however, also demonstrates that there are a number of historical bases for contemporary postural yoga within classical Hinduism. The Europeans did not invent it wholesale, but they changed it from an embarrassment to an occasion for cultural pride, and from a tradition that encouraged the cultivation of 'aversion to one's own body' to another, also rooted in ancient India, that aimed at the perfection of the body. The modern yogis didn't take their methods from European physical culture; they took them *back* from physical culture. Yoga is a rich, multi-cultural, constantly changing interdisciplinary construction, far from the pure line that its adherents often claim for it.

THE TOLERATION OF INTOLERANCE
IN HINDUISM[1]

When India and Pakistan turned on one another in violence after Partition in 1948, Western intellectuals were astonished that the nonviolent, tolerant Hindus could do such a thing. And when India invaded and annexed Goa in December 1961, Western intellectuals were again astonished that the nonviolent, tolerant Hindus could do such a thing. But when, in 1992, Hindus stormed the Babri mosque in Ayodhya that Babur had built over the place where many Hindus believe Rama was born, and over a thousand people died in subsequent riots, they were no longer so astonished. The world had become used to the almost daily bloodshed in India, to the killing of Sikhs by Hindus, Hindus by Sikhs, Muslims by Hindus, Hindus by Muslims, Tamil Hindus by Buddhists, Buddhists by Tamil Hindus, Dalits by Brahmins, Brahmins by Dalits, and on and on. Today, hardly anyone is surprised by reports of violence and hate crimes in Gandhi's India, a predominantly Hindu and overwhelmingly religious society. But what was the source of the earlier belief in Hindu tolerance? Is there any basis for it in the intellectual history of India?

Tolerance, of course, is an English word, expressing the outsiders' view of what they think happens in India. There is no word in any of the Indian languages that corresponds to the English term 'religious tolerance', which covers everything from mere 'endurance of' or 'putting up with' religious difference (as one 'tolerates' pain) to a more active endorsement, even celebration, of religious difference. For tolerance denotes not merely the absence of intolerance but a more positive, welcoming or even encouraging attitude. There is no Sanskrit or Hindi word for 'tolerance' in that sense, as a good to be sought in the world; there are words only for passive and negative ideas of endurance.[2] *Samadarshana* (literally, 'looking upon [all things] as the same') might be a rough Sanskrit equivalent for tolerance,[3] and there are basic Buddhist terms, like *upeksha* ('indifference' or 'forbearing') and *karuna* ('compassion') that are also important in Hinduism. (Here I should make it explicit that I am speaking about Hindu intolerance, not 'Indian' intolerance in general, which would include not only Buddhism and Jainism but Indian Islam and Indian Christianity.)

The concept of tolerance in the positive sense is a product of the Western Enlightenment. Yet, just because Hindus do not have a word for it does not mean that they do not have a set of intellectual concepts that might approximate the Western concept of 'tolerance' and that, more important, might lead to the active embodiment of tolerance—that might make people actually *be* tolerant. It is, I think, the intellectual rather than the political history of India that has given rise to the outsiders', especially Westerners', idea of Hindu tolerance. That is, it is what Hindus have said about themselves—and what Western intellectuals have thought that Hindus believe—rather than what Hindus have done—or, more precisely, what Western intellectuals have *thought* that Hindus have done—that has given rise to the Western idea of Hindu tolerance. And Western ideas about Hindu tolerance are closely tied up with Western ideas about Hindu pluralism[i]: if they can tolerate all those gods (the argument goes), with all those heads and all those arms, if they can entertain all those different concepts of divinity, they must be able to tolerate the different concepts of divinity expressed in different religions.

But we must distinguish between two significantly different sorts of pluralism, sociological and intellectual. Contemporary pluralism is a sociological phenomenon that can itself be approached on two levels, both the fact of the existence of many religions in our world today, and our reaction to that fact. In this latter sense, pluralism is a conscious attempt to harmonize different religious beliefs in a spirit of tolerance and mutual appreciation, in the hope of reducing the kinds of fanaticism that lead to everything from bigotry to holy wars. This is a way in which people come to terms with Otherness and come to treat Others.[4] Pluralism is not a useful word until difference is a problem.

Ancient Hindu pluralisms are of a different sort. They tackle the problem of ontology from several different (plural) angles, branching off from an ancient and still on-going argument about the way the world is, about whether it is basically uniform or basically multiform. This is an intellectual phenomenon, a pluralism of ideas within a single social group that regards all of these ideas, some of which might seem contradictory to us, as valid—though not necessarily *equally* valid.

[i] See 'Are Hindus Monotheists?'

We might subsume under intellectual pluralism the category of internal or individual pluralism, the problem of personal dissonance. More emotional than purely intellectual, internal pluralism might be regarded as a kind of mediating category, between the mental constructs of intellectual pluralism and the physical reality of sociological pluralism incarnate in real, flesh-and-blood people. Internal pluralism is eclectic: one person holds a tool-box of different beliefs more or less simultaneously, drawing upon one on one occasion, another on another. A pivotal example of such individual pluralism can be found in the law text of Manu, which argues, within a single chapter, passionately against and then firmly for the eating of meat.[ii]

The two basic sorts of pluralism, sociological and intellectual, are interconnected in any number of (plural) ways. We might ask if the intellectual pluralism of Hinduism has led to the sort of sociological pluralism that is often the basis of religious tolerance. I will argue that ancient Hindu intellectual pluralism has not, in the past, led to ancient Hindu sociological tolerance, but that it might do so in the future.

THE VEDIC BACKGROUND

The world of traditional, Vedic, worldly Hinduism was plural in several senses. Sociologically, it maintained the pluralist—even if inegalitarian— and relativist caste system, with separate, different dharmas for each social group and individual dharmas for each person (*svadharma*). Intellectually, it recognized a pantheon of many gods. This pluralism, like everything else in the literature of Hinduism, begins with the *Rig Veda*, at the start of the first millennium BCE, and it begins with polytheism.

But the polytheism of the Rig Veda is of a peculiarly monistic hue— monistic in viewing the very substance of the universe as divine, and viewing that substance and that divinity as unitary—as one, and indivisible. Monism, however passive, often conceals a submerged form of intellectual imperialism. Beneath all the flickering images of all the different gods lies *brahman*, the undying divine substratum of the universe. Thus the Rig Vedic poet says, 'The wise speak of what is One in many ways' [RV 1.164.46]. In this view, though pluralism does in fact arise out of the original monism, it has a secondary, illusory status in comparison with the enduring, real status of the underlying monism.[iii] There is, thus, a clear hierarchy that privileges monism over pluralism.

[ii] See 'Eating Karma'.
[iii] See 'You Can't Get Here', 'Are Hindus Monotheists?' and 'Three (or More)'.

It may be argued that there is always some sort of hierarchy in the Vedas, and that, more broadly speaking, you cannot have intellectual pluralism at all without some sort of hierarchy. But then, there is always grammar, and where there is grammar there is subordination. There is implicit hierarchy any time that we use language, and perhaps implicit hierarchy is even more insidious than explicit hierarchy. Any time that we speak, and state our own views to someone else, someone Other, we imply that we believe that what we are saying is better than the alternatives, and in that sense all religious statements are attempts at conversion. Only if we refrain from applying a hermeneutic of suspicion can we regard the absence of explicit hierarchical statements in the *Rig Veda* as a step in the right direction: indeed, even in the Vedic Hymn of the Primeval Male[iv], the *purusha sukta*, we may see the implicit belief that 'we' Aryans are better than 'those' servants (also called aliens or 'other people', Dasyus or Dasas). However, the leap from making a (necessarily hierarchical) statement—as the Vedas do—to insisting that the person to whom we make it renounce his or her opposing views (let alone the further leap to threatening death or other punishment if our view is not accepted) is the leap from tolerance to intolerance. The texts of Vedic Hinduism don't quite take this leap (though, as we will soon see, other forms of Hinduism do). The monistic polytheism of the Vedas, therefore, establishes a base for religious tolerance.

The vague monism of the Vedas was sharpened by the more systematized monism of the Vedanta, beginning in the Upanisads a few centuries later. In these texts, the sense of the unity of ultimate reality (*brahman*) with the souls of all embodied creatures (*atman*) could, theoretically, make people see the unity of all peoples; this is, in fact, one of the arguments of the *Bhagavad Gita* [6.29-30], many centuries later. Certainly, in this sense, a monistic religion is likely to be more tolerant than a monotheistic religion. As David Tracy has remarked, one of the chief dangers in monotheism is an exclusivism that can (though it need not) lead to intolerance by falsely suggesting that the belief in the one-ness of god encourages people to think that truth, too, takes just one form.[5] For the monotheistic, Abrahamic religions assume not only a unitary reality but one that is personified anthropomorphically as a jealous husband; alternative views of the truth, therefore, take on the status of illicit partners.[6] A polytheistic religion, by this argument, might be expected to be more tolerant of the worship of other gods than a monotheistic religion would be. A monistic religion stands in the middle, more tolerant than a monotheistic but less tolerant than a polytheistic religion. The Hindu evidence supports this correlation.

[iv] See 'You Can't Get Here'.

CATEGORIZING THE ONE AND THE MANY

Post-Vedic Hindu cosmogonies attempt to reconcile our experienced, worldly multiplicity with an ideal monistic unity.[v] Beginning with the *Rig Veda* and continuing through the Puranas, Indian cosmogonies have mingled, seemingly at random, abstract entities (the year, the metres, desire) and material entities (the moon, snakes, people.)[vi] Post-Vedic texts set out the various groups in these Hindu cosmogonies in a particular hierarchical order: like the pigs in George Orwell's *Animal Farm*, all ontological categories are equal, but some are more equal than others. Thus, although the three goals of life (*trivarga* or *purusharthas:* kama [pleasure], artha [profit] and dharma) are often said to be separate but equal, there is a tendency to rank dharma first. At the same time, textbooks of erotic love give pride of place to pleasure, political handbooks privilege profit, and dharma texts rank dharma above the other two goals. And later, when release [moksha] is introduced as the fourth goal, there is complete hierarchy: moksha is said, by Vedantists, to be far superior to the other goals, indeed, to be in an entirely different class from the other goals.[vii]

Even within the pluralistic, non-monistic texts of later Vedic Hinduism, the Puranas and the Shastras, the rococo lists were ultimately made hierarchical: not only are the categories different, but one is definitely better than another. We can see the ways in which Hinduism deals with these hierarchies in the triads and quartets based upon the social paradigm of the four *varnas* or classes of society.[viii] Hierarchy also explains the importance of the priest in cosmogonies. The social or, more precisely, socio-religious element—the priest, the sacrificer, the human being in a particular class or stage of life—recurs in Hindu cosmogonies as a defining factor in the basic framework of the cosmos: the sacrificer and priest must perform the rituals that keep the universe going, that make the sun rise and the rain fall. The implications of this priestly presence seriously restrict the apparently fluid pluralism that seems to pervade Hindu cosmogonies, and these intellectual formulations have social repercussions: those at the top often enforce their positions in dramatically intolerant ways.[7] The most obvious manifestation of this in Hindu society was—as it still is—the hierarchy-ridden and sometimes exploitative and violent interaction among the different castes.

[v] See 'Together Apart'.
[vi] See 'You Can't Get Here'.
[vii] See 'Three (or More)'.
[viii] See 'Three (or More)'.

Vedantic monism, too, can be elitist and hierarchical, rather than egalitarian; the Vedantic vision transcends the political world but leaves it intact. That is, the belief that *brahman* is all that is real takes precedence over the belief in the ability of multiple gods to offer help in particular situations; the vision that those situations are ultimately unreal generally siphons off the impulse to take action against social injustices, against poverty and cruelty, that the texts explicitly remark upon.

MONISM, HIERARCHY AND INTOLERANCE

What do we learn from the ancient texts of this monistic/pluralistic Hinduism? We learn that the two sorts of pluralism, sociological and intellectual, are not connected in the way that might seem most obvious, and has indeed seemed obvious to many Orientalists and Western theologians. That is, ancient Hindu intellectual pluralism does not lead to ancient Hindu sociological tolerance[8]; the belief that all the gods are equally real and equally useful to their different worshippers does not lead to the belief that all the castes are equally useful to society. One reason for this may simply be that ancient Hindu pluralism did not ultimately carry the field. As we have seen, intellectual pluralism was successfully challenged and supplanted by two different sorts of non-pluralism that determined the course of subsequent Hindu thinking: the hierarchy of Vedic/Puranic Hinduism and the strict monism of the Vedanta. (I am using the term 'Vedanta' here to designate the strain of Indian philosophy that begins with the Upanishads, climaxes with the great commentaries of Shankara and Ramanuja, and survives in the thought of Vedantas such as Ramakrishna and Vivekananda. And by Vedic/Puranic I mean not merely the Vedas but the entire strain of Hinduism, including the Puranas, that endorses Vedic sacrifice and the worship of a pantheon of gods, as it is carried on to this day in Hindu temples and households.)

Both hierarchical pluralism and monism continued (and continue) to exist in India cheek by jowl in uneasy symbiosis. The pluralistic world, the world of Vedic/Puranic ritual, was primarily orthoprax, not orthodox.[ix] That is, it did not insist on doctrine (*doxis*) as long as ritual and social behaviour (*praxis*) satisfied the standards of the particular group (usually a small caste group). It was intellectually pluralistic in that each sect acknowledged the existence of gods other than their own god(s), suitable

[ix] See 'The Concept of Heresy'.

for others to worship, but whom they did not care to worship themselves. On the other hand, when it came to sociological pluralism, there was a further split. The orthoprax world saw all social roles as equally valid— from the god's eye view: everyone, from Brahmin priest to the burner of corpses, is necessary for a complete social world; and it saw the world of action as cumulatively pluralistic, exemplifying a desirable plenitude: everything that exists and that happens, even suffering and injustice, is necessary to make the universe perfect, in the sense of having everything possible in it. This was plenitude that extended, ultimately, to a proposed solution to the problem of evil, or theodicy, justifying cancer and moral evil as essential cogs in the universal wheel of life. But it gave the *individual* no choice at all in his or her social role, no pluralism of action, though the hierarchy of values assigned to different roles might well have inspired the wish to make such choices. For, though all social roles were equal (in the eyes of god), some were more equal than others (in the eyes of men and women).

The strictly monistic world of the Vedantists, by contrast—the world of philosophy—was primarily orthodox. That is, renunciant sects (including Buddhism and Jainism), monistic both sociologically and intellectually, were far less doctrinaire about the behaviour of the layperson (though certainly not about the behaviour of the monk, which was in many ways far more important) than orthoprax Hinduism was; but they believed that there was only one correct belief. Thus, unlike orthoprax Hindus, these sects proselytized—that is, they went around telling people that they were right and everyone else was wrong.

Later, the monistic view turned itself inside out to generate a different sort of tolerance: it argued not only that all physical and immaterial things were one, but that all *religions* were also one, that Muslims and Christians really worshipped the same god that Hindus worshipped, but just called him Allah or Christ. This led to interesting misunderstandings when Christian missionaries fired their canons across the bows of South Asians.[x]

The monistic view has influenced reformers and rulers through the centuries. Among the more remarkable was the Mughal Emperor Akbar (1542-1605), the descendant of the Babur who built the Babri mosque in Ayodhya. Akbar was a true pluralist; born a Muslim but with a Hindu wife, he entertained a veritable circus of holy men at his multi-religious salons. Alfred Lord Tennyson was inspired by the English translation of an

---

[x] See 'Are Hindus Monotheists?'

inscription by Abul Fazl, Akbar's minister and chronicler, to write a poem entitled 'Akbar's Dream'.[9]

Here is Abul Fazl's inscription for a temple in Kashmir, as he recorded it in the *A'in-i Akbari*, the third volume of the *Akbarnama*, the 'Book of Akbar', the Persian document that Abul Fazl wrote documenting the administration of the Emperor Akbar:

> O God in every temple I see people that see Thee, and in every language I hear spoken, people praise Thee. Polytheism and Islam feel after Thee. Each religion says, 'Thou art one, without equal.' If it be a mosque people murmur the holy prayer, and if it be a Christian Church, people ring the bell from love to Thee. Sometimes I frequent the Christian cloister, and sometimes the mosque. But it is Thou whom I search from temple to temple. Thy elect have no dealings with either heresy or orthodoxy; for neither of them stands behind the screen of Thy truth. Heresy to the heretic, and religion to the orthodox, but the dust of the rose-petal belongs to the heart of the perfume seller.[10]

Tennyson's poem is long, but my favorite passage is this one, a statement by Akbar to Abul Fazl:

> Sit by my side. While thou art one with me,
> I seem no longer like a lonely man
> In the king's garden, gathering here and there
> From each fair plant the blossom choicest-grown
> To wreathe a crown not only for the king
> But in due time for every Mussulman,
> Brahmin, and Buddhist, Christian, and Parsee,
> Thro' all the warring world of Hindustan.
> Well spake thy brother in his hymn to heaven
> 'Thy glory baffles wisdom. All the tracks
> Of science making toward Thy Perfectness
> Are blinding desert sand; we scarce can spell
> The Alif of Thine alphabet of Love.'

Later in the poem he speaks of wanting to 'beat back/ The menacing poison of intolerant priests, Those cobras ever setting up their hoods.' Then he tells Abul Fazl his dream:

> Well, I dream'd
> That stone by stone I rear'd a sacred fane,
> A temple, neither Pagod, Mosque, nor Church,
> But loftier, simpler, always open-door'd

To every breath from heaven, and Truth and Peace
And Love and Justice came and dwelt therein.
But while we stood rejoicing, I and thou,
I heard a mocking laugh 'The new Koran!'
And on the sudden, and with a cry 'Saleem'
Thou, thou—I saw thee fall before me, and then
Me too the black-wing'd Azrael overcame,
But death had ears and eyes; I watch'd my son,
And those that follow'd, loosen stone from stone,
All my fair work; and from the ruin arose
The shriek and curse of trampled millions, even
As in the time before; but while I groan'd,
From out the sunset pour'd an alien race,
Who fitted stone to stone again, and Truth,
Peace, Love and Justice came and dwelt therein.
Nor in the field without were seen or heard
Fires of Suttee, nor wail of baby-wife,
Or Indian widow; and in sleep I said
'All praise to Alla by whatever hands
My mission be accomplish'd!' but we hear
Music: our palace is awake, and morn
Has lifted the dark eyelash of the Night
From off the rosy cheek of waking Day.
Our hymn to the sun. They sing it. Let us go.

Tennyson still cannot resist, through *his* Akbar, an intolerant slur against 'the warring world' of Hinduism (suttee, the mistreatment of widows, child brides and all that), but the poem ends with a hymn to the sun which is Hindu in its inspiration, if—in Tennyson's version of history—Anglican in its execution: for after the 'son' of Akbar has undone all his good works (it was actually Akbar's grandson, Aurangzeb), the 'alien race' that will pour 'from out the sunset' (i.e., the West) to rebuild the shattered pluralistic dream is, of course, the British. (The description of the demolishing of Akbar's dream temple now conjures up the memory of the demolishing of Babur's temple in 1992.)

Logically, the sort of universalism that argues that 'in every temple I see people that see Thee' should have led polytheistic Hindus to the belief that there was no point in trying to convert a Muslim to Hinduism, yet this was not always the case. Vedic/Puranic, orthoprax Hindus certainly made no efforts to convert anyone to Hinduism, arguing that you had to be born a Hindu to be a Hindu. But Vedantic Hindus lapsed back into the shadows of orthodoxy and argued that *their* particular brand of monism was more monistic than thou. Such Vedantins went about proselytizing like mad. (Similarly, Krishna in the *Gita* allows that all other gods are aspects of himself, but still suggests that the *best*—quickest, most secure—way to God is directly through him: 'When their wits are stolen away by their desires, people seek other gods . . . but whatever body a devotee wishes to honour with faith, I confirm that faith in him, making it unwavering. But the reward of those men of small minds is limited. Those who sacrifice to the gods go to the gods, but those who are devoted to me and sacrifice to me go to me' [*Bhagavad Gita* 7.20-23]. And: 'Even those who are devoted to other gods and sacrifice to them, filled with faith, they too really sacrifice to me. For I am the one who enjoys all sacrifices, but they do not recognize me truly, and so they fall away. Those who dedicate themselves to the gods go to the gods, but those who sacrifice to me go to me' [9:23-5].) It might well be argued that this sort of conversion is a form of intellectual violence commensurate with the physical violence of enforced behaviour. For, although proselytizing is not in itself necessarily intolerant, it does close the open-ended door of pluralism.

Medieval, Vedic/Puranic Hinduism (which remains alive and well today in India) is a strange mixture of these two currents which join but never merge, like streams of oil and water. Ritually, Puranic Hindus are Vedic, orthoprax. The fanatics among them kill people (such as Muslims, and women) who challenge or violate rituals: who act wrongly, who do not respect the bounds of the caste system, and so forth. Philosophically, though, a majority of the orthoprax remain heterodox, and view with tolerance, even if disdainful tolerance, the divergent views of other religions. Some of them, however, while remaining Vedic in their practices, are philosophically Vedantic, orthodox, and correspondingly intolerant, also, of deviant doctrines. This gives them yet another reason, exacerbating their orthopraxy reasons, to try to convert (if not to kill) people like Muslims.

THE RIDDLE OF NONVIOLENCE

Tolerance is not the same as nonviolence,[xi] but the two have often been conflated, and one can see why: when intolerance is put into action, it can result in religious violence. The Vedantic emphasis on nonviolence, ahimsa, that Gandhi made so famous in the West, is far from typical of

---

[xi] See 'The Ambivalence of Ahimsa'.

Hindu thinking, let alone Hindu action. Of course, Gandhi did not invent ahimsa; Hindus—Vedic/Puranic, pluralistic Hindus, as well as Vedantic Hindus—have sworn allegiance to the concept of nonviolence at least from the time of *The Laws of Manu*; 'Hindu tolerance' is certainly not an idea imposed upon Hindus by Orientalist, imperialist pressure. But it may well be that Hindus doth protest too much about their tolerance. As Krishna pointed out in the *Bhagavad Gita*, it is quite possible to adhere to the mental principles of nonviolence while killing your cousins in battle.

Nonviolence became a cultural ideal for Hindus precisely because it holds out the last hope of a cure, all the more desirable since unattainable, for a civilization that has, like most others that we know of, always suffered from chronic and terminal violence. Nonviolence was an ideal propped up against the cultural reality of violence. Classical Hindu India was violent in its politics (war being the *raison d'être* of every king), in its religious practices (animal sacrifice, ascetic self-torture, fire-walking, swinging from hooks in the flesh of the back, and so forth), in its criminal law (impaling on stakes and the amputation of limbs being prescribed punishment for relatively minor offences), in its hells (cunningly and sadistically contrived to make the punishment fit the crime) and, perhaps at the very heart of it all, in its climate, with its unendurable heat and unpredictable monsoons.[xii] Violence is as Hindu as curry.[xiii]

It is against this background that we must view the doctrine of nonviolence. Hindu sages dreamt of nonviolence as people who live all their lives in the desert dream of oases. In *The Laws of Manu*, the two views, violent and nonviolent, are juxtaposed in an uneasy tension in the context within which Manu debates most problems: the ritual. Indeed, ahimsa may itself derive primarily from the ritual, from the argument that the priest does not actually injure the animal but merely 'pacifies him' (*sham*, 'to pacify,' is the usual euphemism for the ritual slaughter) and that, therefore, its primary meaning is in fact to do injury without doing injury, a casuist argument from its very inception.[xiv]

In their ambivalent attitude to violence, the Hindus are no different

---

[xii] The monsoon is generally welcomed with joy in India; but I had in mind the times when the monsoon fails and results in famine, or when the monsoon brings massive floods that kill or displace thousands. But I am not in general inclined to blame the extremes of Indian religion on the extremes of the Indian climate.

[xiii] Actually, Indian violence is much older than Indian curry, hot spices being a relatively recent culinary innovation in India.

[xiv] See 'The Ambivalence of Ahimsa'.

from the rest of humanity. It was the neo-Vedantin idealists who gladly embraced the Gandhian hope that the Hindus might set an example for the human race in passive resistance. Swami Vivekananda claimed, wrongly, that 'India is the only country where there never has been a religious persecution.'[11] The naïve self-image of the neo-Vedantins was encouraged by the liberal American transcendentalists (Thoreau was a great one for nonviolence and the *Gita*) and by the Hindus' own desire to prove to the disdainful British that the Hindus were not the lascivious, blood-thirsty savages depicted in the colonial caricature.[xv] We can, therefore, see a kind of pizza-effect in the contemporary Hindu investment in nonviolence: an ancient Hindu idea was appropriated and given new power by Hindus (such as Gandhi) who had been influenced by Western thinkers (such as Tolstoy) who were acquainted with the neo-Vedantins as well as with German idealists who had been reading the Upanishads, making these ideas more attractive both to Westerners and to Hindus still living under the shadow of Western domination. But Gandhi was whistling in the dark.

Hindus remain intolerant of any slur cast against their tolerance. Shortly after Partition, a member of the fundamentalist and anti-Muslim Hindu association, the RSS, remarked that, since Hindus are, as is well-known, the most tolerant people in the world, they deserve to have the land of India to themselves, and, therefore, the (less tolerant) Muslims should be disenfranchized:

> The spirit of broad catholicism, generosity, toleration, truth, sacrifice and love for all life, which characterizes the average Hindu mind not wholly vitiated by Western influence, bears eloquent testimony to the greatness of Hindu culture . . . The non-Hindu peoples in Hindustan . . . must not only give up their attitude of intolerance and ungratefulness towards this land . . . but must . . . stay in the country wholly subordinated to the Hindu Nation, claiming nothing, deserving no privileges, far less any preferential treatment—not even citizen's rights.[12]

Here it is perhaps appropriate to recall that it was an RSS man who killed Gandhi. On the lighter side, the widening gap between the 'tolerant' scriptures and the intolerant interpretation of them was evinced in *India Today* in 1991:

> The recent Indo-Pak seminar to foster bilateral amity might have succeeded to some extent. While the generals on both sides were optimistic, there seemed little amity on the Indian side. Ram Jethmalani

---

[xv] See 'Are Hindus Monotheists?' and 'From Kama to Karma'.

observed that India had always been a tolerant society. After all, the Pandavas were accommodating enough to share one wife. This raised the hackles of journalist Mrinal Pande. She laid into the hapless lawyer by quoting a character in the *Mahabharata* who had pointed out, 'If the *shastras* say this, then the *shastras* are wrong.' This demolished an apologetic Jethmalani's tolerance argument. But it also showed that while Indo-Pak friendship was a possibility, intra-Indian amity might be more elusive.[13]

Here we may note the way in which sexual promiscuity (in this case, the polyandry of Draupadi, the wife of the five Pandavas[xvi]) is used as a metaphor for a debased and rejected pluralism.

The sort of pluralism that has prevailed in Hinduism was thus more of a multiplicity, often a belligerent multiplicity, than the mellow universalism that it has often claimed to be. Thus, for example, Hindus, and Indologists, often cite as an example of Hindu tolerance the story of the incarnation of the Hindu god Vishnu as the Buddha. But a closer look at this myth reveals its hidden agenda: Vishnu became the Buddha in order to teach the wrong-headed doctrine of Buddhism to a group of dangerously pious demons in order to lead them away from the Vedas, disarm them of their sacrificial merit, and kill them.[xvii] In 1990, a garbled version of the myth of the Buddha avatar was used in Pakistani textbooks to support anti-Hindu arguments, explaining the decline of Buddhism as in fact the Hindus do explain it in the myth of the Buddha avatar: 'The Hindus acknowledged Buddha as an avatar and began to worship his image. They distorted his teachings and absorbed Buddhism into Hinduism.' A Hindu critic comments on this passage: 'The message is oblique, yet effective—that Hinduism is the greatest curse in the subcontinent's history and threatens to absorb every other faith.'[14]

Certainly this particular brand of pluralism has not led to tolerance or nonviolence, nor was it able to diffuse the political and economic factors that, in India as everywhere else in the world, erupt in communal violence—in India, the bloodbath of Partition. These same political and economic factors, inflamed and perhaps manipulated by the rhetoric of religious intolerance, resurfaced to demolish Babur's mosque in Ayodhya in 1992, to inspire the killing of Sikhs in Delhi in 1984 and of Muslims in Gujarat in 2002, and to exacerbate the extreme suspicion and hatred that

---

[xvi] See 'The Mythology of the *Kamasutra*'.
[xvii] See 'The Concept of Heresy'.

touched off many other riots. The world of pluralistic divinities and open-ended cosmogonies existed, after all, in the minds of people already shackled by the realities of social oppression and mutual hatreds.

But perhaps we can learn from Hinduism's long and complex history of pluralism some of the pitfalls to avoid, some of the mistakes that we need not repeat. And, on the other hand, perhaps we can emulate some of India's successes, some of the ways in which individuals like Akbar or Gandhi transcended the cultural agendas that had bred as much violence as nonviolence. We can also take heart from movements within Hinduism that rejected both hierarchy and violence, of which the most obviously significant is the bhakti movement that included women and Dalits within its ranks, rejected violent sacrifice, and advocated a theology of love. Yet here, too, we must curb our optimism by noting that bhakti did not overthrow the caste system and that it was in the name of bhakti to Rama that the militant Hindus tore down Babur's mosque.

We learn from the history of Hinduism that would-be pluralists must realize and avoid two dangers, that they walk a razor's edge between denying diversity and hierarchizing it. As for the first danger, the Hindu example suggests that, for those who hope to 'enhance diversity' and celebrate plenitude, to create a world where difference is a value, the hypothesis of an original unity from which all religions derive may not be as useful as the hypothesis of an original and essential pluralism. The Hindu example shows us the perils of universalism. Granted, the universalistic hypothesis makes dialogue possible, for Hindus and others today as well as for ancient Hindus: it shows that all religions share some of the same problems. But we must take the harder but ultimately more rewarding path of going on to acknowledge that various religions offer rather different solutions to the basic human problems, and, indeed, that they also recognize different problems.

On the other hand, when we consider the second danger, the danger of hierarchization, it is evident that, although the rigid social system of ancient Hinduism does make possible a kind of pluralism in which various religions are acceptably different, as are men and women, Brahmins and Dalits, with complementary talents and weaknesses, it renders the Other separate but unequal. And this essential hierarchical modification of the democratic paradigm renders that social system intolerant. Here it may be useful once again to distinguish the essentialist pluralism of Buddhism and Gandhi from the hierarchical pluralism of Hinduism.

There are, moreover, sociological disadvantages even to tolerance itself.

We might view intolerance in a positive sense in contemporary India, where 'good' people who have tolerated intolerance for centuries now no longer tolerate it. For, due to social reforms, there are now many people who won't put up with intolerance against them—and this leads to violence, as their heightened awareness of intolerance leads them to take political action. It may ultimately be argued that a truly tolerant person would also have to accept intolerance as one of the things that it is necessary to tolerate. This being so, since the intolerant would not make an equivalent gesture toward the tolerant, intolerance would ultimately prevail. As William Butler Yeats put it (in 'The Second Coming'). 'The best lack all conviction, while the worst/Are full of passionate intensity.' This is an inevitable result of the intrinsic inequality of tolerance and intolerance. Yet this sort of logic, which dominates political conflict, need not prevail in religious dialogue, which need not play a zero–sum game.[xviii] Even the intolerant might be persuaded to operate with an open–ended, rather than zero–sum, model of religious truth, and under such a model the exclusivist truth of the intolerant need not cancel out the inclusivist truth of the tolerant.

There are no easy answers. The degree of Hindu tolerance for other religions has varied dramatically in different social and economic circumstances. There is tolerance and intolerance in every religion, and we must look at historical factors to explain these changes. Tolerance does not result merely from a set of intellectual ideas; intolerance arises not only when people have bad ideas about other people but, especially, when they don't have enough to eat. (As Bertolt Brecht put it, '*Erst kommt das Fressen, dann kommt die Morale.*' Or, as Marc Blitzstein translated it, 'First feed the face, and then talk right and wrong.') Thus the end of the line of this chapter on the intellectual tradition of tolerance in India is an anti-anti-historical argument; it argues that you cannot entirely explain intolerance by an idea (orthodoxy), that you also need to understand particular historical factors to explain it (orthopraxy).

And there have always been positive signs, reasons to hope. Hindus and Buddhists in the early period shared ideas so freely that it is impossible to say whether some of the central tenets of each faith came from one or the other. The great poet and saint Kabir, who self-consciously rejected both Hinduism and Islam, nevertheless built his own religious world out of what he would have regarded as the ruins of Hinduism and Islam, as did

---

[xviii] See 'Together Apart'.

many of the great Sufi saints. And the same Hindu texts that told of Vishnu's avatar as the Buddha also told of his avatar as Krishna, who does not destroy the cobra Kaliya, even when Kaliya is killing Krishna's friends, but subdues him and removes him to another place; evil is tolerable as long as you can domesticate it or protect yourself from it.[xix] The Other has a right to live, but not to kill us. Similarly, Hindus believe that violent goddesses are needed to deal with evil, and that they, too, must be tolerated.

Is there something in Hinduism that would help the world to develop enduring brands of pluralism? Were there people in Hinduism who developed them? I think there were, and there are. I began by deconstructing the Western misconception that intellectually pluralistic Hindus are sociologically tolerant. But this does not necessarily eliminate pluralism itself as a road to tolerance. In the case of Hinduism, the model is undercut in two ways: first, because not all Hindus were pluralistic, and, second, because, even when they were, factors other than theology may have inspired intolerance. But the sort of pluralism that Hinduism developed and maintained throughout its history, despite the incursions of both intellectual and social forms of intolerance, remains, in my opinion, the best option for religious tolerance in the world at large.

[xix] See 'The Concept of Heresy'.

THE POLITICS OF HINDUISM TOMORROW[1]

HINDU DIVERSITY AND POLITICAL CHAUVINISM

The genius of Hinduism has always been grounded in its malleability and diversity, its ability to grow and change through its receptivity to the ideas and customs of people other than Hindus. This gives it a terrific edge over those branches of the monotheistic religions (Judaism, Christianity, Islam) that are straitjacketed by a single canon (Bible or Qu'ran) and/or a single governing body (Pope or Ulema). Yet a serious threat to the future of Hinduism is posed by a bad habit that some Hindus have recently caught from the extreme fringes of those monotheisms: fundamentalism.

Fundamentalism is as much a political as a religious phenomenon, and so is Hinduism. Hinduism didn't wake up one morning and discover that it had been metamorphosed into a giant political bug during the night. It was not suddenly politicized by the nineteenth century nationalists or the twentieth century Hindutva demagogues.[i] It was, like most religions, born political, in the sense that it was shaped and constantly changed by its relationship with political actors such as kings with the power to bestow land, Buddhists vying for royal patronage, Muslim rulers who did or did not allow the building of temples, and finally by the British Raj and the contending factions after Independence. Even the caste system, that quintessentially Hindu phenomenon, was configured from the start by the Brahmins' and kings' desire to assimilate and control various foreigners (Scythians, Greeks, Kushanas) and marginal people (such as Adivasis) as well as different political, ethnic and economic factions within the body of Hinduism.

Despite occasional conflicts between competing religions, Hindu interactions with Buddhism and Jainism were generally creative and

---

[i] See 'You Can't Make an Omelette'.

constructive on both sides, as ideas such as karma, compassion and non-injury (ahimsa) passed back and forth between the groups, picking up new spins as they moved on. The presence of Muslims in India, too, added momentum to movements such as bhakti, in part by the positive example set by sects such as the Sufis and in part by inspiring Hindus to change in order to survive in the face of negative aspects of the Muslim challenge. Christianity, too, contributed new approaches to already developing Hindu movements for social action in defence of human rights for women and the lower castes.

But the serpent in this inter-religious Eden was the monotheistic itch to convert, which often soured Hindu relations with both Islam and Christianity. (Judaism did not, for the most part, proselytize, and the Jews in any case remained a small minority in India.) A more deadly sting than conversion, however, came from those Protestants within the British Raj who, in the nineteenth century, tried to recast Hinduism as a monotheism.[ii] In lifting up this monolithic form of Hinduism, the British (and the many Hindus who followed them) trampled down and largely wrote off the dominant strain of Hinduism that celebrated the multiplicity of the divine, the plurality of forms of worship. But they could not kill it; indeed, most Hindus of this type didn't even know that they were regarded as either beneath contempt or entirely non-existent.

As monotheistic fundamentalism emerged in the twentieth century, the constricted, sanitized form of Hinduism[iii] caught the fundamentalist virus too, and used the Western weapons of mass cultural destruction—television, the blogosphere—to broadcast its message of repression and hate. The hatred of the fundamentalist Hindus is directed not only against Hindus of the more diverse traditions but also, ironically, against the very monotheisms that started the rot (including the insistence that Hinduism is monotheistic) in Hinduism: Islam and Christianity. These new resentments reinforced older beefs (if I may use that word), many of them stemming from the still gaping wound left in India by the centuries of British occupation.

There is a further irony in the way that Hindu fundamentalism, while protesting that it is a reaction against European pressures, actually learned from the West much of its anti-Western identity politics as well as many Protestant evangelical strategies. Its emphasis on the priority of personal experience (conversion and re-affiliation) justifies a new definition of 'Hindu' that has to do with an experience of Hindu-ness ('If you do not

---

[ii] See 'Are Hindus Monotheists?' and 'The Toleration of Intolerance'.
[iii] See 'From Kama to Karma'.

meditate, you cannot understand the Upanishads,' someone objected after one of my lectures). Hindus of this persuasion have attempted, as Amartya Sen eloquently expressed it, 'to miniaturize the broad idea of a large India—proud of its heterodox past and its pluralist present—and to replace it by the stamp of a small India, bundled around a drastically downsized version of Hinduism'.[2]

HINDUTVA AND HISTORY

What is the relevance of history to this conflict? Sumit Sarkar has pointed out several reasons why control over the writing of history is so central to Hindu nationalism, including the fact that the exponents of Hindutva need the historical myths to rally their own quite diverse people, to establish their own identity as a unique and uniform group.[3] Amanda Huffer has well summarized all that the Hindutva faction (often called the Sangha) have at stake in their revisionist history:

> The accurate historical account would illustrate the Sangha's complacency with British rule in the years leading up to Partition. It would admit to Savarkar's initial agreement with Jinnah's two-nation theory on Nov 15, 1943, and the cover-up thereafter. It would implicate the RSS in the assassination of Mahatma Gandhi. It would reveal the complexities of the Sangha's ambivalent position on the caste system. With regard to ancient Indian history, it would refute the equation of Hindu with Aryan and subsequently deny the ethnic theory of Hindus as a superior race. It would bring to light institutionalized discrimination along the lines of caste and gender in the Hindu tradition. Ultimately, it would undermine the Sangha's claims to eternal righteousness and legitimacy based on an antiquated timeline of Hindu civilization.[4]

All of this gives the advocates of Hindutva an enormous incentive to revise Indian history, as they have done.

There are also lessons to be learned from the academic discipline of the history of religions. If we could prove that human sacrifice was attested in the ancient Sanskrit texts (and humans were, at least theoretically, included in the list of sacrificial victims or *pashus*, in the Brahmanas, c. 700 BCE, along with horses, cows, goats and sheep),[iv] would that justify human sacrifice today? Not logically or legally, but to a certain type of reactionary

---

[iv] See 'Sacrifice and Substitution'.

religious mind, it would indeed; the past is a very important template for the present; we must do in the present what our ancestors did in the paradigmatic past. And for many centuries, people in India have supported their arguments for particular religious ideas by insisting that those ideas come from the Vedas, and that the Vedas date from the dawn of time. The word 'Veda', that for centuries has evoked a beautiful, mysterious, wise ancient text, now often signals a rallying call for fundamentalism, jingoism, chauvinism.

MYTH AND HISTORY

Hinduism is as rich in history as it is in myth, but they are not the same thing; and we have to be careful how we use history and myth to understand each other. In this context I would define a myth as a story that a group of people believe for a long time despite massive evidence that it is not actually true; the spirit of myth is the spirit of Oz: pay no attention to the man behind the curtain. When we read a text that says that a Hindu king impaled eight thousand Jains,[5] we need to use history to understand myth—that is, we need to know a bit of history to understand why such a text was composed and retold many times: that means knowing the reasons for the tensions between Hindus and Jains at that time (such as the competition for royal patronage). But we cannot use the myth to reconstruct the actual history behind the text; we cannot say that the text is evidence that a Hindu king actually did impale Jains.

To take another example, when the *Ramayana* speaks of ogres (*rakshasas*), it may be simultaneously constructing an imaginary world in which evil forces take forms that can destroy us and using ogres as a metaphor for particular types of human beings.[v] But it does not record an actual event, a moment when people from Ayodhya overcame real people in India (tribals, or Dravidians, or anyone else), nor does the story of the building of a causeway to an island that the text calls Lanka mean that Rama and an army of monkeys actually built a causeway[vi] from India to present-day (Sri) Lanka.[6] Such myths reveal to us the history of sentiments rather than events, motivations rather than movements.

But stories, and the ideas in stories, do influence history in the other direction, into the future. People who heard or read that story about the

---

[v] See 'Shadows of the *Ramayana*'.

[vi] Yet this mythical causeway was real enough, in September of 2007, to put an end to a major government project to build a canal through the area where Rama's bridge was said to be.

impaled Jains may well have acted differently towards Jains and/or Hindus (better or worse) as a result. More often than not, we do not know precisely what happened in history, but we often know the stories that people tell about it. In some ways, the stories are not only all that we have access to but all that people at the time, and later, had access to and hence all that drove the events that followed. Real events and sentiments produce symbols, symbols produce real events and sentiments, and real and symbolic levels may be simultaneously present in a single text. Myth has been called 'the smoke of history',[7] and we must constantly strive to separate the smoke of myth from the fire of historical events, as well as to demonstrate how myths, too, become fires when they do not merely respond to historical events (as smoke arises from fire) but drive them (as fire gives rise to smoke). Ideas are facts too; the belief, whether true or false, that the British were greasing cartridges with animal fat[vii] started a revolution in India in 1857.[8] For we are what we imagine, as much as what we do.

To say (as I do) that the *Ramayana* tells us a great deal about attitudes toward various social groups (including women and the lower castes) in the early centuries CE is a far cry from saying that someone named Rama actually lived in the precise city now known as Ayodhya and fought a battle on the precise island now known as Sri Lanka with a faithful band of talking monkeys on his side and a ten-headed demon on the other—or with a band of tribal peoples (represented as monkeys) on his side and a proto-Muslim monster on the other, as some contemporary Hindus have asserted. Rama left no archeological or inscriptional record. There is no evidence that anyone named Rama did or did not live in Ayodhya; other places, too, claim him, in South India as well as North India, for the *Ramayana* was retold many times, in many different Indian languages, with significant variations. There is no second Troy here for a Schliemann to come along and discover. Or, rather, there is a second, and a third, and a nineteenth Troy for anyone to discover.

Placing the *Ramayana* in its historical contexts demonstrates that it is an epic poem created by human authors who lived at various times, and that it shows how the human imagination transformed the actual circumstance of the historical period into something far more beautiful, terrible, challenging and elevating than, perhaps, the circumstances themselves.

[vii] The Great Rebellion, formerly known as the Sepoy Mutiny, was triggered when Indian troops serving under the British feared that the British were greasing cartridges—which the troops had to bite—with pig fat (anathema to Muslims) or cow fat (anathema to Hindus) or both.

Texts reveal histories, but we need to find out about those histories and ground them in solid evidence to read against, not into, the texts' narratives. Reconstructing the ways in which human authors constructed stories, in reaction to earlier texts as well as to historical circumstances, reveals their texts as works of art rather than mere records of actual events.[9]

Though I would characterize myth in general, and Hindu myth in particular, as, to quote David Arnold, 'the positive connotation of something culturally richer and psychologically more revealing than history alone, a portal into civilization's inner self',[10] myth also has, like the supernatural creatures it portrays, its dark side:

> [M]yth-making can be the deliberate, self-interested falsification of history. The myths surrounding the eleventh-century sack of the temple of Somnath are a case in point, but increasingly in America and across the globalized world [there is] a new kind of Hindu mythologizing, in which moral conformity is being imposed on a religion that once had reason to rejoice in its decentred plurality, and where myths, which once survived because of their ability to speak to the human condition, can now be exploited by the power of the internet. The televised *Ramayana* shown in India has, for many ideologues, become the only acceptable form of what were once, and still should be, the many *Ramayana*s. The . . . textual tradition [is] threatened by those who claim to be its guardians, and who would make of something as rich as myth something as routine as religion.[11]

THE HINDUISM OF THE FUTURE

There is hope. Through the ages, most Hindus have gone on worshipping their gods, singing their songs, telling their stories. Hindutva will not have the last word. The good news is that the other sort of Hinduism, the full-screen, pluralist, creative sort, remains in the majority, and it, too, can call up mass media to rally its forces. The film industry—both in Bollywood and among the many fine independent filmmakers of India—has broadcast, throughout India and abroad, powerful tales of inter-religious tolerance and protests against injustice, as have individual Hindu artists and writers, jamming the mindless transmissions of the bigoted blogs.

The Hinduism of the future will have to survive in a multi-cultural, multi-religious India that simply will not be homogenized; it will have to flow with, rather than against, the currents of modernization and globalization. It will have to open its doors wide to welcome change, for in any case, it is too late to shut them. As India's prosperity continues to grow, so too its connections with the wider world, and its participation in global concerns for human dignity, will increasingly nourish native movements working for social reform and for the protection of individual rights, both for women and Dalits within Hinduism and for Muslims, Christians and others whose ancestors made India their home many centuries ago. The Hinduism of the future will continue to be light years ahead of the fundamentalists of all religions in its breadth of vision, depth of spiritual understanding and spellbinding stories.

GODS, HUMANS AND ANTI-GODS

SAGUNA AND *NIRGUNA* IMAGES OF THE DEITY[1]

If you say he exists, he does;
his forms are these forms.
If you say he does not,
his formlessness
is of these non-forms.
If he has the qualities
of existence and non-existence,
he is in two states.
He who pervades is without end.

—Nammalvar[2]

N ammalvar ('Our Alvar'), the last of the great Tamil Vaishnava saints
called Alvars, lived from approximately 880 to 930 CE and is said to
have been born into a Shudra caste, a peasant caste (Vellala), in Tamilnadu.
This verse is part of his greatest poem, the *Tiruvaymoli*, often called 'The
Tamil Veda', a work of 1,102 verses. Here Nammalvar refutes those
(particularly but not only Buddhists) who say that there is no Veda, no god
and no universe.[i] On the contrary, Nammalvar argues, god participates in
'two states', both in the world of forms and existence and qualities (*saguna*)
and in the world of formlessness and non-existence, without qualities
(*nirguna*). For existence and non-existence are themselves the very form of
god, and whether you say he exists or he does not exist, he still exists. Even
where he does not seem to be, he is the inner soul of everything and,
therefore, he exists.

The hypothesis of this chapter is that the *nirguna* image of the deity—the
god without qualities[ii]—in Hinduism is a graft onto Puranic and temple
bhakti that never really took, that the *nirguna* line was taken up by grass-

---

[i] See 'The Concept of Heresy'.
[ii] See 'Are Hindus Monotheists?' and 'You Can't Get Here'.

roots Hindus with a strictly limited degree of success. The logical outcome of merging with a *nirguna* deity—moksha—would be the disappearance of bhakti, with no god to be the object of devotion; the ultimate *nirguna* deity is *brahman*, the impersonal divine substance of which all living things are elements. *Nirguna* bhakti is therefore an Irish bull (or, as the Hindus say, *vandhyaputra*, '[as meaningless as] the son of a barren woman'). Charlotte Vaudeville has elegantly and clearly stated the paradox that is at the heart of this problem: the Sants—North Indian saints—not only wavered between *nirguna* and *saguna* images of the deity, but purposely challenged the very distinction between these categories.[3] This conflict results, at least in part, from the merging of several different Indian traditions (including Sanskrit Vedanta and vernacular bhakti)—a merging that was not always willing or conscious. For *nirguna* bhakti is a concoction that monistic Hindu philosophers imposed upon a *saguna* bhakti tradition that managed, somehow, to absorb it.

It is difficult to imagine a deity who cannot, by definition, be imagined; it can be done, but it is difficult. Hindu philosophers have much more practice, and can bring it off; but what about the rest of India? Nowhere on earth can one find a people more eager than the Hindus to revel in specific, concrete, multitudinous detail. This is immediately obvious from a brief glance at any Sanskrit *kavya* or Puranic *stotra*—the descriptions of jewellery and of trees, the lists of attributes, the enumeration of physical qualities. And in temple architecture, the epitome of a *saguna* entity is surely the South Indian *gopuram* with its staggering, overwhelming baroque superabundance of detail that so nauseated the early European observers with their cool Greek ideals. Where, then, does the *nirguna* image play a role in this side of Hinduism? It begins in the *Rig Veda*, with the hymns of the late tenth book that play word-games with the ineffable that is neither being nor non-being.[iii]

But the down-to-earth Hindus were quick to turn the *nirguna* question into a *saguna* answer. Epic and Puranic Hinduism abound in examples of resistance to the *nirguna* ideal. Avatar is a prime example. Theoretically, one cannot reconcile a *nirguna* deity with avatars; yet the Kabir-panthis tended to treat Kabir as a kind of avatar. Avatar may also colour the *nirguna* Sant tradition both in the tendency to divinize Sants and in the magnetic attraction of the name of God, a cult that impinges upon the very *murti* (idol)-worship and celebration of incarnation that is elsewhere sharply mocked by the Sants. This tension is even more evident in the Puranas, where the Brahmin authors attempted to channel the emotional current of *prema* (love) *bhakti* into the classical furrows of Advaita monism, stubbornly ignoring their basic incompatibility. (The philosopher Ramanuja tackled the problem in a far more sophisticated way; though the Puranas do not quote him as much as they quote a kind of third-rate version of Shankara, Puranic thought owes much to Ramanuja's resolution of *saguna* with *nirguna*.)

The avatar is constantly bumping into his own *nirguna* image; the texts never fully accept this resolution of the *nirguna-saguna* tension. When, in the *Bhagavad Gita*, Arjuna naively asks Krishna to demonstrate his full *nirguna* form and Krishna complies, Arjuna quickly begs him to turn back into the aspect he can handle—his old pal Krishna, the tricky *saguna* charioteer. This request is couched in terms of striking intimacy and specificity, the essence of the *saguna* deity, in sharp contrast with the *nirguna* god that Arjuna has just praised:

> Your strength is infinite, and your power is infinite;
> You achieve everything; you are everything.
> It was madness of me to think of you as a friend,
> to say, 'Hey, Krishnna, Hey Yadava, Hey friend!'
> I did this because I did not know how great you are—
> or else, perhaps, in carelessness because I love you.
> Sometimes I would tease you when we were joking,
> either at table, or sitting, or resting, or playing,
> when we were alone, or together with others.
> Forgive me for that, you who cannot be measured.[4]

Arjuna begins and ends with praise of the *nirguna* god; in between, he lapses helplessly into the *saguna* idiom, to justify himself, to reassure himself, and to remind the god that he loves him.

And when, in the *Bhagavata Purana*, Krishna's mother sees the *nirguna* Krishna inside her child (the *saguna* Krishna), she cannot stand it, and Krishna lovingly deludes her with the emotion of maternal love, giving her back the specific, complicated little boy she adores in place of the ineffable god she cannot understand.[5] Tulsidas, too, is irresistibly drawn by the magnet of the *saguna* deity: though he begins his invocation to Shiva as *nirguna*, *nirvikalpa*, etc., he ends up by describing him as having matted locks, the Ganga in his hair, etc.[6] And this same tendency may also be seen in the relentlessness with which the Puranas attribute to their gods details so minute as to border on the banal, and to contrast these details specifically with the *nirguna* image.

Despite this bias, the *nirguna* philosophy is expounded at great length from time to time in the Puranas, in the typically simplified Puranic version of Vedantic philosophy. But these speeches never seem fully integrated into the main plot-lines; they do not affect the characters who speak them, or cause them to exchange their world-attached, earthy goals for the high ideals inspired by the *nirguna* deity. The Puranas are not so much *by* common people as *for* common people; they are often manipulated by Brahmins to teach people ideas that Brahmins think people should have. The Sants, on the other hand, *choose* to mix *nirguna* and *saguna*.

One can see a similar interaction in the structure of the Hindu temple, in shrines as far removed and different in form as the Minakshi temple at Madurai in South India and the caves at Elephanta in Central India. On the outermost periphery, the quintessence of *saguna* worldliness is expressed in a mind-blowing variety of detail: the temple market, the piles of vermilion powders and rows of shining brass pots, brilliant flowers and garish postcards—the chaotic and noisy world of profane life. But even here there is a sacred tug: for what is being sold is food for gods (*prasada*), and vessels for holy water; this is the borderline of the two worlds. Immediately afterwards, in South India, one encounters the incredible *gopuram*, the epitome of *saguna* detail; now nothing is being bought and sold, and the detail is all god's detail, not humans'. But detail it certainly is: we have moved a little farther into the centre, and the layers concealing the divinity are dropping away. We enter the next courtyard and encounter less colour and shape than in the *gopuram*, but still a lot: carved pillars, images depicting mythological scenes, and the actual human and animal activity of the temple—painted elephants, pious beggars, chanting priests. At Elephanta, we see the elaborate panels depicting the marriage of Shiva and Parvati, their quarrels at dice, Shiva squashing Ravana under Kailasa, Shiva in yogic meditation, the Ganga descending on Shiva's head, the androgynous form of Shiva and Parvati (Ardhanarishvara), Shiva impaling the demon Andhaka, Shiva dancing to create the universe, Shiva dancing to destroy the universe—one's head begins to spin, the mind boggles, the eye cannot absorb it all.

Overwhelmed by these *saguna* manifestations, one flees gratefully to the still centre of the temple, the *garbha-griha* (Sanskrit for 'womb-house'), the innermost shrine, *sanctum sanctorum*—and here one encounters the *nirguna* god. At Elephanta, it is the great Maheshvara image which, whatever it may mean (and no one has ever convinced me that they really understand it), is certainly most striking in its simplicity and lack of detail, in contrast with the surrounding panels. Here is a god who has gathered all his action into himself and remains completely latent, potential; one cannot tell what he is thinking, what he is about to do, or indeed if he has ever done anything or ever will; he is a complete enigma. In the South Indian temples, too, one encounters the simplest of images in the *garbha-griha*, usually a Shiva-*lingam* or Vishnu's *shalagrama* stone, sometimes a small icon completely mummified in layers of cloth, a sinister image but one without qualities, *nirguna*. This stark, aniconic symbol is usually very old, worshipped from time immemorial, far older than anything else in the temple; but in its original existence, outside the temple, it had particular meanings associated with various local cults, a name perhaps, a mythology, a specific function to procure specific human desiderata for the villagers who worshipped it. Only when it was later incorporated into the temple and subjected to Brahminical reinterpretation did it take on the meaning of a *nirguna* deity. And although one has moved from a large physical space (the outer boundary of the temple) to a small physical space (the small cave, cool and dark, reeking of bat urine), the feeling is that one has been moving *outward* all the time, spiritually, into larger and larger spaces, until one encounters in the still centre the *nirguna* image that is the totality of the universe. This is the triumph of the *nirguna* deity in the Hindu temple.

But it is not a lasting triumph. Again and again one encounters a kind of backlash against the serenity and finality of the metaphysical stasis of the central image in the *garbha-griha*. For one thing, people keep taking it out and doing things to it, and banalizing it as they do the Puranic gods: this mysterious, unearthly thing that lurks under the ancient wrappings is changed, fed and treated with almost insulting intimacy—given qualities which make it possible for the worshipper to demonstrate his love for it.[iv] (I use the male pronoun here with reason: for centuries, women were seldom if ever allowed into or near the *garbha-griha*—despite its use of the female metaphor of the womb; even today, some temples forbid women access to this most intimate place in the temple.)

The excursions to which the *garbha-griha* image is subjected may range from the daily routine to the annual festival—the ceremony of the *ratha* (chariot) carrying the image outside the temple. George Michell has

---

[iv] In a similar way, an eye-less, face-less, naked, feature-less child's Teddy bear, reduced by years of hard play to a *nirguna* lump, may be wrapped up in a cloth (like the image in the temple) and *imagined* to have all the qualities the child desires.

referred to the temple *ratha* as a 'mobile temple', in contrast with the 'minimal' temple represented by the formless roadside shrine of rock or tree.[7] The 'minimal' temple is *nirguna*; the orthodox temple is *saguna*; and the 'mobile' temple mediates between them, giving qualities to the formless central image. Even here, the austere splendour of the veiled deity is tempered by the need for anthropomorphic detail. In the temple of Kataragama, in Sri Lanka, the god is taken out once a year; in an inspiration of true anthropomorphism, he is carried past the house of his long-suffering wife and left instead in the house of his mistress, where he spends the night and emerges next morning in a better mood, more inclined to grant favours to his devotees. And what are these favours? Not moksha, nor enlightenment, nor any of the stock-in-trade of the *nirguna* deity; but the small, worldly needs that animate his worshippers: a clear skin after smallpox, a decent crop after a failed monsoon, a husband, a healthy child—all the *details* that make life precious. And these details are reflected in the very image of the god, a god endowed with specific qualities, *saguna*, by the mind of the worshipper if not by the hand of the sculptor.

YOU CAN'T GET HERE FROM THERE:
THE LOGICAL PARADOX OF HINDU CREATION
MYTHS[1]

In the earliest age of the gods, existence was born from non-existence.
—Rig Veda 10.72.2

INTRODUCTION

Creation myths tackle the problem of the ultimate origin of it all, of the beginning of life out of non-life, at three different basic levels: creation of the universe, of the human race, or of the individual human being, the embryo. What sort of origins do we regard as 'our' origins? Scholars often mimic believers in this regard: The search for origins *in* religious texts has also been a scholars' search for the origins *of* religious texts. The idea, seldom expressed but generally operative, is that the earliest texts will somehow be closest to the origins of the world and, therefore, most likely to have the truth about it, just as texts closer to the time of the Buddha are thought to be more likely to have the truth about the Buddha. The scholarly equivalent of the religious quest for origins is the quest for the *Ur*-text, a nineteenth-century obsession that still lingers in many backwaters of the academy. A somewhat more sophisticated corollary to this belief is the assumption that any idea that is shared by a number of cultures has a kind of truth in it. In fact, all that it proves—and this is still something worth knowing, the basis of the discipline of comparative religion—is that human beings in several cultures have had some roughly similar ideas about, say, the origins of the world, and even then we must quickly add that they have had some very different ideas, too. Many patterns extend through many religions on both the cosmic and the social level; but these patterns vary according to the specific historical and social conditions of the cultures that create them. Though myths have a life of their own, they are embedded in human culture, and as science changes, myth changes: astronomy, botany, geography, embryology, methods of measurement—each has its effects upon the formulation of mythological concepts of creation.

The problem that most creation mythologies, including, I think, scientific theories of creation, must face is the basic problem of creation *ex nihilo*, getting from the original putative moment of nothing to the present moment of something. It is not a problem that every culture takes on; the ancient Mesopotamians are not, apparently, bothered by this problem at all, but simply assume that everything was always already there. This may well be; or is it, perhaps, that they did not care to discuss the problem, and preferred to begin at a moment in time when everything was already there?[2] And indeed, if you believe that time is infinite or eternal then there is no problem about finding its beginning. But creation myths do not usually take this cowardly way out, preferring instead to wrestle with the problems of beginnings. Perhaps the mythological mind, unlike the philosophical, just can't accept the mind-boggling concept of a time without beginning or end. Most people, after all, even mythographers, are more interested in what happened to our first ancestors than in more philosophical paradoxes, and many myths are designed not to answer peoples' questions but to make them start asking those questions in the first place. Some myths inspire questions but also constrain the answers by leading people to frame them in specific theological terms.

Many mythologies do tackle this paradox of getting something from nothing, and when they do, the resulting mental gymnastics always remind me of the old joke about the native city-dweller trying to give complicated street directions to an out-of-towner and finally admitting, 'You can't get there from here.' No mythology can get here (the present) from there, and most of them fudge this fact by positing the unexplained sudden appearance of an original something—god, or a kind of chaotic primeval matter—and moving quickly off this highly debatable point into a labyrinth of baroque elaboration, a proliferation of detail: from this original something came water, and then an egg, and then a bird, and then fourteen kinds of snakes, and twenty-nine tribes of human beings, and so forth and so on. This is a false trail that lures the listener or reader away from the opening point, the inevitable weak point, the question that cannot be answered.

For the ultimate moment of transition from pre-creation to post-creation is a moment that no one can actually know, and that presents a logical dilemma that no argument can resolve. Instead, the texts devise indirect strategies to give the false impression that that basic question has been answered when it has not; they try to explain it by adopting various attitudes (ranging from dogmatic certainty to humble confessions of ignorance) and various techniques of obfuscation, all designed to cover up the unavoidable but inadmissible fact of (the origin of) life, the fact that you can't get here from there.

THE ORIGINS OF THE UNIVERSE

In India, texts begin with the *Rig Veda*, a canonical collection of 1,028 hymns composed in the hills of the Punjab, about 1500 BCE, by the inspired priests of a migratory people who rode their horses, and grazed their cattle, down into the Ganga Valley by about 900 BCE. So let me begin with the *Rig Veda*, the oldest Indian text (and hence, presumably, closest to the moment of creation). The first thing to note is that there is no one, single theory of creation in this text, nor in Hinduism as a whole; there are a number of different, more or less compatible, theories, which no one ever tried to fit systematically into a canonical doctrine.

Several models of creation are imagined in a poem that combines the earthy details of a woman giving birth to a baby with philosophical questions about the role of the gods in the creation of the universe. This woman, called Aditi ('Without Limits', 'Infinity'), is the feminine power paired with Daksha, the male principle of virile efficacy (or dexterity, a word that is related to the Sanskrit *daksha*):

> Let us now speak with wonder of the births of the gods—so that some one may see them when the poems are chanted in this later age. In the earliest age of the gods, existence was born from non-existence. After this the quarters of the sky, and the earth, were born from her who crouched with legs spread, and from the earth the quarters of the sky were born. From Aditi, Daksha was born, and from Daksha Aditi was born. After her were born the blessed gods, the kinsmen of immortality . . .[3]

Before we have recovered from the philosophical paradox of existence coming from non-existence, we are assaulted by the paradox of mutual creation: Aditi and Daksha create one another; a later commentary takes pains to explain that by the dharma of the gods, two births can be mutually productive of one another.[4] Then comes contradiction: the earth born from the crouching divinity is also said to be born from the quarters of the sky that are born from her. But along the way a more anthropomorphic image has surfaced, the woman who crouches with legs spread (*uttana-pad*, literally, 'with legs stretched up', more particularly with knees drawn up and legs spread wide), a term that designates a position primarily associated with a woman giving birth. It is later associated with yoga, and might have yogic overtones even in this period.[i]

Another Vedic hymn tries another tack, this time in a more theistic vein, demonstrating that the basic principles of creation prevail whether or not the author of the text believes that one god created the universe. To measure is to make. The Sanskrit verb '*ma*' means both; it means 'to make' not only in the sense of creating *ex nihilo*, or even of fashioning a pot out of clay, but of making something by arbitrarily delineating it from what it is not, as people once 'made' political units such as Bangladesh not by dredging mud up out of the Bay of Bengal but by drawing a line across a piece of land that might have been India or Burma and saying: 'This is now Bangladesh.' This Austinian speech act alters reality. The idea of cosmic measurement was more fully developed in a short hymn addressed to Vishnu:

> Let me now sing the heroic deeds of Vishnu, who has *measured apart* the realms of earth, who propped up the upper dwelling-place, striding far as he stepped forth three times. He alone with but three steps *measured apart* this long, far-reaching dwelling-place. Alone, he supports threefold the earth and the sky and all creatures.[5]

This brief text is the basis of the later myth of the dwarf avatar of Vishnu, who takes three steps not to create the universe but to win it *back* from Bali, the anti-god who had stolen it: with one step he covers the earth, with one the atmosphere, and with the third, heaven. And voilà: Bangladesh.

But the propping apart of heaven and earth, measuring out and establishing the three worlds for all creatures to dwell in, is a central Vedic cosmogonic act,[ii] usually attributed not to Vishnu but to more important Vedic gods like Indra (Vedic king of the gods and god of the sky and rain) or Varuna (god of the vault of heaven, of the waters, and of morality and truth). This time-sharing property of the Vedic gods turns out to be one of a number of ways to keep the existence, and/or number, of the authors of creation an open question in Vedic religion.[iii]

If several gods existed, then, in the life of a single worshipper, how

[i] See 'Assume the Position'.
[ii] See 'Together Apart'.
[iii] See 'Are Hindus Monotheists?'

many gods were there? The *Rig Veda* tell us that some people challenged the existence even of Indra, but the text ultimately affirms him; one hymn remarks: 'He about whom they ask, "Where is he?" or they say of him, the terrible one, "He does not exist,"—believe in him! He, my people, is Indra.'[6] One hymn is addressed 'to Indra, if Indra exists'.[7] [iv]

The doctrine of creation *ex nihilo* ('existence was born from non-existence'), that we saw stated as a known fact in the Aditi poem, is queried in the opening line of another poem that is known, from its first words, as the 'Nasadiya' or 'There was not' poem. This short, linguistically straightforward poem, that explicitly lays out an open-ended attitude to the first things, has provoked hundreds of complex commentaries among theologians and scholars, both Hindu and non-Hindu, for it raises unanswerable questions, piling up paradoxes:

> There was neither non-existence nor existence then; there was neither the realm of space nor the sky that is beyond. What stirred? Where? In whose protection? Was there water, bottomlessly deep? There was neither death nor immortality then. There was no distinguishing sign of night nor of day.
>
> That one breathed, windless, by its own impulse. Other than that there was nothing beyond . . . Who really knows? Who will here proclaim it? Whence was it produced? Whence is this creation? The gods came afterwards, with the creation of this universe. Who then knows whence it has arisen? Whence this creation has arisen—perhaps it formed itself, or perhaps it did not—the one who looks down on it, in the highest heaven, only he knows—or perhaps he does not know.[8]

There is a charming humility in this hymn, an open-mindedness. The last line—'or perhaps he does not know'—seems almost to mock the rhetoric of more typical hymns in the very text in which it occurs, the *Rig Veda*, even in the penultimate phrase here: 'the one who looks down on it, in the highest heaven, only he knows.' The hymn begins, most confusingly, with the statement, 'There was neither non-existence nor existence then'—easy enough to say, impossible actually to visualize—and the hymn ends, open-endedly, with the suggestion, 'perhaps he does not know.' Most important, the hymn asks, 'Who really knows?'—a question about the very nature, perhaps the very existence, of god.

This admission of ignorance becomes even more powerful in the *via negativa* of the Upanishads, philosophical commentaries on the Vedas, from perhaps 600 BCE, which, when asked to describe the Absolute

---

[iv] See 'The Concept of Heresy'.

[*brahman*], can only reply, '*Neti, neti*'—'not like this, not like that.' Indeed, the Upanishads openly contest the Vedic cosmogony; one sage quotes the Vedic line about existence coming from non-existence,[9] but then remarks: 'How can that possibly be?' and argues, instead, that, 'In the beginning, this world was simply what is existent.'[10]

The unanswered cosmic question—'Who really knows?'—recurs in the *Rig Veda*, in another cosmogonic hymn, in which each stanza ends with the questioning refrain, 'Who is the god whom we should worship with the oblation?'; 'He by whom the awesome sky and the Earth were made firm, by whom the dome of the sky was propped up, and the sun, who measured out the middle realm of space—who is the god whom we should worship with the oblation?'[11] And so forth. Later Hindu tradition, troubled by the open-ended refrain of the creation hymn, invented a god whose name was the interrogative pronoun 'Who?'—*ka* (cognate with the Latin *quis*, French *qui*). One text explained it: The Creator asked Indra (the sky god whose existence was sometimes challenged), 'Who am I?', to which Indra replied, 'Just who you just said' (i.e., 'I am Who') and that is how the Creator got the name of Who.[12] So, too, in one Vedic ceremony, when the ritual subject goes to heaven and comes back again, he must say, on his return, 'I am just who I am.'[13] Read back into this Vedic hymn, as it was in the Vedic commentaries,[14] this resulted in an affirmative statement ('Indeed, Who is the god whom we should honour with the oblation') somewhat reminiscent of the famous Abbott and Costello routine ('Who's on first?'). The question becomes the answer. But since the question itself is the origin of self-consciousness, to stop questioning, or to find an answer, is to shut down that self-consciousness.

THE CREATION OF THE HUMAN RACE

The same principles that permeate the mythology of cosmogony operate on the next level of creation, the creation of the human race, or anthropogony. The most explicit Vedic discussion of the origins of the human race, the 'Hymn of the Primeval Male' (the *purusha sukta*), is also the most explicitly hierarchical hymn in the whole of the *Rig Veda*. For, when the texts get down to the nitty-gritty level of the creation of the human race, it is the affirmative rather than the questioning tone that dominates, and the concept of hierarchy that has the last word. Like many myths of the origin of the human race that instil ideals of social hierarchy that they construct as natural, this famous hymn seems to have abandoned all sense of scepticism in order to present a clear-cut social theory in the guise of a myth of creation.

The *purusha sukta* is about the dismemberment of the cosmic male giant (*purusha* later comes to designate any male creature, indeed the male gender), who is the victim in a Vedic sacrifice that creates the whole universe. Out of the Primeval Male, the four classes of society (the *varnas*) are born. This is the central passage:

> The Primeval Male has a thousand heads, a thousand eyes, a thousand feet. With three quarters the Male rose upwards, and one quarter of him still remains here. From this (quarter on earth) he spread out in all directions, into that which eats and that which does not eat. From the Male, the female was born, and from the female came the Male.

★

> When they divided the Primeval Male, his mouth became the Brahmin; his arms were made into the Raja; his thighs the people [Vaishya]; and from his feet the servants [Shudras] were born. The moon was born from his mind; from his eye the sun was born. From his navel the middle realm of space arose; from his head the sky evolved. From his two feet came the earth, and the quarters of the sky from his ear. Thus they set the worlds in order . . . when the gods, spreading the sacrifice, bound the Male as the sacrificial beast. With the sacrifice the gods sacrificed to the sacrifice.[15]

At the top of the four classes created from the dismembered Male are the Brahmins, the class from whom the priests were drawn (and presumably the authors of this particular Brahmin-empowering poem, though not necessarily of all of the Veda). All Vedic priests are Brahmins, though not all Brahmins are priests. Then comes the Raja, the King, generally taken to refer to the class of warriors, policemen and kings (Kshatriyas); and then Vaishyas (the common people, the Third Estate, who produce the food for the first two and themselves). The fourth class, Shudras, servants, are set apart, the outside class within society that defines the other classes. Viewed historically, the hymn takes the three Indo-European social classes (according to the paradigm of Georges Dumézil: king-priest at the top, then warriors and policemen, and then the rest of the people) and adds, at the bottom, a fourth class, servants.[v] The hierarchical distinction is clear from our

---

[v] The fact that the fourth class is already present in Avestan texts implies that such a class—consisting primarily of artisans—may in fact have been Indo-European, which would imply a serious corrective to the Dumézilian model. Yet this class is already an outsider, which substantiates the essence of that model.

relationship with the gods, where we are the bottom quarter: 'All creatures are a quarter of him; three quarters are what is immortal in heaven. With three quarters the Male rose upwards, and one quarter of him still remains here.' And it is mirrored in the structure within that human quarter, where the bottom quarter consists of the servant class. This distinction makes it possible to view the final combination in both cases not as a quartet but as a dualism: all of us (in the first three classes, who are already given several names, such as Aryans or twice-born) vs. all of them (in the fourth class, the non-us, the Others). That the Shudras were an afterthought is evident from the fact that the third class, Vaishyas, is sometimes said to be derived from the word for 'all' and, therefore, literally to mean 'everyone', leaving no room for anyone below them—until someone added a class below them.[vi]

The *purusha sukta* ranks the kings below the priests. The supremacy of Brahmins was much contested throughout later Hindu literature and, in fact, may have been primarily a Brahmin fantasy; there is much evidence of resistance to the concept that the priests and kings ever shared power at all. That is, many texts argue, or assume, that priests never were as high as kings, and others assume that kings never fell below priests. Buddhist literature simply puts the kings at the top, the Brahmins second,[16] and many characters in Hindu texts also defend this viewpoint. If we accept the Dumézilian view that the king shared the first position with the Brahmin in the putative Indo-European world, it appears that the king slips down, in the *Rig Veda*, to share the second position with the warrior. So even in this earliest layer, in a hymn supposedly postulating a social charter that was created at the very dawn of time and is to remain in place forever after, we can see movement, change, slippage, progress or decay, depending upon your point of view. This is another sort of obfuscation that is basic to mythology: the semblance of an unmoving eternity presented in texts that themselves clearly document constant transformation.

In the *purusha sukta*, the 'sacrifice' designates both the ritual and the victim killed in the ritual; moreover, the Primeval Male is both the victim that the gods sacrificed and the divinity to whom the sacrifice was dedicated; that is, he is both the subject and the object of the sacrifice.[vii]

[vi] Indo-European linguists usually derive Vaishya from a different word that means 'settlement' or 'people who live on the land', but some Sanskrit texts cite the derivation from 'all'. See also 'Three (or More)'.
[vii] See 'Sacrifice and Substitution'.

This Vedic bootstraps pattern or chicken-and-egg paradox is a kind of tautology: 'From the Male, the female was born, and from the female came the Male.' The same paradoxical/tautological structure recurs in other cosmogonies we have seen: 'From Aditi, Daksha was born, and from Daksha Aditi was born.' The Creator in many of these texts has the tautological name of Svayambhu, 'self-existing', often translated as 'self-created': he creates himself.[17] This sort of tautology is a major obfuscational stratagem in the game of cosmogony: you *do* explain where something comes from—it comes from something else—and, indeed you explain where *that* comes from too: it comes from the first thing. Two for the price of one. Moving right along . . .

This circular creation appears in later myths as well, such as the oft-retold story of the origins of Vishnu and Brahma:

> When the three worlds were in darkness, Vishnu slept in the middle of the cosmic ocean. A lotus grew out of his navel. Brahma came to him and said, 'Tell me, who are you?' Vishnu replied, 'I am Vishnu, Creator of the Universe. All the worlds, and you yourself, are inside me. And who are you?' Brahma replied, '*I* am the Creator, and everything is inside *me*.' Vishnu then entered Brahma's body and saw all three worlds in his belly. Astonished, he came out of Brahma's mouth and said, 'Now, you must enter my belly in the same way and see the worlds.' And so Brahma entered Vishnu's belly and saw all the worlds. Then, since Vishnu had shut all the openings, Brahma came out of Vishnu's navel, and rested on the lotus.[18]

Each god sees all the worlds (including, as Vishnu points out but Brahma does not, the other god) inside the belly of the other god.[viii] Each claims to be the Creator of the universe, and yet each contains the other creator. This circularity is mirrored by the mutual birth symbolism: Brahma, born from Vishnu as a baby would be born from a mother, is nevertheless connected to Vishnu by the lotus stalk that comes out of Vishnu's navel, functioning as an umbilical cord, which would make Vishnu the baby, connected to the lotus (a symbol of the womb, in India, and always the seat of Brahma) by his own navel, as a baby would be connected to the mother. And, near the end of the myth, Brahma is indeed born for a second time,

---

[viii] In other, related myths, Krishna's mother Yashoda sees herself inside her own baby's mouth (*Bhagavata Purana* 10) and, when Brahma and Vishnu cannot decide which came first, Shiva appears in the form of a giant flaming phallus and humbles them both (*Kurma Purana* 1.25). See 'God's Body'.

this time before our eyes, through Vishnu's navel. The myth of Vishnu and Brahma is also set at the liminal moment when the universe has been destroyed and reduced to a cosmic ocean (dissolution), and is about to undergo a new creation, which in turn will be followed by a dissolution, then a creation, and so on *ad infinitum*—another series of mutual creations.

THE BATTLE BETWEEN THE GODS AND THE ANTI-GODS

Later texts begin to distinguish gods (*devas*) not merely from humans but from anti-gods (or demons, *asuras*), no simple task in India. Indeed, in the Indo-European stage[ix] the *asuras* were not anti-gods at all but simply a particular sort of sky-gods; the great god in the Avesta, the ancient Persian counterpart to the *Rig Veda*, is called Ahura Mazda, the great *asura*, a benevolent spirit. Even in the *Rig Veda*, several gods are still called *asuras* (Varuna, in particular). And, just as benevolent *asuras* became malevolent demons in later India, so, too, benevolent Greek *daemons* (another sort of god) became malevolent *demons* in Christianity, and the *devas* of ancient India and Persia (gods, cognate with *deus* in Latin) became the *devils* of Christianity. These linguistic clues to the fungibility of the moral attributes of the powers that be—to the absence, as it were, of any real moral distinction between gods and anti-gods—were categorically expunged by later Manichaeanism and Hinduism.

But the arbitrary nature of the later distinction between gods and demons, both sons of the Creator, is emphasized by a circular logic that resembles, in form, the tautologies we have already encountered in the Veda: the Creator makes the demons evil because they are evil, and he creates them out of darkness, but he then makes their substance into night. The text that first tells this story, the *Shatapatha Brahmana*, composed a few centuries after the Vedas, in about 700 BCE, replicates the Vedic model of dismemberment, in a modified form: The Creator creates from his mouth not the Brahmins but the gods, and they are not made out of his mouth but simply emerge from it, leaving him intact:

> The Creator was born to live for a thousand years. Just as one might see in the distance the far shore of a river, so he saw the far shore of his own life. He desired progeny, and so he placed the power to produce progeny in himself. From his mouth he created the gods, and they entered the sky. Then with his downward breath he created the demons, and they entered this earth, and there was darkness for him

---

[ix] See 'Hinduism by Any Other Name'.

when he had created them, and so he knew then that he had created evil. Then he pierced them with evil, and it was because of this that they were overcome. Therefore it is said, 'The battle between gods and demons did not happen as it is told in the narratives and histories, for the Creator pierced them with evil and it was because of this that they were overcome.' The daylight which had appeared for him when he had created the gods he made into day; and the darkness which had appeared for him when he had created the demons he made into night. And they are day and night.[19]

This text still maintains a piece of ancient Vedic scepticism to the degree that it challenges traditional statements that the gods conquered the demons in fair combat; instead, it maintains, the Creator corrupted them. Thus, for the first time, the text begins to incorporate into the cosmogony another puzzle of origins that rivals, both in importance and in impenetrability, the puzzle of the creation of something from nothing: the creation of evil from, presumably, good—or at least moral neutrality.[20]

The myth of dismemberment is further developed in *The Laws of Manu*, the most famous of the law books of dharma, the textbooks of the Hindu social system. Its version of creation begins with one variant of the usual image of undifferentiated chaos: 'Once upon a time this (universe) was made of darkness, without anything that could be discerned, without any distinguishing marks, impossible to know through reasoning or understanding; it seemed to be entirely asleep.' But then, *ex nihilo*, a creator god appears, and goes to work: 'First he emitted the waters, and then he emitted his semen in them. That (semen) became a golden egg. He divided the egg into two. Out of the two fragments he made the sky and the earth, and the atmosphere in the middle, and the eight cardinal directions.' And we're off and running. First thing you know, 'He emitted time and the divisions of time, the constellations and planets, rivers, oceans, mountains, rough ground and smooth ground; ascetic heat, speech and sexual pleasure; desire and anger.'[21] Note the casual interleaving of physical things like mountains and mental constructs like the divisions of time, mediated by quasi-physical things like speech and emotions. There is simply no time to ask, 'Where did the creator god come from?' as the Vedic hymn, a thousand years earlier, had asked. The numbers in these myths are part of the technique of obfuscation, lending an air of mathematical precision to what is in fact pure speculation, or, rather, what the legal profession calls a tap dance.

Instead, we progress to the creation of the human race. *The Laws of*

Manu takes up this aspect of creation right after the bit about cracking the egg and before we get into the constellations and human emotions. Manu speaks of innate activities, that is, karmas, inherent in each creature from its birth; an individual is born to be a king, or a servant, or, more precisely, in terms of the actuality of caste rather than the theory of class, a potter or a shoemaker. This is what the text says:

> And in the beginning he made the individual names and individual innate activities (karmas) and individual conditions of all things precisely in accordance with the words of the Veda. And to distinguish innate activities, he distinguished right from wrong, and he yoked these creatures with the pairs, happiness and unhappiness and so forth. And whatever innate activity the Lord yoked each (creature) to at first, that (creature) by himself engaged in that very activity as he was created again and again. Harmful or harmless, gentle or cruel, right or wrong, truthful or lying—the (activity) he gave to each (creature) in creation kept entering it by itself. Just as the seasons by themselves take on the distinctive signs of the seasons as they change, so embodied beings by themselves take on their innate activities, each his own.[22]

During the millennium that separates the Vedic text from Manu, both the authoritative tone and the insistence on social hierarchy grew stronger. The circularity of the innate activities, the circularity of karma, is explicitly set from the time of creation: you must be what you are; you cannot change your qualities. The re-creation of individual characteristics is inevitable, explicitly likened to the natural process of the seasons. To nail down this point, the text reverts to the canon of authority, the Veda, repeating the core of the *purusha sukta*:

> Then, so that the worlds and people would prosper and increase, from his mouth he created the priest, from his arms the ruler, from his thighs the commoner, and from his feet the servant.

And then it takes on gender:

> He divided his own body into two and became a man with one half, a woman with the other half.[23]

And from there on, it's downhill all the way: once women enter the scene, Manu has a great deal to say about the dangers they pose for men.[x]

---

[x] See 'Why Should a Brahmin?' and 'The Control of Addiction'.

This text grounds itself in the past by quoting the *purusha sukta*. But then it goes on to secure the future by inserting into the very earliest stages of creation the birth of the author of the text in question—Manu, the Indian Adam, the ancestor of man: 'And the active female principle emitted me, Manu, the Creator of this whole (universe).'[xi] For Hindu texts tell us that the human race is called '*manava*', 'descended from Manu'. And Manu is going to go on to pronounce the laws of Manu, the laws of the caste system; and the names of the ten great sages, his first act of creation, include the names of the authors of several of the great legal texts. Thus the creation of the world is the creation of the human race, and the creation of the human race is the creation of the social system.

Time inevitably runs down, but it also starts up again: it declines and is reborn over and over again, as each successive doomsday undergoes its sea-change into each successive cosmogony, at the end of which comes doomsday, followed by a period of quiescence or latency, when all is a watery chaos (as it is in the myth of Vishnu and Brahma which we considered); and then the universe is created anew from the waters. And so we are recreated, with no end and no beginning, constantly getting there from here.

[xi] In another important creation myth involving Manu, the 'female principle' is the goddess Saranyu. See 'Saranyu/Samjna'.

TOGETHER APART:
CHANGING ETHICAL IMPLICATIONS OF
HINDU COSMOLOGIES[1]

The basic structures of Hindu cosmology, constantly reinterpreted, served as an armature on which authors in each generation sculpted their musings on the structure of human society. We may read these musings, the frequently retold stories about the primeval egg, about heaven and earth, gods and anti-gods, gods and ascetics, as paper-thin overlays on the ongoing-debates about very real social classes and sectarian and religious conflicts. They merely begin to indicate the rich variety of ways in which the imagined shapes of the cosmos shifted and changed to accommodate, first, an ethics of equilibrium and, later, an ethics of egalitarianism in the visible, everyday world.

COSMOGONIES—OR THEORIES OF THE ORIGIN OF LIFE AND
THE UNIVERSE—OF THE *RIG VEDA*

In the *Rig Veda* (c. 1500 BCE), the Hindu universe was an egg,[i] the two halves of the eggshell forming heaven and earth, with the sun as the yolk in the middle; it was a sealed, perfectly enclosed space with a given amount of good and evil, and a given number of souls. It was a world of balance, an ethics of equilibrium.

Several different cosmogonies are found in the *Rig Veda*,[ii] but two, especially in combination, raise intriguing ethical questions. One is the myth of the separation of heaven and earth; the other is the myth of the marriage of heaven and earth. The separation is usually more abstract than the marriage; in the separation, heaven and earth may not be personified at all, while in the marriage they usually are. Because of the greater

---

[i] See 'You Can't Get Here'.
[ii] See 'You Can't Get Here'.

anthropomorphism of the marriage model, one would expect to find it more susceptible to ethical and psychological glosses than the separation, and this is generally the case. But when the separation is anthropomorphized, and particularly when it is then combined with the marriage, peculiar ethical conflicts arise. For, if the combination of heaven and earth is regarded as a marriage, then what can the separation of heaven and earth be but a divorce? And how can this be held to be auspicious by the same society that, by sanctioning the marriage cosmogony, affirms marriage as auspicious? These are some of the problems raised by the transformations in the myths of separation and marriage of heaven and earth in the *Rig Veda* and, hundreds of years later, by the *Jaiminiya Brahmana*.

We can, I think, see a definite ethical shift in the treatment of cosmogonic themes during this period. The earliest myths, in the *Rig Veda*, regard the separation of heaven and earth as a good thing (for the cosmos), and do not draw any conclusions at all as to its implications for human ethical behaviour. But other *Rig Veda* hymns speak of another kind of separation of heaven and earth, the separation of humans from god, which is directly connected with the first, more mechanistic cosmogonic split. This second split is a bad thing, something to be avoided, with clear implications for human ethical behaviour: humans must act in such a way—offering sacrifice, keeping the laws of the gods, speaking the truth, and so forth—that the gods will not go away.

Only the first of these actions—the sacrifice—remains significant as a way to prevent the cosmogonic separation in the next set of texts, from the Brahamanas (c. 800-600 BCE), and sacrifice, by this time, is largely devoid of its ethical components. Instead, it is a means to power, and the 'reunion' of humans and gods is regarded as a way in which power may flow from humans to gods (through the offering) and from gods to humans (through rain and all that rain symbolizes). Finally, however, the Brahmanas begin to consider a more subtle problem arising from the cosmogonic divorce and to recast it in terms that foreshadow the very different ethical deliberations of later Hindu theodicies.

The myth of separation is told repeatedly in the *Rig Veda*, where kathenotheism—the worship of a series of gods, each regarded as the supreme god at the moment he is addressed—gives credit for the action to various gods on various occasions.[iii] A hymn to Varuna[iv] refers to 'the

---

iii See 'Are Hindus Monotheists?'
iv See 'Are Hindus Monotheists?' and 'You Can't Get Here'.

famous Varuna who struck apart the earth and spread it beneath the sun . . . He stretched out the middle realm of space in the trees . . . Varuna placed the sun in the sky . . . Over the two world-halves and the realm of space between them Varuna has poured out the cask . . . I will proclaim the great magic of Varuna the famous Asura, who stood up in the middle realm of space and measured apart the earth with the sun as with a measuring-stick.'[2] But Prajapati (the creator god, Lord of the Creatures), too, is the one 'by whom the awesome sky and the earth were made firm, by whom the dome of the sky was propped up, and the sun, who measured out the middle realm of space'.[3] And when the poet turns to Vishnu he says much the same thing: 'Vishnu, who has measured apart the realms of earth, who propped up the upper dwelling-place, striding far as he stepped forth three times . . .'[4] Indra, too, is the one 'who made fast the tottering earth, who made still the quaking mountains, who measured out and extended the expanse of the air, who propped up the sky.'[5] And the Soma plant, which was pressed to yield a juice offered to the gods in the sacrifice, is said to be what separated earth and sky, 'He who is the pillar of the sky, the well-adorned support, . . . the one who by tradition sacrifices to these two great world-halves.'[6]

The starkness of most of these verses, coupled with the fact that it does not seem to matter who gets credit for the cosmogonic split, lends an air of abstraction and impersonality to the Rig Vedic myth. Yet some verses describe the separation of heaven and earth with vivid images of human and animal forms, regarding the sun as the child of the sky-father-bull and the earth-mother-cow: 'The son of these parents milks the dappled milk-cow and the bull with good seed; every day he milks the milk that is his seed. Most artful of the artful gods, he gave birth to the two world halves that are good for everyone. He measured apart the two realms of space with his power of inspiration and fixed them in place with undecaying pillars.'[7] The last sentence lands us back in the formulaic, straightforward, abstract version of the myth, but before we get to it we must fight our way through some fairly obscure and riddling verses that bristle with sexual ambiguities: the cow has seed, but one also milks the bull; 'he' (almost certainly the sun, but also perhaps the Creator) is the son of the two parents, but he gives birth to them.

Such sexual paradoxes are a favourite stock-in-trade of the Vedic poets,[v] but their use in this hymn may be a result of the poet's awkwardness in

---

[v] See 'You Can't Get Here'.

grafting a set of symbols onto a myth that was not originally a sexual myth. These images of children and seed at first seem more appropriate to the myth of the marriage than to the myth of the divorce of heaven and earth, a marriage that is not directly narrated at all in the *Rig Veda*. Yet the sky-father and earth-mother are regarded as parents, and as parents who give birth, even in verses that refer to the usual myth of separation: 'The two full of butter . . . sky and earth have been propped apart, by Varuna's law; un-ageing, they are rich in seed . . . You two world-halves, rulers over this universe, pour out on us the seed that was the base for humankind . . . Sky and earth, the all-knowing father and mother who achieve wondrous works—let them swell up with food to nourish us.'[8] Evidently, heaven and earth give birth to the sun by separating, not by uniting; later texts express this through the metaphor of the egg that 'gives birth to' or releases the yolk (the sun) when the upper shell draws away from the lower. Moreover, in this last hymn, as in the earlier hymn about the cow and the bull, it would appear that the 'seed' is not primarily the substance from which children are made but, rather, the substance with which children are fed; the seed is milk.

By contrast, in the Upanishads the seed is unequivocally procreative seed; a man who is about to impregnate his wife should say, 'I am heaven, you are earth; let us embrace and place together the seed to get a male child, a son.'[9] The Vedic hymns cited above refer to earth and sky as separate, and to the children that they have engendered and that they continue to feed; they do not describe the union of the two parents, though they refer obliquely to the begetting of the child. Yet what can 'the seed that was the base for humankind' mean except the seed shed by sky and earth to produce the human race? Presumably, this seed, like the sun, was creatively shed at the moment when the two worlds separated. These ambiguities suggest that the mixing of the metaphors of separation and marriage had begun even at the time of the *Rig Veda*.

These problems are compounded by the existence of two other, secondary myths of cosmogony in the *Rig Veda*, myths that can be seen as forming a kind of prologue and epilogue, a temporal frame, to the two that we have begun to examine (see fig. 1). The first is the myth that distinguishes between cosmogony and theogony; the second is the myth of the departed god (*deus absconditus*).

In the hymn of Aditi and Daksha,[vi] the origin of the universe (cosmogony)

[vi] See 'You Can't Get Here'.

Figure 1. Stages of Hindu Cosmogony

	Separation	Marriage and Mating

I. *Rig Veda*

a. (10.129) 1. Existence/Nonexistence

b. (5.85; 1.160) 2. Heaven/Earth

c. (1.160; 1.164) → 3. Heaven + Earth

d. (1.164; 7.86) 4. God/Man ◄

e. (7.86) → 5. God + Man (Sacrifice)

II. *Jaiminiya Brahmana*

a. (1.145) 4. God/Man ⟶ 5. God + Man (Sacrifice)

b. (1.166) 3. Heaven + Earth

4. Ether/Heaven + Earth ⟶ 5. God + Man (Sacrifice)

3. Heaven + Earth

c. (1.185) 4. Ether/Heaven + Earth ⟶ 5. God + Man (Sacrifice)

d. (3.72) 4. Ether/Heaven + Earth
↓
6. Evil/World ⟶ 7. Evil + Man

e. (1.97) 8. Gods/Demons
↓
4 + 5. God/Man (Sacrifice)
↓
9. Man/Man (Sacrifice)
↓
6. Evil/World ⟶ 7. Evil + Man

KEY

/ = 'separates from'; + = 'joins with'. Letters designate texts; Arabic numerals designate themes. ⟶ designates transition within a single myth.

and the origin of the gods (theogony) seem to have taken place at the same time, and through the actions of an earth-mother, *not*, significantly, in conjunction with the sky-father. Instead of the male sky, this hymn speaks of four female quarters of the sky, who are, moreover, the sisters, not the husband(s), of the earth, for all of them are born from the same mother. This mother is simultaneously highly abstract—she has no name and corresponds to no physical part of the universe—and highly anthropomorphic: all we know of her is her posture, which is that of a woman in the throes of childbirth.

When the Vedic abstractions are fleshed out, they become embroiled in complex human entanglements. In order for heaven and earth to mate, they must first become created as separate entities; only then can they produce their children. Some cosmogonies emphasize one aspect, some another; so, too, some cosmogonies describe androgynes that must 'split' in order to procreate, while others describe androgynes that must 'fuse' to procreate.[10] We thus have a primeval cosmogony (the making of 'distinguishing signs' in chaos), followed by the separation of heaven and earth, followed by the procreative action of heaven and earth, resulting in the creation of the more anthropomorphic gods. The fourth step, following the three above, which is the retreat of the creator god, or the departed god, is also foreshadowed in the *Rig Veda*. One Vedic hymn combines this myth with the theme of the sky-father and earth-mother: 'The sky is my father; here is the navel that gave me birth. This great earth is my mother, my close kin. The womb for me was between the two bowls stretched apart; here the father placed the embryo in the daughter. He who made him knows nothing of him. He who saw him—he vanishes from him.'[11] Apparently the first 'he' in this last phrase is the father, the sky, who vanishes after he has made 'him', the sun, the child born of the mating of heaven and earth. The sun is, however, also said to have been born as the result of the *separation* of heaven and earth.

It thus appears that both the mating and the separation of heaven and earth are procreative in the *Rig Veda*. The sky-father actually mates with the earth, who is apparently his daughter; this accounts (in the same hymn) for the fact that earth and sky separated *after their marriage*: the daughter was ashamed: 'The mother gave the father a share in accordance with the Order, for at the beginning she embraced him with mind and heart. Recoiling, she was pierced and flowed with the seed of the embryo.'[12] Though elsewhere the *Rig Veda* seems to identify the daughter as dawn, here she is evidently earth, the daughter of the sky-father but also his consort (as in the Aditi hymn, where earth is both the mother and the sister of the quarters of the sky). She recoils from him, thus apparently separating heaven and earth forever after.

Here, for the first time, we may see a glimmer of moralizing in the theme of separation, though it is certainly a faint glimmer. On the most elementary level, we can see that the unacceptable results of an incestuous mating, even on the most abstract cosmogonic level, would underscore the prohibition against incest in the human world. On the other hand, we can see that the myth regards incest—again, on the abstract cosmogonic level—as basically necessary. The problem of incest in cosmogonies originally arises from a purely abstract, non-ethical problem: If creation begins with some sort of unity (if only the unity of chaos), and then proceeds to a duality that splits and mates, one is stuck with incest, in human terms. That is, the cosmogony is driven by its own, non-ethical logic into a position that has unethical implications.

We are thus faced with a double paradox, one that applies not only to the incestuous mating but to the original separation: such cosmogonic acts are sinful but necessary, and *both* the mating and the separation are necessary. The worlds must remain separate, but they also must remain together. The paradox of the creative act that is sinful but necessary appears far more explicitly in India in the myths of Indra, whose slaughter of Vritra makes creation possible but also threatens the survival of Indra and hence of the entire cosmos.[13] More broadly still, it is the paradox of the sacrifice: in early texts, the sacrifice is dangerous to the sacrificer but essential to his survival,[vii] and in later texts the slaughter involved in sacrifice is regarded as blatantly evil, yet still necessary.[viii] This is not the place to investigate these problems, which are discussed elsewhere in this book; but it is appropriate to point out their relevance to the question on which this chapter focuses, the question of the ethical implications of Hindu cosmogony.

The double paradox (sinful but necessary, separate but together) reappears in human (albeit theoretical) terms in the dilemma of the *varnas*. The Kshatriya, a warrior and a king, must sin, and must be absolved; this problem is expressed in the myths of Indra. The Brahmin, too, has his paradox: he must remain outside the world in order to retain his sacred powers, but inside the world in order that those powers may bear fruit for the sacrificers for whom he acts. The two paradoxes merge in the

[vii] See 'Sacrifice and Substitution'.
[viii] See 'The Ambivalence of Ahimsa'.

Brahmin: his sin is his inability to remain both separate and non-separate. Moreover, together the Brahmin and the Kshatriya constitute yet another paradox. The two of them must remain separate, by definition and in order to retain their individual identities and powers; yet the Brahmin and the Kshatriya must intermarry and exchange in order to make it possible for society to function at all.[14] Similarly, the 'renouncer' must remain separate from society (the fertile cosmogonic divorce), but at the same time he must participate in society (the essential mating), for his status as an outsider gives him the valuable authority of impartiality and the wisdom of distance.[15] Hindu society places a complex set of values on remaining separate and remaining engaged.[16] All of these ambivalences of human ethical activity are implicit, *in nuce*, in the Vedic ambivalence toward the necessary, sinful cosmogonic marriage.

As to the myth of the departed god, the *deus absconditus*, a less mysterious and more straightforward form of it appears elsewhere in the *Rig Veda*, where the separation of god and humankind is depicted in moral rather than physical terms. Varuna's primary role was watching over human behaviour and punishing those who violated the sacred law (*rita*). He would snare miscreants in his bonds (*pasha*), which often revealed their presence through disease. In this hymn, Varuna ignores his transgressing worshipper (the nature of the transgression is never specified), though he is not said literally to go away to heaven. Yet, significantly, the withdrawal of Varuna is directly preceded by his own role in separating heaven and earth:

> The generations have become wise by the power of him who has propped apart the two world-halves even though they are so vast. He has pushed away the dome of the sky to make it high and wide; he has set the sun on its double journey and spread out the earth. And I ask my own heart, 'When shall I be close to Varuna? Will he enjoy my offering and not be provoked to anger? When shall I see his mercy and rejoice?' I ask myself what the transgression was, Varuna, for I wish to understand. I turn to the wise to ask them. The poets have told me the very same thing: 'Varuna has been provoked to anger against you.' O Varuna, what was the terrible crime for which you wish to destroy your friend who praises you? Proclaim it to me so that I may hasten to prostrate myself before you and be free from error, for you are hard to deceive and are ruled by yourself alone. Free us from the harmful deeds of our fathers and from those that we have committed with our own bodies. The mischief was not done by my own free will, Varuna; wine, anger, dice, or carelessness led me astray. The older shares in the

mistake of the younger. Even sleep does not avert evil. As a slave serves a generous master, so would I serve the furious god and be free from error.[17]

This hymn begins with the primeval situation, undifferentiated chaos; it describes the beneficial separation of heaven and earth and leaves them amicably separated forever, one assumes. But then it moves on to another, subsequent separation, the separation of Varuna and the worshipper, which could not have taken place at the beginning of time but is necessarily secondary. The separation of Varuna from the worshipper is clearly regarded as an occasion for great sorrow and regret; it is, moreover, a schism that the worshipper fervently hopes to mend, by giving Varuna an offering—the present hymn, as well as some sort of sacrificial offering— that will quell the god's anger and restore the original close friendship. The poem assumes that, on the one hand, one may not be blamed, or perhaps not entirely blamed, for errors committed under the influence of passionate emotions, and, on the other hand, one may be punished not only for conscious errors but also for errors committed unconsciously, in sleep, or even by other people (both one's parents and one's children). This idea becomes much more important in later Hinduism, in texts that characterize the Vedic transaction as one in which the ritual transfers to the sponsor the good karma that the priest generates. Eventually, the idea of the transfer of good karma in a ritual act with effects in this life develops into the idea of the moral consequences of any act, not only in this life but also in future lives, and the more general transfer of karma.[ix]

In a closely related hymn, the worshipper recalls the days in which the gods and mortals lived together happily, before he offended Varuna: 'Where have those friendships of us two gone, when in the old times we could live together without becoming enemies?'[18] These are among the most heart-searching of the Vedic hymns, highly charged with moral and ethical concerns; and they are linked to the originally a–moral theme of the separation of heaven and earth.

COSMOGONIES OF THE *JAIMINIYA BRAHMANA* (C. 600 BCE)

The question might then be asked as to whether these two ends of the spectrum (the abstract separation and the departed god) are simply logical oppositions of a structural kind or represent a chronological development.

[ix] See 'Death and Rebirth'.

A clue to this question might be sought in the further development of the cosmogony, this time in the Brahmanas.

The *Jaiminiya Brahmana* is a particularly fertile place to search for such a development, since it is noteworthy among the Brahmanas for its taste for sex and violence, its tendency to clothe abstract rituals in lurid folktales, and its flair for racy imagery.[19] By examining five different *Jaiminiya Brahmana* versions of the myth of the primal separation and marriage, we can begin to see the ways in which the tradition reinterprets itself in moral and ethical terms that are only dimly adumbrated in the *Rig Veda*, even in those hymns that do reflect the procreative metaphor of the myth. Taken in a certain sequence, the *Jaiminiya* texts can be said to describe the marriage, mating, raising of the children, divorce and rejection of the children (in a sense, the Vedic custody battle). Moreover, each of these stages is further interpreted by the text itself to point a moral about some other, non-sexual, aspect of human life, usually a ritual aspect.

We begin with the marriage:

> These two worlds were together, but then they separated. Nothing from either of the two reached the other. The gods and mortals were hungry, for the gods live on what is given from here [offerings] and mortals live on what is given from there [rain, and from rain, food]. Then the Brihat chant and the Rathantara chant said, 'Let the two of us get married with our very own bodies.' Now, the Syaita chant of fire was the very own body of the Rathantara, and the Naudhasa chant of the Brihat. By means of these they got married. The world there gave dawn to this world as a marriage gift, and the world here gave fog to that world. The world there gave rain and the world here gave the divine sacrifice.[20]

The myth begins with a union and a separation. This initial union is not the stage of primeval chaos, however, but a vaguely anthropomorphic union roughly akin to the mating in the third stage of the Vedic scenario we've discussed earlier. The separation, therefore, corresponds not to the primeval separation (stage 2 of the Vedic scenario), but rather to the subsequent separation (stage 4)—the departed god. The first sort of separation (stage 2) is regarded as a good thing and as an enduring situation in much of the *Rig Veda* and elsewhere—for even to this day we can see that earth and sky are, in fact, separate. But when the two worlds become anthropomorphic they long for one another as a separated couple would— an early example of the theme of *viraha*, or longing for the beloved: and when they become symbolic of the worlds of gods and mortals, that *viraha* takes on all the overtones of theological longing, as it will again in medieval bhakti literature.

Thus the fourth-stage separation becomes a temporary problem that can be solved only by some sort of reunion of heaven and earth. In the *Rig Veda*, this reunion was achieved through a sacrifice; in the *Jaiminiya* it is a sacrifice conceived as a marriage, more precisely, a re-marriage. It is not the literal reunion of the two worlds, the complete merging of one with the other as in the situation before stage 1, for primeval chaos would recur (a situation that is, in fact, welcomed in much later bhakti texts, but that is anathema to the order-obsessed ancient Brahmins). The reunion is, therefore, carefully kept in the realm of the anthropomorphic, rather than the abstract, so that mere contact, rather than complete reintegration, is the goal, even as the earth and sky procreate by moving apart.

How is this goal to be achieved? The 'marriage' is immediately glossed in terms that render inevitable a ritual solution to the problem. As in the *Rig Veda*, the separation of heaven and earth represents a schism between mortals and gods, and the solution to this is the invention (or, rather, the re-invention) of the sacrifice. For the text implies that once, before the separation took place, mortals and gods lived in happy symbiosis, like Varuna and his worshipper in the *Rig Veda*. Elsewhere, the *Jaiminiya* tells of a time when gods and mortals drank the ambrosial Soma together for the last time, before a great battle took place between them. Here, marriage gifts are exchanged, and bodies mingle; but the gifts are natural elements (dawn, fog and rain) plus the sacrifice, and the bodies are twice removed from anything anthropomorphic: the chants (the Brihat, the Rathantara, the Syaita and the Naudhasa) stand in for the hymns that represent the worlds of heaven and earth. Thus the Brahmana makes explicit what lies behind much of the *Rig Veda* but is never directly linked to the myths of separation there: the sacrifice is the 'reunion' that repairs the damage done by the separation from the departed god. The sacrifice is the marriage.

A second passage in the *Jaiminiya* expands upon another theme from the *Rig Veda*: the depiction of the conjunction of the worlds in terms of human mating. What distinguishes this text from the *Rig Veda*, however, is the fact that now there are three worlds, so that the one who is 'abandoned' is not the earth or humankind, deserted by heaven or the gods, but the child of heaven and earth, deserted by both parents:

> The light [n.], the cow [f.] and the lifespan [n.] are the three chants. The cow sheds her seed in the lifespan; from that was . . . born the light. This world is the lifespan; that world is the cow; and the intermediate ether is the light. They [the lifespan and the cow] made

him go in front, as one would a son. This world went up to him and that world went down, and the light went in front of them piled up all around so that we can see. The two of them, wishing to unite, drew the light out to the end [from the middle], just as two parents follow after the son when he goes in front. They became mated chants when they repelled him. The son lies in the middle between the wife and husband. And just as a couple who are about to mate push the son from one side or another, so they did to him. The chants with their plus and minus [convex and concave] are mated for progenerating. So when anyone desires to have many progeny he should sacrifice with these [chants], saying, 'May I have progeny and cattle,' and he gets many progeny and cattle.[21]

The three worlds of the Brahmana period—heaven, earth and the air between—have replaced the two worlds of the early *Rig Veda*. (In their turn, they will later be replaced by the three worlds of Hinduism: heaven, earth and hell.) When the hierogamy is extended to this new Brahmana model, the roles do not fit easily, and the Brahmana compounds the confusion by choosing from its ritual storehouse three items that do not correspond to the genders at all; the metaphor is forced. The cow is awkwardly linked with the masculine, both in terms of the world with which she is identified (heaven, usually male) and in terms of her role in the copulation: to impregnate the lifespan. This identification is particularly bizarre in light of the fact that, elsewhere in the Brahmanas, the cow is said to be the earth, an identity that persists throughout later Hinduism,[x] as in the tale of Prithu milking the earth-cow.[22]

But what is most striking about this passage is the way that the Rig Vedic myth of the begetting of the sun by sky and earth, through the intermediary link of the begetting of (sun-) light by the cow and the lifespan, becomes the begetting of a third world, the ether, by heaven and earth. This myth, of the productive hierogamy, is then half-transformed into the myth of separation, with a difference: in order that the (original) two worlds can unite (to make more worlds), they must first separate, not from one another but from their first child—they must separate from the (new) world. The myth of the child abandoned by his father is one we have seen in the verse about the sky vanishing from the sun; the myth of the child abandoned by his mother is an important Rig Vedic theme that occurs in conjunction with the myths of cosmogony.[23]

---

[x] See 'The Ambivalence of Ahimsa'.

This Vedic theme is then introduced in place of the theme of the separation of the two worlds; the marriage becomes a separation. Finally, the majestic Vedic cosmogony plummets bathetically in two ways: first, the world systems are analogized to particular chants, which is standard operating procedure for the Brahmanas (i.e., they revert to abstraction from anthropomorphism). But then the two worlds become re-anthropomorphized in a most trivial way: they are plagued by awkward sleeping arrangements (an awkwardness which plagues actual sleeping conditions in traditional India). The chants are given sexual organs (the 'extra' syllable of one and the 'missing' syllable of the other corresponding to what a man has and a woman lacks), and their 'mating' is the sacrificial analogue of the marriage of heaven and earth. The greater moral problems of the separation and hierogamy—incest, rejection, the vanishing sky-god—are reduced to the dry linguistic intricacies of the liturgy and the perennial preoccupations of the marriage manuals: waiting till the children fall asleep. Ethics has fallen by the wayside.

The more usual problem posed by these children, however, is the problem of feeding them once they are born; this was already evident in the *Rig Veda*, where the 'seed' that makes the child is analogized to the 'seed-milk' with which he is fed. When the three worlds separate, food separates too:

> Indra gave the ascetics to the wolves. From them when they were being eaten, three boys were left over: Rayovajas, Prithurashmi and Brihadgiri. They praised Indra and he said to them, 'What do you boys wish for, that you praise me?' 'Support us, generous one,' they said. He tossed them between his two shoulders, and they hung on to his three humps.
>
> Now, these [pl.] worlds, which had been together, separated into three parts, and the eating of food separated after them. They hung on to the three humps of these three worlds, that was the eating of food. Then [Indra] realized, 'If they gain control and keep back the eating of food that is the three humps of these three worlds, I will not amass for myself these three humps.' He saw this chant and praised with it, and by this means he gained control and kept the food-eating that was the three humps. And by that means he amassed for himself those three humps.[24]

The food that was the key to the relationship between the two worlds in our first *Jaiminiya* passage (where it was the basis of exchange between gods and mortals) is here transformed from a theological to a physiological image: Indra becomes a foster-mother to three orphans and supports them with the food from the 'humps' on his back, like the breasts of a mother. Indra is the appropriate one to do this, since he is often likened to a hump-backed bull and since, in later Hindu mythology, he nourishes with milk from his thumb a child who has no human mother.[25] But after he has nourished the three boys, in keeping with the reciprocity of the sacrifice, he then fears that they will usurp his powers to give or to hold back food (through his function as the god of rain), and so he undertakes another sort of sacrifice, jealously hoarding the powers for himself. This is a major shift in the ethical stance of the Brahmanas.

For the antagonism between gods and mortals that lurks behind the scenes of the first *Jaiminiya* myth (bolstered by other myths in which mortals willfully withhold food from gods, or gods withhold rain from mortals) is at first displaced in this variant; here, Indra is waging some sort of vendetta against the ascetics, more precisely against a group of ascetics called Yatis. This is a story much repeated, but never fully explained, in the Brahmanas. Indra is said to have committed a number of sins, of which this is the first and the favourite.[26] The boys are, therefore, orphaned as a direct result of Indra's action in killing their fathers; their 'separation from the parents' may be seen as the fallout from one of the earliest skirmishes in the perennial battle between kings and priests, or Vedic gods and Vedantic ascetics, in India. Thus the separation of the three worlds is used to express a schism between Vedic religion and post-Vedic asceticism; and the healing of that schism is expressed through a Vedic image of the parent feeding the child.

What are the ethical implications of this myth? Here, I think, for the first time, one of the gods has become sufficiently anthropomorphic to enable the myth to stand as a model for human ethical (or unethical) behaviour. Indra in this tale does not, as in the *Rig Veda*, literally and definitively prop apart heaven and earth (though even this, as we have seen, does have ultimately ethical implications, when we regard separation and participation as primary categories for human interaction); here he merely murders a group of ascetics and feeds their orphaned sons. Though one can hardly take this as a positive role model, it does, in fact, epitomize and, therefore, begin to make possible an ethical approach to one of the enduring problems of ancient Indian law: the problem of the evil king. For, just as the primeval parents *had* to commit incest (when the once abstract pattern of the One who mated with his own creation became anthropomorphized) and yet ought not to have committed incest, so too the king (symbolized by Indra, king of the gods) *had* to kill, and to oppose asceticism,[27] though it was a sin for him to kill, or to oppose asceticism.[28] The solution at this point in the development of Indian moral law was a simple one—feed the gods, feed the priests, feed the survivors of the inevitable debacle. Crude as this was, it was at least an advance on the earlier Indo-European attitude ('Kill as many as you can, take the food, and run like hell') and did provide a basis for later re-examinations of the ethical quandary of the king.

A fourth *Jaminiya* variant on the motif of separation is the most explicitly ethical in its transformations:

> These [pl.] worlds, which had been together, separated into three parts. They sorrowed as one who is split into three would sorrow. The gods said, 'Let us strike away the three sorrows of these three worlds.' They saw this chant and praised with it, and with it they struck away the three sorrows of these three worlds. And because they struck away the three sorrows of these three worlds, therefore the chant is called the 'Three Sorrows' chant. Whoever knows it strikes away sorrow. They [the gods] caused them [the sorrows] to enter the impotent man, the criminal and the whore. And therefore these [three] are sorrowful, for they have been pierced by sorrow. But this does not happen to the man who knows this.[29]

Whereas the *Rig Veda* assumed that the separation of the worlds produced nothing but good, and other *Jaiminiya* myths eventually explained the incidental (though inevitable) disadvantages of the separation, here the very first thing that we are told is that separation is sorrow. The anthropomorphism implicit in this attitude is patent. Moreover, whereas in earlier variants the gods were directly affected by this sorrow—for they themselves suffered when the soup-lines between heaven and earth were cut—here they are apparently benevolent bystanders, acting not out of self-interest but out of pity and sympathy. Or so the text says.

Yet a more selfish reason for the gods' concern is apparent when we view the myth in the context of the wider corpus of Brahmana tales of which it is a part. For the theme of transferring sorrow (or evil) from one person or thing to another is a major one in the Brahmanas, where the person who most often benefits from this transfer is none other than Indra. When he sins, by killing a destructive dragon who happens to be a Brahmin, his sin (of Brahminicide, Brahmin-killing, the defining sin of Brahmin culture) is passed on to volunteers on earth: water, women, trees and the earth itself, thus freeing Indra from his pollution and enabling him to help his worshippers remain strong and fertile.[30] Thus we may assume that the sorrowing of the three worlds is a situation that harms the gods, that weakens the power of the universe in which their own power must be set. They cannot undo the cause of the sorrow, for they cannot reunite the worlds. Neither could Indra prevent his defilement, for the Brahmin dragon had to be slain.

What the gods can do is mitigate the ill effects of these necessary evils.

The time-honoured way to do this is to palm the evil off on a scapegoat who deserves it anyway: a sinner. Who are these sinners? Significantly, one is excessively neuter, one excessively female and the third excessively male. In the example that I have translated and quoted above, they are 'the impotent man, the criminal and the whore'. The word I have translated as 'impotent man' is *kliba*, which covers a multitude of sexual inadequacies from the Indian viewpoint, including temporary impotence, permanent impotence, castration and homosexuality.[xi] The word for 'whore', *pumshchali*—literally 'man-chaser'—is clear enough. The third word, *kitava*, means a gambler, hence a cheat, hence a drunkard, hence a madman (a thumbnail sketch of the road to ruin in ancient India). We can, I think, assume that the female earth became the whore, the male sky became the criminal and the neuter ether became the impotent man—the rejected child. These analogies fit far more neatly than did the neuter 'light' and 'lifespan' and female 'cow' in the other *Jaiminiya* myth.

But what is the meaning of these analogies? In this variant the author is taking a stance that will become the prevalent one in later Hindu theodicies: that evil recoils upon the evil; that evil, once created, cannot be destroyed but can be distributed; that the structure of the cosmos is moral, so that evil naturally gravitates to those who are doomed to be evil anyway. In this early text, 'evil' is not yet explicated as specifically as it will be in the later law books, where the punishment must fit the crime. Here, evil is still more or less identified with sorrow, the villain of the piece in many of the Brahmanas. The first part of this myth fits a pattern that is dear to the heart of the authors of the Brahmanas: a situation is imagined in which the protagonist is in danger or sorrow or need; he sees the chant that gets him out of that situation; and so the chant is called a danger- or sorrow- or need-dispelling chant. The present text fulfils the requirements of this pattern by the phrase 'Whoever knows it strikes away sorrow', a formulaic structure ('Whoever knows this . . .') which concludes many Brahmana episodes.

[xi] See 'The Third Nature'.

But in this case the text goes on, to tell us *what happened to the evil*—it was 'pierced by sorrow'. This extension destroys the usual pat ending of the myth and starts a chain reaction that leaves many loose ends dangling. What did the whore and the impotent man and the criminal do, in the past, to make them deserve to have these sorrows placed on them? Or, if you accept the aptness of these distributions, what did they do to become a whore, etc., in the first place? What could they then do to get rid of the evil that had been placed in them? If one had to devise an ethical system equipped to deal with questions such as these, questions that arise here for the first time, one would probably end up inventing the theory of karma. Although the *Jaiminiya Brahmana* does not invent such a theory, or even provide the elements from which it was ultimately invented, it does at least paint itself into an ethical corner, so to speak, from which it could only be rescued by the kind of basic rethinking that led, in the Upanishads a few hundred years later, to the new theory.[31] The loose ends dangling from the Brahmanas provided fuel for centuries of later Hindu theodicy.

The predominant Hindu theodicy actually begins right in the *Jaiminiya Brahmana*, in a myth that takes the structural motifs of the cosmogonic divorce entirely out of the context of the ancient myth and transforms that myth into a tale of the departed god type. Here, as in the previous example, the text shows concern for the fate of evil itself, but now that evil is not taken from the worlds, but put *into* them:

> The gods and anti-gods were striving against one another. The gods emitted [from themselves] a thunderbolt, sharp as a razor, that was a male (*purusha*). They hurled this at the anti-gods, and it scattered the anti-gods, but then it turned back to the gods. The gods were afraid of it, and so they took it and broke it into three pieces. When it had been shattered into three pieces, it stood right up. Then they took hold of it and examined it, and they saw that the divinities had entered into that man in the form of hymns. They said, 'The divinities have entered into this man in the form of hymns. When he has lived in this world with merit, he will follow us by means of sacrifices and good deeds and asceticism. Let us therefore act so that he will not follow us. Let us put evil [*papman*] in him.' They put evil in him: sleep, laziness, anger, hunger, love of dice, desire for women. These are the very evils that attach themselves to a man in this world.
>
> Then they enjoined Agni [fire] in this world: 'Agni, if anyone escapes evil in this world and wants to do good things, trick him and harm him utterly.' And they enjoined Vayu [wind] in the ether in the

same way, and Aditya [the sun] in the sky. But Ugradeva Rajani said, 'I will not harm mortals whom I have heard these three highest gods harm. For the person whom these divinities harm is harmed and harmed indeed.' But the divinities do not harm the person who knows this, and they do trick and utterly harm the one who tricks and harms the person who knows this.[32]

The world split in three survives in the *Jaiminiya Brahmana* only in the reference to the appointment of three divinities as watchdogs in each of the three worlds; indeed, a reader of this myth might well see no cosmogony in it at all, were that reader unaware of the supporting corpus of myths that we have seen. The cosmogonic theme is, however, further enhanced by the reference to the splitting apart of a male (*purusha*), a variant of yet another Rig Vedic theme of creative separation[xii]—the dismemberment of the Primeval Male (Purusha), narrated in the *purusha sukta*.[33]

Structurally, the myth in the *purusha sukta* falls into line with those of the *Jaiminiya Brahmana* that we have considered, but there the resemblance ends. Ethically, they are worlds apart. For where the dismemberment of Purusha was done with his apparent consent to the self-sacrifice, and for the benefit of the universe, the dismemberment of the thunderbolt-man is done in order to destroy him and to protect the gods. By this time the concept of sacrifice as a force that joins together the powers of gods and mortals, through the exchange (of rain and offerings) that reunites the severed worlds, has been transformed into the concept of sacrifice as a force that has the potential to drive gods and mortals apart, by making mortals so good, and hence so powerful, that they rouse the jealousy of the gods.[34]

This jealousy appears first in the gods' fear of the weapon they have created, that rebounds against them as such weapons so often do in mythology (as in life); they separate the weapon from itself, into three parts like the dismembered cosmos, in order to destroy it. When this fails, they divide up something else—not the thunderbolt-man, but evil itself. The same evil that was said, in the *Jaiminiya Brahmana* myth of the 'Three Sorrows,' to result from the separation of the three worlds and to be taken away from them to be put into people, is here said to be created (apparently *ex nihilo*, or perhaps left over from the previous cosmic divorce) and put into people in order to cause sorrow to humankind. The

[xii] See 'You Can't Get Here'.

dynamic is still technically the same: the sorrow, or evil, is taken out of the triple world (or away from the frightened gods) and put into humankind.

The myth of the thunderbolt-man adds to the three sorrows-evils of the previous text (impotence, gambling, lust) three more: sleep-laziness (a rough equivalent of impotence), anger-love of dice (the gambler's problems) and hunger-desire for women (lust). If there be any doubt in our minds that the gods are behaving unethically, and presenting mortals with the seeds of all their future ethical problems, the text tells us of a human being (identified unmistakably as such by the formulaic patronymic—Ugradeva Rajani—of human sages) who expressly refuses to behave as badly as the gods behave. Thus we are given the reason for both the generally unethical behaviour of humankind (the gods made humans prey to the vices that destroy them) and the possibility of ethical behaviour among mortals, for it is possible for people like Ugradeva Rajani to resist, if not to counteract, the efforts that the gods make to ruin us when we try to do good things.[xiii]

COSMOGONIES OF THE PURANAS (C. 350–750 CE)

Ethically, this is a world of limited good, or a zero sum game, an ethics of equilibrium: if someone is saved, someone else has to be damned. For Brahmins to be pure, Dalits have to be impure; if you win, I lose. Since evil is a substance, space is a problem. That is, the Hindu universe or 'egg of Brahma' is conceived of as a sealed, perfectly enclosed space with a given amount of good and evil, and a given number of souls. This means, among other things, that evil, once created, cannot get out of the universe; the best you can do is just move it over to some spot where it will do the least possible harm, as the fire that fused Shiva's anger and Kama's erotic power was temporarily stashed in the doomsday mare at the bottom of the ocean.[xiv] (And as Krishna moved the serpent Kaliya to another place.)[xv]

A set of examples of some of the ways in which ethical order interacts with cosmogony and changes it is provided by the Puranas, in two sets of myths that I can but briefly summarize here.

The closed structure of the universal egg began to prove problematic when many Puranic myths acted as pamphlets for a particular shrine, magnifying its salvific powers, presumably to drum up business by boasting that anyone—even women and people of low castes—could go straight to

---

[xiii] See 'The Concept of Heresy'.
[xiv] See 'The Submarine Mare'.
[xv] See 'Death and Rebirth'.

heaven after any contact with the shrine; or when a good anti-god produces an excess of goodness (virtue, piety, ascetic heat) in the world of the anti-gods.[xvi] This is an ethics of egalitarianism, and in both of these instances, it poses a problem for an ethics of equilibrium: there is too much goodness collected in one place (the wrong place). And so, in the first instance, there is no night, nor any job for the god of hell, or heaven becomes so crowded that the gods (read: Brahmins) in some myths worry that people in heaven will have to stand with their hands above their heads, like people in a rush-hour subway.

Given the original shape of the cosmos—closed—there are only a few ways in which the second situation can be remedied: the anti-god can be corrupted or entirely destroyed or turned into a god, so that he can be transported to the world of the gods, and the rest of the anti-gods then lapse back into their properly evil ways. To keep heaven a more exclusive club, the gods take measures to destroy the shrines—flooding them or filling them with sand, or simply corrupting people (as in the Buddha avatar[xvii]) so that they stop going to the shrine.[35] This is what happens in the early myths, and such episodes may be coded comments on actual historical incidents: both Hindu and Muslim rulers did indeed, before, after and during this period, destroy great Hindu shrines.[36]

But under the influence of a major shift in Hindu concepts of ethical order these problems begin to be met in an entirely new way. Later Puranas composed in the tradition of bhakti, or devotional religion, blast through this impasse. One form of this sort of cosmological transformation may be seen in two different versions of hell, first with a *Mahabharata* king (Yudhishthira) who cannot transfer his personal good karma and then with a Puranic king (Vipashchit) who can.[xviii] Another is the mythology in which sinners are given good karma that they don't deserve, but since now it is a god, rather than a human king, who transfers his powers, his compassion and forgiveness, the god, unlike the king, loses nothing by it, none of his good karma.

The world of limited good then gives way to a world of infinitely expansible good karma and bhakti; the generous donor keeps it all while the sinners benefit from it too, just as, in the avatar, the god remains entire in heaven even while he gives a portion of himself to the avatar on earth. These texts are saying that even if you lack bhakti you can be saved from

[xvi] See 'The Scrapbook'.
[xvii] See 'The Concept of Heresy'.
[xviii] See 'Death and Rebirth'.

your sins; the god has enough bhakti for both of you. In several of the late Puranic texts, when a shrine offers universal access to heaven, raising the gods' hackles, Shiva intervenes, preserves or restores the shrine, and takes everyone to 'the abode of Brahma'.[37] When the god of hell, Yama, complains that women, Shudras and dog-cookers (Dalits) are all going to heaven through one particular shrine, the Shaiva shrine of Somnatha, putting Yama out of work, Shiva replies that they have all been purified by the sight of the shrine, and he dismisses Yama without another word.[38]

To the complaint that heaven is full of evil people, Shiva simply replies that the people in question are no longer evil, ignoring the other half of the complaint, that heaven is full, or that Yama is on the dole. Apparently, Shiva's new heaven cannot be filled; these texts imagine a new heaven that can stretch the envelope to accommodate everyone.[39] Similarly, where the shrine in the early myths would be destroyed, or limited so that only a small group of the elect could use it to get to heaven (the equivalent of taking only the one good anti-god and making him into a god), in the later myths the shrine lets everyone go to heaven—which has now become infinitely expandable.

Ultimately, the mythology dispenses with the topography of both heaven and hell in favour of an open-ended system—what Mircea Eliade referred to as *briser le toit de la maison* ('Break open the roof of the house'), cracking open the egg of the closed universe—in which it is possible to escape evil forever. Examples of such a development may be seen in the myths of the good anti-god who goes to heaven (Virochana or Prahlada)[40] and in the stories of crowds that are allowed to enter heaven (from shrines such as Somanatha and Dvaraka).[41] It also appears in the mythology of grace given to unredeemed sinners.[xix]

In all of these cases, it appears at first that certain ethical developments are forestalled by the given set of cosmogonic circumstances, the bounds of the arena in which the ethical battle must take place; the shape of the universe seemed to constrain the ethical possibilities. But as the centuries go on, and those possibilities grow intense, these developments do take place after all (major developments that involve a challenge to the caste system and a major reformulation of the doctrine of eschatology and salvation), and in order to accommodate them the shape of the arena itself is changed. In this way, cosmogony and ethical order can remain divorced, as it were, for long periods; ethical order develops in its own sphere, in

[xix] See 'The Scrapbook'.

complete isolation from a cosmogony that thus becomes successively more and more outmoded or irrelevant or even inconsistent with that order, until, one day, the two join again in a marriage that changes them both.

And when the cosmos changes its shape, this, in turn, can change the way that human beings treat one another, at least in theory, and perhaps in practice. A breakthrough in ethics may lead to a breakdown in cosmogony, and to a regeneration; both of these stages may result in new myths, or, more often, new versions of old myths. The payoff is still in the next life: most of these texts are not saying that a Dalit can act like a Brahmin in this life, merely that he, too, can be freed from this life. But some of them seem to imply that people of all castes can change their forms of worship in this life and thus gain a better rebirth. And here again we must acknowledge that these stories are not merely about Dalits, but also about the relationship between all humans and their salvation.

Certain cosmogonies are designed to introduce order, and, therefore, certainty, into our perception of the cosmos, and when they break down they must be replaced by equally reassuring cosmogonies. But other cosmogonies (the chaos-affirming ones) are designed to assert or even to inspire uncertainty on the level at which traditional cosmogonies inspire certainty; they may inculcate ambiguity rather than certainty—many kinds of ambiguity, including ethical ambiguity. Even when a cosmogonic myth provides us with an orderly way of viewing the world (and all cosmogonic myths do this, to one extent or another), that world may not in itself be orderly. Yet the very fact that ambiguity or disorder is expressed by the cosmogonic myth lends a kind of centripetal movement to these conceptions, which otherwise would remain in the centrifugal realm of private dreams and lonely fragmentations. Even the cognitive upheavals caused by the need to reimagine the whole shape of the universe offer to those who embrace them some sort of shared conceptual system, an assumed principle of what is most important on some deeper level. Thus even the denial of order becomes in itself an assertion of a different kind of order, and even the myths of chaos offer the structure of their formality as *myths*— linguistic, cognitive, shared, sacred views of the world—and thereby constitute a framework on which new ethical understandings may be built.

GOD'S BODY, OR, THE *LINGAM* MADE FLESH: CONFLICTS OVER THE REPRESENTATION OF SHIVA[1]

Until February of 2010, the *Encyclopaedia Britannica* entry on Hinduism included this sentence about the god Shiva: 'In temples and in private shrines, Shiva is [. . .] worshipped in the form of the *lingam*, or phallus, often embedded in the *yoni*, the symbol of the female sexual organ.' That definition was based on the one established by the standard, nineteenth century Sanskrit dictionary of Sir Monier Monier-Williams, which defines the *lingam* (or *linga*—the 'm' is optional) as 'the male organ or Phallus (esp. that of Siva worshipped in the form of a stone or marble column which generally rises out of a yoni, q.v., and is set up in temples dedicated to Siva|).' But in February of 2010, in response to a number of complaints from Hindu readers, *Britannica* replaced their original sentence with the following rather cumbersome paragraph:

> In temples and in private shrines, Shiva is worshipped in the form of the *lingam*, a cylindrical votary object that is often embedded in a *yoni*, or spouted dish. Together they symbolize the eternal process of creation and regeneration. Since the late 19th century, some scholars have interpreted the *lingam* and *yoni* as being aniconic representations of the male and female sexual organs, respectively.

This change was a response to a dispute about the symbolism of the *lingam* that has been going on for many centuries: Is its primary meaning inexorably tied to the physical body (iconic), or is it abstract (aniconic)? The *Britannica* hedged.[i]

The Shiva-*lingam* is well known throughout India, a signifier that is understood across barriers of caste and language, a *linga franca*, if you will.

---

[i] In the interest of full disclosure I must confess that I serve on the *Britannica*'s International Board of Editors, and that the *Britannica* staff consulted me in making this revision.

But what is signified? Many Hindus have, like Sigmund Freud, seen *lingam*s in every naturally occurring elongated object, including the so-called self-created *lingam*s, *objets trouvés* such as stalagmites, the most well-known being the ice stalagmite inside the Amarnath cave in Kashmir, which is a popular Hindu pilgrimage site. But recently, many Hindus, especially bloggers on the Hindu internet (sometimes called the Hindernet), have insisted that the *lingam* has nothing at all to do with any part of the body of any human or any god, and the *Britannica* acted in response to that groundswell, or, rather, air-swell. Where did this argument come from?

This question about present-day Hindu sensibilities is greatly illuminated by setting it in the context of the history of the usages of the word *lingam* in ancient texts and the evidence of material images of the Shiva-*lingam* in Indian art, as well as the historical role of foreign empires in the formation of contemporary attitudes to the *lingam*.

THE INDUS VALLEY

The story begins in the Indus Valley Civilization in what is now northwest India and Pakistan, a culture (dating from well before 2500 BCE) with rich archeological remains but no deciphered script. The textual silence has allowed scholars to draw wild conclusions, often politically motivated, about the nature of the many physical objects discovered there. Some people have seen a kind of proto-*lingam* on one of the many carved stones found there, rectangular sections of soapstone about the size of a postage stamp, which were used as seals or stamps. Sir John Marshall began it all, in 1931, in his magisterial three-volume publication, *Mohenjo-daro and the Indus Civilization*, which devotes five pages of a long chapter entitled 'Religion' to seal 420:

> There appears at Mohenjo-daro a male god, who is recognizable at once as a prototype of the historic Siva . . . The lower limbs are bare and the phallus (*urdhva-medhra*) seemingly exposed, but it is possible that what appears to be the phallus is in reality the end of the waistband.[2]

Urdhva-medhra ('upward phallus') is a Sanskrit term for an erect phallus, like the Greek-based English term 'ithy-phallic'. The mute image on the seal suggested to Marshall an early form of the Hindu god Shiva, because both Shiva and the figure on the seal are seated in a possibly yogic posture and have horns, multiple faces, surrounding animals, and an erect phallus. Marshall's suggestion was taken up by several generations of scholars, who made much of this tiny bit of soapstone; the millimetre of the putative erection on this seal (the *whole seal* is barely an inch high) has, like the optional inch of Cleopatra's nose, caused a great deal of historical fuss. The 'upward-phallus-or-is-it-perhaps-just-his-waistband-or-the-knot-in-his-dhoti?' has a lineage in Indian art history that comes to rival the 'snake-or-is-it-perhaps-just-a-rope?' in Indian philosophical idealism, as a trope for the power of illusion. And there *is* a general resemblance between this image and later Hindu images of Shiva. The Indus people may well have created a symbolism of the divine phallus. But even if this is so, and we cannot know it, it does not mean that the Indus images are the source of the Hindu images, or that they had the same meaning.

THE VEDAS AND THE UPANISHADS

The word *lingam* does not occur in the *Rig Veda*, the most ancient Hindu text (c. 1500 BCE), nor does the god Shiva. But the deity Rudra, in many ways an antecedent of Shiva, does make a brief appearance, and the male organ, by another name (*kaprith*, perhaps meaning 'expanding' or 'extending pleasure'), also appears in the Veda, in an obscene hymn[ii] about a sexual competition between a male monkey and the god Indra.[3] Indra is a virile god, a distant cousin of Zeus and Jupiter, who bequeaths to Shiva some aspects of his mythology, including myths of castration.[4] The male organ also appears, by yet another name (*shishna*, 'piercer' or 'tail'), in two Vedic hymns imploring that same god, Indra, to strike down 'those whose god is the phallus' or 'those who play with the phallus' (*shishna-devas*).[5] Some scholars have suggested that this phrase may refer to an 'early Indus cult' of the *lingam*.[6] But there is no evidence that the Indus Valley people had such a cult, let alone that the people who composed the *Rig Veda* knew about it, or that they disapproved of it instead of assimilating it to their own worship of their own phallic god, Indra—no lawyer would go into court with such shaky evidence.

The word *lingam* appears in the Upanishads (mystical texts from around 600 BCE) only in its general sense of a sign, as smoke is a sign of fire. But the male organ does appear, under yet another name, in one of the oldest Upanishads, which calls it 'the Thing' (*artha*).[7] The same text[8] also describes the female organ in considerable detail, analogizing the Vedic oblation of butter into the fire to the act of sexual procreation.[iii]

[ii] See 'Indra as the Stallion's Wife'.
[iii] See 'From Kama to Karma'.

THE *MAHABHARATA*

Gradually the word *lingam* took on the more particular meaning of a sign of gender, then the sign of the male gender, and finally the sign of the male gender of the god Shiva. In the *Mahabharata* (c. 300 BCE to 300 CE), we first encounter the word *lingam* unequivocally designating the sexual organ of Shiva:[iv]

> The creator, Brahma, wishing to create creatures, said to Shiva, the first being, 'Create creatures, without delay.' Shiva said, 'Yes,' but seeing that all creatures were flawed, he who had great ascetic heat plunged into the water and generated ascetic heat. Brahma waited for him for a very long time and then created another creator, a Prajapati ('Lord of Creatures'). The Prajapati, seeing Shiva submerged in the water, said to his father, Brahma, 'I will create creatures, if there is no one who has been born before me.' His father said to him, 'There is no other male (*purusha*) born before you. This is just a pillar (or, Shiva who is called The Pillar) submerged in the water. Rest assured, and do the deed.' And so the Prajapati created creatures. They were hungry and tried to eat the Prajapati, until Brahma provided them with food, plants and animals, and then they began to procreate and increased in number.
>
> Then Shiva stood up from the water. When he saw those creatures of various forms, increasing by themselves, he became angry, and he tore off his own *lingam* and threw it down on the ground, where it stood up just as it was. Brahma said to him, hoping to conciliate him with words, 'What did you accomplish by staying so long in the water? And why did you tear out this *lingam* and plant it in the ground?' Then Shiva, becoming truly furious, said to Brahma, 'Since someone else created these creatures, what will I do with it? The creatures can go on recycling forever, eating the food that I obtained for them through my ascetic heat.' And Shiva went to his place on the mountain, to generate ascetic heat.[9]

The 'flaw' in the creatures seems to be their need for food, though later retellings say that Shiva hoped to produce, through his ascetic heat, creatures who would never die; to that degree, his powerful asceticism makes him *more*, not less, creative. What is significant for our question here

---

[iv] Shiva in this text is called Harikesha [the Tawny-Haired], the Lord of the Mountain, the Eldest, the Lord Rudra, Bhava, and the Guru of the World; I have simplified the text by calling him Shiva throughout, and I have also condensed it somewhat, but added nothing.

is the ambiguity of the word for pillar (*sthanu*): it is a name of Shiva, signifying the immobile, ascetic, de-sexualized form of the *lingam*; but it also designates an inanimate pillar, which is what Brahma implies in his answer to the Prajapati, not exactly lying but drawing on the wrong meaning of the word in order to avoid admitting that there is, in fact, already another creator at work, precisely what the Prajapati did not want. Shiva in this myth is both a potentially procreative phallus (a fertile *lingam*) and a pillar-like renouncer of sexuality (an ascetic *lingam*). The word *lingam* has the same double edge as the word 'Pillar.' Shiva's castration does not render him asexual but, rather, extends his sexual powers to the universe, just as his destruction of Kama, the god of erotic love, actually releases the power of Kama into the world at large.[10]

THE GUDIMALLAM *LINGAM*

A *lingam* that scholars generally regard as the earliest physical depiction of the god Shiva was made sometime between the third and first centuries BCE, in Gudimallam in southeastern Andhra Pradesh. Its anatomical detail is highly naturalistic (apart from its size: just under five feet high), and on the shaft is carved the figure of Shiva, also naturalistic, two-armed, holding an axe in one hand and the body of a small antelope in the other. His thin garment reveals his own sexual organ (not erect), his hair is matted, he wears large earrings, and he stands upon a dwarf. The details of its carving define this image unequivocally as an iconic representation of the male sexual organ; the hypothesis that it is a form of the god Shiva is suggested by the iconography of the axe, antelope, matted hair and dwarf, and supported by the three horizontal lines, the sign of Shiva, that were painted on it some time after its original creation. Visitors to the Gudimallam *lingam* in the early twenty-first century noted that while the large *lingam* as a whole remains entirely naked, with all its anatomical detail, a chaste cloth was wrapped around the small image of the naked Shiva on the front of the *lingam*, a kind of loincloth (or fig leaf) simultaneously covering up the middle of the figure in the middle of the *lingam* and the middle of the *lingam* itself. Here is a tradition driving with one foot on the accelerator and the other on the brake.

STORIES ABOUT THE SHIVA *LINGAM* IN LATER SANSKRIT TEXTS

There is convincing textual evidence that people in ancient India associated the iconic form of the *lingam* with the male sexual organ. A verse from the 'Garland of Games' of Kshemendra, a Brahmin who lived in Kashmir in the eleventh century CE, refers to the human counterpart of the divine Shiva-*lingam*: 'Having locked up the house on the pretext of venerating the *lingam*, Randy scratches her itch with a *lingam* of skin.'[11] The first *lingam* in this verse is certainly Shiva's, and there is an implied parallelism, if not identity, between it and the second one, which could be either a leather dildo (of which a number are described in the *Kamasutra*[12]) or its human prototype.

The human and divine levels of the *lingam* were explicitly compared in a rather different way in the *Skanda Purana*,[v] which argued that all creatures in the universe are marked with the signs of the god Shiva and his consort, since all females have *pindas* (the term for the base in which the sculpted form of the *lingam* is set) and join with males, who have *lingam*s (like the Shiva-*lingam* set in the *pinda*).[13] In a sixteenth century Marathi text, the Kali Yuga (the embodied spirit of the present Dark and Evil Age[vi]) grasps by one hand his *lingam* (representing unrestrained sexuality, a synecdoche for wrong action of all kinds) and by the other hand his tongue (symbolic of lascivious speech), and he says, 'I will be defeated only by those who guard their *lingam* and their tongue.'[14]

The nineteenth-century sage Ramakrishna used to worship his own male organ because, he said, it reminded him of the Shiva-*lingam*; he had learned this '*jivantalingapuja*,' or worship of the living *lingam*, from his guru.[15] As related by Mahendranath Gupta, Ramakrishna described what he called his madness: 'When I experienced that divine madness, I used to worship my own sex-organ as the Siva-phallus.'[16] A satire on this experience appears in Paul Scott's *Staying On*, when Mr Bhoolabhoy, an Indian Christian, deplores the near certainty that he is about to make love once more to his horrid wife:

> 'Indeed I am lost,' he thought. 'She will make me do it. I am not a Christian at all. I am a Hindu and she is my goddess. Every orgasm is an offering to her, and every erection is a manifestation in me of *Shiva-lingam*.' He shut his eyes so that he could not see his idol. He tried to conjure a different image. It would not come.[17]

The many Sanskrit myths that explain the origin of the worship of the Shiva-*lingam* can be divided into those that do regard the *lingam* as a part of the god's sexual anatomy and those that do not. Of the texts in which the

[v] See 'The Scrapbook'.
[vi] See 'The Concept of Heresy'.

lingam is obviously the phallus of Shiva, like the myth about the Pillar that we have already considered, some—most, but not all, told by worshippers of Shiva—regard the *lingam* as an entirely glorious form in which Shiva appears and accepts worship. But other texts—some, but not all, told by worshippers of gods other than Shiva, particularly Vishnu—regard the *lingam* as an object of scorn and shame.[18] These texts are early evidence of the discomfort caused by the phallic meaning of the symbol, though they do not yet attempt to deny that meaning.

That discomfort can be traced back to ascetic and renunciant traditions that began in the Upanishads, alongside the very passages that praised the sexual act as inherently sacred. And this ascetic strain, often misogynist, often expressing a deep anxiety about the human body, challenged the other sort of Hinduism, the one that gloried in the body both for its fertility and for its eroticism. The two traditions remain in tension to this day.[vii]

The stories of Shiva in the Pine Forest occur in two sets of variants along this divide. In both sets, Shiva enters the Pine Forest naked, often 'with his seed drawn up' ('upward seed', a variant of 'upward-phallus'), either in order for his seed not to fall down in the act of procreating, or in order to procreate, or both at once—another striking instance of the sort of ambiguity that haunts this debate. The women of the Pine Forest fall madly in love with him, which infuriates their husbands, and Shiva's *lingam* falls to the ground. But sometimes it falls as a result of the sages' curse (when the text regards the *lingam* as shameful), and sometimes through Shiva's own volition (when the text regards the *lingam* as a source of desirable power).[viii] In both cases, dire consequences follow, and the sages, having learned their lesson, agree to worship the Shiva-*lingam* forever after.[19]

Lingam-worship is cast in a definitely negative vein in a group of stories in which the sage Bhrigu visits the gods Brahma, Vishnu and Shiva in turn; the first two welcome the sage, but Shiva happens to be alone with his wife and refuses to be disturbed. The furious sage curses Shiva to be worshipped in the form of the thing that he seems to care most about, the *lingam*.[20] But *lingam*-worship is a positive factor, and Shiva is superior, rather than inferior, to Brahma and Vishnu, in another myth in which the *lingam* doesn't seem to have anything at all to do with any part of the male anatomy. In this myth, usually called 'the epiphany of the *lingam*'

[vii] See 'Three (or More)', 'From Kama to Karma' and 'Medical and Mythical Constructions'.
[viii] See 'The Submarine Mare'.

(*lingodbhava*), Shiva appears in the form of the pillar in the water that he takes in the *Mahabharata* story of self-castration, and indeed this episode of the epiphany is often told as a direct sequence to that story of self-castration.[21] While Brahma and Vishnu are arguing as to which of them fathered the other,[ix] Shiva appears before them as a pillar of light and flame, infinitely high and infinitely deep; the two gods try in vain to find its top and bottom, Brahma in the form of a goose and Vishnu in the form of an aquatic boar, and sometimes Brahma lies and says he's found the top when he hasn't, for which he is cursed never to be worshipped in India any more. Then Brahma and Vishnu humbly prostrate themselves before Shiva, recognizing that he had created both of them, as well as everything else in the universe.[22] There is nothing sexual about this *lingam*, though it is perhaps significant that it is the star witness in a debate about fatherhood.

THE *LINGAM* IN VERNACULAR TEXTS

Later Sanskrit and vernacular texts depict the Shiva-*lingam* alternatively, and in combination, as a part of his body and as an abstract symbol of the god, worshipped with offerings of fruit and flowers. Hindus for many centuries have seen their god(s) simultaneously in two forms: the true form of god is without any qualities (*nirguna*), unimaginable; but out of compassion for us, and so that we can love him, the god also manifests himself in a form with qualities (*saguna*),[x] perhaps as a human with two arms, or with particular features (a blue skin for Krishna, a third eye for Shiva). Each is real in its own way; sometimes you reach for one, sometimes for the other. In this way, too, many Hindus have regarded the *lingam* as both abstract, without (sexual) qualities, and particular, with (sexual) qualities.

The *lingam* can also be real, and human, and particular, without being sexual. A number of South Indian texts in Tamil tell of a miracle: a stone image of Shiva, with a face, bleeds in response to, or to test, the devotion of a pious worshipper. Some versions of this story refer to this image simply as 'the Lord', that is, Shiva, but other versions assume that what is meant is a statue of the Lord, a *lingam*. The many representations of this episode in both paintings and sculpture depict the form of a Shiva-*lingam* with a face and eyes. Such an image seems to be assumed, but never named as such, in this story about Shiva told in the *Periya Puranam*, a popular South Indian Tamil text from the twelfth century:

[ix] See 'You Can't Get Here'.
[x] See '*Saguna* and *Nirguna*'.

One day, Kannappar, the chief of a tribe of hunters, found [a stone] Shiva in the jungle. Filled with love for the god and pity that he seemed to be all alone, Kannappar resolved to feed Shiva. He kicked aside the flowers that a Brahmin priest had left on the head of Shiva and gave him the flowers that he had worn on his own head. His feet, and his dogs' paws, left their marks on Shiva. He stayed with him all night, and left at dawn to hunt again.

In order to demonstrate to the Brahmin priest the greatness of Kannappar's love, Shiva caused blood to flow from one of his own eyes. To staunch the flow, Kannappar gouged out his own eye with an arrow and replaced the god's eye with his. When Shiva made his second eye bleed, Kannappar put his foot on Shiva's eye to guide his hand, and he was about to pluck out his remaining eye when Shiva stretched out his hand to stop him, and placed Kannappar at his right hand.[23]

Since at least the seventeenth century, the common Tamil term for Shiva's *lingam* has been *kuRi* (mark, or sign), a direct translation of the original, non-sexual meaning of *lingam*. (*An-kuRi* and *peN-kuRi*—'male sign' and 'female sign' represent the Sanskrit *pum-lingam* and *stri-lingam*.) The term *kuRi* is still common today as a respectable or medical term for the sign of sex. But the *Periya Puranam* never uses the term *lingam* (or *kuRi*) at all, merely saying: 'The eyes of the Lord were bleeding.' Nevertheless, many scholars subsume the Kannappar story under the category of bleeding *lingams*,[24] and the Tamil tradition assumes that the stone has the form of a *lingam*. Yet that stone has nothing to do with any part of Shiva's body but his eyes.[xi]

THE *LINGAM* AND MUSLIM RULERS

The *lingam* took on a new role in Hinduism after Muslim rule began, in the eleventh century CE. Many great temples were built at this time, but one large and influential twelfth-century South Indian Hindu sect differed from earlier renouncers in spurning not only houses but stone temples. These were the Lingayats ('People of the *Lingam*')—also called Charanas ('Wanderers') because they prided themselves on being moving temples, itinerant, never putting down roots—and Virashaivas ('Shiva's Heroes').[25] Their founder preached a simplified devotion: no goal but to be united, at death, with Shiva, and no worship but that of a small *lingam* worn around

---

[xi] Of course, Freud would have something to say about the upward displacement of the genitals to the eyes, as in the blinding of Oedipus—standing in for his castration—but we need not follow there.

the neck.[26] This *lingam* was never said to have any sexual connotations; instead, the entire body of the worshipper represented the earthly body of the god, as the temple did for more conventional Hindus.

But several of the Delhi Sultans, those who were particularly devout and iconoclast Muslims, regarded the *lingam* as sexual and anthropomorphic, and took pride in destroying as many *lingam*s as they could. In 1026, Mahmud of Ghazni attacked the temple of Somnatha, which held a famous Shiva *lingam*; this much, at least, seems to be historical fact. But then comes the mythologizing. According to some versions of the story, including early Turko-Persian triumphalist sources, Mahmud stripped the great gilded *lingam* of its gold and hacked it to bits with his sword, sending the bits back to Ghazni where they were incorporated into the steps of the new mosque.[27] Medieval Hindu epics of resistance created a counter-mythology in which the stolen image came to life (another bit of evidence that it was regarded as a living thing, a body in itself) and eventually, like a horse trotting back to the stable, returned to the temple to be re-consecrated.[28] Other sources, including local Sanskrit inscriptions, biographies of kings and merchants of the period, court epics and popular narratives that have survived, give various versions of the event.[29] In South India, some three hundred years later, Ala-ud-din Khilji's forces attacked the temple of the Dancing Shiva in Chidambaram and with 'the kick of the horse of Islam', as the Indo-Persian poet Amir Khusrau put it, destroyed the *lingam*s there.[30] The seventeenth-century Mughal emperor Aurangzeb, notorious for his chauvinism, particularly hated Varanasi (Benares) because it was the centre of *lingam*-worship, which he regarded as the most abominable of all abominations.[31] This foreign attitude to the *lingam* was to have serious repercussions for the attitude of the Hindus themselves.

(One bit of comic relief in this area is P.N. Oak's argument, in *Tajmahal: The True Story*, first published in 1965,[32] that the Taj Mahal is not a Islamic mausoleum but an ancient Shiva temple, which the Mughal emperor Shah Jahan commandeered from the then Maharaja of Jaipur; that the term 'Taj Mahal' is a corrupt form of the Sanskrit term '*Tejo Mahalaya*,' signifying a Shiva temple; and—the crowning argument—that persons connected with the repair and maintenance of the Taj have seen the Shiva *lingam* and 'other idols' sealed in the thick walls of the monument and in secret chambers below its marble basement.)

THE *LINGAM* IN THE RAJ

British historiographers made much of the Muslim destruction of Hindu temples and *lingam*s, in order to claim that the British had rescued the

Hindus from oppression by Muslims. And many of the British in India, particularly at the start, in the eighteenth century, appreciated all forms of Hindu culture, including its art forms and its eroticism. But the puritanical Protestant ministers who evangelized India after 1813 were not amused by the copulating couples on the walls of the temples of Khajuraho (built between 900 and 1100 CE in Madhya Pradesh).[xii]

What the British missionaries most despised was what they regarded as the obscene idolatry of the *lingam*. The British in general regarded the Hindus, as they regarded most colonized people of colour, as simultaneously over-sexed and impotent, and the British presence had a negative effect on the self-perception that Hindus had of their own bodies.[xiii] For, still reeling from the onslaught of the Muslim campaigns against *lingam*s, the Hindus who worked with and for the British internalized their colonizers' scorn.[33] Thus the British taught the Hindus to be ashamed of the sexual meanings of the *lingam*.

When Sir Richard Francis Burton published the first English translation of the *Kamasutra* in 1883,[xiv] he and his co-translator, Foster Fitzgerald Arbuthnot, also British, 'adroitly managed to escape the smell of obscenity' by using what they presented as 'the Hindu terms for the sexual organs, *yoni* and *lingam*' throughout their translation.[34]

English, unlike Sanskrit, lacks a common register for the sexual organs between the obscene and the medical. To the extent that nineteenth-century writers regarded the words themselves, not the actual things that they designated, as obscene, the foreign words, Sanskrit words, devoid of any English connotations at all, were able to make an end-run around the obscene thought—not to mention the obscenity laws. The term *lingam* was perceived as 'neither erudite nor earthy, neither gross nor gynaecological'.[35] Arbuthnot elsewhere even attempted to coin the word 'yonjic' to match 'phallic'.[36]

But this decision of Burton's to use *lingam* and *yoni* to represent the sexual organs in the *Kamasutra* was problematic in several ways. First of all, these terms do not represent the text, which only rarely uses *lingam* to refer to the male sexual organ and never refers to the female sexual organ as a *yoni*. Where the *Kamasutra* does use *lingam*, the context suggests, and the commentator affirms, that it is gender-neutral, used in its basic lexical sense and meant to apply to both the male and female sexual organs: 'The sexual

---

[xii] See 'From Kama to Karma'.
[xiii] See 'Medical and Mythical Constructions'.
[xiv] See 'From Kama to Karma'.

organ is called the 'sign' (*lingam*), because it is the sign of femaleness and so forth.'[37] Instead, the *Kamasutra* generally uses several other words for the sexual organs, primarily a gender-neutral term that can be translated as 'pelvis' or 'between the legs' (*jaghana*) or other terms (such as 'the instrument' [*yantra* or *sadhana*]) that are neither coy nor vulgar. (The exception is the final section of the *Kamasutra*, Book Seven, about the use of drugs and sex-tools, which has an entirely different tone from the rest of the text and is probably a later addition; this section of the text does use *lingam* for the male sexual organ several times.[38]) Yashodhara, the thirteenth-century commentator on the *Kamasutra*, sometimes uses *lingam* and *yoni* to gloss other terms that the *Kamasutra* uses for the sexual organs, but he also uses various other words. So for Burton to use the terms *lingam* and *yoni* consistently to translate, as it were, other Sanskrit words for the sexual organs was to create a weird linguistic back-formation.

Second, by Burton's time, the terms *lingam* and *yoni* had taken on strong religious overtones, as both Indian English and Indian vernacular languages used these words primarily to designate the stone icons of Shiva and his consort. The exclusive application of these two terms to human genitals, therefore, may have had, at the very least, inappropriate overtones and, at the most, blasphemous implications for some Hindus. Yet Burton and Arbuthnot *knew* the religious meaning of the *lingam*. Arbuthnot wrote that, 'There is in Hindostan an emblem of great sanctity, which is known as the Linga-Yoni.'[39]

Finally, the terms *lingam* and *yoni* had Orientalist implications for most English readers.[xv] The use of any Sanskrit term at all in place of an English equivalent anthropologized sex, distanced it, made it safe for English readers by assuring them, or pretending to assure them, that the text was not about real sexual organs, *their* sexual organs, but merely about the appendages of weird, dark people far away. This move dodged 'the smell of obscenity' through the same logic that allowed *National Geographic* to depict the bare breasts of black African women long before it became respectable to show white women's breasts in *Playboy*. (Indeed, in some instances *National Geographic* actually darkened the skin colour of a partially naked Polynesian woman 'in order to render her nudity more acceptable to American audiences'.[40]) The use of the term *lingam* enabled the authors to pretend that the book was not obscene because it was about India, when they really thought it was about sex, and knew that English readers would

---

[xv] See 'I Have Scinde'.

think so too. And so Sir Richard Burton is the one who really made *lingam*, in English, into a dirty word. No wonder that the Hindus recoiled from that implication. One begins to see why some Hindus began to be very sensitive about the interpretation of the word *lingam*.

CONTEMPORARY HINDU ATTITUDES TO THE SHIVA *LINGAM*

The history of the word *lingam*, and the history of the shift in its contexts, demonstrates that we are dealing not just with two bodies of separate texts, one interpreting the *lingam* sexually and one theologically, but with a tension within each of a number of texts, the same tension between the erotic and the ascetic that characterizes so many other aspects of Hinduism in general and the god Shiva in particular.[41]

Nowadays, many Hindu texts treat the *lingam* as an aniconic pillar of light or an abstract symbol of god, with no sexual reference. To them, the stone *lingams* 'convey an ascetic purity despite their obvious sexual symbolism'.[42] There is nothing surprising about this. The *Skanda Purana* text that argued that all human beings are born marked with the signs of Shiva and his consort on their bodies—the *lingam* and *pinda*—implies that humans are born marked with the symbol of their faith, as a Christian might be born with a birthmark in the shape of a cross, or might receive the mark of the stigmata on her palms. Arbuthnot actually wrote a book about what he called *The Masculine Cross*,[43] that is, the Shiva *lingam*. But by the late nineteenth century, for many Hindus, a Hindu *lingam* was no more a sexual organ than a cross was a Roman instrument of execution.

To continue this parallel, some Christians see in the cross a vivid reminder of the agony on Calvary, while others see it as a symbol of their god in the abstract or of Christianity as a religion; this dichotomy corresponds to that between the anatomically detailed *saguna*, phallic *lingam* (such as the Gudimallam *lingam*) and the abstract, *nirguna*, elongated-object *lingam*, which have different resonances for worshippers.[xvi] But some Hindus, particularly those who advocate a sanitized, 'spiritual' form of Hinduism,[xvii] do not merely see the *lingam* as an abstract, *nirguna* symbol but go on to object to, and attempt to censure, the interpretations of those who view it in more somatic terms, as a *saguna lingam*. They would be the counterparts of Christians who would refuse to acknowledge that the cross ever referred

---

[xvi] Protestants generally favour the abstract or *nirguna* cross, Catholics the *saguna* crucifix (which has the image of Christ on it).

[xvii] See 'You Can't Make an Omelette' and 'The Politics of Hinduism'.

to the crucifixion of the historical Jesus. There is nothing new in the tension between abstract and earthy interpretations of the *lingam* in India; what is new is the insistence that one of them, the earthy one, is *wrong*, and must be silenced.

THE GENERAL PROBLEM OF *LINGAM* SYMBOLISM

To read all the myths of the *lingam* as the revisionist Hindus would insist on doing would be a travesty. If we return to the central episode of the myth about the creation of the *lingam*, and translate the word *lingam* as such Hindus would have us do, this is what we get:

> Shiva stood up from the water. When he saw those creatures of various forms, increasing by themselves, he became angry, and he tore off his own *abstract symbol of god* and threw it down on the ground, where it stood up just as it was. Brahma said to him, 'Why did you tear out your *abstract symbol of god* and plant it in the ground?' And Shiva replied, 'Since someone else created these creatures, what will I do with my *abstract symbol of god*?'

And so forth.

Foolish as this story sounds if we limit ourselves to the non-sexual meaning of the *lingam*, we would be equally wrong to distort the story of Kannappar's *lingam* with the bleeding eye by translating 'the Lord' in that text as the 'male organ of Shiva':

> One day, Kannappar, the chief of a tribe of hunters, found *the male organ of Shiva* in the jungle; filled with love for the god and pity that he seemed to be all alone, Kannappar resolved to feed *the male organ of Shiva*. He kicked aside the flowers that a Brahmin priest had left on the head of *the male organ of Shiva* and gave him the flowers that he had worn on his own head. His feet, and his dogs' paws, left their marks on *the male organ of Shiva* . . . [and so forth]

This story is about the presence of the god in a very physical, but not at all sexual, form.

To conclude by returning to the beginning, let us recall that the word *lingam* primarily means a sign. And we know that signs, like symbols, are always reversible, never reducible. Like myths, symbols change all the time; the greatest of all the survival tactics of a myth, or of a great symbol, is its ability to stand on its head. This flexibility allows a myth or a symbol to be shared by a group (who, as individuals, have various points of view) and to survive through time (through different generations with different points of view).[44] This is certainly true of the *lingam*. Ernst Kantorowicz wrote about the two bodies of medieval European kings, the body politic and the body natural.[45] In the same way, we can speak of the sexual *lingam* and the theological *lingam*. In order to include the full range of its meanings in our understanding of it, it might be best either to leave the term *lingam* untranslated, unglossed, like dharma—now an English word— or to settle for the broadest possible meaning, perhaps just 'a symbol of the god Shiva'.

To paraphrase a line often, wrongly, attributed to Sigmund Freud, sometimes a *lingam* is just a *lingam*, but more often, it is both a *lingam* and a cigar.[46] We need to be aware of both the literal and the symbolic levels of the *lingam*, the historical and the contemporary meanings, simultaneously. Ambivalence towards the *lingam* was built into the Hindu tradition from that first moment when the Upanishads sketched out a parting of the ways, two divergent paths. But that ambivalence remained a matter of peaceful coexistence until the bigoted or the prudish among two of India's non-Hindu rulers intervened: some Muslims destroyed *lingam*s, and the British made the Hindus ashamed of them. The history of interpretations of the *lingam* in India reveals the ways that the actions of the state—in this case, the Muslim dynasties and the British, who viewed the *lingam* negatively— have deeply affected native Hindu perceptions of the body of their own god. And this set the stage for the final blow, when yet another bigoted and prudish political movement, the twentieth-century Hindutva[xviii] faction, condemned and outlawed what they regarded as unacceptable aspects of their own religion, such as the sexual aspects of the Shiva *lingam*. But in this renewed battle over god's body, the god himself may deny either side victory. For Shiva—the ascetic god of the yogis as well as the erotic god of the Tantrics; the Lord of dance who dances the dance of both destruction (the *tandava*) and pleasure, hence, creation (the *lasya*); the thoroughly male god who also becomes a woman—has always gloried in ambivalence. The contrasting aspects of the *lingam*, phallic and abstract, like all the other contrasting aspects of the god, are not in conflict but always simultaneously present, each illuminating the other.

[xviii] See 'You Can't Make an Omelette' and 'The Politics of Hinduism'.

SACRIFICE AND SUBSTITUTION: RITUAL MYSTIFICATION AND MYTHICAL DEMYSTIFICATION IN HINDUISM[1]

Sacrifice might be minimally defined as the act of giving up something in order to receive something of greater worth. Sacrifice is central to Hinduism throughout its history, and though it has meant very different things to different Hindus at different times, it has always involved a transaction between humans and gods. In the Vedic period, there was full reciprocity: the gods needed humans to offer sacrifice to them, usually in the form of butter or the pressed essence of the Soma plant, but also in the form of animals (usually goats, sometimes horses), while humans needed the gods' goodwill to be sure of good crops, healthy children and success in war. The gods themselves sometimes sacrificed to themselves,[i] while the offerings that humans made sustained not merely the gods but the whole universe. In later periods, the gods sometimes became jealous of humans and interfered with their sacrifices,[ii] while, still later, actual sacrifice was abandoned or internalized and transformed into other forms of religious expression.[iii]

The Sanskrit texts detailing the philosophy as well as the actual performance of the sacrifice are so detailed that Vedic sacrifice was often taken as the paradigm for the category of sacrifice anywhere in the world, a fundamental category in the study of religion that sometimes functioned as a kind of placeholder for all religious ritual, or as the foundation of all morality and ethics. Sacrifice has even been identified as the origin of civilization itself in the classical works of modern sociology and psychology by Émile Durkheim and Sigmund Freud, and there is a certain sense in which all life—human and non-human, cultural and natural—might be

---

[i] See 'You Can't Get Here'.
[ii] See 'The Concept of Heresy'.
[iii] See 'The Ambivalence of Ahimsa'.

regarded as a series of deaths and rebirths, that is, as a continuous process of sacrifice.

But the operation of the ritual of sacrifice, it seems, depends on a kind of sleight of hand or self-deception, a shell game of displacement and replacement. Sacrifice is defined in relation to three crimes from which it is otherwise indistinguishable—suicide, murder and deicide (or the killing of gods); and it becomes distinguishable from them only by a confusion of roles and a set of characteristic acts of substitution. This apparently sacrilegious conclusion has been reached not only by the major modern theorists of the sacrificial ritual but was also reached, long ago, by the philosophers and mythologists of the sacrifice or *yajna* in ancient India.

SACRIFICE AND SUBSTITUTION AMONG THE THEORISTS

Substitution, the use of a 'stand-in' in place of an original that then 'represents' it, is at the very heart of sacrifice. Henri Hubert and Marcel Mauss, in their *Sacrifice: Its Nature and Function*, contended that 'the very nature of sacrifice' is 'dependent, in fact, on the presence of an intermediary, and we know that with no intermediary there is no sacrifice'.[2] Among other intermediaries so crucial to, even definitive of, the sacrificial ritual (including the priest who acts as a buffer and guide between the sacred and profane realms) is the ritual victim. The victim represents or 'becomes' (and thus substitutes for) both the invisible divine recipient of the offering and the human being who makes the offering. 'Through this proximity the victim, who already represents the gods, comes to represent the [sacrificer] also. Indeed, it is not enough to say that it represents him: it is merged in him. The two personalities are fused together.'[3] Every sacrificial victim, then, symbolizes both the god and the worshipper; every sacrifice is both an ersatz self-sacrifice and a dramatization of the killing of god(s). It is, according to these authors, through the victim that the 'communication' between the sacred and profane realms, between gods and men, is effected. By standing in for both the sacrificer and the deity, the victim draws them together.

Scholars of Vedic religion have also noted that sacrifice seems to be a kind of symbolic self-sacrifice; as Ananda K. Coomaraswamy puts it, 'To sacrifice and to be sacrificed are essentially the same.'[4] 'The only authentic sacrifice,' Sylvain Lévi has similarly, if more caustically, observed, 'would be suicide.'[5] Literal self-sacrifice, as we shall see, does indeed appear in Indian ritual and mythological texts as the defining instance of the ideal— and, therefore, rarely realized—sacrifice. Or, second best, we read of a *sarvamedha*, the 'sacrifice of everything', in which the sacrificer gives away all and then, 'dead to the world', retires to a renouncer's life in the wilderness.[6]

In a very basic sense, then, anything that one sacrifices is a surrogate for the ultimate paradigm underlying all sacrifices—the sacrifice of oneself. The least symbolic is the suicidal human sacrifice, in which the symbol stands for itself. It was this that led Joseph de Maistre to argue that the theory of sacrificial substitution could not apply to human sacrifice, since 'One cannot kill a man to save a man.' Yet, as René Girard points out in mocking de Maistre's 'bold and wholly unsubstantiated assertion', that is precisely the purpose of human sacrifice.[7] In order not to die, we kill another animal; in order not to lose something, we give it away.

Jan Heesterman takes a different approach to the close affinities between suicidal self-sacrifice and the 'authentic' Vedic sacrifice of the self, noting that the latter turns on substitution and the nature of the victim chosen as surrogate:

> What emerges from the ritual and from ritualist speculation is that self-sacrifice as such is invalid . . . Sacrifice, on the other hand, cannot be valid by immolating just any victim that presents itself. The person, animal or substance that is immolated must be that part of the sacrificer that defines him as such, namely the goods of life he has acquired by risking his own life . . . Without this bond uniting the sacrificer and his victim, sacrifice would be as invalid as self-sacrifice is *per se*.[8]

Insofar as self-sacrifice *qua* sacrifice remains 'symbolic', a substitute victim, which nevertheless must be 'identified' with what it signifies, is obviously required. Lévi has thus termed sacrifice a 'subterfuge'.[9] But the substitution of another for the self does serve to distinguish sacrifice from suicide, martyrdom and all other literal forms of self-death.

Some theorists have also emphasized the other side of sacrificial substitution—displaced violence towards another. In this view, sacrifice is defined not in relation to other forms of self-death, but rather in relation to other forms of murder (homicide as well as deicide); and in either case it is by virtue of the substitute that sacrifice is set apart from—i.e., made 'sacred' in relation to—these other, 'profane' killings. Girard, in *Violence and the Sacred*, speaks of a 'double substitution' in the ritual. Following Freud,[10] Girard places substitution at the very centre of sacrifice and sees violence (repressed and expressed) as the key to the ritual. He writes of a 'fundamental truth about violence; if left unappeased violence will accumulate until it overflows its confines and floods the surrounding area. The role of sacrifice is to stem this rising tide of indiscriminate substitution and redirect violence into "proper" channels.'[11] The cycle of violence is short-circuited by the double substitution which at once conceals and represents the real victim as it transfers the violence from the real victim to a surrogate and then again to a ritual substitute. This byzantine chain of displacement is summed up thus:

> The ritual victim is never substituted for some particular member of the community or even for the community as a whole: *it is always substituted for the surrogate victim.* As this victim itself serves as a substitute for all the members of the community, the sacrificial substitute does indeed play the role that we have attributed to it, protecting all the members of the community from their respective violence—but always through the intermediary of the surrogate victim . . . Ritual sacrifice is founded on a double substitution. The first, which passes unperceived, is the substitution of one member of the community for all, brought about through the operation of the surrogate victim. The second, the only truly 'ritualistic' substitution, is superimposed on the first. It is the substitution of a victim belonging to a predetermined sacrificial category for the original victim. The surrogate victim comes from inside the community, and the ritual victim must come from outside.[12]

Girard's hypothesis finds a certain amount of support in ancient Indian ritual texts, as we shall soon see. For now, we might point to the earliest sources describing the Vedic horse sacrifice, in which there actually are double victims (indeed, two doubles): the horse, the ultimate victim, is accompanied by a most literal scapegoat—a goat—that is slaughtered with him,[13] and, later, by a dog, a ritually unclean animal, onto whom the evil of the sacrificer is projected.[14] Indeed, this doubling of the horse is sometimes still more complicated: instead of two other animals, two *groups* of animals, wild and tame, are bound to the stake, and the tame are killed while the wild are set free. As the process of substitution escalates, the number of victims subsidiary to the horse increases to as many as 111 and 180.[15] This is doubling to the nth degree.

The victim, Girard notes, is identified with the deity, and is for this reason, among others, regarded as sacred. But he also notes that a paradox then arises: 'Because the victim is sacred, it is criminal to kill him—but the victim is sacred only because he is to be killed.'[16] The second surrogate, the 'ritualistic' substitute victim, is often an animal; but Girard strangely regards this as a matter of no consequence: 'In the general study of sacrifice there is little reason to differentiate between human and animal victims . . . Strictly speaking, there is no essential difference between animal sacrifice and human sacrifice, and in many cases one is substituted for the other.'[17] This assertion, however, seems to be contradicted by myths of human sacrifice that go to great lengths to explain precisely why the sacrifice of an animal is *not* the same as (though it may well be the substitute for) the sacrifice of a human. Thus, for instance, in the Brahmana tale of Shunahshepha,[18] the boy who is about to be sacrificed protests, 'They are going to slaughter me as if I were not a human being,' and eventually makes them sacrifice a Soma plant instead.[19]

All the general conclusions regarding sacrifice, then, coincide. For all, sacrifice is defined by substitution. It is, in the first place, a substitute for an impossible or prohibited real act, such as the actual coalescence of the divine and the human, a real suicide, or plain, unritualized violence and murder—and all substitutions *within* a sacrificial ritual are, therefore, substitutions for a prior, and definitive, substitution of a ritual act for an unritualized killing. Secondly, all theorists considered here emphasize the critical importance of the victim to the sacrificial process, and all see this victim as a multivalent substitute and symbol for a pair of opposites: the sacred and the profane, god and the human, recipient and giver, father and son, society as a whole and its individual members. The substitute victim is, as a symbol, a representative of two (or more) different and even contradictory things or beings. And because it is a symbol, it is not critical to the efficacy of the sacrificial process itself who or what is selected to act as the symbol. It could be, and in the comparative view, is, almost anything: humans (of any number of culturally constituted types), animals, vegetables, non-sentient physical objects, physiological functions (as in the 'sacrifice of breath' in the Upanishads), even ideas ('individuality', 'desire', 'faith', 'truth', etc.) can and do function as the symbolic victim.

This is not to say, however, that within particular cultures and particular religious traditions the choice of the appropriate victim is left to the whims of individuals. Far from it. The appropriate sacrificial victims are, as Girard says, 'predetermined'. Still, the fact remains that substitute victims of all kinds populate the sacrificial arena. The proliferation of surrogates in sacrificial rituals, such as we have seen in the multiplication of subsidiary victims in the ancient Indian horse sacrifice, may be compared to the proliferation of variants or fragments (or overlapping mythemes) in the myths that so often gloss, or expound upon, these sacrifices. In both cases, this fragmenting and proliferation is necessitated by the worshipper's inability to deal with the problem directly. In the myth, it indicates that one cannot state the problem outright, and hence introduces a series of fragmentary statements (such as unglossed bits of symbolism or unexplained actions).[20] In the ritual, it means that one hesitates to sacrifice oneself or another directly, and hence interposes a series of surrogates.[iv]

If substitution is in fact the key to the sacrifice, then the only thing that the victim will never stand for is itself (more precisely, itself alone: a goat may symbolize goats in general as well as a goat-god or the owner of the goat). Seen in these terms, the theory of sacrifice is merely a branch of the more general theory of symbolism, and any and every insightful approach to symbolism will help us to understand the sacrifice (and vice versa).[v]

One may also, of course, turn for insights into the nature of sacrifice and substitution to the rituals and myths of sacrificial traditions themselves. More important: we can use the insights from the great theoreticians of sacrifice to help understand some of the more puzzling aspects of the ancient Indian texts, which explore at some depth, and sometimes in unexpected ways, the theoretical intricacies of sacrifice.

VEDIC THEORIES OF SUBSTITUTION IN SACRIFICE

In the texts of the Vedas, as well as in subsequent Hindu thinking about sacrifice, we encounter people inside one particular religious tradition wrestling with the complexities, even conundrums, of sacrifice and substitution. Vedic ritualism was first and foremost an exercise in and the product of a philosophy of resemblances and connections. Supposedly similar or resembling entities and phenomena were linked by 'connections' (*bandhus* or *nidanas*) and human beings could, therefore, claim to understand and to exert an influence on the natural, supernatural and social realms from within the confines of their ritual world: what the sacrificer did to the sacrificial offering was thought to have a direct effect on the natural force—such as the sun, or the rain—symbolized by the god to whom the offering was made . Put otherwise, ritual action on wholly accessible things and beings was said, by means of the connections, to work simultaneously and sympathetically on their natural, supernatural and social analogues.

[iv] One obvious place to begin a comparison of ritual substitutions would be with the transition from the actual sacrifice of a scapegoat and a Passover lamb in ancient Judaism to the historical sacrifice of Jesus interpreted as a substitution for that lamb; and, subsequently, the ritual sacrifice of a wafer and a cup of wine as a substitute for the actual crucifixion of Jesus. See Doniger O'Flaherty, *Other Peoples' Myths*, Chapter Five

[v] This being so, Freud's *Interpretation of Dreams* is as important as his *Totem and Taboo* for the question of sacrifice and substitution.

Vedic ritualism in its entirety, like 'sacrifice' as a category within the study of religion, is thus based on and made possible by substitution. The Vedic ritualists assume that it is not possible to have direct contact with the supernatural forces (the gods of sun or rain) that are the transcendent prototypes and, therefore, the ritual must use immanent counterparts or symbols (fire or the Soma juice) for the 'real thing'. So it was critical for the ritualists to know the answer to the question posed succinctly in the *Rig Veda*: 'What was the transcendent prototype (*prama*), what was the immanent counterpart (*pratima*), and what was the connection (*nidana*) between them?'[21]

At the most general level, the sacrificial ritual as a whole is a counterpart of the transcendent Cosmic One, Prajapati (the creator god) or Purusha,[vi] who has created the ritual as a *pratima* or counterpart or image of himself. Thus the texts repeatedly tell us that 'the sacrifice is Prajapati',[22] or that 'Prajapati is the sacrifice', or that he emits the sacrifice from himself, or 'makes his *atman* (soul)' the sacrifice, or *is* the *atman* of the sacrifice.[23] The sacrifice and Prajapati are counterforms of each other, and the creator god is no different from the cosmic whole. So it is that 'this all', which is Prajapati, corresponds to (or results from) the sacrifice itself.[24] Furthermore, because both the sacrifice and the year are counterparts of the same prototypical Prajapati, they are themselves linked on a common chain of resembling surrogates: the sacrifice has 'the same measure' (*sammita*) as the year.[25]

The components of the sacrifice are said to be resembling forms of cosmic prototypes (each element of the ritual being vertically connected to transcendent correlatives), and the sacrifice as a whole is the counterpart to the prototype that is Prajapati, the universe: 'Two levels, but one being,' as Paul Mus has put it.[26] The sacrifice operates with 'images' (such as the twelve days of a certain sacrifice) while Prajapati's body or self comprises the 'originals' (the twelve months of the year), but both participate in the same ontological essence. Counterparts are only in this sense to be regarded as 'substitutes'. They 'stand for' or 'represent' their originals in that they are more or less incomplete images or emanations of them. A series of resembling forms, from the prototype to its least complete manifestation, comprise the elements within a set. The *pratima* of Prajapati is the year, the cosmic whole on the temporal plane; and the counterpart of the year is the sacrifice of twelve days' duration because 'the year has twelve months, and

---

[vi] See 'You Can't Get Here'.

this is the *pratima* of the year'.[27] A sacrifice lasting a whole year would of course be more fully the form of Prajapati conceived of temporally, but one of twelve days can also serve the purpose, albeit less completely.

The doctrine of counterparts makes possible both ritual efficacy—the manipulation of ritual counterparts in order to influence cosmic prototypes—and ritual efficiency: 'The gods said, 'Find the sacrifice that will be the counterpart for one of a thousand years, for what man is there who could get through with a sacrifice lasting a thousand years?'[28] Human beings can participate in rituals of cosmic dimensions by means of resembling sacrifices gauged to the human condition—again, not with the completeness of the original but with the efficacy and efficiency of the counterpart. Sacrifice itself, then, is in Vedic philosophy a substitute for a cosmic operation that always lies outside the grasp of human practitioners. From this point of view no less than from the point of view of the modern theorists, sacrifice is always a substitute for an unattainable (or even undesirable) ideal.

The sacrifice in Vedism is also, as Paul Mus writes, a counterpart and a personal substitute for the man who offers it.[29] And a Brahmana says much the same thing: 'The man is the sacrifice because it is the man who offers it. And each time he offers it, the sacrifice takes the shape of the man.[vii] Therefore the sacrifice is the man.'[30] In this instance, the sacrificial ritual functions as a kind of representation of the very life of the sacrificer; the ritual substitutes for the real life of the one who offers it.

The sacrifice is thus regarded as the counterpart not only of the creator god and of the cosmos as a whole but also of the sacrificer himself. But if the sacrificer is in this way connected to the sacrifice—which is, it will be remembered, a counterpart of the creator god—it is not surprising that the sacrificer is also said to be 'nearest to' the prototypical Prajapati.[31] Man and god are 'identified' explicitly in Vedic ritualism;[32] the sacrificer, like the sacrifice, is a manifest counterpart of the ineffable creator god.

In relation to others, however, the sacrificer himself functions as a prototype with his own counterparts. A chain of potential substitutes for the sacrificer is thus created. An animal, more nearly resembling the sacrificer than vegetable oblations, in its turn stands as the prototype in relation to the lesser forms within the series. In this manner, the baked cake is the counterpart of the sacrificial animal (*pashu*),[viii] and, following the

---

[vii] In an account of a sacrifice sponsored and performed by the gods, the list of sacrificial fees given to the divine priests includes the gift of a man to Prajapati (TB 2.2.5.3; cf. PB 1.8.14)
[viii] See 'The Ambivalence of Ahimsa'.

chain, also therefore the counterpart of the sacrificer.[33] The sacrificer and his oblation are in this way analogues of one another. And because of their affinity, the sacrificer is said to offer a form of himself when he offers clarified butter, the sacrificial cake, or an animal; for 'by virtue of the counterpart, it is the man'.[34] Or, again, the relation of resemblance between the sacrificer and the animal victim within his sacrifice is sometimes described as one in which there is a metaphysical connection (*nidana*).[35]

But all counterparts, all representatives, are not created equal, and are not regarded as such; sacrificial victims are also not all equal in their ability to represent the prototype. The technical texts on the ritual, when listing the possible replacements for any given original component of the sacrifice, do so with a clear order of preference based on the strength of the resemblance of the species to the genus,[ix] and also with an explicit hierarchy of rewards: 'In any performance (wherein optional injunctions are prescribed), the higher the choice the higher the fruit.'[36]

The hierarchical nature of the lists of substitutes is perhaps most obviously exemplified in the discussion of substitutes for the sacrificial fee offered to the officiating priests by the sacrificer. The standard fee for a sacrifice is comprised of a cow, some gold and a garment[37]—obviously a gift of some expense (and in some sacrifices the gifts are far more costly). If these items are 'unavailable', the text continues, a much more modest (and inferior) substitute is prescribed: a gift of edible fruits and roots. 'If even this is not [within reach of the sacrificer],' the teacher concludes (perhaps with some exasperation), 'he should not offer the sacrifice.' Just as one could not offer a sacrifice to the gods without providing some (indeed, almost any) oblation in the fire for them, so one is prohibited from sacrificing without offering something to the Brahmin priests, the 'human gods'. And it may not be out of place here to recall who the creators of these ritual rules were.

Such a hierarchical gradation of counterparts which may function as substitutes for an original can also be observed when one looks at lists of sacrificial victims or *pashus*. One such enumeration is found in a passage whose purpose is to explain the etymology of the term '*pashu*':

[ix] Observe, for example, the progression in the list of substitutes for fire if, perchance, it has gone out and cannot be regenerated: one may, in that case, use an ordinary (*laukika*) fire, or offer in the right ear of a female goat (because, according to SB 7.5.2.6, Prajapati created the goat from his ear), in the right hand of the Brahmin (where the 'oblations' of sacrificial gifts are also placed), on a cluster of *darbha* grass, or one may offer the oblation in water (ApSS 9.3.3-16; BhSS 9.4.5-9.5.5; HSS 15.1.51-64; etc.)

Prajapati turned his attention to the forms of Agni. He searched for that boy[x] who had entered into the [various] forms [of Agni]. Agni became aware [of this and thought], 'Father Prajapati is searching for me. I will take a form unrecognizable to him.' He saw those five sacrificial victims: man, horse, bull, ram and goat. Because he saw (*pashyat*) [them], they are therefore *pashus*. He entered these five sacrificial victims and became these five sacrificial victims.[38]

Later in that same text, another passage makes it clear that the order in which the *pashus* are listed is not accidental, but rather is one calibrated to the relative 'excellence' of each victim:

He offers the man first, for man is the first of the *pashus*; then [he offers] the horse, for the horse comes after the man; then the bull, for the bull comes after the horse; then the ram, for the ram comes after the bull; then the goat, for the goat comes after the ram. In this way he offers them, in hierarchical succession according to their relative excellence.[39]

A man (*purusha*) is thus proclaimed as the highest and most desirable of all possible sacrificial victims; in Vedism, as in sacrificial theory elsewhere, the paradigmatic sacrifice is self-sacrifice. Not only is man listed first in the various enumerations of the *pashus*, he is also extolled by texts that place him closest to the deity, to Prajapati. The human *pashu*, being 'nearest to' Prajapati, is therefore the best substitute for the primordial victim, the creator god himself.[40] The superiority of the human victim is underlined in one account by claiming that he is 'all *pashus*', that is, he encompasses them all by virtue of his hierarchically superior rank (and note again the order in which the *pashus* are listed):

Prajapati at first was one. He desired, 'May I emit food, may I be reproduced.' He measured out the *pashus* from his breaths. From his mind [he measured out] the man; from his eye, the horse; from his breath, the bull; from his ear, the ram; from his voice, the goat. And since he measured them out from his breaths, they say, 'The *pashus* are the breaths.' And since he measured out the man from his mind, they say, 'The man is the first, the most potent of the *pashus*.' The mind is all the breaths, for all the breaths are firmly established in the mind. And since he measured out the man from his mind, they say, 'The man is all *pashus*,' for they all become the man's.[41]

---

[x] The 'boy', who plays no appreciable role in this version of the myth, is an echo of the important Rig Vedic myth in which the child of Agni is lost, searched for, and found (RV 5.2).

In relation to the other *pashus*, however, the sacrificer himself functions as the prototypical victim, with the other animals as inferior substitutes for or counterparts of man. The question of whether human beings were ever actually sacrificed in ancient India has long exercised scholars, and continues to do so. Bruce Lincoln, in *Myth, Cosmos, and Society*, argues that 'In practice humans were probably never offered in India, the *purushamedha* ('sacrifice of a man') remaining only a priest's fantasy of the sacrifice to end all sacrifices.'[42] There is, however, in addition to the textual references to human sacrifice,[43] also physical evidence of its performance, such as archeological remains of human skulls and other human bones at the site of fire-altars, together with the bones of other animals, both wild and tame (horse, tortoise, pig, elephant, bovines, goats and buffalos).[44] It is also possible that the ceremony known in the Vedas as the horse sacrifice originally involved the sacrifice of a man as well as a horse.[45]

The fact that there are surrogates for the human sacrificer/victim, in turn, makes it possible to conceive of the sacrifice as categorically different from suicide—indeed, as precisely a ritual inversion of suicide. It may now be viewed as an act that 'redeems' the sacrificer from death and increases his longevity:

> When he sacrifices with the animal sacrifice, he renews the fires. And along with renewing the fires, the sacrificer renews himself, and along with the sacrificer, his house and *pashus*. The redemption of his self (by offering the animal substitute) is for his longevity. For while he is sacrificing, the fires of the sacrificer hunger for meat. They turn their attention to the sacrificer himself; they long for the sacrificer. People cook meat taken at random in various other fires, but these (sacrificial fires) look for no other meat than that of him to whom they (the fires) belong. He who sacrifices with the animal sacrifice redeems himself— a male for a male. For the *pashu* is a male, and the sacrificer is a male. This meat is the best food. He becomes the eater of the best food.[46]

In this passage, there is a frank recognition that, according to the principles of Vedic ritualism itself, the sacrifice (or, more exactly, the sacrificial fire) anticipates the sacrificer himself as the victim: the fires 'long for the sacrificer'. And the animal stand-in, as it is again quite frankly recognized in the text, is a ransom for the life of the sacrificer.[47] Hubert and Mauss, as pointed out above, make this role of the victim that on which the communication between the sacred and profane turns:

> The destructive consequences of the rite partly explain this strange procedure. If the religious forces are the very principle of the focus of

life, they are themselves of such a nature that contact with them is a fearful thing for the ordinary man . . . That is why between these powers and himself he interposes intermediaries, of whom the principal is the victim. If he involved himself in the rite to the very end, he would find death, not life. The victim takes his place. It alone penetrates into the perilous domain of sacrifice, it dies there, and indeed it is there in order to die. The sacrifier [= sacrificer] remains protected: the gods take the victim instead of him. *The victim redeems him.*[48]

The sacrifice *is* a sacrifice, and not a suicide (or a 'murder' of the sacrificer by the fire), because of this displacement and replacement made possible by the substitute victim.

In yet another narrative concerning the types and relative ranking of the sacrificial victims, the familiar hierarchical order—from man, the highest form of *pashu*, to the goat, the lowest on the scale—is reiterated. The enumeration appears in the course of relating how the quality that constitutes all of these animals as worthy of sacrifice entered into and then left them, creating in its wake new but defective forms of each. In this text, however, we are also introduced to another component of the Vedic theory of sacrifice and substitution. For although it is clear that the *pashus* are hierarchically ranked, the lowest on the hierarchical ladder is also said here to be the victim most often used, and in some ways, the best victim:[xi]

> The gods offered man as sacrificial victim. Then the sacrificial quality passed out of the offered man. It entered the horse. Then the horse became fit for sacrifice and they dismissed him whose sacrificial quality had passed out of him. He [the former man, now devoid of the sacrificial quality] became a defective man (*kimpurusha*).[xii] They offered the horse, and the sacrificial quality passed out of the offered horse. It entered the cow . . . It [the former horse] became the wild *bos guarus* (*gauramriga*). They offered the bull . . . The sacrificial quality entered

---

[xi] Centuries later, this identification of the 'easiest' with the 'best' became an argument in both devotional and Tantric Hinduism. (See 'The Concept of Heresy.') But it would certainly be unwise to assert that the latter simplification, designed to appeal to all sorts of worshipper, can be derived from the hierarchical principles of the Vedic ritual reasoning. It is, rather, virtually an inversion of Vedic principles.

[xii] Various translations have been offered for the *kimpurusha*, ranging from 'monkey' or 'dwarf' to 'savage' or 'mock-man' (for which see Eggeling's note on SB 1.2.3.9), or 'horizontal androgyne', half equine and half human (Doniger O'Flaherty, *Women, Androgynes*, 216 and 309). It seems probable, however, that in Vedic texts the term *kimpurusha* (or *kinnara*) refers to tribal people.

the ram . . . It [the former bull] became the *bos gavaeus* (*gavaya*). They offered the ram . . . The sacrificial quality entered the goat . . . It [the former ram] became the camel. It [the sacrificial quality] stayed the longest in the goat; therefore the goat is the *pashu* most often used [as sacrificial victim]. They offered up the goat, and it (the sacrificial quality) passed out of the goat. It entered this (earth), and therefore this (earth) became fit for sacrifice. They dismissed him whose sacrificial quality had passed out of him. He [the former goat] became the wild *sharabha*.[xiii] These *pashus* whose sacrificial quality had passed out of them became unfit for sacrifice. Therefore one should not eat them.[49]

The curious fact, and the one that the theorists have not sufficiently prepared us for, is that in this myth the least 'excellent' of the *pashus*, the goat, is presented as not only the one 'most often used' but also the one most saturated with the quality that constitutes a sacrificial victim as such.

This peculiar virtue of the least desirable and hierarchically most inferior victim is corroborated in other texts as well. One, for example, distinguishes the goat by claiming that it possesses the essences of all the other (and hierarchically superior) *pashus*—thus turning on its head the earlier cited text which claimed, in accord with the expected, that man, the highest *pashu*, encompasses all other victims:

> In this *pashu* [the goat] is the form of all *pashus*. The form of man [incorporated in the goat] is what is hornless and bearded, for man is hornless and bearded. The form of the horse is what possesses a mane, for the horse possesses a mane. The form of the bull is what is eight-hoofed, for the bull has eight hoofs [four cloven hoofs]. The form of the ram is what possesses ram hoofs, for the ram possesses ram hoofs. The form of the goat is the goat. Thus, when he offers this [goat], he offers all those *pashus*.[50]

The least worthy animal substitute is here said to recapitulate all members of the class of substitutes. Nor does this process of concentrating the sacrificial quality into lower and more easily expendable objects in the category stop with the goat.

When, according to the myth, the sacrificial quality finally left the goat after its longish residency, 'it entered this earth. They searched for it by digging. They found it as those two, rice and barley. Thus even now they find those two by digging.' And further, these lowly victims, these

---

[xiii] A kind of deer; later, a mythical beast with eight legs.

vegetable '*pashus*', are said to 'possess as much potency as all the sacrificed *pashus* would have'.[51] A variant tells much the same story:

> They follow it [the sacrificial essence] into this [earth]; it, being followed, became rice. When they offer the rice cake in the animal sacrifice, [they do so thinking,] 'May our sacrifice be done with a *pashu* possessing the sacrificial quality; may our sacrifice be done with a fully constituted *pashu*.' His sacrifice becomes one done with a *pashu* possessing the sacrificial quality; the sacrifice of one who knows this becomes one done with a fully constituted *pashu*. When the rice cake [is offered], it is indeed a *pashu* which is offered up. Its stringy chaff, that is the hairs; its husk is the skin; the flour is the blood; the small grains are the flesh; whatever is the best part [of the grain] is the bone. He sacrifices with the sacrificial quality of all *pashus* who sacrifices with the rice cake.[52]

How are we to understand these claims for the lowest *pashus*—the very lowest being no more than simple vegetables—as the recapitulation and apparent equal of the highest sacrificial victims? It would seem that here the hierarchical order of things has been overturned and rendered meaningless. Indeed, in the same text in which the *pashus* are enumerated, and sacrificed, 'in hierarchical succession according to their relative excellence',[53] it is also declared that the five 'all should be the same, they all should be equal, for all these are the same, all these are equal, in that they are called "Agnis", in that they are all called "food"; because of that they are the same, because of that they are equal'.[54]

What are we to make of this apparent contradiction? On the one hand, the goat is not equal to the other *pashus*; on the other hand, the goat is said to be not only their equal but, indeed, in some sense the best of all victims. But rather than the inversion of a hierarchical order of mutually resembling entities, what we encounter here is a feature of that very system. For if there is no question that the substitute in Vedism is not the full equal of the original, it is also recognized that the original, more often than not, is wholly inaccessible. The inaccessibility of the original does not logically make the goat equal, let alone better; but it does make its use inevitable. And in order to justify this unavoidable reality, the texts simply *say* that the goat is just as good or—on the principle that one might as well be hung for a sheep as for a lamb, as it were—even better. Here is another example of unavoidable ritual obfuscation; we will encounter still others before the end of the argument.

We have seen that sacrifice as a whole is but a replica of cosmic processes quite out of reach of direct human control. We have also seen that the best victim (the deity and/or the sacrificer himself) is precisely the one that cannot be used in the sacrifice if it is really to remain a 'sacrifice' and not a crime. Yet another example of this phenomenon of the inaccessibility of what should be used in sacrifice—an inaccessibility that thereby necessitates a substitution—is the employment of the Putika plant and others in place of the Soma plant.[55] This substitution, already allowed in the earliest Vedic texts,[56] may have been required because the original Soma was unknown, or often unavailable, or possibly never existed at all.[xiv] Soma became a kind of transcendent prototype early on; in this case, as in others, both the 'original' and the 'substitute' were counterparts of an inaccessible substance.

Extolling the substitute as the 'equal' of the original is, one might say, a stratagem for constituting it as a proper substitute. So it is that, according to the ritual texts, a replacement is to be treated just as the original would have been. All the characteristic features, and all the preparatory rites that make the substance fit for sacrifice, are transferred to the substitute.[57] The mantras recited for the original also remain unchanged when there is a substitute: references in the prescribed verse to the original (e.g. 'Soma' or 'goat') are kept even when a substitute is being used (e.g., Putika for Soma, or a rice of barley cake for a goat).[58]

But while the substitute thus comes to function as if it were the original, the fact that it is a substitute and not the original is never forgotten. If the replacement for an original should for some reason become unusable in the course of the performance of the sacrifice, the secondary substitution should be made on the basis of its resemblance to the original, and not on the basis of a similarity to the substitute.[59] 'There can be no substitute for a substitute,' as S.C. Chakrabarti notes.[60] This point may constitute a Vedic exception to Girard's general rule. In this theory of sacrificial substitution, it will be recalled, the 'ritual substitute' stands in for a 'surrogate victim' or scapegoat which is itself a substitute for a 'real victim.' The Vedic rule, by prohibiting substitutes for substitutes, seems to disallow Girard's formula.

Substitution in Vedic ritualism, in any event, is regarded as something of a necessary evil. While the texts make it clear that the ritualists know how a perfect sacrifice would be done, they also realize that such perfection is out of reach in rituals performed by human beings. The important thing,

---

[xiv] Wasson and Doniger conclude that the Soma was originally a mountain mushroom called the fly agaric, which eventually became inaccessible to the ritualists as they moved away from the Himalaya. That an 'original' Soma never existed at all is a speculation that has not been put forward by Indologists, and perhaps deserves consideration.

however, is that the sacrifice continue to be performed, even if it is a mere facsimile of the genuine article. And so, the texts declare, *nitya* or obligatory sacrifices may be done with any number of substitutions, as long as they are done: 'Thus, with a root, some fruit, honey or meat, the obligatory sacrifices are to be performed continually. And [thereby] one does not interrupt the obligatory sacrifices.'[61]

We may be here observing, by the way, one of the early roots of the later Hindu theory of *apad dharma*,[xv] where the normal duties of the various castes are suspended in 'times of distress' or 'times of emergency'. Indeed, the laws of dharma and the laws of ritual are both extremely complex, detailed, and demanding; perhaps for this very reason the law-makers provided various escape hatches to allow for their all-too-human frailty and the vagaries of life. Substitutions may be made before beginning an obligatory sacrifice, and the reasons for doing so include, as in the case of *apad dharma*, various exigencies in times of distress or the unavailability of certain required materials.[xvi] Or they may be made after the sacrifice has already been started (e.g., when certain of the necessary materials have become spoiled, lost, or otherwise rendered unusable).[62]

Substitution in the Vedic ritual texts entails not only a subsequent assumption of equivalency (making the best of a bad situation, the substitute is treated in the ritual as if it were the original), but a process of *simplification*: the replacement is in every case a simplified, more easily attainable, less expensive version of the original. In all instances, the chain of acceptable substitutes moves from the most complex, highly valued and rare, to the simpler, less costly and more common. Such chains always end with the *minimally acceptable*. And this is precisely what is assumed in and lies behind those Vedic texts that speak of the 'identification' between the lower and the higher.

Furthermore, this sort of minimalism presented as equivalency is not simply a quirk of one aspect of the sacrifice but, rather, is a frequently encountered aspect of Vedic ritualism. The presentation of the smaller, the less adequate and the abbreviated as the 'equal' of the larger, the fully appropriate and the unabridged is an integral feature of the philosophy of

---

[xv] See 'Eating Karma' and 'Why Should a Brahmin?'

[xvi] The 'times of distress' that may preclude the performance of the Agnihotra are the times when there is a disturbance within the whole country, when one is afflicted with disease, when one is away on the journey, living at a teacher's house, when there are unfavourable conditions of place, time and materials, or when there are 'circumstances in which other things are unavailable'. See, e.g., BSS 29.8.

hierarchical resemblance that underlies the whole Vedic ritual system; and, indeed, one might even more generally say that the whole of ritual symbolism is also founded on such a notion. Claims of equivalency between sacrifices of clearly different hierarchical values, for example, are frequently made. We have already encountered ritual substitutes for the sacrifice of a thousand-year duration, and in a real sense all Vedic sacrifices were substitutes for hypothetical and prototypical cosmic rituals. The phenomenon of 'equivalency', when it deals with sacrifices within the realm of human possibility, most often takes the form of 'equating' lesser rituals to the Soma sacrifice. [63]

Vedic resemblance, in sum, allows for basically two different kinds of substitutions, two kinds of ritual condensations, both of which entail a kind of synecdochic reductionism (whereby a part of the whole represents the whole), but differ as to what kind of part is made to represent the whole. The first type of this synecdoche, which is readily understandable in hierarchical terms, is the encompassment of the condensed essences of the lesser within the greater—a condensation *upward*, so to speak. We have observed above such a claim for the human victim, which is said to encompass within it all other *pashus*; a similar claim is made for the Soma sacrifice, which is supposed to contain within it all other sacrifices, both the lower and the higher.[64] Elsewhere the Soma sacrifice is said to be the 'the most perfect' (*sampannatama*) of all Vedic rituals on account of its all-encompassing nature.[65] Other rituals are similarly advertised. The rites within the ritual that builds the fire-altar, the Agnicayana, are assimilated to all the rituals of the Vedic repertoire, and thus 'he obtains all the sacrifices with the Agnicayana'.[66] The Rajasuya (consecration ritual) has the same capacity: 'He who offers the Rajasuya envelopes all sacrificial rituals.'[67] Such great rituals make their claim to superiority in part by virtue of the fact that they encompass within them the condensed kernels of all other Vedic sacrifices.[68]

The second form of condensation within Vedic resemblance is less obviously in harmony with hierarchical presuppositions, and is less often accounted for in theoretical discussions about sacrifice and substitution. This is a condensation *downward* of the essences of the superior which are then reprised within inferior 'equivalents'. Claims of equivalency between 'great' prototypes and their condensed counterparts can, however, also be explicated in terms of hierarchical resemblance. They serve to unite Vedic ritualism from top to bottom, and vice versa. Such homologies are not intended to *collapse distinctions*, but rather to *strengthen connections* between interrelated entities and phenomena. In this system, even the smallest and relatively weakest may function as a resembling counterpart to the greatest and most complete. The inferior is not here regarded as an *equivalent replacement* for, but rather only as a *condensed representative* of, its superior relative within a class.

The Vedic texts, then, are a rich lode of data on sacrifice and substitution. There is, first, a recognition among the authors of these texts that the act of sacrifice is essentially a substitution for a prototypical, cosmic act that humans cannot precisely reduplicate but can only more or less adequately replicate. Second, there is also an admission that sacrifice is an act of displacement of violence onto a substitute victim that prevents the real victim of the sacrificial ideology, the sacrificer and/or deity, from suffering the consequences of the sacrificial ideal. Third, the Vedic material also exemplifies the confusion of identities necessary to the sacrificial operation and to the series of substitutions integral to sacrifice. The sacrifice as a whole, the deity, the sacrificer, the animal and the vegetable victims are all thoroughly conflated.

But, fourth and most importantly, the Vedic 'science of ritual' also emphasizes that hierarchical distinctions are never lost in the process of sacrificial conflations and surrogations. Sacrificial substitution is guided, and indeed made possible, by ontological and metaphysical resemblance; but the difference between prototypes and counterparts, and between counterparts of differing degrees of resemblance to the prototypical original, is never forgotten or denied.

SACRIFICE AND SUBSTITUTION IN HINDUISM

These many varieties of religious substitutions in the Vedic texts are themselves 'simplified' and reduced in later Hinduism in two basic ways that then serve as justifications for new Hindu practices.

The first of these is the argument by necessity. As we have seen, the Vedic texts describe substitutions of a most practical sort: if one could not for some reason obtain a certain substance, another could be used in its place. The Veda itself came to be regarded as, on the one hand, something that *could be* used as a substitute and, on the other, something for which there *had to be*, by necessity, a substitute. Thus, the Veda, in the concrete form of a manuscript or printed text, could be treated as a physical object of veneration within a temple, the sacred scripture functioning in this way as a kind of stand-in for an image of the deity. Since, however, the content of the text has long been unknown to all but a small minority of Hindus, and is largely irrelevant to Hindu doctrine and practice, other scriptures that claimed to be simplified versions of the Veda were by necessity substituted for the original.[69]

Further, the ritual described in the Veda also came to be regarded as an inaccessible original. In later Hinduism the mere *recitation* of the Veda, with or without comprehension of meaning, is regarded as the simplified equivalent of the actual performance of a Vedic sacrifice.[70] Indeed, in a sense it might be said that all subsequent Hindu ritual is a substitute for the Vedic sacrifice; Hinduism is, from this point of view, a necessary substitution for a religion rendered impossible by the decline of human ability in the Kali Yuga or Dark Age.[xvii] Hinduism, in other words, might be regarded as a gigantic exercise in *apad dharma*, a way of proceeding in an 'emergency'— the Kali Yuga.

One may view sacrifice in the history of post-Vedic Indian religion not so much as a ritual act or set of acts but rather as a category that acts to provide explanatory power, traditional legitimacy and canonical authority in Indian history.[71] Sacrifice is perhaps one of only two such categories which can perform such a canonical function in Hindu religious life, the other being the closely related category, Veda.

Vedic sacrifice thus provides a basic category that Hinduism inherits and continues to cherish—but not always uncritically. Where in Vedism all sacrificial substitution is justified on the grounds of necessity, in Hinduism at least some substitutions are rationalized on an ethical basis. This is the second form of the justification of Hindu beliefs and practices, the argument by morality. Thus, while in Vedic ritual texts, the vegetable offerings may have to serve as the substitute victim because of, say, economic necessity, in Hinduism offerings of rice and barley are claimed to be *better* than those of animals, because they avoid the sin of killing.[xviii]

Not only was the sacrifice of animals discontinued in upper-caste Hindu temples, the entire mythology supporting that ritual was turned on its head. The Epics and Puranas contain Hindu myths in which the Vedic concept of the sacrificial victim as symbolic of the sacrificer, or of the god, or of both, was not ignored but, on the contrary, was taken so literally that it called the Vedic hand, as it were, and revealed the hidden deception inherent in the symbolic identifications. Two striking myths of this genre illustrate this assertion, the first very well known to Hindus throughout the ages as well as to scholars of Hinduism, and the second rather obscure in both Hindu and academic circles.[72]

[xvii] See 'The Concept of Heresy'.
[xviii] See 'The Ambivalence of Ahimsa'.

The myth of the sacrifice of Daksha enacts a new fantasy, a new paradox of sacrifice:

> Daksha had unwillingly given his daughter Sati in marriage to the god Shiva. One day, Daksha performed a sacrifice to which he invited all his daughters and sons-in-law and grandchildren, but he did not invite Shiva or Sati. When Shiva refused to attend the sacrifice, since he had not been invited, Sati insisted on going there without him. After she arrived, she rebuked the sages who were there, but Daksha continued to revile Shiva and to look upon Sati with hate. In anger and humiliation, Sati killed herself by burning her body in the fire of her own power of yoga.
>
> When Shiva learned of this, he tore out a clump of his matted hair, from which a horrible demon was born. He instructed the demon to burn up the sacrifice of Daksha and all who were there. The demon and his demonic throng seized the sacrifice, which had taken the form of a wild animal to flee, and beheaded it. They mutilated the other gods, desecrated the goddesses, and polluted the sacrificial fire with excrement and filth. Then the demon found Daksha hiding in terror behind the altar; he dragged him out, tore off his head, and cast it into the fire into which oblations were placed.
>
> The gods went to Shiva and praised him, begging him to restore Daksha and all the others, and promising to give him a share in the sacrifice. Shiva restored them all, giving Daksha the head of a goat, the sacrificial animal. Daksha arose and rejoiced. Though he had hated Shiva in the past, his mind was now clear. He praised Shiva, who gave Daksha permission to complete his sacrifice, in which a full share was given to Shiva.[73]

The 'theoretical' identification of the sacrificer and the victim hypothesized by our theorists, and the all-too-demanding expectation, discussed in the Vedic ritual texts, that the sacrificer will offer himself, is literally realized and enacted in this myth. Because Daksha is both the victim and the sacrificer, when Shiva beheads Daksha he simultaneously ruins the sacrifice (by injuring the sacrificer) and accomplishes the sacrifice (by injuring the victim). Moreover, the oft postulated identity of the priest and the god is also actualized literally here: Shiva himself (or rather, his *surrogate*, the demon) performs the act of immolation. The 'sacrifice of Daksha' is a theological pun (in English as in Sanskrit: *Daksha-yajna*), a sacrifice that Daksha thinks is 'by' Daksha but that he comes to learn is 'made of' Daksha when he substitutes for the sacrificial beast.

Some myths, such as the Brahmana myth of Shunahshepha, establish the paradigm of the sacrifice of an animal or a vegetable through the rejection of human sacrifice: a human is slated to be sacrificed as a surrogate for the animal victim (that is in itself a surrogate for the human sacrificer), and this sacrifice is at the last minute prevented.[xix] The myth of Daksha is a reversal of such a myth. Its narrative begins at a time when animal sacrifice had long been established, and then moves back to the primitive time (which might have never really existed at all) when human sacrifice had not yet come to be replaced by animal sacrifice; the myth moves behind the symbolic sacrifice of a goat to the actual sacrifice of the sacrificer.

The myth of Daksha demystifies the mystification of the Vedic sacrificial ritual; it lifts the curtain of liturgy to expose the trick trapdoors and two-way mirrors of the enacted metaphor. What happens to Daksha is not what happens to the ordinary worshipper. For when the sacrificer identifies himself with the victim, as he does explicitly in this as in many if not all sacrifices, he does not mean that he is *really* the victim; after all, the victim gets killed, but he doesn't. By actually sacrificing Daksha, Shiva reminds him (and the hearer/reader of the myth) that the victim in the ritual is merely a surrogate for the sacrificer. Unlike the ordinary worshipper, Daksha gets caught up in the literal dramatization of the metaphor, or rather the collapse of the metaphor, in a ritual that entirely deconstructs its own symbolism: in Daksha's sacrifice, the victim does not 'stand for' the sacrificer; he *is* the sacrificer.

By making the ritual literal rather than symbolic, the myth about the ritual totally inverts it; what happens here is what is always supposed to happen but never does happen, never should happen, and, one might say, never *can* happen in an actual sacrifice. Only at the end, when the goat's head is used in place of Daksha's head, does the myth re-approach what happens in an actual ritual. In this way, the myth of Daksha demythologizes the ritual by imaginatively realizing the symbolic identifications that are essential to the efficacy of the ritual operation only insofar as they remain symbolic.

THE VEDIC HORSE SACRIFICE DECONSTRUCTED

There are other examples of this demystification of the sacrificial ritual in Indian mythology, other explorations of what happens when sacrificial ideology becomes real. In one of these, the myth collapses together not the

---

[xix] The Biblical story of Abraham and Isaac offers a strong parallel.

victim and the sacrificer but the victim and the recipient of the sacrifice, the god.

In the Vedic horse sacrifice,[xx] the slaughtered stallion was said to 'be' both the sacrificing king (to whom the stallion transferred his powers) and the god Prajapati.[74] A ritually consecrated stallion was killed after a chariot race; the chief queen then pantomimed copulation with the stallion, to the accompaniment of verses (spoken by priests) which include a lot of obscene banter about the size and character of the horse's phallus.[75] The queen acts as an intermediary who transfers to the king the seed of the stallion, and with it the royal and magical powers of the stallion.[76] Even the liturgical texts themselves regarded this ritual as obscene and therefore prescribe a 'perfumed' verse to be recited at the end, to wash out the mouths of the participants.[77] (Brihaspati, author of the Charvaka heresy,[xxi] is said to have mocked the Vedic ritual in which 'the sacrificed wife takes the phallus of the horse.'[78])

Georges Dumézil noted that the Indians were embarrassed by the obscenity of the horse sacrifice and that this embarrassment led to its desuetude.[79] Dumézil remarked upon the association of the Indian horse with virility,[80] and noted that the ancient sacrificial texts insisted that no part of the horse should be mutilated (hence the killing by suffocation). Willibald Kirfel asserted that the Vedic horse was originally killed by being beheaded with a slaughtering knife,[81] perhaps because death by this method produces an erection, which (the accompanying text says) the stallion should have.[82] The presence of the several queens introduced into the Indian ritual represented not merely a sexual factor but a political factor, the jockeying for favour among the queens that became a metaphor for political intrigue, 'co-wife' (sa-patni) being a synonym, in Sanskrit, for 'enemy'. The politics of sex are matched by the eroticism of political power.

When Ralph T.H. Griffith translated the texts of the ashvamedha into English in 1899, he left out the episode of the queen and the stallion,[83] and he remarked: 'This and the following nine stanzas are not reproducible even in the semi-obscurity of a learned European language.'[84] That learned language was, of course, Latin, into which other lewd bits of Sanskrit were traditionally translated; when such passages were encountered in Latin texts, such as Catullus, they were simply left in Latin, in the midst of the

---

[xx] See 'The Ambivalence of Ahimsa' and 'The Mythology of Horses'.
[xxi] See 'The Concept of Heresy'.

English translation.[xxii] An eighteenth-century variant of the ritual does not mention the queen's copulation with the stallion, an omission that Dumézil suggests may be due to the fact that the text was edited by a canoness who 'purified' several episodes. The 'indecency' of the ancient rite may survive, however, Dumézil suggests, in another passage of the same eighteenth-century text, which tells the tale of a perverse king who killed a group of Brahmins for laughing when the queen's skirt was tossed up by the wind.[85]

Dumézil cites the post-Vedic myth of Indra ('who is rather a debauched god'), who 'one day took advantage of the occasion [of the horse sacrifice] and substituted himself, quite alive, for the dead stallion, lying with a certain queen whom he had taken a fancy to'. This is the story:

> Janamejaya was consecrated for the sacrifice, and his queen approached the designated stallion and lay down beside him, according to the rules of the ritual. But Indra saw the woman, whose limbs were flawless, and desired her. He himself entered the designated stallion and mingled with the queen. And when this tranformation had taken place, Indra said to the priest in charge of the sacrifice, 'This is not the horse you designated. Scram.'
>
> The priest, who understood the matter, told the king what Indra had done, and the king cursed Indra, saying, 'From today, Kshatriyas [the class of kings and warriors] will no longer offer the horse sacrifice to this king of the gods, who is fickle and cannot control his senses.' And he fired the priests and banished the queen. But then Vishvavasu, the king of the Gandharvas, calmed him down by explaining that Indra had wanted to obstruct the sacrifice because he was afraid that the king would surpass him with the merits obtained from it. To this end, Indra had seized upon an opportunity when he saw the designated horse, and had entered the horse. But the woman with whom he had made love in that way was actually Rambha, a celestial nymph; Indra had used his special magic to make the king think that it was his wife, the queen. The king of the Gandharvas persuaded the king that this was what had happened.[86]

Janamejaya is already familiar with shadow sacrifices, nightmare sacrifices; he had performed a surreal sacrifice of snakes, instead of horses, at the very beginning of the *Mahabharata*.[87] Here at the very end of the Epic, his sacrifice goes wrong in yet another way: he implicitly defies the god simply

---

[xxii] If the translators of *Catullus* had known Sanskrit, they might have translated those bits of *Catullus* into Sanskrit in revenge, but this does not seem to have happened.

by doing the extravagant sacrifice at all, which makes him the object of the god's envy, and then at the end he explicitly defies the god by excluding him from the sacrifice because the god has spoilt it by taking the form of the animal.

In Hindu mythology, Indra, the king of the gods, is one of several gods designated as the recipients of the horse sacrifice, but he is unique in that he is himself a performer of horse sacrifices, famed for having performed more horse sacrifices than anyone else and jealous of this pre-eminence. (He steals the sacrificial horse of King Sagara to prevent Sagara from surpassing his record.[88])[xxiii] He thus (unlike the usual human worshipper) combines the roles of sacrificer and recipient. In the story of Janamejaya's wife, Indra adds to these roles that of the victim.

MYTHS AS TRUTH–TELLING

The story of Janamejaya, which *ends* with an exclusion of the deity and a refusal to worship him, is thus in many ways an inversion of the story of Daksha, which *begins* with the exclusion of the god Shiva and ends with the promise that Daksha will in fact sacrifice to Shiva, after Shiva has both ruined and accomplished the sacrifice by making the sacrificer take the form of the animal. The epilogue of the Janamejaya story, in which the king is persuaded that it was all an illusion, is a common device used to undo what has been done in a myth, a kind of godhead *ex machina*. But it is also a recapitulation of precisely what the central episode of the myth has just done: it has revealed and unmasked the illusion implicit in the sacrifice, the illusion that the sacrificial horse, is in fact, the god Indra, and not merely a horse. Where the myth of Daksha reminds us that we would not like it if the *sacrificer* really did become the sacrificial animal, as the ritual texts say he does, the story of Janamejaya reminds us that we would not like it if the *god* really did become the sacrificial animal either, as the ritual texts also say he does.

These myths are hard-hitting exposés of substitution in sacrifice, demythologizing within the structure of mythical discourse the ritual assumption that the sacrificial animal is a surrogate for the worshipper (Daksha) or the god (Indra). It may appear paradoxical that myths, which live in the realm of the imagination, should provide the tools to uncover the illusory nature of rituals, which actually happen. But of course it is *all* taking place in the imagination: the Hindu myths are not actually dealing

---

[xxiii] See 'The Submarine Mare'.

with the Vedic ritual at all, but merely demystifying the Vedic *myths* about the Vedic ritual by *imagining* what ritual ideology would be like if realized, mythically. Here, as so often, the myth, in fact, tells the truth about a painful paradox that other social forms—in this case, ritual—have had to keep in the dark. These myths move back behind the Vedic sacrifice to a mythical time in which the sacrificial animal was *really*, not just symbolically, something more than just an animal.

Texts such as the myths of Daksha and Janamejaya represent moments when a tradition says two different things at once: 'We used to do that, but now we do this. We used to do sacrifice, but now we don't anymore; we are, therefore, better than the old religion that we have evolved out of. On the other hand, what we do now is essentially the same as what we did; what we do now is really sacrifice still, but a better kind of sacrifice.' Hindus, Buddhists and Jains all rejected the Vedic sacrifice, especially the animal sacrifice; but Hindus also dressed up their new doctrines and religious activities in the guise of the Vedic sacrifice. The previous sacrificial tradition was in this way made to appear as relatively inferior to newly revealed 'sacrifices'. But even anti-sacrificial traditions often found it necessary to call up the ancient category of sacrifice as a form of legitimation of the new in the guise of the old. New doctrines and practices were lent the air of archaic authority by being encoded in the vocabulary of sacrifice. Sacrifice, then, may function to conceptualize and articulate the new in terms of the old. The category serves to traditionalize innovations.

The rice cakes do not, in fact, so much replace the offering of animal flesh as supersede it. That is, in the earliest records of the ancient Vedic horse sacrifice, the killing of the stallion was accompanied by an offering of balls of rice. The sacrifice was thus ambivalent from the very start; it involved not only an animal surrogate for a human victim but also the substance that first complemented and ultimately came to replace that animal surrogate. Indeed, so intense is the symbolism linking the rice cake with the sacrificer that, already in the Vedic period, even the *symbol* could be repugnant: the Vedic texts state that one must not perform the twelve-day ceremony (involving the oblation of rice cakes) for another person, because by eating the victim—in this case, the rice cake—one would be eating the sacrificer's flesh.[89] The confusing complexity of such transformations was beautifully, if perhaps unconsciously, expressed by Evans-Pritchard, when he spoke of his intention to limit his discussion of sacrifice to blood sacrifice, but then remarked: 'On the other hand, I include as coming within the sense of bloody sacrifice offerings of cucumbers, for they are consecrated and immolated as surrogates for oxen.'[90]

CONCLUSION

We have seen how Vedic ritualism and the Hindu myths about the Vedic sacrifice explore the mysteries of sacrifice: the *mysterium fascinans et tremendum* of an act that is separated from profane, criminal acts of suicide and murder only by a convenient compromising of its own ideological principles. Sacrifice, we have observed, is an act that is always a shadow of itself. It is always an act of surrogation, an imitation of an ideal, a counterpart of an unrealizable prototype. Furthermore, it is an act whose own claims for itself, when taken literally and seriously, become the nightmares of mythology. Sacrifice, in sum, is paradoxically an act that becomes indistinguishable from suicide, murder and deicide only when it substitutes for its own ideal form.

In one sense, then, sacrificial substitution is absolutely necessary for the integrity of the category 'sacrifice'. It is substitution, in other words, that defines sacrifice as sacrifice. Substitution makes sacrifice possible: the surrogate victim that stands in for the sacrificer and the deity redeems the act from criminality. Sacrifice is thus an act that necessarily compromises its own principles through substitution. Further substitutions—substitutes for substitutes—are similarly compromises, and are treated as such in traditions like Vedism; that is, surrogates, necessary though they may be, are regarded as inferior to originals (which are unattainable or undesirable). Substitutions in sacrifice may always be necessary; but, making the best of a bad situation, the substitute may also come to be valued higher than the original as substitution by necessity is recast as substitution by morality.[xxiv] The inversion of the worth of the vegetable oblation as one moves from Vedism to Hinduism—from the hierarchically inferior to the ethically superior—is one case in point of such a phenomenon.

The Hindu myths about the Vedic sacrifice argue with a paradoxical logic, looking back on their sources in a self-deceptive way. The tradition is saying, 'It is a rice cake, and therefore a moral improvement on human or animal sacrifice, but it is also flesh, with all the power of the sacrifice that it came to replace; we are doing the same thing, but we are doing it differently.' And this phenomenon might be generalizable far beyond the Indian context, and far beyond the context of the fortunes of sacrifice in Indian history.

[xxiv] See 'Together Apart'.

THE SCRAPBOOK OF UNDESERVED SALVATION:
THE *KEDARA KHANDA* OF THE *SKANDA PURANA*[1]

THE SCRAP PURANA

Scholars of Hinduism often assume that the Sanskrit Puranas (composed between c. 250 and 1350 CE) were made, like camels in the old joke, by a non-communicating committee, or that, like the elephants in another old joke, they continued to be perceived blindly by different members of the tradition as a composite of several distinct, non-communicating sorts of texts, to which anyone was entitled to add a snake here (the trunk, a hymn of praise), a rope there (the tail, a local folktale) and so forth. And indeed there is some truth in this, as in most wrong ideas. Certainly the authors of the Puranas did not share our respect for the integrity of an inherited written script. For one thing, they worked as often from oral as from written texts, and, for another, their tradition was one that encouraged improvisation.[i]

In this world of ever-shifting Puranic sands, the *Skanda Purana* is surely the shiftiest, or perhaps the sandiest, of all. The longest and most sprawling of all the Puranas, though it was usually grouped with the Maha- rather than the Upa-Puranas, it was regarded even by the native Indian tradition as a 'scrap-bag'; its name forms a pun to this effect in Tamil, where it is the 'scrap' Purana (*Kantal-Puranam*). Its open-endedness has proved most useful to Indian authors through the ages; whenever the author of a Purana (called a Pauranika) came upon a story that seemed to be, or ought to be, old, but did not seem to have any known provenance, he could remark, without fear of contradiction, 'It's in the *Skanda Purana*,' just as family members assure one another, when looking for a misplaced object, 'It's probably in that old closet in the attic.' Many a naive Indologist (myself

---

[i] See 'Impermanence and Eternity'.

included) has wasted days searching in the extant editions of the *Skanda Purana* for stories said to be there, but not there now. I got my own back once, however, by resorting to this ploy myself when, having misplaced the source of a quotation that I distinctly remembered copying out of some now irretrievable Puranic text, I finally decided to use it anyway and to attribute it to the *Skanda Purana*.[2]

Certainly, different parts of the *Skanda Purana* were added at different periods (even the formidable Ludo Rocher despairs of dating this text[3]), and divergent traditions, composed in increments over several centuries, were brought together in the present redactions. The text often betrays its chequered past, despite its constant attempts to integrate each new view. But this is its strength, not its weakness. The *Skanda Purana* is, in a very real sense, a *living* Purana, one of the few living Puranas still extant in Sanskrit, and certainly one of the most popular.[4] Why has it survived where other Puranas have become literary dinosaurs? Clearly, it has served someone's purposes, perhaps even several conflicting purposes. On the one hand, it has proved a means whereby the Sanskrit tradition could encompass rival traditions, could 'kill by embracing', as the saying goes. Or, to look at it from the other standpoint, it has been a door through which the local, vernacular Puranas could enter into the so-called mainstream tradition. It has enabled the vernacular tradition to legitimize itself by claiming to be a part of an infinitely expansible Sanskrit text.

The *Bhagavata Purana* represents a revolution in the Puranas, establishing bhakti over ritualism as a means to salvation.[5] The *Skanda Purana* goes one step further than the *Bhagavata* and surpasses bhakti itself. In this, the *Skanda* is a counter-revolutionary text, which undoes bhakti (or deconstructs it, to use the more modern word) by reabsorbing the *sthalapurana* traditions into the conservative ritualist tradition of the *Mahabharata*. Or, if you prefer, it revalidates Epic ritualism through a consistent reformulation of traditional Puranic myths. It also introduces into many traditional myths a cynical and feminist point of view that is, in its own quiet way, subversive.

PAURANIKAS AND INDOLOGISTS

We must not, therefore, follow most Sanskritists in regarding the *Skanda Purana* as not only authorless but mindless. The scraps were not thrown into the scrap bag without any consideration of their relevance to what was already in the bag. The divergent traditions were synthesized and arranged in a new plan devised by the compiler of this one text.[6]

We generally believe, and not without reason, that the mission of

Indologists is rather different from the mission of the authors of the texts that they study. Indologists comb through the texts of ancient India in search of pieces of a new puzzle that they hope to construct (and, perhaps, to solve) from the fragments of the rather different, often insoluble, puzzles posed by the texts themselves. And so we go about, snipping a few pieces from the *Rig Veda*, a few from the *Mahabharata*, and so forth, in order to produce our new Purana, our own monograph on 'Horses in Ancient India' or, more narrowly, 'Evidence for the Use of the Stirrup in Ancient India'. Naturally, our agendas are different from theirs; most basically, of course, they were usually composing texts related to worship, while we compose texts related to academic tenure or the narcissism of publication. But there are also a number of less obvious, more intellectual agendas that we as Indologists may very well share with the authors of the texts that we study.

THE *KEDARA KHANDA*

A case in point: the redactor of the *Kedara Khanda*[ii] (the first book of the first section, the *Maheshvara Khanda*, of the *Skanda Purana*[iii]) seems to me to have had an agenda very like that of many Indologists. That is, he sifted through the texts of his own tradition and selected those myths that seemed to him to have certain themes in common. And then, in retelling them, he added bits and pieces of his own interpretation to make their inherent correspondences more blatantly apparent and, in some cases, to use them in entirely new ways. This process could well stand as a mirror for the academic discipline of Indology. True, the author's plan is coloured by a devotional agenda—he is setting out to magnify his god, Shiva—but there, too, I wonder how far he is from the spirit of those anthropologists who regard the people among whom they do their fieldwork as 'their' tribe.

Other Puranas, of course, have unifying themes, though these are often of a more traditional character. For instance, many Puranas weave their

---

[ii] Rather than tackle the *Skanda Purana* as a whole in this brief essay, let me confine myself to the *Kedara Khanda*. We are justified, I think, in taking this book as a self-contained literary work.

[iii] Ludo Rocher confirms what has long been suspected, that the *Kedara Khanda* was composed at a time and place distinct from the other *Khandas* of the *Skanda Purana*, even from the other portions of the *Maheshvara Khanda*. Another text, also called the *Kedara Khanda* and said to be a part of the *Skanda Purana* (but not of the *Maheshvara Khanda*), was published by the same press (Bombay: Venkatesvara Steam Press). This is an entirely different work, much longer than the text that I am using here.

stories around the central theme of the place in which they were composed: all the great events of the mythical past are said to have taken place here.[iv] Or there may be a theme of pilgrimage: as the author moves through a sacred geography, he tells us what happened in each special place along the way.[v] Or there may be a genealogy: stories are told about each of the ancestors in a long line.[vi] Or, finally, there may be episodes in the biography of a single god. This last technique works best for gods who have quasi-human lives, like Krishna, but it is also done for other gods, including Vishnu and Shiva, whose life cycles, however supernatural, nevertheless touch down at many of the human rites of passage (birth, marriage, the occasional adultery, and, in some texts, even a kind of temporary death).

What is unusual about the first book of the *Skanda Purana* is that it seems to organize its stories about abstract themes, rather than a concrete person or a place; it has an intellectual agenda. The principle of organization is neither spatial (geographic) nor temporal (the life-story narrative), but thematic. One might have expected, from the title, some kind of geographical focus upon the temple of Kedaranatha in the Himalaya, said to be 'the highest . . . and coldest of the holy places'.[7] But this is not the case; the scope of the text, both in its sources and in its claims, is pan-Indian and often Vedic. Thus, instead of producing yet another local, self-aggrandizing *sthalapurana*, this text does what we always thought only Indologists did: it looks at its own mythological tradition, selects from it, rearranges it, and restructures it into a thematic essay.[vii]

It does this in two ways: it winds a set of old stories together into a new text, adding just enough to each story to make its point, and it adds new stories that are not found elsewhere. The text puts a particular spin on each tale that it retells, and that spin, picking up the impetus already present within the older story, like a good judo player, throws the separate stories together into an orchestrated constellation of new movement. The new stories add up to make a statement that will go on to be echoed in many vernacular texts: the grace granted to the 'accidental devotee' or 'immoral

[iv] This is particularly true of the so-called *sthalapuranas* of vernacular traditions (see Shulman, *Tamil Temple Myths*), but it also applies to several Sanskrit Puranas, or, more usually, sections of Sanskrit Puranas.

[v] This way of organizing myths is already found in the *Mahabharata*, which groups several cycles of stories around journeys to holy places.

[vi] There are the solar and lunar lineages of the great Puranas, but also the minor lineages of other Puranas.

[vii] See the appendix to this chapter for an outline of the contents of the *Kedara Khanda*.

or undeserving devotee' through the worship of the *lingam*, the symbol of the god Shiva.[viii] And the old stories are retold in a satirical and quasi-feminist vein. Both of these new projects involve major reversals of conventional moral expectations, positioning marginal figures (sinners, women) at the centre of the grace of God. Let us consider the two projects one by one.

THE UNDESERVING DEVOTEE OF THE *LINGAM*

The theme of the 'undeserving devotee' or 'accidental devotee' is not unique to the *Kedara Khanda*. It appears in the *Padma Purana*[8] and in the appended prologue to the *Shiva Purana*, in the story of Devaraja.[9] (The Devaraja story glorifies the text that tells it: it is by hearing the *Shiva Purana*, accidentally and without paying any attention to it, that Devaraja is saved from the consequences of his sins.) And it is common in vernacular texts, particularly in South India. But where most of the other texts tell just one story, often (like the Devaraja story) as a kind of extreme *phalashruti* (advertisement for the benefits of reading/hearing the work in question), the *Kedara Khanda* tells a number of interrelated stories of this genre and even uses it as a kind of armature on which to build the text as a whole.

The theme of the undeserving devotee implicitly repositions ritualism, apparently 'mindless' ritualism, over bhakti. It argues that feelings, emotions, intentions, do not count at all; that certain actions are efficacious in themselves in procuring salvation for the unwitting devotee. In this it mirrors another sort of bhakti, one that is, significantly, characteristic of the Shaiva Siddhanta philosophies of South India: the bhakti of the kitten, who goes limp to let god the mother cat pick him up by the scruff of the neck, in contrast with the bhakti of the baby monkey, who holds on tight to god the mother monkey.[ix]

But the accidental devotion of the *Kedara Khanda* is far from a return to Vedic ritualism. For knowledge (an essential criterion of Vedic ritualism[x]) does not count any more than emotion, in this line of argument; the actions have an automatic efficacy, like the elements of a magic formula or the words in a mantra. But the deity is not automatically compelled to respond; he (or, in the case of the goddess, she) is the one moved by emotion, moved by love, even unrequited love, for the unrepentant sinner.

[viii] See 'God's Body'.
[ix] See 'Zoomorphism'.
[x] See 'The Concept of Heresy'.

The particular inflection of this motif that is presented in the *Kedara Khanda*, the theme of 'great sinners who were saved from hell by an accidental act of *lingam* worship', incorporates (and reverses) an old story, told elsewhere, not of a sinner, but of a *good* man, a devotee of Shiva, who is saved from death (Yama) or Kala ('Time') by Shiva in the form of Yamantaka ('the ender of Yama') or Kalantaka ('the ender of Kala'). The *Bhagavata Purana* calls him 'Markandeya', and depicts him worshipping the *lingam*, from which Shiva emerges. Other Puranas call him Shveta and depict him, too, as worshipping the *lingam*, from which Shiva emerges to destroy Kala.[10] In yet other texts, however, Shveta is not worshipping the *lingam* at the critical moment, though he is still rescued by Shiva,[11] and this is also true of the *Kedara Khanda* version, which regards Kala as the master of Yama:

> King Shveta was, from birth, a virtuous king and a devotee of Shiva; he told the truth and ruled with dharma, and everyone in his kingdom was happy. No one grieved for the death of a son, and there was no disrespect and no murder, nor any poverty. Yama and Kala came to take him one day when he was worshipping Shiva. Then Shiva, the Destroyer of Kala, saw Kala, and he looked at Kala with his third eye and burnt him to ashes in order to protect his devotee. Shveta awoke from his meditation to see Kala burnt in front of him. He praised Shiva and asked him what had happened, and Shiva told him, 'Kala eats all creatures, and he came here to eat you in my presence and so I burnt him. You and I will kill evil men who violate dharma, heretics who wish to destroy people.' But Shveta said, 'This world behaves properly because of Kala, who protects and creates by destroying creatures. If you are devoted to creation, you should revive Kala, for without him there will be nothing.' Shiva did as his devotee suggested; he laughed and revived Kala with the form he had had. Then Kala praised Shiva the Destroyer of Kala, he who made Kama disembodied and destroyed the sacrifice of Daksha,[xi] and who pervades the universe with the form of the *lingam*. And Kala told his messengers, 'The devotees of Shiva, with their matted hair and rosaries and Shaiva names, wear the garb of Shiva. Even if they are parasites who terrify people, even if they are evil and do bad things, you must not bring them to my world [of death].' (32.4-96)

[xi] See 'Sacrifice and Substitution'.

Despite its general advocacy of *lingam* worship, the *Kedara Khanda* does not specify what sort of worship Shveta is engaged in at the moment when death comes for him. Instead, this text assimilates the killing of Yama to the burning and revival of Kama, which it has just narrated (*Kedara Khanda* 21.68-126; see below).

This not a tale of grace given to a sinner. On the contrary, it shares the old bhakti assumption (itself based upon the older Vedic assumption) that if you love god and serve him he will love you and serve you.[12] But within the body of narratives about sinful *bhaktas* we can note a crucial shift in the attitude to the virtue, or lack of it, of the devotee who is to be saved. (1) First comes the story of the good *bhakta*, a good man, a devotee of Shiva, whom Shiva saves from death. There are many other stories of this type,[13] in which the criterion (which Shveta embodies) is a combination of virtue and Shiva-bhakti. (2) Midway, the criterion shifts to virtue, with no reference to sectarian orientation, when Shiva proposes that, usurping the task of the now-defunct god of the dead, he and Shveta should punish evildoers and heretics (even, supposedly, evildoers who are also Shiva worshippers). (3) But then the evil *bhakta* is exonerated: the god of death is forced to spare all worshippers of Shiva, even if they are evildoers or evil-thinkers: heretics[xii] and liars too go to heaven if they worship Shiva [5.101]). Thus, the paradigmatic story of virtue rewarded is subtly twisted into a tale of (possibly virtueless) devotion rewarded.

Finally, in another story in the *Kedara Khanda*, we encounter a man who is neither good nor (consciously) a *bhakta*:

> A thief, who killed Brahmins, drank wine, stole gold and corrupted other men's wives, lost everything in a game of dice. That night, he climbed on the head of a Shiva-*lingam* and took away the temple bell [inadvertently ringing it]. At that moment, Shiva sent his servants from Kailasa to that temple. When the thief saw them, he wanted to run away from the head of the *lingam*, but Virabhadra, Shiva's servant, said, 'You fool, what are you afraid of? Shiva is pleased with you today.' And they put him in the heavenly car and brought him to Kailasa and made him a servant of Shiva (8.1-13).

The thief himself is unaware of the theological twist that makes him, as Shiva tells his servants, 'the best of all my devotees' (8.8). But the god saves him despite himself. The thief's brush with accidental bhakti does nothing at all to change him; presumably, he goes on dicing, womanizing and

---

[xii] See 'The Concept of Heresy'.

drinking until he dies. Although in some stories the accidental act of worship changes the worshipper, more often the sinners remain unreformed like this, and therefore go to heaven. For now the heaven of the god can accommodate not only all reformed sinners but even *unreformed* sinners, and, as we shall soon see, people of all classes.[xiii] Indeed, this heaven is *particularly* partial to unreformed sinners. This is a world of not only unlimited good but undeserved good, of what might be called accidental grace.

None of these sinners reforms as a result of his accidental encounter with the god; no one sees the light, or turns over a new page; all go on sinning until they die, presumably of syphilis, cirrhosis or impalement. But the mere encounter is enough to save them. You don't even have to know how to do the ritual, but you do it 'naturally', almost like the 'natural' (*sahaja*) acts of Tantric ritual. In this sense, at least, these stories present a Tantric argument for the efficacy of a ritual useful for sinners in the Kali Age.[xiv] The narratives seem counter-intuitive and were perceived as perverse by some subsequent Hindu commentators.

Three variants on this theme are collected together in a single chapter of the *Kedara Khanda*. The first story in the series is the tale of Indrasena:

> Indrasena was a king who was crazy about hunting, a cruel man who nourished his own life-breath by the life-breaths of others. He was a thief and an adulterer, a drunkard and Brahmin-killer, and a seducer of his guru's wife. When he died, Yama's messengers bound him and brought him to Yama, but then Yama rose, bowed his head to Shiva, reviled his own messengers, and set Indrasena free from his bonds. He promised to send him to glorious worlds, saying, 'For you are a great devotee of Shiva.' Indrasena said, 'I don't know Shiva. I've always been addicted to hunting.' Then Yama said, 'You always used to say (when hunting), 'Get that! [*ahara*]. Strike him! [*praharasva*]' [phrases containing 'Hara,' the name of Shiva]. And by the ripening of that karma you have been purified.' Then Yama's messengers took Indrasena to Shiva, who embraced him and made him his servant, named Chanda. (5.64-85)

Directly after this story we are told another brief vignette of accidental grace:

[xiii] See 'Together Apart'.
[xiv] See 'The Concept of Heresy'.

An evil thief was killed by the king's men. A dog came to eat him, and accidentally, unconsciously [*chaitanyena vina*], the dog's nails made the mark of Shiva's trident on the man's forehead. As a result, Rudra's messengers took him to Kailasa. (5.92-95)

The dog, instead of the sinner, performs an accidental act of worship; the three scratches of his nails, part of his foot, the lowest part of this lowest of creatures, form the triple lines of Shiva's trident (*trishula*). The dog who intends to eat the thief (and perhaps succeeds; the text does not say) unthinkingly blesses him.[xv]

The bard then tells another, longer story:

A Kirata [a mountaineer and hunter, regarded as a member of a Dalit caste], addicted to hunting, devoid of discrimination, harming living creatures, one day came upon a *lingam* in the forest when he was parched with thirst. He worshipped the *lingam* by spitting cheekfuls of water onto it and placing the flesh of wild animals on it with his left hand, and vowed to devote himself to heaven from that day forth. He, too, was translated to heaven, even before his death. There he took on the same form as Shiva, and the goddess laughed and said, 'He is certainly just like you, with your own form and movement and laughable qualities. But you are the only one that I serve.' When the Kirata heard what the goddess said, he immediately turned away his face, while Shiva was watching, and said, 'Forgive me, Shiva, and make me your doorkeeper.' And Shiva did. (5.111-97)

This story[xvi] makes a new point: the Kirata is not unconscious of his act of worship, but he is unconscious of the normal rules of worship. The gifts that he offers are hideously unclean from the traditional point of view, but Shiva accepts them in the spirit in which they are offered. The character of the Kirata resonates with one of the earliest and most famous myths of Shiva, the *Mahabharata* story of the combat between Arjuna and Shiva, when Shiva took the form of a Kirata, vanquished Arjuna, and then revealed himself and gave Arjuna the magic weapons that he sought.[14] This identification alerts us to one of the implications of the theme of accidental devotion: that, since the god himself is an outsider, violent and iconoclastic, he is partial to worshippers who are, as the goddess mockingly remarks,

[xv] See 'Dogs as Dalits'.
[xvi] Probably based upon the Tamil story of Kannappar in the *Periya Puranam*. See 'God's Body'.

like him. (The laughter of the goddess at Shiva's expense is a theme that we will encounter often in this text.)

Another undeserving devotee appears in the *Kedara Khanda*'s version of the Vaishnava story of the generous demon Bali.[xvii] The transformation is achieved not by making Bali, the arch Vishnu-worshipper, a Shiva-worshipper, but by giving him a former life as a Shiva-worshipper. Thus Bali's tale is supplemented by the tale of Kitava ('Rogue'), which forms a bridge between our basic theme—great sinners who were saved from hell by an accidental act of Shiva-worship—and a closely related theme—demons (*asuras*, anti-gods) who worshipped Shiva's *lingam* and usurped Indra's throne. There are two variants of Kitava's tale narrated in the *Kedara Khanda*.[15] Conflating the categories of '(human) sinner' and 'demon', Kitava both gets saved and usurps, and does one of them (the usurping) twice, once as the human sinner Kitava and once when he becomes reincarnate as the demon Bali. Here is the new episode, the episode of Kitava:

> In a former life Bali had been Kitava, and one day when he was bringing flowers and betel and sandalwood and so forth to his whore, running to her house, he had stumbled and fallen on the ground and passed out for a moment. An idea had occurred to him as he regained consciousness, as a result of his former karma and his great pain and misery: 'Let the perfume and flowers and so forth that fell on the ground be given to Shiva.' And as a result of that good deed, after his death when Yama's minions took him to hell, he won the place of Indra for a brief period, while Indra, suffering from Brahminicide, was in hiding.
>
> Indra and the other gods were miserable, but Kitava and his servants, delighting in the worship of Shiva, were very happy. Then Narada said to Kitava, 'Bring Indrani [Indra's wife] here.' But Kitava, the darling of Shiva, laughed and said, 'I should not speak to Indrani, or have anything to do with her, honoured sir.' And then he started to give things away; he gave Indra's elephant Airavata and the other things to Agastya and the other sages. But when the brief period allotted to him in heaven was over, the former master, Indra, returned to heaven, and Indrani rejoiced.
>
> Then the fool, Indra, said to Indrani, 'Did Kitava make love with you? Tell me truly.' The guiltless woman laughed and said to Indra, 'You think everyone else is just like you. Kitava is a noble person, free of passion, by the grace of Shiva.' When Indra heard her words he was ashamed and silent. But when he saw that Kitava had given away all his things, he went down to Yama and complained against him.

[xvii] See 'The Concept of Heresy'.

Yama said to Kitava, 'Giving is prescribed on earth, where actions bear fruit. But no one is supposed to give anything to anyone in heaven, you fool, and so you should be punished, because you have not behaved according to the textbooks.' But Yama's servant argued that all of Kitava's evil deeds had been burnt to ashes by the grace of Shiva and that, because of the greatness of his giving, Kitava did not belong in hell, and Indra returned in embarrassment to heaven. (18.52-116)

This story may be read as an embellishment of the story of Nahusha that appears in the text just before this one (15.61–89), for Nahusha falls from the position of Indra when he lusts after Indrani.

Most directly, the tale of Kitava is an expansion of the story of Bali, a demon who is punished for his excessive giving, a famous story that the text has just alluded to (18.41-44). But Kitava is not punished for his excessive giving; on the contrary, Yama's servant expressly says that Kitava obtained his position through giving, and Kitava merely withdraws when his term in office is up. Though Kitava never actually worships the *lingam*, the flowers and incense that he 'dedicates' to Shiva on the doorstep of the brothel (the literal *limen* like the liminal door of the temple) would normally be placed on the *lingam*. And bhakti, even accidental bhakti, renders all conventional power struggles irrelevant.

The objections that Yama makes elsewhere to the emptiness of hell as a consequence of the democratization of bhakti are not only not addressed here but inverted: it is Yama who persuades Indra that Kitava should not go to hell. Yama's objections are explicitly stated, and answered, in a later part of the text, where what amounts to accidental bhakti poses a problem that is then inverted to make it not the problem but the solution:

When sinners merely looked at Skanda they became purified, even if they were the most evil dog-cookers. Yama took Brahma and Vishnu and went to Shiva and praised him and said, 'By the greatness of the sight of Skanda all people are going to heaven, even if they are evil. What should I do about distinguishing between what should and should not be done? For those who are truthful and peaceful, free of lust and anger, virtuous sacrificers, are going to the same place that all the dog cookers and violators of dharma are going to. They have all left my place; what is there for me to do now?' Shiva replied, 'People who have evil within them often do meritorious deeds, and their purification takes place in the mind-and-heart. Women and fools and Shudras and the lowest dog cookers are born in evil wombs because of their previous lives, but nevertheless, by fate and their former deeds, they become purified human beings. Do not be amazed at this . . .' And Yama became enlightened. (31.2-77)

Looked at from the point of view not of the worshipper but of the god of hell, universal salvation is a problem.[16] Here, Yama is simply talked out of it. But, as if unsatisfied by this pat solution, the author is then, finally, inspired to tell the story that is the granddaddy of the genre of the devotee saved from hell, the story of Shveta, the *virtuous* devotee, with which we began this analysis. The text then immediately reverts to the sinful and accidental devotee, and tells the final, and by far the most elaborate, story in this series, the penultimate story in the whole book:

Once upon a time there was a certain Kirata named Chanda [Fierce], a man of cruel addictions. He killed fish with a net and various wild animals with arrows, and in his fury he killed birds and Brahmins, too,[xviii] and his wife was just like him. One night, on the dark fourteenth of Magha, on the great Night of Shiva [Shivaratri], he was hunting a hog. He hadn't caught anything all day, and at night he was up in a sacred *bilva* tree,[xix] awake without blinking an eye. In order to get a better view of his prey, he cut off many *bilva* leaves and thus, unknowingly, effortlessly, even though he was angry, he did puja [worship] to a Shiva-*lingam* that was under the *bilva* tree. And he spat mouthfuls of water, which chanced to fall on that Shiva-*lingam*, and by the force of fate, that too became a Shiva puja, by bathing the *lingam*. Then he got down from the tree and went to the water to fish.

His wife stayed up all night worrying about him, and then she followed his tracks, for she was afraid that he had been killed. At dawn she went to bring him food, and saw him by the river. They both bathed, but just as they came out a dog arrived and ate all the food.[xx] She got mad and started to kill the dog, saying [to her husband], 'This evil one has eaten our food, yours and mine. You fool, what will you eat? Tomorrow you will be hungry.' Then Chanda, dear to Shiva, said to her, 'I am satisfied by knowing that the dog has eaten the food.

[xviii] There is a pun here on twice-born (*dvi-ja*): birds reborn from the egg, and Brahmins reborn at initiation. (Teeth are also called 'twice-born'.)
[xix] The leaves of the *bilva* tree are used in the worship of Shiva.
[xx] By eating the food, the dog, an unclean animal, inadvertently made the Kirata and his wife participants in the act of giving food (and fasting), a part of the puja prescribed for the Night of Shiva, Shivaratri. This is not mentioned in the text itself, but the table of contents helpfully points it out.

What use is this body, anyway? Stop being angry.' So he enlightened her.

Then Shiva sent his messengers with a heavenly chariot. His servants said that they had come to take the Kirata to the world of Shiva, with his wife, because he had worshipped the *lingam* on the Night of Shiva. But the Kirata said, 'I am a violent hunter, a sinner. How can I go to heaven? How did I worship the Shiva-*lingam*?' They said, 'Shiva is pleased with you.' Then they told him how on the Night of Shiva he had cut the *bilva* leaves and put them on the head of the *lingam*, and stayed awake (as had his wife), and they had both fasted. They brought the couple to heaven, with great celebration. (33.1-64)

This is truly a story of amazing grace. By eating the food, the dog inadvertently causes the Kirata and his wife to give up food, a part of the puja prescribed for the Night of Shiva, as is staying up all night. This story recapitulates and integrates in a single tale the three separate stories that we have encountered: *lingam* worship by mouthfuls of water from a Kirata, inadvertent worship by a hunter named Chanda, and salvation for a man touched by a dog.

It also includes the man's wife in the process of his salvation. Let us therefore turn to the theme of women in the *Kedara Khanda*.

THE FEMINIZATION OF VISHNU

The very first triad of stories about undeserving devotees introduces the corollary to the theorem of Shiva-worship that will be the basis of the rest of the book: that it is the worship of the *lingam*, rather than any other form of Shiva worship, that opens all doors and rights all wrongs. Implicit in this assertion is another dogma that the *Kedara Khanda* shares with many other Shaiva Puranas: that Shiva subsumes Vishnu within him. But here the *Kedara Khanda* begins to weave its own secondary agenda, a quasi-feminist agenda. It retells the familiar story of the argument between Brahma and Vishnu—about who has fathered the other—which is settled when Shiva appears in the form of the *lingam* of flame and Brahma and Vishnu compete to find the top and the bottom of this enormous pillar.[xxi] As a result of lying about having seen the top of the *lingam*, Brahma is cursed never to be worshipped again; this is also said in other Puranas. But this time Vishnu, who did not lie, is also subjected to a change in worship status:

[xxi] See 'God's Body'.

> When the *lingam* raged out of control, Brahma and the sages praised
> Shiva, and he, pacified, told them to ask Vishnu for help. They praised
> Vishnu, and he laughed and said, 'In the past I saved you from demons,
> but I can't save you from this *lingam*.' Then a voice in space, reassuring
> the gods, said to Vishnu, 'Envelop this *lingam*, Vishnu, become the
> base [*pinda*], and save everyone that moves and that is still.' And the
> lord assented to this in his mind. (7.1—21)

Since, in other versions of this story, it is the goddess, or Shiva's Shakti,
who is called in to support and control the *lingam* by taking the form of the
pinda base (also called the *yoni*, 'vagina', or *pitha*, 'seat'), the assignment of
this role to Vishnu in this text amounts to the feminizing of Vishnu, the
subordination of Vishnu to Shiva, through the incorporation of Vishnu
into the goddess's role in the worship of the *lingam*.

And the text goes on to tell us that the whole universe is made of Shiva
and Shakti; the clear proof of this is the fact that all men have the *lingam*
and all women the *pinda* (8.18—19). This affords incidental support to the
argument about the 'naturalness' (and hence the possibility of accidental
performance) of *lingam* worship: every human being is walking around
with the essential materials for worship. Moreover, the lack of vertical
distinction between the male god and human males, on the one hand, and
the female goddess and human females, on the other, is then given a
horizontal counterpart: there is no distinction between Shiva (the male
part of the *lingam*) and Vishnu (its female base, the *pinda*).

A similar feminization takes place in the telling of the story of the
churning of the primeval ocean,[xxii] which follows the standard plot until the
moment when the devastating *halahala* poison appears. Then the text continues:

> Vishnu and Brahma and the others, pervaded by the poison, sought the
> help of Heramba (Ganesha), who propitiated Shiva until the supreme
> Shakti appeared in the form of the *yoni*. Ganesha praised Shiva united
> with Shakti, and the *lingam*, pleased by Heramba's praise, swallowed
> the poison. (10.7-11, 39-56)

This episode does not appear in the extant Sanskrit *Mahabharata* version of
the churning of the ocean (where Shiva in his anthropomorphic form,
rather than as the *lingam*, swallows the poison, and Ganesha does not yet
exist), but it resonates with another Epic episode that is subsequently
related by the *Kedara Khanda*:

[xxii] See 'The Submarine Mare'.

When the Soma appeared from the churning, the demon Vrishaparvan stole it and carried it down to the underworld. At the behest of the gods, Vishnu took the form of Mohini, a beautiful enchantress, bewitched the demons, took back the Soma, and gave it to the gods. (12.1—74)

Where the *Mahabharata* describes the feminization of Vishnu as Mohini in just two verses,[17] and later Puranas add an episode in which Shiva is enchanted by this enchantress and embraces her (giving birth to Hariharaputra—'the son of Vishnu and Shiva'),[18][xxiii] the *Kedara Khanda* inserts into the story a wonderfully cynical conversation between Mohini and Bali, king of the demons:

> Bali said to Mohini, 'You must distribute the elixir [Soma] right away.' She smiled and said to Bali, 'A smart man shouldn't trust in women. Lies, violence, deception, stupidity, excessive greed, impurity and cruelty are the natural flaws of women. Like sadistic jackals among beasts of prey, like crows among birds and like swindlers among men—that's how women should be recognized by wise men. How can I make friends with you? Consider who you are, and who I am. Therefore you should think about what should and should not be done . . .' Bali replied, 'The women you have been talking about are common women, whom common men like. But you do not belong among those women you have been talking about. No more talk; do what we ask. Distribute the elixir; we will take what you give us, I promise you.' (12.18-28)

The self-hating misogyny of Mohini's speech repeats the serious statements of many other texts, beginning with the *Rig Veda*, which puts similar words into the mouth of Urvashi ('There are no friendships with women; they have the hearts of jackals'[19]), and continuing in Manu ('The bed and the seat, jewellery, lust, anger, crookedness, a malicious nature and bad conduct are what Manu assigned to women.'[20]) But in the *Kedara Khanda*, this can only be a satire on Hindu misogyny, as becomes apparent from a survey of the subversive role of women in this text.

PRIMITIVE FEMINISM IN THE *KEDARA KHANDA*

It is worth noting the strong human women in this text, women like Chanda's wife. When the gods murder Dadhicha to take his body to make their weapons, his wife, Suvarcha, curses the gods and does not mince her words: 'O you gods, you're worse than anyone, impotent and greedy.

[xxiii] See 'Transsexual Transformations'.

Therefore you gods who dwell in heaven will have no progeny' . . . So, too, when the dwarf (Vishnu) has taken only two steps and has had Garuda bind Bali with the nooses of Varuna, Bali's wife, Vindhyavali, goes into action. She goes to the dwarf and asks him to step on the heads of her child, herself and Bali; he does so and sets Bali free to live in Sutala, where he promises that he, Vishnu, will dwell as Bali's doorkeeper (a significant reversal of the Shaiva pattern, where the devotee becomes the doorkeeper). (17.7–14, 19.32–58)

But it is the goddesses Indrani and Parvati (or Devi; the Goddess) who best express the powers of women; after all, they are *called* 'power', Shachi and Shakti. We have already seen some instances of the text's quasi-feminism in the goddess's mocking remarks about the resemblance between Shiva and his devotees and in Indrani's mockery of Indra. Other stories are also told about the goddess and about Indrani, in other traditional episodes that become, through the strength of character attributed to the women, much less traditional. Thus, whereas in the *Mahabharata*, when Nahusha usurps the throne of Indra, Indrani weeps and seeks the help of Brihaspati and Indra, who tell her how to trick Nahusha so that he loses the throne and is cursed to become a snake,[21] in the *Kedara Khanda* she dries her tears and thinks up the plot all by herself:

> When Narada urged the gods to install Nahusha on the throne of Indra (who was once again recuperating from Brahminicide), Shachi, hearing the words from the mouth of Narada, burst into tears and retired into the inner apartments of the palace. The gods installed Nahusha as king of the gods, and he summoned Indrani to come to him. Indrani laughed and said, 'If he lusts for me, another man's wife, let him come to get me in a non-vehicular vehicle.' When Nahusha, deluded with lust for Indrani, heard what she had said, he considered what might be non-vehicular and decided that it was a Brahmin rich in asceticism. So he harnessed two of them to his palanquin, and as he drove them on he shouted, 'Go! Go!' [*sarpa sarpa*], and so Agastya, one of the sages drawing the palanquin, cursed him to become a serpent [*ajagara*, also known as a *sarpa*].
>
> Shachi then sent the gods to search for Indra, and she cursed Brihaspati: 'Because you brought two surrogates to me [Nahusha and Yayati, Nahusha's son] while Indra was still alive, someone else will do what you should do while you are alive; he will have your marital luck and beget a famous son in your 'field' [i.e., your wife].[xxiv] Go and look

---

[xxiv] See 'Medical and Mythical Constructions'.

for Indra with the rest of the gods; if you don't, I'll give you another curse.' When he heard what Shachi said, Brihaspati went with the other gods. (15.62—89, 16.1-10)

Indrani's curse refers to the well-known ancient story of the adultery of Tara, Brihaspati's wife, with Chandra (the moon), resulting in the birth of Budha, the great king.[xxv] To my knowledge, no other text suggests that this affair took place as the result of a curse of vengeance for Brihaspati's role in pandering for Indra's surrogates with Indrani. (Indeed, the *Mahabharata*, following the *Brihaddevata*, tells of a more direct possible cause for Brihaspati's cuckolding: Brihaspati raped the wife of his brother, Utathya.[22] This, too, the *Kedara Khanda* ignores in favour of its own set of connections, though other texts do connect Brihaspati's rape of Utathya's wife, Mamata, with his own cuckolding by Chandra, his pupil.[23])

But of all the goddesses and women, Parvati is the great heroine of the *Kedara Khanda*, and she is assisted by Rati, the wife of Kama and goddess of sexual pleasure, after Shiva has burnt Kama to ashes:

> As Parvati wondered how she could get Shiva into her power, Rati said to her, 'Do not despair, Parvati; *I* will revive Kama.' And having consoled Parvati in this way, Rati began to engage in asceticism. Narada then came to Rati and asked whose she was. Furious, Rati said, 'I know you, Narada, you're a virgin boy, for sure. Go back wherever you came from, and don't delay. You don't know anything, and all you do is make quarrels. You are the first among lovers of other men's wives, rakes, and low adulterers, people who do not work, parasites.'
>
> When Rati had reviled him in this way, Narada went and told the demon Sambara to abduct Rati. Sambara, deluded by lust for Rati, asked her to come with him, and wanted to grab her by the hand, but she said, 'If you touch me, you will be burnt.' He took her to his house and put her in charge of the kitchen, where she was known as Mayavati. (21.100-25)

Now, several texts say that, after the death of Kama, Rati was reborn as Mayavati.[24] And one says that, after Rati had become Mayavati, Narada visited her and told her, to her benefit, what she was to do.[25] But the *Kedara Khanda* alone blames Narada for the degradation of Rati—her becoming a demon's maid—inflicted in revenge for her spirited denunciation of him (which manages somehow to imply simultaneously that he is sexually innocent and lascivious).

[xxv] See 'Transsexual Transformations'.

THE DECONSTRUCTION OF SHIVA

Parvati herself takes complex revenge against Shiva in the final myth told in the *Kedara Khanda*, right after the tale of the Kirata, a myth that not only recapitulates all the myths of *lingam*-worship that recur in this text but goes on to satirize them. (And we might see in Parvati's masquerade as a mountain woman, a Shabari, a variant of the theme of the mountaineer who worshipped the *lingam*.) The story begins as a variant on the well-known,[26] though not particularly early, theme of the dice-game quarrel of Shiva and Parvati:

> One day the sage Narada came to visit Shiva and Parvati on Kailasa and said, 'There would be greater pleasure for the two of you in playing dice than in making love.' They began to play dice and began to argue, and, as the hosts of Shiva joined in the quarrel, Shiva's servant, Bhringi, reminded Parvati of the time when Shiva had burnt Kama, and the time when Shiva had been reviled at the sacrifice of Daksha and Sati committed suicide. Then Parvati got mad and said to Bhringi, 'You're always trying to come between us. But how can there be any separation between us two? I will give you a curse: be without flesh.'
>
> Then, in fury, she put her hand on the serpent Vasuki and took it down from Shiva's neck, and [then she took] many other things, ornaments, and the crescent moon, and elephant skin, and then, laughing, she took even his loincloth. When all the troops of Shiva averted their faces in modesty, Shiva said, 'All the sages are laughing at this joke, and Brahma and Vishnu. How can you, born in a good family, do this? If you have won, then at least give me back my loincloth.' Then she laughed and said, 'Why do you need a loincloth, you hermit? You were naked enough when you went into the Pine Forest, begging for alms and seducing the sages' wives. The sages made your loincloth fall down there. And that's why I took it from you in the game of dice.'
>
> Hearing that, Shiva was angry and looked at her in fury with his third eye. Everyone was terrified, but she laughed and said, 'Why are you looking at me with that third eye? I'm not Kala or Kama, nor am I Daksha's sacrifice. I'm not the triple city, or Andhaka. You're wasting your time with that third eye on me.' She said a lot of things like this to him, and he set his heart on going to a deserted spot in the forest.
>
> When Shiva had gone to the forest, Parvati was tormented by longing in separation (*viraha*). Still, she laughed and said, 'I beat him and reduced him to poverty. What can't I do? Without me he is ugly;

I made him beautiful. Watch me play a new game with him now.' And with that, she set out to go to Shiva, taking the form of a magnificent mountain woman [Shabari], dark and slender, with lips like *bimba* fruits, and she went where Shiva was meditating. He woke up and saw her and was filled with lust. He took her by the hand, but as soon as he touched her, she vanished. Then he, who was the destroyer of mistaken perceptions, himself was enveloped in a mistaken perception. Unable to see her, he was tormented by longing in separation.

But then he saw her again, and he asked who she was and she said, teasing him, 'I am seeking [my/a] husband,[xxvi] a man who is omniscient, independent, unchanging and the best lord of the universe.' He replied, 'I am a suitable husband for you, but no one else is.' She smiled and said, 'You are indeed the husband that I seek. But let me tell you something. You are devoid of virtue.[xxvii] For a woman chose you before and won you by her great inner ascetic heat, and you abandoned her in the wilderness.' Shiva denied that he had abandoned a woman with great inner ascetic heat. When he continued to insist that she marry him, she said he must ask her father, Himalaya.

She took him to her father, stood with him at the door, and said, 'This is my father. Ask. Don't be ashamed. He will give me [to you], there is no doubt about that. Don't hesitate.' Shiva bowed to Himalaya and said, 'Best of mountains, give your daughter to me today.' Hearing this pitiful speech, Himalaya stood up and said to Shiva, 'What kind of a joke is this? It doesn't befit you. You're the one who gives everything in the universe.' Just then Narada arrived, laughed, and said, 'Contact with women always leads to the deception [*vidamba*] of men. You are the lord of the universe. You should speak as befits you.' Thus enlightened by Narada, Shiva woke up and laughed and said, 'You spoke the truth, Narada. Mere contact with women is the downfall of men. Today she deluded me and brought me here; this act was like [a rape] by a ghoul. Therefore I won't stay near this mountain; I'll go to another part of the forest.' Then Shiva vanished, but they all praised him, and he came back. Drums sounded, and all the gods, Indra and the others, sent a rain of flowers, and the great Shiva reigned there with Parvati. (34.20—153, 35.1-58)

[xxvi] There is a significant double entendre here, both 'I am looking for my husband' and 'I am seeking a husband'.

[xxvii] Another pun, on *guna* ('virtue' or 'quality or characteristic'): 'You are devoid of virtue' can also mean, applied to the supreme godhead, 'You have no qualities' (*nirguna*). See '*Saguna* and *Nirguna*'.

The arguments about the supremacy of Shiva versus Shakti recapitulate arguments that have been made throughout this text about Shiva versus Vishnu and Vishnu as Shakti, beginning with the reviling of Shiva at the sacrifice of Daksha. Indeed, this episode, the final story in the *Kedara Khanda*, refers several times to the first story of Daksha's sacrifice, in which Sati, as usual, defends Shiva with great spirit and reminds her parents and the gods of his great deeds:

> [Sati said:] Once upon a time, Brahma, you became five-headed in your pride, and Shiva made you four-headed—do you remember? Once upon a time, he wandered begging in the Pine Forest, and you cursed him, and his mere limb filled the whole universe, which became a *lingam* at that moment. How can you have forgotten? (3.10-14)

Her words predict several myths that will be told, seriously, later in the book[xxviii]; but she refers to the same myths in this final episode only to mock them, turning the text itself on its head in the end.

Parvati argues, against Bhringi, that Shiva and Shakti are one, despite their quarrels (just as, we have seen, Shiva and Vishnu are one, despite the quarrels of their devotees). In this way, the text evokes, without narrating it here, the myth of Bhringi: Bhringi had wanted to worship Shiva without worshipping Parvati, and in punishment for his disrespect for the female side of God, she deprived him of the female side of every person: the flesh.[27] By reviving the quarrel with Bhringi at this point, the text implicitly analogizes it not only to the old myth of the sacrifice of Daksha but to the new myth, created by the *Kedara Khanda*, of the integration of Shiva with the feminine, both with Shakti and with the feminized Vishnu.

There are also several different sorts of references here to Shiva's burning of Kama and of Kala/Yama; these references bring out a parallelism between the two incidents that is reflected in two parallel epithets of Shiva (Kamantaka and Yamantaka, or Kalantaka) but is seldom explicitly remarked upon in Sanskrit texts. The myth of Kama is also recapitulated in the episode of Shabari as a whole, which is a satire on the well-known myth that we have already heard in this text, the episode in which Parvati, having been rejected by Shiva as a lovely young girl, returns to him in another form, as an ascetic woman, when he is meditating, inspires him with love, and causes him to ask her father for permission to marry her.

[xxviii] See 'God's Body'.

One particular argument of the *Kedara Khanda* version of that episode is particularly relevant here:

> When Parvati asked permission to serve Shiva while he mediated, he said to Himalaya (her father), 'This slender young girl with her terrific hips and her sweet smile must not come into my presence.' But Parvati laughed and replied, 'You should consider who you are, and who Nature [*prakriti*] is.' When he retorted, 'I will destroy Nature with my ultimate inner ascetic heat, and I will stay here without Nature,' she said, 'How could you transcend Nature? What you hear, what you eat, what you see—it's all Nature. How could you be beyond Nature? You are enveloped in Nature, even though you don't know it. But if you are, in fact, beyond Nature, then what do you have to fear from me?' Shiva laughed and let her stay. (20.15-26)

So, too, in the final episode, Parvati reminds him that he literally cannot exist without her.

And, finally, when Parvati teases Shiva, she deconstructs the whole mythology of the *Kedara Khanda* and even myths that are not told here, other myths of the third eye such as the ancient myth of the burning of the triple city and the later myth of the impalement of the demon Andhaka. Best of all, by forcing Shiva to play what amounts to a game of strip poker, Parvati offers a superb satire on the central myth in this book, the story of the falling of Shiva's *lingam* in the Pine Forest. In her mockery of her husband, Parvati equates the loincloth with the *lingam*, teasing him about the time the sages caused his 'loincloth' to fall. In fact, the sages caused his erect penis to fall; does this mean, therefore, that when she takes his loincloth she symbolically castrates him, too? Shiva himself implicitly mocks and feminizes himself, when he says that he has been treated like the victim of a marriage of the ghouls, which Manu defines thus: 'The lowest and most evil of marriages, known as that of the ghouls, takes place when a man secretly has sex with a girl who is asleep, drunk or out of her mind.'[28] Shiva seems to be saying that he was out of his mind (presumably with a combination of ordinary lust and the extraordinary illusory powers of the goddess) when Shabari seduced him. Where Parvati is at first said to be 'tormented by longing in separation', she turns the tables until he himself is 'tormented by longing in separation'.

Thus Shakti demonstrates that she, too, can play the 'departed god' trick[xxix]—now you see me, now you don't—just as Shiva did in the stories

---

[xxix] See 'Together Apart'.

of Daksha's sacrifice and the Pine Forest. In doing this, she is usurping the top place, just as he had done to Vishnu. By giving the upper hand to Parvati, the text is parodying the basic, assumed paradigm of the worshipper as female and the god as male (a reversal that we may also see in the feminizing of Vishnu). So, too, by making Shiva the fool who, despite his delusion, 'accidentally' wins his own wife (his own deity), the text reverses the conventional roles of god and worshipper. As David Shulman has put it, 'The god, too, ends up acting out the logic of reversal no less than his human counterparts.'[29]

When Shiva, too, becomes a 'departed god' again near the end of the story, ludicrously embarrassed by his public humiliation in proposing to his own wife, just as Indra had been embarrassed (and separated from his wife) by the more serious sin of Brahminicide, the gods bring him back with praise. That praise that brings god back to us, the husband to his wife, the wife to the husband, is the *raison d'être* of the *Kedara Khanda* of the *Skanda Purana*, as it is of all Puranas. 'The people who recite with supreme faith this marvellous glorification of Shiva, this Shiva text that Shiva loves, and the people who listen to it with devotion and delight, they go to the ultimate level of existence' (35.64, the final verse of the *Kedara Khanda*).

But the *Kedara Khanda* differs from other Puranas in its inclusive attitude to 'the people' who listen and recite the Purana. By granting the grace of God to unregenerate sinners and to women, the *Kedara Khanda* is salvaging two human groups that more conventional Puranas have marginalized and excluded: women and (male) sinners who do not consciously worship at all. The justification for including both is the same: the worship of the *lingam* and *yoni* is so 'natural' (because we are all carrying around the materials for the liturgy) that it can be carried out mindlessly, by people who do not know what they are doing when they worship god. So, too, women in this text represent 'Nature' (*prakriti*) in opposition to 'culture' (the elaborate ritualism of other Puranas, from which women are excluded). This is, as we have seen, the argument by which Parvati gains access to Shiva so that she can ultimately conquer him: he cannot live without Nature. This being so, it is through natural, accidental or unconscious, acts of worship that sinners and women find their way to him.

In salvaging these discarded pieces of society, the *Kedara Khanda* also salvages discarded pieces of Puranic lore, off-beat stories, precious scraps, all bottom-fished from the great ocean of Indian stories. We, the readers, thus participate in a double salvation when we read the *Kedara Khanda*: of ourselves (women and sinners) and of the scraps of stories.

APPENDIX: THE CONTENTS OF THE *KEDARA KHANDA*

This is how Ludo Rocher describes the entire contents of the *Kedara Khanda*:

> The *Kedara Khanda* (1.1) begins with the destruction of Daksha's sacrifice. It devotes several chapters to the churning of the ocean, and proceeds to describe the birth and activities of Parvati, up to her marriage with Shiva. The description of Karttikeya's birth is followed by that of his successful fight with the demon Taraka. The *Khanda* ends with the story in which Shiva loses everything to Parvati in a game of dice, their temporary separation, and their reunion.[30]

This is, more precisely, a summary of those parts of the contents of the text that are known from other Sanskrit texts as well, and it forms a consecutive narrative sequence, an integrated story. But it does not provide us with an armature on which to build all the rest of the book. For there is more, far, far more. Here, in brief, is what is in the *Kedara Khanda*:

1.1.1. Introduction: The sages in the Naimisha Forest question Lomasha about Shiva.

1.1.1–4 Shiva destroys Daksha's sacrifice.

1.1.5 Indrasena, a very evil man, says 'Hara' unconsciously and is saved from hell. A Kirata (mountaineer and hunter) is taken to Shiva's heaven.

1.1.6 The Pine Forest sages cause Shiva's *lingam* to fall.

1.1.7 The *lingodbhava*: the flame *lingam* appears to Vishnu and Brahma.

1.1.8 A man steals a bell and is saved from hell. Ravana worships Shiva and Vishnu becomes incarnate as Rama.

1.1.9 The demon Bali takes Indra's throne. The gods and demons churn the ocean for Soma.

1.1.10 Vishnu and Brahma and the others, pervaded by the *halahala* poison, seek help from Ganesha, who invokes the supreme Shakti in the form of the *yoni*, and praises Shiva in the form of the *lingam*, united with Shakti. This united form then swallows the poison.

1.1.11–14 Vishnu appears as Mohini, and the gods get the Soma.

1.1.15 Indra kills Vishvarupa and suffers from Brahminicide. Nahusha takes Indra's throne but is undone by his lust for Indra's wife.

1.1.16–17. His Brahminicide dispelled, Indra kills Vritra and incurs Brahminicide again.

1.1.18 Kitava (Bali in a former life) is saved from hell and takes Indra's throne.

1.1.19 Indra wins his throne back from Bali, with Vishnu's help.

1.1.20–31 Shiva burns Kama, marries Parvati, and begets Skanda.

1.1.32 Shveta, the devotee of Shiva, is saved from hell.

1.1.33 A Kirata is saved from hell.

1.1.34 The goddess tricks Shiva at dice and almost into adultery by becoming a mountain woman (Shabari).

WOMEN AND OTHER GENDERS

WHY SHOULD A BRAHMIN TELL YOU WHOM TO MARRY?: A DECONSTRUCTION OF *THE LAWS OF MANU*[1]

A virtuous wife should constantly serve her husband like a god, even if he behaves badly, freely indulges his lust and is devoid of any good qualities.

—Manu 5.144

The female sex (and, for that matter, sex in general) has never found favour with any of the world's religions, or with their priests and prophets (which should make us stop and think a little about religion in general, but that's another book.) How much of this misogyny do we see in Hinduism? To what extent was marriage—and, more broadly, sexual activity—legislated by religious law in ancient India? How did the authors of the religious texts justify their authority? To what extent was that authority actually recognized and that law actually enforced? We may begin to answer these questions by considering *The Laws of Manu*,[i] long regarded as the most authoritative textbook of Hindu religious law (*dharmashastra*).

WOMEN IN MANU'S *DHARMASHASTRA*

Manu is notorious for his attitude to women,[ii] whom he holds responsible for men's desire.[iii] He regards women as a sexual crime about to happen:

> Drinking, associating with bad people, being separated from their husbands, wandering about, sleeping and living in other people's

---

[i] See 'Medical and Mythical Constructions'.
[ii] Manu is also excoriated nowadays for his attitude to people of the lower castes—people still burn copies of Manu at protests against caste injustices—but that topic is beyond the scope of this chapter. See 'Medical and Mythical Constructions'.
[iii] See 'The Control of Addiction'.

houses are the six things that corrupt women. Good looks do not matter to them, nor do they care about youth; 'A man!' they say, and enjoy sex with him,[iv] whether he is good-looking or ugly. [9.12-17]

Therefore, men should watch women very carefully indeed:

A girl, a young woman, or even an old woman, should not do anything independently, even in her own house. In childhood a woman should be under her father's control, in youth under her husband's, and when her husband is dead, under her sons'. She should not have independence. [4.147-9; 9.3]

This lack of independence meant that, in Manu's ideal world, a woman had very little space to manoeuvre within a marriage, nor could she get out of it:

A virtuous wife should constantly serve her husband like a god, even if he behaves badly, freely indulges his lust and is devoid of any good qualities. A woman who abandons her own inferior husband . . . is reborn in the womb of a jackal and is tormented by the diseases born of her evil. [5.154-64]

And she is not set free from this loser even when he dies:

When her husband is dead she may fast as much as she likes, living on auspicious flowers, roots and fruits, but she should not even mention the name of another man. Many thousands of Brahmins who were chaste from their youth have gone to heaven without begetting offspring to continue the family. A virtuous wife who remains chaste when her husband has died goes to heaven just like those chaste men, even if she has no sons. She reaches her husband's worlds after death, and good people call her a virtuous woman. [4.156-66]

Not only may she not remarry, but her *reward* for not remarrying is that she will be her husband's wife 'in the hereafter', which, 'if he behaves badly, freely indulges his lust and is devoid of any good qualities', may not have been her first choice.

The good news, at least, is that Manu does expect her to live on after her husband dies, not to commit suicide on her husband's pyre, becoming a *sati*. Yet Manu's fear that the widow might sleep with another man was an

---

[iv] The *Mahabharata* repeats this sentiment (M13.38.17) and adds: 'As soon as she sees a man, a woman's vulva becomes moist.' (M 13.38.26)

important strand in the later argument that the best way to ensure that the widow never slept with any man but her husband was to make sure that she died with him. The man, of course, can and indeed must re-marry. [4.167-9] All that there is to set against all of this misogyny is Manu's grudging 'keep the women happy so that they will keep the men happy' line of argument: 'If the wife is not radiant she does not stimulate the man; and because the man is not stimulated the making of children does not happen. If the woman is radiant, the whole family is radiant, but if she is not radiant the whole family is not radiant.'[3.60-63] Well, it's better than nothing. I guess.

But we must not forget the gap between the exhortations of the texts and the actual situation on the ground. The records of donations to Buddhist stupas offer strong evidence that contradicts the *dharmashastras'* denial to women of their rights to such property.[2] In this period, many women used their personal wealth to make grants to Jain and Buddhist orders. Hindu women, too, could make donations to some of the new Hindu sects, for they received from their mothers and other female relatives 'women's wealth' (*stri-dhana*), and they were often given a bride price on marriage, the opposite of dowry (Manu is ambivalent about this), and their children, including daughters, could inherit that. [9.31, 191-5] Most often, women's wealth consisted in gold jewellery, which they could carry on their bodies at all times; though men controlled land, cattle and money, women had some resources—diamonds have always been a girl's best friend. This one claim to independence made Manu nervous: he warns against women hoarding their own movable property without their husbands' permission. [9.199]

THE BRAHMIN'S AUTHORITY OVER SEX

Here we may pause to reiterate our opening question: Why should a Brahmin legislate such things? There are two sides to this question: Why should a Brahmin want to interfere in this area, and why should people *allow* him to do so? As for the first side, sex is among the most basic of human needs, the key to the survival of human life within the lineage or species. To control sex means to control everything else that stems from it—politics, power, everything. And, as for the second side, the fact that this force is so deeply embedded in the human organism means that it is, like death, an area of great vulnerability, mystery, danger; it is ultimately inaccessible to reason or science. This is the shadowy place in which people feel a need for religion, where Brahmins are invited to enter or offer to enter.

Manu presents both 'because' arguments (explicit dogmas or appeals to authority) and 'this is why' arguments (implicit rationalizations or appeals to persuasion) for the Brahmins' hegemony over all women. The necessity of the purity of women is established by the 'because' argument of the other world and the life after death: only a son born of the right sort of woman can give the food that feeds the ancestors:

> Two kinds of sons are born in other men's wives, 'the son of an adulterous woman' and 'the son of a widow': the former is [born] while the husband still lives and the latter after the husband has died. But . . . they cause the offerings to the gods and ancestors to be lost to those who give them, both here on earth and after death. [3.174-5]

And the afterlife effects of a woman's misbehaviour redound not only upon her male relatives but upon herself as well:

> A woman who violates her [vow to her dead] husband because she is greedy for offspring is the object of reproach here on earth and loses the world beyond. [5.161]

It is, therefore, very important to keep women pure so that they can bear the right sorts of sons to feed the ancestors. Or one might put it this way: the importance of inheritance law in a patrilineal society leads to an emphasis on the chastity of women.

Marriage, therefore, may also be regulated through both 'this is why' and 'because' arguments. The list of women whom one can marry makes a lot of sense—at first:

> A woman who is neither a close relative on her mother's side nor belongs to the same ritual lineage on her father's side, and who is a virgin, is recommended for marriage to twice-born men. When a man connects himself with a woman, he should avoid the ten following families, even if they are great, or rich in cows, goats, sheep, property, or grain: a family that has abandoned the rites, or does not have male children, or does not chant the Veda; and those families in which they have hairy bodies, piles, consumption, weak digestion, epilepsy, white leprosy, or black leprosy. A man should not marry a girl who is a redhead or has an extra limb or is sickly or has no body hair or too much body hair or talks too much or is sallow; or who is named after a constellation, a tree, or a river, or who has a low-caste name, or is named after a mountain, a bird, a snake, or has a menial or frightening name. He should marry a woman who does not lack any part of her body and who has a pleasant name, who walks like a goose or an

elephant, whose body hair and hair on the head is fine, whose teeth are not big, and who has delicate limbs. [3.5-10]

It does not take a particularly profound knowledge of ancient Hindu culture to make sense of most of this. But are we justified in claiming that the items that do not at first make sense to us (What's wrong with red hair, or being named after a tree or a river?) are 'because' factors? We must assume that if we knew enough about the culture, we would at least know why something puzzling to us made sense to them, though it is likely that we may still find it irrational in light of our present assumptions about the world.

In discussing the begetting of children, Manu begins with remarks about fertility that may well be grounded in observation, but he moves quickly into the more convenient sphere of the logical but unverifiable:

> The natural fertile season of women is traditionally said to last for sixteen nights, though these include four special days that good people despise. Among these [nights], the first four, the eleventh, and the thirteenth are disapproved; the other ten nights are approved. On the even nights, sons are conceived, and on the uneven nights, daughters; therefore, a man who wants sons should unite with his wife during her fertile season on the even nights. [3.46-8]

There is a nice symmetry to this paragraph, but, as Sudhir Kakar once calculated, if a man avoids his wife on all the nights that Manu disapproves of, he can make love to her on minus three days every month.

There is also, perhaps, some human truth in the psychological portrait of children born of 'mixed marriages': 'From those [four] . . . bad marriages are born cruel sons, liars who hate the Veda and religion'. [3.41] In a society such as Manu's, which is constitutionally required to mistreat such children, they would indeed be likely to become sociopaths. But are class considerations 'because' or 'this is why' arguments? It depends, of course, on how natural one regards class to be. This is what Manu says:

> Not a single story mentions a Shudra woman as the wife of a Brahmin or a ruler, even in extremity. Twice-born men who are so infatuated as to marry women of low caste quickly reduce their families, including the descendants, to the status of Shudras. A Brahmin who climbs into bed with a Shudra woman goes to hell; if he begets a son in her, he loses the status of Brahmin. No redemption is prescribed for a [twice-born] man who drinks the saliva from the lips of a Shudra woman or is tainted by her breath or begets a son in her. [3.14, 16-17, 19]

By saying that this is so, Manu makes it so, even as Manu, the Son of the Creator, makes women lustful and malicious.

The 'other world' argument (which I classify as a 'because' argument because of its unfalsifiability) also applies to sons born of the right and wrong women through the right and wrong sorts of marriage (the Brahma marriage being the highest, the others increasingly undesirable):

> If a son born to a woman who has had a Brahma marriage does good deeds, he frees from guilt ten of the ancestors who came before him, ten later descendants, and himself as the twenty-first. A son born to a woman who had a marriage of the gods [frees] seven ancestors and seven descendants, a son born to a woman who had a marriage of the sages [frees] three [of each], and a son born to a woman who had a marriage of the Lord of Creatures [frees] six [of each]. [3.37-8] [But] the ancestors and the gods do not eat the offerings to the gods, to the ancestors and to guests that such a man makes with [a Shudra woman], and so he does not go to heaven. [3.18]

And that, O best beloveds, is why a man should not sleep with a low-born woman.

RATIONAL AND IRRATIONAL ARGUMENTS IN MANU

To appreciate fully the specific arguments about sex, it will be useful to set forth some of the general principles of authority and argument in *The Laws of Manu*. The three main criteria are eyewitness perception, inference (or reason) and the teachings found in various religious texts. And 'if [the question] should arise, "What about the laws that have not been mentioned?" [the reply is]: "What educated Brahmins say should be the undoubted law."' [12.105-6] In fact, Manu has an even higher card to play in the game of authority, which he plays, significantly, in the context of the control of women: 'The bed and the seat, jewellery, lust, anger, crookedness, a malicious nature and bad practices are what Manu assigned to women.' [9.17] Manu is, as his own text makes explicit, not merely the primeval lawgiver but also the son of the Creator and, hence, a creator himself. He thus assigns these qualities to women in both capacities, by making them originally and by recognizing them in his laws.

Manu's assumptions about Brahmin authority are revealed in many different ways, but they can, as we have seen, be usefully classified into 'because' and 'this is why' arguments. The 'because' arguments are like the non-arguments that every parent uses when he or she cannot or will not explain something to a child who asks why something should be done as the parent says: 'I am bigger than you and I run this show and I tell you it is this way and this is all I am going to tell you.' Paradoxically, whenever Manu actually *says* 'this is why' (or 'therefore') and supplies a reason, he cites an irrational, or unfalsifiable, argument: 'The gods like it that way' or, more often, 'It is in the Veda.' He gives a reason, but it is a 'because' reason; the case is closed.

(In his long lists, by contrast, Manu really does seem to use genuine 'this is why' arguments, in that he gives, or rather assumes, ethical, moral or medical reasons, rational or empirical reasons, for doing something. Yet, on close examination, his lists do not explicitly explain anything. He does not, for instance, tell us why a leper or an arsonist should not be invited to the funeral meal; he assumes we can work that out for ourselves.)

In a certain sense, the 'because' arguments may be better arguments than the 'this is why' arguments precisely because of their power to mystify, to shut off any possibility of challenge. And yet, it is not fair to claim that the items that do not at first make sense to contemporary readers are 'because' factors. Perhaps Manu was, at many points in his text, striving to accommodate what he perceived to be a 'because' argument to a 'this is why' argument. That different parts of *The Laws of Manu* were added at different times, and that divergent traditions were brought together in the final redaction of Manu, is certain. The themes and lists in *The Laws of Manu* are inherited pieces of the *bricolage* of ancient Indian culture. The text encompasses as much as possible; its goal, like that of Hindu culture itself, is not consistency but totality.

It is, then, particularly hard for us to 'crack the code' of Manu if we think that there is one code; in fact, there are several different (and not necessarily incompatible) codes, any one of which may be invoked to justify a particular verse, and none of which can explain the 'system' as a whole. It is really not a code at all, except perhaps in the sense that it is a shorthand to be deciphered or, like the genetic code, an encapsulation of the whole culture *in nuce*. But the gymnastics that Indian commentators go through to justify some of these items (often in blatant disagreement not only with one another but also with the patent meaning of the original verse) indicate that they, too, sometimes no longer know why it makes sense. In those cases, for them as for us, the answer is just 'because'.

LAW IN EXTREMITY

Manu himself implicitly acknowledges the ultimate inadequacy of all arguments, both 'because' and 'this is why', by providing us with a mechanism that effectively deconstructs his own system. This is the mechanism of *apad*, which may be translated as 'in extremity'—an emergency, when normal rules do not apply.[v] *Apad* is further supplemented by other loophole concepts such as adversity (*anaya*), distress (*arti*) and near-starvation (*kshudha*). In a famine, according to Manu, a father may kill his son. [10.105][vi] *Apad dharma* is the ultimate 'this is why' argument, the bottom line of realism in Hindu law.

The concept of *apad* recognizes the inevitability of human fallibility: Don't do this, Manu says, but if you *do*, this is what to do to fix it. This two-edged sword is, after all, the rationale for any system of legal punishments and religious restorations: the system is designed primarily for people who disobey it. When, for instance, Manu both condemns and recommends the appointment of a widow to sleep with her dead husband's brother, he does mean both things: he is saying that this is what one has to do in an emergency, but that it is really a very bad thing to do, and that if you do it, you should not enjoy it, and you should do it only once. If you have to do it, you must be very, very careful. Ideally, a man should not sleep with his brother's wife, but there are times when he cannot help doing it, and then Manu is there to tell him how to do it. This is what one does when caught between a rock and a hard place, between the Devil and the deep blue sea; it is the best one can do in a no-win situation to which there is no truly satisfactory solution. The Sanskrit term for the rock and the hard place is *apad*.

The emergency escape clause is further bolstered by recurrent references to what is an astonishingly subjective standard of moral conduct:

> The root of religion is the entire Veda, and [then] the tradition and customs of those who know [the Veda], and the conduct of virtuous people, and what is satisfactory to oneself. [2.6] The Veda, the tradition, the conduct of good people, and what is pleasing to oneself—they say that this is the four-fold mark of religion, right before one's eyes. [2.12] If a woman or a man of lower caste does anything that is better, [a man of higher caste] should do all of that diligently, and whatever his mind and heart delight in. [2.223] Whatever activity satisfies him inwardly when he is doing it should be done zealously; but he should

---

[v] See 'Sacrifice and Substitution' and 'Eating Karma'.
[vi] See 'Eating Karma'.

avoid the [activity] which is the opposite. [4.161] A person should recognize as lucidity [*sattva*] whatever he perceives in his self as full of joy, something of pure light which seems to be entirely at peace . . . When he longs with his whole [heart and mind] to know something and is not ashamed when he does it, and his self is satisfied by it, that [act] has the mark of the characteristic of lucidity. [12.27, 37]

Thus, the elaborate web of rules, which, if followed to the letter, would paralyze human life entirely, is equally elaborately unravelled by Manu through the escape clauses. Every knot tied in one verse is untied in another. The constrictive fabric that he weaves in the central text, he unweaves in the subtext of *apad*. The need for *apad* might be taken as an indication of the ultimate failure of Manu to provide a code of human conduct that can be realistically applied. But it must be conceded that emergencies are the stuff that human life, and certainly human law, are made of.

If Manu himself acknowledged the need to escape from his system, how seriously did other Hindus take it? Many a young man must have seduced, or been seduced by, his guru's wife (a situation that must have been endemic, given both Manu's paranoid terror of it and its inevitability in a world in which young women married old men who had young pupils). How likely was such a young man, afterwards, to 'sleep on a heated iron bed or embrace a red-hot metal cylinder . . . or cut off his penis and testicles, hold them in his two cupped hands and set out toward the southwest region of Ruin, walking straight ahead until he dies'? [11.104-5] Would any but the most dedicated masochist turn down the milder alternatives that Manu, as always, realistically offers: 'Or he may carry a club shaped like a bedpost, wear rags, grow a beard, concentrate his mind and carry out the "Painful" vow for a year in a deserted forest. Or, to dispel [the crime of violating] his guru's marriage-bed, he should restrain his sensory powers and carry out the "Moon-course" vow for three months, eating food fit for an oblation or barley-broth.' [11.106-7]

How do we know that anyone ever did any of this? How was the *Laws of Manu* used?

The Hindus themselves have always taken Manu seriously in theory. By the early centuries of the Common Era, Manu had become, and remained, the standard source of authority in the orthodox tradition for social and religious duties tied to class and stage of life. The text attracted no fewer than nine complete commentaries, attesting to its crucial significance within the tradition, and it is cited far more frequently than any other *dharmashastra* in other ancient Indian texts. In the realm of the ideal, *The*

Laws of Manu is the cornerstone of the Brahmin vision of what human life should be, a vision to which some Hindus have always paid lip service and to which, in many ways, many still genuinely aspire. It influenced expectations, tastes and judgments, beneath the level of direct application of given cases.

However, whether this status extended beyond the texts to the actual use of Manu in legal courts is another matter. One could not actually run a country using Manu alone; Hindus soon developed, for that purpose, a network of local authorities (panchayats) that actually decided legal disputes. The existence of numerous alternatives to Manu in Hindu traditions indicates that Manu's was only one voice among many. In addition to the many other *dharmashastras*, there are the many commentaries, both on *The Laws of Manu* and on the other dharma texts, which openly debate almost every point. And then there are the alternative systems, both within Hinduism (including such antinomian movements as the bhakti devotional sects and the Tantric cults) and, alongside it, in the Indian subcontinent (Buddhism and Jainism in the early days; Islam, Sikhism and Christianity later; modern reform movements still later).

But administrators in British India, beginning with Warren Hastings, wanted to use Manu as the basis of a legal system, whether or not it was in fact used in that way in India at that time. Under the British, Manu became instrumental in the construction of a complex system of jurisprudence in which 'general law' was supplemented by a 'personal law' determined by religious affiliation. Manu's text certainly does not deserve the pride of place that the British gave it as an applied legal text. Only a small part of *The Laws of Manu* deals with what we would call law. The rest is a code of a very different sort, an encyclopaedic organization of human knowledge according to certain ideal goals, a religious worldview. But as a document actually capable of adjudicating the day-to-day decisions that human beings have to make about a subject as important as sex, it could not be, and (if we read it carefully) did not claim to be, the law.

And yet, despite the absence of anything like an authoritative legal status, *The Laws of Manu* deeply infiltrated Hindu culture, building into it many negative assumptions about the lower castes and about women that sharply restricted their freedom, regulated their behaviour and blocked their access to social or political power. Memorized by generation after generation of young men, it also penetrated the thinking of people who could not read a word of Sanskrit but picked up the ideas out of the great maelstrom of Hindu oral literature. Manu lives on in the darker shadows of Hinduism.

SARANYU/SAMJNA:
THE SUN AND THE SHADOW[1]

O ver the years, I have found myself drawn back, time and again, to one particular figure from Hindu mythology who has survived in the texts for well over two millennia: Saranyu. She stands at the watershed of the Indian goddess tradition and is relevant to us even today, especially in the context of ideas about gender, class/caste and race. It is a complex story, with many strands for us to keep track of as we follow it through many texts and many centuries.

SARANYU IN THE VEDAS

The story of Saranyu begins *in nuce* in the *Rig Veda*. Since this text purposely conceals the story, it is helpful to have a brief summary of the plot before we try to decipher the riddling text:

> Tvastri ('the Fashioner', also named 'the All-Maker', Vishvakarman) was the artisan of the gods. His daughter, Saranyu, married Vivasvant ('the Shining One'), the Sun, and gave birth to twins, Yama and Yami. Then she put in her place a female of-the-same-kind (*savarna*), took on the form of a mare herself, and fled. The Sun took the form of a stallion, followed her, and coupled with her. From that were born the twin equine gods called the Ashvins.

Now, this is how the *Rig Veda* plays with the story:

> Tvastri is giving a wedding for his daughter': people come together at this news. The mother of Yama, the wedded wife of the great Vivasvant, disappeared. They concealed the immortal woman from mortals. Making a female of-the-same-kind [*savarna*], they gave her to Vivasvant. What she became bore the twin equine gods, the Ashvins, and then she abandoned the two sets of twins—Saranyu. [RV 10.17.1–2]

The cryptic form of the text is explained by Maurice Bloomfield's excellent suggestion that the passage 'belongs to the class of Vedic literary endeavours which are styled in the Vedas themselves as "mystical utterances" (*brahmodya* or *brahmavadya*); it is a riddle or charade.'[2] He gives as evidence the fact that no explanations are given for the hiding away of Saranyu, or who it was that bore the Ashvins; instead, a series of hints is presented and, at the end, her name, the answer to the riddle. As the later Indian tradition attempts to unlock the riddle of Saranyu, it draws upon many deep-seated, often conflicting, ideas about human and divine sexuality and masquerade. Although it is useful to begin with a straightforward philological approach to establish our textual footing, following in the steps of the old boys, Bloomfield and co., it is now time for us to go on to raise questions of gender that did not concern them.

In the *Rig Veda*, the female is explicitly an immortal, while her husband is a mortal (one of those from whom 'they' hid her). Her name means something like 'flowing', perhaps a hint of a connection with a river goddess and with the concept of impetuosity.[3] As Saranyu flows through Hindu mythology, the Puranic versions impart increasing degrees of intentionality and feeling to this person/force. Saranyu's double is said to be of-the-same-kind (*savarna*)—of the same sort, or type, or appearance, or of the same colour or class, *varna*. As we shall see, significant changes in this story arise out of the changing meaning of *varna*. Bloomfield suggests that the double may be 'a like one, *double entendre*: one like Saranyu in appearance, and like Vivasvant (the Sun) in character or caste . . . like Saranyu in appearance, i.e., her double, and also one who is suitable in her character to the mortal Vivasvant—more suitable than the divine Saranyu, we may perhaps understand.'[4] This disparity results, in part, from the fact that the double woman is mortal, like the Sun, whereas Saranyu is immortal. The double produces no children, but Saranyu in her own persona produces a single, mortal child whose name (Yama) means 'twin' and who is immediately referred to as one of a set of twins. At the same time, as the mare she produces the twin Ashvins (half horse and half human, like the Greek Dioscuroi or the Roman Gemini), who are liminally immortal: at first denied the privilege of sharing the elixir of immortality (Soma, the juice pressed from the Soma plant), they eventually get it.

That Saranyu's husband and child are mortal is as clear as anything in this riddle. Yama is in many texts said to be the first mortal [RV 10.14.2; AV 18.3.13], and the Sun is explicitly said to be a mortal, to have been born to die, in contrast with his seven immortal brothers. [RV 10.72.8-9; SB

3.1.33] These same texts also state that the Sun was, even in the womb, inadvertently mutilated and consciously abandoned by his own mother. Thus, the theme of rejection by the mother can be traced back from Yama, rejected by his mother, to Vivasvant, Yama's father, who is rejected by *his* mother. And that same rejection is taken to explain why the Sun is deformed. The gods cut off his excess flesh and it became an elephant (or a human: there is a pun on *hastin*, 'one with a trunk' and 'one with a hand'). [SB 3.1.3.4] He is called Martanda ('dead in the egg' or 'born of a dead egg'). Indeed, the daily rising and setting of the sun was seen by many cultures as the continual process of death and rebirth.

Though someone other than Saranyu herself makes the female of-the-same-kind, she herself abandons both the twin (Yama) and the equine twins (Ashvins); there are no other children. But Yaska, glossing the Vedic verses in his *Nirukta* [12.10] (c. 500 BCE), adds another significant child:

> Tvastri's daughter Saranyu gave birth to twins from Vivasvant. Putting in her place another female, a female of-the-same-kind (*savarna*), [and] taking on the form of a mare, she fled. Vivasvant, taking the corresponding form of a horse, followed her and coupled with her. From that were born the two Ashvins. Of the female of-the-same-kind Manu was born.

In the earlier text, 'they' (the gods, we assume) substituted someone else for Saranyu, with or without her consent. Here she explicitly produces the substitute herself. This is a significant shift, which raises a question that we would do well to bear in mind throughout this inquiry: Who is the agent? Does the woman masquerade of her own will, or does someone else force her to do it? This also brings us to the critical question of points of view: Who *wants* this to happen? *Who* makes it happen?

Yama has, by the time of Yaska's *Nirukta*, explicitly become twins in the dual (*yamau*), and he has now been joined by another child, Manu, born of the female of-the-same-kind.[5] The mortality of Yama is closely related to the nature of his brother Manu, the ancestor of the human race.[i] Although Manu is not mentioned in the riddle verse about Saranyu, the *Rig Veda* refers elsewhere to a Manu who is the father of the human race, identifying him in at least one passage [8.52.1] with a patronymic that makes him the son of Vivasvant. But Manu is also given the name (a matronymic?) of

---

[i] See 'You Can't Get Here', 'Medical and Mythical Constructions' and 'Why Should a Brahmin?'

savarni or *savarnya* [10.62.9 and 11]—the latter implying that, already in the *Rig Veda*, our ancestor was the son of the female of-the-same-kind or was himself someone of-the-same-kind.

That Saranyu and her double are regarded as the mothers of the two ancestors of the human race is even more significant a fact than might at first appear—for Saranyu and her double mark the dividing line between abstract goddesses who have children and anthropomorphic goddesses who do not. Before her, Aditi (the mother of the Sun, and of Indra) and Tvastri (Saranyu's father, and later said also to be the father of Indra) produce immortal children, as do Sky and Earth and a few other deities. But Saranyu is the first goddess to unite with a (mortal) god in order to give birth to children and, through her double, to human children. After Saranyu, many celestial nymphs (*apsaras*) produce children with mortal men, and some goddesses give birth to divine children by themselves, through a kind of parthenogenesis (as Parvati gives birth to Ganesha), but never anthropomorphically and never through sexual union with a god. There are stories in later texts explaining why the goddesses are all barren; their infertility is sometimes said to result from a curse uttered by Parvati.[6] But this is an afterthought, designed to account for what had already long been taken for granted, namely, that immortals, simply because they are immortal, do not have children; if you don't die, there is no need to reproduce yourself. Or, to put it the other way around, as the myth often does, if you have sex, you must have death. (This is also the message of the loss of Eden.) And, contrariwise, if you are immortal, you can't have sex (or, at least, procreative sex). This explains why it is that, although Hindu gods and goddesses often marry—the *hieros gamos* is, after all, a major mythological theme—they do not usually procreate with their spouses. Instead, gods seduce mortal women, and celestial nymphs, rather than goddesses, seduce mortal men. The Saranyu myth marks the transition between these two patterns: mating with a liminal husband who is both a mortal and a god, she herself functions like the Vedic goddess Aditi and produces a god (Yama, god of the dead), while her double, functioning like one of the later celestial nymphs, produces a mortal (Manu, the founder of the human race).

The story of Saranyu and Manu is narrated in greater detail in the *Brihaddevata*, a text composed some centuries after the *Nirukta*:

> Tvastri had twins, Saranyu and a three-headed son. He willingly gave Saranyu in marriage to Vivasvant, and Saranyu bore him Yama and Yami, who were also twins. Out of her husband's sight (*paroksham*),

Saranyu created a female who looked like her (*sadrisha*); tossing the couple of children (*mithunau*) to this female, she became a mare and went away. But in ignorance of this, Vivasvant begat Manu upon her, and Manu became a royal sage, who was like Vivasvant in his energy. Then Vivasvant became aware that Saranyu had departed in the form of a mare, and he went quickly after her, having become a horse. Saranyu, knowing that it was Vivasvant in the form of a horse, approached him for coupling (*maithuna*), and he mounted her. But in their haste the semen fell on the ground, and the mare smelled that semen because she desired to become pregnant. From that semen that was inhaled twins were born, the famous Ashvins. (6.162–63, 7.1–6)

Now, just as the theme of maternal rejection is extended backwards from Yama to his father the Sun, so in this text twinhood is extended backwards from Yama to his mother Saranyu, whose twin brother has three heads where she has three forms. Moreover, Saranyu's twins are given twin nomenclatures: *yamau*, as in the earlier texts, but now also *mithunau*, literally 'a couple', providing a pun for her own 'coupling'.

Saranyu's ambivalence toward her husband here splits the story into two contrasting sexual episodes. As a goddess, she leaves him (we are not told why); as a mare, she receives him. By conceiving through her nose rather than her genitals, the mare expresses the upward displacement of language (for surely these are talking horses): life and creativity spring from the head, not the loins.[ii] But she is also placing smell, the reliable animal criterion for the appropriate sexual partner, above vision, the flawed human (and, apparently, divine) criterion. Whereas vision made the Sun mistake the wrong female (created 'out of his sight', *paroksham*) for his wife, and made the mare at first mistake him for someone else, ultimately smell allows Saranyu the mare both to recognize her true mate and to conceive by him.

The statement that the Ashvins were conceived from the nose (*nasat*) may also have been inspired by a desire to account for their Vedic epithet of Nasatyas, which Herman Lommel interprets as 'Nose-beings', in harmony with the traditional Indian interpretation of the name.[7] 'Nasatya' is elsewhere said to mean 'not false' (*na-a-satya*, literally, 'not-not-true' or 'not-not-real')—an interesting assertion in light of the fact that they are the 'true' sons of Saranyu, in contrast with their not-equine, and not-immortal, brothers.[iii]

[ii] See 'Zoomorphism'.
[iii] Herman Güntert derives *nasatya* from *nes*, 'to save', and translates it as 'saviour'.

SARANYU IN THE *HARIVAMSHA*

In several later variants, the goddess is named not Saranyu but Samjna, which means, significantly, 'sign' or 'image' or 'name'.[iv] At the same time, Samjna's surrogate is no longer said to be of the same kind or type but is rather her *chaya*, her mirror image or shadow—a creature who is not exactly like her but is her opposite in terms either of inversion (the mirror image) or of colour (the shadow). This is the version given in the *Harivamsha*, an appendix to the great epic, the *Mahabharata*, composed in about the fifth century CE:

> Vivasvant was born of Kashyapa and married Samjna, the daughter of Tvastri. She had beauty and youth and virtue, and she was not satisfied by the form of her husband, the greathearted one called 'Dead-Egg'. For the form of Dead-Egg, the Sun, was burnt by his own fiery glory in all his limbs, and so became unlovely. 'Let him not be dead while he is still in the egg,' his father, Kashyapa, had said in love and ignorance, and so he became known as 'Dead-Egg'. But the Sun's fiery glory was constantly excessive, and with it he overheated the three worlds.
>
> The Sun produced a daughter and two sons: Manu and the twins Yama and Yamuna. But Samjna, seeing that the form of the Sun had a dark colour (*syamavarna*), unable to bear it, transformed her own shadow (*chaya*) of-the-same-kind (or colour, *savarna*). Her own shadow became a Samjna that was made of magic illusion. Samjna said to the female of-the-same-kind, 'I am going to my father's house; you stay here in my house. Treat my three children well, and do not tell this to my husband.' The female of-the-same-kind replied, 'Even if I am dragged by the hair, even if I am cursed, I will never tell your husband. Go wherever you like, goddess.' Somewhat embarrassed, the wise woman went to her father's house. But her father reviled her and kept telling her, 'Go back to your husband.'
>
> And so she took the form of a mare, concealing her form, and grazed in the land of the northern Kurus. But the Sun, thinking, 'This is Samjna,' produced in the second Samjna a son who was his equal. And because the Sun thought, 'This one looks like (*sadrisha*) the former Manu,' his name was 'Manu of-the-Same-Kind' (*savarna*). But the earthly (*parthivi*) Samjna gave extra affection to her own child and did not behave in the same way to the older children. Manu put up with her, but Yama could not put up with her. In his anger and childishness, and through the force of future destiny, Yama threatened

---

[iv] In one verse (8.1) of the *Harivamsha*, she is called not Saranyu but Surenu ('Lovely Dust').

Samjna with his foot. Then the mother of-the-same-kind, who was very unhappy, cursed him in anger: 'Let that foot of yours fall off.'

But Yama, terrified by the curse and agitated by Samjna's words, reported this to his father. 'Turn back the curse!' he said to his father. 'A mother should behave with affection (*sneha*) to all her children, but this one rejects us and is good to the younger one. I lifted my foot at her but I did not let it fall on her body. If I acted out of childishness or delusion, you should forgive that.' The Sun said, 'You must have had very good cause indeed if anger possessed you who know dharma and speak the truth. But I can't make your mother's words fail to come true. Worms will take flesh [from your foot] and go to the surface of the earth. Thus your mother's words will come true, and you will be protected from the blow of the curse.'

Then the Sun said to Samjna, 'Why do you show excessive affection [to one] among your children when they are all equal?' She avoided this question and said nothing to the Sun, and he wanted to curse her to destroy her. Therefore, she told everything to the Sun, and when the Sun heard this he became angry and went to Tvastri. Tvastri assuaged the Sun's anger and trimmed him on his lathe, removing his excessive fiery energy. Then he was much more handsome.

He saw his wife the mare, and, taking the form of a horse, he coupled with her by joining with her in her mouth, for she was struggling since she feared it might be another male. She vomited out that semen of the Sun from her nose, and two gods were born in her, the Ashvins, the healers. Then the Sun showed her his lovely form, and when she saw her husband she was satisfied.

But Yama was greatly tormented in his mind by his karma, and as the overlord of the ancestors, the king of dharma, he ruled over these creatures with dharma. And Manu of-the-Same-Kind will rule in the future during the era of Manu of-the-Same-Kind. His brother, Vivasvant's second son, became [the inauspicious] planet Shanaishcara ['slow-moving', Saturn]. Yami, the younger of the two (twins), became the famous river, the Yamuna. [*Harivamsha* 8.1–48]

There are several significant developments in this expanded text. The double is still called the *savarna* (the female of-the-same-kind), as in the earlier versions, but she is also the *chaya* (shadow or reflection) and *sadrisha* (the look-alike). More important, there is real ambiguity now about the person whom the Shadow looks like: Samjna or the Sun? Samjna in this text perceives herself as literally of a different class from that of her husband. We have noted that *varna* may mean 'kind' in the sense of mortal vs. immortal and might, therefore, be translated as 'class'. Over the centuries, the word *varna* came primarily to denote 'class' in a sociological rather than a purely morphological sense,[v] reflecting the hardening of the lines between the social classes (called *varnas*) and the increasing concern about skin colour (also designated by *varna*). This shift in the meaning of *varna* may explain why the *savarna* ('same sort') of the Veda and Yaska becomes a *sadrisha* ('look-alike') or a *chaya* ('shadow') in the *Brihaddevata* and the *Harivamsha*. The latter refers to the 'dark colour' of the Sun and the 'same colour' of the double woman, implying that Samjna rejected the Sun because of his blackness and created an appropriately black mate for him (*chaya* here perhaps indicating the dark shadow rather than the bright reflection)—someone who, being dark like him, was of-the-same-kind as he. The counterintuitive idea that the sun is black seems to have occurred to several ancient Indo-Europeans, perhaps as a result of the black spots we see when we stare directly at the sun or of the sun's black colour during its underworld journey, when it is night on earth. The *Harivamsha* implies that the sun gave himself a suntan: 'He was burnt by his own fiery glory in all his limbs.' In later texts, Yama is often described as a black man (with red eyes); in the *Amar Chitra Katha* comic, which we shall soon encounter, Yama is depicted as dark brown with thick red lips. Presumably, he inherits this colour from his father.

MORTAL AND IMMORTAL

But the more important meaning of *varna* in the story of Samjna is 'sort' in the sense of mortal vs. immortal. Thus the *Harivamsha* refers to the shadow as 'earthly' (*parthivi*), belonging to the earth, in contrast with the other, the heavenly mother. The mortality and/or mutilation of the Sun (and, more significantly, of the sons of the Sun) is a pivotal point of the myth in all its variants. Some versions, such as the *Harivamsha* passage cited above, argue that Samjna, herself a goddess, left the Sun because he was inadequate for her (mutilated and mortal, or black); some, such as the *Markandeya* passage to be cited below, that she left him because he was too glorious for her, a fact that resulted in his mutilation. The mare's motives are correspondingly reversed: in the *Brihaddevata* she receives the stallion willingly, while in the *Harivamsha* she tries to avoid him. Whereas the *Brihaddevata* took conception through the nose as testimony that she *did* want to conceive by him and turned her face towards him as a willing

---

[v] See 'You Can't Get Here'.

human woman would, the *Harivamsha* takes it as testimony for just the opposite reaction, and she turns her face towards him (and her haunches away) as an unwilling mare would. In neither case does she present her hindquarters to him. And the reason that she avoids him in the *Harivamsha* is that, unlike him, she is (in this case, wrongly) suspicious of the identity of her sexual partner; she does not trust her eyes.

There is also a significant development in the nature of the mother of the human race: while Yaska and the *Brihaddevata* explicitly state that Manu was the son not of the first wife, the true wife, but of the replica, the *Harivamsha* says that the first wife bore Manu (presumably Manu the son of Vivasvant, Vaivasvata) and the twins. This text also says that the second wife, the double (no longer called Savarna), bore *another Manu*, a double of Manu, called Manu Savarni; the subsequent evolution of the text indicates that we are the descendants of the second Manu, not the first. Thus we are descended not only from a replicated mother (as we were even in the *Brihaddevata*) but now from a replicated Manu, as well.

The name of the second Manu is a pun. The shadow of Saranyu is now called not only the *savarna* (the female of-the-same-kind), as in the earlier versions, but also the *chaya* (shadow) and *sadrisha* ('look-alike'). Therefore, Manu's usual epithet, 'Of-the-Same-Kind' (*savarni*) is explicitly interpreted not with reference to her but in the sense of 'Of-the-Same-Kind [as his brother]'—although we know that he is also, implicitly, 'Born of the Female of-the-Same-Kind.' In the earlier text, the epithet 'Of-the-Same-Kind' was a matronymic, because Manu's mother was the double and there was no other Manu for him to resemble. But now that the epithet has also become descriptive of a sibling relationship, Manu himself is the double, and the other Manu is given the patronymic (Vaivasvata) that was originally Manu's. Finally, since in this text Manu is given this epithet by the Sun—who, as usual, thinks that the double is the real Samjna (both he and Yama refer to her as Yama's mother)—the Sun cannot name her child, Manu, after a resembling mother, but he can name him after his resemblance to the previous child. Manu's epithet of Savarni thus reveals yet another punning meaning: he is the son of the woman of-the-same-kind as his father. This makes Manu not merely a double but a triple: he is of-the-same-kind as his replicated mother, his older brother (son of the true mother) and his (dark, mortal, lower-class) father.

Indeed, by changing the name of the mother from Saranyu to Samjna, this text makes both the mothers of the human race unreal, for the name of the first wife (Samjna) means 'the sign' or 'the image' or 'the name', and the name of the second wife (Chaya) means 'the shadow'. Samjna is the Signifier. (Her name contains the verbal root *jna*, cognate with the Greek *gnosis* and English *know*.) Since the word or name is the double of the thing or person, Samjna is her own double from the start. And perhaps it is relevant to note here that *chaya* is also used in Sanskrit to refer to a commentary on a text. Thus, if Samjna is the text, Chaya is the commentary; if Samjna is the dream, Chaya is the secondary elaboration. Yet it should be recalled that names and images in India are regarded as in many ways isomorphic with—corresponding exactly to—reality or even able to *create* reality.[8]

This consideration not only distinguishes the Sanskrit term from its Greek and Latin cognates but gives greater force and meaning to the female who is 'just' an image. Samjna may even be a riddle term for Sandhya, another name for the Dawn; the shadow woman is then evening twilight, and the sun has two wives.[9] The parallels between Samjna and Sandhya are striking, for each is the wife of the sun, ambivalent and incestuous.[10] Each also designates a linguistic symbol: just as 'Samjna' means 'sign' or 'image', so 'Sandhya' becomes the term for the 'twilight speech' of later Hindi poetry, a speech marked by riddles, inversions and paradoxes.

A feminist might well read this myth as a powerful astronomical image of male domination, inasmuch as the female images are regarded by the texts as mere reflections of the energy of their husband, the Sun. (Here it is relevant to recall that in both the Vedas and the Puranas, despite the fact that the Sun is mortal and Samjna immortal, the Sun is worshipped and Samjna is not.) And this interpretation is supported by other expressions of domination, as well. One manuscript of the *Harivamsha* inserts a short passage[11] describing Samjna's thoughts while she contemplates becoming a mare, thoughts about the nature of women's subordination to men:

> She became very worried, and thought, 'To hell with this behaviour of women.' She kept blaming herself and her own womanhood: 'No one should remain a woman, ever; to hell with this life with no independence. In her childhood, youth and old age she is in danger from her father, husband and sons, respectively.[vi] It was stupid of me to abandon my husband's house; I did the wrong thing. Even though I have not been recognized, I have suffered now in my father's house,

---

[vi] This is a satire on the famous verse in Manu (5.148): 'In childhood a woman should be under her father's control, in youth under her husband's, and when her husband is dead, under her sons'. She should not have independence.' See 'Why Should a Brahmin?'

and there she is, the female of-the-same-kind, with all her desires fulfilled. I have lost my husband's house because of my naive stupidity, and it is no better here in my father's house.'

And with that, she decides to become a mare, perhaps because mares, unlike human women, are free—both to reject unwanted stallions and to indulge in their unbridled sexuality.[vii] This passage strikes a contemporary reader as a strange mix of a quasi-feminist perception of male persecution and a male chauvinist justification for that persecution, projected (by the male author of the text) into the mind of the victim (the woman). Yet the Sun is surely a most pathetic victimizer, and the real energy (perhaps even the real power) in all versions of the myth seems focused on the tricky females. If this myth is about victimization, then it is certainly equally, if not more, about subversion.

SARANYU IN THE *MARKANDEYA PURANA*

The basic story is retold in the *Vishnu Purana*,[12] and other Puranas add other details and reverse certain sequences (such as the statement that, even after he has been trimmed on the lathe, the Sun is unacceptable to Samjna, who leaves him after the birth of the Ashvins).[13] As the version of the Saranyu legend given in the *Markandeya Purana* differs from the *Harivamsha* text only in certain details, it will be sufficient merely to note these differences rather than retell the whole myth. The *Markandeya* uses the story of Samjna to introduce the *Devi Mahatmya*, one of the earliest, and still one of the most important, texts about the worship of the goddess, Devi. This use of the story is a most significant move, for it comes at a moment when the dominant (male) Sanskrit tradition is just beginning to incorporate into its texts the corpus of stories about female divinities (a.k.a. goddesses), who had long been alive and well and living in the non-Sanskritic, vernacular traditions. In aid of this appropriation, the old Vedic myth—about a goddess, Saranyu, who was no longer worshipped even in the *Rig Veda* and a sun god who was worshipped both in the *Rig Veda* and at the time of the Puranas—serves as a bridge to, and perhaps a validation of, the new Puranic myth about a goddess, Devi Mahishamardini, who enters the Sanskrit tradition in this text and is now widely worshipped.[14] For despite the fact that no known ritual (that is, no known worship) was dedicated to Samjna/Saranyu, her myth is very important indeed, given

[vii] See 'The Submarine Mare'.

that she is the ancestor of the human race. In the context of a Purana that is so concerned with dynasties, this Ur-mother is clearly crucial.

The *Markandeya* tells the story of Samjna/Saranyu twice (chapters 103–5 and 74–75). Neither variant says anything about the Sun's ugliness or dark colour; instead, the text [74.8] tells us that Samjna could hardly bear her husband's splendour (or semen: *tejas*) and that she also feared his anger. When her father threw her out of his house, she took the form of a mare, 'not wanting the sun's heat, and frightened of his energy/semen'. [74.23] That the word for 'energy' (*tejas*) is also a word for 'semen' is surely relevant: Saranyu in her anthropomorphic form avoids the Sun's 'energy', while in her mare form she avoids the stallion's semen.

When the look-alike curses Yama, the curse is subtly different from that of the *Harivamsha*, for it makes explicit that it is the foot that is the object of the curse: 'Since you threaten your father's wife with your foot, your foot will fall' [103.20], or 'Your foot will fall to the earth' [74.29]. In both *Markandeya* variants, the father, Vivasvant, also specifies that worms will take flesh from Yama's foot and fall to earth.

The pun or riddle about the foot ('Worms will take flesh and go to the surface of the earth; thus your mother's words will come true, and you will be protected from the blow of the curse'), as well as the mutilation that it so vividly describes, is a recurrent theme in this corpus. The Sanskrit curse and counter-curse turn upon a double pun, for 'foot' (*pada*, cognate with Latin *pes*, *pedes*, French *pied*, and English *foot*) has two other meanings that are relevant here. *Pada* also means 'a quarter, a part' (that is, only one of the four assumed feet), so that the counter curse invokes a kind of implicit synecdoche, *pars pro toto*: Yama will lose not his whole body but only part of it, the part that the worms will take away. And *pada* also means a word or a line or measure of poetry (that is, only one of the four assumed quarters of a verse), a meaning that 'foot' also has in English. Thus the trick of the part (*pada*) and of the word (*pada*) is what saves Yama's foot (*pada*).

The *Markandeya* prefaces one of its retellings of the story of Samjna with a brief but stunning sequence:

> Samjna was the daughter of Tvastri and the wife of Martanda, the Sun. He produced in her Manu, called Manu Vaivasvata, since he was Vivasvant's son. But when the sun looked at her, Samjna used to shut her eyes, and so the sun got angry and spoke sharply to Samjna: 'Since you always restrain (*samyamam*) your eyes when you see me, therefore you will bring forth a twin (*yama*) who will restrain (*samyamanam*) creatures.' Then the goddess became agitated by terror, and her gaze

flickered; and when he saw that her gaze darted about, he said to her again, 'Since now your gaze darts about when you see me, therefore you will bring forth a daughter who will be a river that darts about.' And so because of her husband's curse Yama and Yamuna were born in her. [74.1–7]

Where Manu is named after his father, and is blessed, Yama is named after his mother, and is cursed; for he is named not after her name but after her evil deeds. The pun here is not on feet but on eyes. Here, a pair of rather awkward puns on the actions of the mother's eyes (restraining and darting) makes Yama 'the Restrainer' (one of his famous epithets), instead of lame. The injured eye here replaces the injured foot.

In both *Markandeya* variants, unlike the *Harivamsha*, the look-alike cleverly avoids calling herself a mother and merely claims, correctly, to be Yama's father's wife. But Yama suspects her, judging not by appearances (as his father does) but by actions. He says, 'I do not think she can be my mother, for a mother does not behave badly even toward badly behaved sons.' [103.22–32] His father, however, persists in referring to her as a mother, although he adds that he will modify the curse 'because of his affection for his son'. But finally, he, too, 'realizes that the look-alike is not the true mother', even though, in this version, she does not break her promise to remain silent. And he says, 'Surely you are not the mother of these [children]. You are some Samjna or other who has come here. For how could a mother curse a son even among children with no good qualities?' [103.27–32]. In the other version, the Sun's words are given to Yama, who says, 'Daddy, this great wonder was never seen by anyone, that a mother rejects her calf-love (*vatsalya*) for her son and gives him a curse. This woman does not act like a mother to me as Manu told me she did (to him); for a mother would not act with no good qualities even toward sons who had no good qualities.' [74.31–32] (In the *Amar Chitra Katha* comic book version of the myth, Yama says to his father, 'Father, that woman is not our mother!' His father replies, 'I agree. A son may change in his affections but a mother never ceases to care.' And the Sun realizes, 'The children are right. She must be an impostor.')

When the look-alike still avoids giving an answer to his question about whether she is the mother of his children, the Sun thinks about it and realizes the truth. [103.33] He summons the look-alike Samjna and says, 'Where has she gone?'—a question that seems to imply that he knows the look-alike is not the real Samjna. But the look-alike nevertheless continues, at first, to say what Samjna had told her to say: 'I am Samjna the daughter of Tvastri, your wife, and these are the children you begat in me.' Subsequently (as in the *Harivamsha*), when he is about to curse her, she tells him all the details of what had happened. [74.33—35] In both variants, he goes to Tvastri, who puts him on the lathe and trims away his excessive energy, which he makes into weapons (as in the *Harivamsha*). Finally, the text tells us:

> Then Vivasvant's body was beautiful, and had no excessive fiery energy. He went to his wife, the mare, in the form of a stallion. But when she saw him approaching she feared it might be another male, and so she turned to face him, determined to protect her hindquarters. Their noses joined as they touched, and the seed of the Sun flowed from his two nostrils into the mare and came out of her mouth, and in that way the equine twin gods called the Ashvins were born. And as the seed stopped flowing (*retaso'ante*) a son named Revanta was born, mounted on a horse. Then the Sun showed her his own form, and when she saw that it was peaceful she was full of joy, and she took on her own form and was full of love, and he took her home. [105.1–13]

And only after we are told what became of Manu the son of Vivasvant, Yama, Yamuna, the Ashvins and Revanta, do we learn about the children of the shadow. The bard says, 'Now learn from me the places assigned to the children of the shadow Samjna: the firstborn son of the shadow was the equal of the eldest-born Manu, and so he obtained the name (*samjna*) "Of-the-Same-Kind" (*savarnika*).' [75–35] It is striking, and surely no accident, that the name of the mother, Samjna, is here used, finally, in its lexical sense of 'name'.

THE FATHER OF THE BRIDE

All three of these Puranic variants (the *Harivamsha* and the two *Markandeya* passages) give new prominence to an old, silent character: the father-in-law, Tvastri, who at first receives Samjna when she flees from her husband, then forces her to leave his house, and finally mutilates her husband in order to make him acceptable to her. Tvastri is the artisan of the gods, the blacksmith, who is in many Indo-European mythologies crippled and consequently abandoned by his wife, or cuckolded; thus, in Greek mythology, Hephaestus's wife, Aphrodite, betrays him with Ares. Here it is Tvastri's son-in-law (Vivasvant) and his grandson (Yama) who are crippled and abandoned by their wife/mother, while his son (the three-headed Trishiras) is beheaded. This is an unhappy family: the Sun is rejected and mutilated by his mother; Yama is tormented by his karma; the female of-the-same-kind is miserable; and the first children (Manu Vaivasvata, Yama and Yamuna) are rejected by the first mother and mistreated by the foster mother. Only the child of-the-same-kind, Manu Savarnika, is not rejected: he alone is treated well by the mother of-the-same-kind.

The aggression of the bride's father against her husband in the Puranic corpus has been thought to lend weight, retrospectively, to the possibly incestuous connection that some Indologists have seen between Tvastri and Saranyu in the Vedic corpus.[15] Adalbert Kuhn argues that 'the anger of the gods regarding the wedding of the father and the daughter also explains why the gods hide Saranyu and slip a look-alike under Vivasvant'.[16] There is also the argument that the incestuous connection between Tvastri and Saranyu is further supported by the parallel between the story of Saranyu fleeing from the Sun in the form of a mare and the myth of Ushas fleeing from her incestuous father, Prajapati, in the form of a mare; he becomes a stallion, who mounts her; when she becomes a cow, he becomes a bull, and so forth, in order to produce various races of offspring.[viii] [BAU 1.4.1–6]

But if the theme of father-daughter incest is questionable, the theme of brother-sister incest appears here unmistakably. For Yama and Yami commit incest in the Iranian tradition, and in the *Rig Veda* [10.10] Yami tries, in vain, to persuade Yama to go to bed with her. The theme of the substitute mother (who rejects her husband because he is too far away from her, being mortal when she is immortal) is closely conflated with the theme of the resistant brother (who rejects his sister because she is too close to him, being his sibling).[17]

SARANYU: THE CLASSIC COMIC BOOK

Interesting bowdlerizations[ix] may be seen in the *Amar Chitra Katha* story of 'Surya', which is 'Retold from the *Markandeya Purana*'.[18] Here, the incestuous implications of the aggression of the bride's father against her husband in the Puranic corpus are veiled in the sanitized comic book version, but the presence of Samjna's father remains pivotal. When Tvastri (here called Vishwakarma, from his Sanskrit epithet of Vishvakarman, 'All-maker') kicks her out, he says, 'A woman's place is by her husband.'

[viii] See 'The Submarine Mare' and 'Zoomorphism'.
[ix] See 'From Kama to Karma'.

Before this, when Vishwakarma suggests that she marry Surya, he also says, 'Think well. Are you sure you will be able to bear his brilliance in all seasons?' To this she replies, veiling her face from him, 'I am sure, father'—and she has a dreamy look in her eyes when she muses, 'I was wondering how long I would be able to revel in Surya's warmth.' One of the women who dress her for her wedding remarks, 'Let me darken your eyes. You will need protection from his glances,' whereupon another woman adds, 'Glare, you mean.' But Sanjna (which is how the comic book spells her name) replies, 'Need protection from Surya's glances? Me?'

When Manu grows up, we are told, 'Surya and Sanjna were proud of him.' The delighted father remarks, 'He is brilliant!' to which his mother replies, 'Like his father!' Thus the Sanskrit pun on *tejas* as 'brilliance' or 'semen' is given a third twist—'brilliance' in the contemporary sense of intellectual power. And the cosmic question of resemblance is reduced to the cliché compliment/complement of fathers and sons: 'Chip off the old block.' But Surya's brilliance reverts to its cosmic, solar meaning soon enough, when he says to his wife, 'Come Sanjna, sit by me.' Here, as usual, the *Amar Chitra Katha* editor bowdlerizes what was a more intimate sexual contact in the Sanskrit text. But even this contact is too much for Sanjna, and the text elaborates upon the theme of closing the eyes: 'Sanjna, what's the matter?' 'My lord! Why do you glare at me so! Lord! I cannot open my eyes.' He says, 'Sanjna! Look at me! I am your husband! Sanjna! Will you repel me?' 'I am sorry, my lord.' 'Then listen carefully. Since you closed your eyes on me, the sustainer of all living beings, the son you bear now shall be Yama, the god of death.' Since the pun on 'restrain' is lost here, the curse makes no sense, except through an implicit connection between blindness and death.[x]

But the sexual squeamishness of the *Amar Chitra Katha* cannot cope with the subsequent equine issue. Sanjna's only reason for turning into a mare is avoidance: 'I cannot face Surya. I will turn myself into a mare. Then no one will find me.' When Surya goes to Vishwakarma in search of her, Vishwakarma says, 'I have divined that she turned herself into a mare.' On the way to find her, they ask a passer-by, 'Have you seen a mare go by?' 'Yes! A quaint one . . . by the river.' Surya then says, 'Why do you call it a quaint one?' 'I speak the truth, sir. *This mare talks!*' To which Surya

---

[x] There may also be a resonance with the episode in the *Mahabharata* where a woman who closes her eyes in her husband's embrace gives birth to a blind child. See 'Women in the *Mahabharata*'.

makes the wonderful reply, 'It must be Sanjna.' The talking horse[xi] is persuaded to resume her own form, and there is not a whisper about the mating of horses or the birth of the Ashvins.

The shadow (*chaya*), like the Sun, is interpreted literally and naturalistically in the comic book; she is both a reflected image and a shadow. At first, the shadow is Sanjna's reflection in the water, which Sanjna draws out. But when Sanjna remarks, 'You, Chaya, are safe from the glare of Surya,' Chaya replies, 'I shelter all who fear it'—a reference to the Shadow as shade, which is, on the literal level that this text favours, indeed safe from the sun. Chaya is happy with Surya, although she thinks, 'Poor Sanjna had to give up all this. Will she ever return? I must not forget that I am only Sanjna's shadow.' Thus, in a single speech she expresses the banal, all-too-human materialism of the second wife and the reminder that she is merely a natural phenomenon, a shadow.

As in the Sanskrit text, the shadow is a good mother only to her own children (two sons and a daughter): 'But alas! She did not care for Sanjna's children in the same manner.' This time we learn more about the stepdaughter, who is (as in the Sanskrit) cursed by Surya because of the sins of her true mother. But despite the generally naturalistic bent of this text, the stepdaughter's curse is not naturalistic (a darting river) but psychological (a fickle woman, more appropriate to the nature of both her mother and her stepmother): 'You tremble before me? Then you shall bear a daughter too. And she, Yamuna, shall be as fickle as you.' Now, as the Shadow beats Yamuna, Yamuna thinks, 'How I wish I were motherless.' Still the text tries to salvage Sanjna's good-motherhood, or at least her good-wifehood. The Shadow says to Surya, 'I am Chaya, the shadow of Sanjna. She did not want to leave you uncared for. So she sent me here instead.' And when Sanjna turns back from mare into goddess, the first thing she says is, 'My lord! How are our children?' to which he replies, 'Manu, Yama and Yamuna will know a mother again.'

And finally everyone is a good mother. Sanjna says, 'I shall never again wander away from home,' and Surya adds, 'Chaya shall be forgiven and shall live with us.' 'So Surya and Sanjna went back to his abode in the skies and lived there in happiness with Chaya and the children.' And all the children, of both generations, are depicted in a final family snapshot. This text has travelled a long way from the Sanskrit corpus in which the tragic story of Samjna and Manu attributes the origin of the human race to an abandoning mother.

[xi] See 'Zoomorphism'.

SARANYU : KUNTI = YAMA : KARNA

The theme of the abandoning mother, the wife of the sun, resurfaces in a transformation in a myth that is central to the *Mahabharata*:

> The princess Kunti was given the boon of invoking a god to give her a child, and she tried out her boon on the sun god, merely out of curiosity. The sun god split himself into two by his power of yoga, so that he came to her but still went on shining in the sky. As soon as Kunti saw him, she begged him to go back, pointing out that she was still a child, but he insisted on having her, threatening that if she did not give in to him, he would burn to death 'your foolish father, who does not know of your misconduct'. Karna was thus born, but to conceal her own misdeeds, Kunti threw the boy into the Horse River (*ashvanadyam*), lamenting, 'Fortunate is the woman from whose breast you will drink. What dream will she have?' Then she returned to the palace, sick with sorrow and in fear of awakening her father. Karna was retrieved by a charioteer whose wife adopted him.
>
> Now, Karna was born with golden armour and earrings grafted right onto his body. He always competed with Arjuna, one of Kunti's five 'legitimate' sons, the Pandavas, who feared Karna's invincible armour. In order to help Arjuna, one day Indra [the father of Arjuna] came to Karna in disguise as a Brahmin and begged the armour from him. Indra suspected that the sun god had warned Karna that Indra would come in disguise, but Karna did not refuse the request, though he asked in return for a magic spear that Indra had. Then Karna said, 'I will strip off the earrings and the armour and give them to you, but let me not look disgusting with my body flayed.' Indra replied, 'You will not look disgusting, and there will be no visible scar on your body. You will look like (*tadrisha*) your father in glory (*tejas*) and in colour (*varna*)'. Karna sliced the armour from his body, which was streaming with blood, along with the earrings, and gave them to Indra. [M 1.104, 3.290–94, and 5.138–42.]

The sun god forces himself upon Kunti, in part by threatening to harm her father (an echo of the old incestuous connection that some scholars have seen between Saranyu and Tvastri). Karna's foster mother is first imagined by Kunti, with envy, and subsequently described; the equine mother survives only the form of the 'Horse River' that receives the child—a body of water not mentioned elsewhere in the epic, to my knowledge. And just as Surya is the only god who forces himself upon Kunti, so Karna is the only one of the Pandavas who is mutilated. His mutilation is, moreover, an inversion of Yama's mutilation: in the epic, which abounds in multiple fathers rather than multiple mothers, Karna and Arjuna have the same mother (Kunti) but different fathers (the Sun and Indra), and one father (Indra) mutilates the son of the other father. In addition, Karna is restored to the condition of *looking like* his father in two respects essential to the myth of Saranyu: glory (or semen: *tejas*) and colour (*varna*)—precisely the qualities for which Saranyu rejected Karna's father.

CONCLUSION

As anthropogonies, these stories are saying that the primeval children, our ancestors, were abandoned by their mother. And on the metaphysical level the myth of Saranyu/Samjna seems to be saying that we, the descendants of Manu, are the children of the image—the children of *maya*, not the children of the real thing. These myths embody the Vedantic view that we are born into illusion, live in illusion, and can only know illusion. Clearly, this is a deeply religious story, not merely (or, perhaps, not even primarily) a story about men and women, or parents and children, or skin colour. For, in addition to psychological questions regarding incest, stepmothers, rejected children and unwanted husbands, the Saranyu story raises theological questions about the origin of the human race and of human death, about appearance and reality, about the relationship between male and female divine powers, and about the nature of the relationship between humans and the divine. The metaphysical question of the origin of the human race is posed in the fate of Saranyu's second son, Manu, and the metaphysical question of death is posed in the mythology of Saranyu's first son, Yama. But that is yet another story, best left for another time.

THE CLEVER WIFE IN INDIAN MYTHOLOGY[1]

Many cultures tell the story of a husband who challenges his wife to get a child fathered by him, though he spurns her bed; and she succeeds by tricking him into an attempted adultery. Stith Thompson, the Linnaeus of folklore, included in his wide survey of folktale motifs this cycle of myths known to folklorists as 'The Clever Wench' or 'The Clever Wife'. Thompson gives it the evocative title of 'AT 891D', subtitled 'The Rejected Wife as Lover.' The story, which has a very long shelf life indeed, always embodies a paradox about a child and often poses a riddle about a ring[i]:

> The central task requires the production of an heir by the wife, and the supplementary tasks all involve obvious symbols of male and female sexuality—the obtaining of rings, swords, or the husband's stallion, the digging of a well . . . the filling of a trunk. In several of the tales, the wife in fact disguises herself as a man, gains access to her husband, beats him at cards and offers to provide him with a woman . . . To fulfil the female part of the bargain and to put to rest their husbands' sexual anxieties, the women . . . take on the roles of lower-class, powerless, or degraded women--a cowherd's daughter, a slave, an imprisoned princess, a poor Florentine maid—women who, like whores, can be used contemptuously to supply sexual satisfaction and abandoned with ease without concern for consequences or heirs.[2]

The word 'clever' in the woman's title originally carried a negative, misogynist value, as the British upper classes used to apply it to a man (usually of a lower class, or Jewish) who was too glib and not to be trusted, an arriviste, not a true gentleman ('Too clever by half'), or as Americans in World War II used it in the jingoist phrase 'Damn clever, the Japanese.' In Hindi folklore, tales of 'clever wives' are usually about women who

---

[i] See 'Rings of Rejection'.

manage to commit adultery without getting caught. But there is far more to it than that.

THE STORY OF MULADEVA'S CLEVER WIFE

One of the earliest recorded variants of the story, probably the ultimate source of Shakespeare's *All's Well That Ends Well*, is the tale of Muladeva and the Brahmin's daughter, the final tale in Somadeva's *Kathasaritsagara*, or 'Ocean of the Rivers of Story', composed in Sanskrit in Kashmir in the tenth or eleventh century CE. It's a massive text, which shared its streams of story with yet another narrative ocean, the *Arabian Nights*, and this particular story is the ultimate riddle in a great book of riddles. The protagonist, named Muladeva, tells it in the first person:

> I went to Pataliputra with my friend Shashin, to test the cleverness of the people there. I met a young boy who was crying over a bowl of warm rice, and I chided him for his foolishness, but he replied, 'You are the fool, not I. I am crying in order to cool my rice and to clear my head of phlegm.' Embarrassed by our own lack of cleverness, we went on. Then we saw a beautiful girl gathering mangoes, and we asked her for some. 'Do you want to eat them warm or cool?' she asked. Wishing to understand this mystery, I said to the girl, 'Let us eat the warm mangoes now, and afterwards the others, my lovely one.' Thereupon she threw some mangoes on the ground, in the dust. When we had removed the dust by blowing on them with our mouths, we ate them. Then she laughed and said, 'First I gave you the warm mangoes, which you must have had to cool with your breath. Now catch these cool ones in your clothes, since you don't have to cool them with your breath.' And with this she threw some mangoes into the hems of our clothes. We took them and went away from that place, embarrassed. And I said to Shashin, 'I must certainly marry that clever girl. I must pay her back for making such fun of me.'
>
> We found out her father's house and went there in disguise. He promised to give me whatever I asked if I would stay there for four months, and when, at the end of the four months, I asked him for his daughter he said, 'I have been deceived! Well, so be it. What fault can there be, since he is virtuous.' And he gave her to me in the proper way. That night, in the bridal chamber, I laughed and said to my wife, 'Do you remember those warm and cool mangoes?' When she heard that she recognized me, and she smiled and said, 'City slickers trick country hicks like that.' Then I said to her, 'I hope you're happy, you city slicker. This country hick is going to abandon you and go far

away, I promise you.' To which she, too, made a promise: 'I swear that you will be bound and brought back to me by means of a son fathered by you.' When we had made these mutual vows, she turned her face from me and went to sleep, and I put my own ring on her finger while she slept. Then I went back to my native city, Ujjain, in order to test her cleverness.

When the Brahmin's daughter awoke in the morning she did not see me but she found the ring with my name on it, and she realized, 'He has kept his promise and abandoned me. Well, I will keep my promise, too, and abandon all regrets. His name, on this ring, is Muladeva, a famous trickster. Everyone says he lives in Ujjain. That's where I'll go.' She lied to her father, saying, 'My husband has already abandoned me. How can I live without him? So I will go on a pilgrimage, to torment this cursed body.' Unwillingly, he gave her his permission.

She went to Ujjain, dressed as a courtesan named Sumangala, set up an establishment, and became famous there. But she turned away all of her suitors, including my friend Shashin, and I became curious and went to see her. I entered and saw my own darling, whom I did not recognize, because she was wearing the clothes of a courtesan. But she recognized me again, and received me like a trickster courtesan. Then I passed the night with her, the most beautiful woman in the world, and I became so bound to her by passion that I could not leave the house. She, too, was bound to me through sexual passion, and never left my side until, after some days, the blackness of the tips of her breasts showed that she was pregnant. She then forged a summons from the king, and left me to return to Pataliputra. Though I was in love with her, I did not follow her, because I supposed that she belonged to someone else.

She gave birth to a son, and when he was twelve years old another boy said to him, 'No one knows who your father is, for someone or other fathered you when your mother was wandering around in foreign lands.' The boy, embarrassed, asked his mother, 'Mommy! Who is my father, and where is he? Tell me!' And his mother, the Brahmin's daughter, thought for a moment and said to him, 'Your father is named Muladeva. He abandoned me and went to Ujjain.' When she told him the whole story, the boy said, 'Mommy, I will bind him and bring him back, and so I will fulfil your promise.'

He went to Ujjain and recognized me from the description his mother had given him. Then he stole my bed right out from under me while I was asleep, lowering me gently onto a pile of rags on the floor.

When I woke up I felt a mixture of embarrassment, laughter and amazement. I went to the market place and wandered around, and I saw the boy selling the bed. I asked him, 'What price will you take for this bed?' But he replied, 'You can't buy it for money, O crown-jewel of tricksters, but by telling me a marvellous tale never heard before.' I said to him, 'I will tell you a marvellous tale never heard before. If you understand it and admit that it is true, you may keep the bed. But if you do not, you must be the son of a lover and you must give me the bed. Now, listen. Once when there was a famine, a certain king watered the back of the boar's beloved with spray from the chariots of the snakes, and with the grain that grew there he put an end to the famine.' The boy laughed and said, 'The chariots of the snakes are clouds; the boar's beloved is the earth, whom Vishnu loved in his incarnation as a boar; the rain from the clouds made grain grow on earth.'

And then that boy, who was a trickster, said, 'I will tell you a tale never heard before. If you understand it and admit that it is true, I will give you the bed. But if you do not, you will be my slave.' I agreed to this, and then the boy trickster said, 'Once upon a time, O lord of tricksters, a certain little boy was born here. As soon as he was born, he made the earth tremble by the weight of his foot, and then, when he grew big, he put his foot into another world.' I didn't understand what the boy said, and I replied, 'This is a lie. There is absolutely no truth at all in it.' Then the boy said to me, 'Didn't Vishnu, as soon as he was born, take the form of a dwarf and make the earth tremble at the strides of his feet? And then, when he grew big, didn't he put his foot into the world of heaven? So I have conquered you, and you are my slave.'

Then he bound me and took me back to his mother in Pataliputra. When she saw him she said to me, 'My husband, today my promise has been fulfilled. You have been bound and brought here by a son fathered by you.' And then she told the whole story, in front of everyone. Then her relatives all congratulated her on having achieved her wish through her own wisdom and on having the stain on the family honour wiped away by her son. And I, having achieved my goal, lived there with my wife and son for a long time, and then returned to Ujjain. So you see, your majesty [the story is being told to King Vikramaditya], there really are in this world some women of good family who love their husbands; not all women misbehave always.[3]

There is a fine symmetry to this story. The encounter between Muladeva and his wife is framed by stories about children who ask riddles: one little boy embarrasses Muladeva in the beginning, and another at the end; the final riddle is about a little boy, and about growing up. Both the first child and the woman pose riddles about food—cooked rice and mangoes, hot and cold food—and hot and cold emotions: the little boy cools his cooked rice by weeping, and Muladeva's future wife laughs about cooling warm mangoes by blowing on them. Other Indian variants, folk variants, of this particular story (for the story of Muladeva found its way into—more probably, back into—Indian folk literature) use other riddles here. In one, she asks him about a two-petalled flower, and although he gets the answer right—the eye—he vows to take vengeance on her, a low-caste woman, for her impertinence in daring to 'crack riddles' with him, a prince.[4]

The final set of riddles concerns two variants of the myth of the creation of the world by the god Vishnu:[ii] the giant Vishnu masquerades as a dwarf, just as Muladeva's Brahmin wife masquerades as a courtesan; and Vishnu grows bigger and conquers the world, just as Muladeva's son grows up and conquers his father. Thus, the text tangles cosmogony in a myth of sexual substitution. But the basic riddle of the myth of Muladeva is posed by the situation itself, the quandary of the rejected wife: how can you get a child if your husband won't sleep with you?

Muladeva is the most famous thief and trickster in ancient India, the subject of many stories in both folk and courtly literature; even the Brahmin's daughter knows his name. But he appears throughout the *Kathasaritsagara* not only as a thief, but as a thief of love, particularly noted for his devious erotic adventures. In another of the riddle-tales in the same text, Muladeva gives a lovesick friend a pill that turns him into a woman[iii] so that he can gain access to the harem.[5] Muladeva has been identified with the Gonikaputra ('Son of a Courtesan') whom Vatsyayana, the author of the *Kamasutra*, cites frequently as an earlier authority on the erotic science.[6]

Muladeva is also said to be the author of 'Muladeva's Verse': 'What man would enter a house from which no lovely, full-breasted, wide-hipped woman looks out on the street (for him), a house that is a prison without chains—unless he is made of stone?'[7] In the story of the Brahmin's daughter, Muladeva himself is precisely the man in his verse, the man who rejects the beautiful woman in his house. He knows all the answers, but he does not know their meaning; he knows how to turn another man into a

---

[ii] See 'You Can't Get Here' and 'Together Apart'.
[iii] See 'Transsexual Transformations'.

woman, but not how a woman can turn into another woman. The word in 'Muladeva's Verse' that I have translated as 'made of stone' is *jada*, which covers a range of meanings including 'numb', 'senseless', 'inanimate', 'stupefied' and 'impotent.'

What identifes Muladeva's son as the true son of his father is his cleverness, usually his skill as a thief, his father's profession; he inherits his dud dad's ability to steal, which is the proof of his paternity. The boy, an even greater trickster than his father, proves his identity not merely with words but with the bed, the scene of the crime, in a most literal bedtrick that matches his mother's: he steals the bed out from under his sleeping father. In one variant, the boy plays another literal bedtrick: he sneaks into his father's bedchamber, spreads sleeping powder, steals all the jewels, and finally, 'He even undid the legs of the couch which were inlaid with precious coral, and instead put under the bed the strong plantain stalks! To add insult to injury. Then he disappeared into the night.'[8] Muladeva explicitly says that if the boy can't answer the riddle, he will prove himself to be a bastard ('the son of a lover', *jarajata*), which is what he at first appears to be. In one variant, the son becomes a famous thief who cannot be caught;[9] even when he is the son not of a thief but of a king, the old motif hangs on atavistically. We are told that his mother, herself a princess, rejects her own father's offer to put the boy on the throne and determines instead to make him a thief (he can even steal a man's pyjamas when the man is wearing them), so that he can win his father's throne, and she can win his father.[10] Often the son also bears a striking physical resemblance to his father, particularly when the father is not a thief but a king; in one tale, the boy 'was struck to recognize himself in the face and shape of the prince', and when the king's father saw the two of them he said, 'Our son and this boy are as if one and the same person!'[11] In another variant, the unknown son pretends to be his father the king, wearing his ornaments, and the king says, 'This indeed is not my son. What of that? There is a little like my son's face.' In this case the resemblance extends to mind as well as body: the king decides that his known son is a fool and makes the unknown son sovereign in his place. Another variant hints that the father is insecure in his paternity; as usual, she obtains tokens (a cap and a picture, in this version) when she sleeps with him in disguise, and then: 'On the husband's arrival, he was not pleased to see the baby, but she showed him the cap and the picture, and told him the whole story ... So all ended happily.'[12] Or, all's well that ends well—as Shakespeare was to re-christen this tale.

The son's active role in capturing his absent father makes this story, from the son's point of view, a variant of the myth of the boy who seeks his true but unknown father. The boy's cleverness, however, identifies him as the true son not just of his father the thief but, even more, of his mother the clever wife. In the folk variants she plays an even stronger role than in the Sanskrit text; she teaches him 'how to change his appearance, how to climb ropes, how to steal'.[13] She is the riddler and trickster, who uses her head, as well as her body, to trap her man, both at the start of their courtship and in its final resolution. Muladeva's ring functions quite literally as a fetter—not for his wife, as he thinks when he puts it on her finger, but for himself, when the boy ties him up and drags him home. Though the wife's relatives refer at the end to a stain on the family honour, she knows all along that her honour is clean, despite appearances, just as she knows that she is not a courtesan, despite appearances—or even, perhaps, despite practices (though the Sanskrit text carefully specifies that she turned away all of her customers). Yet the myth in which the woman intentionally manipulates her husband by pretending to be a glamorous courtesan often shades off into darker stories in which a rejected woman (often, but not always, a wife) actually sinks into more sordid forms of prostitution and, without her intending any disguise, is so disfigured by her sufferings that her husband does not recognize her when he presents himself as a paying customer.

In other South Asian variants, the rejected wife engages in only slightly more respectable professions: she becomes a street-juggler,[14] a dancing girl,[15] or a rope-dancer,[16] and sleeps with her husband non-professionally. Sometimes, she steals the man's ring. Yet Muladeva grudgingly admits at the end that she is an exception to the general rule of these appearances; the moral that he explicitly culls from this story is one of grudging misogyny: not all women misbehave all the time. A Kashmiri folk variant of this story begins with a man who refuses to marry until his family assures him that 'all women are not alike'—that some are like trees that give welcome shade, while others are like bitches that bite your heels as you go in and out at the door.[17] Muladeva's wife is of the shade-tree variety.

Thus, all of the members of Muladeva's family are tricksters; the 'mutual vows' that Muladeva and his wife exchange are not, as in our parlance, marriage vows, but vows to deceive. Muladeva's son mockingly calls him 'the crown jewel of tricksters', but Muladeva is out-tricked not only by his tricky boy, but by his tricky wife (who is described, at one point, through the pun of a 'trickster courtesan'—that is, one who pretends to be a courtesan, and also a courtesan who tricks people) and, ultimately, by Vishnu, the supreme trickster. At various points, Muladeva and his wife see through one another's tricks. She does not, apparently, recognize him when he comes in disguise and lives in the house for four months, but she recognizes him on the wedding night, not at sight, but at speech: the riddle about mangoes. Muladeva fails to recognize her at the crucial meeting in Ujjain, simply because he cannot mentally process the fact that his wife— whom he has, after all, only been in bed with once, and then did not consummate the act—is a courtesan; no other reason is given. In one variant, he 'of course had not recognized her since she was dressed up completely as a juggler's girl';[18] another simply says, 'The husband did not recognize his wife because of her dress and makeup.'[19] Yet, in the Sanskrit text, he knows that his 'courtesan' is pregnant because he sees her nipples darken, a sharply observed, earthy fact that will be, with much else, jettisoned in the European retellings. She recognizes him much earlier than he recognizes her, and teaches her son to recognize him when he does not recognize his son. Only at the end does he recognize her, through her deeds and her words: the promise fulfilled.

We never learn her name, nor her father's or her son's; she is just the Brahmin's daughter. But, significantly, she gives herself a name when she becomes a courtesan; does this mean that her masquerading identity as a courtesan is her only true independent identity? Muladeva, of course, has a name, indeed a notorious name, which is all that she gets from the ring in this text. But the ring plays a far more important role in other Indian variants: sometimes, before the disguised wife will sleep with her husband, on three separate occasions, over three years, in three different cities, she demands that he give her his pearl necklace, diamond necklace and ring,[20] or his ring and handkerchief,[21] or his diamond necklace, signet ring and breast-ornament,[22] and she produces them, along with the grown child, years later. In a Moroccan variant, he gives his disguised wife first his ring, then an anklet and finally a necklace; years later, when he is about to marry another woman, the first wife produces three children, each carrying one of the three pieces of jewellery, and each named after the town in which she seduced her husband, the names being regarded as part of the proof, too.[23] (Sometimes just the three children named after towns, devoid of jewellery, are the proof.[24]) Thus, where the ring in the tale of Muladeva reveals the father's name only to the mother, in other tellings it reveals to the whole world the father's connection with both his wife and his son.

The ring that reveals the name of the father was folded into a modern folk variant of the great Sanskrit epic, the *Mahabharata*. In this story, the hero Arjuna travels widely and marries several women, one of whom, Vasudanta, is a half-cobra princess, a Nagi, from Nagaloka, the underworld kingdom of the Nagas; Arjuna, as is his wont, abandons mother and son and does not see them again until the son grows up to be a warrior, who then joins his father in the great doomsday battle. A Hindi variant of that episode was narrated in the Himalaya by Bacan Singh in 1986:

> Arjuna said to his wife Vasudanta, 'My mother has sent these bumblebees [as messengers]—I must go to Hastinapura.' Vasudanta said, 'The male of the species is very bad. You will forget me and marry again. Give me your token.' Now, Arjuna had a special ring that enabled him to travel very quickly, and his ten names were written on it. He left it with her, and therefore it took him twelve years to reach Hastinapura. And the child Nagarjuna was born in Nagaloka and grew to be twelve years old . . . He laughed and played with the people of the city. The other children teased him, calling him a bastard. He went crying to his mother and told her how the other children teased him. He said, 'Mother, who is my father?' and she said, 'You have no father . . .' She said, 'Look at this ring. There's a copper plate inside: read it. On it is written that your father is Arjuna, who lives in Hastinapura.'[25]

This telling, which closely parallels several aspects of the Muladeva story, uses the ring to plug up, as it were, or at least to embed, in a known cultural context, some of the moral holes that came to be perceived in Arjuna's story by a much later culture that knew about copper-plate engravings and male chauvinism. The other children tease the child by calling him '*cor-jar-putra*,' the equivalent of 'bastard' but more literally 'son of a thieving lover', which is precisely what the boy is in the Muladeva story. The ring is the woman's surety that her husband will return, when she voices concerns that other women in her position might also have had. But the ring that solves one problem opens up another; as William Sax, the anthropologist who collected and translated the story, remarks in a footnote, 'It is odd, to say the least, that Arjuna gave up his ring and thus took so long to reach Hastinapura. This detail is anachronistic: it facilitates the aging of Nagarjuna, so that he will be an adult when Arjuna confronts him, but what did Arjuna's family do for twelve years while they waited for him?' This lacuna would normally have been filled by the machinations of the forgotten wife; for the anachronism was created by combining two rings: the magic ring of swift flight (which Arjuna ought to keep) and the seal ring of paternal identity (which the wife either keeps or gets, and from which she learns the husband's name and city, as Muladeva's wife does). This is one of the perils of intertextuality: Arjuna must travel on foot for twelve years, leaving his ring of swift flight to serve a different purpose for his wife.

Who is asking the riddle? Who is testing whom in these stories? Often (as in the Muladeva story) the wife sets the task herself, and not only satisfies her own conditions, but out-riddles her husband and makes a fool of him. Her cleverness is, in many variants, the problem as well as the solution: humiliated when she trumps his riddles, he vows to marry her precisely in order to take revenge. Thus, in a version that was translated (into French) from spoken Arabic in the Nile valley in 1893, 'He could find no better way to pay her back than to marry her.'[26] And her cleverness often inspires her to set up the riddle in revenge; when he vows, 'As a punishment for your impertinence—cracking riddles with me!—I shall marry you! But right from that moment I'll throw you into solitary confinement!' she replies, 'If indeed you will marry me, then I shall bear you a son without you even knowing it, and I shall make him flog you with a whip!'[27] Or, when he vows, 'Someday I will marry you and punish you greatly,' she replies, 'When I have borne you a son, I will tie you to your horse's leg and have you beaten,'[28] or she vows that she will bear him a son who will tie him in a sack and beat him.[29] In the Muladeva story, she is the one who turns her back in bed first, and in another variant, too, it is she, rather than he, who gets up and sleeps in a separate bed when she realizes that he has tricked her by spying on her when he was disguised as her cook.[30]

But the man usually sets the task for his wife, and he does this as part of his more general rejection of her. In an oral Arabic variant, 'When the prince entered the nuptial chamber he did not touch his wife at all, nor spoke even a single word to her, but, on the contrary, distanced himself from her with contempt.'[31] In one Indian variant in which there is no initial antipathy between them, and hence no reason for revenge, the husband is the one who makes the wager; as he goes away on a business trip he casually remarks, 'When I return I expect to find you have built me a grand well; and also, as you are such a clever wife, to see a little son!'[32] (In a Moroccan variant, the well is already there, and he throws her into it.[33]) The unmotivated rejection appears already in the opening banter in a Kashmiri version of the tale; when the king of Kashmir, carried away by hunting, meets a beautiful girl deep in the forest, the first words he says to her are, 'Ha ha! Certainly! A wife like you, whom after marrying I could put aside here in this jungle!' to which she replies, 'Of course, I'd marry somebody like you and get a child; and the boy should marry your daughter!' When he sends for her and marries her and then puts her in his harem and ignores her, she tells her mother that she supposed it was on account of her retort that the king of Kashmir thus treated her.[34] But he had stated his intention to abandon her before she ever said a word. Throughout the corpus of these myths, no matter who actually sets the terms of the test, the man always has the power, and he always leaves her. But even when he sets the terms, she takes charge; she is able to trick him into coming back, and she always wins in the end.

THE REJECTED WIFE

Do these stories have a happy ending? Does the clever wife really get what she wants? I wonder.

Sometimes the clever wife's husband comes to love her after she has his child. The logical paradox, the 'Catch-22', is to get the child before he loves her; once she solves that riddle, she wins. But do we accept the statement that he loves her after she has borne him a male child? That depends very much on the very different cultural and individual expectations of the women in different variants of the tale. She may win his body for a night, long enough to make a child, but often she wants more than that. The woman who marries the king of Kashmir comes to him in disguise because, 'It happened, however, that she loved him,'[35] and at the end of another Kashmiri variant, the husband capitulates completely and declares, 'You are the master, I am the pupil. Forgive my conceit, love me again thoroughly.'[36]

The wife is undesirable for many of the reasons we have considered, but also, and perhaps primarily, because the husband knows that she is his wife, that he must desire her; this is why he rejects her, and why he subsequently accepts her when he thinks she is not his wife. Often, the upper-class wife attempts to overcome her husband's paralyzing respect through a change in class (she dresses like a whore) or culture (she dresses like a foreigner); but when the wife is of a lower class, that, too, as we have seen, may be the reason for her rejection. The clever wife is usually 'foreign', not merely in the explicit political sense (she may wear the costume of another culture— Muladeva's wife goes from Pataliputra to Ujjain), but in the psychological sense of alienation or defamiliarization: she makes herself strange to her husband, and hence desirable, no longer the boring legitimate partner, but fresh again. In several well-known Hindu myths, after a god has impregnated a woman (Kunti, Satyavati), he restores her virginity,[37] as some husbands re-sealed the boxes that belong to the clever wives; this is what the fantasy of the wife-as-mistress does for the husband. Too high or too low, too clever by half, she seems to begin in a no-win situation. Her only way out is to escape from all of these superficial labels and turn her cleverness from a liability into an asset. Becoming someone else, she makes him see who she really is.

If the wife's goal is to win back her husband's heart forever, then it is she who seems self-deceived. She has won her husband's respect for her perseverance and ingenuity, but this is likely to be a temporary victory. In some texts, even, perhaps, the tale of Muladeva's wife, the husband is, in the end, quite pleased to have such a clever wife, precisely the quality for which he rejected her in the beginning. Other texts may reflect a cultural suspicion that intelligence, like complexion, can be partly inherited, even from the distaff side, so that it's a good idea for the dynasty in a world of dangerous court intrigues to find a really smart wife. But some texts are either ignorant of these genetic factors or, as was the case in classical Indian legal texts,[iv] assume that only the father, not the mother, hands on his character traits to the child.[38]

PATERNAL INSECURITY

Whatever the genetic theory, the mother, too, has concerns for heredity. The clever wife may or may not hope to satisfy her desire for her husband's love but she almost always hopes to satisfy her desire for a child. The question of inheritance, which is generally viewed as a male problem—'Give me lots of sons just like me'—is also a female problem: 'Let my children inherit.' If the wife is willing to settle for a child that her husband acknowledges as his own, with all the rights and privileges thereto, then all may indeed end, more or less, well.[39] Muladeva's wife is using her husband to get a baby, perhaps even stealing his substance to give her what she wants; but she is also using the baby to get the husband. Often the rejected wife wants both at once, and in fact, the husband often wants a baby, as well as an erotic partner. In one story where the husband is about to remarry and he sees the three sons he has unknowingly begotten, playing near him, preparatory to confronting him, he thinks, 'If I had such lovely children I would never remarry.' When their mother proves to him that

---

[iv] See 'Why Should a Brahmin?' and 'Medical and Mythical Constructions'.

they are his, they transform the celebration from a wedding to a triple circumcision.[40] Folklore tends to emphasize the goal of fertility and babies, literature the goal of love; but in some stories of both genres, the two goals are inseparable.

The usual legal process is for a woman to get a ring and then get a baby; the usual physical process is first sex, then baby. To have the baby but not the ring is, of course, the defining situation of every unwed mother, the fate worse than death that has haunted women throughout recorded history. The narrative paradox seems to reverse this process, requiring the woman to have a baby in order to get both the ring and the sex, but in fact, here, too, the sex must come first; it merely appears to come second. The clever wife gets a child as the result of her masquerade, and is then legally and physically acknowledged by her husband.

And the father wants to be sure that the kid is his. Paternal nervousness is well expressed in the saying, *pater semper incertus est*, as Roman law remarks drily—which means, I think, both that the father is uncertain in his mind and that fatherhood is an uncertain thing. The ghost of this sentiment hovers over these stories of clever wives, which regard the ring as proof of paternity, against all logic, because the father in the stories (and telling the stories) wants something hard, like a piece of jewellery (which, after all, can get lost but not so easily broken as a heart), to prove what can in fact never be proven: that the child is his own. (Nowadays, DNA can offer a kind of proof of paternity, and is resorted to by an astonishing number of nervous men, fifteen per cent of whom turn out to have good cause to be nervous. But not even DNA can prove chastity or fidelity, or cure sexual jealousy.) The stories pit male fears about legitimacy against women's knowledge about sexuality, and men's power against women's cleverness.

But there is more than paternal nervousness at issue in these tales. Two different female virtues are at stake here: on the one hand, the subversive virtue of actively resisting, fighting for what you want (usually the legacy of your child), honestly or dishonestly; and, on the other hand, the noble, passive virtue of being innocent of sin (though often wrongly accused). The clever wife, though usually spurned for her wit at the start of the story, is praised for it at the end; defending her marital fidelity with a subversive intelligence, she proves that she has innocence as well.

RINGS OF REJECTION AND RECOGNITION IN ANCIENT INDIA[1]

A piece of circular jewellery—a ring or a necklace, sometimes a bracelet or an anklet—plays a central role in three separate but related bodies of mythology in classical Sanskrit literature, each of which deals with the theme of sexual rejection and recognition. The first cycle tells of a woman who is married but rejected by her husband before she is able to get pregnant; the second tells of a woman who is impregnated before a public marriage has taken place and is then denied by her husband; and the third tells of a woman who disguises herself as a non-wife and is identified as a legal wife by her necklace. The ring (or necklace) identifies the woman in the first case as a married woman who has been (legally) impregnated, in the second case as a pregnant woman who is legally married, and in the third as a desired woman who is the legally designated, though not yet married, wife. In all three cycles, circular jewellery resolves the paradox of marital sexual rejection: the husband desires both an erotic encounter and a legitimate child, but not from the same woman. Let us consider these cycles separately and then together, to see how the ring or necklace is not simply multivalent but bi-polar, ambivalent, signifying, like so many symbols, two opposite things at the same time.[2]

The first is the tale of the clever wife, which I have discussed elsewhere in this volume.[i] So let us now consider the second and the third, before comparing all three.

THE RING OF SHAKUNTALA

For the clever wife, the ring is the solution to the problem of her legitimation, when she uses it to prove who impregnated her. For Shakuntala, the ring is both the problem (when she loses it) and the

---

[i] See 'The Clever Wife'.

solution, when she finds it again); but now the ring is also the solution (the excuse) for her husband, king Dushyanta (also called Duhshanta).

The ancient story of Shakuntala and the lost ring of memory is told in a famous Sanskrit play—*Abhijnana-shakuntalam*—by the poet Kalidasa, in the fourth century CE, but it is based upon a story in the *Mahabharata* (composed between about 300 BCE and 300 CE) in which there is no ring:

> When King Duhshanta was hunting in the forest, killing all the animals, he came to a hermitage where he met Shakuntala and persuaded her to marry him by the *gandharva* rite of private, mutual desire; but she made him promise that the son she bore to him would become king. Then he left, promising to send for her. Shakuntala gave birth to a boy and brought him to court, saying to Duhshanta, 'This is your son.' When the king heard her words, he remembered perfectly well, but he said, 'I do not remember. Whose woman are you? I don't remember ever having had anything to do with you. I do not recognize this son that you have. Women are liars. Who will trust what you say? Your son is too big, and too strong, to have been born as recently as you claim.'
>
> She left in fury, and a disembodied voice from the sky said, 'The mother is the father's leather water-bag; the son belongs to the man who begets him. The mother brings forth a son and her own body is split into two. Support your son, and do not reject Shakuntala.' Then Duhshanta said to his courtiers, 'I knew all of this perfectly well, knew that he was my own son. But if I had accepted him as my own son just from her words, there would have been doubt among the people.' Then he accepted his son and forgave Shakuntala for the harsh words she had spoken to him in her anger.[3]

Duhshanta's sexual viciousness is foreshadowed by his excessive hunting and hardly mitigated by his statement that he rejected Shakuntala because of his fear of public disapproval, an argument that rings equally hollow when Rama uses it to reject Sita in the *Ramayana*.[4] Either he does not remember her or, much more likely, he does not want to remember either her or his awkward promise about the succession. But a divine voice forces him to acknowledge his son, whose extraordinary size and strength had previously led the king not to accept him as divinely blessed but to reject him as begotten by some other, previous lover. That voice's statement about the importance of mothers is hardly feminist; it is of the 'hen is a way for an egg to make another egg' school of embryology. But its surprisingly violent image of a woman in childbirth—split in two—evokes sympathy for mothers and suggests the classic, violent response of a woman to a double-dealing man: become two women, as clever wives do when they masquerade as mistresses. Surely we must hear an ironic voice, perhaps even a woman's voice, in the text's statement that the king magnanimously forgave *her* for speaking to him in anger.

Stanley Insler likens Duhshanta to Yavakri, the demonic rapist (who appears, too, in the *Mahabharata*):[5] he compares the 'forced rape' that Yavakri commits and his destruction by a 'fake wife' with what he regards as the virtual rape of Shakuntala at the hands of the 'false' Duhshanta. Insler calls it a rape because Shakuntala was 'completely innocent until the arrival of the king and therefore highly susceptible to the king's advances . . . The Gandharvan [marriage is] motivated by desire and lust, and the tale thus continues the old theme of rape with a new twist.'[6] But we need not single out the particular story of Yavakri to find a counterpart to the tale of Shakuntala; hundreds of other stories in Indian literature, and beyond, share these features of rape and masquerade as well as many other details that make them even closer parallels.[7]

When the Buddhists told the story of Shakuntala, in Jataka texts composed perhaps as early as the fourth century BCE, they used different names and introduced the theme of a ring, not a ring of memory but a ring that served both as a proof of identity and as a kind of child support:

[King Brahmadatta of Benares was wandering in his pleasure groves when he saw a woman and fell in love with her. He seduced her and she conceived.] He gave her the signet ring from his finger and dismissed her with these words: 'If it be a girl, spend this ring on her nurture; but if it be a boy, bring ring and child to me.' [She gave birth to a boy, and the children teased him, calling him 'No-father'. He asked his mother about his father, and she told him. At his wish, she took him to the palace and said], 'This is your son, sire.' The king knew well enough that this was the truth, but shame before all his court made him reply, 'He is no son of mine.' 'But here is your signet-ring, sire; you will recognize that.' 'Nor is this my signet ring.' Then said the woman, 'Sire, I have now no witness to prove my words, except to appeal to truth. Wherefore, if you be the father of my child, I pray that he may stay in mid-air; but if not, may he fall to earth and be killed.' So saying, she seized the Bodhisattva by the foot and threw him up in the air. [The child, suspended in the air, told the king he was his son. The king received him in his arms and made him heir to the throne.][8]

This text is one of very very few, among thousands of retellings of this tale, that mentions the commonsense fact that a ring doesn't actually prove anything at all unless other people recognize it. (In fact, another Buddhist Jataka reverts to the more conventional assumption that the ring is an absolute proof: when the seducer, this time the king's Brahmin chaplain, says to the child, 'I gave your mother a token, where is it?' the boy hands him the ring, which the Brahmin recognizes and acknowledges.[9]) It also perpetuates the gender bias in the hard-headed value of a ring: if the child is a boy, it's all well and good to use the ring to secure his patrimony, but if it's a girl, you might as well use it for her dowry. These rational moments lead, however, back into irrational religion, an act of truth reminiscent of Sita's fire ordeal in response to Rama's rejection and of the voice from the sky in the *Mahabharata* tale of Shakuntala: a miracle, a suspension of the law of gravity, which proves the identity of the child and epitomizes the liminality of the child torn between two parents. The king here quite blithely accepts the possibility that his son may crash and die. The Buddhist text spells out, as the *Mahabharata* does not, the king's embarrassment and his total disregard for the child as well as the mother.

The poet Kalidasa had his work cut out for him to transform the king (whom he calls Dushyanta) from a lying rapist to a sympathetic lover, and he fell back upon the tried and true device of the magic ring and the curse of forgetfulness:

> King Dushyanta met Shakuntala in the forest, and they fell in love. She did not yet know that he was the king (he told her he was the king's minister in charge of religious affairs); then he offered her his signet ring with his name engraved on it, and when her friends read the name on the ring and acted surprised, he said, 'Do not misunderstand; the ring is a gift from the king.' Shakuntala refused the ring at first, but eventually, after she had found out that he himself was the king, she slept with him (by the *gandharva* rite of mutual desire). He placed his ring on her finger as he left to return to court, telling her to count off one day for each letter of his name, and at the end he would send for her.
>
> One day, Shakuntala, lost in thoughts of the king, ignored the hot-tempered sage Durvasas, who cursed her: 'Since you were so lost in thought of someone so that you had no mind for anyone else, he will not remember you even when you try to awaken him, just as a drunk does not remember the story that he told before.' Shakuntala didn't hear the curse, but her friends did, and persuaded the sage to limit it;

he said: 'The power of the curse will cease the moment she presents some ornament as a token of recognition.' When the king failed to send for her, and Shakuntala discovered that she was pregnant, she set out for court, and her friends advised her, 'If the king is slow to recognize you, be sure to show him the ring inscribed with his name.'

Meanwhile, at court, the king's neglected chief queen was singing a sad song: 'How have you forgotten your love?' When the king saw Shakuntala, who was veiled, he wondered who she was; when he was told that she was bearing his child, he was full of doubt; and when she removed her veil, he said, 'Did I take this beauty before, or not? No matter how hard I try, I cannot remember ever making this woman my own. And how can I accept her when she shows clear signs of pregnancy and I have doubts about being the one who sowed the field,[ii] as it were?' Shakuntala thought to herself, 'When his passion has undergone such a change, what good would it do even if I were to make him remember? But I must prove my own purity.' And she said to the king, 'If you have doubts, thinking that I am another man's wife, I will dispel your doubt by this token of remembrance . . . O god, my finger does not carry the ring!' Her chaperone said, 'It must have been lost when you went into the water at the shrine.' The king smiled and said, 'This is why people say that women are so cunning.' But he continued to waver: 'Am I deluded, or is she lying? This is my quandary. Which is worse for me, to be a wife-abandoner or a man defiled by the touch of another man's wife?'

The chaplain made a helpful suggestion: 'Since it has been predicted that the king's son will be a sovereign of the world, wait until Shakuntala has the child and see if he has the marks of sovereignty.' The king agreed, but Shakuntala ran away and was snatched up to heaven by the celestial courtesan who was her mother. The king lamented, 'Though I do not remember the sage's daughter, or any marriage, still my aching heart contradicts me.'

Sometime after this, a fisherman found the king's ring inside a fish and brought it to the palace. As soon as the king saw the ring, he remembered that he had married Shakuntala and that he had denied her in the delusion that overcame him when she had lost the ring. But one of the women in his court argued, 'Such a passion should not need a token of remembrance or recognition.' To which the king replied, 'So, let me blame the ring.'

[ii] For the metaphor of the seed and the field, see 'Medical and Mythical Constructions' and 'Why Should a Brahmin?'

One day, in heaven on a mission for the gods, Dushyanta met the child that Shakuntala had borne. The boy was playing with a lion cub. When a bystander remarked, 'Miraculous, astonishing, the speaking resemblance between this boy and you,' the king began to suspect that it was his own son. The boy had lost his bracelet while playing with the cub, and the king picked up the bracelet, to the astonishment of the bystanders, who recalled that it was a magic bracelet that no one but the boy or his parents could pick up; if anyone else touched it, it would change into a serpent and bite them. The sceptical king asked, 'Have you yourself ever been eye witnesses to this transformation, with your own eyes?' To which two women among the bystanders replied, 'Many times.' But the king was convinced only when the boy said, 'You are not my father; Dushyanta is my father.' Then Shakuntala entered and said, 'Even after I heard that the bracelet didn't turn into a serpent, I was afraid to believe it.' But when she saw the king she said, 'He is not like my husband. Who is he, who defiles by the touch of his limbs my son, who was protected by that bracelet?' The boy said, 'Mommy! This stranger embraces me and calls me his son.' Then Shakuntala and the king began to argue:

King: 'My dear, it is only fair that you should turn my cruelty to you against me, as I see that you now refuse to recognize me. The darkness of my delusion has been pierced by the light of memory . . .'

Shakuntala: 'It must have been the ripening of my past deeds that made you, who had been so compassionate, become so cold. But how did you come to remember unhappy me? Ah, I see your ring.'

King: 'Yes, it was by getting back this ring that I got back my memory. It does seem to me strange that, through a loosening of my memory, I denied Shakuntala and then, afterwards, as a result of seeing the ring, I understood that I had formerly married her.'

Shakuntala: 'Thank goodness! My husband did not refuse me without any reason. But I don't remember being cursed. Could I have been cursed without knowing it, when my mind was distracted by the separation? Is that why my friends advised me to show the ring to my husband?'

Then a god explained it to her: 'Your husband rejected you because of the curse that obstructed his memory; the reflection [chaya] does not assume a shape on the surface of a mirror when its brightness is masked by dirt, but it easily finds its place there when it is cleaned.'

The twist here consists in the fact that although the king gave Shakuntala the ring to make her remember *him*, its loss makes him forget *her*; the magic of the loss of the ring on her finger is projected, as it were, into his mind many miles away, like the ointment that, according to ancient Indian theory, you put on your eyes to keep other people from seeing you.[10] The shadow and clouded mirror-reflection symbolize the loss of the image, of the memory.

The king lies about the ring at the start (denying that it is his, just as he will later deny that Shakuntala and her son are his), and then he forgets it; the curse is a very convenient and rather suspicious excuse, as the cynical ladies in the court point out: 'Such a passion should not need a token of remembrance or recognition.' The king's reply, 'So, let me blame the ring', is about as close to an admission of guilt as that sort of ruler, indeed that sort of man, will ever get. The king has done this before, as we know from the neglected queen who sings of forgotten love. Shakuntala, who has begun to understand him better, offers him an easy out: 'It must have been the ripening of my past deeds that made you, so compassionate, become so cold.' She is also persuaded that 'when his passion has undergone such a change', it would be no use to try to remind him of it. Yet she pretends not to recognize him at first, subjecting him to his own treatment, a very mild version of the trickster tricked.

Dushyanta's loss of memory is notorious in later Sanskrit literature: when a woman named Kalingasena is seduced by a man disguised as a king, and the real king later denies having had her, she says to him, 'Did you marry me by the *gandharva* ritual and then forget me, as Dushyanta forgot Shakuntala, long ago?' But the king replies (in that case honestly), 'Truly, I never married you at all; I just came here now.'[11] The ring, in Kalidasa's play, is doubled by the magic bracelet that identifies the boy's parents (an item that, in mass production, would put an end to all paternity suits). And the king is sceptical about this trick, too (as is Shakuntala, who won't believe the evidence of the bracelet until she sees the king with her own eyes), but eyewitnesses shut him up.

The woman must produce the hard evidence of *both* the ring *and* the son to win her husband back. Unlike Duhshanta in the *Mahabharata*, who with calculating commonsense rejects the son who is unnaturally big and strong for his alleged age, Dushyanta recognizes his son by that very same unnatural, supernatural behaviour—his courage in playing with a lion. But there are other signs of recognition as well. Bystanders note the 'speaking resemblance', literally 'forms that talk together', between the boy and his father. The hard evidence is undermined and the 'soft' evidence of somatic memory is validated: when the king first fell in love with Shakuntala, who was apparently of another class (not royal), he had hoped that she might, in fact, turn out to be of his own class, and had reasoned: 'Surely she is fit to be the wife of a man of royal birth, since the heart of a nobleman like me yearns for her; for the inner inclinations of good people are their authority to distinguish doubtful objects.' [1.19] He now responds instinctively in the same way to his son, even when his memory does not know that it is his son: 'How is it that I feel love for this little boy as if he were the son born of my own loins? If my limbs thrill so to his touch, what bliss must he give to the man from whose body he grew?' [7.19] And earlier, his 'aching heart' had remembered his marriage to Shakuntala even when his memory had not ('Though I do not remember the sage's daughter, or any marriage, still my aching heart contradicts me . . .' 5.31). This tension between heart and memory, body and mind, is correlated to the tension between illicit love and marital love in all of these stories, a tension that takes a different twist in the third cycle, to which we will now turn.

THE RING OF COINCIDENCE

The cynicism that Kalidasa's play expresses explicitly toward the evidence of the bracelet and implicitly toward the proof of the ring is ultimately undermined by the text: both the ring and the bracelet tell the truth. This cynicism is more forcibly expressed, though again contradicted, in another story about the conflict between the erotic woman and the married woman—King Harsha's *Ratnavali*, composed in the eighth century CE. The *Ratnavali* is part of a complex cycle of classical Sanskrit texts surrounding the mythical figures of King Udayana, his queen, Vasavadatta, and a series of co-wives.[12] We may read the Shakuntala story as another instance of this general theme, in which Shakuntala is the new co-wife who threatens the chief queen, a queen who grieves, much like Vasavadatta, over the waning of her husband's love.

Several episodes in Harsha's *Ratnavali* turn upon the symbolism of jewellery. The play enacts this story:

> It was predicted that King Udayana, married to the jealous (with good reason) Queen Vasavadatta, must marry Ratnavali ('The [Lady with the] Jewelled Necklace'), the daughter of the king of Simhala. Udayana's prime minister spread a rumour that Vasavadatta had died in a fire [so Ratnavali could be brought to the kingdom] but while Ratnavali was sailing to Kausambi, the ship was wrecked. Ratnavali was rescued from

the water by a merchant and given to the minister, who recognized her by the jewel necklace which she always wore. He put her in Vasavadatta's service as a handmaid named Sagarika ('Oceanic'). Vasavadatta tried to keep the king from seeing Sagarika, who was very beautiful, but Sagarika saw him and fell in love with him. One day the king found a portrait that Sagarika had painted of him with herself and declared his passionate love for the unknown maiden who had painted it. Then Sagarika and the king met, but she ran away and the king said, 'My beloved, who is like a jewel necklace, slipped out of my hand before I could get her around my neck.' Vasavadatta entered; the jester hid the portrait, as the king told him to do, but then he dropped it and the queen saw the portrait, recognized Sagarika, and asked the king who the other woman painted next to him was. The king smiled nervously and said, 'Don't get the wrong impression, your majesty. Trust me. I painted this girl out of my own imagination and never saw her before (*adrishtapurva*).' The jester added, 'I swear by my sacred thread, this is the truth, if we ever saw such a woman before.' The queen's companion added, 'Your majesty, this sort of coincidence does happen.'

But the queen left in anger, with a headache, and sent her servants to have Sagarika put in prison. As she was led to prison, Sagarika gave the jewel necklace to her friend to give to a Brahmin; the friend gave it to the jester, who realized that Sagarika must be of noble birth. Just then the chief counsellor of Ratnavali's father, the king of Simhala, arrived, with his escort; he had accompanied Ratnavali on the voyage and had survived the shipwreck but thought that Ratnavali had died. The counsellor saw the necklace on the jester and thought he recognized it as Ratnavali's but then decided that this might be sheer coincidence.

He told king Udayana that the king of Simhala had sent Ratnavali to him, but she had been shipwrecked and drowned. Then Sagarika appeared, and the counsellor from Simhala said to the escort, looking at Sagarika, 'She looks just like the princess.' And the escort said, 'This very thought was in my mind.' The counsellor asked about Sagarika, and Vasavadatta replied to the king, 'Your minister told me that she had been rescued from the sea; that's why she was called Sagarika.' Then the counsellor, recalling the necklace, decided that this must in fact be Ratnavali, and he said aloud, 'Princess Ratnavali! How did you fall into such misfortune?'

Vasavadatta asked the escort, 'Is this Ratnavali?' and when he said, 'It is,' she embraced Ratnavali and said, 'My sister!' The king said, 'Is this the daughter of the king of Simhala, a man of high birth?' The jester said, 'As soon as I saw the jewel necklace I knew that this was the property of no common person.' Vasavadatta had Ratnavali's chains taken off and embraced her. The minister entered and explained how he had set it all up, including putting Ratnavali/Sagarika in the harem so that the king would see her and fall in love with her. Vasavadatta smiled, adorned Ratnavali with her own ornaments, took her hand and joined it with the king's, and said, 'My lord, accept this Ratnavali.' Vasavadatta addressed Ratnavali as 'Queen', and they all lived happily ever after.

Thus Vasavadatta, the chief queen, apparently forgets her sorrow and anger and accepts Ratnavali as her co-wife. And the king gets them both; Hindu kings are, after all, no different from kings the world over.

Consider the necklace. It suggests, if it does not prove, Ratnavali's identity.

The king likens Sagarika to a jewel necklace, not realizing that 'jewel necklace' is really her name, Ratnavali. This is a kind of Freudian slip, suggesting that on some deep level the king may suspect that Sagarika is in fact Ratnavali. The necklace, like the ring, invites this sort of buried recognition, and, like the ring, is associated with a hidden name: the Oceanic girl at first is *like* a necklace, and is known to *have* a necklace (by which Udayana's minister recognizes her before the play begins, and her father's counsellor half-recognizes her at the end), and finally is recognized as being *named* a necklace.

The necklace is at first taken as evidence, but is then ruled inadmissible. The argument about coincidence deflects the power of the jewellery clue so that it isn't the essential clue after all, but just evidence to corroborate the more profound recognition when it comes. The counsellor at first invokes coincidence to explain away the striking resemblance between the necklace last seen on Ratnavali and now seen on the jester: princesses have so many jewels that 'It is not hard to find a coincidence (literally, a conversation) of ornaments', like the 'speaking resemblance' that identified the true son of King Dushyanta in Kalidasa's *Shakuntala*. But in the end the counsellor decides, 'Since the necklace on the jester's neck bears such a strong resemblance, and since this girl came from the ocean, it's clear that this is Ratnavali, the daughter of the King of Simhala.'

The question of coincidence has already been raised on another occasion, too: trying to explain the fact that the king claims to have painted a woman he has never seen, the queen's companion refers to it as a coincidence, *ghunakshara*, literally an alphabet letter eaten into a page by a bookworm. The jester tries to explain the portrait away with a pun, remarking that he and the king never 'saw such a woman before'; he uses the term *adrishtapurva*, which can mean either that such a woman was never seen before, that she is marvellous and unique, which is the truth, or that the king never saw Sagarika in real life, which is a lie.

Other forms of jewellery and clothing, too, are used to perpetrate other sorts of disguises and machinations. Thus the king bribes Sagarika's friend with his own earring and rewards the jester with his own bracelet; the queen gives Sagarika's friend her own clothes and adorns Ratnavali with her own ornaments.

But the truth that the necklace reveals from the start is not Ratnavali's particular identity (which is finally established by her face, her resemblance to herself) but her class. She is the daughter of a foreign king, masquerading as someone of a lower class, the princess as the pauper. Here again, like the Jataka text that used the magic ring to provide for the rearing of a child, the text suddenly plays a harsh rational light on a traditional romantic theme: *anyone* who has a fabulous necklace of emeralds and rubies must be a princess, if not necessarily the particular princess you are looking for. And Sagarika's class is eventually the key to her individual identity, just as it was a clue to Shakuntala's ('Surely she is fit to be the wife of a man of royal birth, since the heart of a nobleman like me yearns for her; for the inner inclinations of good people are their authority toward doubtful objects'). Class precipitates Vasavadatta's fury against Sagarika: on one occasion, the queen overhears the king remark to Sagarika that he values the queen only for her 'naturally noble birth', while genuine passion inspires his feelings for the apparently lower-born Ratnavali-as-Sagarika. Then Vasavadatta, the queen, steps forward and rejects the king's efforts to conciliate her by throwing himself at her feet; through clenched teeth she says, 'Get up, get up, your majesty. Why should you suffer even now by serving a woman who is "of naturally noble birth"?'

Here is a new (or *is* it new?) plot use for the ring of recognition, further enhanced by the near-homonym, in Sanskrit, between the word for noble birth (*abhijana*, the quality that the king instinctively recognizes in Shakuntala) and recognition (*abhijnana*, the word used in the title of Kalidasa's play about Shakuntala). Thus, although the necklace is not, as in the folk tradition, the single clue by which all stands or falls, it is still an essential piece in a more complex puzzle.

THE SYMBOLISM OF THE RING

Some rings, such as signet rings, are extensions of the hand; they have the personal emblem of the owner, the stamp of approval. In this way they are signifiers, semiotic objects with the ring of truth. The signet ring (the semiotic ring) is a sign of both identity and memory, particularly the memory of love; it is, as A.K. Ramanujan remarks, 'truly a "memento"'.[13] The ring carries a sense of identity; it may remind the wearer of the giver because it actually has something of him/her in it. The signet ring of identity is closely related to the ring of love, as Heinrich Zimmer has suggested: 'A ring is a symbol of the personality, and to bestow a ring implies the surrender of one's being. To bestow one's ring is to bestow a power, the authority to speak in one's name.'[14]

But when the ring is lost, it may make the wearer forget both love and identity, both the wearer's identity and the beloved's. The two-way power of rings, which serve as much to make people forget the truth about someone's identity as to prove true identity, may explain why they are so often doubled: sometimes a single ring plays a double function, simply by being first present then absent, first lost then found. The ring is often made to take the blame: its loss, or, on the other hand, its evil power, clouds the memory of the husband.

These two layers of symbolism, of personal identity and recognition on the one hand and of sexual union on the other, unite to make the ring the pivot of myths about the identity of a sexual partner. More specifically, the ring plays a role in stories told in ancient India about the tension between illicit eroticism and legal marriage and progeny.

Why do narratives so often connect circular jewellery, particularly rings, with women's sexuality? The sexual symbolism of finger rings is not subtle; the ring's obvious sexual meanings may have been suggested by the analogy between putting your finger through a ring and putting one sexual organ into another. But rings also have intricate historical and sociological implications. The ring gives the woman her authority; the marriage ring validates the married woman's chastity, and the ring of love makes public a lover's private promises. The ring also gives a woman some degree of financial independence; for most of recorded history, jewellery has been the only property that women have been allowed to own, and we have seen the hard-headed acknowledgement of its usefulness in building a dowry. Jewellery has, moreover, the advantage of being portable property: if a woman wanted to leave her husband, few legal or economic sanctions were available to her, but she was usually allowed to keep the jewellery that she had brought into the marriage (her dowry), and sometimes also the jewellery that she had been given in the course of it. The ancient Indian tales build upon these deep symbolic resonances of rings, adding to the cross-cultural theme of memory and forgetfulness the particularly Hindu resonances of the theory of karma[iii] and the Indian folk wisdom of the ways that a woman can manoeuvre to keep her husband and legitimize her child within the constraining structures of Hindu patriarchy.

[iii] See 'Death and Rebirth' and 'Forgetting and Re-awakening'.

THE THIRD NATURE: GENDER INVERSIONS IN
THE *KAMASUTRA*[1]

Then the woman abandons her own ways and changes to what the man has a
natural talent for, doing the slapping, while the man abandons his own way, of
slapping the woman, and takes up her ways, moaning and screaming.

—Yashodhara on the Kamasutra 2.7.22

The *Kamasutra*, composed around 300 CE, has surprisingly modern
ideas about gender and unexpectedly subtle stereotypes of feminine
and masculine natures. It also reveals relatively liberal attitudes to women's
education and sexual freedom, and far more complex views of homosexual
acts than are suggested by other texts of this period. To appreciate the
Kamasutra's liberalism toward women, it is useful briefly to recall the
attitudes to women in two important texts that precede it.[i] Though
women are not the worst of all the addictions,[ii] they are the only universal
one, and the authors of the *shastras* apparently found them more fun to
write about than any of the others. We have discussed in another context[iii]
the attitude to women in the *dharmashastra* of Manu, the flag-bearer for the
Hindu oppression of women. Kautilya, the author of the *Arthashastra*, is far
more liberal. He takes for granted the woman with several husbands,[2] who
poses a problem even for the permissive *Kamasutra*.[3] Kautilya is also more
lenient than Manu when it comes to divorce and widow remarriage; he
gives a woman more control over her property, which consists of jewellery
without limit and a small maintenance;[4] she continues to own these after
her husband's death—unless she remarries, in which case she forfeits them,
with interest, or settles it all on her sons.[5] In these ways and others, Kautilya

[i] See 'Three (or More)'.
[ii] See 'The Control of Addiction'.
[iii] See 'Why Should a Brahmin?'

314

allows women more independence than Manu does. But both of them greatly limit women's sexual and economic freedom.

WOMEN IN VATSYAYANA'S *KAMASUTRA*

If we listen to the alternative voice of the *Kamasutra*, we hear a rather different story.

The *Kamasutra*, predictably, is far more open-minded than Manu about women's access to household funds, and about divorce and widow remarriage. The absolute power that the wife in the *Kamasutra* has in running the household's finances[6] stands in sharp contrast with Manu's statement that a wife 'should not have too free a hand in spending'[7] and his cynical remark that, 'No man is able to guard women entirely by force, but they can be safely guarded if kept busy amassing and spending money, engaging in purification, attending to their duties, cooking food and looking after the furniture.'[8] And when it comes to female promiscuity, Vatsyayana is predictably light years ahead of Manu. Vatsyayana cites an earlier authority on the best places to pick-up married women, of which the first is 'on the occasion of visiting the gods' and others include a sacrifice, a wedding, or a religious festival. Secular opportunities involve playing in a park, bathing or swimming, or theatrical spectacles. More extreme occasions are offered by the spectacle of a house on fire, the commotion after a robbery, or the invasion of the countryside by an army.[9] Somehow I don't think Manu would approve of the man in question meeting married women at all, let alone using devotion to the gods as an occasion for it, or equating such an occasion with spectator sports like hanging around watching houses burn down.

The *Kamasutra* assumes a kind of sexual freedom for women that would have appalled Manu but simply does not interest Kautilya. Vatsyayana is a strong advocate for women's sexual pleasure. He tells us that a woman who does not experience the pleasures of love may hate her man and leave him for another.[10] If, as the context suggests, this woman is married, the casual manner in which Vatsyayana suggests that she leave her husband is in sharp contrast to the position assumed by *The Laws of Manu*:[iv] 'A virtuous wife should constantly serve her husband like a god, even if he behaves badly, freely indulges his lust and is devoid of any good qualities.'[11] The *Kamasutra* also acknowledges that women could use magic to control their husbands, though it regards this as a last resort.[12] Vatsyayana casually

---

[iv] See 'Why Should a Brahmin?'

mentions, among the women that one might not only sleep with but marry,[13] not only 'second-hand' women (whom Manu despises as 'previously had by another man') but widows: 'a widow who is tormented by the weakness of the senses . . . finds, again, a man who enjoys life and is well endowed with good qualities'.[14]

Vatsyayana dismisses with one or two short verses the possibility that the purpose of the sexual act is to produce children; one of the things that make sex for human beings different from sex for animals, he points out, is the fact that human women, unlike animals, have sex even when they are not in their fertile period.[15] Given the enormous emphasis that the traditional texts of Hindu religious law—dharma—place on having sex *only* to produce children,[v] the *Kamasutra*'s attitude here is extraordinary. It is also extraordinary in assuming that women would, and should, know this text.[vi]

Vatsyayana also presents an argument in favour of female orgasm far more subtle than views that prevailed in Europe until very recently indeed, and certainly worlds above the attitudes of his predecessors, whose cockamamie ideas he quotes. He also knew about the G-spot (named after the German gynaecologist Ernst Graefenberg),[16] and he tells the man how to recognize when a woman has reached a climax—or, perhaps, if we assume (as I think we should) that the text is intended for women, too, he is telling the woman how to fake it.[17] He argues that women have orgasms just like men; Yashodhara, commenting on the *Kamasutra* in his thirteenth-century work *Jayamangala*, supports Vatsyayana's position with a poem of unknown provenance:

> A woman's sensual pleasure is two-fold:
> the scratching of an itch and the pleasure of melting.
> The melting, too, is two-fold:
> the flowing and the ejaculation of the seed.
> She gets wet just from the flowing,
> and her sensual pleasure of ejaculation comes from being churned.
> But when a woman is carried away by her sexual energy,
> she ejaculates at the end, it is said, just like a man.[18]

From this, Vatsyayana concludes: 'Therefore the woman should be treated in such a way that she achieves her sexual climax first.'[19]

---

[v] See 'Why Should a Brahmin?'
[vi] See 'Reading the *Kamasutra*'.

Vatsyayana's discussion of the reasons why women become unfaithful rejects the traditional patriarchal party line that one finds in most Sanskrit texts, a line that punishes very cruelly indeed any woman who sleeps with a man other than her husband (cutting off her nose, for instance). We've encountered Manu's assumption[vii] that every woman desires every man she sees ('Good looks do not matter to them, nor do they care about youth; "A man!" they say, and enjoy sex with him, whether he is good-looking or ugly'[20]). The *Kamasutra* takes off from this same assumption, but then limits it to *good-looking* men and modifies it with an egalitarian, if cynical, formulation: 'A woman desires any attractive man she sees, and, in the same way, a man desires a woman. But, after some consideration, the matter goes no further.'[21] The text does go on to state that women have less concern for morality than men have, and does assume that women don't think about anything but men. And it is written in the service of the hero, the would-be adulterer, who reasons, if all women are keen to give it away, why shouldn't one of them give it to him?

But the author empathetically imagines various women's reasons not to commit adultery (of which consideration for dharma comes last, as an afterthought), and the would-be seducer takes the woman's misgivings seriously, even if only to disarm her:

> Here are the causes of a woman's resistance: love for her husband, regard for her children, the fact that she is past her prime, or overwhelmed by unhappiness, or unable to get away; or she gets angry and thinks, 'He is propositioning me in an insulting way'; or she fears, 'He will soon go away. There is no future in it; his thoughts are attached to someone else'; or she is nervous, thinking, 'He does not conceal his signals'; or she fears, 'His advances are just a tease'; or she is diffident, thinking, 'How glamorous he is'; or she becomes shy when she thinks, 'He is a man-about-town, accomplished in all the arts'; or she feels, 'He has always treated me just as a friend'; or she cannot bear him, thinking, 'He does not know the right time and place,' or she does not respect him, thinking, 'He is an object of contempt'; or she despises him when she thinks, 'Even though I have given him signals, he does not understand'; or she feels sympathy for him and thinks, 'I would not want anything unpleasant to happen to him because of me'; or she becomes depressed when she sees her own shortcomings, or afraid when she thinks, 'If I am discovered, my own people will throw me out'; or scornful, thinking, 'He has gray hair'; or she worries, 'My

[vii] See 'Why Should a Brahmin?'

husband has employed him to test me'; or she has regard for dharma.
[5.1.23, 25-6, 28-9, 31-35, 37-41]

Vatsyayana here brilliantly imagines the resistance of a woman who is tempted to commit adultery, in ways that rival the psychologizing of Gustave Flaubert and John Updike. This discussion is ostensibly intended to teach the male reader of the text how to manipulate and exploit such women: 'A man should eliminate, from the very beginning, whichever of these causes for rejection he detects in his own situation.' [5.1.43] But, perhaps inadvertently, it provides a most perceptive exposition of the reasons why women hesitate to begin an affair.

And the *Kamasutra* is equally informative about women's (more precisely, courtesans') thinking about ways of ending an affair. It describes the devious devices that the courtesan uses to make her lover leave her, rather than simply kicking him out:

> She does for him what he does not want, and she does repeatedly what he has criticized. She talks about things he does not know about. She shows no amazement, but only contempt, for the things he does know about. She intentionally distorts the meaning of what he says. She laughs when he has not made a joke, and when he has made a joke, she laughs about something else. When he is talking, she looks at her entourage with sidelong glances and slaps them. And when she has interrupted his story, she tells other stories. She talks in public about the bad habits and vices that he cannot give up. She asks for things that should not be asked for. She punctures his pride. She ignores him. She criticizes men who have the same faults. And she stalls when they are alone together. And at the end, the release happens of itself. [6.3.39-44]

A little inside joke that may not survive the cross-cultural translation is the word used for 'release'—*moksha*—which generally refers to a person's spiritual release from the world of transmigration;[viii] there may be an intended irony in its use here to designate the release of a man from a woman's thrall. The rest comes through loud and clear, however: the woman employs what some would call passive-aggressive behaviour to indicate that it is time to hit the road, Jack. There is no male equivalent for this passage, presumably because a man would not have to resort to such subterfuges: he would just throw the woman out. The woman's method is

---

[viii] See 'Three (or More)'.

an example of what James Scott has taught us to recognize as the 'weapons of the weak', the 'arts of resistance'.[22]

WOMEN'S VOICES IN THE *KAMASUTRA*

Passages such as the woman's thoughts about beginning an affair, or a courtesan's thoughts about ending one, may express a woman's voice, or at least a woman's point of view. The *Kamasutra* often quotes women in direct speech, expressing views that men are advised to take seriously, and it is clearly sympathetic to women, particularly to what they suffer from inadequate husbands. [5.1.51-4] But if parts of the text are directed toward women, is it also the case that they reflect women's voices? Certainly not always. For, while the *Kamsutra* quotes women in direct speech, we also encounter the paradox of women's voices telling us, through the text, that women had no voices.

Male texts may merely engage in a ventriloquism that attributes to women viewpoints that in fact serve male goals.[23] The *Kamasutra* not only assumes an official male voice (the voice of Vatsyayana) but denies that women's words truly represent their feelings. Women's exclamations of pain ('Stop!' or 'Let me go!' or 'Enough!' or 'Mother!' [KS 2.7.1-21]) are taken not as indications of their wish to escape pain being inflicted on them, but merely as part of a ploy designed to excite their male partners. This is what we now recognize as the rape mentality: disregarding a woman's protests against rape.[ix] Vatsyayana lists rape as one of the worst, but still acceptable, of the eight wedding devices [3.5.26-7], and takes for granted the type of rape that we now call sexual harassment, as he describes men in power who can take whatever women they want:

> A young village headman, or a king's officer, or the son of the superintendent of farming, can win village women just with a word, and then libertines call these women adulteresses. And in the same manner, the man in charge of the cowherds may take the women of the cowherds; the man in charge of threads [presumably the supervisor of women engaged in sewing and weaving] may take widows, women who have no man to protect them, and wandering women ascetics; the city police-chief may take the women who roam about begging, for he knows where they are vulnerable, because of his own night-roamings; and the man in charge of the market may take the women who buy and sell. [5.5.7-10]

[ix] See 'Zoomorphism'.

These women, at least, have absolutely no voice at all, let alone agency.

We must admit that we find women's voices in the *Kamasutra* carrying meanings that have value for us only by transcending, if not totally disregarding, the original context. Were we to remain within the strict bounds of the historical situation, we could not notice the women's voices speaking against their moment in history, perhaps even against their author. Only by asking our own questions, which the author may not have considered at all, can we see that his text does contain many answers to them, fortuitously embedded in other questions and answers that were more meaningful to him. Adam Gopnik has made this point well, with reference to some of the Western classics: 'A lot of the skill in reading classics lies in reading past them . . . The obsession with genetic legitimacy and virginity in Shakespeare; the acceptance of torture in Dante—these are not subjects to be absorbed but things you glide by on your way to the poetry.'[24] We need to read past the outer husk of the *Kamasutra*'s obsessions, not only to get to the precious kernel within—the vivid depictions of sexual psychology—but to get to our own obsessions.

GENDER IN THE *KAMASUTRA*

We can learn a lot about conventional and unconventional Hindu ideas of gender from the *Kamasutra*. Vatsyayana tells us that, 'By his physical nature, the man is the active agent and the young woman is the passive locus. The man is aroused by the thought, "I am taking her," the young woman by the thought, "I am being taken by him." [2.1.10] These gender stereotypes—the passive woman, active man—underlie other gender arguments in the text, too. Vatsyayana tells us what he thinks of as typically female behaviour: 'dress, chatter, grace, emotions, delicacy, timidity, innocence, frailty and bashfulness.' The closest he has to a word for our 'gender' is *tejas*, a Sanskrit term designating light and heat, rather as we might say, 'It is what someone shines at,' or, perhaps, 'natural talent' or 'glory':

> A man's natural talent is
> his roughness and ferocity;
> a woman's is her lack of power
> and her suffering, self-denial and weakness. [2.7.22]

And the commentator, Yashodhara, explains that people can sometimes deviate from these norms:

Sometimes, but not always, there is an exchange when they make love, out of the pull of passion or according to the practice of the place. Then the woman abandons her own ways and changes to what the man has a natural talent for, doing the slapping, while the man abandons his own way, of slapping the woman, and takes up her ways, moaning and screaming. But after a short time, they change back. And in the absence of passion or this particular technique, they do it just as before, and there is no occasion to switch.

The *Kamasutra* tells us that people do switch genders sometimes when they engage in the sexual position with the woman on top, which is heavily laden with gender implications for women. What we call the 'missionary position' is also the assumed norm in most Hindu texts.[x] But when the *Kamasutra* describes this position among all the other, more exotic positions that 'take practice', the commentator scornfully remarks, 'How does he penetrate her in this position? It is so easy that there is nothing to worry about!' [2.6.17] Most Sanskrit texts refer to the position with the woman on top as the 'perverse' or 'reversed' or 'topsy turvy' position (*viparitam*), the wrong way around. Vatsyayana, however, never uses this pejorative term. Instead, he refers to the woman-on-top position only with the verb 'to play the man's role' (*purushayitva*). Vatsyayana acknowledges that people do, sometimes, reverse gender roles [2.7.23], and this switch of 'natural talents' is precisely what happens when the woman is on top: 'She does to him in return now whatever acts he demonstrated before. And, at the same time, she indicates that she is embarrassed and exhausted and wishes to stop.' [2.8.6] Yashodhara spells out the gender complications:

> All of this activity is said to be done with a woman's natural talent. The acts he demonstrated before are acts that he executed with roughness and ferocity, the man's natural talent; she now does these acts against the current of her own natural talent. She hits him hard, with the back of her hand and so forth, demonstrating her ferocity. And so, in order to express the woman's natural talent, even though she is not embarrassed, nor exhausted, and does not wish to stop, she indicates that she is embarrassed and exhausted and wishes to stop.

Now, since Vatsyayana insists that the woman 'unveils her own feelings completely when her passion drives her to get on top' [2.8. 39], the

---

[x] Indeed, it begins in the *Rig Veda*, which, in describing the original creation of the universe, imagines the missionary position: male seed-placers, giving-forth above, and female powers below receiving beneath. *Rig Veda* 10.129.5; see 'You Can't Get Here'.

feelings of the woman when she plays the man's role seem to be both male and female. Or, rather, as the commentator explains, when she acts like a man, she pretends to be a man and then she pretends to be a woman. Thus Vatsyayana acknowledges a woman's active agency and challenges her stereotyped gender role.

The poet Amaru wrote a verse about a girl who forgets herself, and forgets her womanly modesty, as she makes love on top of her male partner, but then, as her memory returns, and with it her sense of shame, she suddenly becomes aware of her own body and releases [*mukta*] first her male nature and then her lover.[25] The thirteenth-century commentator Arjunavarmadeva glosses the verse, in part, like this:

> An impassioned woman in the woman-on-top position abandons, first, maleness, and, right after that, her lover. What happened? She perceived her own body, which she had not recognized at all while she was impassioned. Only later is there any mention of the distinction between being male or female. She is described as becoming modest only at the onset of memory.[26]

The sequence here seems to be that she takes on a male nature, loses her natural female modesty, suddenly regains her memory, regains her modesty, recognizes her female body, lets go of her male nature and lets go (physically) of the man. The interrelationship between gendered actions (male on top, female on the bottom), gendered natures (males rough, females modest) and gendered bodies, together with the loss and recovery of a sense of one's own body balanced against the holding and releasing of the body of a sexual partner, is complex indeed.[xi]

SAME–SEX MEN

What about more extreme challenges to gender roles? What, for instance, does the text have to say about people who engage in homosexual acts? Classical Hinduism is in general significantly silent on the subject of homoeroticism, but Hindu mythology does drop hints from which we can excavate a pretty virulent homophobia. The dharma textbooks, too, either ignore or stigmatize homosexual activity. Male homoerotic activity was

---

[xi] It becomes even more complex when we recall that 'release' (*mukta*) is from the same root as *moksha*, the same word that, on the one hand, as we have seen, Vatsyayana uses for the courtesan's technique of getting rid of an unwanted lover and, on the other hand, in a religious context, signifies ultimate liberation from the wheel of rebirth.

punished, albeit mildly: a ritual bath[27] or the payment of a small fine[28] was often a sufficient atonement.

But the ascetic aspects of Hinduism create a violent dichotomy between marriage, in which sexuality is tolerated for the sake of children, and a renunciant priesthood, in which asceticism is idealized and sexuality entirely rejected, or at least recycled. In this taxonomy, homosexual love represents what Mary Douglas has taught us to recognize as a major category error, something that doesn't fit into any existing conceptual cubbyhole, 'matter out of place'—in a word, dirt.[29] Traditional Hindu mythology regards homosexual union not, like heterosexual marriage, as a compromise between two goals in tension (procreation and asceticism), but as a mutually polluting combination of the worst of both worlds (sterility and lust). The myths, therefore, seldom explicitly depict homosexual acts at all, let alone sympathetically.

The Sanskrit word *kliba* has traditionally been translated as 'eunuch' but almost certainly did not mean 'eunuch', since eunuchs—in the sense of men intentionally castrated, particularly in order to serve as guardians in the royal harem—did not exist in India before the Turkish presence in the ninth century and, therefore, cannot be recorded in texts such as the *Mahabharata*, composed long before that date. Men were castrated in punishment for various crimes in ancient India (and animals were gelded to control them), but such men were not employed as eunuchs. '*Kliba*', rather, includes a wide range of meanings under the general rubric of 'a man who does not act the way a man should act', a man who fails to be a man, a defective male.[30] It is a catch-all term that traditional Hindus coined to indicate a man who is in their terms sexually dysfunctional (or in ours, sexually challenged), including someone who was sterile, impotent, castrated, a transvestite, a man who had oral sex with other men, who had anal sex, a man with mutilated or defective sexual organs, a hermaphrodite, or, finally, a man who produced only female children. Often it has the vaguely pejorative force of 'wimp' or, more literally, 'limp-dick'. Thus, when Krishna, the incarnate god in the *Bhagavad Gita*, wishes to stir the martial instincts of the conscience-stricken human hero Arjuna, he says to him, 'Stop behaving like a *kliba!*'[xii]

The *Kamasutra* departs from the dharmic view of homosexuality in significant ways. It does not use the pejorative term *kliba* at all, but speaks instead of a 'third nature' (*tritiya prakriti*, a term that first appears a few

---

[xii] See 'Indra as the Stallion's Wife'.

centuries earlier, in the *Mahabharata*) or perhaps a 'third sexuality' in the sense of sexual behaviour:

> There are two sorts of third nature, in the form of a woman and in the form of a man. The one in the form of a woman imitates a woman's dress, chatter, grace, emotions, delicacy, timidity, innocence, frailty and bashfulness. The act that is [generally] done in the sexual organ is done in her mouth, and they call that 'oral sex'. She gets her sexual pleasure and erotic arousal as well as her livelihood from this, living as a courtesan. That is the person of the third nature in the form of a woman. [2.9.1-5]

The *Kamasutra* says nothing more about this cross-dressing male, with his stereotypical female gender behaviour, but it discusses the fellatio technique of the closeted man of the third nature in considerable sensual detail, in the longest consecutive passage in the text describing a physical act, and with what might even be called gusto:

> The one in the form of a man, however, conceals her desire when she wants a man and makes her living as a masseur. As she massages the man, she caresses his two thighs with her limbs, as if she were embracing him. Then she becomes more boldly intimate and familiar . . . pretending to tease him about how easily he becomes excited and laughing at him. If the man does not urge her on, even when he has given this clear sign and even when it is obvious that he is aroused, she makes advances to him on her own. If the man urges her to go on, she argues with him and only unwillingly continues. [2.9.6-11]

And so forth, and so on. This is a remarkably explicit analysis of the mentality of the closet, the extended double entendre of an act that is cleverly designed to appear sexually innocent to a man who does not want, or does not want to admit that he wants, a homosexual encounter, but is an explicit invitation to a man who is willing to admit his desire for such an encounter. And a massage is a massage in the *Kamasutra*: 'Some people think that massaging is also a kind of close embrace, because it involves touching. But Vatsyayana says: No. For a massage takes place at a particular time set aside, has a different use, and is not enjoyed by both partners in the same way.' [2.2. 27-8] Or is it? Consider this: 'But when a woman who is giving the man a massage makes sure he has understood her signals and rests her face on his thighs as if she had no desire but was overcome by sleep, and then kisses his thighs, that is called a kiss [of] "making advances."' [2.3. 31] And this: '"Gooseflesh" is made when nails of medium length are brought close together and moved over the chin, breasts, or lower lip, so lightly that they leave no line but by the mere touch cause the thrill of gooseflesh and make a sound as they strike one another. A man can do this to the woman he wants, in the course of massaging her body . . .' [2.4.12-13]

The legitimacy of this person of the 'third nature' is supported by a casual remark in the passage describing the four sorts of love, and the contexts in which they arise. One of the four types is called 'The love that comes from erotic arousal', and it is said to arise from the imagination, not in response to any object of the senses: 'It can be recognized in the course of oral sex with a woman or with a person of the third nature, or in various activities such as kissing.' [2.1. 42] The commentary expands upon this but, significantly, leaves out the reference to the person of the third nature and refers only to a female partner: 'Erotic arousal also comes from kissing, embracing, scratching, biting, slapping and so forth; at the moment of sexual pleasure, the person performing these acts experiences a mental love, and *the woman* for whom they are done also experiences a mental, rather than merely physical, love, because of the imaginative power of passion directed to each spot that is being stimulated.' Here, as so often, the commentary has closed down one of the options.

One remark, in a passage warning the bridegroom not to be too shy with his shy bride, suggests that some people disapprove of men of the third nature: '[Certain scholars] say, "If the girl sees that the man has not spoken a word for three nights, like a pillar, she will be discouraged and will despise him, as if he were someone of the third nature."' [3.2.3] So, judgmentalism appears to creep in after all. But when we look closer we see that the people who make this judgment are the 'scholars' with whom Vatsyayana almost always disagrees, as he does here, for he goes on to remark: 'Vatsyayana says: He begins to entice her and win her trust, but he still remains sexually continent. When he entices her he does not force her in any way, for women are like flowers, and need to be enticed very tenderly. If they are taken by force by men who have not yet won their trust they become women who hate sex. Therefore he wins her over with gentle persuasion.' [3.2.4-6] This is the sort of man whom the wrong sort of scholar, but not Vatsyayana, might fear that some people might stigmatize as someone of the third nature. It is evidence, all the more impressive for being so casual, of the prevalent homophobia of that time and place.

Men of the third nature are always designated by the pronoun 'she', basically because the word 'nature' is feminine in Sanskrit (as it, and most abstract nouns, are also in Latin and Greek). Indeed, the idea of a third gender, rather than a binary division, may come from the basic habit of Indo-European languages to assign three genders—neuter as well as masculine and feminine—to all nouns. Yet the very use of the word 'third'—which clearly implies a previous 'first' and 'second'—demonstrates that Vatsyayana is thinking primarily in binary, more precisely dialectic, terms: two opposed terms modified by a third.[xiii] But there is another, better reason why Vatsyayana uses the female pronoun for a person of the third nature, and that is because of her perceived gender: he lists the third nature among *women* who can be lovers. [1.5.27] This use of the pronoun 'she' can also be seen as an anticipation of the practices of some cross-dressing gay men of our day.

SIR RICHARD BURTON ON THE 'THIRD NATURE'

The *Kamasutra* passage about people of the 'third nature' has been largely unknown outside Sanskrit circles because it was mistranslated in the version of the text that has been used by English-language readers (and, through translation, French readers) for over a century: the translation by Sir Richard Francis Burton.[xiv] Burton's translation misses the entire point about same-sex eroticism because he renders 'third nature' as 'eunuch' throughout. He also leaves out, entirely, the line that includes the 'third nature' in the list of women who are sexually available. (KS 1.5.27) It would appear that he used the word 'eunuch' in its broader sense, to designate not a guardian in the harem but a man who had been castrated for one reason or another. Perhaps he confused the men of the third nature with *klibas*, the elastic category that includes both castrated men and homosexual men. Or with the Hijras, usually castrated transvestites, many of whom earn a living as male prostitutes in South Asia today, as they did during Burton's time, and are often called 'eunuchs'.[31] The Hijras, who have been part of South Asian society, but as marginal people, for centuries, do correspond rather closely to the first type of 'third nature', the cross-dressing female type that is dismissed after just a sentence or two,

---

[xiii] Vatsyayana actually analogizes men and women to grammatical terms, in the discussion of gender stereotypes considered above, which does not take account of the third nature at all: 'By his physical nature, the man is the active agent (the subject) and the young woman is the passive locus (the locative case, in which the action takes place).' [2.1.26] (The object is the sexual act.)

[xiv] See 'From Kama to Karma'.

but not to the second type, the closeted male type, to which Vatsyayana devotes considerable attention.

Burton had written about the Hijras in the notes to his translation of the *Arabian Nights*, but there is no evidence of their existence at the time of the *Kamasutra*, nor is there anything about such a group in the *Kamasutra*. Why, then, did Burton use the word 'eunuch'? Why did he not recognize the text's reference to sexually entire men who happened to prefer having (oral) sex with other men? Did he read the text as implying that this was the only option available to them due to some sort of genital malfunction? This cannot be the case, since Burton had undertaken at least one study of a male brothel (in Karachi)[32] staffed by 'boys and eunuchs'.[33] And his famous 'Terminal Essay' to the *Arabian Nights*, published in 1885, includes an 18,000-word essay entitled 'Pederasty' (later republished in his collection of essays entitled *The Erotic Traveller*) that was one of the first serious treatments of the subject in English, though he stated that Hindus held the practice in abhorrence.[34] No, Burton's 'eunuchs' are, rather, the product of 'Orientalism': the depiction of 'Orientals' as simultaneously oversexed and feminized.[xv] The word 'eunuch' was frequently used in British writings about the Orient, conveying a vague sense of sexual excess, cruelty and impotence. Burton simply followed the tradition in his translation of the *Kamasutra*.

SAME–SEX WOMEN

What about homoerotic women? Vatsyayana is unique in the literature of the period in describing lesbian activity. He does this at the beginning of the chapter about the harem, in a brief passage about what he calls 'Oriental customs'. [5.6.2-4] (The use of the term 'Oriental'—or 'Eastern'— for what Vatsyayana regards as a disreputable lesbian practice in what was soon to be a colonized part of the Gupta Empire—indeed, the Eastern part—suggests that 'Orientalism' began not with the British but with the Orientals themselves.) These women use dildos, as well as bulbs, roots, or fruits that have the form of the male organ, and statues of men that have distinct sexual characteristics. But they engage in sexual acts with one another only in the absence of men, not through the kind of personal choice that drives a man of the third nature: 'The women of the harem cannot meet men, because they are carefully guarded; and since they have only one husband shared by many women in common, they are not

---

[xv] See 'I Have Scinde'.

satisfied. Therefore, they give pleasure to one another with the following techniques.' [5.6.2] Yashodhara's commentary helpfully suggests the particular vegetables that one might employ: 'By imagining a man, they experience a heightened emotion that gives extreme satisfaction. These things have a form just like the male sexual organ: the bulbs of arrow-root, plantain and so forth; the roots of coconut palms, bread fruit, and so forth; and the fruits of the bottle-gourd, cucumber, and so forth.' One can imagine little gardens of plantain and cucumber being cultivated within the inner rooms of the palace, the harem.

The *Kamasutra* makes only one brief reference to women who may have chosen women as sexual partners in preference to men: the text says that a girl may lose her virginity with a girlfriend or a servant girl, and the commentator specifies that 'They take her virginity by using a finger.' [7.1.20] Manu and Kautilya say that a woman who corrupts a virgin will be punished by having two of her fingers cut off [Manu 8.369-70, AS 4.12.20-22]—a hint of what Manu and Kautilya—like Yashodhara—think lesbians do in bed. Vatsyayana never uses the verb 'to play the man's role' when he describes lesbian activities [5.6.1-4], nor does he ever refer to women of this type as people of a 'third nature.' But the commentator's belief that the children produced when the woman is on top might be 'a little boy and little girl with reversed natures' [2.8.41] refers to the view that the 'reverse' intercourse of parents might wreak embryonic damage, resulting in the reversed gender behaviour of the third nature—significantly, for a girl as well as a boy, the female type not spelt out by the text's discussion of the 'third nature'.

BISEXUALITY

In addition to male and female homosexual acts, there are a few oblique, passing remarks that suggest bisexuality.[xvi] The female messenger may have had bisexual behaviour in mind when, praising the man's charm, she says, according to the commentator, 'He has such luck in love that he was desired even by a man.' [5.4.15] So, too, in the *Buddhacharita* [4.12], composed in roughly the same period as the *Kamasutra*, the court chaplain encouraging a group of women to seduce the Buddha tells them, 'By your knowledge of the telltale signs of emotion, your flirtation, your perfect beauty, you are able to enflame the passion even of women, so how much more is this so of men?' In the *Kamasutra*, two verses embedded within the passage about fellatio performed by women describe men who engage in

---

[xvi] See 'Bisexuality' and 'Transsexual Transformations'.

oral sex not by profession, like the men of the 'third nature', but out of love:

> Even young men, servants
> who wear polished earrings,
> indulge in oral sex
> only with certain men.
> And, in the same way, certain men-about-town
> who care for one another's welfare
> and have established trust
> do this service for one another. [2.9.35-36]

These men, who seem bound to one another by discriminating affection rather than promiscuous passion, are called 'men about town', *nagarakas*, the term used to designate the heterosexual heroes of the *Kamasutra*. In striking contrast with men of the third nature, always designated by the pronoun 'she', these men are described with nouns and pronouns that unambiguously designate males, yet they are grouped with women. Perhaps, then, they are bisexuals.

The commentator on the *Kamasutra* even makes Dattaka, the author of the part of the text commissioned by the courtesans, a serial bisexual.[xvii] [1.1.11] The double knowledge of bisexuals such as Dattaka is the special expertise of serial androgynes such as the female-to-male bisexual Chudala,[xviii] who says, when she is a woman, that a woman has eight times as much pleasure (kama) as a man, which could also be translated as eight times as much desire. Yashodhara may well have this mythology in mind when, glossing Vatsyayana's statement [2.1.36] that 'It is commonly said: "The man runs out of fluid before the woman runs out of fluid," he remarks: 'He runs out of fluids first because the woman has eight times as much fluid as a man. And so it is commonly said: 'A fair-eyed woman cannot be sated by men.' [Y on 2.1.14]

Thus, despite the caution with which the text broaches this topic of homosexuality, and even more cautiously, bisexuality, it is possible for us as readers to excavate several alternative sexualities latent in the text's somewhat fuzzy boundaries between homoeroticism and heteroeroticism. This sort of reading suggests various ways in which the *Kamasutra*'s implicit claim to sexual totality—everything anyone could ask to know about sex—might be opened out into a vision of gender infinity.

[xvii] See 'The Mythology of the *Kamasutra*'.
[xviii] See 'Transsexual Transformations'.

BISEXUALITY AND TRANSSEXUALITY AMONG
THE HINDU GODS[1]

Before we consider the evidence and significance of bisexuality in Hindu mythology, it would be useful to talk a little about the term itself. Does the word 'bisexual' refer to what one does or what one is? It makes a difference. Bisexuality refers, in common English parlance, primarily to the nature of a person's sexual partners; thus the Britannica Online defines bisexuality actively, as 'in human sexuality, sexual interest in and attraction to members of one's own and the opposite sex. A bisexual is a person with both heterosexual and homosexual desires.' That is, a bisexual does something bisexual. But Merriam Webster gives as the first meaning the existential definition, 'possessing characteristics of both sexes, hermaphroditic', and only as the second meaning the active definition, 'sexually oriented toward both sexes'. That is, a bisexual *is* something bisexual, primarily, and only secondarily someone who *does* something bisexual.

This subtle distinction takes on more obvious dimensions in mythological formulations, which, in the case of ancient India, easily and happily imagine supernatural creatures that are bisexual in the existential sense but must construct highly elaborate plots to allow bisexual relationships in the active sense. Mythological androgynes come in two forms: splitting (the more prevalent form) and fusing.[2] Sometimes androgynes do both, first fusing and then splitting, or the reverse, but they remain only existentially, rather than actively, bisexual.

The image of a male (for Hindu androgynes are often primarily male, not equally male and female) who splits off half of his body in order to make a woman to be his mate appears first in India in the famous cosmogony in the *Brihadaranyaka Upanishad* [1.4.3]: 'He was of the same size and kind as a man and woman closely embracing. He caused himself to fall [*pat*] into two pieces, and from him a husband and a wife [*pati* and *patni*] were born. Therefore, Yajnavalkya has said, "Oneself is like a half-fragment."[3] In this instance, existential bisexuality not only does not facilitate active bisexuality but, on the contrary, necessarily limits subsequent sexual activity to heterosexuality. This choice, which seems entirely logical in the text in question, is revealed to be, on the contrary, a limited choice that eliminates other logical possibilities, when we compare this story to one that it closely resembles, the scenario imagined by Aristophanes in Plato's *Symposium*, in which the initial bisexual couple does indeed give rise to heterosexual human couples, but they are from the start supplemented by two other mythical creatures that give rise to male homosexuals and female homosexuals. Neither the Indian text nor the Greek text, however, imagines a divine or human individual who is actively bisexual, that is, who has both male and female partners.

Nor does the fusing androgyne fare much better in India. The god Shiva and his consort Parvati are often depicted as an androgyne, 'The Lord Who Is Half Woman' (Ardhanarishvara), but the myths that explain how they came to be fused often describe a quarrel or conflict between them, rather than sexual desire,[4] and a famous Sanskrit poem suggests that when they are in this form, Shiva is distressed because he cannot see Parvati (let alone touch her).[5] Here is yet another way in which existential bisexuals are, by definition, precluded from becoming active bisexuals.

Later Hindu mythology attempts, though in a most roundabout way, to visualize the possibility of divine bisexuality. The Hindu gods are more often serially than simultaneously bisexual, more precisely transsexual, transformed physically into the other sex. The Vedic Indra on occasion changes both gender and species.[i] Each of the two great male gods, Vishnu and Shiva, is transformed into a female in a famous cycle of myths, and both goddesses and supernatural women become male in certain texts. Serial transformation, which in a sense appears to be chronological, first one sex and then another, is really existential: it is an attempt to recover a lost possibility, to express an ambiguity that is present from the start, revealed when it seems to be transformed. Many Hindu myths attest to both the existential *perception* of the self as bisexual (as having a body of one sex and a mind/soul/personality/gender of another) and active bisexual (or transsexual) *transformations*, from male to female (known as MTF in the trade these days) or female to male (FTM).

With these concepts in mind, let us consider a few myths about bisexual

---

[i] See 'Indra as the Stallion's Wife'.

or transsexual Hindu gods and supernatural beings, leaving for the next essay considerations of human beings who go through similar transformations.

THE COUPLING OF VISHNU/MOHINI AND SHIVA

In the *Mahabharata*, the gods and anti-gods churn the ocean to obtain the ambrosia, the Soma juice that maintains their immortality, and the anti-gods claim it as theirs. Then, just three verses tell this story:

> Vishnu took on an enchanting [*mohini*] illusion, the marvellous body of a woman, and he went to the anti-gods. As their minds were bewitched and their hearts set on her, they gave the ambrosia to him in his female form. The goddess who was made of the illusion created by Vishnu gave the ambrosia to the gods but not to the anti-gods. A fight broke out, and Vishnu gave up his incomparable female form and attacked the anti-gods.[6]

Vishnu uses sex to destroy a demonic enemy (an old Hindu trick: celestial nymphs routinely use their wiles to destroy individual powerful ascetics[7]). Vishnu presumably takes on merely the outer form of the anti-god; he never forgets that he is Vishnu; he retains his male memory and his male essence and resumes his own form after returning the Soma to the gods. But when the story is retold and greatly expanded in the *Brahmanda Purana* (350-950 CE), several centuries after the *Mahabharata*, Vishnu *resumes* his Mohini form at Shiva's express request on a second occasion, and although Vishnu still remembers who he really is, Shiva seems to forget that the enchantress is Vishnu:

> When the anti-gods stole the elixir of immortality from the gods, Vishnu meditated on the great goddess [Maheshvari], and by concentrating on nothing but her he took on her form: a beautiful enchantress. She seduced the anti-gods and returned the ambrosia to the gods. When the sage Narada saw what the enchantress Mohini had done, he went to Mount Kailasa, the home of Shiva. Shiva asked Narada, 'What has happened to the ambrosia? Who has won it, the gods or the anti-gods? What is Vishnu doing about it?' Narada told him how Vishnu had taken the form of Mohini, deluded the anti-gods, and brought the ambrosia back to the gods. Shiva dismissed Narada and went with Parvati to see Vishnu, unknown to anyone, even his sons Nandin, Skanda and Ganesha.
>
> Vishnu rose to greet Shiva and Parvati, and Shiva asked Vishnu to

show him the form he had taken before, enchanting everyone. Vishnu smiled a little and again meditated single-mindedly on the goddess; then he vanished, and Shiva saw a gorgeous woman [described in fifteen more or less boilerplate verses]. Immediately Shiva ran after her, abandoning Parvati, who stood with her head lowered in shame and envy, silently. He grabbed her [Mohini] with some difficulty and embraced her again and again; each time she shook him off and ran away, but Shiva grabbed her again, overpowered by desire. From that violent coupling his seed fell upon the ground, and the god Mahashasta was born. The goddess who enchants everyone disappeared, and Shiva turned back and went to his mountain with Parvati.[8]

Is the 'difficulty' with which Shiva catches and embraces Vishnu/Mohini somehow connected with the fact that Vishnu/Mohini is not really a woman? In this text, composed in honour of the goddess, whose worship had developed during the centuries after the brief *Mahabharata* story, Vishnu does not have to produce the woman out of his own power of feminine illusion, but is able to do so by meditating on an already existing goddess. This somewhat weakens the original idea that Vishnu himself actually becomes transformed, for there Mohini does not go on to have an enduring separate existence; she is absorbed back into Vishnu. But the existence of the goddess as a separate person gives a kind of feminine reality to the creature, who now actually mimics a real female, and perhaps that is what inspires the author to imagine that she inspires Shiva with desire. The statement that Vishnu 'smiled a little' before agreeing to Shiva's request suggests that he, too, knew that this was one of those boons that the asker would come to regret.

In this and other variants of this myth, Shiva's seed—shed on the ground, with no reference to a male or female partner—gives birth to a child, here called Mahashasta ('The Great Chastiser'), but variously identified as Skanda, Hanuman, Aiyanar, or 'Hariharaputra' ('the son of Vishnu and Shiva'). These later texts may have added the encounter of Vishnu and Shiva to the Mohini myth precisely in order to justify the theological love child, the quasi androgyne Hariharaputra, to join Vishnu and Shiva physically as well as theologically. Yet Vishnu retains his male memory and his male essence, playing first the active role with the anti-gods and then the passive role with Shiva. In this inadvertent masquerade Mohini is the victim rather than the aggressor—though the text is *very* careful to tell us that the seed fell short of its goal, perhaps implying that no actual sexual act was consummated. Moreover, Shiva himself expressly loses his memory (though not his sex or gender) in one variant of his seduction of Mohini, in which, at the end, 'When the seed was shed, Shiva realized his delusion, became cool, and turned back from his evil act.'[9] Is the delusion the loss of control that lets Shiva desire Mohini, or the loss of the memory of the fact that the woman he desires is a man, Vishnu? The text does not say. The extreme case of this agenda occurs in a Telugu variant of the story, in which, after Shiva has grabbed Mohini, in the middle of the act Mohini turns back into Vishnu, and Shiva does not stop.[10] This ambiguity adds yet another nuance to the more general question of the depth of the transformation.

SHIVA IN THE MAGIC FOREST

Although Shiva's motives in desiring Mohini seem straightforwardly heterosexual, his own connection with androgyny also facilitates these shifts, and when it comes to transsexuality[ii] he is far more active than Vishnu; in the Tamil tradition, for instance, on one occasion, Shiva takes the form of the mother of a woman alone in childbirth.[11] The story of a magic forest sacred to Shiva and/or Parvati, in which men become women, undergoes numerous sea changes in many retellings. The *Ramayana* gives one reason for the transformation: 'When Shiva was making love with Parvati, he took the form of a woman to please Parvati, and everything in the woods, even trees, became female.'[12] That is, *first* comes the statement that Shiva turned into a woman, and only afterwards, as a *result* of that transformation, does the rest of the forest change gender. Yet all the subsequent texts that retell this story—and it is retold often—reverse that causal sequence and specify either that Shiva accidentally became female after the whole forest was cursed, or that he alone of creatures in the forest did *not* became female, being explicitly excepted by Parvati. The idea that Shiva became a woman with Parvati in the forest, explicit in this text, may well have been implicit in all the others that follow, some of which specify neither that Shiva was transformed nor that he was not. The fourteenth-century Vedic commentator Sayana, for instance, simply says that when making love with Shiva, the goddess said, 'Let any man who enters here become a woman,'[13] leaving ambiguous the question of whether Shiva himself became a woman.

The *Brahmanda Purana* is stunningly inconsistent on this point:

[ii] See 'Transsexual Transformations'.

Once upon a time, Shanaka and other young boys came to see Shiva, and they saw him making love with the goddess in a hidden place. They all turned back, embarrassed, and the beloved goddess said to her beloved god, to do what he would like, 'Let any man who enters my ashrama become a woman as beautiful as a celestial courtesan.' Then all the creatures, goblins and beasts became females, sporting with Rudra [Shiva] like celestial courtesans. Rudra became a woman, together with the goblins.[14]

The first part of this passage imagines Parvati creating women who then become Shiva's sexual partners, the whole point of which requires that he remain absolutely male. But then the text says that he, too, became a female. What are we to make of this—or, for that matter, of the paradoxical statement in the *Ramayana* that Shiva himself becomes a woman while making love with Parvati? Are we to assume that he carries on in that form? Or that he stops? If he continues, this raises the same ambiguity that we considered in the myth of Mohini: if Shiva is merely superficially transformed into a female, but remains essentially male, we might expect him to continue despite the transformation. This interpretation is supported by one Hindu view of gender, the view that when the body changes, the mind and the memory remain the same and that gender is not fluid or superficial but embedded in memory. But if it is a complete transformation, a change of inner essence, and Shiva does not stop, it would involve him in a rare but not unprecedented situation[iii] in the Sanskrit literature of Hinduism[15] and a parallel to those variants of the myth of Mohini in which Shiva continues to desire Mohini when she changes back into Vishnu in inner essence as well as superficial form. This would support the other Hindu view of gender, also expressed in many of these Sanskrit texts, as fluid and superficial, changing completely when the body changes.[iv]

Sometimes Shiva himself becomes female for a different reason:

The gods begged the goddess Kali to rid the earth of demonic kings, and she agreed to become incarnate as Krishna. Shiva prayed to Kali and was given permission to become incarnate as Radha, the mistress of Krishna, in order to make love in reverse. At Shiva's wish, Radha's husband became impotent immediately after marriage.[16]

By becoming a human woman—in order to remain heterosexual when his wife has switched her own sex (to become Krishna)—the god simultaneously changes species and gender.[v] This involves two negative transformations, vertical and horizontal: Shiva becomes both human (vertically worse) and female (horizontally worse, in the Hindu view).

THE TRANSSEXUALITY OF THE WORSHIPPER OF PARVATI

A Tamil text from the late sixteenth-century imagines a human man who changes to a woman under the combined influence of the goddess Parvati and her agent on earth, a pious devotee. Although the protagonist in this myth is a human being, the fantasy of sexual transformation is built entirely out of divine imagery:

> Two Brahmin boys learned that a certain pious woman named Cimantani would give lavish gifts to Brahmin sages who came to her with their wives, for she imagined the sage as Shiva and the sage's wife as Parvati. With some misgivings, one of the boys dressed up as a woman; women expert in the arts of adornment came to make him up. They made him breasts out of some other substance, plastered him with kunkum and sandal paste, hung a pearl necklace around his neck and fashioned a long braid so black it put night to shame. His eyes they shaded with kohl; stuck earrings in his ears; and draped him in a sari that was worth at least as much as the entire cosmos.
>
> In short, by the time they were finished he looked as ravishing as Mohini, the female form assumed by Vishnu. They arrived at the palace of Cimantani, whose eyes were too long to be hidden by her hands. When she saw the young man and his friend, who had taken on woman's form, Cimantani came toward them, offered the guest offering, worshipped them, and invited them to sit down together with all the other Brahmins. While she was ministering to these guests, she took a good look at the faces of the two boys and realized at once that they were, indeed, both males. Although she was a rather compassionate person, she frowned.
>
> Then she hid her face. She always thought of whoever came to her, in whatever guise or mode (*ettirattanum*), as Shiva and Uma. So now, too, holding to the order of the Vedas and the Agamas, she performed puja in devotion (*patti*) and fed them all a rich meal of milk, fruit, honey, sweet drinks, rice and snacks, served on golden plates. Then she presented them with fragrant garlands, sandal paste, flawless clothes and jewels, white camphor and areca nut. She praised all the Brahmins as Shiva and Uma and then gave them leave to depart.

[v] As Indra does, in 'Indra as the Stallion's Wife'.

On the way back, the boy who had dressed as a woman turned into a woman—exactly like the guise he had worn—all because of Cimantani, who had imagined them as Uma and Shiva. 'He' totally forgot that he used to be a man. What is more, he now turned to his companion with the idea of making love, like a woman. The Brahmin lad, still not realizing how fully his inseparable friend had become feminine, turned, a little scornful, to study 'his' face. Not an iota of the masculine was left in it. Amazed, he saw that everything about his friend had melted into a lithe, vine-like grace. Her luminous, budding breasts, smeared with sandal paste; her long, thick curls, black as night; her face radiant as the full moon and—like fish darting through the moon—the long eyes shooting lethal looks; the red glow of her body, like an unfolding bud; her bangled wrists, delicate fingers, bejewelled belt, the perfection of her loins . . . She smiled and said, 'My dear husband! Listen. I used to be your friend Camavan. Now I'm a woman named Camavati. In fact, I'm your wife. Desire to make love to you drove me to speak. Embrace me. Have a good look with your own eyes. I am a woman. I am *not* a man.' With this, she revealed her whole body to her lord.

He took a good look. He saw, to his astonishment, that no other woman in the whole wide world had such a beautiful body as this courtesan. He realized that all this had happened because of the imagination exercised by Cimantani in her heart. He protested and tried to resist her, but she was by now very disturbed by Kama's arrows and far beyond thinking about what was or wasn't right. She took his wrist and raped him, then and there, to her great satisfaction. He, on the other hand, felt no pleasure. In fact, he was deeply distressed. But eventually the two of them married, by the grace of the goddess.[17]

In dramatic contrast with the gods who are transformed into women only temporarily, and with many human men who are cursed to become women and move heaven and earth to be transformed back into men,[vi] this Brahmin boy ends up a woman forever, and is apparently perfectly satisfied with this outcome. The thin line that divides transvestism (the transformation of the surface, the gender) from transsexuality (the transformation of the body, the sex) is often breached, and here it is entirely erased: the surface masquerade becomes, through divine magic, a transformation in depth. The text is inconsistent about the memory of the transformed man: he is said not to remember who he had been, but then he declares who he had been. His partner, too, at first vehemently refuses to accept his friend's sexual transformation but is eventually persuaded, enough to marry her.

[vi] See 'Transsexual Transformations'.

THE TRANSSEXUALITY OF CHUDALA

A brilliant example of female to male transsexuality, and back again, is the story of Queen Chudala, which is narrated at great length and with many labyrinthine triple crosses in the *Yogavasishtha*, a philosophical Sanskrit text composed in Kashmir between the tenth and twelfth centuries:

> Queen Chudala and her husband King Shikhidhvaja were passionately in love, like two souls in one body. In time, the queen became enlightened and acquired magic powers, including the ability to fly, but she concealed these powers from her husband, and when she attempted to instruct him he spurned her as a foolish and presumptuous woman. Yet he remarked that she seemed to have regained the bloom of her youth, and he assured her that he would continue to make love to her. Eventually, the king decided to seek his own enlightenment and withdrew to the forest to meditate; he renounced his throne and refused to let her accompany him, but left her to govern the kingdom.
>
> After eighteen years she decided to visit him; she took the form of a young Brahmin boy named Kumbha ('Pot') and was welcomed by the king, who did not recognize her but remarked that Chudala-as-Kumbha looked very much like his queen, Chudala. After a while, the king became very fond of Chudala-as-Kumbha, who instructed him and enlightened him, and she began to be aroused by her handsome husband. And so Chudala-as-Kumbha went away for a while. When she returned, she told the king that a sage had cursed her to become a woman, with breasts and long hair, every night. That night, before the king's eyes, Chudala-as-Kumbha changed into a woman named Madanika, who cried out in a stammering voice, 'I feel as if I am falling, trembling, melting. I am so ashamed as I see myself becoming a woman. Alas, my chest is sprouting breasts, and jewellery is growing right out of my body.'
>
> Chudala-as-Kumbha-as-Madanika slept beside the king every night in the same bed like a virgin, while Chudala-as-Kumbha lived with him during the day as a friend. After a few days Chudala-as-Kumbha said to him, 'Your majesty, I sleep beside you every night as a woman. I want to marry you and to enjoy the happiness of a woman.' He consented to this, and so one day Chudala-as-Kumbha bathed ceremonially with the king, and that night Chudala-as-Kumbha-as-Madanika married him. And so the couple, whose previous state of marriage was concealed, were joined together. They lay down on the marriage bed of flowers and made love all night.
>
> Thus they lived as dear friends during the day and as husband and

wife at night. Eventually, she changed from Chudala-as-Kumbha-as-Madanika to Chudala. The king said, 'Who are you and how did you get here? In your body, your movements, your smile, your manner, your grace—you look so much like my wife.' 'Yes, I am truly Chudala,' she said, and then she told him all that she had done. He embraced her passionately, and said, 'You are the most wonderful wife who ever lived. The wife is everything to her husband: friend, brother, sympathizer, servant, guru, companion, wealth, happiness, the Vedic canon, abode and slave. Come, embrace me again.' Then he made love to her all night and returned with her to resume his duties as king. He ruled for ten thousand years and finally attained release.[18]

Chudala wishes to be her husband's mistress both in the sense of lover and in the sense of teacher, schoolmistress. She has already played the first role but is now denied it, and he refuses to grant her the second role.

But the queen wants to get her husband into bed as well as to enlighten him; the story is, after all, not merely a parable of enlightenment but a very human, very funny story. And the text is not so antinomian as to image a consummated male homosexual relationship. Eventually, Chudala manages to enjoy her husband as a male friend by day and as a lover and wife by night, and she does this by getting him to marry her again. The double woman whom she creates—Chudala-as-Kumbha-as-Madanika—is her real self—the negation of the negation of her femininity; the jewellery that actually grows out of her body is what she would have worn as Queen Chudala at the start of the story, and the description of her transformation—'I feel as if I am falling, trembling, melting'—is surely a double-entendre for female orgasm. This double deception works well enough and may express her full fantasy: to be her husband's intellectual superior under the sun and his erotic partner by moonlight. But since the two roles belong to two different personae, she wants to merge them and to play them both as her original self. That is, she wants to reintegrate herself and abandon her double, and in the end, she does. The playful juggling of the genders demonstrates both the unreality of appearances and the falsity of the belief that one gender is better than the other; the male and female forms of Chudala are, in a sense, all alike in the dark. Moreover, the woman is wiser than the man, enlightens the man, and so forth. This extraordinary openness to gender bending in ancient India may be an indirect benefit of the rigid social order: since social categories are taken for granted, there is more room for role-playing. But not, when we look closer, all that much room. Chudala has to become a man herself—like a Bodhisattva—to teach her husband, and she has to become a woman again to sleep with him. Moreover, the relationship between Chudala and the king is never the relationship of a real husband and wife. She functions like a goddess, giving him her grace and leading him up the garden path of enlightenment, setting up a divine illusion and then revealing herself to him as the gods reveal themselves.

CONCLUSION

Myths in which gods change their sex are often coded human bisexual fantasies. The stories about the gods have their human models and their human moments. To the extent that they are composed by humans and clearly reflect human attitudes, we might, with caution, use them to attempt to formulate hypotheses about ancient Hindu attitudes to various sexual acts. But myths about transsexual deities are also stories about the way the world is, about the ambiguity of all existence. On that level, they may express a desire that transcends not only appearance but even gender itself, a desire that desires the soul no matter what bits of flesh may be appended to various parts of the body.

When male deities are magically transformed into women but change only their superficial physical genitalia, they do so usually in order to kill a male enemy; this is the case with Vishnu as Mohini. The man retains his male memory, and it is this male consciousness that kills—or, at least, fights. But when the transformation is deeper and the male takes on a female memory, it is this female consciousness that enjoys sex; this is the case with Shiva and Mohini, and in all those myths in which the mind and memory change, too, change their gender when the body changes its sex. This double pattern reaffirms gender stereotypes: males kill, females make babies. But it also suggests that male memory is the killer. Female-to-male transformations reinforce this pattern: the retained female memory makes love, as in the myth of Chudala.

Bisexual desire is not an inevitable component of the myths of sex change, but in Hindu texts like the story of Queen Chudala, the change may be effected in the service of heterosexuality and occasionally bisexuality. Some of these myths may, therefore, be read as tales about bisexual desire. The Hindu texts challenge our own ideas about gender; they tell us that the desire for sexual pleasure both with and as members of both sexes is real, though ultimately unrealizable by all but the magically gifted—or cursed. Some of them may express a wish for androgyny and offer, in subversion of the dominant homophobic paradigm, closeted images of a happily expressed and satisfied bisexual desire. The episode of Chudala as the master of enlightenment, and some variants of the magic forests of Shiva and Parvati, epitomize this playful, relaxed attitude toward gender boundary-jumping.

TRANSSEXUAL TRANSFORMATIONS OF SUBJECTIVITY AND MEMORY IN HINDU MYTHOLOGY[1]

Many myths in the Epics and Puranas involve human beings who undergo either transvestism (dressing as someone of the other gender) or transsexuality (transformation into someone of the other sex).[2] Vedantic philosophy produced many male-to-female dream doubles, of whom the most famous is Narada, who became a woman and lived a full life but eventually returned to his life as a man.[3] We have considered the role of bisexuality and transsexuality in Hindu myths involving the gods.[i] Now let us shift our attention to transsexual myths that shed light upon the nature of human identity, and let us concentrate on key episodes in the two Hindu epics (also taking into consideration later refractions of those myths in other texts).

In the great Sanskrit epic the *Mahabharata*, composed between about 300 BCE and 300 CE, several people lose their subjectivity, often their memories, to become someone else, sometimes as the result of a curse, sometimes out of a desire to become other. Nala is transformed into a deformed dwarf; Arjuna disguises himself as a transvestite who may or may not be impotent; Yayati becomes a younger man. In the other great Sanskrit epic, the Valmiki *Ramayana* (which I will call, henceforth, the *Ramayana*), composed within roughly the same period, the transformations generally take place on both a higher and a lower register: the demons, or anti-gods (*asuras*), create spectacular illusions, but the human characters in general do not undergo nearly so many transformations[ii] as their counterparts in the *Mahabharata*.[4] One story on the margins of the *Ramayana*, however, depicts the transformation of a human being—Ila, not one of the central

[i] See 'Bisexuality' and 'Indra as the Stallion's Wife'.
[ii] See 'Shadows of the *Ramayana*'.

342

characters—in ways strikingly similar to the transformations of a slightly more central character in the *Mahabharata*—Amba. Both are stories of sexual transformation: in one, a man becomes a woman (MTF, male to female), and in the other, a woman a man (FTM, female to male). Let us consider these stories of male and female sexual transformation one by one, and then together.

THE TRANSFORMATION OF ILA

The *Mahabharata* tells us, rather cryptically, that a woman named Ila gave birth to Pururavas and became both his mother and his father. [M 1.70.16. 33-69] In the *Ramayana*, Ila's birth is sexually ambiguous, and his/her adult sexual life is so problematic that it sometimes becomes convenient, in discussing this myth (and others in this chapter), to use at ambiguous moments the otherwise awkward modern non-sexist pronoun s/he to describe him/her. The story takes place in the magic forest in which Shiva turns all the males, including himself, into females. We have considered the implications of this transformation for the god;[iii] now let us consider what it does to the mortal:

> One day, King Ila, the son of Kardama, went hunting and killed thousands of animals, but still his lust for hunting was unsatisfied.[iv] As he came to that place where Shiva was making love with Parvati, he was changed into a woman, and when she approached Shiva to seek relief from her misery, Shiva laughed and said, 'Ask for any boon except manhood.' Ila pleaded with Parvati, who said: 'Shiva will grant half of your request and I the other half. In that way you will be half female, half male.' Rejoicing at this wonderful boon from the goddess, Ila said, 'If you, whose form is unrivalled by any copy, are truly pleased with me, let me be a woman for a month, and then a man again for a month.' 'So be it,' said Parvati, 'but when you are a man, you will not remember that you were a woman; and when you are a woman, you will not remember that you were a man.' 'So be it,' said the king, and for a month he became the most beautiful woman in the world.
>
> During that first month, she was wandering in the forest [outside the magic grove] with her female attendants, who had formerly been men, when she came upon King Budha, the son of the moon, immersed in a lake and immersed in meditation. She was struck by his stunning

---

[iii] See 'Bisexuality'.
[iv] See 'The Control of Addiction'.

good looks and started splashing the water; he noticed her and was pierced by the arrows of lust. He thought to himself, 'I have never seen a woman like this, not among goddesses or snake women or demon women or celestial courtesans. If she is not married, let her be mine.' He asked her followers whose she was, and they replied, 'This woman with superb hips rules over us; she has no husband and wanders with us in the woods.' When he heard this speech, whose meaning was hidden, Budha used his own magic powers and discovered the entire truth of what had happened to the king. He transformed the women into centaurs [kimpurushas], and they ran away. Then he smiled and said to Ila, 'I am the son of king Soma; look upon me with loving eyes, and make love with me.' In that deserted place, deprived of all her attendant women, she spoke pleasingly to him, saying, 'Son of Soma, I am free to do as I wish, and so I place myself in your power. Do with me as you wish.' Hearing that astonishing speech from her, the king was thrilled, and he caused Ila to enjoy the exquisite pleasures of love-making—for a month, which passed like a moment.

But when the month was full, Ila awoke in bed [as a man] and saw Budha immersed in the water, immersed in meditation. He said to Budha, 'Sir, I came to this inaccessible mountain with my attendants. But now I don't see my army; where have all my people gone?' When Budha heard these words from Ila, whose power of recognition had been destroyed, he replied with a persuasive, conciliating speech: 'Your servants were all destroyed by a hailstorm, and you were exhausted by your terror of the high winds and fell asleep on the grounds of this hermitage. Don't be afraid; live here in comfort, eating fruits end roots.'

Though the wise King Ila was encouraged when he heard those words, he was greatly saddened by the death of his servants, and he said, 'I will renounce my own kingdom; I cannot go on for a moment without my servants and wives. Please give me leave to go. My eldest son, named Shashabindu, will inherit my throne.' But Budha said, 'Please live here. Don't worry. At the end of a year, O son of Kardama, I will do you a great favour.' And so Ila decided to stay there.

Then, for a month she became a woman and enjoyed the pleasure of making love ceaselessly, sleeplessly, and then for a month he increased his understanding of dharma, as a man. In the ninth month, Ila, who had superb hips, brought forth a son fathered by Budha, named Pururavas. And as soon as he was born, she placed him in the hands of Budha, for the child looked just like him and seemed to be of the same class. And then when she became a man again, Budha gave him the pleasure of hearing stories about dharma, for a year.

Then Budha summoned a number of sages, including Ila's father, Kardama, and asked them to do what was best for him/her. Kardama suggested that they propitiate Shiva with a horse-sacrifice and ask his help. Shiva was pleased by the horse-sacrifice; he came to them, gave Ila his manhood, and vanished. King Ila ruled in the middle country of Pratishthana, and his son Shashabindu ruled in their country of Bahli. [R 7.87–90].

The story of Ila is told in many of the medieval Sanskrit texts called the Puranas, since s/he founded both of the two great Indian dynasties, the lunar and the solar, and dynastic succession is a central concern of the Puranas. The myth tells of the joining of the descendant of the Sun (Ila, grandson of Vivasvant, the Sun) with a descendant of the Moon (Budha, son of Soma, the moon; his son is named Shashabindu, 'Hare-marked', an epithet of the moon, in which the Hindus see a hare where other cultures see a man). The sexual labyrinths of the text may have been generated, at least in part, through a desire to account for the joining of two great dynasties, each claiming descent from a male cosmic body (for both the sun and the moon are usually male in Sanskrit), without demoting either partner to the inferior status of a female. The solution: to imagine two cosmic patriarchs, and to turn one—only temporarily, of course—into a woman. (The parallel desire, to have a child born of both the gods Shiva and Vishnu, was resolved by turning Vishnu, temporarily, into a woman, Mohini.[v]) The form of the curse in the *Ramayana* is no accident; the founding of the lunar dynasty is linked, by natural association, with the monthly vacillation between female and male. On the other hand, the fact that one person, Budha, has the power and the knowledge and undiminished masculinity throughout the episode, while the other, Ila, does not, would seem to privilege the status of Budha and the lunar dynasty over Ila and the solar dynasty; and that may well have been one of the intentions of this text.

There are scattered references here to the problem of recognition, all refractions of the central problem, namely, that when s/he is transformed into a woman, Ila does not recognize himself. One aspect of recognition is resemblance: Does one self resemble another? Thus, in praising the goddess, Ila says that her form is 'unrivalled by any copy' (*pratima*, a reflected image); Budha says that he has never seen 'a woman like this'; and their child is said to look just like him or to 'seem to be of the same class or

---

[v] See 'Bisexuality'.

kind' (*savarna*).[vi] When Ila does not recognize himself after he has been restored to his primary form as a man, he is said to be someone whose power of recognition (*samjna*) has been destroyed; as a woman, in his secondary form, she is not himself, but only his (female) shadow or inverted mirror image (*pratima*).

But recognition also involves memory, and part of the curse (or is it the boon that balances the curse?) is to make Ila forget one gender when s/he is immersed in another. In the initial transformation, in the enchanted forest, Ila apparently does retain his memory, for he asks the gods to change him back; at this stage, he would seem to have the body of a woman and the mind of a man. When, however, the transformation has settled into monthly alternations, Ila forgets who she is; her servants tell Budha the story that we must assume Ila, too, believes, that she is a woman without a husband, wandering in the woods. Ila doesn't remember her pleasure in bed when he is a man. In fact, Parvati explicitly states that s/he will not remember the altered states; is this because normally one would, or normally one would not, remember? Budha doesn't tell Ila who she is, though he knows this through powers of his own; he withholds Ila's memory from her/him and keeps him/her in his power. By cutting him/her off from the knowledge of his/her true identity and then seducing him/her, Budha is in effect raping a sleeping woman, engaging in what Hindu law classifies as the 'marriage of a ghoul', which 'takes place when a man secretly has sex with a girl who is asleep, drunk, or out of her mind.'[5] (Modern governments, too, have legal sanctions against the rape of an insane woman.) In this case, she is quite literally out of her mind, and into someone else's, and the text does not rest until s/he is restored to his/her manhood (*purushatva*) again—this being the 'favour' that Budha cryptically promises to do for him at the end of the year.

Ila is disempowered by the loss of both sex and class: in one stroke s/he is deprived of political power, class (servants) and gender. As soon as s/he becomes a woman, even while s/he still has servants (class), s/he loses his/her ownership of his/her self; Budha asks her followers not who but whose she is. (This is the standard way of inquiring about a woman's identity in ancient India, to which the standard answer consists of her father's name, if she is unmarried, or her husband's, if she is married.[vii]) This is the question that the followers answer with 'hidden' meaning. And of course s/he also

[vi] See 'Saranyu/Samjna'.
[vii] See 'Why Should a Brahmin?'

loses his/her political power, both because s/he forgets that s/he is a king and because a woman cannot (except in extraordinary circumstances) be a king. When Budha pulls out from under him/her the one remaining prop, his/her servants, she finds herself alone with him in the middle of the forest, helpless. Naturally, she gives in to his sexual demands.

But even when Ila becomes retransformed into a man, he remains helpless for reasons of class that remain even when gender has been restored. Thus he remarks, 'I cannot live without my servants and wives.' He has lost a significant part of his identity by losing his social world. Men, in this worldview, are dependent on women for services, and women are dependent on men for protection. But they are also mutually dependent for sex. We have already been told that Ila is, as it were, 'asking for it'. We know that she lusted for Budha before he lusted for her, and, indeed, that even as a man, Ila suffered from the fatal and quasi-sexual lust to hunt. One text makes explicit this connection between hunting (especially hunting people whom you have mistaken for animals)[viii] and gender transformation: 'One day, a female goblin [*yakshini*] who wanted to protect her husband from King Ila took the form of a deer expressly in order to lure him into the magic part of the forest. King Ila entered the wood.'[6] It is surely significant that Ila is hunting females—whether demon or deer—when he is lured into the forest where he will be cured, at least temporarily, of his passion for hunting.

Budha keeps Ila captive not only by lying to her but by giving her pleasure, as she gives pleasure to him (the verb for sexual enjoyment, *ram*, is consistently used in the causative both for him and for her). Even when she becomes a man, Budha gives him the pleasure of hearing stories, using the same verb, *ram*, for sexual pleasure and for what Roland Barthes has taught us to call the pleasure of the text. But in this mutual dependence, the woman is far more dependent on sex than the man is. Thus, in a parallel story about a man, Bhangashvana, magically transformed into a female, when Indra (the king of the gods) asks him/her which sex s/he would like to remain forevermore, s/he says that s/he would prefer to remain a woman, since as a woman s/he had greater pleasure in sex— which also makes her love the children she had as a woman more than the children she had as a man. [M 13.12.1-49] (In other texts, as we have seen,[ix] it is said that a woman has eight times as much pleasure, or,

---

[viii] See 'Control of Addiction' and 'Zoomorphism'.
[ix] See 'The Third Nature'.

sometimes, eight times as much desire—not the same thing at all—as a man.)[7] The Buddhist transsexual Soreyya also has children both as male and as female and prefers the children of his female persona to those of the male. (No one seems to have dared to ask him which way sex was better.)[8] Yet, even this greater pleasure does not ultimately weigh in the scale of gender against the disadvantages of being a woman: Ila chooses not to remain female.

In some variants of this myth in the Puranas, Ila begins life not as a male but as a female, which puts a special spin on the story:

> Ila's parents had wanted a boy; but the priest had made a mistake, and so a girl was born instead, named Ila. The priest then rectified his error, and she became a man, named Ila. One day when Shiva and Parvati were making love, the sages came to see Shiva. Parvati was naked, and when she saw them she became ashamed and arose from Shiva's embrace, tying her waist-cloth around her loins. The sages, seeing that the couple were making love, turned back. Then, to please his beloved, Shiva said, 'Whoever enters this place will become a female.' Some time later, Ila reached this spot and became a woman, and all the men in his/her entourage became women, and all their stallions became mares. Queen Ila, as she had become again, married and gave birth to King Pururavas. Eventually she begged Shiva to change her back to a man, named Sudyumna, and s/he was allowed to be a woman for one month and a man for one month. Finally, s/he went to heaven as someone who had the distinguishing signs of both men and women.[9]

It might be argued that, even here, Ila begins as a male, since it was the original desire of his parents (like most Hindu parents) to have a boy. But since his first physical form is that of a female, his final physical transformation (after he has become a man) is in effect a transformation back into her original physical nature. The text, therefore, constantly fights its way upstream against the current of Ila's tendency to revert to female type and requires constant interventions from male powers (gods or Brahmins) to keep making her male. Even in heaven, s/he still has both sets of distinguishing marks [lakshana], which here cancel one another out and therefore distinguish nothing.

Another variant of this myth, also in a Purana, reverses the force of both memory and gender:

> Ela, who would have been king of the lunar dynasty, came to the Sahya mountain, greedy for hunting, but when he entered the forest

he became Ila, an identical image/shadow of Ela, and when his soldiers saw Ila from a distance, they fled in terror. Ila became a female companion and servant of the goddess Parvati. Though s/he learned that if she bathed in the river as a woman she would be released from her female form, Ila said s/he preferred to be a female slave to Ganga (the river) and Gauri (Parvati). Ganga and Gauri, however, quickly replied, 'To hell with birth as a woman; it's nothing but pain and grief,' and so Ila entered the water and bathed in a special pool and emerged as King Ela, a man. The face that had been as beautiful as the moon was now bearded and deep-voiced, and the female sex that she had acquired through the curse of Parvati was now a male sex (lingam).[10]

This text makes brutally explicit the fact that it is a bad thing to be a woman, and clearly implicit the fact that, for once, Ila is conscious of his male past in the midst of his female present and, therefore, able to make a choice. He chooses to be a woman for religious reasons that have motivated many devotees of both the goddess (Devi) and Krishna, in India: male worshippers have imagined themselves as women, and sometimes even dressed as women, in order to be like the goddess or to be the lovers of Krishna, just as Ila wishes to remain the female devotee of Ganga and Gauri. But the women around him quickly enlighten him, and he rejoins his true self, his true gender.

A tale in the *Kathasaritsagara*, or Ocean of the Rivers of Story, is related to the story of Ila and even cites it as a proof text:

A man named Shashin, a friend of the great trickster and magician Muladeva,[x] was in love with a princess who was closely guarded in a harem. Muladeva gave Shashin a pill to put into his mouth (but not to swallow), which turned him into a woman so that he could gain access to the harem. Muladeva himself took another pill that transformed him into an old Brahmin. Once inside the harem, Shashin took the pill out of his mouth, became a man, and made love to his princess. After a while, a prince saw Shashin when he was in his form as a woman and insisted on taking 'her' as his wife; Shashin insisted that the marriage not be consummated for six months, during which she lived in the harem with the prince's first wife, the queen. One night she told the queen the story of Ila and the forest of Parvati, took the pill out of his mouth, and made love to her, too. Eventually, Muladeva married the princess secretly, while Shashin married her officially.[11]

[x] See 'The Clever Wife'.

Shashin, like Shashabindu, is a name of the moon, appropriate for someone who periodically changes form (for six months, too). Since he remains male inside even when his body becomes female, the text can imagine him making love only to women, never to men.

In all the texts of this myth that we have seen, with the exception of the glorification of the Sahya forest, Ila is the passive victim of a curse; he loses his memory when he loses his body. Significantly, Ila's transition to and from her existence as the wife of King Budha takes place, in the *Ramayana*, when Budha is meditating in the water—precisely the condition of the sage Narada's very similar translation into and out of womanhood. Ila's neat trick in both fathering and mothering his/her son is also accomplished by the father of the monkey heroes Valin and Sugriva in the *Ramayana*, who does it serially—first he is the father, and then the mother, and then the father again:

> One day a great monkey named Riksharaja saw the reflection of his own face in a lake. Thinking that it was an enemy mocking him, in his monkey foolishness he plunged into the water, but when he came out of the water he was a beautiful woman. The gods Indra and Surya (the Sun) desired her and were overpowered by lust. Indra shed his seed on her head before he actually managed to consummate the act, and then he turned back; but because Indra's seed is never shed in vain, she gave birth to a king of the monkeys; and because the seed had fallen in her hair [*vala*], he was named Valin. The seed of Surya, when he was overpowered by lust, was sprinkled on her neck; he said not a single good word but regained control and reined in his lust; Sugriva was born from the semen that had fallen on her neck (*griva*). Then the two gods went away, and when the sun rose after that night had passed, Riksharaja resumed his own monkey shape and saw his two sons. He suckled them with honey and took them home. Thus the monkey Riksharaja was the father of Valin and Sugriva, and also their mother.[12]

Like Narcissus in Greek and Roman mythology, the monkey mistakes his reflection for another human being—not, this time, a potential sexual partner, but a mocking enemy. The result is much the same, however: the myth short circuits the Narcissus connection so that the monkey does not mate with his reflection as if it were someone of the other sex, but becomes his sexual reflection, as it were—and mates with someone else. (Indeed, he mates with two other men who double one another, even as his female self doubles his male self.) Here, as so often, the myth reifies and embodies a cliché: we often speak of a single parent as being 'both mother and father' to a child; in Indian myths, it actually happens. Indeed, this story gives new meaning to another cliché: 'single parent'.

Since Riksharaja is a serial rather than a simultaneous androgyne, his male and female parts are never able to meet and mate; the gods must descend, ex machina, to substitute their sperm for that of the usually required male monkey, to allow him to impregnate himself. Riksharaja simultaneously changes gender and species: a male monkey becomes a human (or at least anthropomorphic) woman. But his monkeyness prevails: though two gods more or less artificially inseminate a woman, the resulting children are neither gods nor humans, but monkeys, the true, underlying form of the father. Something of his true self remains in place despite the double transformation.

THE TRANSFORMATION OF AMBA

The transformation of a male into a female, as in the stories of Ila and Riksharaja, is the predominant form of transformation in India. The corresponding transformation of women into men is both rarer and more destructive. A typically lethal transsexual from the *Mahabharata* is Amba, whose story is told in fragments scattered throughout the long text:

> Bhishma had taken a vow of eternal celibacy, to assure his stepmother that he would never have progeny who might challenge her son's right to become king. He went to find wives for his (half) brother Vicitryavirya and abducted Amba and her three sisters from their *svayamvara* (self-choice of a husband/mate). But when he learned that Amba had given her heart to another man who loved her, Bhishma sent her back to her betrothed lover, King Shalva. [1.96.45-53] Shalva, however, refused to accept a woman who had been carried off by another man. Caught in the middle, Amba cursed Bhishma and became an ascetic in order to amass the power to kill him. The river Ganga, Bhishma's mother, tried at first to dissuade Amba and then cursed her to become a crooked river, dried up except in monsoon and teeming with crocodiles. Amba did become a river, but only with one half of her body; the other half remained a woman and propitiated Shiva, saying, 'Because of Bhishma I have come to this eternally miserable state, neither a man nor a woman. I am disgusted with the condition of being a woman and have determined to become a man. I want to pay Bhishma back.' Shiva promised her that she would become a man who would kill Bhishma, and that she would remember everything when she had taken on a new body. Then she entered the fire and died. [5.170-187]

Now, King Drupada, whose wife had had no sons, asked Shiva for a son, but Shiva said, 'You will have a male child who is a female.' In time, the queen gave birth to a daughter, but she and the king pretended it was a son and raised the child as a son, whom they called Shikhandin. Besides the parents, only Bhishma knew the truth, which he learned from a spy, from Narada's report, from the words of the god [Shiva], and from Amba's asceticism. When the child reached maturity, 'he' married a princess; but when the princess found out that her husband was a woman, she was humiliated, and her father waged war on King Drupada. Drupada, who had known all along, pretended that he had been deceived by the queen, and she swore to this.

When Drupada's daughter, Shikhandini, saw the grief and danger she had caused her parents, she resolved to kill herself, and she went into the deserted forest. There she met a goblin [yaksha] named Sthuna ('Pillar') and begged him to use his magic to turn her into a man. The goblin said that he would give her his own sign of manhood [pum-lingam] for a short time, if she would promise to return it to him after the armies left the city; meanwhile, he would wear her sign of womanhood [stri-lingam]. They made this agreement and exchanged sexual organs. When Drupada learned from Shikhandin what had happened, he rejoiced and sent word to the attacking king that the bridegroom was in fact a man. The king sent some fine young women to learn whether Shikhandin was female or male, and they happily reported that he was absolutely male. The father of Shikhandin's bride rebuked his daughter and went home, and Shikhandin was delighted.

Meanwhile, Kubera, the lord of the goblins, found out what had happened and cursed Sthuna to remain female forever and Shikhandin to remain male forever—or, rather (in response to Sthuna's pleas) to remain male until Shikhandin's death, when Sthuna would regain his own form. When Shikhandin returned to Sthuna to keep his part of the bargain, he learned of Kubera's curse and returned to the city, rejoicing. [5.188-93]

In the battle of Kurukshetra, Shikhandin joined the Pandavas' army in order to kill Bhishma, who was in the Kaurava camp.

Now, Bhishma had vowed not to shoot at a woman, anyone who used to be a woman or had a woman's name or appeared to be a woman. [5.193.60-65] Shikhandin attacked Bhishma, but Bhishma, regarding him as someone made of a woman [strimaya], did not return the attack. [6.99.4-7] Arjuna said, 'Put Shikhandin in front; Bhishma has said he won't fight with him because he was born a woman.' [6.103.100] When Shikhandin shot arrows at Bhishma, Bhishma repelled them playfully, laughing as he remembered the femaleness of Shikhandin. But he did not strike Shikhandin, and he [Shikhandin] did not understand. Then Arjuna and the rest of the Pandavas used Shikhandin as a shield in their vanguard, and Bhishma fell under the rain of their arrows. [6.112.80]

Later, in the night raid, Shikhandin attacked Ashvatthaman and struck him between his two eyebrows. Furious, Ashvatthaman attacked Shikhandin and cut him in half. [10.8.58-9] After Bhishma died, Ganga, his mother, lamented, 'At the *svayamvara* in the city of Varanasi he conquered the warriors and carried off the women, and no one on earth could equal him. How is it that my heart did not break when I heard that Shikhandin killed him!' Krishna said, 'Do not grieve; he was killed by Arjuna, not by Shikhandin'. [13.154.19-29]

Amba is caught in limbo between two men, her beloved and the man who abducted her; she is socially, if not physically, raped by Bhishma (for his abduction of her made her second-hand goods from the standpoint of the man she loved) and then rejected by Bhishma as well as by her betrothed lover. In her own view, this makes her neither man nor woman; that is, she equates her liminal sexuality with androgyny. The phrase she uses,'Neither man nor woman', is the phrase often used to describe a *kliba*.[xi] A *kliba*, as we have seen, is not merely an androgyne; where androgyne implies a male-female equality and a creature of mythological status, with power and dignity,[xii] a *kliba* is a defective male, a male suffering from failure, distortion and lack. The term was coined by a homophobic Hindu culture to indicate a man who is in their terms sexually dysfunctional. When a culture does not want to confront an issue, it produces a haze of obfuscating terms that can be used for a wide range of pejorative purposes; *kliba* is such a term. The phrase 'neither man nor woman' is also used to describe a Hijra,[xiii] a kind of transvestite eunuch in contemporary India.[13]

Amba epitomizes the no-win situation of a woman tossed like a shuttlecock between two men, each of whom ricochets between inflicting upon her sexual excess or sexual rejection.[xiv] And when she becomes a man, that is precisely the sort of doubly hurtful man she becomes: the liminal Shikhandin/Shikhandini humiliates her bride, as Bhishma and Shalva together had humiliated Amba, and unsexes (and humiliates) a

[xi] See 'The Third Nature'.
[xii] See 'Bisexuality'.
[xiii] See 'The Third Nature'.
[xiv] See 'The Clever Wife'.

helpful goblin. His/her sexual ambivalence is itself ambivalent, or at least doubled: s/he is a female first masquerading as a male and then transformed into a male. And there are further echoes of Shikhandin's tendency to split in two: before undertaking asceticism herself, Amba chooses as her champion Rama-with-an-Axe, Parashurama, the annihilator of the Kshatriyas, who had cut his own mother in two, just as Ashvatthaman cuts Shikhandin in two when he kills him. And Amba is cursed by the motherly river, Ganga, to become a deadly river, devoid of fluids and teeming with toothy crocodiles, and then is further split between that river and the form of a woman.

Shikhandin does not seem to remember that s/he was Amba, even though Shiva expressly promises her that she will remember (just as Parvati promised Ila that he would not remember—is there a significant gendered difference here?). Shikhandin knows he was Shikhandini, but apparently not that he was Amba. Indeed, since Shikhandin/i has no voice, we don't really know what s/he knows; s/he can't even act but is merely used as a screen. Because s/he does not remember, s/he doesn't 'understand' when Bhishma won't fight with him/her. Despite Shiva's promise, memory here does not survive rebirth, even rebirth as someone of the same sex (though a different gender!). And the killing of Bhishma by Shikhandin is rather anticlimactic and further blurred by its diffusion: Shikhandin does not kill Bhishma outright but merely functions as a human bulwark for Arjuna;[xv] and Bhishma does not die immediately of his wounds but withdraws and dies long, long afterwards. Later, Shikhandin himself takes part in the night raid that violates the injunction against killing someone asleep, just as Budha violates the injunction against violating someone asleep.

But if Shikhandin does not remember, Bhishma certainly does; he has the whip hand over her in this, too, though it seems to be more important to him that Shikhandin was born a woman (Shikhandini) in this life than that she was a woman in a former life (Amba), let alone a woman who died cursing his name and vowing to kill him. Bhishma explicitly notes, but no one seems to care, that Shikhandin was Amba. There is something suspiciously idiosyncratic about Bhishma's vow not to 'shoot at a woman, anyone who used to be a woman, or has a woman's name, or appears to be a woman'.[14] Perhaps he invented the vow to protect her; he changes the

---

[xv] Since, as we are about to see, Arjuna functions as an androgyne in one book of the *Mahabharata*, and Shikhandin's transsexuality makes her a different sort of androgyne, this moment depicts one androgyne hiding behind another.

wording each time he says it, and he says it often in justifying his refusal to fight with Shikhandin.

But this vow opens a loophole clause for Bhishma's enemies in his otherwise complete invulnerability: only a woman can kill him, precisely because he regards a woman as so lowly that he would not stoop to defend himself against her. Thus the text implies that Shikhandin retained her female gender when she lost her female sexuality. Indeed, it is imperative for Bhishma that Shikhandin is in essence (in this case, in gender) a woman, despite her outer male form. This mythological loophole is a variant of the observation that men, by ignoring the differences between women (or others whom they dominate), can be tricked and overcome by them, by what James Scott has called the weapons of the weak. It is also related to a theme that appears elsewhere in the Hindu epics (and in epics from other cultures): the villain blackmails the gods into granting him the boon that he can be killed by no one on a list that he formulates, but he omits people beneath his contempt, one of whom, sneaking under the radar of the protective boon, kills him. Thus Ravana obtained the boon that he could be killed only by a human (Rama) [R 1.14.11], and, closer to our theme, the buffalo demon Mahisha obtained the boon that he could be killed only by a woman (inspiring the gods to create the goddess Durga).[15] In the case of Bhishma, the perfect solution, a creature with the technical status of a woman but the power of a man, is a murderous transsexual.

This ambiguity is also used in the self-definition of Hijras. Serena Nanda relates a story told to her by a Hijra:

> When Ram left Ayodhya to go to the forest, 'the whole city followed him because they loved him so. As Ram came to the banks of the river at the edge of the forest, he turned to the people and said, 'Ladies and gents, please wipe your tears and go away.' But those people who were not men and not women did not know what to do. So they stayed there [for fourteen years, till the end of Ram's exile] because Ram did not ask them to go . . . And so they were blessed by Ram.'[16]

Amba's connection with Hijras has been appropriated by contemporary Indian politics, as Lawrence Cohen has noted in a cartoon that was plastered onto walls near a big political rally in 1993:

> A male figure representing the common man and labelled the *Shikhandin janata* (*janata* means the people and Shikhandin is the gender-bending warrior from the *Mahabharata* epic, who for most Banarsis is . . . like a Hijra or eunuch) is shown bent over and raped at both ends by two

other male figures, orally by a *gandu neta* or politician-bugger and anally by a *jhandu pulis* or useless policeman.[17]

This image is classical in two senses. First, it draws upon a political insight couched in sexual language already documented in an ancient Brahmana text about the horse-sacrifice,[xvi] which speaks of a male who 'thrusts the penis into the slit, and the vulva swallows it up', and glosses this statement: 'The slit is the people, and the penis is the royal power, which presses against the people, and so the one who has royal power is hurtful to the people.'[18] Or, as one might say nowadays, the king fucks the people. Second, Shikhandin himself was, in his previous life as Amba, the very opposite of raped—sexually rejected—by two men, Bhishma and her betrothed lover. A very apt image indeed, but transformed, like Shikhandin himself, from the image of a woman to that of a man. To make the metaphor powerful and meaningful the authors of the Banarsi cartoon transformed the doubly not-raped, but lethally vengeful, Amba into the doubly raped Shikhandin.

Bhishma's mother, shamed at the thought of her son's death at the hands of a man-woman, is consoled by being told that Bhishma was killed not by Shikhandin but by another sort of *kliba*, Arjuna. Let us conclude with a look at this episode from the *Mahabharata*, the masquerade of Arjuna as the androgyne in the court of King Virata, for the story of Amba in many ways plays upon it, and it introduces yet another sort of transformation of the self—transvestism:

> The celestial courtesan Urvashi fell in love with Arjuna and propositioned him, but he said she was like a mother to him and clapped his hands over his ears. Furious, the spurned nymph gave him a curse to be a dancer among women, devoid of honour, regarded as a *kliba*. But Indra, the father of Arjuna, softened the curse and promised Arjuna that he would spend only a year as a dancer and then would be a man again. Years later, when it was time for Arjuna and his brothers to go into exile in disguise, Arjuna put on woman's clothing (though he failed to disguise his hairy, brawny arms) and told his brothers: 'I will be a *kliba*.' He offered his services as a dancing master to the women in the harem of a king. The king was suspicious at first, remarking that Arjuna certainly did not look like a *kliba*, but he then ascertained that 'her' lack of manhood was indeed firm and so let 'her' teach his daughters to dance.[19]

[xvi] See 'Sacrifice and Substitution', 'Indra as the Stallion's Wife', and 'The Mythology of Horses'.

Urvashi here plays the role of the seductive mother, the spurned, vengeful and incestuous goddess who punishes her unwilling son. Urvashi is not literally Arjuna's mother, but she is a female ancestor in the line of the Bharatas, Arjuna's line. Arjuna's response to Urvashi's threats is to disguise his manhood twice over: he pretends to be a *kliba* pretending to be a transvestite. Since the king determines (as the father of Shikhandin's wife determined, though with the opposite verdict) that he lacks manhood (more precisely, in a double entendre, that he has a firm lack of manhood), his disguise must mean here something more physiological than mere transvestism. But what?

This is a paper-thin masquerade meant to be funny, because we all know how virile Arjuna is; he is, in effect, mimicking a drag queen. His assumed name is a phallic joke ('Big-reed', Brihannada), and there are jokes about his big hairy arms; in fact, Arjuna argues that women's clothing is the only thing that will disguise the bowstring scars on both of his arms, which would otherwise reveal his identity as the world's greatest ambidextrous archer (a man who shoots with both hands, a delightful metaphor for a bisexual). Thus, in contrast with Amba, Arjuna does no harm when he is in drag, because he never approaches any man sexually; his womanliness at most reflects some true aspect of his macho womanizing in the rest of the epic.

★

What conclusions can we draw from this corpus of myths and from others related to them? In some texts, a male is entirely transformed into a female, with a female mentality and memory (aspects of gender rather than of sex), the situation that we might expect from the fluidity of gender; this happens to Ila in most texts (except on the Sahya mountain). Yet many texts, probably reflecting the dramatic, even grotesque, asymmetry between perceptions of people of different genders in actual life in ancient India, seem to reflect the very opposite view, a view of gender as astonishingly durable: the male merely assumes the outer form of the female, retaining his male essence, his male memory and mentality (as Ila does in the Sahya text and at the beginning of his transformation in most texts).

There are other Hindu tales of gender-bending, in which gender is sometimes more, sometimes less, basic than other aspects of self-recognition. For example, in one story, a magician puts the soul of a courtesan into the body of a wandering mendicant and vice versa; the resulting confusion is the subject of a Sanskrit farce (the *Bhagavadajjuka*), in which the whore thinks and acts like a yogi, and vice versa. And the poet comments: 'The life's breaths of the woman, placed in the body of this Brahmin, will cause a transformation of his essence [*sattva*] and his behaviour [*shila*].'[20] Here gender clearly remains distinct from the transformed body: the Brahmin behaves like a courtesan, not like a Brahmin. Buddhist mythology, too, teaches that, to become a Bodhisattva, a woman must have not only the body but the mind of a man (though, since Buddhists do not affirm the existence of a soul, she can't have the *soul* of a man).

Most of the transformations in these myths are temporary: the person undergoing the transformation, willingly or as the result of a curse, ends up as s/he was at the start. But even in stories in which, during the period of the transformation, the subject has no memory of the original (and final) state, at the end the subject (or, failing that, someone else) usually remembers, or discovers, the transformation. Here we must note a significant gender asymmetry: no matter whether a man magically becomes a woman, or a woman becomes a man, the transformed person usually forgets the former gender and identity. But in both cases, there is another man present, untransformed, who remembers, and who, therefore, has power over the transformed person. For Ila, it is Budha; for Amba, Bhishma.

Gender often proves remarkably tenacious. Even the Vedantic theory of illusion, which disparages the body in favour of the soul, implies that you may very well remain a male in some essential way even when you happen to take on a female body: even when memory is transformed, the male almost always reverts to his maleness in the end. It is worth noting that very few, if any, gender changes occur in reincarnation; even Amba changes her gender only *after* she has been reborn with the same gender that she had in her previous life: and this stands in strong contrast to the frequent changes of species that take place in reincarnation, in texts like *The Laws of Manu*. Thus a man might more easily be reborn as an ant (presumably a male ant) than as a woman. The two contrasting views of the persistence of gender may be correlated with two contrasting attitudes to women: the texts that view gender as fluid generally depict the transformed male as happy in her female form, for he forgets he is a man, as his memory, like his body, is transformed; while those in which the gendered memory lags stubbornly behind the body depict him as miserable in her female form, for she remembers that she was once a man.

The sexual tension, if not the desire, in these stories is usually within a single person at war with his or her changing self. These are not generally happy stories, or charters for the affirmation of a polymorphous androgyny. Some of these texts perceive sex as so dangerous that they attempt to eliminate the woman, to eliminate the other, to produce the only truly safe sex—when you are alone, a serial androgyne who becomes his own partner.

Occasionally the sex change is effected in the service of a kind of androgyny or bisexuality. Some of these myths may be read as tales about bisexual desire, and many of them, such as the comic episode of Arjuna as the dancing master, are joyous rather than tragic. Chudala *purposely* becomes a man by day and a woman by night,[xvii] condensing into a single day Ila's helplessly alternating month-by-month experience and getting the best of both worlds, male and female. When Dattaka becomes a woman in order to experience the subjective sexuality of women as well as men, in writing his *Kamasutra*,[xviii] he gains a unique two-dimensional sexual knowledge.

Some of these stories are also about empathy: what is it like to be the other? True, empathy can be used as a power play: 'Which way was the sex better?' they asked Bhangashvana, and answer came: 'As a woman.' But often the transformed characters become far more sympathetic to the other that they have experienced. It would certainly be simplistic to overlook the misogynist implications of the argument that women enjoy sex more than men do, but these texts do tell us that sexual pleasure is a serious goal for both sexes, and that it influences the preference for one set of children over another, which is certainly significant. Moreover, they remind us of two truths in tension, a paradox: one Hindu view of gender makes it as easy to slough off as a pair of pants (or a dress), but this view is often challenged by myths in which skin is more than skin deep, in which the soul and the memory, too, are gendered, an intrinsic part of the mortal coil that is not quite so easily shuffled off.

[xvii] See 'Bisexuality'.
[xviii] See 'The Mythology of the *Kamasutra*'.

KAMA AND OTHER SEDUCTIONS

THE CONTROL OF ADDICTION IN
ANCIENT INDIA[1]

*So overpowering are the senses that they can be kept under control only when they
are completely hedged in on all sides. It is common knowledge that they are powerless
without food, and so fasting undertaken with a view to control the senses is helpful.*

—M.K. Gandhi

Mind is at the root of all sensuality . . . Brahmacharya *means control of the senses
in thought, word and deed. There is no limit to the possibilities of renunciation.*

—M.K. Gandhi

ADDICTION AND RENUNCIATION

A profound psychological understanding of addiction (*sakti*,[i]
'attachment', particularly 'excessive attachment', *ati-sakti*) is evident
throughout the history of Hinduism. The lawmaker Manu writes in his
dharmashastra: 'A man should not, out of desire, become addicted to any of
the sensory objects; let him rather consider in his mind what is entailed in
becoming excessively addicted to them.'[2] The Hindu appreciation of the
value of exquisite pleasure (kama) was balanced by an awareness of the
dangers that it posed when cultivated to the point at which it became a
vice (a danger appreciated even by the *Kamasutra*), and a number of
religious disciplines were designed to control sensual addictions. The
renunciant movements of ancient India addressed precisely this problem,
which was of great concern also to the wider tradition. Renunciation and
asceticism were like dykes built to hold back the oceanic tides of sensuality.
While only a small number ever went to the extreme of renouncing the

---

[i] Not to be confused with *shakti*, a feminine form of power.

material world, fasting and vows of chastity were, as they still are, widely accepted, in moderated forms, even among Hindu householders.

Most sorts of renunciation were peaceful, both for the individual renouncer and for the society from which the renouncer withdrew, *hors de combat*, while remaining perceived as broadly beneficial to the community at large. But other kinds of renunciation were violent both to the physical body and to the social body, to the world of families. Hinduism was violent not only in its sensuality but in its reaction against that sensuality—violent, that is, both in its addictions and in the measures that it took to curb those addictions.

Manu's entire text is an intricate regimen for the control of the senses—essential for anyone on the path to moksha, release from the material world of rebirth (for one must detach oneself from all sensual bonds in order to break free from the world), but also a desideratum for people on the path of rebirth (where a pious life demands complete self control). Kautilya's *Arthashastra*, by contrast, tosses off the need for control of the senses with just a few, rather unhelpful lines: 'The conquest of the senses arises out of training in the sciences [*vidyas*] and is accomplished by renouncing desire, anger, greed, pride, drunkenness and exhilaration.' And later: 'Absence of training in the sciences is the cause of a person's vices.'[3] But the *Arthashastra* also prescribes what we would call aversion therapy for a young prince who is addicted to any of the four vices of lust. It advises a king to have a secret agent tempt the crown prince with all four vices, and another secret agent to dissuade him from them.[4] And if that does not work:

> If in the overflowing of adolescence he sets his mind on the wives of other men, the king's agents should turn him off by means of filthy women pretending to be noble women in empty houses at night. If he lusts for wine, they should turn him off by a drugged drink (a spiked drink that makes him nauseated). If he lusts for gambling, they should have players cheat him. If he lusts for hunting, they should have him terrified by men pretending to be robbers blocking his path.[5]

The *Kamasutra*, too, knows how dangerous the senses can be—and likens them to horses: 'For, just as a horse in full gallop, blinded by the energy of his own speed, pays no attention to any post or hole or ditch on the path, so two lovers blinded by passion in the friction of sexual battle are caught up in their fierce energy and pay no attention to danger.'[6] It is, I think, significant that the senses were analogized not to unglamorous tame animals like pigs or dogs, nor to violent wild animals like lions or crocodiles, but to noble, beautiful, expensive horses.[ii] How to guard against that danger? Study the *Kamasutra*, but also use your head.[7]

ADDICTIVE VICES IN THE THREE TEXTS OF THE THREE GOALS OF LIFE

The main arena in which ancient India tackled the subject of addiction for householders, rather than for renouncers, was the corpus of scientific texts known as the *shastras*, particularly the texts dealing with the three Goals of Life (the *purusharthas*): dharma, artha and kama, known collectively as the *trivarga*. (Later, as we have discussed elsewhere, a fourth goal of moksha, release, was added for renunciants, but we will deal in this section only with the earlier triad.[iii]) The *Kamasutra* shares with both the *Arthashastra* and Manu (as well as with other important Indian traditions such as yoga) a strong sense of the need for the control of addiction, though each text has its own reasons for this.

Ancient Indian texts often call the four major addictions that kings were vulnerable to 'the vices of lust', sometimes naming them after the activities themselves—gambling, drinking, fornicating, hunting—and sometimes projecting the guilt and blame from the addict onto the objects of addiction: dice, intoxicants (wine, various forms of liquor, as well as marijuana and opium), women (or sex) and wild animals. The addictions are also called the 'royal vices', and indeed the typical member of the royal or warrior class is 'a drinker of wine to the point of drunkenness, a lover of women, a great hunter—killing for sport', as well as a gambler and (beyond the four classical vices) a slayer of men and eater of meat.[8] That is, it was the king's job to indulge in what were, sometimes for him and always for people of other classes, deadly vices. Kings were allowed to have the vices that kill the rest of us, but even kings could be killed by an excess of them. Addiction to the vices marginalized some rajas by stripping them of their power and status; kings, at least in stories, lost their kingdoms by gambling or were carried away by hunting and landed in dangerous or polluting circumstances. The *Mahabharata* remarks that the four vices are the curse of a king,[9] and indeed all four cause serious trouble in the *Mahabharata* story: Pandu, the father of the protagonists, is doomed by excessive hunting and forbidden sex (Book 1); two kings, Yudhishthira

---

[ii] See 'The Mythology of Horses'.
[iii] See 'Three (or More)'.

and Nala, are undone by gambling (Books 2 and 3); and the entire clan is destroyed by men who break the law against drinking (Book 16). The four addictive vices of desire were also associated with violence, in the double sense of releasing pent-up violent impulses and being themselves the violent form of otherwise normal human tendencies (to search for food, take risks, drink and procreate).

Hunting is of course violent but also shares the quality of 'just one more' that is the tell-tale sign of addiction—there are many stories of hunters who kept going even after they knew they should turn back, until they found themselves benighted or in a dangerous place, or both—as well as the quality of blindness (as in 'blind drunk') that makes the hunter mistake a human being for an animal, with disastrous consequences.[iv] Both Draupadi in the *Mahabharata*[10] and Sita in the *Ramayana*[11] are abducted when their men are away hunting; King Parikshit, obsessed with hunting, impatiently insults a sage who obstructs his hunt and is cursed to die;[12] King Dasharatha, hunting, is cursed to lose his son when he accidentally shoots a boy whom he mistakes for an elephant;[v] and deer appear to King Yudhishthira in a dream, complaining that their numbers are dwindling because of his family's incessant hunting.[13] Dushyanta's excessive hunting foreshadows his mistreatment of Shakuntala,[vi] and King Ila's excessive hunting foreshadows his sexual curse.[vii]

The *Arthashastra* ranks gambling as the most dangerous vice a king can have, more dangerous than (in descending order) women, drinking and hunting.[14] Gambling, in the form of a game of dice, was the metaphor for the disintegrating Four Ages or Yugas,[viii] and a central trope for the role of chance in human life. The Vedic consecration ritual includes a ritual dice game of multiple symbolic meanings: the Four Ages, the risk implicit in the sacrifice itself, the element of chance in getting and keeping power, the royal vice of gambling that must be channelled into political daring, and the king's hope of 'gathering' in all the winning throws of all the other players. The king is regarded as the maker of the Age, and the ceremonial dice game played at his consecration is said, like the gambling of Shiva in Shaiva mythology, to determine what kind of cosmic age will come up next—the Winning Age or the Kali (Dark) Age (the losing throw of the dice).[15] But King Yudhishthira, the eldest of the Pandava brothers, happens

---

[iv] See 'Zoomorphism'.
[v] See 'Shadows of the *Ramayana*'.
[vi] See 'Rings of Rejection'.
[vii] See 'Transsexual Transformations'.
[viii] See 'Three (or More)' and 'The Concept of Heresy'.

to be, as an individual rather than someone in the office of king, a compulsive and unsuccessful gambler, and his enemies take advantage of this: they send in to play against Yudhishthira, on the occasion of his consecration, a man known to be invincible, almost certainly dishonest, and Yudhishthira gambles away his possessions, then his brothers, himself and finally his (and his brothers') wife Draupadi. Only Draupadi's courage and wit and legal knowledge are able to save the Pandavas from slavery, and even so they lose the kingdom and must go into exile for twelve years, and remain disguised for a thirteenth. Thus the human vice of addictive gambling intrudes upon the controlled ritual of gambling.

As for drinking, and intoxication more generally conceived, there were at least twelve types of alcohol popular in ancient India: *sura* (also called arrack, made from coconut or from other fermented fruits or grains, or sugar cane, the drink most often mentioned, particularly as used by non-Brahmins[16]), *panasa* (from jackfruit), *draksha* (from grapes, often imported from Rome), *madhuka* (from honey), *kharjura* (from dates), *tala* (from palm), *sikhshiva* (from sugar cane), *madhvika* (distilled from the flowers of *Mahue longifolia*), *saira* (from long-pepper), *arishta* (from soap-berry), *narikelaja* (from coconut) and *maireya* (now called rum).[17]

Manu twice equates the drinking of liquor with the three major sins of Brahmin-killing, theft and sleeping with the guru's wife.[18] Those verses assume a male subject, however; Manu associates drinking by women with the milder habits of keeping bad company, being separated from their husbands, sleeping, living in other people's houses and aimless wandering.[19] The *Arthashastra* advises the king to appoint only non-drinking counsellors (to guard against loose talk) and to keep his sons from liquor (which might make them cast covetous eyes on his throne).[20] Against enemy princes, however, liquor is a useful weapon: an enemy prince should be weakened by intoxication so that he can be more easily compelled to become an ally.[21]

Finally, addictive lust. The *Kamasutra*, working the other side of the street, as it were, teaches courtesans how to create, and manipulate, sexual addiction in others. Advice to the courtesan: 'A brief saying sums it up: She makes him love her but does not become addicted to him, though she acts as if she were addicted.'[22] And the clear signs of a man's addiction to her are that 'he trusts her with his true feelings, lives in the same way as she does, carries out her plans, is without suspicion and has no concern for money matters'.[23] Once he is hooked, she can control him: 'When a man is too deeply addicted to her, he fears that she will make love with another man, and he disregards her lies. And, because of his fear, he gives her a lot.'[24] The *Kamasutra* also offers advice to anyone, male or female, professional or amateur, on the uses of drugs to put lovers in your power.[25]

Renunciants regarded sex as a snare and a delusion, and married life as a deathtrap. Manu even admits that what makes women so dangerous is the fact that men are so weak:

> It is the very nature of women to corrupt men here on earth; for that reason, circumspect men do not get careless and wanton among wanton women. It is not just an ignorant man, but even a learned man of the world, too, that a wanton woman can lead astray when he is in the control of lust and anger. No one should sit in a deserted place with his mother, sister, or daughter; for the strong cluster of the sensory powers drags away even a learned man.[26]

THE NATURE AND RANKING OF ADDICTION

In the *Mahabharata*, Nala becomes an addictive gambler only after he has been possessed by the spirit of the Kali Age[ix], an indication that addiction in general was perceived as coming from outside the individual. There is no idea here of an addictive personality; the vices, rather than the people who have them, are blamed. The gambler is not doomed by birth, by his character; he has somehow fallen into the bad habit of gambling, and if he made an effort, he could get out of it. Free will, self control, meditation, controlling the senses—this is always possible. So, too, there are no alcoholics, just people who happen, at the moment, to be drinking too much. Anyone exposed to the objects of addiction is liable to get caught. Sex is the only inborn addiction: we are all, in this Hindu view, naturally inclined to it, exposed to it all the time, inherently lascivious.

Manu sums up the shared underlying attitude toward the addictions:

> The ten vices [*vyasanas*] that arise from desire all end badly. Hunting, gambling, sleeping by day, malicious gossip, women, drunkenness, music, singing, dancing and aimless wandering are the ten vices born of desire. Drinking, gambling, women and hunting, in that order [i.e., with drinking the worst], are the four worst, and, though they are universally addictive, each vice is more serious than the one that follows.[27]

The *Arthashastra* basically agrees with Manu on this point:

> Four vices spring from lust—hunting, gambling, women and drink. Lust involves humiliation, loss of property and hanging out with

---

[ix] See 'The Concept of Heresy'.

KAMA AND OTHER SEDUCTIONS   369

undesirable persons like thieves, gamblers, hunters, singers and musicians. Of the vices of lust, gambling is worse than hunting, women are worse than gambling, drink is worse than women.[28]

All this is clear enough; in the *Arthashastra*, as in Manu, drink is the worst vice of lust, women next, then gambling, and hunting the least destructive. But then the *Arthashastra* adds, 'But gambling is worse than drink— indeed, for a king, it is the worst of the vices,'[29] changing the order of vices for a king: now gambling is the worst, then drink, women and hunting last.

There was room for an even wider divergence of opinions. Hunting was classified as a vice only when it was pursued when there was no need for food, just as gambling became a vice when undertaken independent of a need for money, and sex when there was no need for offspring. A Sanskrit text composed just a bit later (in the fifth or sixth century CE, in Kanchipuram) satirizes both the *Arthashastra* and Manu: a young man whose father had banished him for bad behaviour encouraged the king in all his vices; he praised hunting because it makes you athletic, reduces phlegm, teaches you all about animals and gets you out into the fresh air; gambling makes you generous, sharp-eyed, single-minded, keen to take risks; kama is the reward for dharma and artha (the *Kamasutra* says this too[30]), teaches you strategy, and produces offspring (here assumed to be a Good Thing); and drinking keeps you young, uproots remorse, and gives you courage.[31]

In addition to these differences of opinion, the addictions were ranked differently for different people. We have noted throughout this discussion the special case of kings. Both the senses and horses were a Good Thing for high-spirited warrior kings but not such a Good Thing for more bovine priests and householders whose goal was control. And as Brahmins were perceived (at least by Brahmins) as needed to control kings, so asceticism was thought necessary to rein in the treacherous senses. The other classes, too, presented special cases in the consideration of addiction. Hunting, for instance, is not a vice for poor people, who hunt for rabbits or whatever they can find to eat, though tribal hunters were regarded as unclean because of their habit of hunting. To some extent, these vices levelled the playing field. No one was exempt from addiction.

Not even the gods. Though the great gods Vishnu and Shiva are often depicted as entirely immune to the dangers of addiction, and, therefore, able to capitalize upon the addictions of their demonic enemies, there are notable exceptions. In the Puranas, Shiva plays dice with his wife to the point where she strips him of everything he owns, and he is overcome by desire for a woman (when he sees Mohini[x]). In the folk tradition, Shiva is said to be addicted to *bhang* (marijuana); and in the *Mahabharata* he is a famous (though not particularly addicted) hunter, who appears to Arjuna as an angry mountain boar–hunter, a Kirata. As for the minor gods, Indra as the paradigmatic king is of course the paradigmatic addict, particularly notorious for his lust and his drunkenness. The powers of the gods, that dwarf our own meagre abilities, seem not necessarily to include self-control; or perhaps it is just that their addictions, like everything else about them, are larger than (human) life.

[x] See 'Bisexuality'.

READING THE *KAMASUTRA*: IT ISN'T ALL ABOUT SEX[1]

INTRODUCTION: THE POSITION OF THE *KAMASUTRA*

The *Kamasutra* is the oldest extant Hindu textbook of erotic love, and one of the oldest in the world. It was composed in Sanskrit, the literary language of ancient India, probably sometime in the second half of the third century of the Common Era,[2] in North India, perhaps in Pataliputra (near the present city of Patna, in Bihar). The two words in its title mean 'desire/love/pleasure/sex' (*kama*) and 'a treatise' (*sutra*). Virtually nothing is known about the author, Vatsyayana Mallanaga, other than his name and what little we learn from the text. Nor do we know anything about Yashodhara, who wrote the definitive commentary on the *Kamasutra* in the thirteenth century. But Vatsyayana tells us something important about his text, namely, that it is a distillation of the works of a number of authors who preceded him, authors whose texts have not come down to us. Vatsyayana cites them often—sometimes in agreement, sometimes in disagreement—though his own voice always comes through, as ringmaster over the many acts he incorporates in his sexual circus.

Most people think the *Kamasutra* is a book about the positions in sexual intercourse, the erotic counterpart to the ascetic asanas of yoga.[i] Reviews of books dealing with the *Kamasutra* in recent years have had titles like 'Assume the Position' and 'Position Impossible'. A recent cartoon depicts 'The *Kamasutra* Relaxasizer Lounger, 165 positions.'[3] *Cosmopolitan* magazine published two editions of its 'Cosmo *Kamasutra*', offering '12 brand-new mattress-quaking sex styles', each with its numerical 'degree of difficulty', including positions called 'the backstairs boogie', 'the octopus', 'the mermaid', 'the spider web' and 'the rock'n' roll'.[4] One website offered

---

[i] See 'Assume the Position'.

The Kamasutra of Pooh, posing stuffed animals in compromising positions (Piglet on Pooh, Pooh mounting Eeyore, and so forth); another posed Kermit the Frog in action on an unidentified stuffed animal. Palm Pilot had a copyrighted 'Pocket Sutra: The Kama Sutra in the palm of your hand', which offered 'lying down positions', 'sitting positions', 'rear-entry positions', 'standing positions', 'role reversal' and many more. There is a *Kamasutra* wristwatch that displays a different position every hour.

A typical Roz Chast cartoon entitled 'The Kama Sutra of Grilled Cheese' began with '#14: The Righteous Lion' ('place on hot, well-lubricated griddle. Fry until bread and cheese become one') and so forth.[5] Robin Williams included in his act what John Lahr called 'a fantasy of lascivious Olympic figure skating' and Williams himself called 'the Kama Sutra on ice'.[6] The satirical journal *The Onion* ran a parody about a couple whose 'inability to execute The Totally Auspicious Position, along with countless other ancient Indian erotic positions, took them to new heights of sexual dissatisfaction'.[7] A book called *The Popup Kamasutra* failed to take full advantage of the possibilities of this genre; the whole couple pops up. More seriously, Roland Barthes, in *The Pleasure of the Text*, took the *Kamasutra* as a root metaphor for literary as well as physical desire: 'The text you write must prove to me that it desires me. This proof exists: it is writing. Writing is: the science of the various blisses of language, its *Kama Sutra* (this science has but one treatise: writing itself).'[8] The text for sex is thus the sex of the text, too.

The part of the *Kamasutra* describing the positions may have been the best-thumbed passage in previous ages of sexual censorship, but nowadays, when sexually explicit novels, films and instruction manuals are available everywhere, that part is the least useful. The real *Kamasutra*, however, is not just about the positions in sexual intercourse. It is a book about the art of living—about finding a partner, maintaining power in a marriage, committing adultery, living as or with a courtesan, using drugs—and also about the positions in sexual intercourse. The *Kamasutra* was certainly not the first of its genre, nor was it the last. But the many textbooks of eroticism that follow it eliminate most of the *Kamasutra*'s encyclopaedic social and psychological narratives and concentrate primarily on the sexual positions, of which they describe many more than are found in the *Kamasutra*.

CLASS IN THE *KAMASUTRA*

Who was it written for? It is difficult to assess how broad a spectrum of ancient Indian society knew the text first-hand. It would be good to have more information about social conditions in India at the time of the composition of the *Kamasutra*, but the *Kamasutra* itself is one of the main sources that we have for such data; the text is, in a sense, its own context. Much of the *Kamasutra* is about culture, which belonged to those who had leisure and means, time and money, none of which was in short supply for the text's primary intended audience, an urban (and urbane) elite consisting of princes, high state officials and wealthy merchants The production of manuscripts, especially illuminated manuscripts, was necessarily an elite matter; men of wealth and power, kings and merchants, would commission texts to be copied out for their private use. It is often said that only upper-class men were allowed to read Sanskrit, particularly the sacred texts, but the very fact that the texts dealing with religious and social law (dharma) prescribe punishments for women and lower-class men who read the sacred Sanskrit texts suggests that some of them did so.

The *Kamasutra* is almost unique in classical Sanskrit literature in its almost total disregard of class (*varna*) and caste (*jati*). Where classical texts of dharma in India might have said that you make love differently to women of high and low classes, Vatsyayana just says you make love differently to women of delicate or rough temperaments. But, of course, power relations of many kinds—gender, wealth, political position, as well as caste—are implicit throughout the text. The lovers must be rich, yes, but not necessarily upper-class. When the text says that the man may get his money from 'gifts, conquest, trade, or wages, or from inheritance, or from both,' the commentator (Yashodhara) explains, 'If he is a Brahmin, he gets his money from gifts; a king or warrior, from conquest; a commoner, from trade; and a servant, from wages earned by working as an artisan, a travelling bard, or something of that sort.' [1.4.1]

Varna is mentioned just a few times, once in a single sentence admitting that it is of concern only when you marry a wife who will bear you legal sons, and can be disregarded in all other erotic situations [1.5.1]; once when the go-between is advised to tell the target woman stories about 'other virgins of equal caste' [*jati*, 3.5.5]; and later in a discussion of possible sexual partners:

> 'Sex with a coarse servant' takes place with a lower-class female water-carrier or house-servant, until the climax; in this kind of sex, he does not bother with the acts of civility. Similarly, 'sex with a peasant' takes place between a courtesan and a country bumpkin, until the climax, or between a man-about-town and women from the countryside, cow-herding villages, or countries beyond the borders. [2.10.22-25]

Vatsyayana disapproves of sexual relations with rural and tribal women because they could have adverse effects on the erotic refinement and sensibility of the cultivated man-about-town; he would have been baffled by any Lady Chatterji's sexual transports with a gamekeeper. But for all the rest of the discussion of pleasure, class is irrelevant.

THE LIFE OF A MAN (AND WOMAN) ABOUT TOWN

The protagonist of the *Kamasutra*, literally a 'man-about-town' (*nagaraka*, from the Sanskrit *nagara*, city), lives 'in a city, a capital city, a market town, or some large gathering where there are good people, or wherever he has to stay to make a living' [1.4.2]. He has, as we say of a certain type of man today, no visible source of income. His companions may have quite realistic money problems [1.4.31-33]; his wife is entrusted with all the household management, including the finances; and his mistresses work hard to make and keep their money. But we never see the man-about-town at work:

> This is how he spends a typical day. First is his morning toilet: He gets up in the morning, relieves himself, cleans his teeth, applies fragrant oils in small quantities, as well as incense, garlands, bees' wax and red lac, looks at his face in a mirror, takes some mouthwash, and attends to the things that need to be done. He bathes every day, has his limbs rubbed with oil every second day, a foam bath every third day, his face shaved every fourth day, and his body hair removed every fifth or tenth day. All of this is done without fail. And he continually cleans the sweat from his armpits. In the morning and afternoon he eats. [1.4.5-7]

Now, ready to face the day, he goes to work:

> After eating, he passes the time teaching his parrots and mynah birds to speak; goes to quail-fights, cockfights and ram-fights; engages in various arts and games; and passes the time with his libertine, pander and clown. And he takes a nap. In the late afternoon, he gets dressed up and goes to salons to amuse himself. And in the evening, there is music and singing. After that, on the bed in a bedroom carefully decorated and perfumed by sweet-smelling incense, he and his friends await the women who are slipping out for a rendezvous with them. He sends female messengers for them or goes to get them himself. And when the women arrive, he and his friends greet them with gentle conversation and courtesies that charm the mind and heart. If rain has soaked the clothing of women who have slipped out for a rendezvous in bad

weather, he changes their clothes himself, or gets some of his friends to
serve them. That is what he does by day and night. [1.4.8-13]

Busy teaching his birds to talk, he never drops in to check things at the
shop, let alone visit his mother. Throughout the text, his one concern is
the pursuit of pleasure.

That is not to say, however, that the pursuit of pleasure didn't require its
own work. Vatsyayana details the sixty-four arts that need to be learned by
anyone (male or female) who is truly serious about pleasure [2.10.35]:

> singing; playing musical instruments; dancing; painting; cutting leaves
> into shapes; making lines on the floor with rice-powder and flowers;
> arranging flowers; colouring the teeth, clothes and limbs; making
> jewelled floors; preparing beds; making music on the rims of glasses of
> water; playing water sports; unusual techniques; making garlands and
> stringing necklaces; making diadems and headbands; making costumes;
> making various earrings; mixing perfumes; putting on jewellery; doing
> conjuring tricks; practicing sorcery; sleight of hand; preparing various
> forms of vegetables, soups and other things to eat; preparing wines,
> fruit juices and other things to drink; needlework; weaving; playing
> the lute and the drum; telling jokes and riddles; completing words;
> reciting difficult words; reading aloud; staging plays and dialogues;
> completing verses; making things out of cloth, wood and cane; wood-
> working; carpentry; architecture; the ability to test gold and silver;
> metallurgy; knowledge of the colour and form of jewels; skill at
> nurturing trees; knowledge of ram-fights, cockfights and quail-fights;
> teaching parrots and mynah birds to talk; skill at rubbing, massaging
> and hairdressing; the ability to speak in sign language; understanding
> languages made to seem foreign; knowledge of local dialects; skill at
> making flower carts; knowledge of omens; alphabets for use in making
> magical diagrams; alphabets for memorizing; group recitation;
> improvising poetry; dictionaries and thesauruses; knowledge of metre;
> literary work; the art of impersonation; the art of using clothes for
> disguise; special forms of gambling; the game of dice; children's games;
> etiquette; the science of strategy; and the cultivation of athletic skills.
> [1.3.15]

And while we are still reeling from this list, Vatsyayana immediately
reminds us that there is, in addition, an entirely different cluster of sixty-
four arts of love [1.3.16], which include eight forms of each of the main
erotic activities: embracing, kissing, scratching, biting, sexual positions,
moaning, the woman playing the man's part and oral sex. [2.8.4-5] A rapid

calculation brings the tab to 128 arts, a curriculum that one could hardly master even after the equivalent of two Ph.Ds and a long apprenticeship—and one that not many could afford.

Clearly the *Kamasutra* was intended to be useful for the man-about-town. But what about the woman-about-town? The assumption that the intended reader of the *Kamasutra* is male persists even in popular culture today, where Vinod Verma, apparently hoping to rectify this imbalance, published *The Kamasutra for Women: The Modern Woman's Way to Sensual Fulfilment and Health*, applying Ayurvedic techniques to female heterosexual relationships; and in 2002 there was *The Woman's Kamasutra*, by Nitya Lacroix; and then the *Kama Sutra para la Mujer*. But there is no need for such books.[9] The *Kamasutra* is for women. Vatsyayana argues at some length that some women, at least, should read this text, and that others should learn its contents in other ways:

> A woman should study the *Kamasutra* and its subsidiary arts before she reaches the prime of her youth, and she should continue when she has been given away, if her husband wishes it. Scholars say: 'Since females cannot grasp texts, it is useless to teach women this text.' Vatsyayana says: But women understand the practice, and the practice is based on the text. This applies beyond this specific subject of the *Kamasutra*, for throughout the world, in all subjects, there are only a few people who know the text, but the practice is within the range of everyone. And a text, however far removed, is the ultimate source of the practice. 'Grammar is a science,' people say. Yet the sacrificial priests, who are no grammarians, know how to gloss the words in the sacrificial prayers. 'Astronomy is a science,' they say. But ordinary people perform the rituals on the days when the skies are auspicious. And people know how to ride horses and elephants without studying the texts about horses and elephants. In the same way, even citizens far away from the king do not step across the moral line that he sets. The case of women learning the *Kamasutra* is like those examples. And there are also women whose understanding has been sharpened by the text: courtesans and the daughters of kings and state ministers. (1.3.1–11)

In addition to this general expectation, particular parts of the book were evidently designed to be used by women. Book Three devotes one episode to advice to virgins trying to get husbands [3.4.36–47], and Book Four consists of instructions for wives. Book Six is said to have been commissioned by the courtesans of Pataliputra, presumably for their own use. [1.1.11]

THE *KAMASUTRA* AS A PLAY

What is its genre? Beneath the veneer of a sexual textbook, the *Kamasutra* resembles a work of dramatic fiction more than anything else. The man and woman whose sex lives are described here are called the hero and heroine, and the men who assist the hero are called the libertine, pander and clown. All of these are terms for stock characters in Sanskrit dramas—the hero and heroine, sidekick, supporting player and jester. Is the *Kamasutra* a play about sex? Certainly it has a dramatic sequence, and, like most classical Indian dramas, it has seven acts. In Act One, which literally sets the stage for the drama, the bachelor sets up his pad; in Act Two, he perfects his sexual technique. Then he seduces a virgin (Act Three), gets married and lives with a wife or wives (Act Four); tiring of her (or them), he seduces other men's wives (Act Five) and when he tires of that, he frequents courtesans (Act Six). Finally, when he is too old to manage it at all, he resorts to the ancient Indian equivalent of Viagra: aphrodisiacs and magic spells (Act Seven).

THE *KAMASUTRA* AND US

Two worlds in the *Kamasutra* intersect for contemporary readers, both Indian and non-Indian: sex and ancient India. We assume that the understanding of sex will be familiar to us, since sex is universal, and that the representations of ancient India will be strange to us, since that world existed long ago and (for some of us) in a galaxy far away. This is largely the case, but there are interesting reversals of expectations: some sexual matters are strange (for Vatsyayana argues that sex for human beings is a matter of culture, not nature[ii]), or even sometimes repugnant, to us today, while some cultural matters are strangely familiar or, if unfamiliar, still charming and comprehensible, reassuring us that the people of ancient India were in many ways just like us. Consider the description of the man's day: his morning toilet is much like ours, but we do not, alas, schedule in things like teaching mynah birds to speak. It is the constant intersection of these perceptions—'How very odd!', 'Oh, I know just how she feels!'—that constitutes the strange appeal of the *Kamasutra*.

Many readers will recognize the man who tells the woman on whom he's set his sights 'about an erotic dream, pretending that it was about another woman' [3.4.9], and the woman who does the same thing.

[ii] See 'Zoomorphism'.

[5.4.54] Others will feel a guilty pang of familiarity when reading the passage suggesting that a woman interested in getting a man's attention in a crowded room might find some pretext to take something from him, making sure to brush him with her breast as she reaches across him. [2.2.8-9] This is an amazingly intimate thing to know about a culture, far more intimate than knowing that you can stand on one leg or another when you make love. Sometimes the unfamiliar and the familiar are cheek by jowl: the culture-specific list of women the wife must not associate with, which include a Buddhist nun and a magician who uses love-sorcery worked with roots [4.1.9], is followed in the very next passage by the woman who is cooking for her man and finds out 'this is what he likes, this is what he hates, this is good for him, this is bad for him', a consideration that must resonate with many contemporary readers, cooking for someone they love, balancing the desire to please (perhaps with a Béarnaise sauce? Or a curry made with lots of ghee?) with the concern for the rising cholesterol level. The *Kamasutra* is a unique text, but it is firmly situated within the value system of what might be called the ancient 'Hindu way'; it shares more of its values with those of traditional Hindu texts than one might have expected.

Some of it, like the magic formulas, remains truly foreign to us:

> If you make a powder by pulverizing leaves scattered by the wind, garlands left over from corpses, and peacocks' bones, or pulverize a female 'circle-maker' buzzard that died a natural death, and mix the powder with honey and gooseberry, it puts someone in your power. If you mix the same powder with monkey shit and scatter the mixture over a virgin, she will not be given to another man. [7.1.25-30]

And so forth, and so on. A comparison with Viagra is superficially useful here, but it does not get you far enough to take this paragraph seriously on its own terms. Magic and drugs, the life in the harem, the world of courtesans—these parts of the *Kamasutra* make you think, 'How very different these people are from us.'

For the South Asians among us, there are bits of the text that are startlingly familiar from our everyday world. For the rest of us, these become accessible only through rather distant analogies. Betel, for instance, *tambula*, nowadays called paan, is still popular across India (though not used quite in the manner, or for the purpose, prescribed by Vatsyayana). It is a delicacy made of a betel leaf rolled up around a paste made of areca nuts (sometimes called betel nuts), cardamom, lime paste and other flavours, sometimes with tobacco or other stimulants (including, sometimes, cocaine). The finished product, shaped rather like a stuffed grape-leaf, is eaten as a stimulant, to redden the mouth and to freshen the breath. Throughout the *Kamasutra*, lovers give one another betel, take betel out of their own mouths and put it in their lover's mouth. This basic part of the erotic scene in ancient India can best be understood by non-Indians through an analogy with the overtones that champagne has, or the post-coital cigarette.[iii]

On the other hand, the woman's thoughts on such subjects as how to get a lover and how to tell when he is cooling ring remarkably true for every twenty-first-century reader, regardless of his or her culture. Another part of the text that surely speaks to the modern reader is the description of a man who wants to seduce a married woman. In the would-be adulterer's meditations on reasons to do this, there are self-deceptive arguments that still make sense in our world:

> He thinks: 'There is no danger involved in my having this woman, and there is a chance of wealth. And since I am useless, I have exhausted all means of making a living. Such as I am, I will get a lot of money from her in this way, with very little trouble.' Or, 'This woman is madly in love with me and knows all my weaknesses. If I reject her, she will ruin me by publicly exposing my faults; or she will accuse me of some fault which I do not in fact have, but which will be easy to believe of me and hard to clear myself of, and this will be the ruin of me.' (1.5.12-14)

This is a brilliant portrait of a self-serving rascal who has no illusions about himself.

This constant alternation of the familiar and the strange teaches us a great deal about human nature.

THE POSITIONS

Our reaction to the central subject, the act of love, should surely be one of recognition, of familiarity, but no. Here, rather than in the cultural setting, is where we are, unexpectedly, brought up short by the unfamiliar. The *Kamasutra* describes a number of contortions that 'require practice', as the text puts it mildly, and these are the positions that generally make people laugh out loud at the mention of the *Kamasutra*.

What are we to make of these gymnastics? Did people in ancient India really make love like that? I think not. True, they did have yoga, and great

---

[iii] It evokes the cigarette foreplay of Bogart and Bacall in *To Have and Have Not* and *The Big Sleep* or the cigarette sublimation shared by Bette Davis and Paul Heinried in *Now Voyager*.

practitioners of yoga can make their bodies do things that most of us would not think possible (or even, perhaps, desirable).[iv] But just because one can do it is no reason that one *should* do it. (Or, as Vatsyayana remarks, first at the end of his passage about oral sex and same-sex sex[v] [2.9.41], and again at the end of his Viagra passage, 'The statement that "There is a text for this" does not justify a practice.' [7.2.55] I think the answer lies elsewhere: 'Vatsyayana says: Even passion demands variety. And it is through variety that partners inspire passion in one another. It is their infinite variety that makes courtesans and their lovers remain desirable to one another. Even in archery and in other martial arts, the textbooks insist on variety. How much more is this true of sex!' [2.4.25]

The user's-manual approach does not account for positions that do not invite imitation. These may simply be the artist's free-ranging fantasies on a theme of sexual possibilities: they are not instructive but inspiring, and inspired. They represent a literally no-holds-barred exploration of the theoretical possibilities of human heterosexual coupling, much as the profusion of compound animals—heads of ducks on bodies of lions, or torsos of women on the bodies of fish, and so forth—pushed back the walls of our imagination of the variety of known and unknown animal species. It is a fantasy literature, an artistic and imaginative, rather than physical, exploration of coupling.

The text is a virtual sexual *pas de deux* as Balanchine might have choreographed it, an extended meditation on some of the ways that a naked man and a naked woman (or, rarely, several men and/or women) might move their limbs while making love. And though sexual reality may in fact be universal—there are, after all, just so many places that you can put your genitals—sexual fantasy seems to be highly cultural. This, then, is what is new to us in the brave new world of this ancient text.

[iv] See 'Assume the Position'.
[v] See 'The Third Nature'.

THE MYTHOLOGY OF THE *KAMASUTRA*[1]

The *Kamasutra* has become part of the Orientalist mythology of India, the non-Indian's, or even the non-Hindu's, fantasy of the otherness of the sexuality of other cultures imagined as simultaneously over-sexed and impotent. The West's mythology about the *Kamasutra* is based in large part on the Victorian Orientalist fantasies of Sir Richard Francis Burton, who was the first to translate the *Kamasutra* into English, well over a century ago, in 1883.[i] But the *Kamasutra* has a mythology of its own, a corpus of stories that it invokes to explain and to authenticate its ideas about sex and gender. And it is this mythology in the *Kamasutra* that we will explore here.

MYTHOLOGY IN THE *KAMASUTRA*: TALES TOLD TO WOMEN

The *Kamasutra* refers to a number of stories that it regards as so well known that it does not even bother to tell most of them. In many cases, Vatsyayana uses a myth to make a point quite different from its meaning in the texts from which he takes it. Often, he makes different points from the same myth when he cites it in different contexts; this is, of course, standard operating procedure in the world of mythmakers.[2] And the commentator Yashodhara, who lived a thousand years after the *Kamasutra* was composed, tells us the versions that he knows of some, though not all, of these stories. Between the text and the commentary, we can excavate a rich sexual mythology.

The *Kamasutra* tells us how people told the myths, how they regarded them as relevant and didactically powerful. The basic plot of the *Kamasutra* is boy meets girl; boy sets out to get girl into bed, often with the help of a go-between; boy gets girl. In instructing the go-between messenger about ways to persuade a young girl to sleep with a man before he marries her,

---

[i] See 'Reading the *Kamasutra*' and 'From Kama to Karma'.

Vatsyayana says, 'And she tells the girl stories about other virgins of equal caste, such as Shakuntala, who found a husband by their own resolve and made love with great joy.' [3.5.5] The commentator here describes Shakuntala simply as 'the king's wife', and he says nothing at all about her when Vatsyayana mentions her a second time, as one of the women whose stories are to be told by the messenger trying to persuade a married woman (rather than, as in the first case, a virgin) to take a lover. On that occasion, Vatsyayana says: 'As the woman listens, the messenger tells her well-known, relevant stories, about Ahalya, Avimaraka, Shakuntala and others.' [5.4.14] But Shakuntala's story did not work out so well as Vatsyayana implies; Shakuntala suffers greatly in the version of her story told in the *Mahabharata*—the king impregnates her and then publicly denies and insults her; only years later does he acknowledge her. (She suffers less, but still significantly, in the version told by the poet Kalidasa a few centuries later.)[ii]

The commentator does tell us about the other two people in this particular list, Ahalya and Avimaraka, of whom Ahalya is by far the more famous; she is to Indian mythology what Helen of Troy was to Greek, and the *Ramayana* tells her story not once but twice.[iii] All that the commentator says here, where he is using her as the model of the successful adulteress, is: 'Ahalya was the wife of [the sage] Gautama; the king of the gods fell in love with her and she desired him.' [Y on 5.4.14] But Vatsyayana has already mentioned Ahalya in the first chapter, in a very different context indeed, when he remarks that 'Indra, the king of the gods, with Ahalya . . . and many others afterwards were seen to fall into the thrall of desire and were destroyed.' [1.2.34-36] And there the commentator tells a longer story, not a story of encouragement at all, but a cautionary story:

> The king of the gods, Indra, was aroused by Ahalya; for when he saw her in the hermitage of her husband Gautama, he desired her. When Gautama returned with the fuel and sacred grass, his wife Ahalya hid Indra in the womb of the house, but just at that moment Gautama took his wife into the inside of the house, with an invitation to make love. Then he realized, with the magic gaze that he had achieved through yoga, that Indra had come there, and seeing that a third seat had been drawn up for him he said, 'What is this for, since only the two of us, my wife and I, are here?' Then he became suspicious, and by

meditation he saw what had happened; in fury he cursed Indra: 'You yourself will have a thousand vaginas!' And so, even though Indra was the king of the gods, desire brought him to this sorry state, which was regarded as his destruction. Even to this day that mark that makes people call him 'Ahalya's Lover' has not vanished. [Y on 1.2.36]

Unique to this version is the suggestion that Ahalya's husband, Gautama, had intended to make love to her himself. Other versions of the story generally make it quite clear that Gautama is far too ascetic to do justice to his young wife in bed, and that is what makes her vulnerable to the king of the gods; Ahalya knows quite well that, even when Indra is disguised as Gautama, he is not Gautama, precisely because he wants to make love with her. Other variants, moreover, attribute the form of Indra's curse (to have the mark of vaginas all over his body) to the fact that Indra was caught in the 'womb' of Ahalya, not of the house; Gautama catches them *in flagrante*, the telltale piece of furniture being not a 'third seat drawn up' but the bed. Here, however, it appears that Gautama returns *before* Ahalya goes to bed with Indra, and so, of course, she is not punished, as she usually is, by being cursed to turn into a stone.

Unlike most other variants of this myth, moreover, Yashodhara's version does not mention that the king of the gods, Indra, took the form of Gautama to seduce Ahalya, making her, to some extent, less culpable: she did not intend to commit adultery, but was tricked into it, a factor that makes her story less useful for the purposes of the *Kamasutra*'s messenger. The *Kamasutra* commentator's version has been bowdlerized, cleaned up. Vatsyayana regards the story here, when he tells it as a caution to men, in a much more negative mode than when the messenger is later [5.4.14] told to use it to persuade the woman, and Yashodhara's longer gloss in the cautionary passage also adds much more detail, as a warning to a man about the trouble that desire can cause him. Clearly, Vatsyayana uses the tale of Ahalya (and Yashodhara tells it) in one way to warn men about adultery, and in another way to encourage women to it.

The third person in the list of people to be cited by the messenger encouraging married women to commit adultery is a man named Avimaraka; Yashodhara tells his story:

> The fire-priest instructed his wife to care for the fire. Agni, the god of fire, so desired her that he took on a form and arose out of the fire altar. When she became pregnant, her father-in-law, fearing a stain on the family, abandoned her in the forest. She gave birth to a son, whom the general of the Shabaras [a wild, savage tribe of mountaineers] raised as

his own child. That son, in his childhood, played among the herds of sheep and goats and wandered around with them. By drinking their milk he became very strong, so strong that even though he was just a little child, he killed goats and sheep with his bare hands. And for that reason, the general gave him the appropriate name of Avimaraka ['Sheep-killer']. When Avimaraka reached the prime of his youth, one day an elephant attacked the daughter of a king who was sojourning in the forest, and he killed the elephant and saved her. After that she fell in love with him and of her own will gave him her hand in marriage. These stories are relevant to a discussion of the seduction of other men's wives. [Y on 5.4.14]

Avimaraka is the hero of a Sanskrit play by Bhasa that follows this general plot-line.[iv] Since, however, Avimaraka is neither a woman nor an adulterer, it is not immediately clear how his tale is, as Yashodhara claims, relevant to a discussion of the seduction of other men's wives. Avimaraka does, according to Yashodhara, benefit from two seduced women, one married and seduced by someone else (this woman is his mother) and one unmarried and seduced by him. Is he dragged in through his association with these women who transgress sexual boundaries, because Vatsyayana could not think of any more women who benefited from adultery? Indeed, of *any* such women at all, since it is not at all clear how Shakuntala or Ahalya benefited from it, either?

I think, rather, the point is that Avimaraka was so handsome that the power of kama overcame all the objections that a princess might have had to marrying a man who appeared to be a Dalit (a tribal Shabara), a man who killed animals with his bare hands. In fact, the story may be based on a folk tale in which Avimaraka really was a Dalit, a point that Bhasa, and the commentator on the *Kamasutra*, erased in order to make the play more acceptable to a court audience.[3] In place of that story, these authors simply substituted a variant of the widespread myth of a boy of noble blood who is raised by animals, or the herders of animals, until he grows up and returns to claim his royal heritage. This is the story of Karna and of Krishna in India, as well as Kipling's Mowgli, and of Oedipus, Moses, Tarzan and many others.[v]

[iv] Bhasa glosses 'Avimaraka' as 'killer [*maraka*] of a demon who took the form of a sheep [*avi*]' and leaves out the whole episode of the genuine sheep. The *Kathasaritsagara*, too [112.89], leaves out the sheep from its telling of the Avimaraka story. But one of the Buddhist Jatakas (the *Kunala Jataka*, #536) gives yet another connection with the sheep: the abandoned child drank sheep's milk in some way that killed the sheep.

[v] See 'Zoomorphism'.

Thus, even while the author of the *Kamasutra* pretends to give advice to persuade women to transgress, the actual content of the stories is designed to warn them, as they are explicitly said to warn men, to look before they leap. Vatsyayana manifests his ambivalence about sexual freedom at many points in his book, particularly in the verses at the end of each chapter, which often raise doubts about matters that he has recommended in the prose passages. So, too, the stories that he refers to may be intended to raise doubts in the minds of the women being tempted to commit adultery, even while they are expressly said to be intended to quell such doubts.

MYTHOLOGICAL BACKGROUND

In addition to these stories designed to be told to women within the text, Vatsyayana tells some stories to the reader as part of a more general mythological background.

The very first chapter begins, after a few lines of introduction, with a classically mythological passage:

> When the Creator emitted his creatures, he first composed, in a hundred thousand chapters, the means of achieving the three aims of human life [religion, power and pleasure]: Manu the son of the Self-born One made one part of this into a separate work about religion, Brihaspati made one about power and Nandin, the servant of the Great God Shiva, made a separate work of a thousand chapters, the Kamasutra, which Shvetaketu Auddalaki cut down to five hundred chapters. And then Babhravya of Panchala cut this down further to a hundred and fifty chapters. [1.1.5-10]

Manu the son of the Self-born One, the Creator, is, of course, the Indian Adam, a mythical creature but not a god; indeed, he defines the beginning of the human species, and is the mythical author of *The Laws of Manu*.[vi] The other two authors are gods. Brihaspati is the guru of the gods, the secretary or minister of defence, as it were, for Indra, the king of the gods, and, in his spare time, he is the planet Jupiter. He is also the putative author of a Machiavellian handbook of politics that is the source of the extant text known as the *Arthashastra*, the textbook of political science, the book 'about power' to which the text refers, composed perhaps a century, or less, before the *Kamasutra*. The *Arthashastra* is usually attributed to a human

---

[vi] See 'Three (or More)' and 'Why Should a Brahmin?'

being, Kautilya or Chanakya, the prime minister of the Mauryan king Chandragupta, in the fourth and third centuries BCE. To make the divine Brihaspati the author of the *Arthashastra* is to bring heaven down to earth (or, if you prefer, earth to heaven).

The third author, Nandin, is the ultimate source of Vatsyayana's *Kamasutra*, even as Brihaspati is the source of the *Arthashastra*:

> Nandin is not some other person named Nandin, for the scripture says: 'While the Great God Shiva was experiencing the pleasures of sex with his wife Uma for a thousand years as the gods count them, Nandin went to guard the door of their bedroom and composed the *Kamasutra*.' [Y on 1.1.8]

Yashodhara is here making explicit the fact that the Nandin in question is actually a god, not merely a human named after a god (as people often are, in India and elsewhere). Nandin, a bull or a bull-headed deity, is the son of the Great God, Shiva, and is often stationed to guard the door to the bedroom of his parents. In the earthly parallel to this situation, a statue of Nandin often guards the door to a temple of Shiva (and Uma). It is most appropriate for a bull, and for the god Shiva, to be associated with the textbook of sex and pleasure.

The text then turns from gods to semi-mythical sages from ancient times, beginning with Shvetaketu, who is cited often in the *Kamasutra* as a sexual authority and who also has a mythology of his own, as the commentator, Yashodhara, reminds us:

> Once upon a time, there was so much seduction of other men's wives in the world that it was said:
>
>> 'Women are all alike,
>> just like cooked rice, your majesty.
>> Therefore a man should not get angry with them
>> nor fall in love with them, but just make love with them.'
>
> But [Shvetaketu] forbade this state of affairs, and so people said:
>> '[Shvetaketu] forbade common people
>> to take other people's wives.'

Then, with his father's permission, Shvetaketu, who had amassed great ascetic power, happily composed this text, which distinguishes those who are eligible or ineligible for sex. [Y on 1.1.9]

This story is told at greater length in the *Mahabharata*.[vii] Shvetaketu is well-known as a hero of the Upanishads, the ancient Sanskrit philosophical texts that make the case for renunciation; in those texts, his father teaches him the central doctrines of Indian philosophy. It is surprising to find Shvetaketu here in the *Kamasutra*, cited as an expert sexologist, and this seeming incongruity may have inspired Vatsyayana to allude to, and Yashodhara to tell, this story here: it explains how a sage became simultaneously chaste, an enemy of male adultery, and an authority on sex.

Finally, the text mentions another mere human being: 'Dattaka made a separate book out of the sixth part of this work, about courtesans, which the courtesans de luxe of Pataliputra commissioned.' [1.1.11] But the commentary recites (or invents? I have not been able to find them in other sources) two stories about Dattaka, the second of which makes him supernatural, if not divine:

> One day Dattaka had the idea of learning the finest ways of the world, best known by courtesans. And so he went to the courtesans every day, and learned so well that they asked *him* to instruct *them*. A woman speaking on behalf of the courtesans said to him, 'Teach us how to give pleasure to men.' And because of that commission he made a separate book.

So the story goes. But another quite plausible story is also widely believed:

> Dattaka once touched Shiva with his foot in the course of a festival to bless a pregnant woman, and Shiva cursed him to become a woman; after a while he persuaded Shiva to rescind the curse and became a man again, and because of that double knowledge he made the separate book. If he had simply made a separate work out of what Babhravya had said, how would his own book have demonstrated such originality that people would say that he knew both flavours? But if the author of the *Kamasutra* had known that he had such double knowledge, then he would have said, 'Dattaka, who knew both flavours, made a separate book.' [Y on 1.1.11]

To touch anyone, let alone a god, with your foot, is an act of great disrespect and a common source of curses in India. And men are often, for a number of reasons, turned into women, and back again, in Hindu and Buddhist mythology; Narada, Bhangashvana and Ila[viii] are the most famous

---

vii See 'Women in the *Mahabharata*'.
viii For Ila and Bhangashvana, see 'Bisexuality' and 'Transsexual Transformations'.

of the serial androgynes.[4] The 'double knowledge' of Dattaka refers to the comparative knowledge of sexuality, seen from both sides of the bed. It is an inspired move on the part of Yashodhara to make the author of this text a bisexual, who 'tastes both flavours' (I use 'bisexual' here both in its now popular sense of a person of fixed gender who has both male and female sexual partners, and in its other sense—of an androgyne or hermaphrodite). Yet this is also a move that greatly mitigates the strong female agency in the text: where Vatsyayana tells us that women had this text made, Yashodhara tells us that an extraordinary man knew more about the courtesans' art than they knew themselves.

All in all, there is a supernatural pedigree for the authors of this earliest of all books. And there is also a supernatural pedigree for the very process of its recension, the boiling down of an enormous divine text into a manageable human text:

> Shvetaketu cut [the text] down to five hundred chapters. And then Babhravya of Panchala cut this down further to a hundred and fifty chapters . . . Charayana made a separate book about general observations, Suvarnanabha about sex, Ghotakamukha about virgins, Gonardiya about wives, Gonikaputra about other men's wives and Kuchumara about erotic esoterica. When many scholars had divided it into fragments in this way, the text was almost destroyed. Because the amputated limbs of the text that they divided are just parts of the whole, and because Babhravya's text is so long that it is hard to study, Vatsyayana condensed the entire subject matter into a small volume to make this *Kamasutra*. [1.1.9-14]

The word for 'scholars' (*acharyas*), normally a term of great respect, almost always has a pejorative tone in the *Kamasutra*, perhaps best translated as 'pedants'. The texts cited here no longer exist, but almost certainly existed at the time of Vatsyayana, since he and, later, Yashodhara often quote directly from them. Other Hindu texts are also said to have been reduced from a supernatural source in this way,[5] perhaps on analogy with the human body, for, according to classical Hindu physiology, it takes ten drops of food to make a drop of digestive fluid, ten drops of that fluid to make a drop of blood, ten drops of blood to make a drop of semen.[ix] The *Kamasutra* was produced in this same way. A close parallel to this reasoning occurs in a Buddhist text about the woman who prepared milk-rice for the Buddha when he ended his long meditation after achieving enlightenment.

[ix] See 'Medical and Mythical Constructions'.

She milked a thousand cows, and fed the milk to five hundred cows; then she milked those five hundred cows and fed the milk to two hundred and fifty, and so on, until she fed the milk of sixteen cows to eight. She used the milk of those eight cows to prepare the milk-rice for the Buddha.[6]

Vatsyayana himself seldom refers to the great gods, though he seems to assume their presence. We have seen him refer to Shiva, a famously erotic god,[7] and to Indra, the king of the gods and a god who, like Shiva, has a significantly phallic mythology. Indra's wife, Indrani, appears only in the name of a particular sexual position [at 2.6.11], which can be translated as 'Junoesque' but is literally 'of Indrani'. Indrani resembles Juno, the wife of Jupiter, king of the Roman gods (or Hera, wife of the Greek Zeus), in many ways, including her own enormous sexual appetite and her jealousy about her husband's notorious adulteries.

Vatsyayana first refers to Indra in this not particularly erotic verse:

> Fate made Bali into
> an Indra, king of the gods,
> and fate hurled Bali back down,
> and fate is what will make him an Indra again. [1.2.29]

And the commentary tells the story: Even though Bali was unworthy, because he was a demon, and should have been spurned, he ascended to the throne of Indra, king of the gods, and established himself there until the wheel of fortune turned around, and he was thrown out of that seat and hurled back down into Hell.[x] But when the wheel of fortune turns back around again, it will once again send him out of Hell and back onto the throne of Indra. And so people say:

> Time ripens and cooks all beings,
> time absorbs all creatures,
> time is awake when all are asleep,
> for no one can fight against time. [Y on 1.2.29]

The commentary on the first book of the *Kamasutra* also mentions Indra, in passing, in the context of a myth about the divine embodiments of the three goals of life—dharma, artha (power) and kama (pleasure):[xi]

> The three aims of human life are the three divinities in charge of this work; if they were not divinities it would not be right to bow to them. And there is textual evidence that they are in fact divinities. For the

[x] See 'The Concept of Heresy' and 'The Scrapbook'.
[xi] See 'Three (or More)'.

historian tells us: 'When King Pururavas went from earth to heaven to see Indra, the king of the gods, he saw Dharma and the others embodied. As he approached them, he ignored the other two but paid homage to Dharma, walking around him in a circle to the right. The other two, unable to put up with this slight, cursed him. Because Kama had cursed him, he was separated from his wife, Urvashi, and longed for her in her absence. When he had managed to put that right, then, because Artha had cursed him, he became so excessively greedy that he stole from all four social classes. The Brahmins, who were upset because they could no longer perform the sacrifice or other rituals without the money he had stolen from them, took blades of sharp sacrificial grass in their hands and killed him. [Y on 1. 1.1–14]

This passage builds upon the Rig Vedic myth which tells us that Pururavas, a mortal king, fell in love with the celestial nymph and courtesan Urvashi; when he broke his promise to her, she left him (though, according to other versions of the myth, they were later reconciled). Elsewhere, Yashodhara refers, briefly, to this myth when he remarks that 'power, when it overrides all else, impedes religion and pleasure (as it did for Pururavas)'. [Y on 1.2.41]

But Vatsyayana himself usually takes Indra in general as a sign for the excesses and dangers of uncontrolled desire. We have seen Indra mentioned in the midst of a list of males—human, divine and demonic—who suffered from uncontrolled passion; here is the full passage:

It is said that many men in the thrall of desire were destroyed, even when accompanied by their troops. For instance, when the Bhoja king named Dandakya was aroused by a Brahmin's daughter, desire destroyed him, along with his relatives and his kingdom. And Indra the king of the gods with Ahalya, the super-powerful Kichaka with Draupadi, Ravana with Sita, and many others afterwards were seen to fall into the thrall of desire and were destroyed. [1.2.34–36]

The commentary tells these stories, or, rather, some of these stories. We have already encountered the story of Ahalya and Indra; another supernatural item in this list of males undone by lust is 'Ravana with Sita'. This is the most famous of all tales of destructive lust, from the *Ramayana* [c. 200 BCE to 200 CE], which is perhaps why Yashodhara does not bother to tell the story of the abduction of Sita, wife of Rama, by the demon Ravana, and the subsequent destruction of Ravana.[8] Yet in his commentary on 6.1.17, Yashodhara mentions Ravana again, when he expands on the reasons for passion, including 'fear of death, like the fear that afflicted (the celestial nymph) Rambha because of Ravana, who said to her, "If you do not satisfy my desire, I will kill you."' The *Ramayana* tells how Ravana raped Rambha by threatening to kill her, but she cursed him so that he could never rape another woman again—a story that is told to explain why he could never do that to Sita.[xii]

In this same list, Vatsyayana also mentions 'Kichaka with Draupadi', referring to a story about Draupadi, the heroine of the *Mahabharata*[xiii] who had five husbands, the five sons of Pandu, under circumstances extenuated in various ways by various texts (both in the original Sanskrit version and in various retellings in Sanskrit and in vernacular languages) but never sufficiently to protect her from frequent slurs against her chastity. Yashodhara tells only part of the story: 'As for Kichaka, he is said to have been super powerful because he had the strength of a thousand elephants; but even he was destroyed by desire, for Bhima killed him when he lusted after Draupadi.' [Y on 1.2.36] 'Killed him' is putting it mildly: Bhima, dressed as a woman, beat Kichaka to such a pulp that when people found his mangled corpse the next morning they said, 'Where is his head?', 'Which are his hands?'[9]

The commentator mentions Draupadi again, a bit later, when Vatsyayana quotes another scholar (or pedant) who said that any married woman who is known to have had five men can be seduced without moral qualms [1.5.30], for 'five men or more' (*pancha-jana*) is an expression for a crowd, a group of people (as in the *panchayat*, the quorum of a village). And Yashodhara adds: 'If, besides her own husband, [a woman] has five men as husbands, she is a loose woman and eligible for everyone who has a good reason. Draupadi, however, who had Yudhishthira and the others as her own husbands, was not eligible for other men. How could one woman have several husbands? Ask the authors of the *Mahabharata*!' So, once again, the same character appears in two different passages that make two different points for two different genders: Draupadi with Kichaka is a warning for lustful males, but Draupadi with her five husbands is a challenge for chaste females.

To return to the list of males undone by passion, we are left with one more mortal, a king named Dandakya, and Yashodhara tells his story:

Dandakya was out hunting when he saw the daughter of the Brahmin Bhargava in his hermitage. Overwhelmed by passion, he took her up

---

[xii] See 'Shadows of the *Ramayana*'.
[xiii] See 'Women in the *Mahabharata*'.

in his chariot and carried her off. When Bhargava returned with the
fuel and sacred grass that he had gone off to fetch, and did not see her,
he meditated to learn what had happened and then he cursed the king.
As a result, Dandakya and his entire family and kingdom were covered
by a dust-storm and died. Even today they sing about that place, the
Dandaka Wilderness. [Y on 1.2.35]

Yashodhara also refers to Dandakya just a few lines later, as an example of
a man for whom 'pleasure destroys the other two [goals] when it involves
women of a higher class, or other excesses'. [1.2.41]

All of these seductions involved tricks, which the *Kamasutra* does not
mention: Indra pretended to be Ahalya's husband; Kichaka was foiled (and
killed) when a man took the place of the woman he intended to seduce;
and Ravana masqueraded as an ascetic to abduct Sita, while (in many
tellings after the first Sanskrit version) a shadow Sita took the place of the
Sita that Ravana thought he had abducted.[10] All illusory seductions, they
were all the more deadly for that.

These divine figures are scattered through the mythology of the first of
the seven books of the *Kamasutra*, but they generally do not appear after
that. Vatsyayana never explicitly refers to Krishna, but one verse seems to
suggest a famous myth of Krishna:

> They play the 'plough-handle' game, sing,
> and dance in the Lata way;
> they look at the circle of the moon
> with eyes moist and flickering with passion. [2.10.12.]

And Yashodhara makes explicit the connection:

> It is said of the 'plough-handle' (Hallishaka):
> The 'plough-handle' is a dance
> with the women in a circle
> and one man the leader,
> like Krishna with the cowherd women. [Y on 2.10;12]

The incarnate god Krishna danced in a circle with the cowherd women,
and by his magic powers created doubles of himself so that each woman
thought she was dancing with him and making love with him.

STORIES OF WARNINGS TO HUMANS

The rest of the mythology of the *Kamasutra*, which punctuates the entire
text, consists primarily of warnings against the abuse of the power of sex,

warnings that we have already seen applied to mythological figures and that now reappear in the human realm. For example, in warning against the use of certain violent forms of slapping (called the 'wedge', the 'scissor' and the 'drill'), Vatsyayana says:

> The King of the Cholas killed Chitrasena, a courtesan, by using the 'wedge' during sex. And the Kuntala king Shatakarni Shatavahana killed his queen, Malayavati, by using the 'scissor'. Naradeva, whose hand was deformed, blinded a dancing-girl in one eye by using the 'drill' clumsily. [2.7.28-30]

And Yashodhara explains:

> He embraced Chitrasena so tightly, at the start of their love-making, that she suffered greatly, because she was so delicate. And even when he realized her condition, and knew that she had to be handled delicately, he was so blind with passion that he did not take account of his own strength and destroyed her by using a 'wedge' on her chest.
>
> Shatakarna's son Shatavahana, born in the territory of Kuntala, saw his queen, Malayavati, one day when she had not long recovered from an illness and did not have her full strength, but was dressing for the festival of Kama. Passion arose in him and he made love to her, but his mind was carried away by passion and by using an excessively powerful 'scissor' on her chest, he killed her.
>
> Naradeva was the general of the Pandya king. His hand had been deformed by a blow from a sword. When he saw Chitralekha, a dancing girl, dancing at the king's residence, his passion was aroused, and when he made love with her, blind with passion, he used the 'drill' clumsily because of his lame hand; he missed her cheek and instead hit her eye, blinding her in that eye. [Y on 2.7.28-30].

The kings who commit these excesses are all from South India, where Vatsyayana (a North Indian) generally locates sexual excess. In contrast with such figures as Ravana and Ahalya, these kings are not well-known to Sanskrit mythology.

Another excessive king is an adulterer:

> 'For when Abhira, the Kotta king, went to another man's home, a washerman employed by the king's brother killed him. And the superintendant of horses killed Jayasena the king of Varanasi.' So it is said. [5.5.29]

The 'it is said' may cast some doubt on this pair of adulterers, but not necessarily so. Yashodhara tells a bit more (which I have indicated in added italics), but not a lot more :

> *In Gujurat* there is a place named Kotta, whose king, named Abhira, went to another man's house *in order to sleep with the wife of Vasumitra, the head warrior.* There, a guard employed by his brother, *who deserved the kingdom,* killed him. Jayasena the king of Varanasi [too] *had gone into another man's house to make love with that man's wife.* [Y on 5.5.29]

The commentator has added the details of individual people and places, and the sexual purpose of the housebreaking. Evidently these kings do not have the licence that many European kings, for instance, were able to make use of licentiously. Elsewhere, Vatsyayana insists:

> Kings and ministers of state
> do not enter into other men's homes,
> for the whole populace sees what they do
> and imitates it.
> The three worlds watch the sun rise
> and so they too rise;
> then they watch the sun moving
> and they too start to act. [5.5.1-2

But then Vatsyayana descends from the ideal to the actual: 'Therefore, because it is impossible and because they would be blamed, such men do nothing frivolous. But when they cannot help doing it, they employ stratagems.' [5.5.1-4] So much for the mythology of warning.

THE FANTASY OF THE HAREM

All of this, even the part about the gods, is fairly realistic, even banal. But there is another genre of myth that enters into the discussion, and that is the genre of fantasy literature, erotic adventure literature, Romantic literature, best known from fairy tales: the prince who falls in love with the inaccessible princess, sneaks into the harem at night, and eventually wins her. This fantasy appears, disguised as sensible advice, in a section of the *Kamasutra* devoted to adultery:

> He disguises himself as a guard and enters at a time that she appoints. Or he goes in and out clothed in a bedspread or a cloak. Or he makes his shadow and his body disappear by means of a magic trick: He cooks the heart of a mongoose, the fruits of a fenugreek plant and a long

gourd, and snake eyes, over a fire that does not smoke. Then he rubs
into this the same measure of the collyrium used as eye makeup. When
he has smeared his eyes with this, he can move about without a shadow
or a body. And on the nights of the full moon, he can move about by
the light of many lamps, or by a subterranean passage. [5.6.22-26]

The assumption was that, normally, your eyes projected the vision of you
to someone else's eyes; light rays bounce off you onto the person looking
at you. But the ointment blocked that path of transmission, as one might
jam a radio station.[xiv] (So, too, a god or demon could project a false image
of himself or herself, but if he fell asleep or died, thus failing to keep the
magic projector going, you would see the true form.) The commentary on
this passage does not give the sort of explanation one might have hoped
for; all it says is: 'Some people make the body disappear, but not the
shadow. But only those who make both disappear are not seen.' Hindu
mythology tells stories of people who, like Sita, disappeared, leaving
behind a shadow or reflection, a kind of after-image, which other people
mistook for the person who had disappeared.[11] Evidently there are magic
spells that enable one to do this, and those are not the spells that should be
used in this situation. The fantasy of sneaking into the harem is yet another
myth that informs the imagination of the *Kamasutra*.

[xiv] A similar mechanism was proposed in one of the James Bond movies, by the bloke that
always offered Bond fiendishly clever weapons: a car had a mechanism that made it become
invisible simply by taking a photograph of what was *behind* the car and then projecting it in
front of the car so that the viewer seemed to see the background through the car, as it were.
(René Magritte imagined this, too, in his painting called 'The Human Condition', in which
an easel in front of a window held a painting that showed what you would have seen if you
had just looked out of the window.)

FROM KAMA TO KARMA: THE RESURGENCE OF PURITANISM IN CONTEMPORARY INDIA[1]

THE PROBLEM OF CONTEMPORARY INDIAN PURITANISM

A pervasive and often violent moral policing has taken over parts of the Indian world today. A typical instance of this occurred in 2007, when a twenty-three-year-old student of Fine Arts at Baroda University named Chandramohan Srilamantula mounted an exhibition for other students and staff. He had previously received awards for his work, including the Lalit Kala Akademi National Exhibition award in 2006; later he won first prize in the 2009 Bhopal Biennale. In the 2007 exhibition, one painting depicted a crucified Christ with explicit genitals and a toilet beneath the cross; another, entitled 'Durga Mate', was of a nude woman attacking, with a trident (the weapon of Shiva), a baby issuing from her womb. Christian leaders lodged protests against the first painting, and a group of Hindu chauvinist activists belonging to the VHP (Vishwa Hindu Parishad) and BJP (Bharatiya Janata Party)[i] vandalized the exhibition and roughed up Chandramohan for the second painting.[2] This group was led by Niraj Jain, who has been known to brandish a revolver and once threw eggs[ii] at the Gujarat Education Minister for including them in school midday meals.[3] The police stood by and then arrested not the vandals but the artist. (He was later released.) When the acting Dean of the Faculty of Fine Arts, Shivaji Panikkar, refused to close down the exhibition, the Vice-Chancellor, Manoj Soni, suspended him. Panikkar, stating that he feared for his life, went into hiding. Students and spokespersons of the Indian art community held protests throughout India, claiming that the closing of the exhibition was a direct assault on the rights of freedom of expression.

---

[i] See 'You Can't Make an Omelette'.
[ii] See 'You Can't Make an Omelette'.

In commenting on this event, the well-known editor, columnist and critic Anil Dharker remarked:

> What has made the artists come together in protest is that this attack isn't an isolated one, but one more in a series now increasing in both frequency and wantonness . . . The Mumbai Police stood by when Shiv Sainiks attacked cinema theatres showing a Deepa Mehta film [*Fire*, which showed a lesbian relationship in a middle-class Hindu family] . . . Recently, the Mumbai cops did some moral policing of their own, arresting young couples found in 'compromising position' (policespeak for young men and women having their arms around each other).[4]

Dharker went on to list several more instances, but even these few are representative of broad patterns of attacks by various Hindutva groups, whose members are known as Hindutvavadis ('Those who talk about Hindutva').[iii]

The protest against Chandramohan Srilamantula was one of a number of campaigns against artists and writers who linked Hindu deities with sexuality, or talked openly and frankly about sexuality. In 1996, Hindutvavadis began terrorizing M.F. Husain for his paintings of naked Hindu goddesses. In 2006, after death threats and legal cases, Husain, whom many regarded as India's greatest living artist, and who was then ninety-one years old, was forced into exile in Dubai; he died in London in 2011. Some Hindutvavadis forced Deepa Mehta to leave Varanasi, where she was making a film about the mistreatment of Hindu widows in Varanasi (*Water*, 2005): on 30 January 2000, 'fundamentalist thugs' from the BJP, together with Uttar Pradesh government officials, destroyed the film sets and later threatened the cast and crew; on 6 February 2000, the state of Uttar Pradesh ordered a suspension of production, and Mehta finished the film in Sri Lanka.[5] An essay written in 1991 by A.K. Ramanujan, a world-famous scholar of Indian literature who had been awarded the Padma Shri honour by the government of India in 1976, was included in the 2006 BA, History, syllabus of Delhi University. Entitled 'Three Hundred Ramayanas: Five Examples and Three Thoughts on Translations', it was about some of the many versions of the *Ramayana* that contradict the versions of Valmiki and Tulsidas. A student wing of the BJP opposed its inclusion in the syllabus, and in Oxford University Press's in-print catalogue,

---

[iii] See 'You Can't Make an Omelette'.

on the grounds that it hurt Hindu sentiments. In October 2011, the academic council of Delhi University voted to remove the essay from its syllabus. A widely publicized international protest against the censorship of Ramanujan's essay met with qualified success.

The Hindutvavadis often blame Western influence on the people whom they censor, while, ironically, many of the Hindutvavadis' own actions closely resemble censoring frenzies in the United States. But the Indian incidents are better seen as part of a separate logic of Hindu Puritanism, which has a long history of its own.

THE EARLY HISTORY OF HINDU EROTICISM AND ASCETICISM

When a group of students and artists at Baroda University attempted to stage a protest demonstration for Chandramohan at the Faculty of Fine Arts, they organized an exhibition of photographs taken from the explicitly erotic sculptures that adorn the temples at Khajuraho, in Madhya Pradesh.[6] In choosing Khajuraho, they were making an implicit historical statement: the art heritage of India is rich in erotic themes, of which the images on the Khajuraho temples (built between 900 and 1100 CE) are a famous example. What happened to that tradition? How did India get from there to the scandal in Baroda?

Erotic religious imagery is as old as Hinduism. The earliest Hindu sacred text, the *Rig Veda* (c. 1500 BCE), revels in the language of both pleasure and fertility.[iv] The Upanishads, that followed a few centuries later, analogized the Vedic oblation of butter into the sacrificial fire to the act of sexual procreation: the worshipper in a sexual embrace with his wife imagines each part of the act as a part of the ritual of the oblation: the firewood is the vulva; the smoke, the pubic hair; the flame, the vagina; and the embers and sparks are the acts of penetration and climax.[7] Presumably anyone making the offering into the fire could also imagine each action as its sexual parallel. This is a very early instance of the interpretation of human sexual matters in terms of non-sexual, sacred matters (or, if you prefer, the reverse). Sensuality continued to keep its foot in the door of the house of religion throughout the history of India.

But the Upanishads also introduced into India the concept of two paths, one the path of family life, society and children, the other the path of renunciation, solitary meditation and asceticism. The tension between the two paths, the violent (sacrificial), materialistic, sensual and potentially

[iv] See 'Indra as the Stallion's Wife'.

addictive path of worldliness on the one hand, and the non-violent (vegetarian), ascetic, spiritual and controlled path of renunciation, on the other,[v] was sometimes expressed as the balance between bourgeois householders and homeless seekers, or between traditions that regarded karma—the accumulated record of good and bad deeds—as a good or a bad thing, respectively.

The tension remains in the Tantras, a large body of texts, composed between about 650 and 1800 CE, which proposed strikingly transgressive ritual actions, violating all the taboos of conventional Hinduism, such as drinking wine and menstrual blood, eating meat and engaging in sexual activity with forbidden women. These Tantras thus collapsed the Upanishadic metaphor, saying that the ritual sexual act is not just *like* a ritual (as it is in the Upanishads) but is itself a ritual, the equivalent of making an offering into the fire. Other Tantras, however, situated within the anti-erotic tradition of Hinduism, insisted that the ritual instructions were never intended to be followed literally, but were purely symbolic. They argued that 'wine' really meant a meditational nectar, that 'flesh' meant the tongue of the practitioner, and that the sexual act stood for 'the supreme essence'.[8] This was a very early form of censorship, and a very mild form, for it merely proposed an alternative, anti-erotic interpretation of the text but did not attempt to muzzle the other, erotic interpretation. Far from the spirit that bowdlerized the intentionally obscene horse sacrifice,[vi] this tradition spawned works of art like the 'Century' of the poet Amaru, a hundred poems that are simultaneously erotic and ascetic.

And so the two paths of Tantra, meditation and ritual action, lived side by side, sometimes coexisting in a single worshipper, sometimes within a group, as, for instance, in some texts that say that beginners actually do the ritual, while advanced practitioners just meditate. The split-level connotations were present from the start. Given the attention that Indian literary theory pays to double meanings, to words and indeed whole literary works that simultaneously mean two different things,[9] it seems wise to assume that the Tantrics were capable of walking and chewing imaginary gum at the same time.

The erotic tradition continued to thrive in Hinduism. Many poems to gods in the medieval devotional tradition of bhakti imagine the god as a lover, often an unfaithful lover, and depict the relationship with all the sensual details of good erotic poetry. The poet Kshetrayya, who may have

[v] See 'Three (or More)' and 'The Control of Addiction'.
[vi] See 'Indra as the Stallion's Wife' and 'Sacrifice and Substitution'.

lived in the mid-seventeenth century, and who worshipped a form of the god Krishna, imagined a courtesan speaking to her customer who is both her lover and her god. Kshetrayya's songs survived among courtesans and were performed by male Brahmin dancers who played female roles. His poems speak of such down-to-earth matters as a woman's concern to find a drug or a magic potion to abort the child that she conceived from her lover—the god and her customer.[10]

SIR RICHARD BURTON'S VERSION OF THE *KAMASUTRA*

In addition to these religious texts that incorporated eroticism, there were more worldly texts that treated the erotic *tout court*, of which, of course, the *Kamasutra* is the most famous. There is nothing remotely like it even now, and for its time it was astonishingly sophisticated; it was already well known in India at a time when the Europeans were still swinging in trees, culturally (and sexually) speaking. The *Kamasutra*'s ideas about gender are surprisingly modern, as we have already seen, and its stereotypes of feminine and masculine natures are unexpectedly subtle.[vii] It also reveals attitudes to women's education and sexual freedom, and non-judgmental views of homosexual acts, that are strikingly more liberal than those of other texts in ancient India—or, in many cases, contemporary India.[viii] The *Kamasutra* was a revolutionary document for such people, and for women. It exerted a profound influence on subsequent Indian literature, particularly in court life and in the privileged, classless society that it describes at great length. But, at the same time, the dharma texts like Manu's *dharmashastra*, with their deep suspicion of women and eroticism, retained their stranglehold on much of Hindu society. And then came the British.

One reason why the *Kamasutra* plays almost no role at all in the sexual consciousness of contemporary Indians is that it is known, in both India and Europe, almost entirely through the flawed English translation by Sir Richard Francis Burton. This translation was published in 1883, a time when the Hindus, cowering under the scorn of the Protestant proselytizers, wanted to sweep the *Kamasutra* under the Upanishadic rug. The journalist Curt Gentry, writing in the *San Francisco Chronicle* at that time, suggested that the publication of Burton's *Kamasutra* translation 'might act as a useful corrective to the prevailing cliché of India as a land of asceticism'.[11] And in many ways, it did. Burton did for the *Kamasutra* what Max Müller did for

[vii] See 'The Third Nature' and 'The Mythology of the *Kamasutra*'.
[viii] See 'The Third Nature'.

the *Rig Veda* during this same period; his translation had a profound effect upon literature across Europe and America. But it did not bring the sexual freedom of the *Kamasutra* into Hindu consciousness.

Victorian British attitudes to Hindu eroticism ricocheted between the pornographers and the prudes, and Burton, a connoisseur of eroticism in Arabic as well as Indian culture, was certainly not a prude. His main contribution was the courage and determination to publish the work at all; he was the Larry Flynt of his day.[ix] W.H. Auden didn't think much of him: 'thus, squalid beery Burton stands/for shoddy thinking of all brands.'[12] Marina Warner calls him 'the Frank Harris of the desert and the bazaar'.[13] To get around the censorship laws, Burton set up an imaginary publishing house, The Kama Shastra Society of London and Benares, with printers said to be in Benares or Cosmopoli.[x] Even though it was not legally published in England and the United States until 1962, the Burton *Kamasutra* soon after its publication in 1883 became 'one of the most pirated books in the English language', constantly reprinted, often with a new preface to justify the new edition, sometimes without any attribution to Burton.[14]

This lack of attribution is actually quite appropriate, for the Burton translation is not primarily the work of Burton. It was far more the work of Forster Fitzgerald ('Bunny') Arbuthnot, whose name appears on the title page with Burton's only in some editions, though Burton later referred to the *Kamasutra* translation as 'Arbuthnot's Vatsyayana'.[15] In fact, the translation owed even more to two Indian scholars whose names do not appear on the title page at all: Bhagavanlal Indrajit and Shivaram Parashuram Bhide. (There is a pre-post-colonial irony in the fact that Arbuthnot later tried to get the censors off his trail by stating, in 1885, a half-truth that he almost certainly regarded as a lie: that the translation was done entirely by Indian pundits.)[16] It really should, therefore, be known as the Indrajit-Bhide-Arbuthnot-Burton translation, but since Burton was by far the

---

[ix] His translation of the *Arabian Nights* was notorious. He generally made the tales more salacious than they were, stealing most of them from other translators like Richard Payne and adding many of his own, thumbing his nose at the prevailing prudery of Victorian Britain, with what Marina Warner describes as 'glee and a fair deal of invention, projection, and transference'. One reviewer epitomized the European translators of the *Arabian Nights* as 'Galland [ ] for the nursery, Lane for the library, Payne for the study, and Burton for the sewers'.

[x] The title page read: 'The Kama Sutra of Vatsyayana, Translated from the Sanscrit. In Seven Parts, with Preface, Introduction and Concluding Remarks. Cosmopoli: 1883: for the Kama Shastra Society of London and Benares, and for private circulation only.'

most famous member of the team, it has always been called the Burton translation.

In many ways, it should be called the Burton mistranslation. For, in crucial passages, the Sanskrit text simply does not say what Burton says it says. The Burton translation robs women of their voices, turning direct quotes into indirect quotes, thus losing the force of the dialogue that animates the work and erasing the vivid presence of the many women who speak in the *Kamasutra*, replacing these voices with reported speech rephrased by a man. Thus, where the text says that, when a man is striking a woman, 'She uses words like "Stop!" or "Let me go!" or "Enough!" or "Mother!"'[17] Burton translates it like this: 'She continually utters words expressive of prohibition, sufficiency, or desire of liberation.' Moreover, when the text says that this may happen 'When a man [is] in the throes of passion', and 'If a man tries to force his kisses and so forth on her', Burton says it happens 'When the woman is not accustomed to striking', reversing the genders and reversing the point.[18]

Burton also erodes women's agency by mistranslating or erasing some passages in which women have strong privileges. Take this passage (here translated more or less literally) about a wife's powers of recrimination:

> Mildly offended by the man's infidelities, she does not accuse him too much, but she scolds him with abusive language when he is alone or among friends. She does not, however, use love-sorcery worked with roots, for, Gonardiya says, 'Nothing destroys trust like that.'[19]

Burton renders it:

> In the event of any misconduct on the part of her husband, she should not blame him excessively, though she be a little displeased. She should not use abusive language toward him, but rebuke him with conciliatory words, whether he be in the company of friends or alone. Moreover, she should not be a scold, for, says Gonardiya, 'There is no cause of dislike on the part of a husband so great as this characteristic in a wife'.[20]

What is wrong with this picture? In the first place, Burton mistranslated the word for 'love-sorcery worked with roots' (*mulakarika*), which he renders as 'she should not be a scold' (though elsewhere he correctly translates *mulakarika*). Second, 'misconduct' is not so much a mistranslation as an error of judgment, for the word in question (*apacara*) does have the general meaning of 'misconduct', but in an erotic context it takes on the more specific meaning of 'infidelity', a choice that is supported by the remedy that the text suggests (and rejects): love-magic. But the most serious problem is the word 'not' that Burton gratuitously adds and that negates the wife's right to use abusive language against her straying husband, a denial only somewhat qualified by the added phrase, that she might 'rebuke him with conciliatory words'. Was this an innocent error or does it reflect a sexist bias? We cannot know. A more serious disservice to the *Kamasutra* was done by Burton's mistranslation of the passages about people of the 'third nature'.[xi]

The so-called Burton translation is widely read in Europe and America. It is free (at first poached from the illegal editions, then long out of copyright) and recognizable as what people think the *Kamasutra* should be. Indeed, it is quite a wonderful text: great fun to read, extraordinarily bold and frank for its time, and in many places a fairly approximate representation of the Sanskrit original. It remains precious, like Edward Fitzgerald's *Rubaiyat*, as a monument of English literature, but it is certainly not a monument of Indian literature.

An adolescent girl in Vikram Chandra's story 'Kama' says, 'Sister Carmina didn't want to tell us. It's the *Kama Sutra*, which she says isn't in the library. But Gisela's parents have a copy which they think is hidden away on the top of their shelf. We looked it up there.' And the adult to whom she tells this says, 'You put that book back where you found it. And don't read any more.'[21] In India today, urban, affluent, usually anglicized people will give a copy of the *Kamasutra* (in English translation) as a wedding present, to demonstrate their open-mindedness and sophistication, but most people will merely sneak a surreptitious look at it in someone else's house.

DETUMESCENCE UNDER THE BRITISH

A Supreme Court ruling from 1862 states that 'Krishna . . . the love hero, the husband of 16,000 princesses . . . tinges the whole system (of Hinduism) with the strain of carnal sensualism, of strange, transcendental lewdness.'[22] Given this view of everyday Hinduism, it is hardly surprising that Evangelical Protestants greatly preferred the other path of Hinduism, the philosophical, renunciant path.[xii]

Influenced by British Protestantism, and embarrassed by aspects of their faith that the colonial rulers found abhorrent or ridiculous, the highly

---

[xi] See 'The Third Nature'.
[xii] See 'God's Body'.

Anglicized Indian elite during the Raj developed new forms of Hinduism, particularly the movement known as the Bengal Renaissance or the Hindu Renaissance.[xiii] Following the British lead,[xiv] these Hindus largely wrote off the dominant strain of Hinduism that celebrated the passions of the gods. Eventually, these movements grew into the form of Neo-Vedanta called Sanatana Dharma (Eternal or Universal Dharma) that is embraced by many Hindus to this day. Sanatana Dharma is the banner of Hindutva, which presides over the censorship of art, film, literature and social behaviour.

The British lion, even after its official death in India in 1947, dealt another blow to Indian freedom of expression through the Film Censor Board, which, from the early 1950s, implemented a policy basis that had roots among the British (who had worried more about sedition than about sex). The Film Censor Board's concern for visual pedagogy, nationalism and publicity cast a shadow that extended over Indian visual arts and literature as well as film.

Hindu attitudes to sexuality were further confused by the very public, and very contradictory, sexuality of one of the most important Hindus of the twentieth century, Mahatma Gandhi. Gandhi's insistence on celibacy among his disciples caused difficulty for some of them, as did his habit of sleeping beside girls young enough to be called jail-bait in the US, to test and/or prove his own celibate control. His celibacy drew not so much upon the Upanishadic and Vaishnava ascetic traditions, which were the source of many of Gandhi's practices, as upon the hydraulic Tantric techniques of internalizing power, indeed creating quasi-magical powers, by first stirring up the sexual energies and then withholding semen. Gandhi was a one-man model of the perennial Hindu attempt to harness sexuality.

In the nineteenth and twentieth centuries, liberal Indian intellectuals, who noticed the shift in attitudes to Hinduism's erotic past from appreciation to embarrassment, tended to explain contemporary Hindu prudery in terms of power and patronage from the past. As James McConnachie summarized the situation, 'Erotic literature had been the creation of poets and princes, the argument ran, and as "lascivious" Hindu despots had given way to "fanatical" Mughal overlords, the patronage on which erotic literature depended had withered and died.'[23] V.S. Naipaul in his book *Half a Life* offers his own, rather jaded, version of this accusation:

[xiii] There is some irony in the fact that Bengal was the place that nourished Tantra and the erotic tradition of the loves of Krishna and Radha.

[xiv] See 'Are Hindus Monotheists?'

. . . [I]n our culture there is no seduction. Our marriages are arranged. There is no art of sex. Some of the boys here talk to me of the *Kama Sutra*. Nobody talked about that at home. It was an upper-caste text, but I don't believe my poor father, brahmin though he is, ever looked at a copy. That philosophical-practical way of dealing with sex belongs to our past, and that world was ravaged and destroyed by the Muslims.[24]

And then (the twisted, chauvinist argument goes) came the British missionaries, adding insult to injury. Thus nationalists blamed India's sexual conservatism on 'an unholy combination of imposed Muslim religiosity and imported British "Victorianism"'.[25]

There is some truth in that general historical argument, but it has three serious flaws. First, as for the Muslims, it ignores the enthusiasm for the erotic arts on the part of such Muslims as the Lodi dynasty in the sixteenth century, who commissioned one of the last great works of Sanskrit eroticism, the *Ananga Ranga*,[26] and the Mughals (particularly Akbar and Dara Shikoh) who had textbooks of Hindu erotic arts and religious texts translated from Sanskrit to Persian and illustrated with Persian painting techniques. The Nationalists dismissed all of this, ungenerously, as 'the last, valedictory flourishing of a tragically deracinated tradition'. Second, blaming the British for Hindu prudery allows the very real memory of missionary Puritainism and the racist snobbery of the Raj club culture to overpower the equally important role of other sorts of Brits in the rediscovery of India's erotic heritage.[27] Most of all, blaming the Muslims and the British ignores the history of native Hindu anti-eroticism. For, as we have seen, India had its own home-grown traditions of prudery in opposition to its own sensuality.

THE FALL OF KAMA AND THE RISE OF KARMA

Nowadays, on the public scene, 'a Hindu-nationalist Health Minister can insist that the "Indian traditions" of abstinence and fidelity are more effective barriers against HIV than condoms; and . . . the 1860 Penal Code [still in effect] defines all extramarital sex as criminal'.[28] Many Hindus, in India but also increasingly in the American diaspora, advocate a sanitized, 'spiritual' form of Hinduism (and, in India, a nationalist and anti-Muslim form). For such Hindus, the problem is not (as it was for some liberal Indian intellectuals) how to explain how India lost its appreciation of eroticism but, on the contrary, how to maintain that Hinduism was always the pure-minded, anti-erotic, ascetic tradition that it became, for many upper-class Hindus, in the nineteenth century.

One way to make this argument was to swing to the other side of the pendulum and blame the British not for *suppressing* Indian eroticism but for *causing* it. Under Nehru, the Indian government retained Macaulay's *Indian Penal Code* of 1860, forbidding several acts 'against nature'[xv] that Nehru condemned by saying, 'such vices in India were due to Western influence'.[29] The irony is that in aping the Muslim and British scorn for Indian sexuality, contemporary Hindus who favour censorship are letting foreign ideas about Hinduism triumph over and drive out native Hindu ideas about—and pride in—their own religion and in the diversity and tolerance that have always characterized the world of the mind in Hinduism. Among the other bad habits they picked up from the West, from seeds sown, perhaps, during colonization but flowering only in the more recent contacts with American imperialism, was the Protestant habit of censorship. Never before has the old tension between the erotic and ascetic strains of Hinduism taken the form of one path telling the other path that it has no right to exist.

But the India of the ancient erotic past is not so easily stamped out. Even in the nineteenth century, most Hindus continued cheerfully on the path that celebrated the earthier aspects of life. And now they live on in 'a reported two thirds of young adults who would have casual, pre-marital sex before an arranged marriage'[30], and who, since 1991, can buy condoms called *KamaSutra*—and chocolate-, vanilla- and strawberry-flavoured condoms, too, marketed freely on Indian television channels, circa 2012. And through all this, many hundreds of folk songs and stories—often sung or told by women—have remained robustly bawdy. Clearly the attempt to transform the culture of the *Kamasutra* into what many people, Hindus and non-Hindus alike, mistakenly refer to as the *Karmasutra* (presumably a Vedantic text about reincarnation) has not succeeded.

[xv] Section 377 prohibits 'sexual relations against nature with a man, woman, or animal, whether the intercourse is anal or oral'.

HORSES AND OTHER ANIMALS

THE AMBIVALENCE OF AHIMSA[1]

You do not really die through this, nor are you harmed.
You go to the gods on paths pleasant to go on.

—Rig Veda 1.62
(from a hymn to the sacrificial horse)

Religion, and particularly mythology, which is my beat, deals with questions that can't be answered, problems that can't be solved. The problem of our relationship to animals is one of those religious problems, and it is, therefore, shot through with ambivalence. We have always killed animals to live, often despite feeling that there was something wrong about it. We like to have pets because they make our lives so much better, draw us deeper into nature, make us live longer, lower our blood pressure, as all the surveys show; but animal neuroses are now a major industry, because we drive our pets mad keeping them the way we do, cooped up and alone much of the time. In general, religion, in India and elsewhere, has often papered over or sidelined the natural human ambivalence about the treatment of animals. Against the religious rhetoric of lions of Judah and the good shepherd, against the occasional St Francis or the not so occasional Jain saint, we must confront the truly appalling track record of religions in the lives of animals on the planet Earth.

At last, during the past decades, people the world over have taken up the cause in so many arenas, besides the immediate issues of meat and pets: the culling of wild horses, the importing of ivory, the treatment of farm animals, and above all, perhaps, the realization that so many species are endangered. After all the creatures we have abused over the centuries—slaves, women, homosexuals, children—animals are the last frontier of compassion. Indeed, two of these groups—slaves and horses—have often been linked together in works calling for reform: recall the colour of the horse in Anna Sewell's novel *Black Beauty*, written in 1877 by a woman who was born in 1820 and whose mother was a devout abolitionist. In nineteenth- and twentieth-century English and European literature, the image of a man cruelly beating a horse who had fallen under an impossible burden became an immediately recognized symbol of human evil.

Hinduism has dealt vividly and explicitly, and over the longest historical period of any culture, with the agonizing religious question of how to treat animals. India knew, long ago, that, in a sense, all of us, humans and animals, are a single endangered species. Yet, contrary to widespread misconceptions, Hindus have not always been vegetarians, nor are most of them vegetarians today.[i] (Indeed, since the human species is by nature carnivorous, what is surprising is that there ever were vegetarians, not that we were all, once, and generally remain, meat-eaters.) Nor are Hindus particularly kind to animals. This chapter will consider the history of Hindu ambivalence to animals, in order to gain some insights into the problems that people throughout the world are now facing in their concern for animals.

VEDAS, C. 1500 BCE

Hindu uneasiness about the ritual slaughter of animals may be traced back to Vedic texts about the killing of a stallion.[2] The most dramatic sacrifice you could manage, short of human sacrifice (which was imagined in ancient India, though perhaps never performed[ii]), was to kill a stallion, an animal visibly bursting with life. When you watch a dog die, even a very old, very sick dog, the moment between the time when it is alive, perhaps asleep, and when it is dead, is a terrible, vivid moment, one that makes an indelible impression on a child, or even a grown up. Imagine what it must be like to see a young stallion killed.

One Vedic poem describes the horse sacrifice in strikingly concrete, indeed rather gruesome detail:

---

[i] According to the 2004 Survey Report conducted by the Indian Census, 25 per cent of persons aged 15 years and above were reported to be vegetarian. But according to the 2006 *The Hindu*-CNN-IBN State of the Nation Survey, 40 per cent of the respondents were vegetarian (a figure that includes those who eat eggs); 55 per cent of Brahmins are vegetarian, and in land-locked states such as Rajasthan and Haryana, where seafood is not available as a food source, over 60 per cent are vegetarians. Gujarat, the birthplace of Gandhi and home to a sizable Jain population, is predominantly landlocked, but only 45 per cent vegetarian.

[ii] See 'Sacrifice and Substitution'.

Whatever of the horse's flesh the fly has eaten, or whatever stays stuck to the stake or the axe, or to the hands or nails of the slaughterer—let all of that stay with you even among the gods. Whatever food remains in his stomach, sending forth gas, or whatever smell there is from his raw flesh—let the slaughterers make that well done; let them cook the sacrificial animal until he is perfectly cooked. If someone riding you has struck you too hard with heel or whip when you shied, I make all these things well again for you with prayer. Let not your dear soul burn you as you go away. Let not the axe do lasting harm to your body. Let no greedy, clumsy slaughterer hack in the wrong place and damage your limbs with his knife. You do not really die through this, nor are you harmed. You go to the gods on paths pleasant to go on.[3]

The poet thus intermittently addresses the horse (and himself) with the consolation that all will be restored in heaven, words in which we may see the first stirrings of ambivalence about the killing of a beloved animal, even in a religious ceremony. There was also a concern that the victim should not bleed or suffer or cry out (one reason why the sacrificial animal was strangled before being dismembered). The euphemism for the killing of the horse, 'pacifying' (shanti), further muted the growing uneasiness associated with the killing of an animal. Moreover, unlike goats and other animals that were sacrificed, many in the course of the horse sacrifice, the horse was not actually eaten (though he was cooked and served to the gods). Perhaps this taboo arose because of the close relationship that the Vedic people, like most Indo-Europeans,[4] had with their horses, who not only speak, on occasion,[5] but often shed tears[iii] when their owners die. Still, they did slaughter the stallion.

THE BRAHMANAS, C. 900 BCE

A few centuries later, in the Brahmanas, commentaries on the Vedas, when the sacrificial narratives come to the point of actually killing the victim, the prose becomes heavily euphemistic and mystifying.

They then go back again (to the altar) and sit down turning towards the *ahavaniya* fire, 'so that they should not be spectators of its being made to acquiesce (to its own death)'. They do not kill it by striking it on the forehead, like humans, nor behind the ear, for that is the way (of killing) among the ancestors. They either keep its mouth closed

[iii] Drona's horses shed tears when he is about to die [M 7.192.20]; when the Buddha departs, his horse Kanthaka weeps [*Buddhacharita* 6.33-5; 8.3-4, 17].

(and thus suffocate it), or they make a noose (and strangle it to death). Thus he does not say, 'Kill! Put it to death!' for that is the way of humans. (Rather, he says) 'Make it acquiesce! It has passed away!' for that is the way of the gods. For when he says, 'It has passed away,' then this one (the victim of the sacrificer) passes away to the gods. Therefore he says, 'It has passed away.'[6]

The reluctance to face the horrific reality of human beings killing animals in the sacred ritual leads the Brahmins to imagine that they are operating in the morally pure universe of the divine: they do not 'kill' like humans but, like the gods, they make the victim 'acquiesce' to its own death or 'make it pass away'.

There are many Hindu myths about sacrifice, some of which depict the ritualization of the paradox of the hunting of the tame animal.[7] This paradox may be designed to restore to the grim and often guilt-laden butchery of tame animals some of the glamour and martial eroticism characteristic of hunting. It is by no means clear that all hunters or sacrificers experience guilt or regret at the death of the animal. But some evidently do have some misgivings, by their own testimony (or at least the testimony of their Brahmin priests). The sacrificial experts of ancient India included a rationale of ritual killing specifically aimed at obviating such guilt.

The Brahmanas also recorded a story justifying our treatment of animals:

In the beginning, the skin of cattle was the skin that humans have now, and the skin of a human was the skin that cattle have now. Cattle could not bear the heat, rain, flies and mosquitoes. They went to humans and said, 'Let this skin be yours and that skin be ours.' 'What would be the result of that?' humans asked. 'You could eat us,' said the cattle, 'and this skin of ours would be your clothing.' And so they gave humans their clothing. Therefore, when the sacrificer puts on a red hide, he flourishes, and cattle do not eat him in the other world; for [otherwise] cattle do eat a human in the other world.[8]

The transaction in the other world is here interpreted as the reversal of a reversal: humans and cattle traded places long ago, and, as a result, cattle *willingly* undertook to supply humans with food and clothing. But cattle also, apparently, won the boon of eating humans (and, perhaps, flaying them) in the other world, presumably a place where people go after dying, though the text never spells it out like that. Nakedness, by reducing humans to the level of the beasts, establishes a reciprocal relationship, rendering human beings vulnerable to the sufferings of beasts—being eaten—when they enter the other world. But when a man puts (back) on his 'original' cattle hide he somehow undoes the bargain, which allows him to masquerade as someone who does not (yet) eat cattle, and thus to escape the consequences of his carnivory.

Another narrative elsewhere in this same text adds more detail to the basic idea of reciprocity between humans and animals in the other world:

> Bhrigu went beyond this world to the world beyond. There he saw a man cut another man to pieces and eat him; and then a man eating another man, who was screaming; and then a man eating another man, who was soundlessly screaming. He returned from that world and told his father [Varuna] what he had seen. His father explained that when people who lack true knowledge and offer no oblations cut down trees for firewood, or cook for themselves animals that cry out, or cook for themselves rice and barley, which scream soundlessly, those trees, and animals, and rice and barley take the form of men in the other world and eat those people in return. 'How can one avoid that?' asked Bhrigu. And Varuna replied that you avoid it by putting fuel on the sacred fire and offering oblations.[9]

This text is not just about animals, since trees and barley play an equally important role, but more broadly about all the things used in preparing food (vegetables, animals and fuel), about consumerism in a very literal sense. Being eaten in the other world is not a punishment for sins but rather a straight reversal of the inevitable (and not condemned) eating in this world. Other texts of this period confirm this: 'Just as in this world men eat cattle and devour them, so in the other world cattle eat men and devour them.'[10] And, 'Whatever food a man eats in this world, that [food] eats him in the other world.'[11]

This experience in the other world is, therefore, as certain as death itself, and just as unpleasant. The soundlessly screaming rice and barley resurfaced in the writings of the great Indian botanist Jagadish Chandra Bose, who moved George Bernard Shaw deeply with his demonstration of an 'unfortunate carrot strapped to the table of an unlicenced vivisector'.[12] The silent screams in the Sanskrit text have the quality of a nightmare. This is a world in which even vegetarianism is sinful, and the only way to remain without sin would be to starve to death.

Nowhere, however, does the text suggest that people should stop eating animals (or rice, for that matter, or refrain from burning fuel). It is possible to avoid the unpleasant consequences of eating; the solution is to perform the proper rituals, to restore anyone who has eaten something alleged to produce unfortunate consequences—if left unrestored. Dangers arise in the context of profane eating and are warded off by sacred feeding (the oblations offered to the gods). Indeed, the two are inextricably linked by the belief that it is wrong to take food without offering some, at least mentally, to the gods; in the broadest sense, all human food consists of divine leftovers (later known as prasad, 'grace'). The text is not saying, 'Do not eat animals, for then they will eat you,' but, rather, 'Be sure to eat animals in the right way, or they will eat you.' The proper sort of 'avoidance' makes the meat safe to eat, as if it were kosher or halal.

Religion in this period makes it possible for us to slaughter animals; it washes away our fears and our guilt. Manu[iv] says, 'The Self-existent one himself created sacrificial animals for sacrifice; sacrifice is for the good of this whole (universe); and therefore killing in a sacrifice is not killing.'[13] By defining the sacrifice as nonviolent, Manu *made* it nonviolent. To this day it is often argued in India that the meat of animals killed for the table is poison because such animals die in fear and anger, while animals killed for sacrifice are happy to die, and so their meat is sweet.[v] Such texts betray that old human longing to have one's animal and eat it.

UPANISHADS AND BUDDHISM (C. 600 BCE)

People in ancient India did eat meat, both the meat of sacrificial animals and any other meat they could hunt or breed; hundreds of texts insist on this. But the ideals of nonviolence and vegetarianism were already in the air by the time of the Brahmanas and Upanishads and soon gained momentum as the practice of renunciation spread. Most Indian traditions of renunciation advise the renouncer to avoid eating meat,[14] and renouncers were likely to be vegetarians: to renounce the flesh is to renounce flesh. Moreover, since the renouncer renounces the sacrificial ritual (karma), he thereby loses one of the main occasions when it is legal to kill animals.[15] Even in the Vedic ritual, vegetable offerings (rice and barley) were the minimally acceptable lowest form of the sacrificial victim, the *pashu*,[vi] but

---

[iv] See 'Why Should a Brahmin?'

[v] This sort of self-deception seems to me little better than the comfort a small child offered to herself when forced to acknowledge that she liked to eat chicken even though she loved chickens: 'We're really only eating the inside of the animal. The outside of the animal is still running around, happy.' (Personal communication from Lorraine Daston—who knew the child in question; 18 April 2012.) Or, as the case may be, the inside of the inside of the animal is in a Vedic heaven.

[vi] See 'Sacrifice and Substitution'.

the original animal victim lingers on in the way that the Vedic texts treat even the rice cake like an animal: 'When the rice cake (is offered), it is indeed a *pashu* that is offered up. Its stringy chaff, that is the hairs; its husk is the skin; the flour is the blood; the small grains are the flesh; whatever is the best part (of the grain) is the bone.'[16]

Here and throughout the Hindu texts, the underlying concern is not necessarily for what being eaten does to the animal but for what eating the animal does to the human:[vii] flesh heats the passions and is, therefore, dangerous for the ideal Hindu person, who is always in control of his emotions.[viii] Moreover, in later Hinduism, the strictures against eating and killing continued to work at odds, so that it would have been regarded as better (for most people, in general: the rules would vary according to the caste status of the person in each case) to *kill* a Dalit (Untouchable) than to *kill* a Brahmin, but better to eat a Brahmin (if one came across a dead one) than to eat a Dalit (under the same circumstances). The degree of purity/pollution in the food that is eaten seems to be an issue distinct from the issue of the amount of violence involved in procuring it. It makes a difference if you find the meat already killed or have to kill it, and this would apply not only to Brahmins vs Dalits (admittedly an extreme case) but to cows vs dogs as roadkill.

The story of Bhrigu in the other world does not yet espouse vegetarian doctrines but it probably contributed to their rise. For the idea of reversals in the other world was easily ethicized (in Jainism and Buddhism as well as some Hindu sects) into the belief that the best way to avoid being eaten in the other world was not merely to eat animals in the proper (sacrificial) way but to stop eating them altogether. Gradually, many branches of Hinduism banished all animal sacrifices. While in Vedism substitutions for the prototypical victim (the sacrificer and/or the deity) were inserted on the basis of necessity, in later Hinduism the substitute of a rice cake for a sacrificial animal is often couched in terms of morality, that is, in terms of non-injury, or ahimsa.[ix]

There may also have been an element of necessity in later cases, though of a different nature from earlier ones. Vegetable sacrificial substitutes may have been necessitated in post-Vedic Hinduism by the need to answer the challenge posed by the anti-Vedic polemic of Buddhism, which had converted many powerful political leaders. The Buddhists and Jains, too,

---

[vii] See 'Eating Karma'.
[viii] See 'The Control of Addiction'.
[ix] See 'Sacrifice and Substitution'.

may have had moral reasons to abolish the sacrifice (as they said they did); but they may also have wanted to make a clean break with Hinduism by appropriating, in a transformed version, the definitive element of Vedic self-definition—sacrifice.

Buddhist and Jain traditions unveiled their new doctrines and religious activities in the guise of 'higher' or 'truer' forms of the Vedic ritual, which was in this way made to appear as relatively ineffectual in comparison with newly revealed, and entirely bloodless, 'sacrifices'.[17] It was politic, too, for the Buddhists to promote a religion that did not need Brahmins to intercede for individual humans with gods, indeed that denied the efficacy of gods altogether, and this, more than compassion for furry creatures, was the final move that distinguished Buddhists and Jains from Hindu renunciants, who may not have employed Brahmins themselves but did not deny their authority for others. (The stricter code of the Jains, which forbade them to take any animal life, prevented them from farming, which killed the tiny creatures caught under the plough; Jains were, therefore, forced to become bankers and get rich.)

Post-Vedic Hindu traditions may have found it expedient, and also convenient, to adopt much the same strategy. But when we fold this mix back into the broader issues, we must distinguish among killing animals, tormenting animals, sacrificing them, eating them and, finally, worshipping them. Nonviolence, pacifism, compassion for animals and vegetarianism are not the same thing at all. It is usual for most individuals to eat meat without killing animals (most non-vegetarians, few of whom hunt or butcher, do it every day) and equally normal for an individual to kill people without eating meat (what percentage of hitmen or soldiers devour their fallen enemies?). Vegetarianism and killing may have been originally mutually exclusive: in the earliest period of Indian civilization, in places where there was no standing army, meat-eating householders would, in time of war, like volunteer firemen, become soldiers, and consecrate themselves as warriors by giving up the eating of meat.[18] They either ate meat or killed.

Nevertheless, the logical assumption that any animal that one ate had to have been killed by *someone* led to a natural association between the ideal of vegetarianism and the ideal of nonviolence toward living creatures. The transformation in attitudes to eating meat developed at this time in India in part through the sorts of philosophical considerations evident in the texts and in part through changes in methods of livestock breeding, grazing grounds and ecology that resulted from the transition into the urban life of the Ganges Valley, as well as from the social tensions exacerbated by these changes. The breeding of animals in an urban setting may have introduced both less humane grazing conditions and a heightened awareness of those conditions (though some urban dwellers may have been, like many contemporary city-dwellers, insulated from farming conditions). The new uneasiness about killing animals may also have been a reaction to the increasing number of animals sacrificed in more and more elaborate ceremonies. Sacrifice was still violent, and sacrifice was still power, but a murmur of protest and discontent was growing steadily stronger, soon to find its voice, faintly in the Upanishads and loudly in the *Mahabharata*.

ASHOKA, C. 304-232 BCE

An important moment in the history of ambivalence toward the killing of animals in India came during the reign of the emperor Ashoka, in the third century BCE. Ashoka cared deeply about animals and included them as a matter of course, along with humans, as the beneficiaries of his shade trees and watering places. In place of the royal tradition of touring the kingdom in a series of royal hunts, he inaugurated the tradition of royal pilgrimages to Buddhist shrines, thus substituting a Buddhist (and Hindu) virtue (pilgrimage) for what the Hindus viewed as a vice of addiction (hunting). One of his many rock inscriptions says, 'Our Lord the king kills very few animals. Seeing this the rest of the people have also ceased from killing animals. Even the activity of those who catch fish has been prohibited.'[19] Ashoka's own particular philosophy, his *dhamma*, became prototypical, since the people are to follow the king's example; the implication was, 'This is what I eat in my kitchen; you should eat like that, too.' Elsewhere Ashoka urges 'abstention from killing, and nonviolence [*avihimsa*] to living beings'[20] and remarks that it is good not to kill living beings.[21]

The very word that Ashoka uses—*avihimsa*, a variant of the more common ahimsa—is a hedging, ambivalent word. It means, literally, 'the absence of the desire to kill', and is, therefore, a kind of double negative, a 'when did you stop beating your wife' kind of word. (The Indian nationalist leader Bal Gangadhar Tilak [1856-1920] translated ahimsa, in the *Gita*, as 'harmlessness',[22] another double negative.) Ahimsa describes an emotion, rather than a moral law; it tells us how we should feel towards animals, not how we should treat them.

But Ashoka never did discontinue capital punishment or torture, nor legislate against either the killing or the eating of all animals. This is what he said about his own diet: 'Formerly, in the kitchens of the Beloved of the

Gods, the king Piyadasi, many hundreds of thousands of living animals were killed daily for meat. But now, at the time of writing of this inscription on *dhamma*, only three animals are killed, two peacocks and a deer, and the deer not invariably. Even these three animals will not be killed in future.'[23] Why go on killing these three? Perhaps the Emperor was particularly fond of roasted peacock and venison.[24] Perhaps he was trying to cut down on meat, the way some chainsmokers try to cut down on cigarettes. But his personal tastes cannot explain the other, longer list of animals that the edicts 'protected' from slaughter, including parakeets, mynah birds, red-headed ducks, *chakravaka* geese, swans, pigeons, bats, ants, tortoises, boneless fish, skates, porcupines, squirrels, deer, lizards, cows, rhinoceros, white pigeons, domestic pigeons and all four-footed creatures that are neither useful nor edible; also nanny goats, ewes and sows lactating or with young, and kids, lambs and piglets less than six months old. Cocks are not to be made into capons. One animal is not to be fed to another. On certain holy days, fish are not to be caught or sold; on other holy days, bulls, billy-goats, rams, boars and other animals that are usually castrated are not to be castrated; and on still others, horses and bullocks are not to be branded.[25]

How are we to understand these lists? Ashoka is hedging, stopping short of embracing nonviolence entirely but merely mitigating some of the brutality to animals in his kingdom. He recommends restraint towards living beings in the same breath that he recommends the proper treatment of slaves,[26] but evidently it is all right to kill some of the creatures some of the time. In particular, Ashoka allows for the slaughter of the domesticated animals (*pashus*)—male goats, sheep and cattle, the animals most often used both for sacrifice and for food. There is no ecological agenda here for the conservation of wildlife, nor can the lists be explained by the privileging of certain animals for medicinal purposes. What there is, is the expression of a man who finds himself between a rock edict and a hard place, a man who has concern for animals' feelings (give them shade, don't castrate them—sometimes) but recognizes that people do eat animals. It is a very limited sort of nonviolence.

MANU

The ambivalence of ahimsa reached its heyday during the period, around the turn of the Common Era, when the great dharma texts were consolidated. The most famous of these, *The Laws of Manu*, offers many different lists involving animals: situations in which lawsuits arise between humans and livestock; punishments for people who injure, steal, or kill various animals; animals (including humans) that Brahmins should not sell; classes of beings one should and should not eat; and vows of restoration for anyone who has, advertently or inadvertently, injured, stolen, killed, or eaten (or eaten the excrement of) various animals.[27] But Manu is torn between an ethics of sacrifice and an ethics of vegetarianism.

Manu tells you what you *can't* eat:

> Do not eat the first milk of a newly-calved cow, or meat that has not been consecrated; or the milk of a cow within ten days of calving, or the milk of a camel or of any animal with a whole, solid hoof, or of a ewe, or of a cow in heat or a cow whose calf has been taken from her; and avoid the milk of women, the milk of all wild animals of the wilderness except the buffalo. Do not eat carnivorous birds or any birds that live in villages, wildfowl, moorhen, the parrot and the starling; birds that strike with their beaks, web-footed birds, birds that scratch with their toes, and birds that dive and eat fish; or meat from a butcher or dried meat; or the heron or the crane, the raven or the wagtail; or (animals) that eat fish, or dung-heap pigs, or any fish.[28]

And it goes on like this for quite a while. Such lists rival Ashoka's edicts in unfathomable taxonomic principles, and Manu shares many of Ashoka's qualms: clearly, you can eat a great number of animals if you know your way around the rules; you may eat this, but not that.[x]

The Indian examples lead me to another hypothesis: I think these hedging lists are a way of dealing with moral ambivalence; if we list a number of animals we *don't* eat, we will feel okay about the ones we do eat—we will feel that we are obeying the law, doing something rational and permitted, when we eat certain animals. Jonathan Z. Smith argued that religious canons were formed in the same way as dietary restrictions: you could, theoretically, eat anything, but you arbitrarily limit what you can eat and then cook it in such a way that it resembles the things you have forbidden yourself.[29] Manu even has a line about this: 'If he has an addiction (to meat), let him make a sacrificial animal out of clarified butter or let him make a sacrificial animal out of flour.'[30] Clearly Manu has sympathy for the addicted carnivore with his veggie-cutlets.

---

[x] Manu rivals Leviticus too. Why don't Jews eat lobster or bacon? People used to say it was for health concerns, trichinosis from pigs, hepatitis from shellfish. And then Mary Douglas, in *Purity and Danger*, said, no, it's because certain animals are category errors, matter out of place, hence, dirt. See also 'Eating Karma'.

The hypothesis that inconsistent dietary laws are proof of unresolved ambivalence is supported by other evidence in Manu, for we find him, like Ashoka, beginning to hedge, and to offer excuses:

> Wild animals and birds that are permitted to be eaten may be killed by priests for sacrifices and for the livelihood of dependents. For Agastya did this long ago. Indeed, in the ancient sacrifices of the sages that were offered by priests and rulers, the sacrificial cakes were made of edible wild animals and birds. You may eat meat that has been consecrated by the sprinkling of water, or when priests want to have it, or when you are properly engaged in a ritual, or when your breath of life is in danger. Someone who eats meat, after honouring the gods and ancestors, when he has bought it, or killed it himself, or has been given it by someone else, does nothing bad. A priest should never eat sacrificial animals that have not been transformed by Vedic verses; but with the support of the obligatory rule, he may eat them when they have been transformed by Vedic verses. Herbs, sacrificial animals, trees, animals (other than sacrificial animals) and birds who have been killed for sacrifice win higher births again. A twice-born person who knows the true meaning of the Vedas and injures sacrificial animals for these (correct) purposes causes both himself and the animal to go to the highest level of existence. On the occasion of offering the honey-mixture (to a guest), at a sacrifice, and in rituals in which the ancestors are the deities, and only in these circumstances, should sacrificial animals suffer violence, but not on any other occasion; this is what Manu has said.[31]

And so forth. In other words, there are lots and lots of *religious* reasons why you can eat meat. Indeed, you *must* eat meat, precisely for religious reasons: 'When a man who is properly engaged in a ritual does not eat meat, after his death he will become a sacrificial animal during twenty-one rebirths.'[32] And finally we get the ultimate blatant denial: 'The violence [*himsa*] to those that move and those that do not move which is sanctioned by the Veda—that is known as ahimsa.'[33]

The dizzying lists of permitted and forbidden animals also serve the function of obfuscation, one of the great parlour tricks of any mythology: neatly sidestepping the unstated moral question—How can we bear to torment and/or kill animals?—the texts snare the reader or hearer in the great sweep of detail—the webbed feet, the milk of a camel—until the question disappears under a great pile of fins and feathers.

Manu even expresses a more general philosophy of carnivorousness:

The Lord of Creatures fashioned all this universe to feed the breath of life, and everything moving and stationary is the food of the breath of life. Those that do not move are food for those that move, and those that have no fangs are food for those with fangs; those that have no hands are food for those with hands; and cowards are the food of the brave. The eater who eats creatures with the breath of life who are to be eaten does nothing bad, even if he does it day after day; for the Creator himself created creatures with the breath of life, some to be eaten and some to be eaters.[34]

There is a similar verse in the *Mahabharata*: 'The mongoose eats mice, just as the cat eats the mongoose; the dog devours the cat, and wild beasts eat the dog.'[35] Such a justification of violence lies behind a later text in which the Brahmins tell the king, 'Violence is everywhere and, therefore, whatever the Jain renouncers say is blind arrogance. Can anyone keep alive without eating? And how is food to be got without violence? Is there anyone on earth who does not have a tendency towards violence? Your majesty! People live by violence alone . . . If a person thinks of his good qualities and thinks badly of others—then also he commits violence.'[36] It is ironic that in this very text, the 'violence' of thinking badly of others—what we would call intolerance—is committed against Jain renouncers, who are (blindly and arrogantly) accused of 'blind arrogance'.

The problem becomes still more complex when Manu goes on to speak passionately in favour of vegetarianism, of the benefits of *not* eating meat.[37] Manu transforms five of the earlier Vedic sacrifices (animal sacrifices in which violence is assumed) into five Hindu vegetarian sacrifices that avoid violence. He also argues that these five householder sacrifices are restorations for the evils committed by normal householders in domestic 'slaughter-houses' where small creatures are, often inadvertently, killed (an idea that now seems more Jain than Hindu, but in its day was widely shared): 'A householder has five slaughter-houses, whose use fetters him: the fireplace, the grindstone, the broom, the mortar and pestle, and the water jar. The great sages devised the five great sacrifices for the householder to do every day to redeem him from all of these (slaughter-houses) successively.'[38]

At first, Manu reflects the Vedic view of limited retribution in the Other World: 'A twice-born person who knows the rules should not eat meat against the rules, even in extremity; for if he eats meat against the rules, after his death he will be helplessly eaten by those that he ate. "He whose *meat* in this world do I eat/will in the other world *me eat*." Wise men say that this is why meat is called meat.'[39] But then Manu switches to the post-Vedic view of transmigration, rather than an Other World, and to vegetarianism with a vengeance: 'As many hairs as there are on the body of the sacrificial animal that he kills for no (religious) purpose here on earth, so many times will he, after his death, suffer a violent death in birth after birth. You can never get meat without violence to creatures with the breath of life, and the killing of creatures with the breath of life does not get you to heaven; therefore you should not eat meat.'[40]

One line of Manu seems quite modern in its concerns for the meat-packing industry: 'Anyone who looks carefully at the source of meat, and at the tying up and slaughter of embodied creatures, should turn back from eating any meat.'[41] And finally, for those who think that meat comes ready-made plastic-wrapped: 'The one who gives permission, the one who butchers, the one who slaughters, and the one who buys and sells, the one who prepares it, the one who serves it, and the eater—they are killers.'[42]

Manu offers far fewer pro-meat than anti-meat verses (three pro- and twenty-five anti-), and by the laws of Indian logic the view that he puts forth first (for the eating of meat) is the 'opponent's view', the *purva paksha*, the straw man, and the view that he states second, and finally (for vegetarianism), is where his heart lies. Yet he ends up firmly on the fence: 'There is nothing wrong in eating meat, nor in drinking wine, nor in sexual union, for this is how living beings engage in life, but disengagement yields great fruit.'[43] These activities are permitted under the specified circumstances, but it is better to refrain from them altogether. There is a chain of food and eaters that both justifies itself and demands that we break out of it: it happens, but it must not happen.[44] The question is simply how one is going to live, and kill to live, until death.

The minor tremors, tiny fault-lines in the Vedic ritual armour, eventually gave way to a major Hindu earthquake. But this disquieted conscience concerning sacrificial slaughter does not completely come out of the ritual closet until Hinduism is in full spate, in the Puranic period. At that time, it takes the form of a corpus of Hindu myths about Vedic sacrifice and about cows—myths that simultaneously legitimate Hindu practices by presenting them in the guise of Vedic paradigms while they undercut, often by quite sharp satire, the entire rationale for one of the pillars of the Vedic sacrifice: the killing of animals.[xi] Moreover, as the sociologist M.N. Srinivas pointed out, vegetarianism is the most important habit that the lower castes took

[xi] See 'Sacred Cows'.

upon themselves when they wanted to move up the social ladder through the process known as 'Sanskritization'.[45]

GANDHI

In Gandhi's hands, nonviolence came to mean not just opposition to blood sacrifice but opposition to the British, without spilling their blood any more than an adherent of traditional ahimsa would spill the blood of a sacrificial animal. People called his policy of 'holding on to truth' (*satyagraha*) passive non-resistance (some would call it passive aggressive non-resistance), but he himself resisted the term 'passive', arguing that *satyagraha* was an active measure.[46]

Gandhi was well aware that there has never been true nonviolence in India (or anywhere else, for that matter). He once remarked, 'Indeed the very word, nonviolence, a negative word, means that it is an effort to abandon the violence that is inevitable in life.'[47] He could not simply pick up off the rack a nonviolence already perfected by centuries of Hindu meditation; it was a much-disputed concept. He had to reinvent nonviolence before he could use it in an entirely new situation, as a political strategy, against the British Raj. Writing about the *Gita*, Gandhi granted:

> It may be freely admitted that the Gita was not written to establish ahimsa ... [I]f the Gita believed in ahimsa or it was included in desirelessness, why did the author adopt a warlike illustration? When the Gita was written, although people believed in ahimsa, wars were not only not taboo, but no one observed the contradiction between them and ahimsa.'[48]

PRESENT-DAY INDIA

In addition to rethinking the nature of the Vedic animal sacrifice in myths, later Hinduism took further steps to come to terms with the ritual killing of animals. We have seen that in the Vedic sacrifice vegetable oblations were the minimally acceptable lowest form of the sacrificial victim, the *pashu*. Under the influence of Buddhism or, more generally, of the doctrine of ahimsa that became a part of both Hinduism and Buddhism, a revisionary attitude toward the use of vegetable offerings came to the fore, one which continues to the present day. The carnivorous Vedic gods were generally replaced by strictly vegetarian Hindu deities who are said to accept no blood offerings, but only rice, fruits, flowers and so forth. The vegetable offerings are obviously not animal victims; they are, however, often symbols of the now objectionable blood sacrifices of the Vedic past. The deity in the centre of the Hindu temple (an aspect of Shiva or Vishnu or a goddess) is often a strict vegetarian who accepts no blood offerings, only rice, or rice cakes, as well as fruits, flowers and so forth, while there may be another deity, outside the temple, to whom blood sacrifices are made. Sometimes the vegetarian deity in the inner shrine is a god, and the carnivorous deity outside is a goddess.

Nowadays, throughout India, the Brahmin priest often sacrifices a goat made of dough and papier-mâché, as several ritual texts allow.[49] But the flesh-eating Vedic god may still cast his shadow on the vegetarian sacrifice; the whole coconuts that the deity fancies bear a suspicious resemblance to human heads (a resemblance that is sometimes explicitly mentioned in the accompanying liturgy and in myths about human sacrifice). When a Vedic sacrifice was recently performed in India under the auspices of Western scholars,[50] and objections were raised against the slaughter of goats, rice cakes alone were used. But the rice cakes were wrapped in leaves, tied to little leashes, and carefully 'suffocated' before they were offered, a clear atavism from the Vedic sacrifice in which, as we know, a living animal was suffocated.[xii] When a Vedic sacrifice was performed in London in 1996, there was not even a vegetable substitute for the sacrificial beast; the beasts were 'entirely imagined'. The priest didn't walk around the imaginary victims, or tie them to a (real or imaginary) stake, as one would do with a live animal, but he did mime suffocating them, and sprinkled water where they should have been. But when a Vedic sacrifice was performed in India in 1955, and public protest prevented the sacrificers from slaughtering a goat, another sacrificer protested the revisionist ritual by offering the same sacrifice—with animal victims—on the outskirts of town.[51]

The role of politics in the seemingly humanitarian and/or religious aspects of the treatment of animals cannot be overrated. Just as cow protection became a political, anti-Muslim cause, so did vegetarianism become one of the banners of Nationalism and, in our day, of Hindutva.[xiii] On my visit to New York on the occasion of the National Book Critics Circle Awards in 2009, the Hindus who picketed against me there made sure that the media coverage included the fact that they would afterwards go and eat vegetarian samosas, as if their vegetarian habits gave them the moral high ground over me, as if it gave *all* Hindus, all vegetarians, the

[xii] See 'Sacrifice and Substitution'.
[xiii] See 'You Can't Make an Omelette'.

high moral ground. Ironically, one of the objections by Hindu readers of that ilk to my book *The Hindus* was that it was demeaning to Hindus because I spent so much time talking about dogs and horses.

Clearly the ambivalence of ahimsa has been dichotomized, but never resolved. Every human and every animal dies, every human and every animal must eat, and eating requires that someone or something (since vegetables are part of the continuum of life, too) must die. The replacement of animal with vegetable offerings obviates neither the need to represent the rice cakes as real animals nor the necessity to 'kill' them in the sacrifice. The ambivalence toward the killing of an animal in Hinduism is another manifestation of the paradoxical conflict between the need to offer oneself to the god and the need to stay alive, which is a variant on the more basic paradox at the heart of all sacrifice: one must kill to live.[xiv]

[xiv] See 'Sacrifice and Substitution'.

ZOOMORPHISM IN ANCIENT INDIA: HUMANS MORE BESTIAL THAN THE BEASTS[1]

S anskrit texts are rich in anthropomorphism, projecting human qualities upon animals, but they more particularly abound in zoomorphism, imagining humans as animals. Anthropomorphism, though more common than zoomorphism in India (as elsewhere), tells us comparatively little about animals; an anthropomorphic text assumes a basic identification, such as lion as king, and then, although the object of discourse is, theoretically, an animal, the text imagines the animal as behaving the way the human does, betraying the fact that the author is interested only in kings and not at all in lions. Zoomorphism is more complex: although this time a human being is the explicit object, the bestial qualities imputed to the human usually reveal an observation of animals that is more detailed (if no more accurate) than that of anthropomorphism, and the text teaches us simultaneously what sort of person the author thinks that animal is like and what sort of animal the author thinks that sort of person is like. And where anthropomorphism simply leaps over our knowledge that most animals cannot speak, zoomorphism seizes upon language as a point of potential difference between humans and animals, and worries that point in various ways, imputing human speech to certain individual animals, and to certain individual humans, either muteness or the ability to understand animals.

Let us begin with a quick survey of the relatively straightforward texts of anthropomorphism in India and progress to the more challenging texts of zoomorphism.

ANTHROPOMORPHISM

Sanskrit literature abounds in animal imagery. India is famous for its beast fables, in which animals stand for human types and point human morals: the lion as king, the cunning jackal as his chief minister, clever monkeys and foolish donkeys, the ongoing battle of the crows against the owls. The most famous collection of these stories is the *Panchatantra*, probably composed about 500 CE but drawing upon much older Buddhist sources. These tales, known to Europeans from Aesop's fables, were tracked to their lair by nineteenth-century German folklorists: a Pahlavi (literary Persian) translation perhaps as early as 550 CE was translated first into Syriac and then into Arabic c. 750, whence it entered European literature through Moorish contacts in Spain and elsewhere. The *Panchatantra* is a textbook of political science, probably intended for the education of princes, but its cast of characters was widely diffused into all levels of Indian literature, from folktales in the vernaculars to court poetry in Sanskrit. The heron or the cat, for instance, is a widespread image of the religious hypocrite.[i] Animals also serve as metaphors more broadly in Indian culture: the dominant metaphor, indeed cliché, for anarchy is the law of the fishes (*matsya-nyaya*): the big fish eat the little fish.

Indian mythology also used fish as a metaphor for an alternative consciousness. One tale, in a Sanskrit text, assumes that we can know about the happiness of fish, but that this very understanding may lead to the problem of human involvement:

> There was once a sage named Saubhari, who spent twelve years immersed in a pond. In that pond there lived a great fish who had many children and grandchildren. The young fish played around the great fish all day, and he lived happily among them. Their games began to disturb the sage's meditations; he noticed them and thought, 'How enviable is that fish, always playing so happily with his children. He makes me want to taste that pleasure, too, and to play happily with my own children.' And so the sage got out of the water and went to the king to demand a bride. He married the king's fifty daughters and had a hundred and fifty sons, but eventually he realized that his desires were self-perpetuating and hence insatiable, and that he must return to the meditations that the fish had disturbed. So he abandoned his children and his wives and returned to the forest.[2]

The Hindu sage's empathetic assumption is right: the fish are happy, taking pleasure in the same thing that humans take pleasure in, playing with their children. We might ask if the sage could have been made aware of the pleasures of child-rearing by a vision not of fish but of humans and their children, but the text implies that the sage has left human company and

---

[i] See 'The Concept of Heresy'.

hence would not see human children. Moreover, the sage understands the fish (where he might not have understood his fellow men and women) because he has become, in effect, a kind of animal himself: fish-like, he lives underwater, in a trans-human condition made possible by his extraordinary ascetic powers. But the sage is mistaken in believing that he personally can be happy like a fish, or rather that such happiness is desirable for him: he comes to learn that though other people may be like fish (in enjoying their children), he himself is not like them, and hence, though fish-like (in being non-human), he is not like a fish (in procreation).

TALKING ANIMALS, LISTENING HUMANS

A liminal space between anthropomorphism and zoomorphism is marked out by a mythological cluster about talking animals and humans who commit the fatal error of mistaking sexual humans for animals.[3] This corpus is found in both of the great Sanskrit epics, the *Ramayana*[ii] and the *Mahabharata*. These myths argue that we often mistake animals for people, and the reverse, in sexual (or quasi-sexual) situations. They also imply that people become animals, and therefore in a sense unrecognizable, in the sexual act that Shakespeare's Iago imagined as a 'beast with two backs' [*Othello* 1.1]. Already in the Upanishads, the Creator's daughter takes the form of a series of animals, beginning with a mare, in her vain attempt to flee from her father's incestuous attacks [BAU 1.4.1-6], and the Vedic goddess Saranyu becomes a mare to flee from her husband's unwanted sexual demands. [RV 10.72][iii] The ultimate result of this conflation is that human hunters often mistake other humans for animals, particularly when they are mating—a mistake that has fatal consequences not only for the animals but for the unlucky hunter.

Near the beginning of the *Mahabharata* [M 1.109], Pandu, the father of the Pandavas, is cursed to die in the embrace of his own wife because he killed a sage whom he mistook for a stag when the sage was mating with his wife (they had taken the form of a stag and a doe to do this, because they were too embarrassed to do it as humans). Elsewhere in the *Mahabharata* [M 1.173], another king who has been cursed to become a man-eating demon devours a sage who is making love to his wife (still in human form) and the wife, furious because she had not 'finished', curses the king to die if he embraces his own wife. These mistakes are not limited to the sexual

[ii] See 'Shadows of the *Ramayana*'.
[iii] See 'The Submarine Mare' and 'Saranyu-Samjna'.

arena. Later in this text [M 8.20], the warrior Karna kills a young calf by mistake (presumably mistaking it for a wild animal) and is cursed to fail in a crucial battle. And at the end of the story [M 17.5], the incarnate god Krishna dies when a hunter named Old Age mistakes him for an animal and shoots him in the foot, the only part of him that is mortal, like Achilles' heel or the spot on Siegfried's back.

In the *Ramayana*, Rama's father, king Dasharatha, out on a hunt, mistakes a boy for an elephant and is cursed by the boy's parents to lose his own son. [R 2.57-8] Later, when Ravana plots to capture Sita, he gets another demon to take the form of a marvellous golden deer, who captivates Sita and inspires her to ask Rama to pursue it for her. Rama suspects that it is a demon in disguise (he wishes that he could talk to it), but Sita insists. The deer leads Rama far away from Sita, and, when Rama kills the deer, and it assumes its true demonic form, Rama realizes that he has been tricked and has thereby lost Sita, whom Ravana has captured in Rama's absence. [R 3.41-44] Thus, once again, the killing of a human (here a demon) in animal form causes the hunter to suffer the curse of separation from his partner.

The theme of language first enters this corpus on the outside frame of the *Ramayana*, where we learn that the author, the poet Valmiki, was searching for a poetic language in which to tell the story when he went to bathe in a river. There he saw a hunter kill the male of a pair of mating cranes (Indian saras cranes), and when the hen grieved, Valmiki cried out, 'Hunter, since you killed one of these birds at the height of its passion, you will not live very long.' Then Valmiki realized that he had instinctively uttered this curse in verse, in a meter (the meter in which both the *Ramayana* and the *Mahabharata* are composed) that he called the *shloka*, because it was uttered in sorrow (*shoka*). [R 1.1-2] With this link added to the narrative chain, the corpus of stories combines five major themes: succumbing to the lust for hunting; mistaking a human for an animal and killing the 'animal'; interrupting the sexual act (by killing one or both of the partners); understanding the language of animals; and creating a poetic language. Killing an animal interrupts the sexual act, the animal act, killing sex, as it were, and producing in its place the characteristic human act, the making of language.

Another tale in the *Ramayana* also ties together the themes of the interruption of sexuality, the curse of separation from a beloved, the deadly nature of erotic love, and the language of birds:

A king, the father of Rama's evil stepmother, had been given the boon
of understanding the cries of all creatures, but he was warned that he

must not tell anyone about it. Once when he was in bed with his wife he heard a bird[4] say something funny and he laughed. She thought he was laughing at her, and she wanted to know why, but he said he would die if he told her. When she insisted that he tell her nevertheless, he sent her away and lived happily without her for the rest of his life [R 2.32].[5]

As an indirect result of his ability to comprehend the language of birds, this king hears a bird talking when he is in a sexual situation and laughs, which exposes him to the danger of death and separates him from his mate. This story is in many ways the inversion of the story of Valmiki, who sees a bird who is killed in a sexual situation, hence separated from his mate, which makes him cry and inspires him to invent an unusual language of humans. Or, to forge another link, this king (Rama's step-grandfather, as it were) is forced to become separated from his wife, just as Rama's father is cursed to become separated from his son Rama. The two episodes are related: the stepmother, daughter of the woman who wanted to know why the bird laughed, is the paradigmatic evil co-wife, who uses sexual blackmail to force Rama's father to disinherit Rama, an act that is regarded as directly responsible for the father's death; so she does kill her husband, as her mother failed to do.

Significantly, the man in this story is allowed to understand the speech of animals, and the woman is not. This is in keeping with the underlying Hindu misogyny of the Sanskrit mythological texts that depict men as more gifted with special powers than women are; it may also reflect the actual sociological fact that men in India were allowed to read and speak Sanskrit, while in general women were not.[iv] In a broader sense, as we will see, all hyper-sexualized women are represented as talking animals—but not as talking *with* animals. In this corpus as a whole, there are logical links between, on the one hand, killing a human (who has human speech) whom you mistake for an animal (which lacks human speech) or who has become an animal (to express the bestial sexual impulse) and, on the other hand, becoming a human who has a uniquely poetic language. That is to say, these stories express the idea that the possession of human speech is a prerogative that may deprive humans of their sexuality but may deprive animals of their lives—and may deprive of their lives humans who resort to

---

[iv] There are exceptions to this rule, such as an explicit statement in the *Kamasutra* (1.3.11) that some women were capable of reading such texts, but in general it prevailed. See 'Reading the *Kamasutra*'.

animal sexuality. Or, to put it differently, there are logical links between, on the one hand, sexual transformation (humans becoming animals in the sexual act, regarded as an animal act) and, on the other hand, linguistic transformation (the creation of speech which distinguishes humans from animals and, sometimes, women from men). Sexuality makes humans into animals; language makes animals into humans.

ZOOMORPHISM

We have now seen one reason why, in Hindu myths, humans become animals: to partake of animal sexuality. But there are other reasons why humans—and even gods—become animals, and this takes us deeper into the realm of zoomorphism. The god Dharma takes the form of a dog in the *Mahabharata*;[v] the god Vishnu becomes incarnate as several animals (including a fish, tortoise, boar, half-lion and horse-head); and the god Indra becomes a stallion in order to seduce a queen.[vi] And mortals become animals too.

Humans are animals in several different senses in the *Kamasutra* of Vatsyayana.[vii] Here, humans are distinguished from animals precisely by their sexuality, in the argument that the author puts forward to justify his text [KS 1.2.16-20]:

> Scholars say: 'It is appropriate to have a text about religion (dharma), because it concerns matters not of this world, and to have one about power (artha), because that is achieved only when the groundwork is laid by special methods, which one learns from a text. But since even animals manage sex (kama) by themselves, and since it goes on all the time, it should not have to be handled with the help of a text.' Vatsyayana says: Because a man and a woman depend upon one another in sex, it requires a method, and this method is learnt from the *Kamasutra*. The mating of animals, by contrast, is not based upon any method, because they are not fenced in, they mate only when the females are in their fertile season and until they achieve their goal, and they act without thinking about it first.[viii]

Yashodhara's thirteenth-century commentary on the *Kamasutra* expands upon these ideas:

> Even animals like cows, whose intellects are shrouded in torpor, visibly manage sex without instruction from a textbook; how much

[v] See 'Dogs as Dalits'.
[vi] See 'Indra as the Stallion's Wife'.
[vii] See 'Reading the *Kamasutra*'.
[viii] See 'Three (or More)'.

more must this happen among humans, whose intellects consist primarily of passion? As it is said:

> For desire is satisfied without instruction,
> and does not have to be taught.
> Who is the guru for deer and birds, for the methodology
> to give and take pleasure with those they desire?

And desire goes on all the time, because the qualities of wanting and hating are always there in the soul. These scholars are people who talk about religion, power and release (dharma, artha and moksha). There is no guarding or any other form of concealment, because the females of the species are loose. Animals mate only during their fertile season. Humans who want children, however, do it during a woman's fertile season but also outside her fertile season, in order to enjoy and please the woman. So animals and humans are not the same. And so the law book says:

> You may have sex with a woman in her fertile season
> —or any time when it is not expressly forbidden.

And animals engage in sex just until they achieve a climax; they do not wonder, 'Has he reached his climax or not?' and, therefore, wish to mate a second time. And so, since the goal of animals and humans is not the same, animals need no method for sex. Animals, moreover, do not first think, before engaging in sex, 'What will happen to religion, power, sons, relatives and the prosperity of our faction?' Sex just happens to animals in their own way.

The commentator here alludes to the Hindu belief that matter consists in three 'strands' (torpor, passion and lucidity; *tamas*, *rajas* and *sattva*), and that different creatures are made up of different proportions of these strands: cows have an abundance of torpor, where human beings abound in passion. (Only higher creatures like gods have a preponderance of lucidity.) He also belittles the views of scholars who substitute moksha (the fourth human goal, according to another paradigm) for kama (the third and final human goal in this paradigm).[ix] Here again human language is explicitly contrasted with animal sexuality: humans, whose sexuality is more complex, more repressed ('fenced in', as the text puts it), require language, where animals do not.

Humans, therefore, have a different sexuality from animals, and need a text for it, where animals do not. But when we move from the world of

[ix] See 'Three (or More)'.

science to the world of metaphor, within this same text, the *Kamasutra*, it appears that some humans are very much like animals *precisely* in their sexuality. The text offers a sexual typology according to size:

> The man is called a 'hare', 'bull' or 'stallion' according to the size of his sexual organ; a woman, however, is called a 'doe', 'mare' or 'elephant cow'. And so there are three equal couplings, between sexual partners of similar size, and six unequal ones, between sexual partners of dissimilar size. Among the unequal ones, when the man is larger there are two couplings with the two sexual partners immediately smaller than him and one, when he is largest, with the smallest woman. But in the opposite case, in a coupling when the man is smaller, there are two sorts of couplings with the two women immediately larger than him and one, when he is smallest, with the largest woman. Among these, the equal couplings are the best, the largest and the smallest are the worst, and the rest are intermediate. Even in the medium ones, it is better for the man to be larger than the woman. Thus there are nine sorts of couplings according to size. [KS 2.1.1-4]

As usual, the commentary is enlightening:

> The sexual organ is called the 'sign' [*lingam*], because it is the sign of femaleness and so forth. From texts and from experience it is known that the male organ is convex and the female organ concave. If the man's penis is small, like a hare's, he is called a 'hare'; if medium, a 'bull'; if large, a 'stallion'. The word 'however' indicates that women are distinct; they have a different nomenclature because they have a different sexual organ. Knowing this, scholars called them 'doe' and so forth instead of 'hare' and so forth.

The horse, hyper-sexualized, is the only animal that appears in both male and female form, though these two are not regarded as equal; the stallion is the largest male, while the mare is merely a middle-sized woman. Yet, in Hindu mythology, the mare is regarded as sexually enormous, bigger than the bull (with whom the *Kamasutra* pairs her) and an image of repressed violence: the doomsday fire is lodged in the mouth of a mare who wanders on the floor of the ocean, waiting for the moment when she will be released, to burn everything to ashes.[x] Moreover, the largest woman—the 'elephant cow'—is encouraged to employ the one sexual position associated with a mare, one involving dangerous tightness, not daunting enormity:

[x] See 'The Submarine Mare'.

'In the "mare's trap", which can only be done with practice, she grasps him, like a mare, so tightly that he cannot move.' [KS 2.6. 21] And the cow does not appear here as one of the three sexual types at all, though she epitomizes the 'animal' position in sexual intercourse, the equivalent of the English term 'doggy-style': 'When she gets on the ground on all fours and he mounts her like a bull, that is "sex like a cow."' [KS 2.6. 39] Clearly the six paradigmatic animals are chosen for their size rather than their established cultural symbolism, but the disparity in their sizes reveals their deeper symbolic implications for the relationship between men and women. The nomenclature as a whole also constantly implies that, despite the text's insistence that the sexuality of animals is different from that of humans, there is a very basic sense in which sex, even when done according to the book, as it were, is bestial.

Thus there are two different, conflicting agendas embedded in these passages: ideally, 'equal is best', but in fact the man has to be bigger. This is because women are by nature bigger, in the sense that their sexuality, according to almost all Hindu texts that refer to the subjects of procreation/ sex, women, marriage and so on, is bigger; they are harder to satisfy. Just as elephants are bigger than stallions, so, as the commentator points out in the context of an argument about female orgasm, women have far more desire than men: 'Women want a climax that takes a long time to produce, because their desire is eight times that of a man. Given these conditions, it is perfectly right to say that "a fair-eyed woman cannot be sated by men", because men's desire is just one eighth of women's.' [on KS 2.1.19] Here he is quoting a well-known Sanskrit saying:

> A fire is never sated by any amount of logs,
> nor the ocean by the rivers that flow into it;
>   death cannot be sated by all the creatures in the world,
>   nor a fair-eyed woman by any amount of men.[xi]

In another text, a serial female-to-male bisexual[xii] says, when she is a woman, that a woman has eight times as much pleasure (kama) as a man, which could also be translated as eight times as much desire.[6]

Later in the *Kamasutra*, the greater animality of women is assumed in a passage that makes them, in contrast with men, creatures both explicitly likened to animals and said to speak a meaningless animal language:

[xi] See 'Why Should a Brahmin?' and 'The Third Nature'.
[xii] See 'Transsexual Transformations and 'Bisexuality'.

There are eight kinds of screaming: whimpering, groaning, babbling, crying, panting, shrieking, or sobbing. And there are various sounds that have meaning, such as 'Mother!' 'Stop!' 'Let go!' 'Enough!' As a major part of moaning she may use, according to her imagination, the cries of the dove, cuckoo, green pigeon, parrot, bee, nightingale, goose, duck and partridge. He strikes her on her back with his fist when she is seated on his lap. Then she pretends to be unable to bear it and beats him in return, while groaning, crying, or babbling. If she protests, he strikes her on the head until she sobs, using a hand whose fingers are slightly bent, which is called the 'out-stretched hand'. At this she babbles with sounds inside her mouth, and she sobs. When the sex ends, there is panting and crying. Shrieking is a sound like a bamboo splitting, and sobbing sounds like a berry falling into water. Always, if a man tries to force his kisses and so forth on her, she moans and does the very same thing back to him. When a man in the throes of passion slaps a woman repeatedly, she uses words like 'Stop!' or 'Let me go!' or 'Enough!' or 'Mother!' and utters screams mixed with laboured breathing, panting, crying and groaning. As passion nears its end, he beats her extremely quickly, until the climax. At this, she begins to babble, fast, like a partridge or a goose. Those are the ways of groaning and slapping. [KS 2.7.1-21]

It is worth noting that these women make the noises of birds, never of mammals, let alone the mammals that characterize the three paradigmatic sizes of women. Birds, as we have seen, are implicated in the Hindu mythology of fatal sexuality linked with language. Moreover, one of the birds whose babbling the sexual woman imitates—the parrot—appears elsewhere in the *Kamasutra* as one of the two birds who can be taught to speak like humans: teaching parrots and mynah birds to talk is a skill that both a man and a woman should learn, and that a man can use to lure a woman to his home (the ancient Indian equivalent of coming up to see his etchings). [KS 1.3.15, 1.4.8, 6.1.15]

The passage about slapping and groaning inculcates what we now recognize as the rape mentality—'her mouth says no, but her eyes say yes'—a dangerous line of thought that leads ultimately to places where we now no longer want to be: disregarding a woman's protests against rape. And this treatment of women is justified by a combination of the official naming of women after over-sized animals, with over-sized desire, and the expectation that in the throes of passion women will become animals and lose their human speech. Thus, the commentator assures us, speaking of the woman who has the most sexual energy (of three types) and lasts longest (also of three types): 'The passion even of a long-lasting woman whose sexual energy is fierce is quelled when she is slapped.' [KS 2.7.11] The behaviour of the woman—making animal noises—is a ritualized action regarded as appropriate for her gender.

In the *Ramayana*, the fact that Hanuman can speak Sanskrit, and that monkeys in general can speak human languages, forces humans to apply human ethical considerations to monkeys alone among animals.[xiii] The natural zoomorphism of women is the other side of the coin of this liminal anthropomorphism of the epics, in which some animals speak human languages and some humans—males, in contrast with females—are privileged to understand the language of animals. In the full spate of sexuality, women lose their human language and become like animals. To compare this scenario with the paradigm of the death of copulating animals, we might say that, in an inversion of the myth of the creation of poetic language by the violent interruption of sex, violent sex implies the suspension of language.[7] Men may, sometimes, become like women who have become like animals, moaning and screaming instead of using male human speech. But a modern feminist would say that it is not at such moments of role reversal but when men expect women to behave like animals, while they themselves behave like men, that the men are truly behaving like animals.

BEYOND SEXUALITY:
LANGUAGE AND COMPASSION FOR ANIMALS

Language is the place from which compassion springs. It is difficult, though not impossible, to torment—or eat—the people we speak with. Elaine Scarry made the first point, in reverse, when she argued that torture takes away speech,[8] and Lewis Carroll made the second when the Red Queen, having introduced Alice to the roast ('Alice—mutton: Mutton—Alice'), commanded: 'It isn't etiquette to cut any one you've been introduced to. Remove the joint!'[9] This compassion-inducing language need not be even the sign language of chimps, let alone the whistles of dolphins or the body language of primates; it may be no more than the silent language of the eyes. Emmanuel Levinas once said that the face of the other says, 'Don't kill me'.[10] This is the language that inspires empathy, the language that is denied by people who defend the right to treat animals as mere things, through a self-serving tautology.[11]

The belief that all animals may be in some sense less other than they

---

[xiii] See 'Shadows of the *Ramayana*'.

seem to be is the source of the ever-enchanting myth of a magic time or place or person that erases the boundary between humans and animals. The time of this animal paradise finds a close parallel in the myth that tells of the time when gods walked among people or people walked among gods. The place, like the magic place in the Looking-Glass forest where things have no names, where Alice could walk with her arms around the neck of a fawn, is like the high mountains where people mingle with the gods. And the particular individual with these special powers finds a parallel in the myth of a particular person (often a shaman or a priest) who has the special ability to traffic with the gods. Famous examples of such people who live at peace among animals would include Enkidu in the epic of *Gilgamesh*, Francis of Assisi and the many mythical children who are taken from their human parents and raised as cubs by a pack of animals, like Romulus and Remus, Mowgli and Tarzan—and, by extension, Krishna (among the cows).

Anthropomorphism and zoomorphism are two different attempts to reduce the otherness between humans and animals, to see the sameness beneath the difference. But sameness, just like difference, may lead to the inhuman treatment of both humans and non-humans.[12] The ethical decision to treat animals according to the basic standards of human decency is one that must be taken regardless of whether we prefer to emphasize the qualities that they share with us—such as their sexuality—or those that they do not—their language. Hindus made this decision again and again throughout their history, insisting on the equal consciousness, the equivalent if not identical souls, of humans and animals despite the very different paths that the two groups walk on this planet.

THE MYTHOLOGY OF HORSES IN INDIA[1]

Horses are not indigenous to India, and while there is some evidence that they were found in the Indus Valley Civilization, it is slender: among the many other animals, from monkeys to rhinos, that figure abundantly on Harappan seals, the horse (probably imported even back then) rarely if ever appears. It became an important—even central—figure only in the Vedic age. The most widely accepted, though by no means unchallenged,[i] theory now is that the horse was brought to India, along with the Sanskrit language, by the Indo-Europeans.[ii] The history of the mythology of horses in India demonstrates the ways in which the people of India first identified horses with the people who migrated to their part of the world, or invaded them, on horseback, and then identified themselves with the horses, in effect positioning themselves as their own exploiters.

The horse was a charismatic symbol throughout the history of Hinduism. The horse, rather than the cow, was the animal whose ritual importance and intimacy with humans kept it from being regarded as food,[2] though not from being killed in sacrifices. In the Vedic period, horses were essential not only to drawing swift battle-chariots but to herding cattle, always easier to do from horseback in places where the grazing grounds are extensive.[3] We have noted the importance of the Vedic horse sacrifice[iii] and the founding Vedic myth of a goddess who takes the form of a mare.[iv] And we will soon see a rigged bet about the tail of a horse begin a tragic feud in the *Mahabharata*,[4] and the image of a submarine mare resurface in myths of passion and destruction.[v] Horses pull the chariot of the sun, and

---

[i] The long-held assumption that the Aryans invaded India has been qualified and re-evaluated in different ways by Thomas R. Trautmann, *Aryans and British India*, and Klaus K. Klostermaier, *A Survey of Hinduism*, taking into account contemporary Indian scholarship.
[ii] See 'Three (or More)'.
[iii] See 'Sacrifice and Substitution' and 'The Ambivalence of Ahimsa'.
[iv] See 'Saranyu-Samjna'.
[v] See 'The Submarine Mare'.

horse-headed figures—the twin Ashvins, Vishnu in his Veda-rescuing form of Hayagriva, the centaur-like Kimpurushas—gallop through Hindu mythology. The paradox of the Hindu horse lies in its persistence as an image of glamour and power among people who could not afford to own horses.

THE HORSE IN ANCIENT INDIA

Most of the peoples who entered India rode in on horseback and then continued to import horses into India: the people formerly known as Indo-Europeans (who brought their horses with them), the Turkish people who became the Mughals (who imported Arabian horses from Central Asia and Persia, overland and by sea) and the British (who imported thoroughbreds and hunters from England at first, and then Walers from Australia). In the *Rig Veda*, the horse represented the 'Aryas', as they called themselves, against the indigenous inhabitants of India, the Dasyus or 'slaves', whom they associated with the serpent Vritra. This is a mythology in which the horse that conquers the snake represents 'us' against 'them'.[vi] The political symbolism of the Vedic royal horse sacrifice is blatant: the king's men 'set free' the consecrated white stallion to wander for a year before he was brought back to the home and killed. During that year, he was guarded by an army that 'followed' him and claimed for the king any land on which he grazed. The king's army, therefore, drove the horse onward and guided him into the lands that the king intended to take over. Thus the ritual that presented itself as a casual equine stroll over the king's lands was in fact an orchestrated annexation of the lands on a king's border. No wonder the Sanskrit texts insist that a king had to be very powerful indeed before he could undertake a horse sacrifice.[5]

Horses move around in search of new grazing land, which they need constantly because, unlike cows, they pull up the roots of the grass or eat it right down to the ground so that it doesn't grow back, thus quickly destroying grazing land, which may require some years to recover. The horse is constantly in search of new territory. And the ancient Indian horse-owners mimicked this behaviour, as they responded to the need to provide grazing for their horses once they had captured them and kept them from their natural free-grazing habits. They rode over other peoples' land and took it over for their own herds. This spirit was expressed in their very vocabulary; the word *amhas* ('constriction')—from which comes our 'anxiety'—expressed the terror of being hemmed in or trapped; and the

---

[vi] As in the icon of St George, on horseback, killing the dragon.

word *prithu* ('broad and wide') is the word for the earth (Prthivi, the feminine form) and the name of the first king, the man whose job it was to widen the boundaries of his territory.[6]

It was not merely, as is often argued, that the horse made possible conquest in war, through the chariot; the horse came to symbolize conquest in war, through its own natural imperialism. But it is not easy for a stallion to find good grazing land in South Asia, for he is not well adapted to conditions in most of the area. He is uncomfortable in the humid heat of the Indian plains, and during the monsoon rains his hooves soften in the wet soil and pieces break off, resulting in painful, recurring sores. The Deccan Plateau and Central India provide suitable grazing land, but this becomes parched between May and September.[7] Though the Indian soil apparently has enough lime and calcium to support cattle, it is not good soil for horses; contemporary breeders now add calcium, manganese, iron and salt to the horses' diet. After Independence, Indian breeders found some places suitable for breeding (though I heard Hindu and Parsi stud owners complain, still in 1996, that Pakistan got the best grazing land). Today, in Punjab, Maharashtra and Karnataka there is some horse-breeding, and Pune, Mumbai and Calcutta are breeding centres for thoroughbred horses. But the difficulties in breeding *large* horses are perennial. Kathiawar horses are good for long distances in the desert but are slightly built, not big or fast or strong enough for cavalry; the same is largely true of Arabian horses. And if no new stock is imported, the size of imported horses in India diminishes dramatically in just a few years. As one breeder told me, wistfully, 'If we had pasturage all year round, the horses would be an inch taller.'[8] Marco Polo, in the thirteenth century, noted the sorry state of horses in Malabar:

> No horses being bred in this country, the king and his three royal brothers expend large sums of money annually in the purchase of them . . . [I]t is my opinion that the climate of the province is unfavourable to the race of horses, and that from hence arises the difficulty in breeding or preserving them . . . A mare, although of a large size, and covered by a handsome horse, produces only a small ill-made colt, with distorted legs, and unfit to be trained for riding.[9]

It is not strictly true that there were 'no horses . . . bred' in Marco Polo's time. Horses were bred successfully in North India long before the Turkish invasions in the tenth century of the Common Era, and they continued to be bred under the Mughals. Later, the British established a stud in Bengal, bred some horses in the Punjab, and encouraged breeding in North India; at first they tried to establish a Bengal stud by importing 'good thoroughbred English stallions together with a supply of big, bony, halfbred English hunting mares to serve as a breeding-stock', and a small 'committee for the improvement of the breed of horses in India' was established in 1801.[10] But horses continued to be imported in large numbers, for several reasons.

The difficulties presented by the land and climate of India were compounded by the allegation, by people who may or may not have known what they were talking about, and who may or may not have wanted to slander the Hindus, that Indian kings and their servants simply did not know how to care for horses properly. A Vedic text mentions a horse who is set free so that he can eat ghee (clarified butter),[11] and the *Arthashastra* recommends the feeding of ghee to mares and foals, and a mash including meat and liquor for working horses.[12] Feeding ghee to horses is a really bad idea. Marco Polo said that 'For food they give them flesh dressed with rice and other prepared meats, the country not producing any grain besides rice'; moreover, 'in consequence, as it is supposed, of their not having persons properly qualified to take care of them or to administer the requisite medicines perhaps not three hundred of these [five thousand] remain alive, and thus the necessity is occasioned for replacing them annually.'[13] Or, in another version of the text, only a hundred remain out of two thousand; 'they all die because, they say, they have no grooms to come to them in sickness and know how to give a remedy; nor do they know how to care for them . . . they die from bad care and keeping.'[14] Rudyard Kipling expressed in *Kim* his scorn for 'native' horse management: 'They were camped on a piece of waste ground beside the railway, and, being natives, had not, of course, unloaded the two trucks in which Mahbub's animals stood among a consignment of country-breds bought by the Bombay tram-company.'[15] Note here, too, the reference to country-breds, an acknowledged if inferior breed.

In addition to the difficulties of grazing, and possible mistakes in feeding, there was a third reason for the failure of horses to thrive in India. Marco Polo suggested that it was no accident that there were no 'properly qualified' people to look after horses in India: 'The merchants who bring these horses to sell do not allow [the grooms] to go there, nor do they bring their [own] grooms, because [they wish] the horses of [the] kings to die in numbers soon, on purpose that they may be able to sell their horses as they will; from which they make very great wealth each year.'[16] South

Indians even today speak of the Arab trick of keeping not grooms but farriers out of India, so that the poor horses were simply ridden until their hooves wore down and they died, a kind of 'planned military obsolescence [which] added to the popular notion of the horse as an ephemeral, semi-divine creature (and made for steady business at the Arab end)'.[17] And this practice had important repercussions upon the history and mythology of the horse in India.

After each initial conquest, the rulers replenished their herds of horses with new stallions and mares imported from outside India, and this constant importing of new bloodlines made Indian horses extremely expensive. Ancient Sanskrit and Tamil sources (such as the *Arthashastra* and Cankam texts) observe that horses had to be imported, probably from Parthia. Sanskrit inscriptions from the ninth and tenth centuries tell us the northern route,[18] which is also described in Kipling's *Kim*, set in Northwest India: through Kabul, Peshawar, Pindi, Kangra, Ambala, Delhi and Gwalior, the route through which the Aryans and, later, the Turks entered India.

But from the earliest recorded period in Indian history there was, in addition to the overland route from Central Asia, also a southern route, by sea from Arabia. South Indians, particularly in the vicinity of Madurai, still tell stories about the Pandyan kings' energetic importation of horses,[19] and there is much more information about the lust for horses among later dynasties such as the Nayaks and the Vijaynagara kings. Both foreign and Indian sources testify that South Indians imported as many as 14,000 horses a year valued at 2,200,000 dinars of 'red gold',[20] and a sixteenth century South Indian king of Vijayanagara is reputed to have imported 13,000 horses annually for his own personal use and for his officers.[21] During this same period, 10,000 Arabic and Persian horses were imported into Malabar every year.[22] In Marco Polo's time, a horse cost five hundred saggi of gold, or one hundred marks of silver.[23] When the Europeans arrived in India in the Mughal period, the horse was a very expensive animal indeed, the best ones costing up to the equivalent of $10,000.[24] Heavy losses at sea are the primary reason for their high cost;[25] since horses cannot throw up, sea-sickness is almost always fatal, and 'shipping such fragile and valuable cargo in a pitching East Indiaman on a six-month journey halfway round the world' was a costly and risky venture. British horses also became more scarce, and even more expensive, when so many of them were used, and killed, in the Napoleonic Wars.[26]

Since horses were so expensive, no native village tradition of horses developed in India as it did among the natives of Ireland or Egypt, where farmers kept horses, or even in Southeast Asia, where horses were and still are used in a number of ways. Stall feeding, essential during the dry months, is out of the question for subsistence farmers, and in any case, the horse is rarely used as a work animal in India. It does not pull the plough, it seldom carries a pack, and except in Sind and the Punjab, it is not ridden much either. The only common use for the horse in India was, formerly, for military purposes, and nowadays, for pulling carriages.[27] Throughout Indian history, horses have belonged only to people who were not merely economically 'other' than the Hindu villagers—aristocrats—but politically and religiously other. The horse represented political power, military power, economic power; the tax-collector, or the punitive military expedition, rode into the village on horseback.

MUSLIM HORSES

Since the beginning of the invasions of India by the Arabs, the Turks, and then the Mughals, Muslims have played the role of good-and-evil foreigners in the horse mythologies of India. Hindus as well as Muslims worship at the shrines of Muslim 'horse saints'.[28] A trace of mystery, perhaps also of resentment, but also of glamour, hedges one of the best-known South Indian stories about Muslim/Arab horses, a story often retold, in Tamil, Telugu and other Dravidian languages.[29] This version is from a South Indian text composed in Sanskrit in the early sixteenth century:

> Vatavur had spent on the worship of Shiva the money given him by the king to buy horses. Shiva appeared to Vatavur and said, 'I will bring excellent horses; go to Madurai.' Days passed and no horses arrived. The king imprisoned Vatavur, who prayed to Shiva. Then Shiva, transforming a whole pack of jackals into horses, himself put on the costume of a horse-dealer. Having taken the form of a supreme horseman, he himself chose a horse that was splitting open the earth with his hoof in order to adorn the form of him [i.e. of Shiva] with the snakes [that lived underground], and the dust on Shiva's face was blown away by the hissing of the snakes that he wore in his hair. The king had the horses brought to his palace. He spent the whole day throwing to the horses food such as chickpeas [canaka]. Then the sun set. The horses went back to their jackalhood, gobbled up all the horses of the king, and went to the forests, like lions, their mouths smeared with blood. The grooms reported the various evil deeds of the horses.[30]

The false horses eat the other horses, as jackals would; but since they appear to be horses, they appear to be cannibals. The transformation into jackals might be regarded as a transformation from tame to wild, jackals being the untamed form of dogs; or from pure to impure, jackals, like other scavengers, being polluted and polluting, in contrast with the pure horse. Both of these categories would place the jackals with snakes as inversions of horses—and here we should note the presence of snakes in the metaphors describing the demonic, divine horses of Vatavur. Many Hindu myths depict Shiva as the ultimate other, a Dalit.[31] It is thus not really surprising to find him depicted here as a Muslim, or at least no more surprising than it is to find the god Dharma, the incarnation of Hindu religious law, incarnate as a dog (an animal that caste Hindus regard as an unclean scavenger[vii]) at the end of that great Sanskrit epic, the *Mahabharata*.[32] The statement that these horses eat other horses reveals this as a myth told by people who do not know horses, for such people generally fear the horse's mouth, with its big teeth. This is a dangerous misconception, for, as every horseman and horsewoman knows, though horses can indeed bite, it is the other end of the horse that poses the real danger—the back hooves—and horses are in any case strict vegetarians. The devouring equine mouth is a projection onto the horse of the violence that we inflict upon *it* in taming it, through the use of the bit in the mouth.

A different sort of Indian horse-story, from North India, tells us that seventy-two riders, including one woman, came from the sea and landed in Kutch; these people, called Jakhs, saved the local villagers from the depredations of a demon; the horses were then sent to Delhi, and on the way they fertilized the local mares;[33] or, according to another variant, the riders blessed childless women, including the queen, with children.[34] In most versions, the riders kill not a demon but a human, a tyrant named Punvro (or Punvaro), who had cut off the hands of the architect who had built the city of Patan (or Padhargadh) so that he might not construct anything like it for another prince.[35] Throughout the twentieth century, villagers in Kutch continued to make statues of the seventy-two horses and offer sweet rice to the horsemen and ask them for boons.[36]

Most versions of this myth emphasize the skin-colour of the invaders; they are 'white-skinned foreigners said to have come in the thirteenth century from Anatolia and Syria',[37] or 'white-skinned, horse-riding foreigners from Central Asia', or Greeks, Romans, Scythians, or White

[vii] See 'Dogs as Dalits'.

Huns, 'tall and of fair complexion, blue or grey-eyed'.[38] According to Stella Kramrisch, they stand for the Turks:

> Harking back to other, untold memories from Inner Asian horse-herding cultures, these apocalyptic horsemen transmute the fear generated by Muslim invasions into India into a liberating legend in which the evil power does not come from outside but is local, embodied in the tyrant Punvaro.[39]

These invaders are liberating Muslims; but another interpretation sees them as people liberated *from* Muslims, as 'Zoroastrians from the northern parts of Iran, who, during the whole of this period, were emigrating to India in search of the religious toleration which Islamic persecutors denied them in their own country'.[40]

Let us table for the moment the question of whether the invaders are liberating Muslims or liberated anti-Muslims, and ask, who is Punvaro? This myth may have grafted onto an apparently historical ruler the myth of the tyrant who cuts off the hands of artists, calling upon not 'untold memories' of Inner Asia but another, historically specific, myth about the British, who treated the weavers in Bengal so cruelly (there is abundant testimony about this)[41] that they were widely believed, apparently on no evidence, to have cut off the weavers' thumbs, or, on the basis of one piece of dubious evidence, to have so persecuted the winders of silk that they cut off their own thumbs in protest.[42] [viii] The legend lives on today in a contemporary story about an artisan from Kutch who made a diabolically clever box with a gun inside it, which fired when anyone opened the box; he gave it to the Marquess of Dalhousie,[ix] who gave it in turn to his adjutant (that is to say, his subaltern) to open; the adjutant was killed, and

---

[viii] The thumb-cutting story is found only in contemporary British accounts from the 1770s, when there was fierce rivalry between various factions of the East India Company's servants in Bengal and their supporters in London. The silk-winders' incident, reported by Wilhelm Bolts, a highly disreputable and probably unreliable witness, writing against his rivals in the Company, found its way into Edmund Burke's attacks on Warren Hastings and then into Indian writings in English in the late nineteenth century. The weavers were caught between the rapacity of the Indian agents who served as middlemen and the young Englishmen for whom they worked. But no contemporary Bengali writers, Hindu or Muslim, seem to have mentioned it, perhaps because they attached little importance to what happened to weavers, who were low-caste Muslims and Hindus.

[ix] James Andrew Broun-Ramsay, 1st Marquess of Dalhousie KT, PC (22 April 1812 – 19 December 1860), styled Lord Ramsay until 1838 and known as The Earl of Dalhousie between 1838 and 1849, was a Scottish statesman, and a colonial administrator in British India. He served as Governor General of India from 1848 to 1856.

Dalhousie had the craftsman's hands cut off.[43] The myth of the weavers' thumbs may also have grown out of the famous *Mahabharata* story of Ekalavya,[x] a dark-skinned, low-caste boy whose skill at archery rivalled that of the noble heroes, the Pandavas; to maintain the Pandavas' supremacy as archers, their teacher demanded that Ekalavya cut off his right thumb.[44]

The myth of Punvaro, in Kramrisch's gloss, turns history on its head, telling us that the Muslims saved the good citizens of Kutch from the British, an inversion of the self-serving British sentiment still repeated widely in Chennai (Madras) today, that the British, especially the early East India Company, liberated Hindus in South India from Muslim control and played not merely a neutral but a positive role in establishing an even-handed attitude to all religions in its new territory. In discussing this argument, Joanne Waghorne invoked the equestrian metaphor, beginning with the title of her article: 'Chariots of the God/s: Riding the Line between Hindu and Christian.'[45]

Thus, different versions of the equestrian myth cast different actors as the native villain and the invading heroes. This Kutch tradition may or may not know the ancient Vedic myth of the hegemonic horse trampling the native/demonic serpent; we have here the anthropomorphic, and quasi-historical, form of the mytheme: horsemen trampling natives. But the Vedic bias is maintained: the invading horsemen are the heroes. The Vedic horsemen are replaced by Muslims or Anatolians, even by Dalits and Tribal peoples in some variants,[46] while the Dasyus, or Vedic Others, are replaced by a demon, a Patan tyrant or, by implication, the British. This plasticity kept the myth alive in widely varying contexts[47] which express, in very different ways, the connection between horses and aliens or foreigners. The confusion of the villains and the heroes in the story of Punvaro is no accident; the myth is rife with obfuscation, as well as a kind of inverted subversion, subversion from the top down: it speaks of the assimilation of the values of the conquerors by those who are conquered, expressing, as it were, the snake-eye view of horses, but in a positive light. Certainly it is a myth about, and probably by, invaders, that manipulates the native symbolism of horses and snakes in such a way as to make the invaders the heroes, the natives the villains, in a myth that then took root within the folklore of the natives. It's all done with mirrors, which is to say, with myths.

We must take account of the people who constructed this myth, who perpetuated it, recorded it, translated it, selected it. The popular legends

[x] See 'The History of Ekalavya'.

HORSES AND OTHER ANIMALS   447

concerning these events were 'first collected on the spot and written down by Major (later Sir Alexander) Burnes in 1826; copied with minor variations by Mrs Postans (1839) and later writers and finally embodied in the "standard" account of Kutch (otherwise a generally reliable source) in Volume V of the *Gazetteer of the Bombay Presidency* in 1880.'[48] It is not hard to guess why the British might have wanted to preserve this myth. But we are still hard-pressed to explain the acceptance and perdurance in Hindu India of other forms of this equine mythology, such as the myth of the jackal horses, which has been subject to far less British mediation and still expresses a surprisingly positive attitude to the equestrian conquerors of India.

BRITISH HORSES, AND KIPLING'S *KIM*

The myth of the liberating invader riding his stallion continued to cast its ole white magic over the British. Kipling immortalized the white stallion in his novel *Kim*. The very first chapter of *Kim* introduces a message about a war, coded in horses: 'The pedigree of the white stallion is fully established.' Ostensibly, it means that the Muslim horse-trader Mahbub Ali, who is in the service of the British spymaster Creighton, is able to vouch for a valuable horse that the colonel may buy; the coded message on the second level is that a provocation has occurred that will justify a British attack. But the idea of a pedigree implies that you know the horse when you know its father and mother (or dam and sire); the breeding of horses, of 'bloodstock', of thoroughbreds, was at the heart of a theory of the breeding of humans, a theory of race. Kim is even said to have 'white blood', an oxymoron. I need not point out the significance of the colour of the stallion in a book by Kipling (who coined the phrase 'the white man's burden'[xi]). But we might recall that the Vedic stallion of the ancient Hindus, the symbol of expansionist political power, was also white, in contrast with the Dasyus or Dasas, the serpentine natives, who were said to come from 'dark wombs'. [*Rig Veda* 2.20.7] The white stallion also implicitly represents Kim's Irish father, in the metaphor that Creighton and Mahbub Ali apply to Kim, behind his back: Kim is a colt who must be gentled into British harness to play the game.[49] On the other hand, to Kim's face Mahbub Ali uses horses as a paradigm for multiculturalism *avant la lettre*; in response to Kim's question about his own identity (he felt he was a sahib among sahibs, but 'among the folk of Hind . . . What am I?

[xi] See 'I Have Scinde'.

Mussalman, Hindu, Jain, or Buddhist?'), Mahbub Ali answers: 'This matter of creeds is like horseflesh . . . the Faiths are like the horses. Each has merit in its own country.'[50]

In recorded British history, too, horse-breeding, spying and Orientalism combined in the character of William Moorcroft, a famous equine veterinarian. In 1819, the British sent him to Northwest India, as far as Tibet and Afghanistan, on a Quixotic search for 'suitable cavalry mounts'.[51] Moorcroft had seen mares from Kutch that he thought might be suitable for the army, and he was granted official permission 'to proceed towards the North Western parts of Asia, for the purpose of there procuring by commercial intercourse, horses to improve the breed within the British Province or for military use'.[52] But he also 'collected information not only on military supplies but also on political and economic conditions obtaining at the peripheries of the Empire',[53] and shortly before his mysterious final disappearance, in 1824, he was briefly imprisoned in the Hindu Kush on suspicion of being a spy.[54] Moorcroft had delusions of Orientalism; he told a friend that he would have disguised himself 'as a Fakeer' rather than give up his plan,[55] and after he was lost, presumed dead, in August of 1825, legends circulated about 'a certain Englishman named Moorcroft who introduced himself into Lha-Ssa, under the pretence of being a Cashmerian', or who spoke fluent Persian 'and dressed and behaved as a Muslim'.[56] According to his biographer, Moorcroft was thrilled by the stories he heard 'from the north-western horse-traders—swarthy, bearded men like Kipling's Mahbub Ali'.[57] But Kipling created Mahbub Ali fifty years after the publication of Moorcroft's papers, and aspects of the characters of Creighton, Mahbub Ali and Kim himself may have been inspired by Moorcroft. Clearly, horses were deeply implicated in the British subjugation of India.

THE GIFT HORSE

Despite all of these negative political associations, the religious symbol of the horse became imbedded in the folk traditions of India and then stayed there even after its referent, the horse, had vanished from the scene, even after the foreigners had folded their tents and gone away. To this day, horses are worshipped all over India by people who do not have horses and seldom even see a horse, in places where the horse has never truly been a part of the land. In Orissa, terracotta horses are given to various gods and goddesses to protect the donor from inauspicious omens, to cure illness, or to guard the village.[58] In West Bengal, clay horses are offered to all the village gods, male or female, fierce or benign, though particularly to Dharma Thakur, the sun god. At Kenduli in Birbhum, clay horses are offered on the grave of a Tantric saint named Kangal Kshepa, and Bengali parents offer horses when a child first crawls steadily on its hands and feet like a horse.[59]

In Tamil Nadu, as many as five hundred large clay horses may be prepared in one sanctuary, most of them standing between fifteen and twenty-five feet tall (including a large base), and involving the use of several tonnes of stone, brick and either clay, plaster, or cement.[60] They are a permanent part of the temple and may be renovated at ten- to twenty-year intervals; the construction of such a massive figure usually takes between three and six months. In Balikondala, votive horses, or *thakuranis*, are provided as vehicles for the gods to ride at night to protect the fields and visit the infirm; and there are terracotta horses in the Shaivite temple on the edge of the village.[61] New horses are constantly set up, 'while the old and broken ones are left to decay and return to the earth of which they were made'.[62] The horses are said to be ridden by spirit riders who patrol the borders of the villages, a role that may echo both the role of the Vedic horse in pushing back the borders of the king's realm and the horse's association with aliens on the borders of Hindu society. But the villagers do not express any explicit awareness of the association of the horses with foreigners; they think of the horses as their own.

A Marxist might view the survival of the mythology of the aristocratic horse as an imposition of the lies of the rulers upon the people, an exploitation of the masses by saddling them with a mythology that never was theirs nor will ever be for their benefit, a foreign mythology that produces a false consciousness, distorting the native conceptual system, compounding the felony of the invasion itself. A Freudian, on the other hand, might see in the native acceptance of this foreign mythology the process of projection or identification by which one overcomes a feeling of anger or resentment or impotence toward another person by assimilating that person into oneself, *becoming* the other.[xii] Though there is much to be said for these interpretations, I would want to augment them by pointing out that myths about oppressive foreigners and their horses sometimes became a *positive* factor in the lives of those whom they conquered or dominated; and that the horse did not supplant but rather supplemented the continuing worship of other, more native animals—such as snakes.

[xii] This process of identification has been seen as a factor in the ways in which Hindus assimilated British attitudes to Hinduism in the nineteenth century. See 'Are Hindus Monotheists?' and 'From Kama to Karma'.

The corpus of Hindu myths that depict the Turks and Arabs bringing horses into India seems to have assimilated the historical experience of the importation of horses not only to the lingering vestiges—the cultural hoofprints, as it were—of Vedic horse myths, but also to the more widespead theme of 'magical horses brought from heaven or the underworld'. The myth is, like the horse, a gift from the sea, or from the sky—from another world. And like all great symbols, the horse is often susceptible to inversion as well as subversion: the horse of the conquerors becomes the horse of the conquered. This mythology lends the horse, over and above its natural allure, all the glamour and pathos of the interior room as watched by the child outside, pressing her nose against the windowpane. This is an otherness not loathed but admired, not despised but coveted; it is an otherness that has been assimilated into the native system of values. The villagers who recognize that the horse belongs to those who have political power may be worshipping the horse in order to gain some of that power for themselves. But this is not all that is happening.

Several parallel power relationships are expressed through the symbolism of the horse in contrast with the serpent, on the one hand, and the rider, on the other. Rider is to horse as horse is to snake: power, and domination, travels down the line. First comes the power structure between humans and horses; then between people of power and people without such power; between foreigners and natives; and, specifically, between British and Muslims, on the one hand, and Muslims and Hindus, on the other. But who is represented by the horse, who by the serpent, and who is the rider?

For the horse is, after all, a contradictory symbol of human political power. It is an animal that invades other horses' territory but whose first instinct is always not to attack but to run away. Horses are prey rather than predators, as is evidenced by the fact that they have their eyes towards the back of their heads, the better to flee, rather than in the front, like the cats and other hunters. Like the villagers who worship him, the horse has been oppressed and robbed of his freedom by human beings who made up stories about horses. The fragility of the horses is well represented by the fragile, ephemeral medium in which villagers usually represent him: clay. The horse is thus both victim and victimizer, a ready-made natural/cultural symbol of political inversion. The most basic power beyond manpower, horsepower is what we still use as a touchstone, a basis for other sorts of mechanical power. But horses are not machines; people who work with horses know that you are never in control, that you never entirely tame a horse, who remains at some level always wild. There is a cowboy saying about this: 'Never was a horse that couldn't be rode; never was a rider who couldn't be throwed.' This tension, too, nourishes the image of the wild horse as predator and the tame horse as prey.

And, finally, the horse is a potent natural symbol of things other than political power. Though the village terracotta horse may express an implicit wish for the power of those who have horses, its worshippers seem to seek the power of the horse itself—horsepower in the true sense of the word: strength and fertility. But horses are also worshipped for their beauty, which people continue to care about even when it is clearly not in their best interests to do so. Horses are numinous; they captivate the eye, they inspire desire, they have magic. Their allure infects even people who know, on a rational level, that horses aren't good for them. And this allure is what Indian artisans try to capture in their religious images; it is what makes them treat horses like gods.

THE SUBMARINE MARE IN THE MYTHOLOGY
OF SHIVA[1]

$\mathbf{F}$ire and water are natural symbols, individually and in combination, in mythologies throughout the world. They assume a unique meaning in the Hindu context, where tradition has attached particular significance to each element. Together, as an apparent conjunction of opposites, fire and water resolve some of the major paradoxes of Hindu mythology. The most striking instance of this symbolism is the image of the mare who wanders beneath the ocean, breathing fire, which comes to symbolize the latent force of doomsday always poised to break out and destroy the universe. It is the dangerous power of both suppressed lust and ascetic control; and insatiable appetites of all kinds. Since, of all the Hindu gods, Shiva is most closely associated with these forces, the submarine mare plays a particularly important role in his mythology.

THE BACKGROUND SYMBOLISM OF FIRE AND WATER IN INDIA

Fire is a natural image of energy, all the more compelling in a land in which heat is so intense as to become a constantly obtrusive image of power. More specifically, heat in Indian symbolism has two forms, mutually opposed: kama, the heat of sexual desire, and *tapas*, the heat generated by ascetic practices, particularly by chastity. These two forces often meet and interact in mythology: Kama, the god of desire, once attempted to wound Shiva, the god of asceticism, with an arrow; this resulted in a fire called the flame of Kama, composed of two sparks: the fire that Kama kindled in Shiva and the fire from the third eye in Shiva's forehead, with which Shiva, enraged, burnt Kama to ashes.[2] Other texts describe this battle between the two forms of fire and state that Shiva extinguished Kama's fire with the fire from his third eye.[3] Later in this myth, Shiva places his fiery seed in Agni, the god of fire.[4]

Water has certain obvious connotations in India—such as fertility,

452

immortality, peace and the female power of creation—but it is in conjunction with the more central image of fire that water is of particular significance. Thus, in the myth of Shiva and Kama, Agni is unable to bear the seed of Shiva and places it in the river Ganga, whence Kumara, the son of Shiva, is born. The image of fire in water is the ultimate resolution of oppositions; held in suspended union, each retains its full power and nothing is lost in compromise, but there is complete balance. In ritual, fire and water combine to burn away sinful elements and then to wash them away;[5] Willibald Kirfel has pointed out the importance of the balance between fire and water in the human body in Hindu medical texts,[6] as well as their symbolism of male and female, right and left, the sun and the moon.[7] The ascetic yogi submerges himself in water in the winter and surrounds himself with fires in the summer;[8] the yogic adept is said to achieve immortality by burning his body with the fire of Shiva and flooding it with the elixir of immortality of Shiva's wife.[9] As far back as the Vedas, Soma (the elixir) and Agni (fire) are identified with each other; Soma is described as a fiery liquor, or liquid fire.[10]

In Hindu thought, water brought to fire usually results in the burning up of the water. Indra, the Vedic king of the gods, is able to burn water dry,[11] a power that is shared by Shiva's *ganas*, or troops,[12] and by Shiva himself.[13] The seed—fire—is more powerful than the womb—water;[14] yet there are many notable exceptions, in which fire is quenched by water.[15] The final balance is one of suspension: fire never dies, but is merely transformed or controlled, as uranium is by rods of cadmium.

This balance of powers may be traced back to the Vedic conception of Agni in the waters. As Chauncey Blair has described it:

> It is true that water is said at Rig Veda X.I6.13 to extinguish excessive fire in the dead body, and to extinguish the excessive flame of jealousy and fever, but in general the concept of Agni in the waters does not imply destruction of Agni. He is merely hidden, a potential Agni, and no less capable of powerful action.[16]

The image of Agni born in the waters[17] lies at the heart of the cosmogonic myth of the golden seed of Agni that ripens in the cosmic waters to hatch into the universe.[18] Agni hides in the waters until the gods find him;[19] this story is told at length in the *Shatapatha Brahmana*, where Agni hides in a hollow reed,[20] and in the *Mahabharata*, where it is said, 'Agni hid in the waters of the watery Hell [*rasatala*]; these waters, heated by him, were released by (hot) mountain springs.'[21] In many versions of this story, Agni is said to fear the waters, as in this inverted plot when Agni seeks Indra instead of hiding from him:

> Agni searched for Indra, assuming the form of a woman. Finally, only the waters remained to be searched, and Agni was afraid to enter them, for fire is destroyed by water. 'My *tejas* [fiery heat and light] which goes everywhere is extinguished in the waters which are its womb,' he said. At last the gods strengthened Agni with magic spells and persuaded him to enter the waters.[22]

Agni's antipathy for water appears in another myth in which he hides in the waters but is found by the gods nevertheless; he then spits upon the waters and curses them for being an unsafe refuge.[23] Elsewhere it is said, 'When [the worshipper] throws Agni into the water he does what is improper; he now makes amends to him so that Agni may not injure him.'[24]

The opposing view, that fire is stronger than water, also appears in Hindu mythology:

> King Mathava carried Agni in his mouth. He did not speak, fearing that Agni might fall from his mouth. A priest mentioned butter and Agni fell to the ground. Agni went burning along the river Sarasvati and burnt up all the rivers until he reached the Sadanira river flowing from Himalaya, and he dwelt east of that place.[25]

Finally, the text explains the mutual interaction of the two powers: 'Water is food; water produces food. Therefore, he supplies the fire with food. Water, moreover, is female and Agni is male; so that he thereby supplies the latter with a productive mate.'[26] Fire and water express the related appetites of hunger and desire, and are mutually productive.

FIRE AND WATER IN THE MYTHOLOGY OF SHIVA

In post-Vedic mythology, the ambiguous figure of Shiva combines the two powers: Shiva is in fire and in water;[27] he is born from the golden egg placed in the waters;[28] his terrible form is fire, while his auspicious form is water.[29] A Sanskrit poem expresses the interplay of fire and water in Shankara (Shiva), who is said to have swallowed a deadly poison (*halahala*, produced after the churning of the primeval ocean) and to bear the crescent moon and the river Ganga on his head:

> He who, though gifted with the power
> to stomach deadly poison, to burn to ashes Love

and metamorphose doomsday's fire
to his glowing forehead-eye,
still bears the ambrosial moon,
the mountain daughter and the heavenly stream,
so wondrous is his skill of policy;
may he, great Shankara, protect you.[30]

Often, Shiva himself is Agni, and his wife—'the mountain daughter', Parvati, the daughter of Himalaya—is Soma;[31] her task is to control either aspect of his fiery power: as a female ascetic (*yogini*) she limits the fire of his lust, and as his mistress (*kamini*) she regulates his asceticism.[32] The latter is more frequently portrayed:

May the water of Shiva's sweat,
arising from Gauri's embrace,
which Kama employs as his liquid weapon
when he fears the fire of Shiva's eye, protect you.[33]

In many myths, Shiva's fiery lust is controlled by submersion in water. There is precedent for this in the *Atharva Veda* hymn that refers to the submersion of Kama himself: 'The love that the gods poured within the waters, greatly burning, together with longing—that I heat for thee by Varuna's ordinance.'[34] The commentator Sayana interpreted this verse to mean that the gods poured Kama into the water in order to quench him or, for his own benefit, to cure him of the fever of love; Maurice Bloomfield suggests that the gods did it to punish Kama for his attacks upon themselves.[35] In either case, the fever of lust is controlled by water. The *Mahabharata* draws the human parallel: 'Let a man in whom passion has arisen enter the water.'[36] Shiva begs Parvati to cure him in this way: 'Draw me out of Kama as if from a fire, and save me with the Soma of your body'.[37] Yet here again, fire proves more powerful than water.

Shiva seeks relief in the waters of two rivers, just as Agni seeks relief from the fiery seed in the Ganga:

When Sati [the first wife of Shiva] had died, Shiva wandered about until Kama wounded him with the arrow of madness. Shiva then fell into the Kalindi river and the waters were burnt up and became as black as collyrium. And still Shiva found no peace.

Then, when Parvati departed to perform asceticism, as Shiva had instructed her to do, Shiva was overcome with desire. He wandered over the earth and sprinkled his body with water, but he was still tortured by desire and found no peace. One day he saw the Yamuna river and he plunged in, trying to assuage the torture of his fever, but the waters of the river became black by contact with the fire of Shiva's body.[38]

In both of these myths, the water does not quench the fire but is burnt instead. A similar failure to extinguish the flame of Kama is recorded in the *Brahmanda Purana*:

> After Kama had been burnt by Shiva and revived by the goddess, he attacked Shiva with his arrows. Shiva abandoned his *tapas* and lost all control. Tortured by desire, sighing, heated, burning with Kama's arrows, he could not assuage the heat of his body with the coolness of the crescent moon or the Ganga, nor by the Soma dripping from the crescent moon, nor by lying in snowy waters. He could not extinguish the flame of the bodiless Kama in his body.[39]

Eventually, the fire of Shiva's semen, carried by Agni, is placed in a thicket of reeds, as Agni himself is placed in a hollow reed in the *Rig Veda* and the Brahmanas, and Kumara is born from it.[40]

The unquenchable fire of Shiva appears in a more symbolic form in the myth of the Pine Forest, in which the sages dwelling in the forest castrate Shiva; his phallus, or *lingam*,[i] falls to the ground and blazes out of control, destroying all in its path, until the sages worship it. In one version of this myth, the *lingam* comes to rest in a river;[41] in another, the sages beg Parvati to take the form of a *yoni* (the female sexual organ) to receive the *lingam*, which they sprinkle with consecrated water in order to make it peaceful.[42]

This is a reflection of actual ritual practice; according to William Crooke, 'the *lingam* of Mahadeva, a thirsty deity, who needs continued cooling to relieve his distress, must be kept continually moist to avoid drought'.[43] The Abbé Dubois described a similar practice of placing over the 'idol' of Shiva a vessel filled with water: 'In this vessel a little hole is pierced, so that the water may, by falling on him drop by drop, refresh him and abate the burning heat that consumes him.'[44] The same principle operates in present-day Hinduism, for the goddess of the fever of smallpox is cooled with water and fanned with branches.[45] The flaming power of the idol is thus controlled but never quenched by the ritual immersion. Kalidasa expressed this in a verse combining the symbols of Parvati as water and Shiva as fire with the central image of their balance: the mare at the bottom of the sea:

[i] See 'God's Body'.

United with Parvati, Shiva passed the days and nights of a thousand years as if it were a single night. But the joys of love-making did not satisfy his thirst, just as all the floods of the ocean do not quench the fire blazing within.[46]

THE SUBMARINE DOOMSDAY FIRE

In many versions of the myth of Shiva's conflict with Kama, the fire that blazes from Shiva's third eye to burn Kama—or, in some variants, the fire from Shiva's eye combined with the fire of Kama's arrows—yawns wide to burn up the universe.[47] This destructive fire that threatens to become the fire of untimely doomsday cannot be quenched, but it can at least be made to wait for the moment appropriate for destruction. And so the gods place it in the mouth of a mare (*vadava*) at the bottom of the ocean; inextinguishable flames issue from her mouth. Agni Vadava-vaktra ('the fire of the mare's mouth') drinks the waters of the ocean and lets them out again; eventually this fire of the underworld will destroy the universe, at the end of an aeon.

Because of its destructive nature, the mare-fire is associated with demonic powers: the anti-god Hiranyakashipu used it to dispel Indra's magic darkness during a battle; Indra then sent Soma and Varuna (gods of water) to extinguish the demon magic of the fire.[48] The mare-fire is also associated with Death: in one myth it is said that the mare was a river, the Vadava ('Mare'), which was given to Death as a wife, and in gratitude to Shiva for this gift, Death established a great *lingam* known as the Mahanala (the Great Fire) at the mouth of the Vadava river.[49]

The mare-fire beneath the sea is a common image. In the *Brihadaranyaka Upanishad*, the universal fire is said to be the open mouth of the sacrificial horse in the sea;[50] a commentary on the lawbook of Manu says, 'Fire is born of water, as is seen in the case of lightning and the (submarine) mare-fire.'[51] It is frequently used as a metaphor for a voracious or insatiable energy: 'Not by anything can the fire of enmity be assuaged; it is inextinguishable, like the submarine fire.'[52] The mare-fire is considered a particularly apt metaphor for the insatiable appetites of a flirtatious woman;[53] but it stands equally well for passion in a man: a character in the *Prabodhachandrodaya*[ii] boasts that he has crossed the ocean of passion, escaped from the whirlpool of affection, and dispelled the mare-fire of anger.[54]

[ii] See 'The Concept of Heresy'.

The mare-fire appears in the myth in which Shiva cuts off the fifth head of Brahma, the Creator; in one version, the head is said to be a horse-head, and in another the demon of Brahminicide who pursues Shiva after the beheading is likened to the fire of the mare;[55] the ocean fears that, if the terrible head is placed within him, he will be burnt dry.[56] In another myth, when the goddess instructs her servant to drink up the inexhaustible flood of the demon Raktabija's blood, she says: 'Open your mouth and drink his blood as if your mouth were the fire of the mare.'[57] In one version of the myth in which the gods churn the ocean to obtain the elixir of immortality, the mare-fire emerges from the sea immediately before the terrible *kalakuta* or *halahala* poison that threatens the gods until Shiva swallows it;[58] the poison is merely another aspect of the destructive fire waiting to come forth from the sea. The poison and the fire appear together in this verse:

> The goddess Sri is fickle, . . .
> and the kalakuta is a deadly poison.
> It is pondering these vices of his family
> that burns the ocean's heart,
> and not the underwater fire.[59]

The circle of the sun surrounded by clouds in the rainy season is likened to the mare's head in the ocean,[60] a simile made more appropriate by the Hindu belief that the sun's horses place his chariot in the Western ocean at night.[61] The sun, which emerges from the clouds to destroy the universe at doomsday, is an obvious prototype for the mare-fire.

The image of the mare is also often used to emphasize the greatness of the ocean;[62] the element of latent power is beautifully expressed in a verse from a Prakrit epic which describes the ocean stirring the submarine fire like a lion that roars and shakes his mane in rage when he is roused from deep sleep by being pierced by an arrow.[63] A Sanskrit verse magnifies both the ocean and the mare, depicting once again the perfect balance of fire and water:

> How marvellous the underwater fire!
> How marvellous the blessed sea!
> The mind grows dizzy thinking of their greatness.
> The first keeps drinking greedily its dwelling
> and yet its thirst by water is not quenched;
> the other is so great it never suffers
> the slightest loss of water in extent.[64]

THE FIERY MARE: SAMJNA AND THE CONTROL OF *TEJAS*

The particular form that the fire assumes—a mare—is by no means as whimsical as it may at first appear. In Vedic religion, the horse rather than the bull or cow was the sacred animal, the sacrificial animal, and the mare in Hindu mythology is associated with all the concepts central to the submarine fire.

The horse—both stallion and mare—is symbolic of fertility.[iii] The Vedic Creator, Prajapati, assumed the form of a stallion to pursue his daughter who had fled from him in the form of a mare, and from their coupling humans and all the animals were born.[65] In the ancient horse sacrifice, the *ashvamedha*, the sacrificed wife pantomimed copulation with the consecrated stallion.[66] That the *ashvamedha* had connotations of sexuality, as well as fertility, for the ancient Indians is clearly evident from the *Harivamsha* episode[iv] in which Indra, overcome by desire for Kashya (the wife of King Janamejaya), enters into the stallion consecrated for the sacrifice and unites with the queen during the ritual.[67] Some aspects of this ritual seem to have survived in later Hinduism, for medieval friezes and miniature paintings depict ritual orgies or scenes in which a woman is mounted by a stallion.[68] A particular connection between the *ashvamedha* and the mare-fire may be seen in the later belief that the submarine fire devours the offerings of the horse-sacrifice.[69] The fertility and potency of the *ashvamedha* horse was enhanced by special ritual laws requiring him to abstain from sexual intercourse during the year preceding the ceremony;[70] this ritual chastity remains in many of the myths of the mare-fire.

The head of the horse is particularly sacred and potent; throughout Sanskrit myth and poetry there appear celestial musicians named Ashvamukhas or Kimpurushas, with human bodies and horse-heads (occasionally vice versa); and their women are voluptuously described.[71] Horse-headed women appear on an erotic frieze at Aihole, apropos of which Philip Rawson remarks, 'The horse-headed female [Yakshini] is a familiar Indian night-time bogey, who carries men off for sexual purposes.'[72] A horse-faced Yakshini of Buddhist mythology was in the habit of eating the men she captured, until she fell in love with one whom she forced to marry her; another Buddhist Yakshini, a beautiful mare named Vadavamukhi ('Mare's Mouth'), with a white body and red feet, was pursued by king Pandukabhaya and plunged into a pond; he grasped her mane, subdued

---

iii See 'The Mythology of Horses'.
iv See 'Sacrifice and Substitution'.

her and rode her into battle.[73] The motifs of beauty and flight into water are typical of mare mythology.

The most famous mare in Indian mythology is the Vedic Samjna (later called Saranyu), who married the Sun and then fled from him, from his unbearable heat (*tejas*) and the heat of his sexuality, taking the form of a mare. Her story is, among other things, the great myth of the channelling of sexual fire.[v] Two basic elements of the myth—the unbearable fiery power of sexuality, and of the fire of the sun, and the practice of asceticism—are linked to Shiva by the belief that Shiva's own creative-destructive *tejas*, released when he was castrated in the Pine Forest, was placed in the sun;[74] in return, Shiva receives from the sun in this myth a portion of that same destructive *tejas* to make his weapon, the trident. (Other scraps from the trimming of the sun are said to have been used to build the great temple of the sun at Konarak; built in the form of a horse-drawn chariot of the sun, and covered with erotic friezes, this temple furnishes yet another link between sexual fire and the horses of the sun.) Moreover, Shiva, like the Sun, is said to have difficulty in finding a wife capable of bearing his *tejas*.[75]

Connotations of fertility persist in the mythological figure of the mare. Lakshmi, the wife of Vishnu and daughter of the ocean, follows in the footsteps of Samjna:

> Vishnu cursed Lakshmi to become a mare because she had lusted for Revanta (the child of Samjna and the Sun) when he was mounted on the marvellous horse Ucchaihshravas. Vishnu promised that she would be released from the curse when she had a son. Lakshmi went to the very place where Samjna had wandered as a mare, performing *tapas*, at the confluence of the Kalindi and Tamasa rivers. Lakshmi, the daughter of the ocean, meditated upon Shiva and did *tapas* for a thousand years, taking the form of a mare; then Shiva came to her and promised that Vishnu would appear to her in the form of a stallion and beget a son upon her. Shiva vanished and sent Vishnu to Lakshmi; he begat a son upon her, stallion mounting mare; they resumed their normal forms and returned home, giving the son to a king who had performed *tapas* to obtain him.[76]

This reworking of the myth of Samjna retains the mare theme in association with the familiar motifs: the sun, the horse of the sun, the ocean, the horse born from the ocean (Ucchaihshravas), the mare performing *tapas*, and the birth of a son.

[v] See 'Saranyu-Samjna'.

THE SYMBOLISM OF THE HORSE

The horse is a natural symbol of power as well as of fertility.[vi] For the Vedic Indians, it was also the emblem of war. Eventually, though, martial power was replaced by any inner power that had to be controlled. We have already noted how the mare-fire is symbolic of appetites that are difficult to tame; the Upanishads also likened the senses to horses that must be controlled or else they become vicious and wild.[77] The *Kamasutra*, too, depicted the passions as horses that must be controlled.[vii]

A striking example of the early association of the horse with the taming of wildness, as well as with fire and water, may be seen in a passage of the *Gopatha Brahmana* in which the four Vedas compete over the taming of a wild horse; the horse is referred to as 'she', although no word for mare is used, and the verb used to represent her taming is the same as the term for the extinguishing of a fire or a passion—*sham*. Finally, the Atharvan, the tamer, prepares the waters of tranquillity and sprinkles these over the horse; flames shoot forth from every limb of the animal, who is henceforth perfectly tame.[78] The horse is tamed as the flame *lingam* of Shiva is later controlled, by submersion in water.

The horse is specifically associated with the ocean and with fire, the two elements of the submarine mare: In the *Rig Veda*, fiery horses draw the chariot of the sun; the flames of Agni are his bay chargers.[79] The seven daughters of the sun are the seven bay mares that pull his chariot, the seven sisters who attend the fiery Soma drink.[80] Agni appears in the *Rig Veda* as a horse; he changes himself into a horse in order to deceive the demons.[81] Prajapati takes the form of a white horse to seek Agni when he hides from the gods; when Prajapati enters the water in this form, Agni burns the horse's mouth,[82] furnishing yet another instance of the combination of the essential motifs of the submarine mare-fire.

The connection between the horse and fire is clear and natural; the link with the ocean is less obvious but equally well-established. In the Vedas, the horse is sacred to Varuna, the god of the waters,[83] and the ocean is the womb of the horse.[84] Stella Kramrisch has discussed this belief:

> The ancient Aryans sacrificed a horse to Varuna, the god of the fertilizing waters. In hymnic intoxication, they knew the horse as Varuna (*Rig Veda* I. 163. 1). To the South Indian Dravidian peasant of today, this hymnic realization of the fiery animal, the horse, of the fiery

---

[vi] See 'The Mythology of Horses'.
[vii] See 'The Control of Addiction'.

spark of life that is in the waters, of the fire that at daybreak seems to arise from the waters as the glowing sun and sinks into their darkness and dies, has become uncannily one with the power of Aiyanar and also with the eerie, fatal Seven Virgins.[85]

In South India, even today, horses are dedicated to Aiyanar, the son of Shiva, and are worshipped together with the *lingam*.[86]

Other myths about horses still retain the same elements in different permutations: demons, the ocean, the sun and the taming of the horse:

> The winged white horse Ucchaihshravas, born from the ocean when it was churned, was taken by the demon chief for his own riding animal. The gods, jealous, implored Prajapati to give them horses too; he created four classes and many sub-castes of horses for them. Daksha, a son of Prajapati, considered the winged horses a nuisance and cursed them to live on earth without their wings. Thenceforth they were ridden by gods and men.[87]

The myth of the submarine mare appears in the Kulu Valley in the form of a legend of a mare who had drowned in a sacred lake in the Himalaya, gaining thereby certain healing powers.[88] (In this context it is interesting to note that the horse-headed Ashvins are the physicians of the gods.)

The tamed horse, retaining its power but in a harnessed form, never entirely tamed, is, then, a perfect symbol of the controlled force of fire under water.

THE MYTHS OF SEARCH: DADHYANCH AND SAGARA

The horse-head, in particular, is connected with the myths of the seeking of fire and the seeking of Soma, the cooling elixir, perhaps because of the natural image of swift flight that the horse suggests.[viii] Moreover, since the horse is an essential part of the Soma sacrifice, its image is associated with the drinking of Soma in the Vedas just as the submarine mare is the great drinker of water:

> Dadhyanch, through a horse's head, told (the Ashvins) (the place of) the mead (Soma). The Ashvins gave a horse's head to Dadhyanch and Dadhyanch told them (the place of) the hidden mead . . . Indra with the bones of Dadhyanch slew nine times ninety (or ninety-nine) enemies; as he sought the head of the horse, which was hidden in the mountains, he found it in Sharyanavat.[89]

[viii] See 'The Mythology of Horses'.

A clearer version of the first part of this myth appears in the *Shatapatha Brahmana*:

> Dadhyanch knew (the secret of) the mead and the secret of the sacrifice: how the head of the sacrifice is put on again and becomes complete. Indra threatened to cut Dadhyanch's head off if he told this secret to anyone. The Ashvins asked him to tell them the secret and made this provision: they first cut off his head and laid it aside, then placed the head of a horse on his neck, and then he told them the secret through the horse-head. Indra cut off that head, the Ashvins brought back his own head and restored it, and all was well.[90]

'The head of the sacrifice' is the head of the sacrificial horse; the elixir of immortality, Soma, revives the sacrificial animal, as the ocean waters feed the fiery head. Sayana, in his commentary, sheds some light on the second half of the Vedic myth: 'When Dadhyanch died, he left behind the horse's head. The gods sought it and found it in Lake Sharyanavat, a lake in Kurukshetra. With the bones of this head, Indra slew the demons.'[91]

The elements of this obscure myth recur throughout the corpus of fire-water myths. The Ashvins who give the horse-head (and the Soma) are the sons of the mare Samjna; the seeking of the horse-head by Indra is the seeking of fire hidden in water; and the bones of Dadhyanch appear in Puranic mythology as the bones of Dadhichi, which are, as we shall see later, a direct cause of the birth of the submarine mare. The search for Soma and for fire, the Sun's search for his wife (Samjna/Saranyu)—all are associated with the flight of the horse.

The seeking of the horse-fire itself is the central theme of the myth of Sagara, which appears in several slightly different versions:

> King Sagara had two wives. In order to obtain sons, he performed *tapas* for a hundred years; then, by the favour of Shiva [or by propitiating Aurva, the author of the submarine fire] he obtained 60,000 sons from one wife and one son, named Amshuman, from the other. After some time, the king performed an *ashvamedha* sacrifice; as the horse wandered over the earth, protected by the king's sons, it reached the ocean which was at that time empty of water, and there it disappeared. (Or: it was snatched away by a wave as it wandered by the ocean. Or: Indra took the form of a demon and stole the horse, for Indra was jealous of his own reputation as the giver of horse-sacrifices.[ix]) The king sent his

---

[ix] See 'The Concept of Heresy'.

60,000 sons to search for the horse; they dug with spades in the earth, destroying many living creatures, digging out the ocean which is the abode of sea-demons. They reached down into Hell, and there they saw the horse wandering about, and they saw the sage Kapila there haloed in flames, blazing with *tapas*. The sons were angry and behaved disrespectfully to Kapila; in fury, he released a flame from his eye and burnt all the sons to ashes. Then Amshuman came and propitiated Kapila and obtained the horse, with which Sagara completed his sacrifice. Sagara made the ocean his son, called Sagara. The ocean took the horse and worshipped with it, and he became the ocean. Years later, after Sagara's death, Bhagiratha, the grandson of Amshuman, propitiated Shiva and Ganga; Ganga fell from heaven to earth, breaking her fall upon Shiva's head, and she flowed over the ashes of the 60,000 sons, reviving them.[92]

The submarine mare appears in many forms in this myth: first, as the power—Shiva or the sage Aurva—who grants the sons as a reward for asceticism; then as the horse that vanishes into the ocean (taken by Indra, the one who sought the horse-head of Dadhyanch) to be churned out of it again, like Ucchaihshravas; then as the submarine fire of Hell blazing from the eye of Kapila, as it blazes from the eye of Shiva; and finally as the ashes of the sons, revived by the floods of the Ganga just as the seed of Shiva is engendered there or the fire of his lust assuaged there. The sage Aurva, creator of the submarine fire, is further connected with the myth of Sagara by the tradition that Aurva was preceptor to Sagara and gave him the fire with which Sagara conquered the barbarians.[93] This fire weapon is the same mare-fire that Aurva gave to the anti-gods.

The same elements appear arranged more briefly and simply in the story of the demon Dhundhu:

King Brihadashva ('Possessing great horses') had a thousand sons, of whom Kuvalashva ('Possessing water-lily horses') was the eldest. When the old king handed over his throne to Kuvalashva and entered the forest, he met the sage Uttanka, who told him that an anti-god named Dhundhu was performing great *tapas* there by his hermitage, in the sands of the ocean, burning like the doomsday fire with flames issuing from his mouth, causing the waters to flow about him in a whirlpool. Brihadashva asked Kuvalashva to subdue the anti-god; he and the other sons dug down into the sand, but Dhundhu appeared from the ocean, breathing fire, and he burnt all but three of the sons with his power of *tapas*. Then Kuvalashva drank up the watery flood with a fiery arrow, and he quenched the fire with water; and he killed Dhundhu, burning him up.[94]

The end of the myth expresses the final balance of the powers: the fire is quenched by water, but the water is 'drunk' by fire. Clearly this is an abbreviated form of the Sagara story, centring upon the burning of the king's sons by a submarine fire. The image of the horse seems to be omitted from the Dhundhu story, but it appears in the form of the names of the kings: Brihadashva ('Possessing great horses') and Kuvalashva ('Possessing water-lily horses'). Moreover, the *Mahabharata* explicitly connects the two stories: 'Dhundhu burnt the sons of Kuvalashva with the fire from his mouth, just as formerly Kapila burnt the sons of Sagara.'[95]

Another myth relates Dhundhu to the submarine mare more explicitly:

> The two demons Madhu and Kaitabha stole the Vedas and took them to the Hell beneath the great ocean. Brahma told Vishnu what had happened, and Vishnu took a horse-headed form and entered Hell. He took the Vedas back to Brahma and then he resumed his own form, leaving the horse-head in the ocean as the dwelling of the Vedas. Then he killed Madhu and Kaitabha, who were the parents of Dhundhu. Vishnu himself is the horse-head that lives in the ocean, devouring oblations.[96]

Thus Dhundhu, the submarine fire, is the very form that Vishnu assumes in order to kill the parents of Dhundhu, who have stolen the Vedas (as the Soma and horses are stolen in other myths); and Dhundhu is in turn killed by the fire-and-water weapons of a 'horse' (Kuvalashva).

THE ORIGIN OF THE SUBMARINE MARE–FIRE: AURVA

The submarine fire is often called the fire of Aurva, from the name of the sage whose anger is its source. 'Aurva' is derived from *urva*, which, in the *Rig Veda*, designates the ocean.[97] In particular, the *urva* is the part of the ocean into which many rivers flow; here it is interesting to note that the later mare-fire usually arises at the confluence of a river and the ocean. Sayana glosses *urva* in this context as the mare-fire in the ocean, used as a metaphor for the fire of lightning inside a cloud;[98] elsewhere he remarks that the submarine mare-fire is here a metaphor for unsated desire.[99]

Two more Vedic occurrences add still other essentials of the later myth. Agni himself is associated with two sages named Aurva and Bhrigu, and in the very same verse is said to be the Agni who dwells in the ocean;[100] Bhrigu is the grandfather of Aurva in later mythology, and the *Rig Veda* associates both with the fire in the ocean. The *Taittiriya Samhita* adds to this cluster of ideas the final element: Agni who dwells in the ocean is called *urva* and symbolized by a horse who had been yoked but is now set free so that he can eat ghee[x] and take his place in the ocean.[101] The horse, tamed and set free, devours the oblations (the waters of the ocean), like the fire in the mare's mouth.

Vedic elements persist in the Puranic myths. F.D.K. Bosch has discussed at some length the 'inverse order' and 'inversion' of the Dadhyanch myth and the myth of Aurva,[102] and parallels between the two are clear. A brief prediction of Aurva's birth appears in the *Mahabharata*:

> A sage named Aurva will be born, blazing like a fire, and he will create a fire of anger to destroy the three worlds and reduce the earth to ashes. After some time he will extinguish the fire, throwing it into the mouth of the mare in the ocean.[103]

The myth is expanded and rationalized elsewhere in the epic:

> The sage Aurva was born from his mother's left thigh, blazing with anger toward the Kshatriya (Warrior) class who had destroyed his family and his father. He performed *tapas* in order to destroy the worlds and the people. His great *tapas* heated all the gods, and the Fathers begged him to be merciful and to control his anger. Aurva said, 'My vow of anger cannot be in vain, or I could not live. Undispersed, my anger would burn me as fire burns a forest, if I were to restrain it with my own *tejas*.' The Fathers said, 'Release it into the waters if you like, and, since the waters are the people, this will fulfill your vow to burn the people.' So Aurva placed the fire in the ocean, and it became the horse-headed fire, which vomits fire from its mouth and drinks the waters of the ocean.[104]

Aurva states the problem of the dispersal of excess destructive ascetic power: he cannot take it back, as Shiva cannot take back the fire from his eye, and so it must be placed in the one situation in which it can do no harm: under water. The problem of dispersal is explicitly the central point of the myth in the *Mahabharata*, which tells it to the sage Parashara in order to persuade him to dispose in a similar manner of his own destructive wrath;[105] the epic here introduces the Aurva story as a conscious multiform.

The Brahmana concept of water as food for fire is central to the myth, as is the theme of the seduction of an ascetic to disperse his *tapas*; the gods

---

[x] For the Indian custom of feeding ghee to horses, see 'The Mythology of Horses'.

persuade Aurva to abandon his vow and to place his *tejas* (i.e. his seed) where it will cease to generate heat, in water (i.e. in a woman). The importance of chastity in this context is indicated by a more explicit description of the *tapas* involved in the birth of Aurva:

> The sage Urva was performing *tapas*; the gods asked him to stop and begin family life. He replied, 'This is the eternal dharma of sages, to live in the forest in a hermitage, in chastity. I will not take a wife, but I will create a son nevertheless.' Then by his *tapas* Urva placed his thigh in the fire and churned it; a halo of flames broke out of his thigh and became a son, named Aurva.
>
> Aurva blazed so fiercely that he terrified the universe; he said, 'Hunger binds me: I will eat the universe.' He grew great, burning all creatures, until Brahma said to Urva, 'Restrain your son's *tejas*, for the good of all people. I will give him a dwelling-place and a food like Soma; he will dwell in the mouth of the mare in the ocean, and he will live upon an oblation of water. This water-eating fire will burn all creatures at the end of the aeon.' 'So be it,' said Urva, and he threw the fire into the ocean.[106]

In this version, Aurva is personified as the son of Urva, rather than an elemental fire; and his blaze of hunger is directly derived from the *tapas* of his father's chastity, a force that becomes dangerous when it is released to become productive.

The *Skanda Purana* tells another myth of Aurva's birth, related to the Vedic tradition of the horse-head of Dadhyanch (here called Dadhichi):

> The gods placed their weapons in the hermitage of Dadhichi for safe-keeping, and Dadhichi made them into liquid and drank their essence. One day Subhadra, his wife, put on his loincloth for a menstrual cloth, and she became pregnant with the seed that was on the cloth. When she brought forth a child, she cursed the father, in ignorance, saying, 'I swear by my chastity: let the man who engendered this child die.' At this time the gods returned to take back their weapons; and Dadhichi abandoned his body so that the gods could make their weapons of his bones.
>
> When Subhadra learned that Dadhichi was the father of her child, she rejoiced; but the child, named Pippalada, wished to kill the gods who had killed his father. He went to Himalaya and did great *tapas* to propitiate Shiva; he churned his left thigh with his left hand and from it a mare appeared, followed by a stallion. The mare was covered by the stallion, brought forth a child, and disappeared. Pippalada then told

the child to devour the gods. The gods sought help from Vishnu, who tricked the fire-child into eating the gods one by one, beginning with the waters. The mare, haloed in flames, asked to be brought to the waters, and no one but Sarasvati could bear the fire.

As Sarasvati carried the fire to the waters, a mountain saw her and asked her to marry him; she refused, and he threatened to abduct her by force. She then agreed to marry him if he would hold the mare-fire while she bathed; he did so and was burnt to ashes. She took up the fire and set out again for the ocean. When they reached the ocean, the mare was full of joy and offered Sarasvati a boon; she said, 'Promise that you will drink the waters through a mouth no larger than a needle.' Then she threw the fire into the ocean, and this is the story of the birth of the Aurva fire.[107]

Although the story refers to the Aurva fire, Aurva does not appear; he is replaced by Pippalada and given a complex reason for his destructive fervour: revenge for the death of his father replaces his fierce chastity. Pippalada appears elsewhere as an incarnation of Shiva,[108] and Shiva himself appears here, as in the *Mahabharata* story, as the one who makes possible the birth of the fire-child. The story of Dadhichi's bones is connected with the horse-head of Dadhyanch in the *Rig Veda*, but this connection is submerged in the *Skanda Purana* and seems to have little to do with the birth of Pippalada except to supply the motive for his anger. The image of the mare, which is introduced only as an afterthought at the end of the *Mahabharata* story of Aurva and is absent entirely from the story of Urva, appears here in an awkward and elaborate form unrelated to the horse-head of Dadhichi-Dadhyanch. The role of chastity is transferred in this version from Urva himself to the two women in the myth: the mother of Pippalada, who swears by her chastity, and the bearer of the fire, Sarasvati, whose steadfast chastity enables her to fulfil her role and dispose of the fire. The tricking of the lustful mountain by Sarasvati is a multiform of the double trick played upon the chaste mare: first, to make the fire drink the waters, and then to reduce the size of the mouth to a needle (which, with Vishnu's gift to the ocean of inexhaustible waters, supplies an explicit rationalization of the eternal balance of food [water] and eater [fire]).

Sarasvati's place in the myth is clear; like the Ganga and the ocean, she is the only receptacle for the fire. This is the role that she plays in the control of Shiva's fire as well; for when he went to do *tapas*, after making love to Parvati for a thousand years, he plunged into the Sarasvati river for a year and a half.[109] In anthropomorphic form, Sarasvati is the goddess of wisdom and art, and the wife of Brahma. The sexual nature of the fire-water episode may be seen in the fact that when the fire is placed in the ocean (which is masculine), it is a mare; but when it is placed in the river Sarasvati or the Ganga (which are feminine), it is considered to be masculine; even in the Pippalada myth where it is born from a mare, a stallion is introduced as well, and the resulting child is masculine.

The plight of Sarasvati is elaborated upon in the *Padma Purana*, which here omits the whole story of the origin of the fire in the mouth of the mare:

> Formerly the gods said to Sarasvati, 'You must take this fire and throw it into the ocean of salt so that the gods will be free of fear; otherwise the fire will burn everything with its *tejas*.' Sarasvati asked her father, Brahma, what she should do, and Brahma asked her to protect the gods. She wept bitterly, but she set out, accompanied by Yamuna and Gayatri, and she went to Uttanka's hermitage. There she received the fire in a golden pot and took it to the ocean.[110]

Nothing is said of the origin of the fire; but it comes from the hermitage of Uttanka, the place from which the submarine fire of Dhundhu originates, and there may be a confusion between the two myths here. But the *Brahma Purana* retells this same episode in a version of the story of Pippalada and Dadhicha (sic) which gives a more specific rationalization of the presence of the mare in the story:

> Pippalada the son of Dadhicha performed great *tapas* in order to kill the slayers of his father. When he was able to see the third eye of Shiva, he gained from Shiva the power to kill the gods. The pippala (fig) trees said, 'Your mother was said to be a mare', and when Pippalada heard this he became angry, and from his eye an evil spirit came forth blazing in the form of a mare with a deadly tongue; she had the form of a mare because he had been thinking of a mare. He told her to eat the gods, but she began to eat him, since he had been made by the gods; in terror, Pippalada fled to Shiva, who told the spirit not to take any creature within the distance of a league from that place. Then the mare set out full of fire to burn the universe, terrifying the gods, who sought refuge with Pippalada; but Pippalada could not restrain the mare. As she came to the confluence of the Ganga, she was implored by the gods to begin with the waters of the ocean and then to devour everything. The fire said, 'How can I reach the ocean? Let a virtuous maiden place me in a golden pot and lead me there.' The gods asked the maiden Sarasvati to do this, and she asked them to join her with four other rivers, the Yamuna, Ganga, Narmada and Tapati. The five rivers put

the fire in a golden pot and brought it to the ocean, they threw it into the ocean and it began to drink the waters little by little.[111]

The fire is called a mare until the chaste maiden and the rivers are first mentioned; thenceforth, it is called a fire (masculine), placed in the golden pot that is the receptacle of the golden seed of Shiva and submerged in the Ganga like that seed.[112] Shaiva imagery is strong throughout this version: Pippalada becomes able to see Shiva's third eye and then produces the fiery mare with his own eye;[113] the gods then beg Shiva to protect them from the mare created by the fire of *his* eye,[114] and clearly the two eyes function as one, just as Pippalada and Shiva are one. The theme of chastity plays a part here, too; the slur against Pippalada's mother (a mare being perhaps equivalent to a bitch or at least an over-sexed woman,[xi] as is its connotation in the *Kamasutra*[115]) is reminiscent of the mother's own fears of her chastity in the *Skanda Purana* version; and the chastity of Sarasvati—implicit and important in that version—is here made explicit: only a maiden can carry the fire.

Shiva participates in the action of the myth in symbolic forms more often than he appears anthropomorphically. But he plays a more important role in the *Varaha Purana* version of the myth:

> The sage Aurva performed *tapas* until he began to burn the universe. The gods were frightened; and so one day while the sage was doing *tapas* Shiva looked in anger upon Aurva's hermitage and burnt it up. When Aurva saw that it had been burnt, he said, 'Let the one who has burnt this hermitage be burnt by sorrow and wander over the world.' And so Shiva himself was burnt by a great fire and wandered without finding rest. Finally he went with Parvati to Aurva, who promised that Shiva would be released from the curse if he performed the ritual of bathing a host of cows; and he did so and was cured.[116]

Aurva's curse of an unknown enemy, like Subhadra's unwitting curse of her own husband, results in the creation of a fire. Shiva is both the immediate source of this fire—burning the hermitage with his third eye and causing havoc as the demon Dhundhu caused havoc in Uttanka's hermitage—and its first receptacle; he wanders in torture as he wanders under the influence of Kama's fire. Finally, he is released from his pain by a ritual of bathing not himself, as in many myths in which he plunges into a river, but a cow, the animal that had by this time replaced the horse as the

---

[xi] See 'Zoomorphism'.

sacred animal of fertility. The fire that haunts Shiva retains its erotic connotations even in this myth; for Parvati must be present when Shiva is cured, as she is in the Pine Forest.

SHIVA AS THE MARE–FIRE BENEATH THE SEA

In some texts, Shiva engenders the mare-fire with the blaze of his third eye. Certain descriptions of the battle between Shiva and Kama allow Shiva to restrain or distribute in various ways the fire of anger which has reduced Kama to ashes;[117] but as this fire is expressly said to be the fire of doomsday, there is one inevitable resting place for it: the ocean.

> Kama deluded Shiva, arousing him, and when Shiva realized that Kama was attacking him he released a fire from his third eye, burning Kama to ashes. The fire, having come from Shiva's eye, could never return to Shiva; moreover, Brahma had paralyzed the fire in a vain attempt to shield Kama. When Shiva had vanished, the fire began to burn the gods and all the universe. The gods sought refuge with Brahma, who made the fire of Shiva's anger into a mare with gentle [*saumya*, literally, 'like Soma'] flames issuing from her mouth. Then Brahma took the mare to the ocean and said, 'This mare is the fire of Shiva's anger; having burnt Kama, it wishes to burn the whole universe. I gave it the form of a mare; now you must bear it until the final deluge, at which time I will come here and lead it away from you. It will devour your water, and you must make a great effort to bear it.' The ocean agreed to this, and the fire entered and was held in check, burning quietly with its halo of flames.[118]

A very similar myth is told about a conflict with Indra instead of Kama, in which, again, the uncontrollable, unreturnable flame from Shiva's eye is placed in the ocean:

> Once Indra came with the gods to see Shiva on Kailasa; Indra saw a naked yogi there and reviled him and struck him with his thunderbolt; but the thunderbolt was reduced to ashes, and the man's neck turned blue where it had struck, for the yogi was Shiva himself. Then Shiva glanced at Indra with the fire of his third eye and was about to kill him; but Brihaspati begged him to protect Indra and restrain the fire. Shiva said, 'How can I take back the anger that has come forth from my eye? How can a snake put on again the skin that he has sloughed off?' Brihaspati asked him to throw the *tejas* somewhere else, and Shiva took it with his hand and threw it into the salt ocean at the confluence of the Ganga.[119]

This story is linked with the submarine mare when Indra remarks, 'Formerly the ocean was a refuge for . . . the fire in the form of a horse that burnt all creatures.'[120]

In addition to these two myths, there are scattered references to Shiva as the mare-fire throughout Sanskrit literature. The *Mahabharata* says, 'Shiva's mouth is the mare's head.'[121] The three eyes of Shiva are said to be the sun, the moon and fire, while his tongue is the subterranean mare-fire (whose own tongue is fire).[122] The fire of Shiva's anger, the Aurva fire and the fire of Kama combine in a verse that the love-sick King Dushyanta[xii] addresses to Kama:

> Surely the fire of Shiva's anger still burns in you today,
> like the fire of Aurva in the ocean;
> otherwise, Kama, how could you be so hot
> as to reduce people like me to ashes?[123]

Once again the fire of Shiva's angry asceticism has combined with the fire of desire.

Shiva is himself half fire and half water; he is fire and Parvati is water, and they are one. He is the ascetic that rages against the erotic power; and he is the fire of passion that cannot be controlled by asceticism. He is in this the image of the balance of powers in the universe; his flame blazes eternally, unquenched by all the floods of nature, like the mare-fire within the sea.

[xii] See 'Rings of Rejection'.

INDRA AS THE STALLION'S WIFE[1]

Among the many myths with which the *Rig Veda* tantalizes us, dropping a few bold clues but casually neglecting to provide anything like a full report, there is one unsolved mystery that has remained on the books for close to three thousand years: the case of Indra as the wife (*mena*) of the seed-bearing stallion (or bull-stallion, *vrishanashva*). The episode is mentioned several times in the *Rig Veda*, and every time that Karl F. Geldner, for instance, comes to it,[2] he calls it *dunkel* (dark) and refers the reader to its other, equally *dunkel*, occurrences. This darkness remains, in Geldner's view, despite the potential illumination offered by several Brahmana explanations of the incident, some of which Geldner cites in his despairing notes, though he does not seem to take them seriously.

The myth is alluded to in three cryptic *Rig Veda* passages:

> You [Indra] became the wife of the bull-stallion . . . [1.51.13]
> The unfailing [Indra] made a wife for a bull.[10.111.3].
> As a buffalo, [Indra] desired the seductive female born from himself.
> He made the wife of a horse into the mother of a bull. [1.121.2]

The bull-stallion may be half horse and half bull.[3] This mixture of species is supported by the apparent mixture of species of the woman in the third passage, who appears to be first the daughter of a buffalo, then the wife of a horse, and finally the mother of a bull. But it is not necessary to see the bull-stallion as a composite animal; *vrishanashva* designates an animal that freely sheds its seed (a bull, a stallion, or a 'stud', a virile man[4]). It thus might be translated as a seed-bearing stallion. The bull-stallion, however, highlights the overtone of a mixed species, central to the myth.

ANIMALS AND INCEST

The myth of Indra as the bull-stallion depends upon a contrasting opposition between incest and the mixture of species, or, structurally speaking,

473

between a process of procreation in which the partners are abnormally closely related (incest) and a process of procreation in which the partners are abnormally distantly related (mixture of species). They are by no means the same process, nor do they pose the same problems; but juxtaposing them, as the Rig Vedic texts themselves do, forces us to consider the ways in which they may explain one another. And if we read this pattern back into the specific myth of Indra as the stallion's wife it may help us to interpret that myth.

Let us begin with Indra. Indra in the three verses that tell this story is a buffalo who becomes a bull; he makes a female buffalo who becomes a mare and then functions as a cow. By committing incest with his daughter, Indra transgresses the normal barrier between himself and a female who is of the same class or family (*varna*);[5] by blurring the line between mare and cow, he transgresses the normal barrier between species. The concept of 'species' is also covered by the term *varna*,[i] which further extends to the four major classes of human society—classes that, according to the classical system, ought not to intermarry, but that do.[6] In our myth, a mare, the wife of a horse, is magically created as a buffalo (which is, after all, a bovine), then transformed, equally magically, into a mare, and finally given the (magical) power to produce a bull. In one of the Brahmana texts that we will soon encounter, Indra is said to live in the family (*varna*) of the female that he desires, which also means that he is living in the 'species' (*varna*) of a mare.

There is yet another relevant set of links between animals and incest: the different species of animals are said to have arisen as the result of an act of incest, and literal incest among animals is cited as a justification for a kind of symbolic incest among human beings. Several texts, beginning with the Rig Vedic verse about the buffalo that we have already encountered, allude to the myth of primeval incest.[7] The Brahmanas expand upon this theme by stating that when Prajapati tried to commit incest with his daughter, she became a female wild animal (*mrigi*) and he became a male wild animal (*mriga*).[8] The Upanishads say that the daughter who fled from her father was first a human woman, from whom humankind was born; then she transformed herself into a cow, and he became a bull and covered her; and then she became a mare, whereupon he became a stallion and covered her. Continuing in this way, she produces all whole-hooved animals (when she is a female donkey), then goats, sheep, and 'all the pairs,

---

[i] See 'You Can't Get Here'.

down to the ants'.[9] We will return to this particular list of animals; here let us merely note that it is the woman's shame and revulsion that drives her to transform herself into an animal.[ii]

This important theme recurs in the *Mahabharata*, where a certain sage takes the form of a stag, and turns his wife into a doe,[iii] in order to overcome his shame and have intercourse with her.[10] Certain sexual acts, including incest, are literally 'animal' acts, sanctioned among animals but not necessarily among humans. Thus, sexual intercourse is called 'lust fit for cattle' (*pashavyakama*). This is expressed in another way in a Brahmana text that argues that every act of procreation is incestuous, since the father first has intercourse with his wife and then is reborn in her as his own son. This text then goes on to assert, 'All the beasts know this; therefore a son mounts his mother and his sister.'[11] In this context, we might argue that Indra becomes an animal (bull or stallion) precisely in order to perpetuate an act of incest (with his buffalo daughter). The connection between transformation into an animal, the act of incest, and the sexual union between a god and a mortal may be even older than the ancient Indian connection;[12] it may be Indo-European.[iv]

INDRA AND THE SAGE'S WIFE

Sayana, commenting on the *Rig Veda* in the fourteenth century CE, meditates on gender and the animal realm in explaining the third Vedic verse in our story of Indra as the stallion's wife ('As a buffalo, [Indra] desired the seductive female born from himself. He made the wife of a horse into the mother of a bull.'):

> The buffalo is Indra in the form of the sun, and the woman is the dawn (Ushas), or night, born of him. He lusted after her, even though she was born of him, for the sun does look lustfully at the night and the dawn. And then there is another marvel, concerning the wife of the horse. For this is the name of a female, and the female, the mare, became the mother or the producer of a bull. He made a transformation and a reversal. One day, in sport, Indra caused a bull to be born from a female horse. That is what is meant here, and it becomes quite clear in another verse that is spoken by Indra.[13]

[ii] See 'Zoomorphism'.
[iii] See 'Zoomorphism'.
[iv] Plato groups together, as the epitome of what the untamed part of the soul dreams of, the man who 'will not shrink from copulating with his mother, or with any other human or god or wild beast'. (*Republic*, 571 c–d)

According to this interpretation, Indra does not turn the mare into a cow but does make her the mother of a bull, the 'marvel' consisting in the fact that she gives birth to a species other than her own. As for Indra, in the first half of the verse he is a buffalo, but does he remain a buffalo to produce a bull in the mare, or does he turn back into a god, or a stallion, or a bull?

One would give a great deal to know precisely what verse it is that Sayana so blithely regards as rendering this whole mess 'quite clear'. What was Indra's species, and what was Indra's gender? We have already seen, in the context of the connection between animals and incest, that these two questions are closely related: one may change one's species in order to side-step a problem related to one's gender. Let us, therefore, set the species aside and consider the question of the gender, or more precisely the change of gender, of Indra in this myth, bearing in mind that Hindu gods do at times change their gender.[v] And we will soon see that the problem of gender leads us back, this time with a plausible solution, to the problem of species.

A later Vedic text provides a clue to the ambiguity of Indra's gender in the tale of the stallion's wife:

> Nirriti [Disorder, incarnate as a Fury] seizes the woman who has the form of a man and the man who has the form of a woman. Through the sacrifice one frees oneself from Nirriti . . . When Indra became the wife of the seed-bearing stallion (*vrishanashva*), then evil Nirriti seized him. The evil that he expelled became an impotent man.[vi] Whoever thinks that he has been seized by evil, by darkness, should sacrifice this castrated animal for Indra.[14]

There are a number of difficult but significant points in this text, some of which are best clarified by comparison with other relevant texts. Indra begins by changing his sex on purpose, becoming a female, as several Hindu gods will do in later mythology.[vii] The idea that at first Indra retains his ability to change back and forth again, in order to further his amatory escapades—first becoming a woman to get close to the woman, and then becoming a man in order to enjoy her sexually—is added by another text closely related to the one we have just seen:

[v] See 'Bisexuality'.
[vi] The Sanskrit for this term is *kliba*, a pejorative word that covers a wide range of meanings: a man who is sterile, impotent, castrated, a transvestite, a man who had oral sex with other men, who had anal sex, a man with mutilated or defective sexual organs, a hermaphrodite, or, finally, a man who produced only female children. See 'The Third Nature'.
[vii] See 'Bisexuality'.

Indra loved the female anti-god [Asuri] named Vilistenga. He went among the anti-gods becoming a female among females, a male among males. He thought that he had been seized by Nirriti; then he found this castrated animal that was offered to Indra and to Nirriti. He sacrificed an animal in the form that he had.[15]

Despite the initial convenience of serial androgyny, it appears from both texts that what begins as a strength soon turns into a weakness. When Indra becomes a female, he is 'seized by disorder'. The primary disorder is simply the mixing of this set of categories: when a man is not a man, but a woman, order is shattered.[16] But more specifically, Indra becomes like a castrated animal or an impotent man (kliba). Perhaps he gets trapped or stuck in his female form and can't change back to a man again, as happens to some serial human androgynes in later Hindu mythology.[viii] Or it may simply be that to be changed into a woman is to be castrated; here, as so often in Indian mythology, change of sex, androgyny, castration and impotence are closely related.[17] But, in any case, Indra then makes use of both the castrated animal and the impotent man to cure himself and, even more, to transform his weakness back into a strength again. He is restored both by the sacrifice of a castrated animal and by transferring his 'evil' to an impotent man. Let us look at these two methods one by one.

The castrated animal consecrated to Indra is usually a ram.[18] Since the ram is 'in the form that (Indra) had', according to our second text, i.e., since both the ram and Indra lack testicles, the castrated ram is an appropriate offering to the castrated Indra. In the *Rig Veda*, Indra is called a ram,[19] and in the *Ramayana* the testicles of a ram are used to restore Indra after he is castrated in punishment for having seduced Ahalya, the wife of a human sage named Gautama.[ix] In the course of the sacrifice, it is implied, the testicles that the ram loses are somehow transferred to Indra. Moreover, at the end of it all, Indra is stronger than ever: the testicles of a ram are even better than the ones that he had to begin with.

Support for this interpretation may be seen in an obscure and obscene hymn in the *Rig Veda* that refers tantalizingly to the tale, never told, of Indra and Vrishakapi. The name of Indra's alter ego in this hymn is highly significant for our purposes: *kapi* means a monkey, and *vrisha* is yet another form of the word for 'seed-bearing' or 'bull' that is part of the name of Vrishanashva, so that Vrishakapi is 'The Seed-bearing Monkey'.[20] The text

---

viii See 'Transsexual Transformations'.
ix See 'The Mythology of the *Kamasutra*'.

is far too elusive to allow confident interpretation, but it does seem to contain several relevant elements: the monkey is a son of Indra who makes sexual advances to Indra's wife, the monkey's mother; he makes fun of Indra's inadequate virility and boasts of his own; he is castrated, and Indra takes on the monkey's powers while transferring his own sins to the monkey.[x] In a similar way, after the queen pantomimed ritual copulation with the horse during the ancient Indian horse sacrifice, the dead stallion's virility was transferred to the 'cuckolded' king,[21] and Indra himself is said once to have taken the form of the sacrificial stallion in order to sleep with a queen he desired.[xi]

Let us now read this pattern back into the episode of Indra, the castrated animal and Nirriti. First of all, we can surmise that the virile animal is a symbolic form of the virile Indra, for throughout the *Rig Veda* Indra is routinely praised for his powers as a stallion, a bull, a ram. But then Indra temporarily loses his sexual powers; the Brahmanas regard Indra's sexual transformation, however motivated, as evidence of a problem rather than a miracle, as one of the tight spots that Indra gets himself into from time to time (like his Indo-European cousins Zeus and Wotan), rather than as one of his glorious deeds, that are also celebrated in these texts. At this point, the animal is castrated to make it an appropriate offering to the now 'castrated' (i.e., no longer masculine) Indra, and this animal is then sacrificed to Indra. This is what is behind the phrase, 'Through the sacrifice one frees oneself from Nirriti.' And just as the animal's sexual powers are transferred to Indra, so the impotence of both the animal and Indra is transferred to the impotent man, just as Indra's evil was transferred to the monkey. This is the implication of the phrase, 'The evil that he expelled became an impotent man.' Another Brahmana text explains that the impotent man was created from the evil cast off from the middle realm[xii] when the three worlds were separated.[22] Indra often transfers his sin to others, including water, women, trees and the earth.[23]

Thus Indra loses his virility through his contact with the human species, and regains it through his contact with the animal species. He becomes

---

[x] The theme of the monkey as cuckolder endures in Indian folklore. In a tale from the *Tantrakhyana*, first published by Cecil Bendall, a newly-wed bride wanders away from her sleeping husband in a forest, comes across an ithyphallic monkey, is overcome with passion for him, and remains with him until her husband returns to find her still impaled upon the now sleeping monkey and kills the monkey with an arrow, whereupon the wife commits suicide.

[xi] See 'Sacrifice and Substitution'.

[xii] See 'Together Apart'.

female in order to indulge his sexual appetites, and then finds that he must 'become' an animal—the sacrificial surrogate—in order to regain the powers that he has lost through that very indulgence. He pays for his amours but is ultimately strengthened by them. All of this is relevant to the tale of Indra and the stallion. But there is one final way in which the transformation of Indra's gender is connected with the transformation of his species. We have noted that Hindu mythology tends to lump together various different forms of non-masculinity: change of sex, androgyny, castration and impotence. There is yet another term in this series, however, that holds the key to the mystery of Indra and the stallion, and that is infertility or barrenness. This concept will supply the final piece in our Vedic jigsaw puzzle.

FERTILE MARES AND BARREN MULES

The Brahmanas furnish us with evidence that Indra's act in fathering a bull on a mare is not really the 'marvel' that Sayana suggests. For they tell us that the mare has 'double' seed and can accommodate both the stallion and the donkey. Thus one might argue (rather literally) that since the mare gives birth to both foals and baby mules, why not to calves? But this is hardly conclusive. The ancient Indians may not have felt it as convenient as we do to regard horses and mules as members of a single species (equines), and cows (and buffaloes) as bovines. But the general pattern of the mixture of species that emerges from this cycle of myths indicates a general structure of symbolic thinking, rather than a specific policy of animal husbandry, and that pattern makes good sense of our problem text.

This cycle of myths revolves around the relationship between the mare and the seed of a series of male animals other than stallions. The simplest version of this myth goes like this:

> Prajapati created the creatures and then laid hold of them in the twelfth month; therefore the females bear their young for ten months and bring them forth in the eleventh. From these female creatures as Prajapati was laying hold of them, the she-mule went away. Prajapati followed the mule and took away her seed, which he then wiped off on the mare. Therefore the mare has double seed, and therefore the mule is barren, for its seed had been taken away.[24]

Prajapati starts the process of reproduction going and then brings it to its fruition by touching the females, ending their pregnancy and bringing about their parturition. The she-mule departs, apparently in order to go on being pregnant without giving birth; Prajapati then punishes her, appropriately, by making it impossible for her ever to give birth at all. He 'wipes off' the she-mule's seed on the mare, which means that he transfers the seed to the mare, just as the evil cast off by the castrated Indra/ram is transferred to (wiped off on) the impotent man. The point of this first version is that the barrenness of the mule results from (and corresponds to) the double fertility of the mare. The nature of this double fertility is not made explicit in this text (for mares do not usually bear twins, or bring forth twice as often as other animals, or anything of this sort), but another Brahmana tells us that, 'A mare with a foal is the sacrificial fee, for she gives birth to both a horse and a mule.'[25] And that is her double fertility.

The barrenness of the mule is proverbial in India. The mule in Sanskrit is called ashvatara (female, ashvatari), 'a sort of a horse' or 'more than a horse', and a king who fails to subdue his enemy is said to conceal and harbour death, 'just as a she-mule [conceals and harbours] her embryo.'[26] This seems to imply that the mule does conceive an embryo but never brings it forth, perhaps because it is dead, which may be an echo of the ancient myth in which the female mule wants to keep her embryo inside her instead of bringing it forth in the natural manner. Or it may imply that the mule conceives an embryo that kills her when it comes forth, as the unsubdued enemy will kill the king. This second view is explicitly suggested by the commentary on the verse just cited, which asserts, 'It is well known that only by bursting its mother's womb is the offspring of a mule born from her.'[27] This same assertion is made in glossing another passing reference to mules, in which it is said that the anti-god Vatapin 'had utter contempt for ascetic Brahmins and would kill them from within their stomachs, as her foal will kill a mule when it comes to be born'.[28] Vatapin's modus operandi is also highly relevant to our corpus of myths: for his brother Ilvala transformed Vatapin into a goat that he fed to Brahmins and then recalled out of their stomachs; Vatapin came to life and burst out of the Brahmin's stomach, killing him.[29] Similarly, Indra himself was kept in his mother's womb for many years, and finally broke out against her will.[30] The fact that Indra is as stubborn as a mule in refusing to be born may be related to his 'mulish' ability to belong to several different species.

The barrenness of the female mule may thus have either (or both) of two rather different implications. On the one hand, it may imply that the female mule can never conceive at all, or that if she does she cannot bring forth a live foal. One of the Brahmanas lists a 'female mule giving birth' as one of a series of unusual but not impossible prodigies, such as earthquakes or showers of flowers falling from the skies.[31] In this sense, the 'foal of a mule' is a freak, a monster, but not an absolute impossibility like 'the son of a barren woman' that is used to denote a *logical* impossibility.[32] On the other hand, the barrenness of the female mule is often connected with some act of violence that destroys her womb, either before she attempts to conceive (so that she cannot) or after she has conceived (so that the embryo, in the act of being born, destroys the womb and renders the female mule barren after that single birth). Either of these implications may already be present in the Brahmanas' statement that Prajapati took away the seed of the she-mule.

But in explaining the barrenness of the mule, one Brahmana gives us an expanded version of the myth of Prajapati and the mule, a version that explains the mare's doubleness by linking her with another counterpart, the jack donkey, and describes the transfer of seed not from a female mule to a mare but from a male mule to a jack donkey. The passage begins with the same explanation of the eleven-month pregnancy, and then continues:

> When Prajapati was laying hold of all these creatures, the he-mule ran away from them. [Prajapati] followed [the mule] and took his seed, which he then wiped off on the donkey and on the mare and on cattle and on plants. Therefore the donkey has double seed, and therefore the mare has double seed, and therefore cattle are born in twos and twos.[33]

On the surface level, which presents the etiology of certain aspects of animal husbandry, this passage demonstrates how it is that the mule is barren, while the donkey can impregnate either a female donkey or a mare, and a mare can be impregnated by either a stallion or a jack donkey. The double seed of cattle (a term that may include horses or even humans, but here probably designates cows) may refer to twins, which do occur, though equally rarely in cows and mares, but what are we to make of the double seed of plants? This text is conspicuously silent on this issue, but yet another passage is not:

> When Prajapati laid hold of these creatures, the he-mule went away from them. [Prajapati] followed [the mule] and took his seed, which he then wiped off on the donkey. Therefore the donkey has double seed. They also say, 'He wiped it off on the mare.' Therefore the mare has double seed. They also say, 'He wiped it off on the plants.' Therefore plants glisten even though they are not anointed. They also say, 'He placed it in offspring.' Therefore twins are born. Therefore the mule has no offspring, for his seed has been taken from him.[34]

This text explains the double seed of the plants (that 'glisten' with their inner sap or seed in addition to the solid seed with which they propagate themselves) and goes on to correct the stockbreeding error of the previous text by stating that offspring in general, not cattle in particular, may be born as twins. The offspring may have been attracted, along with the plants, from another myth, for they do not naturally fall into line with the other creatures (horses and cattle) more central to this text. And we do not have to look far to find the myth from which they emigrated: it is provided by the cycle in which Indra transfers to several groups of living things, including plants and offspring, his procreative powers in exchange for casting off his evil[35] (even as he casts off the 'evil' of his androgyny, his 'double seed'—male and female—on the impotent man who has no seed, neither male nor female).[xiii] The use of a tree or plant to receive evil is a very old Indian idea; the *Atharva Veda* addresses a 'wiping-off plant' (Apamarga) that removes all sins: 'The sin, the pollution, whatever we have done with evil, by you we wipe that off.'[36]

Two final texts in this series connect the theme of the double seed of the donkey (though not of the mare) not with Indra and the myth of transference but with Agni and two other Rig Vedic myths connected with Agni: the myth of the search for the lost Agni[37] and the myth of the chariot race. In these two texts, as in the myths we have seen, the concept of doubling, exchange and substitution is central, but here the precise nature of these doublings and equations is rather different. The first text is quite brief:

> When the gods were searching for Agni, they saw one animal for two animals, the donkey for the cow and for the sheep. And since they saw one animal for two animals, therefore the donkey, though he is one, has double seed.[38]

The donkey is 'for' the other two animals probably in the sense of being able to serve as a substitute for either of them in the Vedic ritual; for both the cow and the sheep are sacrificial animals, for which substitutes are often mentioned in the Brahmanas.[39] But this 'doubling' does not provide for an exchange in the same way as the 'doubling' of the seed of the mare did. The donkey's double seed is not for the two female animals that he is 'for', the cow and the ewe; it is for the jenny and the mare. The combination of these two different sorts of equivalences yields us four female animals

---

[xiii] See 'Together Apart'.

arranged in two pairs: the sacrificial cow and sheep, and the procreative jenny and mare. The male donkey provides the pivot around which the others move, even as Indra is the pivot for the cow, mare, stallion and bull in the *vrishanashva* cluster.

Four animals in two different pairs appear in the last text in this series, in which the mule provides a more homogeneous substitute for the ram, so that we have three equines and one bovine (two males and two females):

> Agni ran the chariot race using a chariot drawn by female mules. As he drove them on he burned out their wombs; therefore they do not conceive. Dawn (Ushas) raced with a chariot drawn by cows; Indra with horses. The Ashvins raced with donkeys, and the Ashvins won, but they wore out the speed and energy of the donkey. Therefore the donkey is the slowest of all beasts of burden, but they did not take away the strength of his seed; therefore he has potency and possesses a double seed.[40]

The female mules at the beginning are barren; the male donkeys at the end are doubly potent (though not doubly strong); and in the middle we have the contrasting pair of (presumably normally fertile) female cows and male horses. The double seed of the donkey is linked with other special qualities in another text, which does not mention the other animals in the group but simply concentrates on the donkey, though the female mule is also present by implication:

> One gathers things with a donkey, and therefore the donkey is the best of all domestic animals [*pashus*] for bearing burdens. One gathers things with a donkey, and therefore the donkey grows fat beyond all other domestic animals even on bad grazing, for people gather food and the *arka* plant with him. One gathers things with a donkey, and therefore the donkey has double seed but gives birth to the least [fertile] of animals [the mule], for Agni burnt out his womb.[41]

'His' womb must refer to the womb of the mule, not the womb of the donkey (female donkeys being entirely fertile), and it can hardly refer to the womb of the male mule, except perhaps in the sense of 'the place from which the male mule is born', which is, again, contradicted by natural evidence of fertile female donkeys. It must, therefore, refer back to the other myths in which Agni burns out the wombs of the female mules precisely in order that the donkey may have the double seed that is mentioned here. This destruction of the wombs by Agni is transformed in the later mythology into the belief that we have already encountered, that it is the unborn or unbirthable foal of the female mule that destroys its mother's womb.

But let us return to the myth of the chariot race. In our text of that myth there are different sorts of exchanges: the female mules whose wombs are burnt out get nothing in return; the donkeys sacrifice speed for virility. In this, the donkeys' exchange seems at first to have the same structure as that of Indra, who gives fertility to those who take his sin upon them. But Indra does not lose his powers of fertility when he grants them to others; he merely loses his sin. Thus he is a two-time winner even as the mules raced by Agni are two-time losers. The ram who gives his testicles to Indra is also, like the mules, a double loser: he gives up his virility, and he gives up his life.

Thus, in this text, Indra and the mare are unpenalized winners; the mules and the ram are unrewarded losers. These are 'exchanges' only in the most technical sense; in reality, they are thefts, which explain why certain animals have something that other animals lack. The donkeys alone have a genuine and explicit exchange. Yet there may be a kind of exchange implicit in the myths of the mules that we have seen in the other texts, for though the mules have no seed at all, they do have the unusual ability to benefit from a kind of double seed not in their progeny but in their parents: unlike the other animals, they have two different parents— indeed, two different sets of parents, the mule being born of a jack donkey and a mare, the jennet (or female mule) from a jenny donkey and a stallion.

A final task remains before we return to our original Rig Vedic problem, and that is to demonstrate how Indra is connected with these mutually related animals. This is easily enough done. Indra on various occasions is said to have transformed himself into a ram or a buffalo (as we have seen), and, far more often, a horse or a bull; this is the primary manifestation of his *maya*, his magic power of transformation and creation. More precisely, our Rig Vedic verse about the wife of the seed-bearing stallion is cited in several Brahmanas[42] that neatly wedge it in between verses referring to Indra as a ram and a bull:

[One should invoke Indra by calling him] 'O ram of Medhatithi' [RV 8.2.40], because he became a ram and drank the king [Soma]. And, 'O wife of the seed-bearing stallion' [RV 1.51.13], because the Bounteous Indra became the wife of the seed-bearing stallion and lived in that species. And, 'Down-leaping Gaura bull' [TA 1.12.3], for he became a Gaura bull and leaped down into the ocean.

Immediately after this passage comes a group of epithets that deal with the human incarnations of Indra, centring around his role as the lover of Ahalya. Through this conjunction of human and animal realms, we can see a thread that connects all of these brief allusions to myths and that makes sense of our Vedic verses.

The ram is the animal whose testicles are used to restore Indra after Gautama has castrated him in punishment for his seduction of Gautama's wife, Ahalya.[xiv] The ram of Medhatithi is also associated with Indra, who took the form of a ram to attend Medhatithi's sacrifice and who later helped Medhatithi to win two celestial nymphs.[43] Medhatithi is also linked with the themes of castration and change of sex (Indra as the mare) through another story told by Sayana: a curse from the gods turned a man named Asanga into a woman, but the sage Medhyatithi (sic) turned him back into a man again.[44] And the Gaura bull (Indra as the bull) is connected with the mare both through the ambiguity of the bull-stallion (*vrishanashva*) and through the Rig Vedic verse in which Indra causes a mare to give birth to a bull. The paragraph as a whole, therefore, is about sexual transformations, mutilations, or transgressions in the human world on the part of Indra, which are reversed, restored, or expiated, respectively, by animals.

When we combine these various strands of the mythology of Indra's sexual adventures among animals and women in the *Rig Veda* and the Brahmanas, we can discern not exactly a plot but at least the structure of a plot. Indra seduces a married female (Ahalya, or the queen in the horse sacrifice). On the anthropomorphic level, this is a sin, and he loses his powers, which must be restored. But at the same time, on the animal level, this same act is a source of the powers that are being lost: in the form of an animal, Indra (and, through him, the sacrificer, particularly the king) takes on himself the powers of the animal that he cuckolds (stallion or monkey) or castrates (ram).

This is the multifaceted tale of a god, Indra, who partakes of the virility of what Jaan Puhvel has called the Indo-European 'macho trio' (ram, bull and stallion).[45] We have already encountered this trio, embedded in a series in the myth of primeval incest: the fleeing daughter starts as a human and then becomes a cow, a mare, a female donkey, goat and sheep, going on to give birth to everything including ants.[46] There is a fine symmetry to this list, in the context of the myths about species that we have just been considering. At the two ends of the spectrum are humans and 'ants and

[xiv] See 'The Mythology of the *Kamasutra*'.

everything else', the two animal categories that frame the rank and file mammals. Those mammals appear here as the female counterparts of the macho trio: the cow (for the bull or buffalo), the mare and the female donkey (that we have seen to be the two consorts of the stallion) and the goat or sheep (for the ram; the goat and sheep are often joined in a single Sanskrit noun, *ajavi*, goat-sheep, and the two animals, though not of the same species, are very closely related). The list thus encompasses all the defining species of the ancient Indian world, and Indra is closely associated with all of them.

The macho trio, and their female counterparts, constitute the class of animals known in Sanskrit as *pashu* (cognate with the Latin *pecus*). I have translated it as 'cattle' (as in the myth in which cattle bring forth their young in twos), but it more properly designates the domestic animals, in contrast with the wild animals or *mrigas*. Thus, while the Brahmana version of the myth of primeval incest says that the creator's daughter became a wild animal (*mriga*), the Upanishads make a major change by saying that she became each of the three major branches of domestic animals (*pashus*): bovines (cow), equines (mare and female donkey) and extended ovines (sheep and goat). From our standpoint, humans and 'ants and everything else' are equally remote from this central group, but in the Indian view the humans, at least, are a part of it. The *Atharva Veda* says that there are five kinds of *pashus*—and the context indicates that what is meant is domestic animals suitable to be sacrificed:[xv] humans, cows and bulls, horses, goats and sheep; Sayana's commentary on this text adds that the term 'horses' designates all the animals that have a single hoof,[47] the term used in the Upanishadic passage to designate the animals that were produced from the female donkey, *not* from the horse.

Yet there are other definitions of *pashu* that give a separate place to the donkey; another passage in the *Atharva Veda* says that there are seven *pashus*, and Sayana lists the original five, plus the donkey and the camel.[48] The *Mahabharata* puts the finishing touches on the schema by saying that there are seven wild *pashus* (lion, tiger, boar, monkey, bear, elephant and *buffalo*) and seven domestic *pashus* (the usual five, plus the donkey and the *mule*).[49] The buffalo on this list is the wild buffalo, which may suggest that the buffalo in our original Rig Vedic text is meant to supply the wild counterpart for the domestic bull, to imply that Indra is both a wild animal and a domestic animal. That the mule is listed alongside the donkey and the horse with the domestic animals is also significant; I think it implies

---

[xv] See 'Sacrifice and Substitution'.

that the list was conceived along symbolic rather than purely practical lines. The mule may not be a separate species (since it results from the crossing of two species), but it is an animal with a very special symbolic meaning of its own, distinct from that of its two parents.

Finally, we should note the implications of the inclusion of human beings in all of the classical lists of *pashus*. *Pashus* are animals fit to be sacrificed to the gods; they are the livestock of the gods, the food of the gods.[xvi] Human beings are simply the best of these animals; what the 'macho trio' is to men, the larger group of *pashus*, that includes men, is to the gods. When Indra then takes the form of a sacrificial animal or a human being, he is participating in the world that nourishes him and gives him his power, through food or through sex or through death, all of which are implicated in the Vedic sacrifice.

Indra becomes a mare in the species of a stallion. He loses power (symbolized by seed) when he is transformed into a female, *and* he gains power (symbolized by seed) when a castrated ram is sacrificed to him. The implications of Indra's transformation into an animal or another gender are supplementary rather than contradictory. The god undergoes both transformations at once when he becomes the wife of the bull-stallion.

[xvi] See 'The Concept of Heresy'.

DOGS AS DALITS IN INDIAN LITERATURE[1]

Animals play important roles in the Hindu religious imaginary. Gods become incarnate as animals and have animal vehicles; cats and herons are used as symbols of ascetic hypocrisy; yogic *asanas* and sexual positions are named after animals. The process works in two opposite directions at once. On the one hand, the observation of the local fauna provides images with which people may think of their gods; whether or not people get the gods that they deserve, they tend to get the gods (and demons) that their animals deserve. On the other hand, the ideas that people have about the nature of the gods, and of the world, and of themselves, will lead them to project onto animals certain anthropomorphic features that may seem entirely erroneous to someone from another culture observing the same animal. Clearly the two—the animals of the mind and the animals of the terrain—are intimately connected, and both are essential to our understanding of Hinduism.[i]

Texts about the lower castes are sometimes masked by narratives about dogs, standing for the people now generally called Dalits, formerly called Untouchables. Many Dalit groups were also called 'Dog-Cookers' (Shva-Pakas[ii]), because caste Hindus thought that these people ate dogs,[iii] who in turn ate anything and everything, and in Hinduism, you are what you eat.[iv] Some texts covertly critical of the caste system reverse the usual symbolism of dogs and speak of breaking the rules for dogs, treating them as if they

---

[i] See 'Zoomorphism'.

[ii] *Shvan*, 'dog,' is the source of our 'hound', and *paka* (from the Sanskrit *pak/c*, 'cook'), means ripe, cooked, or perfected and is related to the English term borrowed from Hindi, 'pukka', as in 'pukka Sahib', 'well-ripened/cooked/perfected Englishman'.

[iii] The British, too, made this equation, as in the nineteenth-century signs that often proclaimed 'No Dogs or Indians Allowed'.

[iv] See 'Eating Karma'.

were not impure. Moreover, the dog that doesn't bark[v] generates a silence that speaks; it is a good metaphor for the voice of marginalized people that we can sometimes hear only when it does not speak.

Countless terms have been coined to designate these lowest castes, the dispossessed or underprivileged or marginalized groups, including the tribal peoples. Sanskrit texts usually named them by specific castes (Chandala, Chamara, Pulkasa, etc.) or called them 'Low and Excluded' (Apasadas) or 'Born Last' (Antyajas). Much later, the British called them Untouchables, the Criminal Castes, the Scheduled Castes, Pariahs (a word borrowed from Tamil), the Depressed Classes, Outcastes and so forth. Gandhi called them Harijans ('the People of God'[vi]). Beginning in the 1930s and 40s and continuing now, the members of these castes have called themselves Dalits (using the Marathi/Hindi word for 'oppressed' or 'broken' to translate the British 'Depressed'). Post-colonial scholars call them (and other low castes) Subalterns. Many Dalits, particularly but not only the activists, don't consider themselves Hindu; one, Kancha Ilaiah, wrote a book entitled, *Why I Am Not a Hindu*. But his book argues within the categories and mythologies of the very Hindu traditions that he denies; even in rejection, there's Hindu influence.

While no actual reforms took place in Hinduism in this regard till the nineteenth century, there have been protests against the mistreatment of the lower castes from a very early age in India. But such challenges, in Hinduism's religious texts, generally took the form of renouncing caste society and forming an alternative society in which caste was ignored. The Brahmins, after all, did not produce a great literature in a vacuum, and they did not control the minds of everyone in India. They drew upon, on the one hand, their own lives and those of the political actors of their time, and, on the other hand, the lives of the non-literate classes. Because of the constant incursion of oral and folk traditions into Sanskrit texts, Dalits do speak, not always in voices recorded on a page but in signs that we can read if we try.

---

[v] Sherlock Holmes once solved a mystery, the case of Silver Blaze, a race-horse, by using a vital clue of omission. When Inspector Gregory asked Holmes whether he had noted any point to which he would draw the Inspector's attention, Holmes replied, 'To the curious incident of the dog in the night-time.' 'The dog did nothing in the night-time,' objected the puzzled Inspector, the essential straight-man for the Socratic sage. 'That was the curious incident,' remarked Sherlock Holmes. The fact that the dog did not bark when someone entered the house at night was evidence, in this case evidence that the criminal was someone familiar to the dog.

[vi] Many Dalits today reject this term as patronizing.

Certainly the Sanskrit texts argued that the lower castes would pollute any sacred text that they spoke or read, like milk contained in the skin of a dog.[vii] But this probably applied only to a limited corpus of texts, probably Vedic texts, rather than Sanskrit in general. It is also surely significant that there are strong sanctions against lower castes teaching the Vedas, but not necessarily against them learning it. The fact that the Vedas, the most ancient Sanskrit texts (c. 1500 BCE), scorned the horse-headed gods called the Ashvins for teaching the Vedas to the wrong sort of people, should alert us to the possibility that this, too, might be a rule honoured at least sometimes in the breach as well as in the observance. We can ferret out voices of many castes in the ancient texts, and once we have access to the oral and folk traditions, we can begin to write the alternative narrative with more confidence. And dogs play an important role in that narrative.

DOGS IN THE VEDAS

During the period in which the *Rig Veda* was composed (c. 1500-1000 BCE), dogs lived with the family, under the same roof or right outside the house. A watchdog is the object of a sleeping spell spoken by (according to various interpretations) a thief trying to break into a house, a lover on a secret nocturnal rendezvous in his mistress's house, mothers singing it as a lullaby to their children, or the family priest praying for a peaceful slumber for the inhabitants of the house. Some of the verses are:

> White and tawny son of Sarama, when you bare your teeth they gleam like spears in your snapping jaws. Fall fast asleep! Bark at the thief or the marauder, as you run up and back again, son of Sarama. Tear apart the wild boar, for he would tear you apart. But you are barking at those who sing Indra's praises; why do you threaten us? Fall fast asleep![2]

'Son of Sarama' means 'dog', because Sarama, Indra's beloved brindled bitch, is regarded as the mother of all dogs. The story goes that the Panis, tribal people who were the enemies of the Vedic people, had stolen cows from certain Vedic sages and hidden them in mountain caves. The gods sent Sarama to follow the trail of the cows; she found the hiding place, bandied words with the Panis, resisted their attempts first to threaten her and then to bribe her, and brought home the cows.[3] Sarama's two 'four-eyed' sons (probably a reference to the two eyes plus the two round marks

---

[vii] See 'The Concept of Heresy'.

above the eyebrows that many dogs have to this day) 'with flaring nostrils' guard the doors of hell, the domain of Yama, king of the dead.[4]

But by the time of the Brahmanas, texts composed a few centuries later (c. 900 BCE), the growing acknowledgment of class distinctions in this period, and the formulation of more intense rules of purity and impurity, began to find the omnivorous dog a useful symbol of the impure eater, the outsider. Another factor in the fall of the dog's status may have been the progressive decline of the Vedic gods Indra, Yama and Rudra, who were all associated with dogs.[5]

According to the Brahmana descriptions of the Vedic horse sacrifice,[viii] as the stallion stood in water, collateral relatives of the king and queen brought to the stallion a 'four-eyed' dog. Then, when the dog could no longer touch bottom in the water, the son of a whore killed him with a wooden club, saying, 'Off with the mortal! Off with the dog!' For, 'Truly the dog is evil, one's fraternal enemy; thus he slays his evil, his fraternal enemy . . . They say that evil seeks to grasp him who offers the horse sacrifice. He throws the dog beneath the feet of the horse. The horse has a thunderbolt. Thus by a thunderbolt he tramples down evil.'[6] The horse then put his right front hoof on the dead dog, while another spell banished any man or dog who might harm the horse.[7] The association of the dog with an unclean woman (the whore whose son kills him) and with feet, as well as explicitly with evil, is an indication of his status as a kind of scapegoat, more precisely a scape-dog, onto whom the sins of the community were transferred. The sacrifice of a 'four-eyed dog' at the beginning of the horse sacrifice also takes on deeper meaning when interpreted in the context of the ancient Indian game of dice,[ix] for the dice are also said to be four-eyed, that is, marked by four black spots.[8]

Bitches, too, lose cachet between the *Rig Veda* and the Brahmanas. In the Brahmanas, Sarama is still a somewhat positive figure; she still finds the cows that the Panis have stolen, and resists their bribes of food, as in the earlier text. Indra says, 'Since you found our cows, I make your progeny eaters of food,' and the brindled dogs who are Sarama's descendents 'kill even tigers'.[9] But now she eats the amniotic sac that contains the waters— just as dogs (and other animals) do eat the afterbirth—which the text regards as an act of murder. The same ambivalence hedges the curse/boon that her progeny will be omnivorous—it's good to kill tigers, but bad to eat the amniotic sac.

[viii] See 'The Mythology of Horses'.
[ix] See 'The Control of Addiction'.

Sarama is a good dog, but dogs as a species are bad, for they pollute the oblations by licking them in their attempt to eat them. A number of texts, therefore, ban dogs from the sacrificial area. The *Rig Veda* warns the sacrificer to keep 'the long-tongued dog' away,[10] and the textbook of caste law attributed to Manu (first or second century CE)[x] warns that if the king does not enforce the law, crows will eat the sacrificial cakes and dogs will lick the oblations.[11] Several Brahmanas tell of ways to destroy an ogress named Long-Tongue (Dirgha-jihva), who licks the milk offering and curdles it[12] or licks at the sacred elixir, Soma, all the time.[13] Though she is an ogress, not specifically called a dog, her name is the name of a dog in the *Rig Veda* and she does just what dogs are supposed to do: she licks the oblation. This Long-Tongue also just happens to have vaginas on every limb, like another ogress whom Indra destroyed by placing penises on each of his joints and seducing her.[14] And so Indra equips Kutsa's son (Indra's grandson) in the same way. Then:

> They lay together. As soon as he had his way with her, he remained firmly stuck in her. He saw these mantras and praised with them, and with them he summoned Indra. Indra ran against her and struck her down and killed her with his thunderbolt that was made of mantras. Whoever praises with these mantras slays his hateful fraternal rivals and drives away all evil demons.[15]

Long-Tongue's long tongue makes her ritually dangerous, and her equally excessive vaginas make her sexually both threatening and vulnerable (eventually immobilized, in an image perhaps suggested by observations of mating dogs, often similarly paralyzed). Despite her grotesque and bestial sexuality, Long-Tongue does no harm, yet she is destroyed. She is more sinned against than sinning. For the point of the Brahmana is that the dangerous bitch (in either canine or human form) is not, ultimately, dangerous—for the man who knows the mantras.

Dogs are satirically transformed from the lowest to the highest caste in an Upanishadic passage (c. 600 BCE):

> A group of dogs asked a Vedic priest, 'Please, sir, we'd like to find some food by singing for our supper. We are really hungry.' He asked them to return the next morning, and so the dogs filed in, sliding in slyly as priests slide in slyly in a file, each holding on to the back of the one in front of him. They sat down together and began to hum. Then

---

[x] See 'Why Should a Brahmin?'

they sang, 'Om! Let's eat! Om! Let's drink. Om! May the gods bring food! Lord of food, bring food! Bring it! Bring it! Om!' [16]

Apparently the dogs are rewarded, for the passage concludes with a statement that anyone who understands the secret meaning of the word 'hum' (a meaning that the text supplies) 'will come to own and to eat his own food'. To have dogs, the most impure of animals, impersonate Brahmins makes this remarkable satire, so reminiscent of George Orwell's *Animal Farm*, truly Bolshy. For dogs are already stigmatized as eaters of carrion; when someone annoys a sage by asking where the heart is lodged, he replies, impatiently, 'In the body, you idiot! If it were anywhere other than in ourselves, dogs would eat it, or birds would tear it up.'[17] The author of this text may be poking fun at Brahmins or pleading for more sympathy for dogs (and therefore for the lower castes), or both or none of the above.[18]

DOGS IN THE SANSKRIT EPICS

For caste-minded Hindus, dogs are as unclean as pigs are to orthodox Jews and Muslims, and they are, as we have observed before, symbols of the sorts of people that Sanskrit authors sometimes called 'Dog-cookers'. Dogs are also associated with the Adivasis, the so-called tribal peoples of India. Animal attendants, leather workers, people who touch human waste are often referred to as pigs and dogs. The *Mahabharata* (c. 300 BCE to 300 CE) generally upholds the basic prejudice against dogs, as in this story, which also makes clear the analogy between dogs and upwardly mobile Dalits:

> Once there was an ascetic of such goodness that the flesh-eating wild animals—lions, tigers, rutting elephants, leopards, rhinoceroses and bears—were like his disciples. A dog was his companion, devoted, tranquil, living on roots and fruits, with a heart like that of a human being. One day a hungry leopard came there and was about to seize the dog as his prey when the dog begged the sage to save him. The sage turned him into a leopard, and then, when a tiger attacked, into a tiger, and then a rutting elephant, and a lion[xi]. Now that he was carnivorous, all the other animals feared him and stayed away, and finally he wanted to eat the sage, who read his thoughts and turned him back into a dog, his own proper form by birth (*jati*). The dog moped about unhappily until the sage drove him out of the hermitage.[19]

[xi] He also becomes a *sharabha*, a fierce mythical beast, variously described.

This dog even has a human heart, but he must not be allowed to get ideas above his station. The phrase 'his own proper form by birth' can also be translated as 'his own proper form by caste', for *jati* means both birth and caste. Both the dog and the sage are all wrong from the very beginning; the dog violates dog dharma by being a vegetarian, where he should be a carnivore, and the sage is wrong, too, to protect the dog by making him bigger and bigger instead of putting him in safer and safer places. But the sage does not reciprocate the dog's devotion or attachment to him. Where the dog mis-recognizes himself as a human, the sage in the end is as cruel as a dog.[20]

A very different point of view is expressed in another story about dogs in the *Mahabharata*, which occurs at the very end, when king Yudhishthira is walking alone to heaven, and a dog attaches himself to him:

> Yudhishthira walked alone, never looking down. Only a dog followed him—the dog that I have already told you about quite a lot. Then Indra, king of the gods, came to Yudhishthira in his chariot and said to him, 'Get in.' Yudhishthira said, 'This dog, O lord of the past and the future, has been constantly devoted to me. Let him come with me, for I do not wish to be cruel.' Indra said, 'Today you have become immortal, like me, and you have won complete prosperity, and great fame, your majesty, as well as the joys of heaven. Leave the dog. There is nothing cruel in that. There is no place for dog-owners in the world of heaven; for evil spirits carry off what has been offered, sacrificed or given as an oblation into the fire, if it is left uncovered and a dog has looked at it. Therefore you must leave this dog, and by leaving the dog you will win the world of the gods.'
>
> Yudhishthira said, 'People say that abandoning someone devoted to you is a bottomless evil, equal—according to the general opinion—to killing a Brahmin. I think so too.' When the god Dharma, who had been there in the form of the dog, heard these words spoken by the Dharma King, he appeared in his own form and spoke to King Yudhishthira with affection and with gentle words of praise: 'Great king, you weep with all creatures. Because you turned down the celestial chariot, by insisting, "This dog is devoted to me," there is no one your equal in heaven and you have won the highest goal, of going to heaven with your own body.'[21]

Yudhishthira's dog, like Yama's dog, is testing a dead man at the gates of the other world; Yama's dog, like Sarama, is a good dog, a Vedic dog; but now, in the *Mahabharata*, dogs are regarded as polluting. What is most striking about this passage is that the god of Dharma himself becomes incarnate in this animal; it is as if the God of the Hebrew Bible became incarnate in a pig. (In later Hinduism, Dharma occasionally becomes incarnate as a Dalit, a Chandala.)

Clearly animals are being used here, as usual, to make a powerful ethical point; it is a way of arguing about the sorts of humans who should or should not go to heaven (a topic that the *Mahabharata* also explicitly addresses) or even, perhaps, by extension, about the castes who should or should not be allowed into temples. All good Hindus go to heaven, but they do so after dying and being given a different, heavenly body; Yudhishthira is unique in being given the gift of going to heaven in his own body. Perhaps in acknowledging his bond with animals—treating his dog like 'someone who has come to you for refuge' or 'a friend'— Yudhishthira has somehow preserved the animality of his own body (that very animality denied by the sages who regard both dogs and women as dirty) and enters heaven not merely as a disembodied spirit, but as his entire self.[22]

Yudhishthira refuses to abandon a dog who is 'devoted' (*bhakta*) to him. The dog, the loyal dog, is, after all, the natural *bhakta* of the animal kingdom; it's no accident that it's a dog, not, say, a cat, that follows Yudhishthira like that. (Cats, in Hinduism, are depicted as religious hypocrites.[xii]) But bhakti at this period meant little more than belonging to someone, dedicated to someone as a servant or loyal friend; it almost certainly did not yet have the specific overtone of passionate love between a god and his devotee that was to become characteristic of a branch of medieval Hinduism. Yet as the word expanded its meaning, the story of Yudhishthira and his dog often came to be read as a model for that sort of devotion. The commentator approves of Indra's action in rejecting contact with someone—the dog—who is literally untouchable, *a-sprishya*—the Hindu party line at this time, which Yudhishthira here challenges. For Yudhishthira, heaven will not be heaven if he cannot bring his dog with him.

Indra's argument, that dogs would pollute the sacrificial offerings merely by looking at them, let alone touching them, is a common one. Manu warns that if the king did not wield the rod of punishment justly, the dog would lick the oblation and everything would be upside down.[23] Elsewhere, the *Mahabharata*, in speaking of queen Sita, Rama's wife, who has lived in

[xii] See 'Zoomorphism'.

the home of a man other than her husband, compares her to an oblation that a dog has licked.[24] Much of the trouble in the *Mahabharata* begins with a dog that does *not* lick an oblation:

> When Janamejaya and his brothers were performing a sacrifice, a dog, a son of the bitch Sarama, came near. The brothers beat the dog, who ran howling back to his mother and told her that they had beaten him though he had neither looked at nor licked the offerings. Sarama then went to the sacrificial grounds and said to Janamejaya, 'Since you beat my son when he had not done anything wrong, danger will befall you when you do not see it coming.'[25]

As a result of his prejudiced mistreatment of this pup, Janamejaya soon gets into serious trouble with other animals (snakes). Thus the *Mahabharata* both begins and ends with a story about justice for dogs.

In the *Ramayana*, too, the other great Sanskrit epic, roughly contemporaneous with the *Mahabharata*, a dog comes to Rama and complains, first, that dogs are not allowed in palaces or temples or the homes of Brahmins (whereupon Rama invites him into the palace) and, second, that a Brahmin beggar beat him for no reason. Rama summons the Brahmin, who confesses that he struck the dog in anger when he himself was hungry and begging for food; when he told the dog to go away, the dog went only a short distance and stayed there; and so he beat him. Rama asks the dog to suggest an appropriate punishment for the Brahmin, and the dog asks that the Brahmin—whom he describes as filled with anger and bereft of dharma—be made the leader of a Tantric sect. (The dog himself had this position in a former life and regarded it as a guaranteed road to hell.) This granted, the Brahmin feels certain he has been given a great boon and rides away proudly on an elephant, while the dog goes to Varanasi and fasts to death.[26] Clearly, the dog is morally superior to the Brahmin, and Rama treats him with great respect throughout this long and rather whimsical episode.

But in Yudhishthira's case the conflict remains unresolved; the text equivocates. The sudden intrusion of the voice of the author in the first person at the beginning of the episode ('the dog that I have already told you about quite a lot'[27]) is highly unusual, almost unprecedented. It is as if the author has anticipated the end of the story and begins to remind the audience that it is just a story—and not only just a story, but just a test (as they used to say of air raid signals on the radio), one of a series of tests that Dharma set for his son, all of which he passed.[28] For the dog never does go to heaven, never violates Hindu law, because there was no dog; it was all an illusion; in case of a real dog . . . what then? The story shows just how rotten the caste system is, but does not change it. No dogs get into heaven.

DOGS IN THE PURANAS

Centuries later, in the *Skanda Purana* (c. 700–1150 CE), dogs are depicted very differently: they are the means by which sinners obtain a salvation otherwise beyond their reach.[xiii] There is a complex story of salvation by dog in the *Vamana Purana* (c. 450–900 CE), a story about the very evil king Vena:[29]

> Vena went to purify himself at the *tirtha* (bathing place) of Shiva the Pillar (Sthanu), but the gods forbade him to bathe there. Now, there was a dog there who had been a man in a previous life but had been sinful and hence reborn as a dog. The dog came to the Sarasvati river and swam there, and his impurities were shaken off and his thirst slaked. Then he was hungry, and entered Vena's hut; when Vena saw the dog he was afraid. Vena touched him gently and the dog showered him with water from the *tirtha*. Vena plunged into the water, and by the power of the shrine, he was saved. Shiva offered Vena a boon, and Vena said, 'I plunged into the lake out of fear of this dog, for the gods forbade me to bathe here. The dog did me a favour, and so I ask you to favour him.' Shiva was pleased and promised that the dog would be freed from sin and would go straight to Shiva's heaven. And he promised Vena that he, too, would go to Shiva's heaven—for a while.[30]

The unclean dog transfers the water from his body to that of Vena, both by shaking himself (as wet dogs do) and by frightening Vena so much that Vena jumps into the water. I take the text to mean that Vena could jump into the water only after the dog had sprinkled him. Vena cannot enter the shrine himself, for reasons that are spelt out in another version of the story: as he approaches the shrine of Shiva, the wind in the sky says, 'Do not do this rash deed; protect the shrine. This man is enveloped in an evil so terrible that it would destroy the shrine.'[31] This is the Catch 22: the sinner would pollute the shrine before the shrine could purify the sinner; the sick man is too sick to take the medicine. The dog, therefore, intercedes for him: he makes him a little less polluted, so that he becomes eligible for real

---

[xiii] See 'The Scrapbook'.

purification. Vena is not finished yet; there are other rebirths before he is finally freed, but the dog makes it possible for him to proceed on that path. And finally, at the end of the myth, and a millennium or two after Yudhishthira's dog in the *Mahabharata* vanished before he could enter heaven, this dog enters Shiva's heaven, the world of the one Hindu god who does not treat dogs as polluting.

DOGS IN CONTEMPORARY INDIA

According to Hindu texts, dogs are *supposed* to be treated badly, and, as we have seen, usually are; but on many occasions, dogs are, perversely, honoured. One of those occasions today is the Tantric worship of Shiva in his aspect as Bhairava, who often has the form or face of a dog or a dog as his vehicle. All over India, there are Bhairava temples where people offer puja to both statues of dogs and living dogs. In the temple to Kal Bhairava in Varanasi, there are images of Shiva astride a big white dog, as well as black plaster statues of dogs, paintings of dogs, metal dogs, and real live dogs who sleep and wander inside and outside the temple. Pilgrims to Varanasi worship the dogs, both the live ones and the images, and decorate them with garlands of Indian doughnuts and other things delicious to dogs, which the live dogs of course immediately shake off and eat. All of which is evidence either that (some) dogs are more sacred than cows in Hinduism or, perhaps, that Hindu views of animals are far too complex to capture by words like 'sacred' or 'impure'. Other peoples' zoological taxonomies look bizarre only to people who view them through their own rather ethno-centric lenses.

A number of castes[xiv] take hounds with them during their long expeditions when they graze their sheep in mountain forests. They regard dogs as forms of their god, Mallanna (or Mailara), whom hounds follow in his expeditions and who also takes the form of a dog on occasion. In rituals, the priests (or, sometimes, the householders themselves) enact the roles of dogs and drink milk that they regard as fed to Mallanna. Kal Bhairava may be a Sanskritized (and Tantricized) version of this folk-god.

The worshippers of the Maharashtrian horseman god Khandoba (a form of Shiva, often assimilated to Mallanna and called Martanda) sometimes act as his dogs, and bark in the course of his rituals, as Bhairava is said to have told them to do. These devotees are called 'Tigers' in Marathi and

---

[xiv] Such as the Kurnis (a weaver caste) of Karnataka and Kurumas (a shepherd caste) of northern Andhra Pradesh.

Kannada; it is said that they originally *were* tigers, but that through the *darshan* of the god Martanda their bodies became human[32]—a fascinating inversion of the *Mahabharata* story about the dog who got into serious trouble by trying to become a tiger. Forest-dwelling Maharashtrian tribal groups like the Warlis worship and propitiate tigers as the 'sentinel deities' or guardians of the village boundaries, but the word for tiger can also denote a fierce domesticated animal—a watchdog, sheepdog, or hunting dog of the kind that attend Khandoba.[33] The mixing of 'tiger' and 'dog' is chronic in myth, ritual and art; Bhairava's vehicles are occasionally the dog and the tiger or two animals each of which is a mixture of both.

Two pro-dog stories appeared in the news in November 2007, one from Nepal and one from Tamil Nadu. The first (BBC News, Thursday, 8 November 2007) reported on a Police Dog Training School in Nepal that trains dogs for rescue and search, for tracking criminals, explosives and drugs, and for patrol. There are fifty-one dogs, some born on the premises, others from outside. For most of the year, the dogs are not well treated, and many are left to forage for themselves and feed on scraps, but for one day a year, they are honoured and garlanded (presumably with edibles). The article began: 'According to the Hindu scripture, the *Mahabharat*, dogs accompanied Dharmaraj Yudhisthir on his journey to heaven. There is also a Hindu belief that dogs guard the underworld.' Aside from giving Yudhishthira more than one dog, this was a good, historical approach, and the article concluded: 'It's recognized that no animal has a closer relationship with people.' The compassion here is limited to some dogs, some of the time. But it's a start.

The second story, carried by the *Hindustan Times* and CNN from New Delhi (CNN.com Europe, 13 November 2007) is worth reporting in its entirety:

> A man in southern India married a female dog in a traditional Hindu ceremony in a bid to atone for stoning two dogs to death, a newspaper reported Tuesday. [Picture: P. Selvakumar, left, garlands his 'bride', Selvi.] The 33-year-old man married the sari-draped dog at a temple in the southern state of Tamil Nadu on Sunday after an astrologer said it was the only way to cure himself of a disability, the *Hindustan Times* newspaper reported. P. Selvakumar told the paper that he had been suffering since he stoned two dogs to death and strung them up in a tree 15 years ago. 'After that my legs and hands got paralyzed and I lost hearing in one ear,' the paper quoted him as saying. Family members chose a stray female dog named Selvi who was then bathed and clothed

for the ceremony. The groom and his family then had a feast, while the dog got a bun, the paper said.

Again the special moment of compassion is balanced by a memory of more typical cruelty. As we have seen, the tension between cruelty and compassion has marked the entire span of the history of dogs in India.

A contemporary Tamil poem, entitled, simply, 'Dog', turns upon the plantain leaf on which strict South Indian Brahmins eat their meals, as a leaf is disposable and hence not as vulnerable to pollution as a reusable plate would be:

> The Brahmin in the house opposite ours
> Eats late, and tosses
> His leaf on the street.
> Two dogs tear each other apart
> In the deserted street. Their howls
> Wake up dogs sleeping elsewhere
> In town. Others in distant streets
> Follow. Even dogs in the outskirts
> Jump into the fray. The noise travels—
> Beyond the rice-fields and orchards.
> Dogs in the next town take it up.
> It's an endless chain. However,
> If one were to stop and ask
> The last dog the cause of it all,
> I wonder what he would have to say.[34]

The poem sounds the last word on the relationship between Brahmins, dogs and the transmission of history.

SACRED COWS AND BEEFEATERS[1]

SACRED COWS

The belief that the Hindus have sacred cows is attested in no less an authority than the *Oxford English Dictionary* (OED), which defines the term as, primarily, designating 'The cow as an object of veneration amongst Hindus', and cites an 1891 reference from Rudyard Kipling's father, already in the context of Hindu–Muslim conflict: 'The Muhammedan . . . creed is in opposition to theirs [sc. the Hindus] and there are rankling memories of a thousand insults to it wrought on the sacred cow.'[2] But the term soon became globalized as a metaphor, indeed a backhanded anti-Hindu ethnic slur. In US journalism the word came to mean 'someone who must not be criticized', and in American literature, 'An idea, institution, etc., unreasonably held to be immune from questioning or criticism,' a sense in which Margaret Mitchell used it in 1936 in *Gone with the Wind*: 'I think of my brother, living among the sacred cows of Charleston, and most reverent towards them.'

The idea of a 'sacred cow' is an 'Irish bull' (the old British chauvinist term for an oxymoron), which the OED defines as 'A self-contradictory proposition; in mod. use, an expression containing a manifest contradiction in terms or involving a ludicrous inconsistency unperceived by the speaker. Now often with epithet *Irish*; but the word had been long in use before it came to be associated with Irishmen.' The word 'sacred' is in any case a Christian term that can be, at best, vaguely and inadequately applied in India, but cows would not in any case qualify for the adjective: there are no cow-goddesses or temples to cows or icons of cows to which worship is offered, though there are festivals in which people decorate cows and give them fruits and flowers. Since cows are not deities, there is no need for cow statues. Benign bulls are beautifully depicted at the doors of Shiva temples, and there are temples to monkeys, tiger temples, temple elephants, shrines to snakes, and even a temple or two to dogs, who are closely associated with Bhairava (an aspect of Shiva).[i] But not to cows.

'Holy' (or 'sacred') means a lot more than not-to-be-killed. Few of us kill, or eat, our children, but none would argue that they are sacred. Cows are, in fact, one of the few animals that are not the object of worship in India. Yet cows have been, for centuries, cultural symbols of non-violence[ii] and of the passive, bovine aspect of women, in sharp contrast with mares,[iii] whom the mythology depicts as oversexed, insatiable and Fatally Attractive.

COWS IN ANCIENT INDIA

In ancient India, from the time of the oldest religious text, the *Rig Veda* (c. 1500 BCE), cows were eaten regularly, both ritually and for many of the same reasons that people nowadays eat Big Macs. Like most cattle-breeding cultures, the Vedic Indians generally ate the castrated steers, but they would eat the female of the species on certain special occasions such as rituals or when welcoming a guest or a person of high status.[3] The Brahmanas say that a bull or cow should be killed when a guest arrives, a cow should be sacrificed to Mitra and Varuna, and a sterile cow to the Maruts, and that twenty-one sterile cows should be sacrificed in the horse-sacrifice.[4] For 'the cow is food'.[5] The grammarian Panini, who may have lived as early as the fifth or sixth century BCE, glossed the word *go-ghna* (literally, 'cow-killer') as 'one for whom a cow is killed, that is, a guest'. [3.4.73][6] A Dharmasutra from the third century BCE specifies: 'The meat of milk cows and oxen may be eaten, and the meat of oxen is fit for sacrifice.'[7] This textual evidence is further supported, in this period, by archaeological indications such as cattle bones found near domestic hearths, bearing marks of having been cut, indicating that their flesh was eaten.[8]

It is one of the ironies of history that the British, who called themselves Beefeaters, once ruled India. Yet the ancient inhabitants of India in their attitude to cows somewhat resembled not Britons so much as early Texans: the people of the *Rig Veda* (like other members of the Indo-European family) were cattle-herders and cattle-rustlers, who went about stealing other peoples' cows and pretending to be taking them *back*, all in the service of a religion that argued for *Lebensraum*, constant expansion, more

[i] See 'Dogs as Dalits'.
[ii] See 'The Ambivalence of Ahimsa'.
[iii] See 'The Submarine Mare'.

and more grazing land for their horses. They sacrificed cows to the gods and ate them themselves, and they counted their wealth in *pashus* (cattle), cognate with Latin *pecus* (as in 'impecunious'), Spanish *pecos* (as in 'Pecos Bill'). On the other hand, one Brahmana passage forbids the eating of either cow or bull (*dhenu* or *anaduh*),[iv] concluding that anyone who did eat them 'would be reborn as something so strange that people would say, "He committed a sin, he expelled the embryo from his wife."' The text then adds, 'However, Yajnavalkya, said, "I *do* eat [the meat of both cow and bull], as long as it's tasty."'[9]

But one of the 'category error' methods that Hindus used to resolve their ambivalence about ahimsa[v] (nonviolence, or, more precisely, non-injury) was to make an exception for cows. Later texts insist that cows should not be eaten, and some people made a special exception and *did* eat meat but did *not* eat the meat of cows, as Romila Thapar points out: 'Eventually it became a matter of status to refrain from eating beef and the prohibition was strengthened by various religious sanctions. Significantly, the prohibition was prevalent only among the upper castes.'[10] The argument against eating cows was not the sort of economic case that is often made today, and in any case that would have applied to other animals as well. Nor was the appeal of remaining superior to beef-eating Muslim invaders and *mlechas* (unclean invaders, such as the British) relevant in the ancient period, though such concerns did indeed eventually contribute to the cow-protection case. It was more a symbolic argument about female purity and docility, and a religious argument about Brahmin sanctity, that prevailed from the start. And the social-hierarchy reasons for not eating the meat of the cow persisted, as the sociologist M.N. Srinivas pointed out; the lower castes gave up beef when they wanted to move up the social ladder through the process known as 'Sanskritization'.[11]

The *Mahabharata* explained the transition to the non-eating of cows in a famous myth: 'Once, when there was a great famine, King Prithu took up his bow and arrow and pursued the earth to force her to yield nourishment for his people. The earth assumed the form of a cow and begged him to spare her life; she then allowed him to milk her for all that the people needed.'[12] This myth imagines a transition from hunting wild cattle (the earth cow) to preserving their lives, domesticating them, and breeding them for milk, in a transition to agriculture and pastoral life. It visualizes

---

[iv] Since only cows and bulls are prohibited, the text may allow for the eating of castrated bulls, steers or bullocks.

[v] See 'The Ambivalence of Ahimsa'.

the cow as the paradigmatic animal that yields food without being killed. The earth-cow later becomes the wishing-cow (Kama-dhenu), from whom you can milk anything you desire—not just food but silk cloths, armies of soldiers, anything. (The same function was sometimes assigned to wishing-trees [Kalpa-vriksha] or the ocean of milk, from which one can pick or churn whatever is desired.)

COWS IN CONTEMPORARY INDIA

Gandhi's attitude to cows was an essential component of his version of nonviolence.[vi] Gandhi used the image of 'calf love' (*vatsalya*), the calf's love for and from a mother cow, particularly the Earth Cow, Mother Earth, as a key symbol for his imagined Indian nation. He tried to include Muslims in the family, but cow protection was a factor in his failure to attract large-scale Muslim support, for, by the nineteenth century, one of the objects of the cow-protection movement was to force Muslims, who killed cows, to leave India.

The present-day fundamentalist movement of 'Hindutva'[vii] (literally, 'Hindu-tion') has attempted to use the alleged sanctity of the cow to disenfranchise Muslims, some of whom eat beef and/or slaughter the cows that many Hindus—in Kerala and Tamil Nadu, for instance—eat. Such Hindus argue that 'We Hindus have always been here in India, and have Never Eaten Cows; Those Muslims have come in, and Kill and Eat Cows, and therefore must be destroyed.'[viii] And it is not only the beef-eating Muslims (and Christians) who are the target of Hindutva's hate brigade. In 2002, five Dalits were lynched in Jhajjar, Haryana, for skinning a cow; days later, eighty Dalits from the villages of those killed converted to Buddhism, Christianity and Islam.[13]

THE ATTACK ON *THE MYTH OF THE HOLY COW*

In 2001, Dwijendra Narayan Jha, Professor of History at the University of Delhi, published *The Myth of the Holy Cow*, a dry, straight academic survey

---

[vi] See 'The Ambivalence of Ahimsa'.

[vii] See "The Politics of Hinduism' and 'You Can't Make an Omelette'.

[viii] The Hindutva argument resembles in many respects the old 'they-are-eating-our-children-and-poisoning-our-wells' accusation, which was levelled not just against the witches in Europe but, long before that, by the Romans against the Christians, the Christians against the Jews, and the Jews against various enemies. This myth still survives, in transformation, in Stanley Kubrick's film *Dr. Strangelove* in the character played by Sterling Hayden, who feared that the Communists were putting fluoride in the drinking water and hence polluting his 'precious bodily fluids'.

of the history of Sanskrit texts dealing with the eating, or not-eating, of cows. The book marshals indisputable evidence proving what every scholar of India has known for well over a century: that [a] the ancient Indians ate beef; [b] almost as early, the practice of vegetarianism in general, and, somewhat later, the prohibition of beef-eating in particular, spread throughout India, in Buddhism and Jainism as well as Hinduism, and continued alongside an on-going practice of meat-eating; and, finally, [c] several reformers, most famously Gandhi, made vegetarianism, particularly the taboo against eating beef, a central tenet of Hinduism. Professor Jha traces the history of the doctrine forbidding the eating of cows or the killing of cows, soundly and thoroughly covering both the classic texts and cutting-edge scholarship, both Indian and European.

The only shocking thing about this book is the news that someone had found it shocking, had been shocked, shocked by the argument that people used to eat cows in ancient India. Yet the cover of the book proudly proclaims: 'A Book the Government of India Demands be Ritually Burned', and the flyleaf assures us that the book was 'banned by the Hyderabad Civil Court and the author's life has been threatened.' *The Observer* likened the book's reception to that of Salman Rushdie's *Satanic Verses*, and even the more-PC-than-thou *Lingua Franca* felt that the case was sexy/trendy enough to justify a notice that the book 'was pulled from the country's shelves'. Why?

Apparently what makes this a shocking book is the simple fact that it contradicts the Hindutva party line (the right-wing Bharatiya Janata Party [BJP] was in power in India when Jha's book was published). Ironically, the pejorative phrase 'sacred cow' designates precisely the sort of fanaticism that has dogged the attacks on Professor Jha's book. His basic point stands and is proved beyond dispute: the claim that Hindus have never eaten cows is false. But who will listen to him? Have any of the people making the Hindutva arguments—which are not historical or scholarly but religious and political[ix]—read—or, indeed, will they ever read—Professor Jha's book? Michel Foucault and Edward Said, among others, have taught us that scholarship is often deeply implicated in creating the political mess in the first place; but scholarship has demonstrated far less power to clean the mess up. Like the sorcerer's apprentice, or Frankenstein, or the scientists on the Manhattan Project, scholars create imperialist monsters that they cannot control but merely watch, aghast, from the sidelines, crying, 'No,

[ix] See 'The Politics of Hinduism'.

no, put it *down!!!*' Yet the fact that *The Myth of the Holy Cow* was attacked is a good sign, a sign that someone among the Hindutva thugs reads, and worries that the pen may still be, if not mightier than the nuclear arsenal, at least a weapon worth scanning for, like knives at airports, a weapon capable of subversion.

ILLUSION AND REALITY IN THE
HINDU EPICS

IMPERMANENCE AND ETERNITY IN HINDU EPIC, ART AND PERFORMANCE[1]

ORAL AND WRITTEN PRESERVATION

The forms taken by the classics of India challenge many common assumptions about permanence and impermanence as well as the corollary distinctions between written and oral texts. In India, we encounter more oral traditions than written ones, and more fluid traditions than frozen ones. But more than that, we find a reversal of the assumed link between what is written and fixed, on the one hand, and what is oral and fluid, on the other.

Let us define a classic in a rather broad sense, as a work of art (particularly, but not necessarily, a work of literature) that comes to be accepted by a tradition over a great period of time as embodying what is good and true. Traditions pride themselves on their classics, and that pride is based upon two different but related assumptions: that the classics are in a sense eternal—forever fixed, frozen in the amber of carefully preserved written documents—and that they provide a shared communal base for all educated members of the culture. The Hindu examples to follow, however, show us that neither of these assumptions is true.

Each generation is inspired differently by their classics and retranslates them. It may even be that the very defining characteristic of a classic is that it is a work that must be retranslated by each new generation. Still, the core of meaning is preserved, even when the words of the translations change. Classics define themselves as being tied to a fixed core in the distant past, but the ties that bind the classic to its past change all the time. The Sanskrit tradition in India was continuous, unbroken for over three thousand years, but it changed constantly in the course of written retranslation and reinterpretation. And even more radical are the changes that occur through performance. Yet when the classics are transformed in performance, we experience them as a group; this shared moment is an important source of the belief that such works are 'unchanging' classics. Thus even some of the 'written' classics are in fact experienced, in their most important form, orally.

India has two sorts of Sanskrit classics, typified by two great texts, the *Rig Veda* and the *Mahabharata*. The *Rig Veda* is a massive collection of hymns, a text of over 350,000 words (as long as the *Iliad* and *Odyssey* combined) that was preserved orally for over three thousand years; and the great Sanskrit epic, the *Mahabharata*, is a text of over three million words (almost ten times as long as the *Rig Veda*) that was preserved orally and in manuscript form for over two thousand years. The relationship between orality and fluidity in these texts is the reverse of what one might expect if one simply extrapolated from what we think we know of classics.

The *Rig Veda* was preserved orally even when the Hindus had used writing for centuries. They refused to preserve the *Rig Veda* in writing because it was a sacred magic text, whose power must not fall into the wrong hands. Unbelievers and infidels, Dalits and women, were forbidden to learn Sanskrit, the sacred language, because they might defile or injure the magic power of the words; if the sacred chants were to be spoken by such people, it was believed, the words would be polluted like milk contained in the skin of a dog.[i] The text was, therefore, memorized in such a way that no physical traces of it could be found, much as a coded espionage message would be memorized and then destroyed (eaten, perhaps—orally destroyed) before it could fall into the hands of the enemy. This exclusively oral preservation also ensured that the *Rig Veda* could not be misused even in the right hands: You couldn't take the *Rig Veda* down off the shelf in a library, for you had to read it in the company of a wise teacher or guru, who would make sure that you were not injured by its power.

Now, one might suppose that a text preserved orally in this way would be subject to steadily encroaching inaccuracy and unreliability, that the message would become increasingly garbled like the message in a game of 'telephone'; but one would be wrong. For the same sacredness that made it necessary to preserve the *Rig Veda* orally rather than in writing also demanded that it be preserved with meticulous accuracy. The *Rig Veda* is regarded as a revealed text, seen in a vision or 'heard' (*shruti*) by the human seers to whom the gods dictated it. And one does not play fast and loose with revelation. There are no significant variant readings of the *Rig Veda*,

---

[i] See 'The Concept of Heresy'.

no detailed critical editions or textual apparatus. Just the *Rig Veda*. So much for the inevitable fluidity of oral texts.

Correspondingly, the expected fixity of written texts dissolves when we look at the second sort of Sanskrit classic, typified by the *Mahabharata*. Although the epic was preserved both orally and in manuscript, it is so extremely fluid that there is no single *Mahabharata*; there are hundreds of *Mahabharatas*—hundreds of different manuscripts and innumerable oral versions. The *Mahabharata* is not contained in a text; the story is there to be picked up and found, to be claimed like a piece of uncultivated land, salvaged as anonymous treasure from the ocean of story; it is constantly retold and rewritten both in Sanskrit and in vernaculars.[2] A.K. Ramanujan has remarked that no Indian ever hears the *Mahabharata* for the first time[3]; Alf Hiltebeitel has described it as 'a work in progress'[4]; and Milton Singer has seen it as a literature that 'does not belong in a book'.[5] The *Mahabharata* itself describes itself as unlimited in both time and space: 'Poets have told it before, and are telling it now, and will tell it. . . . What is here is found elsewhere, but what is not here is nowhere else.'[6] In contrast with the divine *Rig Veda* that was 'heard' (*shruti*), the *Mahabharata* is regarded as entirely humanly made, 'remembered' (*smriti*) and reconstructed differently by all of its many authors in the long line of literary descent from its first, human author. There is a *soi-disant* critical edition of the *Mahabharata*, with an apparatus of 'interpolations' longer than the text itself, but it has not been able to defend its claim to sit alone on the throne of the Ur-text. For the *Mahabharata* grows out of the oral tradition and then grows back into the oral tradition; it flickers back and forth between Sanskrit manuscripts and village storytellers, each adding new bits to the old story, constantly reinterpreting it. The anonymity of the text makes it appear to be a part of communal experience, like a ritual, like the whole sky; the author is as fluid as the text. So much for the inevitable fixity of written texts.

Once we begin to distinguish between texts that were (or that we think may have been) *composed* orally (in contrast with those that may have been composed in writing), those that were *preserved* orally (in contrast with those preserved in manuscript), and those that were traditionally *performed* orally, we begin to glimpse the complexity of the problem.[7] For both written and oral texts have both fluid and fixed forms.[8] Indeed, it makes far more sense to mark the distinction between fluid texts (whether written or oral) and fixed texts (again whether written or oral) than to go on making adjustments to our basically misleading distinction between oral and written texts.

Our shifting textual sands shift still more when we distinguish between the use of the inside and the outside of written texts. To use the inside means to use the text in a fluid way, as one might use an oral text: to interrupt the recitation in order to ask about the meaning, to write a commentary, to choose only appropriate passages to recite on a particular occasion. However, to use the outside of the text means to use it in a rigid way, to read or recite it without necessarily knowing its meaning at all, to recite it without any care for the choice of an appropriate message. Since many Hindus do not read the *Rig Veda* at all, and no one, Hindu or otherwise, can understand all of it, it has become a canon so deified and reified that one can have it and recite it but seldom *think* with it. Most of the people for whom the *Rig Veda* is canonical can use only the outside of it. Yet the *Rig Veda* has stamped its general world view, its way of thinking in terms of resemblances and hierarchies, upon all subsequent Indian thought.[9]

Indeed, the 'outside' of the text may be used even more rigidly: The book may be set down but never opened, making a silent statement about status or community; or the whole text may be recited from beginning to end so fast that no one can possibly understand it, as a way of gaining merit. On the other hand, memorization is the basic Indian method not merely of preserving the outside of a text but of understanding its inside. Thus it is said that certain people were able to learn to understand Tulsi's *Ramcharitmanas* by reciting it from beginning to end 108 times (an auspicious number), even when they didn't know a single word of Hindi, the language in which it is composed.[10]

In India, it is often the very sanctity of the text that limits its use to the outside. Manuscripts of great importance are venerated like icons and this veneration often takes the form of placing a daub of vermillion on the text. Over the years, the wet heat causes the vermillion to spread until the text becomes a mass of solid red, so that its sanctity makes it literally illegible.[ii] The book itself becomes solely a physical object, a vehicle for meaning not through the decipherment of the individual syllables that it contains but through the vision of the thing that represents the deity. The Sikhs deified their book and called it the Guru Granth Sahib (literally, Lord Book, the Guru), and Hindus revere Tulsi's *Ramcharitmanas* as an incarnation of the god Rama, offering it food, garlands and other traditional elements of

---

[ii] Edward Cameron Dimock of the University of Chicago told me that he once went to great trouble to track down an important manuscript that was kept in an inaccessible temple, only to find that it had been sanctified (and obliterated) in this way.

puja[11] (though not, sensibly, bathing it like other images of god). Bernard Faure describes this process as it relates to the transmission of certain Buddhist texts: 'The text itself thus became a pure surface, an empty mirror whose content did not really matter, a sign of orthodoxy. Its semiotic value takes precedence over its meaning.'[12]

And, just as the oral tradition of the *Rig Veda* is frozen, the so-called manuscript tradition of the *Mahabharata* is hopelessly fluid, in part because of the interaction in India between living oral variants and empty written variants. Indeed, Hindus have long been aware of the constant interaction between oral and written traditions of the *Mahabharata*. They explain that when Vyasa, the author of the *Mahabharata*, was ready to fix it in writing, he summoned as his scribe the elephant-headed god Ganesha, patron of intellectuals and merchants. (In doing this, Vyasa was reversing the roles that had been played by gods and mortals in the redaction of the *Rig Veda*, where gods had dictated the text to mortals, who inscribed it only in their memories.) Ganesha agreed to take Vyasa's dictation, but only on condition that Vyasa would not lag behind and keep Ganesha waiting for the next line; Vyasa in turn stipulated that Ganesha must not write down anything he did not understand. When, in the course of work, the divine amanuensis seemed to be getting ahead of the mortal author, Vyasa would quickly throw in a 'knot' that would make Ganesha pause for a moment. This accounts for the many scribal errors, corrupted lines, and linguistic stumbling blocks in the manuscript tradition of the great epic.[13] The curse of Ganesha torments every scholar who works on a combined oral/written tradition. It is ironic, I think, that the passage narrating the dictation by Vyasa to Ganesha is the very first one that the critical edition relegates to an appendix—indeed, to an appendix to an appendix; the passage that accounts for the irregularities in the epic resulting from its dual oral/ written status is rejected as just such an irregularity or 'knot'.

Many people in India are illiterate; but we are certainly wrong if we assume that illiteracy is an indication of cultural deprivation. When literacy is not widespread, the written word is often the special privilege of an elite, while oral culture—continuous and free-floating—belongs to the folk in general. This was the situation in Europe for many centuries and has generally prevailed in India. In ancient India, however, the *Rig Veda* was kept within the oral tradition on purpose, precisely in order to limit it to an elite, exclusive group; Sanskrit confined certain forms of the Indian classics (particularly sacred texts) to males of upper castes. Yet other parts of the tradition, relying as they do on oral transmission and consumption, float freely in India, and have remained continuous and unbroken for over three thousand years. The oral tradition has made it possible for millions of Indian villagers to be richly, deeply familiar with their own classics.

When printing began to make texts of the *Ramayana* widely available in India, both in Sanskrit and in vernacular translations, this did in fact lead to an increase in private study of the epic, but it also led to a great increase in the practice of public recitations of the *Ramayana*, attended by great crowds of literate people who experienced in the oral presentation something different from what they experienced in reading it silently at home.[14] In present-day India, where literacy is growing steadily, low-caste women are more likely to attend group readings of fixed written texts than group recitations of fluid commentaries on written texts, the latter demanding from them a level of knowledge and participation from which their background may have excluded them. The Indian people as a whole have seldom had access to such fixed oral classics as the *Rig Veda* and only recently—due to increasing literacy and expanding education—have they gained access to their fixed written classics, for example the *Ramcharitmanas* of Tulsidas. They are beginning to gain access to their fluid written classics, which include variants on the *Mahabharata* that are just now being written down. They have always, however, had access to their fluid oral classics: the tales, stories, images and songs that make up the ubiquitous oral tradition.

The Hindus express their awareness of the relationship between *shruti* (the Vedic canon), 'that which is heard', and *smriti* (the later dharma traditions), 'that which is remembered', in yet another way. Beginning with the *Mahabharata*, various texts from the *smriti* tradition are referred to as 'the fifth Veda'.[iii] Philip Lutgendorf has referred to this as 'the proverbial Hindu euphemism for the text one actually knows and loves'[15] and this is true enough. It means that the text that one knows and loves with intimacy is regarded as an integral part of the text that one does not know but that one loves with awe. It means that the fluid tradition (oral or written) is the child—the love child, perhaps—of the fixed tradition (also oral or written).

THE FLUIDITY OF TRUTH

The fluidity of the Hindu oral/written tradition is merely one aspect of the more general fluidity of Hindu attitudes to *all* kinds of truth. There is no Ur-text, for there is no Ur-reality. Hindus may maintain a belief in several

[iii] See 'Three (or More)'.

different, contradictory answers to the same question; they alter their definitions of reality in order to let such contradictions survive.[16] All truths being multiple, it is not surprising that the true version of any story is also multiple. In Sanskrit texts, the bard may recite a myth in a certain way, only to be interrupted by someone in the audience to whom the tale is being recited (an audience that is built into the text), who argues, 'We heard it differently.' When the person in the audience tells that second version, the bard replies, 'That is true, too, but your version happened in a different world-era'—or, in some stories, 'in a different rebirth'.[17] That is, the same event happens over and over again, but it may not happen in exactly the same way each time; and each happening is true. Moreover, what makes an event in India important is not that it happened at a particular time or place, but precisely the fact that it has multiplied, that it has happened many times in many places.

A wonderful example of the degree to which this sort of plurality is both a widely shared cultural assumption and a still-debated open question is the manner in which the Jains told the story of the end of the *Mahabharata*:

> The great Jain sage Hemacandra went about lecturing to great crowds, telling them, among other things, that the Pandavas, the heroes of the *Mahabharata*, had become Jain monks at the end of their lives. Upon learning of this, the Brahmins of that city complained to the king, pointing out that in Vyasa's *Mahabharata*, the Pandavas died in the Himalayas, after propitiating Shiva. 'But these Jains,' they continued, 'who are actually Shudras, since they have abandoned the true works of the Puranas, babble things about the Pandavas which are contrary to the smritis.' The king summoned Hemacandra, who said, 'That the Pandavas renounced the world as Jain monks has been said in our scriptures, and it is equally true that their sojourn in the Himalayas has been described in the *Mahabharata*. But we do not know whether the Pandavas in our scriptures are the same as those in Vyasa's work, or indeed by still other authors in different works.'[18]

The king, who keeps insisting on his duty to remain impartial, ends by praising the open-minded Jain over the exclusive Brahmins.

THE IMPERMANENCE OF MATERIAL ART

Like the fixity of written texts, the fixity of works of art turns out to be a mirage in India. We tend to think of art as permanent, perhaps as the only permanent thing there is. Storytelling is the only way that we know to ward off death; if only we could tell stories forever, like Scheherazade, we would never die at all. We tend to embalm the written word, to accord enduring status to physical incarnations of art. Our libraries are full of books, our museums full of paintings, and these books and paintings are often the only surviving traces of lost civilizations. But in India, by and large, neither books nor paintings are assumed to have that sort of permanence. In India, where the neglect of material objects is an article of Vedantic faith, all material art is fluid. It is the spoken word, not the written word, that is eternal. Sacred literature is eternal in being handed down first from god to mortals and then from one mortal to another (the infinite *parampara*), just as the individual soul survives in eternity by being handed over from one body to another.

This analogy has deep roots in Hindu civilization. The authors of the *Rig Veda* highly valued their freedom and feared any constraint; they wandered constantly and restlessly, always in search of new grazing land for their horses, never staying in one place long enough to build any lasting dwelling.[19] Although they later settled in cities, the old wanderlust never disappeared, and spiritual leaders, both Buddhist and Hindu, soon began to desert the cities and to abandon their material goods, to wander about as mendicants or to live in the forests, away from the constraints of civilization. The city became a metaphor for the body, the perishable prison of the eternal soul, the trap laid by material life (*samsara*); what the soul sought was freedom, moksha.[20]

Given this cultural background, it is not surprising that the physical incarnations of art and literature are not always valued or trusted in India; impermanence is the very nature of *samsara*, the material world. Books are eaten by white ants or rotted away by the wet heat of the monsoon, and the secular literature that is preserved orally lasts no longer than the mind that knows it.[21] When enormous terracotta horses are constructed in South India, the choice of medium is not accidental. As Stephen Inglis writes: 'Clay is the medium of the worship of the ephemeral. The horse, semi-mythical, temporary, fragile, cyclical (prematurely dying/transforming) fits snugly into the cyclical pattern of offering in village Hinduism. Power, especially "outside" power, always advances and recedes.'[22]

Hindu sacred art, in particular, is often purposely consigned to the realm of the ephemeral in order to prevent its profanation, with much the same logic that prevented the preservation of the *Rig Veda* in writing. When great Vedic sacrifices are performed, involving many priests and lasting for many days, large and elaborate ritual enclosures are constructed of bamboo and thatch; at the end of the sacrifice, these enclosures—which have become dangerously charged with sacred power—are burned to the ground.[23] The material traces of a powerful ritual must vanish in order that the power not remain casually at hand when the ritual awareness of it has ended. For the festival of Durga Puja in Bengal, hundreds of more-than-life-sized papier-mâché statues of the Goddess Durga are made and beautifully decorated; at the end of the week-long celebration, the statues are carried down to the Ganga in torchlight parades at night and cast into the dark waters. In Maharashtra, large clay idols of Ganesha are similarly consigned to rivers or the sea at the end of the Ganesha Chaturthi festival. In Benares, too, life-sized clay images of Rama and Sita are made for the Ramlila festivals and then thrown away.

The word used to describe this 'dismissal' or 'throwing out' of the statue is *visarjana* (cognate with *visarga*), the word used to describe the 'emission' of the universe—that is, its creation—by Brahma. In this sense, all fabricated things come into true existence only by being thrown out or thrown away; only when the body is shed is the soul set free. Indeed, one word for 'art' in India is *maya*, often translated as 'illusion'. And the world of *maya* is the world of matter (*prakriti*), of rebirth (*samsara*), which is impermanent; against it the Hindus contrast the world of truth, of ultimate reality (*brahman*), of spirit (*purusha*), of release (moksha), which is eternal.[24] What survives in the disembodied art forms of India survives in the minds that hand it down one to another. A fixed canonical tradition survives like a thread on which successive generations string their new interpretations and translations of the text. On the other hand, a fluid tradition survives like a series of interlocking beads, one fitting into the next, with no connecting physical thread. This lack of a centre corresponds to what has been observed of the concept of the self in India. Some people tend to think of a person as analogous to an artichoke—peel away the leaves of the external, nonessential characteristics until you find the self at the centre. South Asians tend to think of a person as analogous to an onion: peel away the leaves and at the centre you find—nothing.

Painting in India is not always intended to last. The Bengali painter Jamini Roy once remarked that he felt that all his paintings should be thrown into the river after his death; he painted because he was meant to be a painter, and his paintings were simply a part of his life and should die with him.[25] Many artists are interested more in the act of creation than in preserving the object that is created, but this approach may take on a more particular power in the realm of sacred art. This seems especially true for the sacred art of women, so much of whose lives is involved in producing human services that leave no permanent trace. In many domestic celebrations, women trace intricate designs in rice powder—*kolam* (or *rangoli* in North India)—on the floors and courtyards of houses. After the ceremony these are blurred and smudged into oblivion by the bare feet of the family, or, as the women think of it, the feet of the family carry into the house, from the threshold, the sacred material of the design. The material traces of ritual art must vanish in order that the mental traces remain intact forever. So, too, the smearing out of the *kolam* is a way of defacing order so that one has to recreate it; it is a fleeting stay against inevitable confusion. It is as if a choice were made, somewhat like the choice that you make when viewing a beautiful scene in a foreign land: If you photograph it, you have preserved it (more or less) forever, but the act of photographing it may interfere not only with the full experience of it at the moment but with your own power to preserve it in memory.

The women who make these rice-powder designs sometimes explicitly refer to them as their equivalent of a Vedic sacrificial hall (*yajnashala*). Their sketches are referred to as 'writing'—once the only form of writing that women were allowed to have—and the designs are merely an *aide-memoire* for the patterns that the women carry in their heads, as some men carry the Vedas. So, too, the visual abstraction of such designs as the South Indian *kolam* is the woman's equivalent of the abstraction of Vedic literature, based as it is on geometry (the measurement of the sacrificial altar, one reason why mathematics developed so early in India) and grammar (the central paradigm out of which all sacred commentary develops). The rice-powder designs are a woman's way of abstracting religious meanings; they are a woman's visual grammar.[26] The analogy between the *kolam* designs and the Vedic sacrificial hall has further implications of impermanence, for the hall was burnt down after the ritual.

Like these South Indian women, the women painters of Mithila 'write' large, elaborate geometrical and floral rice-paste figures on the clean mud floors just outside or in front of the family home, in preparation for rituals to follow. These, too, of course, disappear with foot traffic, wind and rain. The Maithali women use the same word, 'write', for their paintings on paper, for which they have traditionally used vivid natural dyes that soon fade:

> For the artists, this impermanence is unimportant—the paintings are not meant to last. The act of painting is seen as more important than the form it takes, and elaborately produced marriage sketches may be cast off after use, to be eaten by mice or even used to light fires.

Frescoes on courtyard walls often fall victim to rain, whitewash, or the playing of children.[27]

But all of this has been changing over the past forty years, as the women of Mithila have learned to paint on more permanent paper, with more permanent colours, and to market their paintings throughout India and, indeed, the world:

> The ancient North Indian Mithila wall painting tradition of rural Bihar—historically passed from mother to daughter—has moved from walls to paper, and expanded from sacred imagery to include critical commentaries on contemporary social, political and personal issues. Many Maithili women have been dramatically empowered by the recognition, travel and income generated by the sale of paintings, directly challenging gender relations in this deeply conservative rural patriarchal society. In effect, Mithila painting has evolved from a narrowly domestic ritual tradition to an often stunningly beautiful, highly flexible, alternative contemporary art form. The artists remain committed to its ancient aesthetic, yet it has also become a powerful means of personal expression, a source of regional identity politics, generational and gender conflict, and a site of intense controversy over the uses of tradition and the politics and commodification of 'heritage' in contemporary India.[28]

The themes of the paintings, too, are no longer purely traditional, but include scenes of social criticism—such as rich women bringing their babies to be vaccinated while poor women are sent away—and political commentary—such as scenes of the attack on the World Trade Centre and the Taj Mahal Hotel in Mumbai. This, too, is a vivid example of the impermanence of art in India: even the impermanence sometimes turns out to be impermanent.

Nowadays, many Hindu artists have caught the European taste for preservation; they go abroad to learn from foreign artists and conservators techniques to preserve their work.[29] Indeed, there must have been Hindu artists long ago who wished to preserve their work, for though the earliest religious monuments in India were carved in wood that decayed, sculptors very soon decided to build more lasting temples in stone; stone temples and stupas dating from the pre-Christian era imitate woodcarving techniques, transferred (clumsily, at first) to the more enduring medium. These permanent art forms, however, both sacred and secular, have continued to exist side by side with the transient forms, just as frozen *shruti* exists side by side with fluid *smriti*.

THE SURVIVAL OF MYTH THROUGH PERFORMANCE

In contrast with material art, verbal art has an astonishing survival power in India. Of all literary forms, drama best reproduces the effects of myth, most powerfully through the catharsis of the tragic drama, but also in the surreal humour of great comedy. In our day, drama (or film) often takes the place of the communal ritual that was a frequent (though certainly not inevitable) complement to traditional mythology. Hindu literature is self-conscious about the relationship between myth and life as it is manifest in myths that are enacted in the theatre. The use of aesthetic experience in salvation was the subject of much discussion; by seeing, and therefore participating in, the enactment of the myth of Krishna, one was led unconsciously into the proper stance of the devotee. Moreover, the viewer was not merely inspired to decide what role in the cosmic drama he or she wished to play (mother, lover, brother, or friend of Krishna); one was inspired to discover what role one was playing, had been playing all along, without knowing it.[30] Alf Hiltebeitel has beautifully described the way the real world gradually absorbs the stage in Hindu religious performances: 'The nightlong dramas, acted out on a small patch of ground beneath petromax lanterns, are finally unravelled at dawn on a stage that grows with the morning light to include first the surrounding outlines of village trees and buildings and then, in effect, the familiar world of the day.'[31]

Hindi films still perform many of the functions of mythology for Hindu society. Sudhir Kakar has interpreted popular Hindi film 'as a collective fantasy containing unconscious material and hidden wishes of a vast number of people . . . Hindi films may be unreal in a rational sense, but they are certainly not untrue . . . [They] are modern versions of certain old and familiar myths'.[32] This is more literally true of Bollywood than it is even of Hollywood, for Hindi films are sometimes rather lurid re-enactments of the sacred stories, with matinee idols playing the parts of the gods. In India, even where people do still tell the old stories in the traditional way, films have begun to usurp the position of myths. It is not, therefore, that myths flee from their classical shrines when these crash down under the assault of modern, materialistic can(n)ons, and find refuge in the cool, dark halls of cinema. No, even when the temple is still standing, the myths find another, supplementary home in the medium of film. Old archetypes never die; they just lurk quietly in the background of the sets of Hindi films.[33]

Indeed, where mythological themes are culturally so omnipresent as they are in India, it is particularly easy for a sophisticated filmmaker to select such themes as elements in a film and to feel instinctively that they will magnify the image that he wishes to project, literally, to a mass audience. One film, *Jai Santoshi Ma* (1975), told the story of a goddess named Santoshi Ma (or Mata); the film became so popular that the cult of the goddess spread throughout India. In R.K. Narayan's novel *Mr. Sampath*, a filmmaker decides to re-enact a story of the destruction of Kama, the god of erotic love, by Shiva, the god of yogis;[iv] and the actors playing the parts are swept up helplessly into a parallel re-enactment of the story in their private lives.[34] Clearly films, like the legitimate theatre, present a modern instance of that swinging door through which myth and reality eternally pass one another.

And the myths survive in other modern avatars: *Amar Chitra Katha* ('Immortal Picture Stories') comics present the ancient Hindu classics in a strangely Westernized but still recognizably Hindu form. Although these comics are ostensibly written for children, many adults read them; and for some, they provide the only remaining source of the classical mythology. And there are other, even more unlikely cartoons in which the myths live on. Hindus who may not know from the *Rig Veda* or the *Mahabharata* the story of the aged sage Chyavana, who was rejuvenated so that he could marry a beautiful young girl,[35] may know the story from newspaper advertisements for a patent medicine called Chyavanprash ('Chyavana-food'). The ad begins with a Sanskrit verse that can be translated thus: 'This is the story of the Chyavana food that the sage Chyavana ate; even though he was worn out with old age, he became a joy to the eyes of women.' The verse is followed by a series of cartoon illustrations with descriptions below them, in English, telling the story of Chyavana. This 'rejuvenating tonic', containing gooseberry, is said to be the one that the Ashvins, the divine physicians, gave to the old sage: 'Thus Chyavana was blessed with the special yoga and having consumed it he became a full-grown youth pleasing to the eyes of the women. Kottakkal Arya Vaidya Sala manufactures this potent tonic prescribed by the Divine Physicians in the traditional and conventional manner with scrupulous care and attention.'

One way or another, through oral or written exposure, Hindus know their myths so well that the retelling of the myths takes on the function of communion rather than communication. People listen to stories not merely to learn something new (communication) but to relive, together, the stories that they already know, stories about themselves (communion).[36] In reading written non-classics, one expects and demands surprises; but it is

---

[iv] See 'The Submarine Mare.'

characteristic of oral classics that the audience takes pleasure in predicting what will happen and satisfaction in seeing it happen.[37] No one who has been asked by a young child to tell a story for the umpteenth time will ever preface a tale with the disclaimer of 'stop me if you've heard this one before'. And no one who has been corrected by a child in the retelling of a tale ('No, no, it was the *first* little pig who built his house of straw, not the *second*') will try to 'improve' on an old favourite with new variations.

Many children's books function as classics, and as myths, in a way that no other works do. For these books provide a shared culture, as we give our children the books that we loved when we were children. Here is the one universal *parampara* or unbroken lineage of transmission in our world. And in addition to this shared content, there is the shared form of the transmission, the performance of the classics: reading aloud to children is for many people the only moment when the oral element of the mythological traditions is still actively preserved.

For India, too, is under pressure from the mobs of rationalists and modernizers to demythologize. True, the plays re-enacting the lives of Krishna (Krishna-lila) and Rama (Ram-lila) are still celebrated even in many highly urbanized settings, and people still travel from the cities to the country to see performances in their traditional settings. But as people move from the villages to the cities, the professional storytellers—those who present the dance dramas of the myths or recite the long epics, in Sanskrit or in the vernacular of the district—lose part of their audience. And even more threatening than the possibility that the particular craft of the storytellers will die out is the undeniable fact that, already, the contexts for storytelling are fast dying out—the occasions when stories are told, the moments of quiet work at the loom or during the mending of nets, the long winter evenings around the fire. But children are a safeguard against this loss, too; for however busy one may be, working in a factory or at an office desk, there still comes a moment when food is prepared and eaten, when children are washed and made ready for bed. And, in the city, as in the village, a small voice will say, 'Tell me a story.'

Children represent the only form of physical permanence, the eternal chain of rebirths in an infinity of bodies (the chain of *samsara*, the world of matter and marriage and mating), in contrast with (and often at the sacrifice of) the setting free (moksha) of the immortal soul. We see our physical selves preserved in the bodies of our children; and we see our mythical selves preserved in their memories. For many—all but those who achieve Release—this is the only eternity there is. As the Hindu law book put it, 'You beget children, and that's your immortality, O mortal.'[38]

SHADOWS OF THE *RAMAYANA*[1]

The *Ramayana*, composed by the sage Valmiki in Sanskrit in Northern India, sometime between the second century BCE and the second century CE, is the oldest surviving text of a story that has continued to be retold for over two thousand years, in Sanskrit dramas and poetry, in Hindi, Bengali, Tamil and other retellings, in *Amar Chitra Katha* comic books, on film, on television, on political posters.[2] The earliest recorded version, in the Sanskrit text of Valmiki, establishes the plot of this central episode that I will focus on in this chapter:

> Sita, the wife of Prince Rama, had been born from a furrow of the earth. The demon (Rakshasa) king Ravana stole Sita from Rama and kept her captive on the island of Lanka for many years. Rama enlisted the help of an army of monkeys and finally killed Ravana and brought Sita back home with him. But then he said he feared that his people worried that Sita's reputation, if not her chastity, had been sullied by her long sojourn in the house of another man. He forced Sita to undergo an ordeal by fire: she swore that she had always been faithful to Rama, called on the fire to protect her, and entered the blazing flame; but the god of Fire placed her in Rama's lap, assuring him that Sita had always been pure in thought as well as deed. Rama reinstated her, but when he doubted her again she disappeared forever back into the earth.[3]

The central human characters of the Valmiki *Ramayana*—Rama the perfect prince, Sita his perfect wife, and Lakshmana his perfect brother (later to form the template for the perfect worshipper of the now deified Rama)—were born to be paradigms of goodness (or, in the case of the perfectly demonic demon Ravana, badness). If that were all there was to the *Ramayana*, it would have proved ideologically useful to people interested in enforcing moral standards or in rallying religious fanatics—as it has proved all too capable of doing—but it would probably not have survived as a beloved work of great literature, as it has also done.

Rama is an incarnate god in the original Sanskrit text, though often he seems to forget that he is, and has to be reminded of it,[4] and more often it does not seem to be an issue at all.[i] But even in Sanskrit, god is in the details, and the details of the *Ramayana* are what give it its character. More precisely, each of the major human characters has at least two doubles, a double among the monkeys who help Rama kill Ravana and retrieve Sita, and a double among the demons in the family of Ravana. All the fun is in the monkeys and demons. The humans, and indeed the demons, also have a number of temporary doubles, illusions created at particular moments in the epic to fool someone. And, finally, in the later retellings of the *Ramayana*, the ones that came after Valmiki's Sanskrit text, the doubles proliferate to an even greater extent. These illusory characters are, ironically, more flesh and blood, as we would say, more complex and nuanced than the human characters that they mirror; or, rather, added to those original characters they provide the nuances of ambiguity and ambivalence that constitute the depth and substance of the total character, composed of the original plus the shadow. In addition, a number of myths are introduced as narrative shadows of the central plot, a few inserted in the main story, but most of them added in the first and last books (1 and 7). These myths supply a constant commentary on the central story, within the text, developing over the centuries.

HUMAN SHADOWS

Let us begin with human characters who serve as doubles of other characters within the *Ramayana*, and let us start with the females. There are a lot of females. The childless king Dasharatha obtains a magic porridge, infused with the essence of Vishnu, to share among his queens; he gives half to Kausalya, who bears him Rama; three-eighths to Sumitra, who bears him the twins Lakshmana and Shatrughna (each made of three-sixteenth of Vishnu); and one-eighth to Kaikeyi, who bears him Bharata. When it is time for Rama, the eldest, to ascend the throne, Kaikeyi combines a reminder of past promises with sexual blackmail to force Dasharatha to put her son, Bharata, on the throne instead, and send Rama into exile, where Ravana steals Sita and the plot, as they say, thickens. Kaikeyi is the evil shadow of the good queen, Kausalya. But Kaikeyi herself is absolved of her evil by having it displaced onto the old hunchback Manthara, a servant, who corrupts Kaikeyi and forces her, against Kaikeyi's

---

[i] See 'Forgetting and Re-awakening'.

better judgement, to act as she does. Shatrughna puns on Manthara's name, saying that it was she who churned up (*manth*) for them the ocean of grief, in which Kaikeyi was the sea-serpent (*graha*). [R 2.71.13] And much later, when Sita sees Ravana coming to kill her, she curses Manthara and blames her sinister counsels for bringing about the sufferings that will overwhelm Kausalya, the mother of Rama. On the other hand, when Shatrughna drags Manthara around, he yells curses on Kaikeyi. In this text, even the shadows have shadows.

Turning now to the male human doubles, we have seen that all four brothers are fragments of a single person, incarnations of Vishnu. Lakshmana functions as the shadow of Rama: Rama is called 'Saha-Lakshmana' ('With-Lakshmana') as if the accompaniment of his brother were a constant quality,[5] like the colour of his eyes, and Lakshmana is the one who speaks out what Rama is too well-behaved to say. After Dasharatha has disinherited and banished Rama, and Rama has quietly acquiesced, other people, but never Rama, complain loudly: first, briefly, Rama's mother, and then Lakshmana, who says, 'I don't like this. The king is perverse, old and debauched by pleasures. What would he not say under pressure, mad with passion as he is? Rama hasn't done anything wrong. What son would take to heart the words of a king who has become a child again? Before anyone learns of this, let me help you seize control of the government. I will slaughter everyone who takes Bharata's side. Now that the king has made me and you his enemies, who will help him make Bharata the king?' But Rama replies, 'It is not within my power to defy my father's bidding. I bow my head in supplication; I wish to go to the forest. I appreciate your love and loyalty, but you don't understand the meaning of life; give up your violence and be righteous like me.' Lakshmana can't bear it; he sighs and his eyes bulge. [R 2.21]

On the other hand, the text suggests that Rama—the human avatar who often forgets he is god—might fear that his brother Lakshmana might become another sort of double, that he could replace Rama as protector and spouse. A man's fear of being cuckolded by his younger brother is endemic to South Asian culture; the *niyoga* or Levirate that allows a widow to conceive a child by her dead husband's brother makes the lawmaker Manu very nervous,[6][ii] and the *Kamasutra* warns that a woman who marries the oldest of several brothers is likely to commit adultery with one of them.[7] So it is not surprising to find this theme reflected in this culture's best-known and loved epic. Rama and Sita, after all, are *human* incarnations

---

[ii] See 'Why Should a Brahmin'.

of the gods (Vishnu and Lakshmi) and must, therefore, display human emotions.

This tension between the two brothers is a significant motivation for the plot. In the forest, Rama goes off to hunt a deer, and tells Lakshmana to guard Sita. Sita thinks she hears Rama calling (it is a trick, about which more below) and urges Lakshmana to find and help Rama. Lakshmana says Rama can take care of himself. Sita, in her anxiety for her husband's safety, rages at Lakshmana, saying, 'You are so perverse. You think that if Rama dies you can have me, but I will never let you possess me. Bharata has gotten you to follow Rama as his spy. That's what it must be. And you've stayed here in order to get me . . . while pretending to be a friend. And that's why you won't come to his aid. But I will never have anything to do with any man but Rama.' Lakshmana gets angry and stalks off, leaving Sita totally unprotected; and Ravana comes and gets Sita. When Rama returns, he says to Lakshmana, 'You should not have come here just because an angry woman teased you. Submitting to Sita and to your own anger has caused you to violate dharma.' But Sita's accusation of Lakshmana is unfounded: when Rama, hunting for Sita, finds the cloak and jewels that she dropped as Ravana abducted her, and says to Lakshmana, 'Do you recognize any of this?' Lakshmana replies, 'I have never looked at any part of Sita but her feet, so I recognize the anklets, but not the rest of her things.'

Finally, after Sita has been restored and rejected (about which, more below), Rama is tricked into having to kill Lakshmana. This happens as the result of a rather elaborate (but not atypical, in this epic) set of vows and curses. Death, incarnate, comes to talk with Rama and makes him promise to kill anyone who tries to interrupt them; Lakshmana guards the door. An ascetic arrives and threatens to destroy the world if Lakshmana won't let him see Rama; Lakshmana therefore interrupts Rama and Death, choosing the lesser of two evils: his own death. Rama then says that, for Lakshmana, being separated from him (Rama) would be so terrible that it would be the equivalent of death, and so he satisfies the curse by merely banishing Lakshmana—who then commits suicide. Rama's responsibility for the death of Lakshmana is thoroughly dispelled on the human plane, but, as we are about to see, it bursts out in the animal world.

ANIMALS

Let us, therefore, now consider the animal doubles, primarily the male monkeys, who function as the shadows of Bharata and Rama. There are a number of parallels between monkeys and people in general in the *Ramayana*, both explicit and implicit.[8] The appropriateness of these parallels is supported by such factors as the human characters' assumption that, though they cannot understand the language of the deer (Rama explicitly laments this fact when he runs off after a golden deer that he suspects—rightly—to be a demon in disguise), they do not comment on the fact that they can understand the language of monkeys, who are called 'the deer of the trees'.[iii] Hanuman, the general-in-chief of the monkeys, not only speaks human languages, but speaks Sanskrit. When he approaches Sita, on the island of Lanka [5.30], he anxiously debates with himself precisely what language he will use to address her: 'If I assume a human form and speak Sanskrit like a sage, Sita will think I am Ravana [as she mistook the real Ravana, a notorious shape-changer, for an ascetic sage] and will be terrified. But I must speak with a human tongue, or else I cannot encourage her. Yet she will think I am Ravana, who can take any form he wants. And she will scream, and we will all be killed.' He finally does address her in Sanskrit, and she is suitably impressed. She does not scream.

Monkeys are like people, and special monkeys are the sons of gods, as special people are.[iv] Monkeys function as the shadows of Lakshmana, Rama and Bharata. In the human world, Rama's father Dasharatha has put Bharata, the younger brother, on the throne in place of Rama, the eldest, and exiled Rama to the forest; Lakshmana and Sita go with him. In the forest, where humans understand the speech of monkeys, after Ravana has stolen Sita, Rama and Lakshmana meet Sugriva, who used to be the king of the monkeys and claims that his brother Valin stole his wife and throne. Rama sides with Sugriva and murders Valin by shooting him in the back, an episode that has troubled the South Asian tradition for centuries, to this very day. Why does he do it? Apparently because Rama senses a parallel between his situation and that of Sugriva and, therefore, sides with Sugriva against his brother: each of them has lost his wife and has a brother occupying the throne that was to be his. But if Sugriva is Rama, who is Valin?

The answer to this question lies in the more specific parallels between the things that happen to the monkey brothers and the things that happen

---

[iii] See 'Zoomorphism'.

[iv] Sugriva is the son of Surya (the Sun god), Valin is the son of Indra (king of the gods, god of rain), and Hanuman, the great general of Sugriva's army, is the son of Vayu, the wind. In this, the monkeys resemble the human heroes of the *Mahabharata*, in which Surya is the father of Karna, Indra the father of Arjuna, and Vayu the father of Bhima.

to the human brothers. For instance, when Sugriva first sees Rama and Lakshmana, he thinks Valin sent them, just as Lakshmana, seeing Bharata approach them in the forest, thinks he has come to fight them. Both of them are wrong, overreacting with a kind of paranoia. After Lakshmana has told Hanuman of Rama's troubles, Hanuman says to Rama, speaking of Sugriva, 'He is exiled from his kingdom and is hated by his brother Valin, who has stolen his wife and left him abandoned in the forest.' Now, this is not exactly true of Sugriva; the first point is pretty true (he is exiled), but the second is not (Valin doesn't hate Sugriva; Sugriva hates Valin), and the third is not exactly true either: Sugriva carried off Valin's consort first, and when Valin retaliated, Sugriva fled out of guilt and terror. Nor is any of this true of any single enemy of Rama (if we take Rama as a parallel to Sugriva); it was Dasharatha who exiled Rama and caused him to flee to the forest; there is no enmity between Rama and Bharata, though Bharata occupies Rama's throne; and it was Ravana who carried off Rama's consort. If the monkey king is to be taken as the simian counterpart of Rama, then the usurping monkey brother is a combination of Rama's father, the demon Ravana, and Rama's brother Bharata. If we try to hang on to this as a parallel, it is a pretty messy parallel.

In fact, Rama sides with the wrong monkey: the 'usurping' monkey is, like Rama, the *older* brother, the true heir; the 'deposed' king had originally taken the throne from the 'usurping' brother. Valin, not Sugriva, is the legal parallel to Rama. Yet the main implication of Hanuman's speech is true: Rama sympathizes with Sugriva because each of them has lost his wife and has a brother occupying the throne that was to be his. The situations are the same, but the villains are entirely different—and this is what Rama fails to notice.

The monkeys' access to human language also grants them access to human ethics, or dharma.[v] On another occasion when Rama behaves badly, the monkeys remind him that he is a man (i.e., higher than a monkey), just as he is elsewhere reminded, when he behaves badly, that he is a god (i.e., higher than a man). When Rama kills Valin, hitting him in the back when he is fighting with Sugriva, the dying Valin reproaches Rama, saying, 'I'm just a monkey, living in the forest, a vegetarian. But you are a *man*. I'm a monkey, and it is against the law to eat monkey flesh or wear monkey skin.' Rama defends himself against the charge of foul play by saying, 'What does it matter whether you were fighting me or not,

[v] See 'Zoomorphism'.

since you are nothing but a monkey? And here is the crowning argument: snares and hidden traps are always used to catch wild animals; and I don't think there is anything wrong about this. Even sages go hunting. That is why I struck you while you were fighting with your brother.' But Rama is whistling in the dark here; the text judges him to have violated human dharma in his treatment of the monkey.

Rama is driven to this unethical act because the rage and resentment that he should feel toward his brother and father, but does not, is expressed for him by his monkey double—the deposed monkey king, Sugriva—and vented by Rama on that double's enemy, Valin, who doubles for Rama's brother and father. This is the sense in which the monkeys are the shadows of the human brothers, or rather, side-shadows, to use the term coined by Gary Saul Morson (after Bakhtin): they suggest what might have been.[9] The monkeys are not merely Valmiki's projections, nor projections from Rama's mind; they are, rather, literary fractions, symbolic layers, parallel lives. The monkey story is not accidentally appended; it is a telling variant of the life of Rama.

But it does not mirror that life exactly; it is a mythological transformation, taking the pieces and rearranging them to make a slightly different pattern, as the dreamwork does, according to Freud. Freud (in *The Interpretation of Dreams*) and Ernest Jones after him (in *On the Nightmare*) wrote about the ways in which animals often replace, in dreams, people towards whom the dreamer has strong, dangerous, inadmissible and hence repressed emotions. Or, to put it differently, the dreamer displaces emotions felt towards people whom he cannot bear to visualize directly in his dreams and projects those emotions onto animals. Thus Rama's cultural role as the perfect son and brother prevents him from expressing his resentment of his father and brother, and so the monkeys do it for him. In the magical world of the monkey forest, Rama's unconscious mind is set free to take the revenge that his conscious mind does not allow him in the world of humans.

And just as the shadow Kaikeyi had her own shadow, the hunchback Manthara, so, here, even the metaphorical shadows, the monkeys, have real shadows. Hanuman's shadow is even detachable, like Peter Pan's: a demoness tries to steal it when he is flying across the water to Lanka, and he has to enter her to get it back again. In later tellings, that shadow of his impregnates her, though Hanuman himself, proud of his chastity, is unaware of this.[10] In the case of this unconscious sexual encounter, the shadow is more substantial than its prototype.

DEMONS

Let us now consider demon doubles, beginning with the males. Demons (Rakshasas) are explicitly said to be projected shadows of humans: Lakshmana says to Rama, about the demon Viradha: 'The anger I felt towards Bharata because he desired the throne, I shall expend on Viradha.' [R 3.2.26] Focusing on our central characters, it might be said that Ravana is a shadow of Rama's father, Dasharatha. Ravana's epithet of 'Ten Necks' (Dashagriva) mirrors the name of Dasharatha ('Ten Chariots'), the demon's a natural epithet, the human's a cultural epithet; their characters, too, are similar: both are undone by lust. (Similarly the names of Sugriva and Dashagriva connect the monkey and the demon as two natural creatures in contrast with humans.) Like Dasharatha, Ravana is a destructive father: because of him, his virtuous son Indrajit is killed.

Far more significant, however, is Ravana's role as a shadow of Rama; more precisely, Ravana and his brothers are the shadows of Rama and his brothers. Just as Rama, Lakshmana and Bharata form a sort of triad (Shatrughna being hardly more than the other half of Lakshmana, and Kubera performing a similarly distant function for Ravana), so too Ravana, Vibhishana and Kumbhakarna form a triad. In Freudian terms, Ravana is a wonderful embodiment of the ego—proud, selfish, passionate—while Vibhishana, the virtuous demon, who sermonizes Ravana and finally defects to Rama, is pure superego, all conscience and moralizing, and Kumbhakarna, who sleeps for years at a time and wakes only to eat and fight, is a superb literary incarnation of the id: he sleeps and eats (while Ravana takes care of the lust).

The triad is even more significant in Indian terms, where they might be viewed as representations of the three constituent strands of matter (called the *gunas*, or qualities):[vi] Ravana is *rajas* (energy, passion), Vibhishana *sattva* (lucidity, goodness) and Kumbhakarna *tamas* (entropy, darkness). Ravana remarks, after Kumbhakarna's death, that Kumbhakarna had been his right arm, which is precisely what Rama says of Lakshmana. Ravana also says that Sita is no use to him with Kumbhakarna dead, which is, again, what Rama says when he thinks Lakshmana is dead. But both Vibhishana and Kumbhakarna revile Ravana, in contrast with Lakshmana and Bharata who love Rama.

Turning to the female demons, it is not surprising to find that Sita, too, has a demonic shadow, Ravana's sister, the hideous demoness Shurpanakha.

[vi] See 'Three (or More)'.

In the Valmiki text, Shurpanakha attempts to seduce Rama and is repulsed by Lakshmana, who cuts off her nose. She tells Ravana about Sita, praising her beauty, and thus triggers the war, just as Sita is said to be its ultimate cause. In Kamban's Tamil version of the *Ramayana*, composed in the twelfth century CE, Shurpanakha impersonates Sita for Rama, who sees through the trick:

> The demoness Shurpanakha, the sister of Ravana, well aware of her ugliness, fell in love with Rama, who rejected her and instructed his brother to mutilate her by cutting off her nose, ears and breasts. She then transformed herself into the image of the divine form of Sita. When the real Sita appeared, Shurpanakha told Rama that the other woman [the real Sita] was a deceitful, man-eating demoness who was skilled in the arts of illusion and had adopted a false form. Rama knew who was who but continued to tease Shurpanakha. When Sita ran to Rama and embraced him, Rama rejected Shurpanakha.[11]

The poet makes explicit the demoness's motive; she reasons, 'He will never look at me while she who has no equal is near him./ Best for me to run there fast, take her and hide her away somewhere quickly/ and then I will assume that form that he loves and I will live with him.'[12] But she does not in fact hide Sita away; the two Sitas, the original and the double, stand there side by side.[13] In the *Balaramayana*, a later retelling, Shurpanakha takes the form of Kaikeyi, and another demon takes the form of Dasharatha, and they banish Rama; Dasharatha and Kaikeyi have nothing to do with it at all! Projection here hath made its masterpiece.

ILLUSORY DOUBLES IN THE *RAMAYANA*: THE SHADOW SITA

The deer that lures Rama away so that Ravana can gain access to Sita is not a real deer: Ravana persuades his pal the demon Maricha to appear as a golden deer to lure Rama and Lakshmana away from protecting Sita, and then he himself appears as an ascetic to lure Sita out of the safe area. From the very start of this episode, Sita is fooled and insists that Rama go after the deer; she is also fooled when the demon mimics Rama's voice calling for help, and she insists that Lakshmana go to him, ignoring Lakshmana's wise warning that it is probably just a demonic imitation. [R 3.42.14, 3.43.1-10, 21-3] Demons, of course, are masters of illusion: Ravana's son produces an illusion of Sita being killed in order to dishearten Rama in the battle, [R 6.68.1-28] and Ravana attempts, in vain, to bed Sita by producing the illusion of the severed head of her husband; Sita falls for it but grieves without seeking comfort from Ravana, and the illusory head vanishes when Ravana leaves. [R 6.31]

In later *Ramayanas*, many more illusory doubles spring up, but by far the most important is the shadow Sita. The fifteenth-century *Adhyatma-ramayana* found it necessary to exculpate Sita not only from being present in Ravana's home but from the weakness of asking Rama to capture the golden deer for her. This illusory deer, however, may have inspired the *Adhyatma-ramayana* to create the illusory Sita who now desires the deer:

> Rama, knowing what Ravana intended to do, told Sita, 'Ravana will come to you disguised as an ascetic; put a shadow of yourself outside the hut, and go inside the hut yourself. Live inside fire, invisible, for a year; when I have killed Ravana, come back to me as you were before.' Sita obeyed; she placed an illusory Sita (*mayasita*) outside and entered the fire. This illusory Sita saw the illusory deer and urged Rama to capture it for her.[14]

Rama then pretends to grieve for Sita, pretends to fight to get her back, and lies to his brother Lakshmana, who genuinely grieves for Sita. Sita herself is never subjected to an ordeal at all: after Ravana has been killed and the false Sita brought back and accused, the illusory Sita enters the fire and vanishes forever, while the real Sita emerges and remains with Rama. But Rama seems to forget what he has done; he orders the illusory Sita into the fire as if she were real. Perhaps in order to maintain the power of the narrative, the author has Rama seem to forget about the shadow at crucial moments; only when the gods come and remind him of his divinity (as they do in the Valmiki text) does Fire (incarnate as the god Agni) return Sita to Rama, remarking, 'You made this illusory Sita in order to destroy Ravana. Now he is dead, and that Sita has disappeared.' Thus Rama creates the shadow but suffers as if he had been helpless to protect his wife. And where Sita's desire for the deer in the Valmiki text proves that she can't recognize a substitute deer, in this text she gets a substitute who can't recognize the substitute deer.

In a later Sanskrit text, the shadow Sita goes on to have a life of her own as a woman notorious for having five husbands:

> One day when Sita and Rama were in the forest, the god of Fire came to Rama, took the true Sita, constructed an illusory shadow Sita, with qualities, form and limbs equal to hers, and gave her to Rama. He told Rama not to divulge the secret to anyone; even Rama's brother Lakshmana did not know. Eventually, Rama subjected (the shadow) Sita to the ordeal of fire and Fire restored the real Sita to Rama.
>
> But then the shadow Sita asked Rama and Fire, 'What shall I do?' Fire told her to go to the Pushkara shrine, and there she generated *tapas*

and was reborn as Draupadi. In the Golden Age[vii] she is called Vedavati; in the Second Age, she is [the shadow] Sita. And in the Third Age, the shadow is Draupadi. This shadow, who was in the prime of her youth, was so nervous and excited with lust when she asked Shiva for a husband that she repeated her request five times. And so she obtained five husbands, the five Pandavas.[15]

Here it is Fire rather than Rama who constructs the double; Rama has lost some of his agency. And it is Fire who gives the shadow Sita a sexual future; for when she has saved the original Sita from contact with Ravana, she goes on to be reborn as Draupadi, heroine of the *Mahabharata* and of many contemporary cults—a woman with five husbands, unheard of in polygynous, but never polyandrous, Hinduism.[viii] Significantly, too, Draupadi, like the shadow Sita in some variants, is born out of a fire [M 1.175]; indeed, it may have been this episode in her history that attracted Draupadi from her own epic into Sita's story in the other epic. Or, perhaps, the birth of Draupadi from fire inspired the episode of the birth of the shadow Sita from fire. Tulsi, in the 16th century, greatly expands the story of the shadow Sita and adds yet another double: Shiva's wife Sati, who masquerades (unsuccessfully) as Sita.[16]

Why so many doubles of Sita? As Rama and Sita become gods, the bhakti tradition covers up for them, invoking the double Sita like a *dea ex machina*. The complex doublings of Sita grow in part out of the doctrine of illusion that is woven throughout all *Ramayanas*.[17] But they are also inspired by a deep ambiguity in the attitude to Sita. On the one hand, she is the epitome of female chastity. On the other hand, the highly sexual demoness Shurpanakha is able to double convincingly for Sita.[18] And while Sita must remain an epitome of chastity, which should make it impossible for anyone other than Rama to approach her, Ravana must be able to carry her off in order for Rama to fulfil his mission on earth, which is to kill Ravana.

As history (in the form of epigraphs and inscriptions, proclamations and panegyrics) claimed the epic for its paradigms, religious texts claimed it all the more for the ahistorical realms of eternity. The Hindus developed the shadow Sita over centuries of occupation by an invasive foreign presence. For, in the twelfth century, the *Ramayana* became a paradigm for a certain sort of history in response to the Turkic presence in India;[19] it began to be used to demonize historical figures, to cast them as actors in the *Ramayana*

[vii] See 'Three (or More)'.
[viii] See 'Women in the *Mahabharata*'.

battle. The battle became a holy war, invoked even in our time (1992, to be more precise) to justify the destruction of the Babri mosque in Ayodhya, said to stand over Rama's birthplace.

SHADOWS OF THE PLOT: RAVANA AS SEXUAL PREDATOR

Over the centuries, Sita's fire ordeal has proved problematic for different reasons to different South Asians, from pious apologists who were embarrassed by the god's unfair treatment of his wife, to feminists who saw in Sita's acceptance of the 'cool' flames, in Tulsi's telling, and in the connection with Sati, an alarming precedent for women who become satis. Both North and South Indians identified Rama with the North and Ravana with the South; but the North demonized the 'Dravidian' Ravana, the South the 'Aryan' Rama. And as the *Ramayana* became increasingly problematic, even during the centuries immediately following its recension, another kind of shadowing took place: a number of myths were introduced into the text as shadows of the central plot.

Many of these myths occur in Books 1 and 7, a kind of prelude and postlude that were most likely afterthoughts, composed after the other books. Though only loosely connected to the plot, these myths set the stage by establishing precedents for some of the irregular behaviour that we will encounter once the central story gets under way; their relevance to the main story inspired the storyteller[s] to select them rather than some of the many other myths that were available at that time. The ascetic Rishyashringa, born when his father is aroused by a female antelope, introduces us to intimate contact with animals, preparing us for the lustful monkeys; the demoness Tataka poses a moral dilemma (Should you kill a woman if she is herself a murderess?) that Rama will face with Shurpanakha.

Most relevant of all is the story of Ahalya, which tells us the origin of adultery, and tells it twice. Both times, Indra, the king of the gods, seduces Ahalya, the wife of the sage Gautama. The second time, in Book 7, Indra simply takes Ahalya by force. Though Gautama curses her for being loose, or unsteady, and led astray by her beauty, the text gives no evidence of this. The fact that she was raped should, we might assume, absolve Ahalya of any misdoing: she was helpless. But this argument is never made; perhaps these ancient texts already assumed, like modern sexists, that any woman who is raped is asking for it. When Ravana rapes Rambha—in a story we are about to consider—he is referred to as a 'demonic Indra', and the *Kamasutra* singles out Indra with Ahalya and Ravana with Sita[ix] as

---

[ix] See 'The Mythology of the *Kamasutra*'.

examples of men who were destroyed by uncontrolled desire.[20] Clearly Indra is behaving in a demonic manner.

The first time the story is told, in Book 1, Indra uses another technique that links him with Ravana: illusion. Indra takes the form of Gautama, but merely by putting on the sage's clothing; Ahalya immediately recognizes him but nevertheless willingly goes to bed with him, 'because she was sexually curious about the king of the gods'. Gautama curses her to become invisible; Sita, too, was rendered invisible when she was merely vulnerable to a rape. The complexities of the tale of Ahalya with Indra nuance and to some extent problematize the parallel but not identical complexities of the tale of Sita with Ravana.

But that story, too, has explicit multiple variants, one of which is in the last book, the book of afterthoughts. Rama banishes Sita twice (just as Indra seduces Ahalya twice); the first time, in Book 6, Sita goes into the fire but comes back again; the second time, in Book 7, she plunges down into the earth, her mother, and does not come back again. Was there something unsatisfactory about the first banishment, to inspire all those doubles to go into the fire in Sita's place? Perhaps it moved some poet to add on another, more final and more noble exit for Sita. Book 7 also resolves a puzzle, closely related to the puzzle of Rama's banishment of Sita, that must have baffled readers and hearers: why does Ravana, demonic in every other way, not use force to make Sita submit to him? When Ravana carries Sita off, he tries to seduce her with words and threats, but never by force. Why not? The author of Book 7 explains Ravana's reticence by citing a curse put upon him after his rape of Rambha:

> One day, when Ravana was full of passion, he saw the celestial courtesan Rambha and went mad with lust for her. She reminded him that she was his daughter-in-law, more precisely the wife of Nalakubara, the son of Ravana's brother Vaishravana. But Ravana replied, 'You say you are my daughter-in-law. For those who have but one husband, this argument is valid, but in their world the gods have established a law said to be eternal, that celestial courtesans have no appointed consorts, nor are the gods monogamous.' Then he raped her. When he released her she ran home, trembling with fear, and told her husband, who said, 'Since he raped you brutally, despite your lack of desire for him, he will never be able to approach another young woman unless she shares his desire. If, carried away by lust, he does violence to any woman who does not desire him, his head will split into seven pieces.' When Ravana learned of the curse his hair stood on end and he ceased to indulge in uniting himself with those who had no desire for him.

And the chaste married women whom he had raped rejoiced when they heard this curse.[21]

And that's why Ravana never forced himself on Sita. A Tibetan text of uncertain provenance states that when Sita sent Lakshmana after Rama she not only accused him of having designs on her but added a curse: 'Perhaps the younger brother thinks in his mind that, when the elder brother is dead, he will live together with me. If I do not want it, then, let whoever will touch me be burned.'[22] And it was this curse, uttered by Sita herself, that protected her, not against the innocent Lakshmana but against Ravana, who, when he arrived, 'knew that, if he touched the queen, he would be burned'. Later *Ramayanas* speculated on the reasons why, if Ravana could fool Sita by taking on the form of a Brahmin sage, he could not seduce her by taking on the form of Rama. A Bengali text tells us:

> Someone said to Ravana, 'You are taking various magic forms in order to get Sita. Why don't you take the form of Rama sometime and then approach Sita?' Ravana said, 'When I think of Rama and even the realm of *brahman* seems a trifling thing, how could I think of such a trifling thing as another man's wife? And so how can I take the form of Rama?'[23]

Ravana is saying that when he thinks of becoming Rama, already he thinks *like Rama*, and so he can't carry out a dirty trick like pretending to be Rama. Ravana cannot switch into Rama's form because he would get Rama's mind and memory traces along with his form.[x] He would stop being Ravana—and, presumably, paradoxically, stop wanting to change into Rama. So, too, a twelfth-century commentary on poems of devotion to Vishnu argues that if Ravana would take the form of Rama, he would become virtuous, since Rama is the very incarnation of virtue, dharma; even if he merely pretended to be virtuous, he would be infected by dharma.[24] William Buck expands upon this theme in his English translation, when one of the demons suggests to Ravana, 'Take Rama's form by magic, go to Sita, and she will willingly love you,' to which Ravana replies, 'No, I can't. The transformation would have to be complete; I'd have to take on all Rama's virtues as well to fool her, and then I could do no wrong, I couldn't lie to her and say I was someone I wasn't.'[25]

In these many different ways, the shadows of the central characters of the *Ramayana* raise philosophical, ethical and narrative possibilities that deepen and enrich the meanings of this ancient epic.

[x] See 'Forgetting and Re-awakening'.

WOMEN IN THE *MAHABHARATA*[1]

As soon as she was born, a disembodied voice said, 'This dark, fair-waisted woman, best of women, will be the death of the Kshatriyas. In time, she will do what must be done for the gods: because of her, a great danger will arise for the Kshatriyas.'
—Mahabharata 1.155.44-45

The women of the *Mahabharata* are extraordinarily prominent, feisty and individualistic, in part as a result of changes that were taking place in the social structures at the time of the recension of the text (such as the widespread public recognition of women as donors and renouncers, and their more active role in the pujas of sectarian Hinduism), in part as a result of the infusion of the Sanskrit corpus with stories from village and rural traditions that were less hidebound in their attitudes to women.

THE BIRTHS OF THE AUTHOR AND THE HEROES

The new attention paid to women in the *Mahabharata* emerges clearly from the stories of the births of both its legendary author, Vyasa, and its heroes:

> Once a fisherman caught a fish, found a baby girl in its belly, and raised her as his daughter. A powerful Brahmin sage seduced the fisherman's daughter, Satyavati, as she ferried him across the river. She gave birth to her first son, Vyasa, on an island in the river, and abandoned him (he had instantly grown to manhood). The sage restored her virginity (and removed her fishy smell). [1.57.32-75]

Vyasa is of mixed lineage, not merely Brahmin and Kshatriya (for though Satyavati's mother was a fish, her father was a king; it's a long story) but human and animal (for his grandparents were a Kshatriya, a female fish, and, presumably, a Brahmin man and woman). This double miscegenation will be repeated several times, always with variations, in this lineage.

The birth of Vyasa's natural sons (Satyavati's grandsons) is more complex and problematic:

> Satyavati later married king Shantanu and gave birth to another son, who became king but died childless, leaving two widows, the Kshatriya princesses Ambika and Ambalika. Satyavati, who did not want the lineage to end, summoned Vyasa to father children with his half-brother's widows. Vyasa was ugly and foul-smelling; his beard was red, his hair orange. Since Ambika closed her eyes when she conceived her son, Dhritarashtra, Vyasa cursed him to be born blind. Ambalika turned pale and conceived Pandu the Pale. When Vyasa was sent to Ambika a second time, she sent in her place a slave girl (dasi). The girl gave Vyasa great pleasure in bed, and he spent the whole night with her; she gave birth to a healthy son, Vidura, but since his mother was not a Kshatriya he could not be king. [1.99-100]

Though Hindu law allows the Levirate (niyoga)[i]—the law by which a brother begets children on behalf of his dead or impotent brother (the *Arthashastra* [3.4.27-41] says any male in the family can do it)—it is often, as here, disastrous.[2] Vyasa appears in the *Mahabharata* as a kind of walking semen bank, the author both of the story of the Pandavas and of the Pandavas themselves (just as Valmiki not only invents the poetic form of the *Ramayana*, the *shloka*, but tells the story, and raises—though he does not beget—the poets). The widows reject him because he is old and ugly and smells fishy, a characteristic that he apparently took from his mother when she lost it. He is also the wrong colour, and this, plus the mother's temporary pallor, results in the birth of a child, Pandu, who is the wrong colour—perhaps an albino, perhaps sickly, perhaps a euphemism for his future impotence.[3] Dhritarashtra's mother-to-be closes her eyes (and, presumably, thinks of Hastinapur), and so her son is blind. A slave girl who functions as a dispensable, low-class stand-in gives birth to Vidura, the incarnation of Dharma. Where Rama and his three brothers have three mothers and separate wives but share both a single human father and a single divine father, the five Pandavas have two mothers (and one wife) and one human father but different divine fathers.

In this disastrous Levirate, two wives give birth to three sons (two of whom have, for great-grandparents, a female fish, two Brahmins and five Kshatriyas, while the third has a Kshatriya, a female fish, two Brahmins and

---

[i] See 'Medical and Mythical Constructions'.

four slaves. Are you still with me?). In fact, the arrangement was originally more symmetrical, for there had been a third woman, Amba,[ii] who had been carried off by Bhishma, yet another son of Satyavati's husband Shantanu (it's another long story[iii]); but she departs before Vyasa arrives on the scene, and she eventually dies in a complex transsexual act of revenge against Bhishma (yet another long story[iv]). Ambika's and Ambalika's hatred of their surrogate lover, though much milder than Amba's hatred of Bhishma, results not in their deaths or his but in a confusion over the throne, because the women's recoiling from Vyasa produces physical disabilities in their children that disqualify them from the kingship: blindness, pallor, and low class. This confusion leads to war and ultimately to the destruction of almost all the descendants of Pandu and Dhritarashtra.

The *Mahabharata* goes on to tell us how, in the next generation, Pandu was cursed to die if he ever made love with any of his wives, for having mistaken a mating man for a mating stag. [1.90.64; 1.109.5-30][v] Fortunately, Pandu's wife, Kunti, had a mantra that allowed her to invoke gods as proxy fathers of Pandu's sons: Dharma (who fathered Yudhishthira[vi]), the Wind (father of Bhima), and Indra (father of Arjuna). [1.90, 1.101] Kunti then generously lent her mantra to Madri, Pandu's second wife, who invoked the Ashvins to father the twins Nakula and Sahadeva. Years later, Pandu seduced Madri one day when he was overcome by desire for her; he died, in fulfilment of the stag's curse and in imitation of the stag's death: a fatal *coitus interruptus*, the sweet death transformed into a bitter death.

But Kunti had already had one son, secretly, out of wedlock: when she was still a young girl, she had decided to try out her mantra, just fooling around. The Sun god, Surya, took her seriously; despite her vigorous protests and entreaties, he raped her and afterwards restored her virginity.[vii] She gave birth to Karna, whom she abandoned in shame; a charioteer and

---

[ii] Amba is clearly the basic name, of which Ambika and Ambalika are variants. These are the names of the three queens that Vedic texts describe as pantomiming copulation with the dead stallion who pinch-hits for the king in the horse sacrifice, just as Vyasa is pinch-hitting for his half-brother, the dead king.

[iii] The goddess Ganga marries Shantanu but kills the first seven of their children (actually doing them a favour, for they are immortals cursed to be born on earth); like Saranyu, Urvashi and Sita, she is an immortal woman who leaves her mortal husband when he violates their agreement, in this case by rescuing the eighth child—Bhishma.

[iv] See 'Transsexual Transformations'.

[v] See 'Zoomorphism'.

[vi] Thus Dharma is incarnate in one of the three sons of Vyasa in the generation of the fathers (Vidura), and he fathers one of the sons (Yudhishthira) of another of those fathers (Pandu).

[vii] See 'Saranyu/Samjna'.

his wife adopted him and raised him as their own. [1.104; 3.290-294; 5.144.1-9] Karna is in many ways the inverse of Vidura: where Vidura is an incarnate god, raised royally, and has both a surrogate father (Vyasa) and a surrogate mother (the maid in place of Ambika), Karna is of royal birth, raised as a servant, and has a divine father (Surya), a royal mother (Kunti), and two low-class surrogate parents (the charioteers).

Beneath the sterile or impotent fathers lie angry women. The lineage of the heroes is a series of seductions and rapes: of Satyavati, Amba, Ambika, Ambalika, Kunti and Madri. For Satyavati and Kunti, the seducer or rapist restores the woman's virginity afterwards and the resulting children are abandoned, as if to erase the entire incident, or at least to exculpate the women.

POLYANDRY

Other events in the lives of these women suggest their unprecedented and, alas, never again duplicated freedom.

Polyandry (multiple husbands) is rampant in the *Mahabharata*, and the text offers us, in four consecutive generations, positive images of women who had several sexual partners (sometimes premarital). Satyavati has two sexual partners (her legitimate husband Shantanu and the sage who fathers Vyasa on the island). Ambika and Ambalika have two legitimate partners (the king who dies and Vyasa, through the Levirate). Kunti has one husband (Pandu, legitimate but unconsummated) and four sexual partners (gods, quasi-legitimate). Madri has three partners (Pandu, legitimate and fatally consummated, and two quasi-legitimate gods). Another *Mahabharata* queen, named Madhavi, sells herself to four kings in succession, for several hundred horses each time, and restores her own virginity after each encounter. [5.113-117] But the prize goes to Draupadi, who has five legitimate husbands—the five Pandavas. Her polyandrous pentad is truly extraordinary, for though polygyny (multiple wives) was the rule, and men could have several spouses throughout most of Hindu history (as, indeed, each of the Pandavas, except Yudhishthira, had at least one wife in addition to Draupadi—Arjuna had three more), women most decidedly could not. Since there is no other evidence that women at this time actually had multiple husbands, these stories can only be suggestive, if not incontrovertible, evidence either of women's greater sexual freedom or, perhaps, of men's fears of what might happen were women to have that freedom. Draupadi's hyper-sexuality may simply have validated an ideal that was understood to be out of reach for ordinary women—imagined precisely in order to be disqualified as a viable option. What else, then, can these stories mean?

Hindus at this period were apparently troubled by Draupadi's polyandry, for which the *Mahabharata* gives three different excuses (always a cause for suspicion). First, it says that Arjuna won Draupadi in a contest and brought her home to present her to his mother; as he and his brothers approached the house, they called out, 'Look what we got!' and she, not looking up, said, as any good mother would say, 'Share it together among you all.' [1.182] And so all five brothers married Draupadi. Not content with this rather far-fetched explanation, the *Mahabharata* tries again: Vyasa says that all five Pandavas are really incarnations of Indra,[viii] and Draupadi the incarnation of Shri (the goddess of Prosperity, the wife of Indra and of all kings).[ix] Still not satisfied, Vyasa offers a third explanation:

> The daughter of a great sage longed in vain for a husband; she pleased the god Shiva, who offered her a boon, and she asked for a virtuous husband. But she asked again and again, five times, and so Shiva said, 'You will have *five* virtuous husbands.' And that is why she married the five Pandavas. She objected, saying that it is against the law for a woman to have more than one husband, for then there would be promiscuity; moreover, her one husband should have her as a virgin. But Shiva reassured her that a woman is purified every month with her menses and therefore there would be no lapse from dharma in her case, since she had asked repeatedly for a husband. Then she asked him if she could be a virgin again for each act of sexual union, and he granted this, too. [1.189; 1.1.157]

Like other polyandrous women whose virginities were restored, sometimes after premarital seduction or rape, Draupadi will be restored to purity each month after willing conjugal sex. In this case there is no need to justify or purify her, but there is a perceived need, if she has a different husband each month, to avoid promiscuity—*samkara*, 'con-fusion' or 'mixing', the same word that is used for the reprehensible mixture of classes.

The mythological extemporizings were not sufficient to protect Draupadi from frequent slurs against her chastity. When Duryodhana has Draupadi dragged into the assembly hall (much as Rama summons Sita to the public

---

[viii] This does not contradict the statement that only Arjuna was the son of Indra, since, as we have seen, these are two different processes: Dharma becomes incarnate in Vidura and also fathers Yudhishthira.

[ix] The Puranas [*Markandeya* 5] expand upon this: as a result of his Brahmin-killing, Indra's power goes into five gods, including him, who father the Pandavas.

assembly) and Duhshasana attempts to strip her, despite the fact that she is wearing a garment soiled with her menstrual blood (the same blood that was supposed to purify her), the enemies of the Pandavas justify their insults to her by arguing that a woman who sleeps with five men must be a slut. [2.61.34-36] Yet all her children are legitimate; they are called the Draupadeyas, 'Children of Draupadi', by a matronymic, which may be nothing more than a way of getting around the awkward fact that, though she is said to have one son from each husband, people often lose track of which Pandava fathered which son. So, too, the multiple-fathered sons of Kunti are often called Kaunteyas, 'Children of Kunti', although they are also called Pandavas, since they have a single legitimate, if not natural, father, Pandu.

The later tradition was not satisfied by any of the official excuses; various retellings in Sanskrit and in vernacular languages during the ensuing, less liberal centuries mocked Draupadi. In one twelfth century CE text, the evil spirit of the Kali Age, incarnate, suggests to five gods who are in love with one woman, 'Let the five of us enjoy her, sharing her among us, as the five Pandavas did Draupadi.'[4] Even the permissive Kamasutra[x] quotes a scholar (or pedant) who said that any married woman who is known to have had five men is 'available' (i.e., can be seduced without moral qualms) [KS 1.5.30-31], and the thirteenth-century CE commentator, Yashodhara, cites Draupadi as an exception.

Yet the power of Draupadi's own dharma—her unwavering devotion to her husband(s)—is what protects her when Duhshasana tries to strip her; every time he pulls off her sari, another appears to cover her nakedness, until there is a great heap of silk beside her, and Duhshasana gives up; the implication is that her chastity protects her. [2.61.40-45][xi] The text often reminds us that Draupadi is no mere mortal but a creature from another world; there is a prediction that Draupadi will lead the Kshatriyas to their destruction, fulfilling the gods' intention. [1.155] How different the lives of actual women in India would have been had Draupadi, instead of Sita, been their official role model! Many Hindus name their daughters Sita, but few name them Draupadi. Yet Kunti and Draupadi are two of the panchakanya, the "five virgins" that Hindus remember daily at dawn.

[x] See 'The Mythology of the Kamasutra'.
[xi] Some later versions of this passage remove Draupadi's agency by saying that she called for help from Krishna, who arrived and performed the miracle of the expanding sari. There is a real loss of feminist ground here. In response to the TV Mahabharata series, a company marketed the Draupadi Collection of saris, which presumably did not stretch infinitely.

It is always possible that the *Mahabharata* was recording a time when polyandry was the custom (as it is nowadays in parts of the Himalaya), but there is no evidence to support this contention. Indeed, Pandu tells Kunti another story explicitly remarking upon an archaic promiscuity that is no longer in effect, pointedly reminding her, and any women who may have heard (or read) the text, that female promiscuity was an ancient option no longer available to them:[xii]

> The great sage Shvetaketu was a hermit, people say. Once, they say, right before the eyes of Shvetaketu and his father, a Brahmin grasped Shvetaketu's mother by the hand and said, 'Let's go!' The sage's son became enraged and could not bear to see his mother being taken away by force like that. But when his father saw that Shvetaketu was angry he said, 'Do not be angry, my little son. This is the eternal dharma. The women of all classes on earth are not fenced in; all creatures behave just like cows, my little son, each in its own class.' The sage's son could not tolerate that dharma, and made this moral boundary for men and women on earth, for humans, but not for other creatures. And from then on, we hear, this moral boundary has stood: A woman who is unfaithful to her husband commits a mortal sin that brings great misery, an evil equal to killing an embryo, and a man who seduces another man's wife, when she is a woman who keeps her vow to her husband and is thus a virgin obeying a vow of chastity, that man too commits a mortal sin on earth. [1.113.9-20]

What begins as a rape somehow concludes with a law against willing female adultery, as uncontrollable male sexuality is projected onto the control of allegedly oversexed women. Pandu tells this story to Kunti in order to persuade her that it is legal for her to give him children by sleeping with an appointed Brahmin,[xiii] an emergency plan that prompts her then to tell him about the mantra by which she can summon the gods to father her children; he is thus carefully distinguishing the permitted Brahmin from the loose-cannon Brahmin in the Shvetaketu story. We recognize Shvetaketu as a hero of the Upanishads, the boy whose father teaches him the doctrine of the two paths;[xiv] here, his father defends promiscuity, using cows as paradigms not, as is usual, of motherly purity, but of bovine licence—so cows, of all things, here become the exemplars of primeval

---

[xii] See 'The Mythology of the *Kamasutra*'.
[xiii] Satyavati, too, has to tell several stories to Ambika and Ambalika to persuade them to submit to the same sort of Levirate.
[xiv] See 'Death and Rebirth'.

female promiscuity. (Perhaps because they are so pure that nothing they do is wrong?)[xv]

The *Mahabharata* keeps insisting that all this is hearsay ('People say', 'We hear'), as if to make us doubt it; it invokes a vivid, quasi-Freudian primal scene to explain a kind of sexual revulsion. A Brahmin's right to demand the sexual services of any woman he fancied evoked violent protest in ancient Indian texts. A notorious example is the story of Yavakri, who tried to exert this right on the wife of another Brahmin and was murdered by a witch in the form of the wife, conjured up by the Brahmin. [3.137.1-20].[5] (Draupadi is subjected to sexual harassment by a Kshatriya rather than a Brahmin when she is in disguise as a servant and not recognized as the princess Draupadi. [4.21.1-67]) We may read the story of Shvetaketu in part as an anti-Brahmin (and anti-cow-purity) tract—depicting, as it does, a Brahmin as sexually out of control, and cows as naturally promiscuous animals—as well as an explicit rejection of archaic polyandry. The *Kamasutra* [1.1.9] names Shvetaketu as one of its original redactors, and the commentary on that passage cites this *Mahabharata* story.[xvi]

The persistent polyandry in the lineage of the heroines is therefore, I think, a remarkably positive fantasy of female equality, which is to say a major resistance to patriarchy, and the *Mahabharata* women—Satyavati, Kunti and Draupadi—are a feminist's dream (or a sexist's nightmare): smart, aggressive, steadfast, eloquent, tough as nails, and resilient. Draupadi, in particular, is unrelenting in her drive to help her husbands regain their kingdom and avenge their wrongs.

FIERY WOMEN

Other women in the *Mahabharata* show remarkable courage and intelligence, too, but their courage is often used in subservience to their husbands. The wives of the two patriarchs, Pandu and the blind Dhritarashtra, are paradigms of such courage. Gandhari, the wife of Dhritarashtra, kept her eyes entirely blindfolded from the day of her marriage to him, in order to share his blindness. Pandu's widows vied for the privilege of dying on his pyre. When he died, Madri mounted his funeral pyre, for, she insisted, 'My desire has not been satisfied, and he too was cheated of his desire as he was lying with me, so I will not cut him off from his desire in the house of death.' [1.116.26] This is a most unusual justification for a sati, Madri's intention being not merely to join her husband in heaven (as other satis

[xv] See 'Sacred Cows'.
[xvi] See 'The Mythology of the *Kamasutra*'.

will state as their motivation), but to complete the sexual act in heaven. Yet Kunti, too, wishes to die on Pandu's pyre, without the peculiar justification of *coitus interruptus*, but simply because she is the first wife. One of them must remain alive to care for both their children; Madri gets her way and mounts the pyre.[xvii] Kunti and Gandhari later die alongside Dhritarashtra in a forest fire from which they make no attempt to escape. [15.37] Finally, the four wives of Vasudeva (the father of Krishna) immolate themselves on Vasudeva's pyre and join him in heaven; they were all permitted to die because by this time all their children were dead. [16.8.16-24]

The association of women with fire is worthy of note. Draupadi, who does *not* die on her husbands' funeral pyres (because [a] she dies before them and [b] they don't *have* funeral pyres—they walk up into heaven at the end of the story), begins rather than ends her life in fire: she is born out of her father's fire-altar:

> Drupada performed a sacrifice in order to get a son who would kill his enemy, Drona. As the oblation was prepared, the priest summoned the queen to receive the oblation and let the king impregnate her, but she took so long to put on her perfume for the occasion that the priest made the oblation directly into the fire, and so the son was born out of the fire, not out of the queen. And after the son came a daughter: Draupadi. As soon as she was born, a disembodied voice said, 'This dark woman, best of women, will be the death of the Kshatriyas. In time, this fair-waisted woman will do what must be done for the gods: because of her, a great danger will arise for the Kshatriyas.' They called her the Dark Woman (Krishna), because she was dark-skinned. [1.155.1-51]

Draupadi, born of fire, is significantly motherless, like Sita, who was born of the Earth and returns into the Earth—after she has entered fire and come out of it. Like Sita, Draupadi is an elemental goddess who is often called *ayonija* ('born from no womb') and follows her husband(s) to the forest. In Draupadi's case, the absence of the expected mother is balanced by the unexpected presence of the daughter. Unasked-for, riding into life on the coattails of her brother, Draupadi went on to become the heart and soul of the Pandavas. She also went on, in India, to become a goddess with

---

[xvii] The text regards this as Madri's triumph and privilege, but a feminist might wonder if she gets this dubious honour of committing sati as a punishment for killing Pandu by enticing him (naturally it is the woman's fault) to the fatal coupling.

a sect of her own, worshipped throughout South India primarily by lower castes, Pariahs and Muslims.[6] The *Mahabharata* mentions other dark goddesses, who may well already have had such sects: the seven or eight 'Little Mothers' (Matrikas), dark, peripheral, harmful, especially for children,[7] and the Great Goddess Kali (Maha-Kali). [*Mahabharata* 12, app. 1 no. 28, lines 72-75] Indeed, Draupadi is closely connected with the dark goddess Kali.[8] As in the stories of the births of Pandu and Draupadi, skin colour here has a religious significance but no social meaning, positive or negative.

A partial explanation for the *Mahabharata*'s open-minded attitude toward polyandrous women may come from a consideration of the historical context. The text took shape during the Mauryan and immediate post-Mauryan period, a cosmopolitan era that encouraged the loosening of constraints on women in both court and village. The women of the royal family were often generous donors to the Buddhist community,[9] and women from all classes, including courtesans, became Buddhists.[10] The king used women archers for his bodyguards in the palace, and Greek women (Yavanis) used to carry the king's bows and arrows on hunts. Women served as spies. Female ascetics moved around freely. Prostitutes paid taxes. The state provided supervised work, such as spinning yarn, for upper-class women who had become impoverished, widowed, or been deserted, and for ageing prostitutes.[xviii] If a slave woman gave birth to her master's child, both she and the child were immediately released from slavery.[11] Thus women were major players in both Buddhism and Hinduism during this period, and the *Mahabharata* may reflect this greater autonomy. Indeed, the tales of polyandry may reflect the male redactors' nightmare vision of where all that autonomy might lead.

[xviii] Much of this information about women comes from the *Arthashastra*, which, if not the Mauryan document that people often assume it is, was nevertheless probably composed in the general period of the composition of the *Mahabharata*, by about 300 CE.

THE HISTORY OF EKALAVYA[1]

How does one go about telling the story of Hinduism by including the maverick as well as the mainstream Hindus in the story? The ancient Sanskrit texts, usually dismissed as the work of Brahmin males, in fact reveal a great deal about the lower castes, often very sympathetic to them. Tracing these stories through the centuries, we can see how the attitudes to these marginalized groups constantly shifted.

One important group of oppressed peoples is constituted by the Adivasis ('original inhabitants'), the so-called tribal peoples of India, on the margins both geographically and ideologically, sometimes constituting a low caste, sometimes remaining outside the caste system altogether. As we have seen elsewhere in this book,[i] there have been protests against the mistreatment of the lower castes from an early age in India. Evidence of this can be found, if we look carefully, in the Sanskrit texts: the lower castes leave their traces in upper-caste literature, as themes and voices from oral and folk traditions find their way into the texts. These signs represent a beginning, a prelude to reform; they do change the world, even if only by imagining a world in which people treated Dalits well.

EKALAVYA CUTS OFF HIS THUMB

Let me take as my example the story of Ekalavya. The earliest version that we have is from the *Mahabharata*. It goes like this:

> Drona was the Pandavas' archery tutor, and Arjuna was his star pupil. One day a boy named Ekalavya, the son of a Tribal (Nishada) chieftain, came to them. When Drona, who knew dharma, refused to accept the son of a Nishada as a pupil, Ekalavya touched his head to Drona's feet, went out into the jungle, and made a clay image of Drona, to which he paid the respect due a teacher. He practiced

---

[i] See 'Dogs as Dalits'.

intensely and became a great archer. One day the Pandavas went out hunting with their dog. The dog wandered off and got lost; he came upon Ekalavya, who was black, wrapped in black deerskin, hair all matted, dressed in rags, his body caked with dirt. The dog stood there barking at him until Ekalavya shot seven arrows almost simultaneously into the dog's mouth. The dog, with his mouth full of arrows, went whimpering back to the Pandavas, who expressed their admiration for the man who had accomplished this amazing feat of archery and went to find him. They found him and asked him who he was, and he told them he was the Nishada Ekalavya, a pupil of Drona's. Only then did they recognize him.

The Pandavas went home, but Arjuna kept thinking about Ekalavya, and one day he asked Drona why he had a pupil, the son of a Nishada, who was an even better archer than he, Arjuna. Drona then resolved to do something about this. He took Arjuna with him to see Ekalavya, and when he found him he said to Ekalavya, 'If you are my pupil, pay me my fee right now.' Ekalavya, delighted, said, 'Command me, my guru. There is nothing I will not give my guru.' Drona replied, 'Give me your right thumb.' When Ekalavya heard this terrible speech from Drona, he kept his promise. His face showed his joy in it, and his mind was entirely resolved to do it. He cut off his thumb and gave it to Drona. And after that, when Ekalavya shot an arrow, his fingers were not so quick as before. Arjuna was greatly relieved. [M 1.123.10-39]

This is a brutal story, even for the *Mahabharata*, which tells many a brutal tale. How are we to understand it? First of all, who is Ekalavya? He is a prince among his own people, but that wins him no points with the Pandava princes. The Nishadas here are a low-caste tribal group who embrace Hindu dharma and Hindu forms of worship but are still beneath the contempt of the caste system. For such a person to stand beside the Pandava princes in archery classes was unthinkable; that is what Drona, who 'knew dharma', realized.

In order to protect both dharma and the reputation of his own world-class archery student, Drona claims his retroactive tuition, called the *guru-dakshina*, the gift to the guru. Of course we are shocked; to add insult to injury, Drona really didn't teach Ekalavya at all, and hardly deserves any tuition fees, let alone such a grotesque payment. But where is the author's sympathy? It is hard to be sure. It is arrogant of Ekalavya to push in where he does not belong; someone of his birth and family cannot join the royal archers. But Ekalavya does not act arrogant. His outward appearance invokes all the conventional tropes for Nishadas: he is described as black, wrapped in black deerskin, hair all matted, dressed in rags, his body caked with dirt. He is made of the wrong stuff (or, as we would say, has the wrong genes). He is literally dirt. But his inner soul, reflected in his behaviour, is pious and respectful; he does what the teacher tells him to do; not only is he a brilliant archer, but he is honest and humble. To this extent, at least, the *Mahabharata* likes him and, presumably, pities him; it refers to Drona's command as 'terrible' (*daruna*).

Yet the act by which Ekalavya proves his mettle as an archer is one of gratuitous and grotesque cruelty to a dog, the animal that is in many ways the animal counterpart, even the totem, of a Nishada.[ii] The dog barks at him, betraying the class attitude that dogs often pick up from their masters; the dog doesn't like the way Ekalavya looks and, probably, smells. Does Ekalavya's unsympathetic treatment of this dog cancel out our sympathy for Ekalavya as the victim of inter-human violence? Does it justify Drona's cruel treatment of him—what goes around, comes around, travels down the line—or, at least, remind us of the cruelty inherent in the *sva-dharma* of a hunter? But the text shows no sympathy for the dog, other than noting that the dog was 'whimpering', and, therefore, no condemnation of Ekalavya for his treatment of the dog.

I read the text as deeply conflicted; it assumes that this is the way things must be, but it does not like the way things must be. It paints Ekalavya sympathetically despite itself.

The main point of the Ekalavya story is not about Nishadas; it is about the virtue of devotion to the guru. It is also about feats of archery, the immediate concern of the part of the story in which it occurs, such as Arjuna's skill in shooting the eye of a wooden bird, in archery class, or the eye of a wooden fish, in the contest to win Draupadi (significantly, inanimate forms in contrast with the real dog that Ekalavya wounds). But the subversive subtext may well be about Nishadas; or else why cast the Nishada in the role of the obedient disciple? And here we may note an interesting parallel between Ekalavya and Karna, an illegitimate child abandoned by his Kshatriya mother and brought up by a charioteer.[iii] Like Ekalavya, Karna finds that his lower caste disqualifies him from an archery contest with Arjuna, again under Drona's aegis; like Ekalavya, Karna mutilates himself at the command of someone of higher caste and is later cursed by his guru.[2] Yet the text does not explicitly question the dharma of

---

[ii] See 'Dogs as Dalits'.
[iii] See 'Women in the *Mahabharata*' and 'Saranyu/Samjna'.

either of the archery contests, as it does question aspects of dharma in many other parts of the *Mahabharata* (in the stripping of Draupadi, for instance, or the episode of Yudhishthira and the dog[iv]).

In the face of his defence of the class and caste system, the author of this story saw the humanity in Ekalavya, saw that Nishadas were human beings of dignity and honour. It doesn't necessarily mean that Nishadas tried to break into the professions of Kshatriyas. Nor does it mean that Kshatriyas went around cutting off the thumbs of Nishadas. It means that the author of this text imagined the situation and was troubled by it. The people who heard and, eventually, read the text must have seen that too; maybe some of them, as a result, treated the Dalits whom they encountered with more humanity. The imagination of a better world may have made it a better world. Moreover, during the long history of this story, different people did read the story differently; the reading of the Brahmin imaginary was certainly not the only one.

THE LEGACY OF EKALAVYA

Whatever the spirit in which the tale of Ekalavya was originally told, it continued to be remembered among people crying out for social reform. A glance at later versions of the same story supports some of the hypothetical meanings that we have hunted out of the original telling and suggests, but certainly does not prove, that the seed of those later responses may already have been there in the Sanskrit text, or at least that there may have been other readings of this episode besides the original one we have, with other evidence of moral conscience, to bridge the gap between the first recorded telling and the later versions that explicitly call out for justice.[v]

There is a Jain text from the sixteenth century that begins much like the *Mahabharata* story of Ekalavya, but then gives the protagonist a different tribe (he is a Bhilla rather than a Nishada), and a different name, and veers in a very different direction:

> Arjuna learned the entire science of archery from Drona and became as it were another image (*murti*) of Drona, and honoured him with many gems, pearls, gold, elephants, horses and so forth. The guru said to him, 'Arjuna, choose a boon.' Arjuna replied, 'Sir, if you are satisfied

---

[iv] See 'Dogs as Dalits'.

[v] There is an interesting parallel between this instance of a dormant social conscience and the development of vegetarianism out of an early but widespread expression of guilt about killing and eating animals; see 'The Ambivalence of Ahimsa'.

with me, let there be no one but me who knows such a science of archery.' Thinking, 'The words of great gurus can never fail to come true,' Drona agreed. One day, a certain Bhilla, named Bhimala, living on the banks of the Ganga in the land of Karnata, came and asked Drona to be his guru; obtaining his promise, he went back to his own place and made an image (*murti*) of Drona out of mud, and honoured it with flowers and sandalwood and so forth, and said, 'Drona, give me the knowledge of archery,' and practised the science of archery in front of him. And with his mind and heart full of the emotion of passionate devotion to him (bhakti), the Bhilla after a certain time became like a second Arjuna.

One day, Arjuna, following Drona who had gone in front to take a bath in the Ganga, saw that the mouth of his dog was filled with arrows that had not pierced his upper lip, lower lip, palate, tongue or teeth. Thinking, 'No one but me has such a power,' Arjuna was amazed, and going forward by following along the arrows from his dog's mouth he saw the Bhilla and asked him, 'Who shot these arrows into the dog's mouth?' 'I did.' 'Who is your guru?' 'Drona is my guru.' Hearing that, Arjuna reported this to Drona and then said, 'Hey, master. If people like you leap over the borderlines of words, then what are we wretched creatures to do?'

Drona went there and asked the Bhilla, 'Where is your guru?' and the Bhilla showed him the representation that he himself had made and told him what he had done, saying, 'Arjuna! This is the fruit of my bhakti.' But the sneaky, cheating Arjuna said to him, 'Bhilla, with your great zeal, you must do puja with the thumb of your right hand for this Drona whom you met through us.' The Bhilla said, 'Yes,' and did it. But then Drona said, 'Arjuna! You are a sneaky, cheating city slicker, and you have deceived this artless, honest, unsophisticated forest dweller. But by my favour, even without a thumb these people will be able to shoot arrows.' And as he said this, Drona, the guru, gave the Bhilla this favour and went back to his own place. And so, even today, a Bhilla can shoot arrows using his middle finger and his forefinger.[3]

The entire moral weight has shifted; now it is Arjuna, not Drona, who makes the cruel demand, and Drona who objects to it and who calls Arjuna deceitful and cunning, in contrast with the artless, honest Bhilla, who does *not* hurt the dog, as the text takes pains to tell us. Indeed, Drona has agreed to be the Bhilla's guru at the start, and, at the end, grants him superior skill in archery, despite Arjuna's attempts to nobble him. The image of Drona that the Bhilla makes of mud is now matched by other, flesh-and-blood images: Arjuna *is* the image of Drona, and the Bhilla *is* the image of Arjuna, hence of Drona. Altogether, the Bhilla comes off smelling like a rose, and Arjuna does not.

Another Jain telling of this story, from the seventeenth century,[4] veers back towards the *Mahabharata* reading of the event. The tribal hunter *does* pierce the dog's mouth with his arrows, and Arjuna uses this in his argument to Drona, saying, 'O lord, that hunter in the forest, invoking your name, kills beings. And that agitates my heart. Surely an art shines only when it is practised by the righteous. O lord, only a jewel set in gold attracts the heart of the world, not one set in tin. In the same manner this art when practised by a hunter does not appear proper.' And the text continues:

> So Drona asked the tribal for his thumb. For indeed, arts are fruitful only to those who do what is pleasing to the teacher. Hearing his words, that hunter, brave and courageous, constrained by the weight of his devotion, cut off his thumb and offered it to him. The teacher destroyed his art (of archery) by a pretext but pleased that lowly hunter by offering him his own thumb ring. Then he returned home with Arjuna. Thinking only thus, 'An art that has been imparted to an unworthy person might quickly lead to evil acts. But the same art, when it is associated with one who is well-qualified with accomplishments, yields sweet results,' the venerable teacher, who knows the result of compassion towards beings, took back that art from him, and not out of hatred towards him.

This text does not name Ekalavya, but calls him an alien (Dasyu) and a forest-dweller. This time he does not take pains to save the dog from suffering, and this is Arjuna's excuse to destroy him on what the text admits is Drona's 'pretext' (the rule of the *guru-dakshina*), designed to destroy his art of archery. The text then leans over backwards to justify Drona's action, insisting that he was compassionate and that he did not hate the hunter, and stating that he 'pleased that lowly hunter by offering him his own thumb ring,' a dubious compensation.

Knowing all of this, we can see other possible multiple readings of the story even in the *Mahabharata*. There is a two-way conversation going on between the Hindu and Jain texts, an intertextual conversation. The Jain texts quote the Hindu *Mahabharata*, an example of the widespread intertextuality between religions in India, not just within Hinduism. But Hindus would probably know the Jain version too—a supposition justifiable on the basis of our understanding of the close relationship between Hindus and Jains at this period; and this may have contributed to the eventual use of the story of Ekalavya by Dalits. Indeed, Jains and Buddhists powerfully influenced the evolving social consciousness of Hinduism, both by their own example and by their ongoing, sharp critique of Hindu attitudes to the lower castes and Tribals.[5]

The earlier Jain version of the story, in which the dog is not harmed, is the one retold at the beginning of a film called *Eklavya, The Royal Guard* (2007, Vidhu Vinod Chapra, starring Amitabh Bachchan). Eklavya, whom the film calls an Untouchable Tribal, is the king's bodyguard and has secretly fathered the son and daughter of the impotent king. The film opens with a sequence in which Eklavya tells the story of Ekalavya to the royal children, who are still very young and subject it to an innocent moral commentary. This is how Eklavya tells the story:

> In the ancient times of the *Mahabharata*, a tribal boy wanted to learn the art of archery. He went to the great guru Drona, but Drona refused. He was mentor to princes and kings. How could he teach a low-caste tribal? Ekalavya returned to the jungle. He made a statue of Drona, called it his guru, and practiced archery night and day. One day, Drona was out hunting. Suddenly his dog stopped barking. Seven arrows had sealed its mouth shut. The archer had sent the arrows with such skill that the dog felt no pain and shed no blood. ['No pain, no blood, no pain, no blood,' says the young prince.] Drona was astonished. Who was this skilled, magic marksman? Do you know who it was? ['Ekalavya! His name was Ekalavya. Your name is Eklavya too,' says the princess, and Eklavya answers, 'Yes, my mother named me after that great archer.']
>
> Then Drona was baffled. The Untouchable tribal was superior to Arjuna. He had to be stopped. Drona said, 'Son, you have trained before my statue, claimed me as your guru. You must pay my fee.' Ekalavya smiled and said, 'Whatever you wish, o guru.' You know what Drona demanded? ['What?'] Ekalavya's right thumb. ['His thumb? Why?'] Without his thumb, how would Ekalavya draw his bowstring? He could never outshine prince Arjuna. ['Ekalavya didn't cut off his thumb, did he?'] Ekalavya merely smiled, cut off his thumb, and offered it at his guru's feet. ['No pain, no blood. No pain, no blood.'] No, there was a lot of pain, a lot of blood. But without flinching, Ekalavya fulfilled his dharma, his sacred duty. ['This dharma is wrong! I'd have refused. Ekalavya was wrong. Ekalavya was wrong. This is not good dharma. This is a bad dharma.']

The Jain theme of 'no pain, no blood' is spelt out in the film, though now there is no condemnation of Arjuna as there was in the Jain text; Arjuna does not appear at all, perhaps because by now he has assumed greater sanctity in Hinduism through the prominence of the *Bhagavad Gita*, in which he plays such a central and noble part. It is Drona himself who makes the demand. And that demand is absolutely unacceptable to the children listening to the story.[vi]

It is also absolutely unacceptable to contemporary Dalits, who use the story of Ekalavya for their own purposes. They want him to do what the myths did not reveal him doing: revolt. One poet says, 'I am conscious of my resolve,/the worth of the blood of Ekalavya's finger.'[6] Another writes at greater length:

> If you had kept your thumb
> history would have happened
> somewhat differently.
> But . . . you gave your thumb
> and history also
> became theirs.
> Ekalavya,
> since that day they
> have not even given you a glance.
> Forgive me, Ekalavya, I won't be fooled now
> by their sweet words.
> My thumb
> will never be broken.[7]

And here is another:

> Eklavya!
> The round earth.
> A steel lever
> in my hand.
> But no leverage?
> O Eklavya,
> You ideal disciple!
> Give me the finger you cut off;
> That will be my fulcrum.[8]

[vi] At a presentation of an early draft of this chapter at the School of Oriental and African Studies, University of London, on 30 November 2010, a member of the audience reported on two versions of the story he had recently heard, one from an Assamese man, who said the moral was, 'Don't trust your teachers,' and one from a Nepalese woman, who said it was about the unfairness of the caste system.

Such poems stand as a Dalit critique of Hinduism, rejecting both Ekalavya and Hinduism.

In the realm of social action, too, Ekalavya lives on. There are Ekalavya education foundations in Ahmedabad and Hyderabad. The Ekalavya Ashram in Adilabad, a northern district bordering on Maharashtra, on the banks of the river Godavari, is a non-profit, tribal welfare facility established in 1990. Run by people from the local business community, it serves underprivileged tribal people who cannot afford to educate their children. The cricket ground at Reshimbag in Nagpur has been named the Eklavya Krida Mandal ('The Ekalavya Games Circle'). The ancient story lives on in a new and liberating form.

ON NOT BEING HINDU

'I HAVE SCINDE': ORIENTALISM AND GUILT[1]

L et me begin with a story about General Sir Charles James Fox Napier, who was born in 1782 and in 1839 was made commander of Sind (or Scinde, as it was often spelled at that time, or Sindh), an area at the western tip of the Northwest quadrant of South Asia, directly above the Rann of Kutch; in 1947 it became part of Pakistan. In 1843, Napier manoeuvred to provoke a resistance that he then crushed and used as a pretext to conquer the territory for the British Empire. Napier was criticized in Parliament in 1844 for his ruthless campaign.[2] The British press described this military operation at the time as 'infamous' (the Whig *Morning Chronicle*),[3] a decade later as 'harsh and barbarous' and a 'tragedy', while the Indian press (the *Bombay Times*) accused Napier of perpetrating a mass rape of the women of Hyderabad ('without a shred of evidence', according to Priscilla Hayter Napier, the biographer who married a descendant of Napier).[4] The successful Annexation of Sind made Napier's name 'a household word in England. He received £70,000 as his share of the spoils'[5] and was knighted. In 1851 he quarrelled with James Broun-Ramsay, the Marquess of Dalhousie (Governor General of India from 1848 to 1856) and left India.

In 1844, the following item appeared in a British publication in London, under the title 'Foreign Affairs':

> It is a common idea that the most laconic military despatch ever issued was that sent by Caesar to the Horse-Guards at Rome, containing the three memorable words, '*Veni, vidi, vici*' ['I came, I saw, I conquered'], and, perhaps, until our own day, no like instance of brevity has been found. The despatch of Sir Charles Napier, after the capture of Scinde, to Lord Ellenborough, both for brevity and truth, is, however, far beyond it. The despatch consisted of one emphatic word—'*Peccavi,*' 'I have Scinde' (*sinned*).

The joke here depends upon the translation of the Latin word *peccavi*, which is the first person singular of the perfect tense, active voice, of the verb *pecco, peccare*, 'to sin', from which are derived our English words 'impeccable' (someone who never sins) and 'peccadillo' (a small sin). Thus the double meaning is 'I have Scinde' (that is, 'I have gained possession of a place called Scinde') and 'I have sinned' (that is, 'I have committed a moral error').

The story caught on. In a play published in 1852, a character named Sir Peter Prolix recites, at a dinner party, the following doggerel:

> What exclaim'd the gallant Napier,
> Proudly flourishing his rapier!
> To the army and the navy,
> When he conquered Scinde?—'Peccavi!'[6]

And when Napier died, a year later, G. Lloyd wrote to the journal *Notes and Queries*: 'It is also stated, I do not know on what authority, that the old and lamented warrior, Sir Charles Napier, wrote on the conquest of Scinde, 'Peccavi.'[7] The incident continued to be cited; a 1990 biography of Sir Charles actually entitled *I Have Sind* cites it three times.[8] Stephen Jay Gould cites it: 'Sir Charles Napier subdued the Indian province of Sind and announced his triumph, via telegram, to his superiors in London, with the minimal but fully adequate quote, '*Peccavi.*'[9] According to the *Encyclopaedia Britannica* online, '[Napier] is said to have sent a dispatch consisting of one word, "Peccavi" (Latin: "I have sinned"—i.e., "I have Sindh").'

But all evidence indicates that Sir Charles Napier never dispatched such a message. The passage about Caesar and Napier is not from the *Times* of London but from the comic journal *Punch* (1844, 6:209). Apparently, a girl in her teens, Catherine Winkworth (1827–78), best known for her later translations of most of the classic German Protestant hymns into English, 'remarked to her teacher that Napier's despatch to the Governor General of India, after capturing Sind, should have been *Peccavi* (Latin for "I have sinned"). She sent her joke to the new humorous magazine *Punch*, which printed it as a factual report under Foreign Affairs. As a result the pun has usually been credited to Napier.'[10] The authors of the *Punch* item may have been inspired by another apocryphal historical anecdote, which was linked with the *peccavi* story as early as 1875 and was in circulation for some time before that; it tells us that someone who had witnessed the defeat of the Spanish Armada announced it with one word: 'Cantharides', which is the Latin and pharmaceutical name of the aphrodisiac drug known as 'the Spanish fly'.[11]

The *Britannica* actually hedged ('he is said to have sent'), and a 1952 biography came right out with it, referring to Napier as 'the man who, though *Punch* was responsible, yet was *supposed* to have made the pun "Peccavi"—I have Scinde.'[12] Salman Rushdie retold the story in *Shame*, referring to his 'looking-glass' Pakistan as 'Peccavistan', but he calls the story apocryphal, bilingual and fictional.[13] So it is not Napier's text; but it is a text, a British text, that has a history of its own; it is a kind of nineteenth-century urban legend, a myth. The shift from the text of history to the hypertext of journalism is significant: the idea of the sin was initially a writer's idea, not a general's. With this in mind, let us unpack the myth a bit more.

Besides the two meanings I've mentioned ('I have conquered Sindh' and 'I have committed a moral error'), there is a third, which we discover if we heed the good advice of Marshall McLuhan, who taught us that the medium is the message; for the medium in this case is Latin. That third message signifies something like, 'Let's say it in Latin, which we Oxbridge types, English upper classes, know, and the natives do not, though they know English—which we taught them.' Stephen Jay Gould, who takes the anecdote as history, remarks:

> In an age when all gentlemen studied Latin, and could scarcely rise in government service without a boost from the old boys of similar background in appropriate public schools, Napier never doubted that his superiors . . . would properly translate his message and pun: I have sinned.[14]

Latin here functions as a code which the bearers of the message will not understand, a function that James C. Scott has taught us to recognize as the hidden transcript, which those in power can employ in ways different from the ways devised by the disempowered.[15] The *peccavi* text is explicitly an imitation of another Latin text (*veni, vidi, vici*), but that earlier text was unambiguous, spoken in the speaker's native language; unlike Napier, Caesar did not have to translate 'conquered' into *vici*.[16] It is also worth noting that even *Punch*, which perpetrated the story, glossed *peccavi* in English, realizing that some of their readers might not have been educated in good schools and, therefore, might not know Latin. But when Priscilla Hayter Napier told the story (as history, not myth) she remarked, 'Possibly this was when he sent his celebrated message—"*Peccavi*," which, in the Latin every educated man had then at his command, means "I have sinned".'[17]

In fact, the pun is not merely bilingual but trilingual or even quadrilingual, for the proper name 'Sind/Scinde' is a Hindi word derived, like 'Hindi' itself, as well as 'Hindu' and 'India', from terms that the Persians derived from the Sanskrit 'Sindhu' ('river').[i] *Peccavi* also breaks down into two puns in English, turning on the meanings not only of Sind [Hindi] /sinned [English] /Sindhu [Sanskrit and Persian] but on the almost invisible word 'have', which functions both as a complete verb, meaning 'possess', as one can possess a thing (like India, to take a case at random), and as an auxiliary verb in the perfect tense indicating that the action represented by the main verb (in this case, 'sin') took place in the past, and not in the present. The grammatical fact in this case denies the argument—which will become central to the anti-Orientalist critique—that the subject of the verb *goes on doing it*.

But it is the second meaning of *peccavi*, the second hidden transcript, of 'sin' as a moral error committed (only) in the past, that has been wrongly overlooked (though Rushdie referred to the one-word message as 'guilty'[18]). Though Sir Charles apparently never said (or wrote) *peccavi*, he seems to have had a sense that he had sinned in Sind.[ii] When he was posted there, he wrote: 'We have no right to seize Sind, yet we shall do so and a very advantageous piece of rascality it will be.'[19] 'Rascality' is a rather flip way to refer to the murder of many people defending their own land, but afterwards he wrote, speaking of his ambition, 'I have conquered Scinde but I have not yet conquered myself,'[20] and, 'I strive to curb pride and vanity. Get thee behind me Satan! But it is not easy to make Satan obey when one is a conqueror.'[21] Napier was also capable of equivocating, as when he wrote of the Sind campaign: 'I may be wrong, but I cannot see it, and my conscience will not be troubled. I sleep well while trying to do this, and shall sleep sound[iii] when it is done.'[22]

GUILT AND ANTI-ORIENTALISM

The sense of sin is not usually a part of the discussion of the story of Napier, but it may indicate a moment when some of the British felt moral

---

[i] See 'Hinduism by Any Other Name'.

[ii] That a man of great political power might have intended this subtext is suggested by a remark by President William Jefferson Clinton that *Newsweek* (21 September 1998) chose to reproduce as an enormous headline: 'I have sinned.' (I have since learned from several South Asianist colleagues that they, too, thought at that moment of Sir Charles Napier.)

[iii] This phrase is almost verbatim what Harry Truman said after the bombing of Hiroshima: 'I never lost any sleep over my decision.' (Lifton, *Hiroshima in America*, 176.)

ambivalence about their conquest of India. And this possibility may help us to dig our way out of the ambivalence which we who study India have inherited and which threatens to poison scholarship about the country in our period, bracketed as it is between ante/i-Orientalism before and postcolonialism after. The question is not whether Napier slept sound, but whether we Anglophone non-Indians engaged in the study of India can sleep sound.

Edward W. Said's book *Orientalism*, published in 1978, changed our way of thinking forever. Until then, we had admired the British scholars who had recorded dialects and folklore that otherwise would have been lost to posterity, who had established the study of Sanskrit in Europe and made available throughout India as well as Europe many of the classical texts recorded in that language. We felt indebted to them for our own knowledge of and love of India. But the anti-Orientalist critique taught us that those British scholars, too, had sinned, that they had been caught up in the colonial enterprise, sustained it, fuelled it, facilitated it. It taught us about the collusion between academic knowledge and political power, arguing that we, too, are implicated in that sin when we carry on the work of those disciplines—that it did not stop, like a Latin perfect tense, in the past.

At the heart of the postcolonial enterprise was the argument that scholars, then and now, affect and often harm the people they study. Twentieth-century anthropology had called this ideal into question long before Said challenged the case of Orientalism; even Rudyard Kipling, in his novel *Kim* written in 1901, had made his chief spy, Colonel Creighton, an amateur ethnographer. In a passage that I read as a satire on anthropology as spying, Creighton says, 'As an ethnologist, the thing's very interesting to me . . . The transformation of a regimental badge like your Red Bull into a sort of fetish that the boy follows is very interesting.'[23] The Great Game, as Kipling calls it (perhaps translating the Sanskrit *lila*, the game played by god in creating the illusory world), is not just spying. It is also anthropology—another form of the discipline once known as Orientalism, or more specifically Indology, the study of India, my game. For I would describe myself as a recovering Orientalist.

Kipling is one of the most dastardly of villains in the comic tragedy now playing in contemporary Indology. The White Man's Burden that he named now falls upon our shoulders, to embarrass us in the opposite way: the burden of being White Men (or, as the case may be, White Women) is what hobbles us in our study of Hinduism. Or so Edward Said tells us, and his words are echoed by those who would deconstruct the study of 'the Orient' in general and Hinduism in particular. Since Said's shattering denunciation, Orientalists—Westerners who study Eastern religions and societies—have perceived themselves to be hopelessly tarred by the brushes of racism, colonialism, Eurocentrism and sexism. Some have become so self-aware and self-critical that they have begun to self-destruct; others argue that it is not possible for non-Indians to study India, and, on the other hand, that we ourselves have created the India that we purport to study.

We can no longer think without the postcolonial critique. The Freudian and post-Freudian Marxist agendas tell us to look for the subtext, the hidden transcript, the censored text; the Marxist and to some extent the Freudian assumption is that this subtext is less respectable, more self-serving, but also more honest, more real than the surface text. In India the British surface text—'We are bringing civilization to these savages'—reveals a subtext—'We are using military power to make England wealthy by robbing India.' But there are more than two layers to any agenda, and we must not assume that it's self-interest all the way down. The *peccavi* anecdote suggests that beneath the subtext of self-interest may lie a nobler self-perception, a place where guilt is registered. And perhaps, beneath that, there may be yet another layer, an admiration of India, a desire to learn from India, perhaps even a genuine if misguided desire to give India something in return, like British law, for instance, or railroads.

Or the English language: Dalits in Uttar Pradesh have built a temple to the Goddess of the English Language, with a bronze statue, two feet tall, holding a pen in one hand and the Constitution of India in the other. Chandra Bhan Prasad, the founder of this project, regards this goddess as the symbol of Dalit renaissance, the way out of the illiteracy and poverty that still plagues the Dalit community. And he cites Dr Bhimrao Ambedkar's statement that English was the milk of the lioness, and only those who drink it will roar.[24] And so the language of oppression has become the language of freedom, the roar of the Dalits.

But the sense of guilt that the excavation of the imperialist subtext has generated has taken a terrible toll on the study of the text itself. Anti-Orientalism has led in many quarters to a disregard for the philology and basic textual work that the Orientalists did very well and that still remains the basis of sound scholarship about Hinduism. But the original anti-Orientalist agenda was monolithic in ways that soon came to be modified, by Edward Said himself, among others, and by James C. Scott. We have learned to see not just oppressors and victims but oppressors and resisters, subverters, people who knew, and know, how to wield the weapons of the weak.

Take, for instance, the anti-Orientalist argument that the British 'invented' or 'imagined' India, or Hinduism. I am a mythologist, which is to say that I take metaphors literally, for many myths are simply the narrative embodiment, sometimes an exaggerated embodiment, of metaphors, even clichés.[25] So to me, the expression 'the British imagined India' meant that, before the British got there, there was nothing south of the Himalaya but a black hole, of the Calcutta or stellar variety. And then the British came and sat in a circle, holding hands, eyes squashed shut, chanting a mantra ('Rule Britannia'), until, like Athena from the head of Zeus, like a file called forth from a hard disk, India popped up on the map, on the screen of the world, full grown, complete with the word for Hinduism and *The Laws of Manu* translated by Sir William Jones and the *Rig Veda* in Max Müller's edition. India, brought to you by the people who brought you the Massachusetts Bay Colony and Hong Kong!

This concept always seemed to me profoundly disrespectful of India, which was, like any other place, in the West or the East, quite capable of inventing itself and went right on inventing itself for centuries before, during and after the British presence. Granted, they had imagined themselves, at first, not as citizens of a nation but as people who lived in that place that was different from other places.[iv] And, granted, the anti-Orientalists imagined a rather different sort of imagining by the British, one that conceptualized India for the first time as a *unitary* political entity, rather than a group of independent entities, and Hinduism as a *unified* religion, and so forth. And, granted, the British imagination did distort and constrain the ways in which Indians represented themselves to others and, to a lesser extent, to themselves.[v] But British ideology never entirely replaced the ways in which Indians had traditionally regarded themselves, nor did it erase their knowledge of their own history. The anti-Orientalists themselves have taught us how powerful language can be, and the 'imagining' argument denies agency to the Indian imagination.

FORGIVING KIPLING FOR WRITING WELL

Edward Said, in a long essay that served first as an introduction to *Kim*, in 1987, points out the significance of the moment when the 'white-bearded

---

[iv] See 'Hinduism by Any Other Name'.
[v] See 'From Kama to Karma'.

Englishman' who is the curator of the museum (a figure modelled on Kipling's father, Lockwood Kipling) gives his own glasses to the Tibetan lama to see through. (Said does not, however, note the parallel, and equally significant, gift that the Tibetan gives to the Englishman: an antique box for *pens*, the gift of creating texts.[26]) The metaphor of the gift of glasses can stand not only for the colonizers' distortion of the vision of the colonized but for the distortion of our own vision by any ideology, including the ideologies of both Orientalism and anti-Orientalism. Obsessed with the nineteenth century, the postcolonial critique has forced us to look through monolithic, and hence skewed, spectacles that prevent us from seeing anything but our previous spectacles, the ones bequeathed to us by British Orientalism. It is time to stop merely looking at those flawed lenses and to try to see *through* them, that is, beyond them and also *by means of* them, this time correcting for the Orientalist myopia.

In his surprisingly appreciative essay on *Kim*, Said wrestles with his conflicted feelings about Kipling. On the one hand, he demonstrates how deeply embedded, indeed coded, in *Kim* is the racist and imperialist view for which Kipling became notorious. But, on the other hand, Said speaks of *Kim* as 'profoundly embarrassing'[27]—for Said, and for us, for any readers caught between their warm response to the artistry of the book and their revulsion at the racist terminology and ideology. Said speaks of Kipling as 'a great artist blinded in a sense by his own insights about India', who sets out to advance an obfuscating vision of imperial India, but 'not only does he not truly succeed in this obfuscation, but his very attempt to use the novel for this purpose reaffirms the quality of his aesthetic integrity'. Salman Rushdie, too, has written of his ambivalence toward the good-and-evil Kipling[28] and, I think, modelled the hero of *Midnight's Children* on Kim: a boy with English blood who appears to be both Hindu and Muslim. But Rushdie reverses the point about race: unlike Kim, who turns out to be English (and Protestant) because of his blood, despite being raised as a Hindu and among Muslims, the English blood of the protagonist of *Midnight's Children* doesn't matter at all, nor his Hindu blood; the boy is a Muslim because he is raised as a Muslim.

The ambivalence that Said and Rushdie expressed towards Kipling was matched by that of the poet W.H. Auden, who began the final section of his poem on the death of the poet William Butler Yeats (1940) with these verses:

Time that is intolerant
   of the brave and innocent,
And indifferent in a week
   to a beautiful physique,
Worships language and forgives
   Everyone by whom it lives;
Pardons cowardice, conceit,
   Lays its honours at their feet.

Time that with this strange excuse
   Pardons Kipling and his views,
And will pardon Paul Claudel,
   Pardons him for writing well.[29]

Auden eventually decided not to pardon Kipling and his views; he excised these verses from subsequent editions, but not before thousands of readers in the English-speaking world had memorized the verses, which are very powerful in precisely the way that, as George Orwell pointed out, Kipling's own verse is powerful. Orwell argued that Kipling is a 'good bad poet', who wrote the kind of poetry that you would like to forget but that you remember, almost against your will, more easily, and longer, than good poetry.[30] Rushdie, too, concludes his essay by saying, 'There will always be plenty in Kipling that I find difficult to forgive; but there is also enough truth in these stories to make them impossible to ignore.'[31]

The Auden poem ends with a verse that he did not excise:

In the deserts of the heart
   Let the healing fountain start,
In the prison of his days,
   Teach the free man how to praise.

Imprisoned as we are, as Said taught us to realize that we are, in the twisted ideologies of the founders of our discipline, we must still find ways to praise not only what they praised, but to praise them, too. It is time to go back to the Orientalists with what the philosopher Paul Ricoeur called a 'second naiveté':[32] an innocence that has travelled through loss of innocence to an apparently unchanged but actually quite different sort of innocence. Where, in our first naiveté, we did not notice the racism, and in our subsequent hypercritical reading we couldn't see anything else, in our second naiveté we can see how good the Orientalists are despite the inhumanity of their underlying world views. Works of great scholarship will survive this new reading; others will not. There is much in the colonial scholarship on India that is worth keeping; I am unwilling to throw out the baby with the bath—a judgment call that depends on how good you think the baby is. Considerations such as these might inspire us to appreciate the tarnished but valuable gift bequeathed to us by British Orientalists.

DONIGER O'FLAHERTY ON DONIGER

[The graduate students in the study of South Asia at the University of Chicago publish a newsletter in which they include book reviews solicited from both students and faculty. In the autumn of 1999, they sent out, as usual, a list of books for review, and included one of mine: Splitting the Difference: Gender and Myth in Ancient Greece and India (Chicago: The University of Chicago Press, 1999). The book compared several clusters of myths, from ancient Greece and from ancient India, in which men or women were beheaded, doubled, split in half, or reversed in gender; it compared the myths of the shadow Sita[i] and the shadow Helen of Troy, the seductions of Ahalya[ii] and Alcmena, and the gender-shifting of Ila[iii] and Teiresias.

I asked to review it for the student paper, promising that I would review it critically. I wrote under the name of Wendy Doniger O'Flaherty, assuming the persona of a rather conventional, anal-retentive Sanskritist, of the type I knew only too well, expressing the criticisms that I always feared such people would have of my books. The review appeared in the Chicago South Asia Newsletter 23:3 (Fall, 1999), p. 6.]

This book is itself split: it simultaneously pursues two agendas, which are not always well integrated and, indeed, often work against one another: agenda A is to demonstrate the enduring sameness of certain underlying plots about split women across cultural boundaries (as, for instance, when a woman writes a book under one name and reviews it under another), and agenda B is to show the differences among numerous Indian variants of the same myths (as when an author tells the same myth in every book she writes, but glosses it differently each time). The comparative and Indological agendas join forces in the central argument that patterns of gender remain

---

[i] See 'Shadows of the *Ramayana*'.
[ii] See 'The Mythology of the *Kamasutra*'.
[iii] See 'Transsexual Transformations'.

more stable than patterns of culture; that when the same story is told (as the author demonstrates) of an Indian woman, an Indian man, a Greek woman and a Greek man, the story of the Indian woman more closely resembles that of the Greek woman than that of the Indian man. Both in their objectification by male authors and in their own subjective strategies of subversion, women in Hindu (and, occasionally, Buddhist) stories are more like women in Greek stories than they are like men in Hindu (or Buddhist) stories. Thus the story of the shadow Sita develops in the South Asian tradition in ways that resemble the development of the story of the shadow Helen in the Greek tradition; whatever their origins, common or disparate, and however divergent their historical developments, both Hindu and Greek traditions resorted to the story of the surrogate double to generate a revisionist history of a rape or a seduction in the epic. Though both Sita and Helen are quasi-goddesses, recovering goddesses—one married to a god (incarnated as a human), the other to a mortal—they seem to lack the agency to produce their own doubles, and what divine power they have to begin with is eroded in much the same way in the course of retellings.

The presentations of the individual texts represent a compromise, not always satisfactory, between the two agendas, which are addressed to two different sorts of readers, generalists (A) and specialists (B): neither literal translations nor paradigmatic summaries, the tellings of the myths offer too much detail for the more general reader who wants to cut to the chase of the basic paradigm and too little detail for the serious Indologist who would prefer to have a closer rendition of the text. The reader, particularly reader A, often has to strain to see the forest (or, rather, the luxuriant jungle) of the overarching pattern that is sometimes obscured by an overgrowth of individual textual trees. They are, for the most part, interesting trees (particularly for reader B), but the excursion into Hollywood films, though amusing (and presumably directed at reader A), is not tied carefully enough either to the Indological analysis or to the central argument, nor is the relevance of the Japanese myth of Amaterasu or Freud's analysis of Schreber immediately apparent. The reader has to work too hard to find the path, but it is there: a pattern that tells the persevering reader why it is that women fool men so much more often than men fool women in these stories, why the beheading of women has both different causes and different results from the beheading of men, and why men who become women face problems so different from those encountered by women who become men.

The first few chapters pay at least some attention to historical context (agenda B), but clearly the author's heart is not in this enterprise, and the contextualization becomes sketchier and sketchier and is jettisoned entirely as the comparison spills over beyond India and Greece to the world at large (more precisely, to Victorian England and Hollywood). This broader range of texts then prompts such theological and philosophical questions as why immortals so often prefer mortal lovers and why feet are so often mutilated in the course of the quest for immortality. The trees do, finally, make a coherent jungle of texts that dance in and out of an intricate and finally persuasive pattern and even a conclusion: that gender trumps culture, or, to put it differently, that culture is the shadow of gender.

YOU CAN'T MAKE AN OMELETTE[1]

One of the many reasons why I took up the study of ancient Hinduism and Sanskrit as a freshman at Radcliffe in 1958[i] was to escape from my red diaper childhood; to avoid politics, to hide in an arcane subject far, far from the real (i.e. far left-wing American) world. And indeed that worked for many decades, in which I published several books about Hinduism without stirring up more than the usual academic criticism. But in view of more recent developments, my reasoning seems to have resembled that of the man who, in the 1930s, realized that a great war was gathering in Europe and decided to escape it by moving to a far-off place no one had heard of or cared about—Iwo Jima (smack in the middle of the South Pacific theatre of war).[ii] For writing about the ancient history of Hinduism has now become highly politicized, and the fight raging around the issue of Hindu pluralism in India[iii] has come back to haunt me in the United States.

The problem arises with Hindutva ('Hindu-ness'), a territorial, racial and fundamentalist form of Hinduism; the word was coined by Vinayak Damodar Savarkar in his 1923 pamphlet entitled *Hindutva: Who is a Hindu?* Hindutva has inspired violence against Muslims, violence against Christians, and the pervasive infection of fundamentalism, particularly on the Internet. It has made many Hindus orthodox as well as orthoprax.[iv] There are many ways to define fundamentalism, but, as US Justice Potter Stewart remarked of pornography, I know it when I see it, and in this context I would define fundamentalism as a fanatical disapproval of people, both inside one's own religion and outside, who deviate from a

---

[i] See 'Foreword Into the Past'.
[ii] There is a famous Orientalist parable on this theme that Somerset Maugham told in his play *Sheppey* (1933) and that John O'Hara cited, a year later, as the epigraph for a novel to which he gave the title *Appointment in Samarra*.
[iii] See 'Are Hindus Monotheists?'
[iv] See 'The Concept of Heresy'.

narrowly defined essence of that religion. The three primary advocates of Hindutva ideologies are the Rashtriya Swayamsevak Sangh (RSS, National Volunteers' Organization or National Corps of Volunteers), the Vishva Hindu Parishad (VHP, World Hindu Council), and the Bharatiya Janata Party (BJP, Peoples' Party of India or National People's Party), often known collectively as the Sangha (with perhaps unfortunate, perhaps intended, resonances with the Sangha as the ancient term for Buddhism), and sometimes called the Hindutvavadis.[v]

My encounter with the Hindutvavadis first began in 2002, when a retired Indian businessman started harassing me on the Internet,[2] and again in London on 12 November 2003, when, in the middle of a lecture that I gave at the University of London, chaired by the historian William Dalrymple, a man threw an egg at me.[3] (He missed.) A message that a member of the two-hundred strong audience posted the next day on a mailing-list website[4] referred to a passage I had cited from Valmiki's *Ramayana* in which Sita, the wife of Rama, accuses her brother-in-law Lakshmana of wanting her for himself.[vi] The web message stated:

> I was struck by the sexual thrust of her paper on one of our most sacred epics. Who lusted/laid whom, it was not only Ravan who desired Sita but her brother-in-law Lakshman also. Then many other pairings, some I had never heard of, from our other shastras were thrown in to weave a titillating sexual tapestry. What would these clever, 'learned' western people be doing for a living if they did not have our shastras and traditions to nitpick and distort?[5]

My defence in the news coverage about the egg incident was:

> The Sanskrit texts [cited in my lecture] were written at a time of glorious sexual openness and insight, and I have often focused on precisely those parts of the texts . . . The irony is that I have praised these texts and translated them in such a way that many people outside the Hindu tradition—people who would otherwise go on thinking that Hinduism is nothing but a caste system that mistreats Untouchables—have come to learn about it and to admire the beauty, complexity and wisdom of the Hindu texts.[6]

---

[v] It seems to me it would be far simpler just to add a single 't' to the abstract term, Hindutva, on the model of the way that people involved in bureaucracy are called bureaucrats, and call these Hindus, Hindutvats. Or one might use Khushwant Singh's wonderful term, 'Fundoos'.

[vi] See 'Shadows of the *Ramayana*'.

And, I should have added, the diversity of the Hindu texts. The parts of his own tradition that the website writer objected to are embraced by many other Hindus and are, in any case, historically part of the record. To the accusation that I cited a part of the Hindu textual tradition that one Hindu 'had never heard of', my reply was: 'Yes! And it's my intention to go on doing just that.'

In an article entitled 'India: The War Over History',[7] William Dalrymple reviewed a number of recent books about Indian history whose authors have been attacked—through words, threats, occasionally blows—by reactionary forces in India. He listed some of the most egregious examples of the rewriting of school history books in India and general misrepresentations of the history of Hinduism, a list to which, alas, many new examples have been added, or resurrected, since he wrote, in 2005. And he mentioned the egg affair:

> Last November, I was chairing a lecture on the great Hindu epic, the *Ramayana*, at the School of Oriental and African Studies in London. The lecture had been sponsored by a wealthy Hindu philanthropist, and was given by the celebrated Sanskrit scholar, Professor Wendy Doniger . . . Midway through the lecture, a man stood up, walked threateningly towards the podium and threw an egg at Doniger, which narrowly missed her. During the questions that followed the lecture, Doniger faced a barrage of heated insults from a group who had come with the egg-thrower, and who maintained that as a non-Hindu she was unqualified to comment on their religion. Other SOAS lectures on India have since been broken up in similar circumstances.[8]

Dalrymple alludes to the fact that the man who threw the egg at me also threw eggs at two other (Indian) scholars who had spoken in the same series of lectures in which I spoke. It was, therefore, not really an attack on me, personally, at all.

But the incident that I have come to think of as 'the egg and I' was not the end of the controversy over my representation of Hinduism.[9] I took the episode as a gauntlet that I could not resist picking up, and it inspired me to write *The Hindus: An Alternative History*, which was published in 2009. Critical reaction to the book in sources such as the *New York Times*, the *Times Literary Supplement*, the *Washington Post*, the *Wall Street Journal* and *Atlantic Monthly*, was mixed. Critics complained, justifiably, that the book was stronger in the ancient period (where I know what I am talking about) than in the Mughal, British and modern periods (where I do not, and relied on not always reliable secondary sources), but they enjoyed the writing and they applauded the agenda. Several critics used the word 'courageous', the full significance of which I was then too naive to appreciate. The book was one of the five finalists in non-fiction for the National Book Critics Circle Award.[vii]

In India, *The Hindus* (published by Penguin Books, Delhi), hit the top of the bestseller list in non-fiction for a while and then remained further down on the list for a while longer; it is still selling very well. But at the same time, the book came under attack by the Hindutvavadis. I was not the first, nor the worst; the attacks on Jeffrey Kripal et al. had begun years ago. But the popularity of my book, its visibility in bookstores, and, I think, its intimate and occasionally tongue-in-cheek(y) tone, its emphasis on the earthier and more narrative forms of Hinduism and its de-emphasis on the philosophical and 'spiritual' aspects that the Hindutvavadis prefer,[viii] made it a particularly attractive lightning rod for Hindu rage. Hindu bloggers accused me of hating Hinduism and of sexualizing and/or psychoanalyzing Hindus. They flooded Amazon.com with their lurid opinions of the book. They sent me obscene and, occasionally, threatening emails. Hindus protested outside the US Embassy in Delhi, calling for the book to be banned.[10] And there were counter-protests; Salman Rushdie came to my defence.[11]

I have not stopped writing about Hinduism. *Au contraire*. Even before *The Hindus* was published, I had begun writing the Hinduism volume of the forthcoming *Norton Anthology of World Religions*. As I made the selections, I became more and more aware of the need to provide even more substantial textual evidence for the Hinduism that the Hindutvavadis would deny and censor; and what better way to do it than with an anthology of texts? Such a collection would provide ammunition for the Hindu voices of reason that continue to speak out against the Hindutva domination of the Internet. And so, after rounding up the usual suspects, the texts usually presented as representative of Hinduism, I added a number of lesser-known texts, including texts from Dalits and Tribals,

---

[vii] A few Hindus marched up and down outside the building where the awards ceremony was held, holding placards saying 'Say No to Doniger' before they retired to eat vegetarian samosas, and one of the selectors said that he was tempted to give me the final award to stand up against the protest, if for no other reason, but he actually preferred Richard Holmes' *The Age of Wonder*, which really did deserve the award and rightly won it. The protesters later insisted that their influence had kept me from getting the award, and celebrated it as a great triumph. See Carolyn Kellogg, *L.A. Times*, 11 March 2010, 'Hindu Activists Protest Professor Wendy Doniger's Book'.

[viii] See 'From Kama to Karma'.

from ancient women poets and modern women novelists, that reveal the strength and beauty of this other Hinduism that I continue to celebrate.

Now there's this book. And there will be more. After half a century of studying and engaging with Hinduism, I'm not about to be silenced by a few (bad) eggs.

THE FOREST-DWELLER[1]

In the midst of the great city of Chicago, I live as a forest-dweller. Forest-dwelling is where I am now in my life, and I am satisfied—or, more precisely, grateful—to be there.

Ancient Hindu texts wisely divide life into three basic stages of life: in the first, you study; in the second, you marry and become a householder; and in the third, you go and live in the forest.[i] (It has similarly been said about dogs that in the first stage, they play; in the second, they eat; and in the third, they sleep). The Hindu texts say that when you see your first grey hairs, or your grandchildren, it is time to take your wife or husband and head for the forest, where you live simply but not grimly, and have time to think about things. (Some texts also suggest a fourth stage, of total renunciation, all by yourself, but I am, like most Hindus, temperamentally ill equipped for that sort of thing.)

Forest-dwelling is not necessarily retirement; it is more a state of mind than a plan of action. It is the time in which things do not matter in the same way they did when we were younger, the time when we achieve the attitude prescribed in the *Bhagavad Gita*, 'action without ambition' (*nishkama karma*). I still teach and write as I have done for over forty years, more than ever, in fact, but without the all-consuming hunger for achievement that drove me for so many years. At last I am content with where I am in my life. Race horses usually keep on running after they pass the finish line, no longer running for the prize, nor running quite so hard, running just for the sheer joy of running. I feel like that sort of horse.

I've done most of the things I wanted to do, and I no longer want or need to do them again; I take satisfaction in having done them. I lived for a year in India, for a year in Moscow (during the Cold War!), for ten years in England, other places, too. But I am always happy to come home to my dog. Some years ago, I gave up riding Arabian horses, as I had given up ballet dancing many years before that. For each thing, its season.

[i] See 'Three (or More)'.

I'm not ready to die yet. I still have wonderful students whom I want to see through the final writing of their dissertations, and to guide into their first jobs. There are still a number of books I want to write (a memoir of my mother, perhaps my own memoir) or rewrite (my novel, of which little but the title has survived massive revisions, but it's a good title: *Horses for Lovers, Dogs for Husbands*) or write about (the ancient Indian textbook of politics, the *Arthashastra*) or finish (my half-completed book on the cross-cultural mythology of women and their jewellery). There are still places I'd like to visit—see the penguins in Antarctica, the fjords of Norway, visit Shimla, go back to the west coast of Ireland—novels I want to read, films I want to see, music I want to listen to. But there's something satisfying in the knowledge that, if I were to die today, no one could possibly say of me, 'Tragically struck down in her youth, so much promise unfulfilled.' There's something liberating about living on borrowed time.

There are of course things about aging that I don't enjoy. I hate it when various parts of my body stubbornly refuse to do their jobs. And it irks me that some of the younger generation of scholars in my field regard my work as *vieux jeu*; somehow I went to bed one night an *enfant terrible* and woke up an old fuddy-duddy. Yet I would not for a minute change places with those young scholars, who must make their way with such caution, afraid that, if they say the wrong things, make the wrong enemies at this point, they might be kicked out, denied tenure, their careers blighted. I can say, and write, whatever I really think, one of the privileges of an *éminence grise* (or old fuddy-duddy).

Best of all, I have finally discovered the pleasures of solitude, of sitting on the deck of a house overlooking a freshwater marsh in Cape Cod, with the waves streaming in onto the beach of the Bay beyond, just sitting there, listening to the wind in the trees, looking at the sky, at the water, watching the red-tailed hawks cruising, and the otter making his way up the river, and the doe with her fawn coming to the bank of the river to drink. This, too, is my forest-dwelling.

APPENDIX I

LIMERICKS ON HINDUISM

On Being Hindu

A worshipper of Minakshi
Objected to strict orthodoxy.
He said, 'If I wish to
I'll also praise Vishnu
In person, or else by proxy.'

A Jew with cirrhosis of liver
Jumped into the pure Ganges river.
His sons all drew lots
On the funeral ghats
And the loser was forced to sit Shiva.

There once was a Rig Vedic *hotr*
Whose birth was within the wrong *gotra*.
He made some oblations
To change his relations
And wrote his own family *stotra*.

Gods, Humans and Anti-gods

'A goddess's fury when scorned,'
Said a Babu, 'is not to be borned.'
So this pious Bengali
Made statues to Kali
And argued, 'Four-armed is fore-warned.'

A learned young man from Barbados
Decided to study the Vedas.
For he wanted to see
If Prajapati
Was really the true god who made us.

Women and Other Genders

'In India,' said the Mahatma,
'We honour the thin or the fat ma.
That a wife should be modest
And act like a goddess
We hold not as dogma but catma.'

Kama and Other Seductions

The *Kamasutra*'s Vatsyayana
(An expert on Indian fauna)
Wrote a law of the fishes
For unconscious wishes:
A sexual Matsya Piranha.

A Hindu who didn't like kama
Refused to take off his pajama.
When his bride's lustful finger
Reached out for his *linga*
He jumped up and ran home to Mama.

Horses and Other Animals

There once was a young Bengali
Who covered his dog, a Kali,
With snakes and an eel
Till it looked so surreal
That his friends shouted, 'Hello, Dali!'

There once was a farmer, a Tamil,
Who mated a cow with a camel.
When friends would insist
That the *varnas* were mixed,
He denied it, 'For each is a mammal.'

Illusion and Reality in the Hindu Epics

The yogis and naths and hakkims
Tell their pupils, 'It's not as it seems.
Though you think that your mind
Made up God, you may find
You're a figment of one of *His* dreams.'

'The Indian sage,' said the Pope,
'Theologically is just a dope.
For the world, so it seems,
Is just one of His dreams,
And He can't tell a snake from a rope.'

The story of Parashurama
Is truly a Freudian drama.
He over-reacts
To his dad, takes his axe
And cuts off the head of his mama.

Poor Renuka lost her head
When she saw Kartavirya, and said:
'My dear son will find
One more axe he must grind,
And behead a Pariah instead.'

On Not Being Hindu

A scholar named Coomaraswamy
Learned Sanskrit and Greek from his Mommy.
But the Doctrine Perennis
Became such a menace,
His colleagues all thought he was balmy.

The Sanskritists find it a treat
To tell the tales of the élite,
While folklorists pillage
The lore of the village,
Thus working both sides of the street.

APPENDIX II

ESSAYS ON HINDUISM BY WENDY DONIGER

Under the name of Wendy Doniger O'Flaherty:

1. 'The Post-Vedic History of the Soma Plant', in Robert Gordon Wasson, *Soma: Divine Mushroom of Immortality*, New York: Harcourt Brace, 1968, 95-147.
2. 'Asceticism and Sexuality in the Mythology of Siva.' Parts 1-2. *History of Religions* 8, no. 4 (May 1969), 300-337; 9, no. 1 (August 1969), 1-41.
3. 'The Symbolism of the Third Eye of Siva in the Puranas.' *Purana Bulletin* 11, no. 2 (July 1969), 273-284.
4. 'In Defense of Sir John Marshall.' *South Asian Review* (The Journal of the Royal Society for India, Pakistan and Ceylon; London) 3, no. 1 (October 1969), 75-81. Reprint, *Journal of Tamil Studies* 2, no. 1 (May 1970), 277-287.
5. 'The Symbolism of Ashes in the Mythology of Siva.' *Purana Bulletin* 13, no. 1 (January 1971), 26-35.
6. 'The Origin of Heresy in Hindu Mythology.' *History of Religions* 10, no. 4 (May 1971), 271-333.
7. 'A New Approach to Sanskrit Translation, with an Application to Kalidasa's *Kumarasambhava*, Canto VIII.' *Mahfil: A Quarterly of South Asian Literature* (Asian Studies Center, Michigan State University) 7, no. 3-4 (Fall-Winter 1971), 129-141.
8. 'The Submarine Mare in the Mythology of Siva.' *Journal of the Royal Asiatic Society* (1971.1), 9-27.
9. Review of *Two Plays of Ancient India: The Little Clay Cart, The Minister's Seal*, translated from the Sanskrit and Prakrit, with an introduction by J.A.B. van Buitenen (1968) and Review of *Sanskrit Poetry from Vidyakara's Treasury*, translated by Daniel H.H. Ingalls (1968). *Journal of the Royal Asiatic Society* (1971.1), 78-84.
10. 'Disregarded Scholars: A Survey of Russian Indology.' *South Asian Review* 5, no. 4 (July 1972), 289-304; follow-up in *South Asian Review* 6, no. 3 (April 1973): 224-226.
11. 'In Praise of the Nineteenth-century Hindoo Mythologists.' *South Asian Review* 6, no. 4 (July 1973), 332-335.
12. 'Hinduism', in *Peoples of the Earth*, vol. 12, edited by Christoph von Fuerer-Haimendorf, 20-26. New York: Tom Stacey and Grolier, 1974.
13. 'Bhagavad Gita', 'Bhagavata Purana', 'Bhakti', 'Dharmasastra', 'Mahabharata', 'Nalopakhyana', 'Purana', 'Sastra', 'Smrti', in *Dictionary of Oriental Literature*, vol. 2, South- and Southeast Asia, edited by D. Zbavitel. London: George Allen and Unwin for Czechoslovak Academy of Sciences, 1974.
14. 'The Hindu Symbolism of Cows, Bulls, Stallions and Mares.' *Art and Archaeology Research Papers* (London) 8 (December 1975), 1-7.
15. 'Contributions to an Equine Lexicology, with Special Reference to Frogs.' *Journal of the American Oriental Society* 98 (1978), 475-78.

16. Review article on the *Mahabharata* translation by J.A.B. van Buitenen. *Religious Studies Review* 4, no. 1 (January 1978), 19-28.

17. 'Mediation in the Sant Tradition.' In *Sikh Studies: Comparative Perspectives on a Changing Tradition*, edited by Mark Juergensmeyer and N. Gerald Barrier, 87-89. Berkeley: Graduate Theological Union, Berkeley Religious Studies Series, 1978.

18. 'Sacred Cows and Profane Mares in Indian Mythology.' *History of Religions* 19, no. 1 (August 1979), 1-26.

19. 'Death as a Dancer in Hindu Mythology.' In *Sanskrit and Indian Studies: Festschrift in Honor of Daniel H. H. Ingalls*, edited by Masatoshi Nagatomi, 201-216. Dordrecht: R. Reidel, 1979.

20. 'Hinduism', in *The Encyclopedia of Ancient Civilizations*, edited by Arthur Cotterell, 192-196. New York: Mayflower Books, 1980.

21. 'Hinduism', in *Mythology: An Illustrated Encyclopedia*, edited by Richard Cavendish, 14-33. London: Orbis, 1980.

22. 'Inside and Outside the Mouth of God: The Boundary between Myth and Reality.' *Daedalus* (Spring 1980), 93-125.

23. 'Dionysos and Siva: Parallel Patterns in Two Pairs of Myths.' *History of Religions* 20, no. 1 (August 1980), 81-111.

24. 'Puranic Encyclopedias .' *South Asia Library Notes and Queries* 9 (March 1980), 2-3.

25. 'The Indo-European Mare and the King.' *Slavica Hierosolymitana*, Slavic Studies of the Hebrew University V-VI (1981), 23-33.

26. 'Illusion and Reality in the Yogavasistha.' The Sir George Birdwood Memorial Lecture, London, 20 May 1980. Reprint, *Journal of the Royal Society of Arts* 5294, no. 129 (January 1981), 104-123.

27. 'The Mythological in Disguise: An Analysis of "Karz".' *India International Centre Quarterly* 8, no. 1 (January 1981), 23-29. Reprint, *Debonair* (Bombay), January 1982, 30-34.

28. 'Manifestations of Siva.' *Connaissance des Arts* (May 1981), 72-79; French version, 'Manifestations de Siva,' *Connaissance des Arts* (Paris), no. 351 (May 1981), 80-87.

29. 'Illusion and Reality in the *Yogavasistha*, or The Scientific Proof of Mythical Experience.' *Quadrant: Journal of the C.G. Jung Foundation for Analytical Psychology* (Spring 1981), 46-65.

30. 'Kailasa', 'Linga', 'Nataraja', 'Pasupati', 'Siva' and 'Yoni', in *Abingdon Dictionary of Living Religions*, edited by Keith Crim, Roger A. Bullard, and Larry Shinn. Nashville: Abingdon, 1981.

31. 'The Shifting Balance of Power in the Marriage of Siva and Parvati.' In *The Divine Consort*, edited by John S. Hawley and Donna Wulff, 129-143, notes 342-343. Berkeley: Graduate Theological Union, Berkeley Religious Studies Series, 1982. [Reprinted by Beacon Press, Boston, 1987].

32. 'The Dream Narrative and the Indian Doctrine of Illusion.' *Daedalus* (Summer 1982), 93-113.

33. 'Epilogue' to 'The Last Meal of the Buddha' by R. Gordon Wasson. *The Journal of the American Oriental Society* 102, no. 4 (October-December 1982), 603.

34. 'The Image of the Heretic in the Gupta *Puranas*', in *Essays on Gupta Culture*, edited by Bardwell L. Smith, 107-127. New Delhi: Motilal Banarsidass, 1983.

35. 'Die Wolkenstadt im Himmel', in *Sehnsucht nach dem Ursprung, zu Mircea Eliade*, edited by Hans Peter Duerr, 406-421. Frankfurt: Syndikat, 1983.

36. 'Emotion und Karma: Uberlegungen zu Max Webers Interpretation der indischen Theodizee', in *Max Webers Studie uber Hinduismus und Buddhismus*, edited by Wolfgang Schluchter, 87-103. Frankfurt: Suhrkamp, 1984.

37. 'Siva Erect and Supine', in *Discourses on Siva: Proceedings of a Symposium on the Nature of Religious Imagery*, edited and with an introduction by Michael W. Meister, 289-297.

Philadelphia: University of Pennsylvania Press; Bombay: Vakils, Feffer and Simons, 1984.

38.   'Ethical and Non-Ethical Implications of the Separation of Heaven and Earth in Indian Mythology', in *Cosmogony and Ethical Order: New Studies in Comparative Ethics*, edited by Frank Reynolds and Robin Lovin, 177-199. Chicago and London: University of Chicago Press, 1985.

39.   'The Role of Myth in the Indian Life Cycle', in *Aditi: The Living Arts of India* (Washington, DC: The Smithsonian Institution Press, 1985), 184-201.

40.   'The Case of the Stallion's Wife: Indra and Vrsanasva in the *Ṛg Veda* and the *Brahmanas.*' *Journal of the American Oriental Society* 105, no. 3 (Special issue dedicated to Daniel H.H. Ingalls, 1985), 485-498.

41.   Foreword to *Ganesa: Lord of Obstacles, Lord of Beginnings*, by Paul Courtright, vii-viii. New York: Oxford University Press, 1985.

42.   Articles on Hinduism and sub-topics (Arya Samaj, atman, avatar, Bhagavad Gita, bhakti, Dayananda Saraswati, dharma, karma, mantra, Ramakrishna, shakti, tantra and Thugs) for the *Funk and Wagnalls Encyclopedia*. 1986 edition.

43.   'Horses and Snakes in the *Adi Parvan* of the *Mahabharata*.' In *Aspects of India: Essays in Honor of Edward Cameron Dimock, Jr.*, edited by Margaret Case and N. Gerald Barrier, 16-44 and 172-173. New Delhi: American Institute of Indian Studies and Manohar, 1986.

44.   'On Translating Sanskrit Myths', in *The Translator's Art: Essays in Honour of Betty Radice*, edited by William Radice and Barbara Reynolds, 121-128. Harmondsworth: Penguin Classics, 1987.

45.   'The Interaction of *Saguna* and *Nirguna* Images of Deity', in *The Sants: Studies in a Devotional Tradition of India*, edited by Karine Schomer and W.H. McLeod, 47-52. Berkeley: Berkeley Religious Studies Series; Delhi: Motilal Banarsidass, 1987.

46.   Articles in the *Encyclopedia of Religion*, edited by Mircea Eliade. New York: Macmillan, 1987, s.v.; 'Androgynes' (with Mircea Eliade), vol. 1, 276-281; 'Brahma', vol. 2, 293-294; 'Indian Religions: Mythic Themes', vol. 7, 182-190; 'Indra', vol. 7, 214-215; 'Pralaya', vol. 11, 483; 'Vrtra', vol. 15, 308-309.

47.   'Impermanence and Eternity in Indian Art and Myth', in *Contemporary Indian Tradition: Voices on Culture, Nature, and the Challenge of Change,* edited by Carla M. Borden, 77-90. Washington, D.C. and London: Smithsonian Institution Press, 1988.

Under the name of Wendy Doniger

48.   (with Brian K. Smith), 'Sacrifice and Substitution: Ritual Mystification and Mythical Demystification.' *Numen* 36, no. 2 (December 1989): 190-223.

49.   Foreword to *The Place of the Hidden Moon: Erotic Mysticism in the Vaisnava-Sahajiya Cult of Bengal*, by Edward C. Dimock, Jr., ix-xiv. Chicago and London: University of Chicago Press, 1989.

50.   'The Tail of the Indo-European Horse Sacrifices.' *Incognita* 1, no. 1 (1990): 18-37.

51.   Foreword to *The Ritual of Battle: Krishna in the Mahabharata*, by Alf Hiltebeitel, 13-21. SUNY Series in Hinduism. Albany: State University of New York Press, 1990.

52.   'Il cavallo nella storia e nella mitologia indiana.' *Abstracta* 5, no. 51 (September 1990), 14-17, translated by Giovanni Maria Del Re.

53.   'Why Should a Priest Tell You Whom to Marry?: A Deconstruction of the Laws of Manu.' Stated Meeting Report presented at the 210th Annual Meeting of the American Academy of Arts and Sciences, 9 May 1990. Reprint, *Bulletin of the American Academy of Arts and Sciences* 44, no. 6 (March 1991), 18-31.

54.   'Fluid and Fixed Texts in India,' in *Boundaries of the Text: Epic Performances in South and Southeast Asia*, edited by Joyce Burkhalter Flueckiger and Laurie J. Sears, 31-41.

University of Michigan Papers on South and Southeast Asia, no. 35. Ann Arbor, Michigan: Center for South and Southeast Asian Studies, University of Michigan, 1991.

55. 'Hinduism by Any Other Name.' *Wilson Quarterly* (July 1991): 35-41.

56. 'Pluralism and Intolerance in Hinduism,' in *Radical Pluralism and Truth: David Tracy and the Hermeneutics of Religion*, edited by Werner G. Jeanrond and Jennifer L. Rike, 215-233. New York: Crossroads, 1991.

57. 'Between the Seen and the Unseen: The Ambiguity of Death in Hinduism', in *Death: The Secret of Life, Proceedings of a Cross Cultural Symposium*. 99-109. New York: Cauldron Productions, 1992.

58. 'When God has Lipstick on His Collar: Theological Implications of Divine Adultery.' Kathryn Fraser Mackay Memorial Lecture Series, St. Lawrence University, 23 September 1991. Reprint, Ogdensburg, NY: Ryan Press.

59. 'The Deconstruction of Vedic Horselore in Indian Folklore', in *Ritual, State and History in South Asia: Essays in Honor of J.C. Heesterman*, edited by A.W. van den Hoek, D.H.A. Kolff and M.S. Oort, 76-101. Leiden: E.J. Brill, 1992.

60. 'Rationalizing the Irrational Other: Orientalism and the *Laws of Manu*.' *New Literary History: A Journal of Theory and Interpretation* 23, no. 1 (Versions of Otherness, Winter 1992), 25-43.

61. 'Echoes of the *Mahabharata*: Why is a Parrot the Narrator of the *Bhagavata Purana* and the *Devibhagavata Purana*?', in *Purana Perennis*, edited by Wendy Doniger, 31-57 and notes 259-262. Albany: State University of New York Press, 1993.

62. 'The Scrapbook of Undeserved Salvation: The *Kedara Khanda* of the *Skanda Purana*', in *Purana Perennis*, edited by Wendy Doniger, 59-83 and notes 262-265. Albany: State University of New York Press, 1993.

63. 'When a Lingam is Just a Good Cigar: Psychoanalysis and Hindu Sexual Fantasies', in *The Psychoanalytic Study of Society: Essays in Honor of Alan Dundes*, edited by L. Bryce Boyer et al., 81-104. Hillside, NJ: The Analytic Press, 1993.

64. 'Rationality and Authority in *The Laws of Manu*', in *The Notion of 'Religion' in Comparative Research*. Selected Proceedings of the 16th Congress of the International Association for the History of Religions, edited by Ugo Bianchi, 43-53 Rome: Dipartimento di Studi Storico Religiosi, 1993.

65. 'Reincarnation in Hinduism.' *Concilium: International Review of Theology* 249, edited by J.B. Metz and H. Haring. (May 1993): 3-15. Also in French, Dutch, German, Spanish, and Italian: 'La Reincarnation dans l'hindouism,' translated by Andre Divault, 13-26; 'Reincarnatie in het hindoeisme', translated by L. Meuwissen, 10-22; 'Reinkarnation im Hinduismus', translated by Andrea Kett, 380-388; 'La reencarnacion en el hinduismo', translated by Pedro Rodriguez Santidrian, 15-29 (783-797); and 'La reincarnazione nell 'induismo', translated by Maria Sbaffi Girardet, 16-31 (760-775).

66. 'Masquerading Mothers and False Fathers in Ancient Indian Mythology.' Gonda Lecture, Royal Netherlands Academy of Arts and Sciences, 29 October 1993.

67. Foreword to *Somadeva: Tales From the Kathasaritsagara*, translated from the Sanskrit with an introduction by Arshia Sattar, xliii-xlvi. New Delhi: Penguin Books India, 1994.

68. Preface to *Authority, Anxiety, and Canon: Essays in Vedic Interpretation*, edited by Laurie L. Patton, vii-viii. Albany: State University of New York Press, 1994.

69. 'The Love and Hate of Hinduism in the Work of Jewish Scholars', in *Between Jerusalem and Benares: Comparative Studies in Judaism and Hinduism*, edited by Hananya Goodman, 15-22, notes 280-281. Albany: State University of New York Press, 1994.

70. 'Hindu Pluralism and Hindu Intolerance of the Other', in *Concepts of the Other in Near Eastern Religions*. *Israel Oriental Studies* vol. XIV, ed. Ilai Alon, Ithamar Gruenwald, and Itamar Singer. Leiden and New York: E.J. Brill, 1994, 369-90.

71. 'Begetting on Margin: Adultery and Surrogate Pseudomarriage in Hinduism', in *From the*

Margins of Hindu Marriage: Essays on Gender, Religion, and Culture, edited by Lindsey Harlan and Paul B. Courtright, 160-183. New York: Oxford University Press, 1995.

72. 'The Criteria of Identity in a Telugu Myth of Sexual Masquerade', in *Syllables of Sky: Studies in South Indian Civilization, In Honour of Velcheru Narayana Rao*, edited by David Shulman, 103-132. Delhi: Oxford University Press, 1995.

73. 'Foreword to *Kali's Child: The Mystical and the Erotic in the Life and Teachings of Ramakrishna*, by Jeffrey J. Kripal, xi-xii. Berkeley and Los Angeles: University of California Press, 1995.

74. Foreword to *The Divine and the Demonic: Mahisa's Heroic Struggle with Durga*, by Carmel Berkson, v-vii. Delhi: Oxford University Press, 1995.

75. 'Desire and Illusion: Two Stories from Ancient India.' *Parabola: The Magazine of Myth and Tradition* 20, no. 4 (Winter 1995): 20-33.

76. 'Sexual Masquerades in Hindu Myths: Aspects of the Transmission of Knowledge in Ancient India', in *The Transmission of Knowledge in South Asia: Essays on Education, Religion, History, and Politics*, SOAS Studies on South Asia, edited by Nigel Crook, 28-48. Delhi: Oxford University Press, 1996.

77. 'Saranyu/Samjna: The Sun and the Shadow', in *Devi: Goddesses of India*, edited by John Stratton Hawley and Donna M. Wulff, 154-172. Berkeley and Los Angeles: University of California Press, 1996.

78. 'Tolstoi's Revenge: The Violence of Indian Non-Violence', in *Genocide, War, and Human Survival*, edited by Charles B. Strozier and Michael Flynn, 219-227. Lanham, Maryland: Rowman and Littlefield, 1996.

79. 'Western Dreams about Eastern Dreams', in *Among All These Dreamers: Essays on Dreaming and Modern Society*, edited by Kelly Bulkeley, 169-176. Albany: State University of New York Press, 1996.

80. 'Enigmas of Sexual Masquerade in Hindu Myths and Tales', in *Untying the Knot: On Riddles and Other Enigmatic Modes*, edited by Galit Hasan-Rokem and David Shulman, New York: Oxford University Press, 1996. 208-223.

81. 'Three (or More) Forms of the Three (or More)-Fold Path in Hinduism', in *Madness, Melancholy, and the Limits of the Self*, edited by Andrew D. Weiner and Leonard V. Kaplan. Madison, WI: University of Wisconsin Law School, 1996, 201-212.

82. Articles under 'Hinduism' in the *New Encyclopaedia Britannica (Macropaedia)*, 15th ed., vol. 20 (1997); articles first published, 1990 printing. 'Hinduism: General Nature and Characteristic Features', 519-521; 'The History of Hinduism' (with A.L. Basham and J.A.B. van Buitenen), 521-529; 'Sacred Texts' (with J.A.B. van Buitenen, Edward C. Dimock, A.L. Basham, and Brian K. Smith), 529-549; 'Cultural Expressions: Visual Arts, Theatre, and Dance', 554-555 (with A.L. Basham and J.A.B. van Buitenen); 'Bibliography', 557-558 (with Brian K. Smith).

83. 'When a Kiss is Still a Kiss: Memories of the Mind and the Body in Ancient India and Hollywood.' *The Kenyon Review* 19, no. 1 (Winter 1997): 118-126.

84. 'Medical and Mythical Constructions of the Body in Hindu Texts', in *Religion and the Body*, edited by Sarah Coakley, 167-184. Cambridge, England: Cambridge University Press, 1997.

85. 'The Sanskrit Maverick.' *Radcliffe Quarterly* 83, no. 2 (Summer 1997): 15.

86. 'Sita and Helen, Ahalya and Alcmena: A Comparative Study.' *History of Religions* 37, no. 1 (August 1997): 21-49.

87. 'Myths of Transsexual Masquerades in Ancient India', in *India and Beyond: Aspects of Literature, Meaning, Ritual, and Thought. Essays in Honour of Frits Staal*. Ed. Dick van der Meij. London and New York [Kegan Paul] and Leiden and Amsterdam [International Institute for Asian Studies], 1997; pp. 128-147.

88. 'Jewels of Rejection and Recognition in Ancient India.' *Journal of Indian Philosophy* 26 (1998), 435-53.

89. 'The Dreams and Dramas of a Jealous Hindu Queen: Vasavadatta', in *Dream Cultures: Explorations in the Comparative History of Dreaming* (ed. Guy Stroumsa and David Shulman. New York: Oxford University Press, 1999). 74-84.

90. 'Eating Karma, in Classical South Asian Texts.' *Social Research* 66:1 (Spring, 1999), 151-65.

91. 'Presidential Address: "I Have Scinde": Flogging a Dead (White Male Orientalist) Horse.' *Journal of Asian Studies* 58 (4), November, 1999, 940-60. Available online at www.jstor.org/view/00219118/di015153/01p0195c/0

92. 'O'Flaherty on Doniger.' Review of *Splitting the Difference.* In *Chicago South Asia Newsletter* 23:3 (Fall, 999), 6.

93. 'The Ring of the Forgetful Husband in World Mythology.' The 1999 Adams Lecture at San Diego State University.

94. 'Gli Anelli Magici della Memoria.' Traduzione di Vincenzo Vergiani. *Adelphiana*, Milan. May 30, 2001. 1-36. (The Jane Ellison Harrison Lecture at Cambridge, May, 2000).

95. 'Why did they burn?' A review of three books about widow-burning, by Lata Mani, Catherine Weinberger-Thomas and Mala Sen. The *Times Literary Supplement*, 14 September 2001, 3-4.

96. 'On the *Kamasutra*' in *Daedalus*, Spring, 2002, 126-129.

97. 'Transformations of Subjectivity and Memory in the *Mahabharata* and the *Ramayana*', in David Shulman and Guy Stroumsa, ed. *Self and Self-Transformation in the History of Religions*. New York: Oxford University Press, 2002, 57-72.

98. 'Shadows of the *Ramayana*', in *The Epic Voice*, ed. Alan D. Hodder and Ralph Meagher. New York: Praeger, 2002, 101-128.

99. 'A Burnt Offering.' Review of D.N. Jha, *The Myth of the Holy Cow. Times Literary Supplement* 5183 (August 2, 2002), 9.

100. 'Lost in Translation: Gender in the *Kamasutra*', in *The Magazine*, Oxford World Classics, Issue 5 Spring-Summer 2002, 2-7.

101. 'The *Kamasutra*: It isn't *All* about sex', in the *Kenyon Review*, vol. 24, #1, Winter, 2003, 18-43.

102. 'Fate (Hindu)' and 'Mythology (Hindu)' in *South Asian Folklore: An Encyclopedia*. Ed. Peter Claus, Sarah Diamond, and Margaret Mills. New York: Routledge, 2002.

103. 'Other Peoples' Religions, Other Peoples' *Kama and Karma*', in *The Stranger's Religion: Fascination and Fear*, ed. Anna Lanstrom. Notre Dame, Indiana. Notre Dame University Press, 2004, 79-98.

104. 'Going with the Flow: Why sex has to be put back into Tantra.' Review of David Gordon White, *Kiss of the Yogini*. The *Times Literary Supplement* May 21, 2004, 3-4.

105. Review of Ramesh Menon, *The Ramayana*, in *Parabola*, Fall, 2004,130-134.

106. 'Zoomorphism in Ancient India: Humans More Bestial than the Beasts', in *Thinking With Animals: New Perspectives on Anthropomorphism*. Ed. Lorraine Daston and Gregg Mitman. New York: Columbia University Press, 2005, 17-36.

107. 'Wake Up Calls: Some Ancient Hindu Myths.' *Parabola*, 30:1, February, 2005, 6-10. Reprinted on pp. 212 to 221 of *The Inner Journey: Views from the Hindu Tradition*. Ed. Margaret H. Case. Sandpoint, IND: Morning Light Pres, 2007.

108. 'La bisexualite dans la mythologie de l'Inde ancienne.' Diogene vol. 51, no. 208 (Octobre-Decembre 2004), 58-71; 'Bisexuality in the Mythology of Ancient India.' Diogenes vol. 52, no. 210 (2005), 50-60.

109. 'Do Many Heads Necessarily Have Many Minds? Tracking the sources of Hindu Tolerance and Intolerance', *Parabola* [30:4], Winter, 2005, 10-19.

110. '*Mahabharata*', in *Encyclopedia of Erotic Literature*. (London: Taylor and Francis, 2005).

111. 'The Clever Wife in Indian Mythology', of *Incompatible Visions: South Asian Religions in History and Culture. Essays in Honor of David M. Knipe*. ed. James Blumenthal. Madison: University of Madison-Wisconsin, Center for South Asia, 2005, 185-203.

112. 'From the Translator's Desk: Why I Was Drawn to Ancient Indian Literature', Prentice Hall Literature, *World Masterpieces*. Penguin Edition. Boston, Massachusetts 2007, 164, 176, 181-2.

113. 'A Symbol in Search of an Object: The Mythology of Horses in India', in *A Communion of Subjects: Animals in Religion, Science, and Ethics*. ed. Paul Waldau and Kimberley Patton. Columbia University Press, 2006, 335-350.

114. 'Parvati, Daughter of the Mountain', 77-90, and 'Durga, slayer of the buffalo demon', in *Goddess: Divine Energy*, ed. Jackie Menzies (Art Gallery of New South Wales: Sydney, Australia, 2006), 123-128.

115. 'Reading the *Kamasutra*: The Strange and the Familiar.' *Daedalus*, Spring, 2007, 66-78.

116. 'Kama and the Kama Sutra', in Fedwa Malti-Douglas, ed. *Encyclopedia of Sex and Gender*. Detroit: Macmillan Reference USA, 2007.

117. 'You Can't Get Here From There: The Logical Paradox of Ancient Indian Creation Myths.' Chapter 4 (87-102) of *Imagining Creation*. Ed. Markham J. Geller and Mineke Schipper, forward by Mary Douglas. E.J. Brill: Institute of Jewish Studies/Studies in Judaica, 2008.

118. 'India's Epic [the *Mahabharata*].' For 'The Fifty Greatest Books' series of *The Globe and Mail*, Toronto. 13 September 2008.

119. 'Special Report: If the woman is not radiant, she does not stimulate the man.' *Sunday Times of India*, New Delhi, 8 February 2009, 8.

120. 'Valentine's Day in India.' *Sightings*, University of Chicago, 14 February 2009.

121. 'The Forest-Dweller.' For *Aging Horizons Bulletin*, 28 February 2009.

122. 'Two Passages to India', in *A Narrative Compass: Stories that Guide Women's Lives*. Ed. Betsy Hearne, University of Illinois Press, 2009, 47-54.

123. 'The Battle over Hindu History.' On *Faith* blog, *The Washington Post*, 19 March 2009. http://newsweek.washingtonpost.com/onfaith/panelists/wendy_doniger/2009/03/the_battle_over_hindu_history.html

124. 'An Alternative Historiography for Hinduism.' *The Journal of Hindu Studies* 2009 2: 17-26.

125. 'Seek justice, only if you deserve it.' *Sunday Times of India*, 26 July 2009.

126. 'Politics of Hinduism: Why the Gods Can't Fail', in *India Today*, 15 August 2009 (Independence Day Special).

127. 'How to Escape the Curse.' Review of John Smith, *The Mahabharata*, for the *London Review of Books*, 8 October 2009.

128. 'The History of Ekalavya', in *Tarikh: The History Journal*, 2008-9. Special Issue on Myth and History, 34-36. St. Stephens, Delhi.

129. 'The Mythology of the *Kamasutra*', in *The Anthropologist and the Native: Essays for Gananath Obeyesekere*, ed. H.L. Seneviratne. pp. 293-316. Firenze: Societa Editrice Florentina; Delhi, Manohar, 2009.

130. 'Dogs as Dalits in Indian Literature', in *Antike Mythen: Medien, Transformationen und Konstruktionen*. Eds. Ueli Dill and Christine Walde. Berlin and New York: Walter de Gruyter, 2009, 391-405,

131. 'India's Sacred Extremes.' Review of William Dalrymple, *Nine Lives*. In the *Times Literary Supplement*, 6 January 2010. http://entertainment.timesonline.co.uk/tol/arts_and_entertainment/the_tls/article6977681.ece?&EMC-Bltn=NJXA32F. Reprinted in *International Journal on Humanistic Ideology: Studies into the Nature and Origin of Humanistic Ideas*, vol. 4, no. 1, Spring-Summer 2011, 143-151.

132. 'The Uses and Misuses of Polytheism and Monotheism in Hinduism.' *Religion and Culture Web Forum*, The University of Chicago Divinity School, January 2010. http://divinity.uchicago.edu/martycenter/publications/webforum/012010/monotheism

133. 'Suttee: Self-Sacrifice or Murder?', in BBC History Magazine online. October 2010. http://www.bbchistorymagazine.com/oup

134. 'Is Yoga a Form of Hinduism? Is Hinduism a Form of Yoga?' *Sightings* 12/30/2010 divsightings@gmail.com. Reprinted in *The Christian Post*, 12/30/2010, http://www.christianpost.com/article/20101230/is-yoga-a-form-of-hinduism-is-hinduism-a-form-of-yoga/

135. 'Preface' (pp. vii to xviii), to *Songs of Kabir*, translated by Arvind Krishna Mehrotra. New York: New York Review of Books, 2011.

135. 'Assume the Position: The Real Roots of Yoga.' Review of Mark Singleton, *Yoga Body: The Origins of Modern Posture Practice. The Times Literary Supplement*, 4 March 2011.

136. 'From Kama to Karma: The Resurgence of Puritanism in Contemporary India', in *Social Research, India's World*, vol. 78, no. 1, Spring 2011, eds. Arien Mack and Arjun Appadurai, 49-74. Reprinted as pp.47-70 of *India's World: The Politics of Creativity in a Globalized Society* (New Delhi: Raintree, 2012).

137. 'God's Body, Or, The *Lingam* Made Flesh: Conflicts over the Representation of the Sexual Body of the Hindu God Shiva', in *Social Research, The Body and the State*, Vol. 78: No. 2: Summer 2011, 485-508.

138. 'One Man's Many Lives in a God-Like Unknowing.' Review of Arshia Sattar, *Lost Loves: Exploring Rama's Anguish*, in *Outlook India*, 4 September 2011.

139. 'The Shadow Sita', in *Journal of Vaishnava Studies* (Vol. 20, No. 1, Fall 2011), 103-122.

140. 'The forest-dweller stage of life', pp. 906-7 of *Harvard and Radcliffe Classes of 1962*, fiftieth anniversary report, Cambridge: MA, 2012. Reprinted, as one of 2 selected from the Radcliffe entries, in *The Best Reports of 2012* (Harvard Class Report Office, 2012), 87-89.

LIST OF ABBREVIATIONS

Abbreviations, or abbreviated titles, have been used through the book for the following Sanskrit texts:

Aitareya Aranyaka [AA]
Aitareya Brahmana [AB]
Apastamba Shrauta Sutra [ApSS]
Ashvalayana Grihya-Sutra [AGS]
Ashvalayana Shrauta Sutra [AShS]
Atharva Veda [AV]
Baudhayana Dharmasutra [BD]
Baudhayana Shrauta Sutra [BSS]
Bhagavad Gita [BG]
Brihadaranyaka Upanishad [BAU]
Chandogya Upanishad [CU]
Hiranyakeshin Shrauta Sutra [HSS]
Jaiminiya Brahmana of the Sama Veda [JB]
Kamasutra [KS]
Katha Upanishad [KU]
Kathasaritsagara [KSS]
Katyayana Shrauta Sutra [KShS]
Kaushitaki Brahmana [KB]

Kaushitaki Upanishad [KauU]
Mahabharata [M]
Maitrayani Samhita [MS]
Maitrayaniya Upanishad [MU]
The Laws of Manu [Manu]
Manava Shrauta Sutra [MSS]
Purva Mimamsa Sutra of Jaimini [PMS]
Ramayana of Valmiki [R]
Rig Veda [RV]
Shadvimsha Brahmana [ShB]
Shankhayana Shrauta Sutra [SSS]
Shatapatha Brahmana of the White Yajur Veda [SB]
Shvetashvatara Upanishad [SU]
Taittiriya Aranyaka [TA]
Taittiriya Brahmana [TB]
Taittiriya Samhita [TS]
Vajasaneyi Samhita [VS]

NOTES

ON BEING HINDU

HINDUISM BY ANY OTHER NAME

1. An earlier form of this chapter, under the same name, was published in the *Wilson Quarterly* in 1991.
2. Doniger, *The Hindus*, 28-29.
3. Srinivas, *Social Change*.
4. Herodotus, *History*, 3.97-100 etc. He called them Hindoi.
5. Thapar, *Early History*, 275.
6. W.C. Smith, *The Meaning and End of Religion*, 30.
7. Babur, *Baburnama*, 352.

ARE HINDUS MONOTHEISTS OR POLYTHEISTS?

1. I've worked on this chapter for many years. It began as an essay entitled 'Pluralism and Intolerance in Hinduism' in a volume in honour of David Tracy, in 1991. Then I revised it, in 1994, under the title of 'Hindu Pluralism and Hindu Intolerance of the Other', and again, in 1996, as 'Tolstoi's Revenge: The Violence of Indian Non-Violence'. I rethought it in 2005, as 'Do Many Heads Necessarily Have Many Minds? Tracking the Sources of Hindu Tolerance and Intolerance' and, in 2010, as 'The Uses and Misuses of Polytheism and Monotheism in Hinduism'. I gave yet another version as a lecture at Kalamazoo College, Michigan, in 2010, and then, revised yet again, at Valparaiso University, Indiana, in 2011. And now I have had yet another go at it, though I still don't think I've got it quite right.
2. Doniger O'Flaherty, *Rig Veda*, 80. *ekam sad vipra bahu vadanti*.
3. BAU 3.9.1.
4. Grierson, 'Madhavas'.
5. Ramanujan, 'Myths of Bhakti', 307.
6. Shulman, *Tamil Temple Myths*, 314-15; cited by Ramanujan ('Myths of Bhakti', 298-9).
7. Shulman, *The Hungry God*.
8. Schimmel, *The Empire of the Great Mughals*, 113, citing Akbar.
9. Rocher, *Ezourvedam*, 3, 19. The text was published in *Asiatic Researches*, Royal Asiatic Society, Bengal, 1822.
10. Mitter, 'Rammohun Roy'.
11. Nandy, *The Intimate Enemy*.
12. *Swami Vivekananda and his Guru*, 25.
13. Swami Vivekananda, *The Complete Works*, 1: 348.
14. Huffer, *Guru movements*.

15. *San Francisco Chronicle*, 'A Different Agenda', by Romila Thapar and Michael Witzel, 6 March 2000, about the attempts of Hindus to alter school textbooks in the United States.

16. *Punjab District Gazetteer*, vol. IV A: *Gurgaon District* (Lahore: Civil and Military Gazette Press for the Punjab Government, 1911), 70. No author is attributed. The reference is to the Meos, a group of Muslims in Gurgaon.

17. Derrett, *Dharmasastra*, 51.

THREE (OR MORE) FORMS OF THE THREE (OR MORE)–FOLD PATH IN HINDUISM

1. This chapter is an expanded version of one, by the same title, first published in *Madness, Melancholy and the Limits of the Self*, in 1996.
2. Larson, *Samkhya*, 86-95.
3. Larson, *Classical Samkhya*.
4. Ibid.
5. Dumont, *Homo Hierarchicus*.
6. Brian K. Smith, *Reflections*.
7. BG 18.18-40.
8. Renou, *The Destiny of the Veda in India*; Brian K. Smith, *Reflections*.
9. Manu 6.87-94.
10. Doniger O'Flaherty, *Siva*.
11. Malamoud, 'Sémantique et rhétorique', 142.
12. Ibid., 146.
13. See Dumézil, *The Destiny of a King*.
14. Doniger O'Flaherty, *Origins of Evil*, 94-97 and 128-131.
15. Organ, 'Three Into Four in Hinduism'.
16. *Mandukya Upanishad* 3-7.
17. Erdman, 'The Empty Beat'.
18. BG 2.49, 3.3.
19. Doniger O'Flaherty, *Siva*, 76-77.
20. Dumont, *Homo Hierarchicus*.
21. Heesterman, *The Inner Conflict of Society*.
22. Doniger O'Flaherty, *Siva*.
23. Ibid., 318.

THE CONCEPT OF HERESY IN HINDUISM

1. I constructed this chapter out of three bodies of material: an article I published in 1971 ('Origins of Heresy in Hindu Mythology'); the dissertation I wrote for my D. Phil. in Oriental Studies from Oxford University (1973), under the supervision of R.C. Zaehner (*The Origins of Heresy in Hindu Mythology*); and my 1983 article on 'The Image of the Heretic in the Gupta Puranas'. In this chapter I have deleted the sections that overlap with materials in my book *Origins of Evil*.
2. Renou, *Hinduism*, 46.
3. Conze, *Short History of Buddhism*, 6.
4. *Shiva Purana* (2.1.17-48—2.1.18.38; *Shivapuranamahatmya* 1.1.2.15-40. See Doniger O'Flaherty, *Origins of Evil*, 233 and 237.
5. Staal, 'Über die Idee der Toleranz im Hinduismus', 215-18.
6. Mayrhofer, *A Concise Etymological Sanskrit Dictionary*, 65.
7. There are arguments against it, such as the subsequent appearance of the nasal. I am indebted to Professor Thomas Burrow of Oxford University for pointing out this etymological problem.

8. Seventh pillar edict; cf. Sircar, *Select Inscriptions*, 63, line 15.
9. *Ashokavadana* and *Divyavadana*, cited by Lamotte, *Histoire du Bouddhisme Indien*, 267-69.
10. Basham, *The Wonder That was India*, 295.
11. Renou, *The Destiny of the Vedas*.
12. *Tantravarttika* of Kumarila Bhatta, 127, commentary on Shabarasvamin's *Jaiminiya Mimamsa Sutra* commentary, verse 1.3.
13. *Padma Purana* 6.263.3.
14. *Shankaravijaya* of Anandagiri. See also *Shankaradigvijaya* of Madhava.
15. *Shankaravijaya* of Anandagiri, chap. 23.
16. Ibid., chap. 24.
17. Medhatithi's commentary on the *Manava Dharmashastra*, 4.30.
18. Manu, trans. Bühler, 133.
19. *Mitakshara* of Vijnaneshvara, commentary on Yajnavalkya *Smriti*, 1.130.
20. Vijnaneshvara on Yajnavalkya, 2.192.
21. *Tantradhikaranirnaya* of Bhattoji Dikshita, 25.
22. *Padma Purana* 6.263.3-5.
23. Commentary on *Vishnu Purana* 3.18.95 ff.; cited in *Shabdakalpadruma*.
24. *Kurma Purana* 2.21.32-33.
25. Manu 5.90.
26. Medhatithi and Narada on Manu 5.90; cited in Bühler, 184.
27. Wilson, *Sketches*, 265.
28. Gonda, *Der jüngerer Hinduismus*, 219.
29. *Mattavilasaprahasana*, act 1, prose between verses 8 and 9.
30. *Padma Purana* 6.250.l-23.
31. *Maghamahatmya* of the Uttara Khanda of the *Padma Purana*.
32. KSS 26(3.5).204, -.218, -.249-50.
33. Gonda, *Der jüngerer Hinduismus*, 219.
34. Hazra, *Studies in the Puranic Records*, 67-68; Chattopadhyaya, *Evolution of Theistic Sects*, 69-76.
35. *Kurma Purana* 2.16.15.
36. *Pashupata Sutra* 1.13-17.
37. *Kurma Purana* 2.37.142-48.
38. M, vol. 12, appendix I, no. 28, 1.405.
39. Apararka's commentary on *Yajnavalkya Smriti*, p. 18.
40. Chattopadhyaya, *Evolution*, 69.
41. M 13.17.45 ff.; cf. vol. 13, appendix 1, no. 4, 11. 66-67.
42. *Pashupata Sutra*, 3.6-10.
43. Ingalls, 'Cynics and Pashupatas,' 291.
44. Kaundinya's commentary on *Pashupata Sutra* 3.15.
45. I am indebted to Dr John Marr of the School of Oriental and African Studies for this insight.
46. *Nandisutra*, p. 391, cited in Altekar, *State and Government*, 15; Jaini, 'Jina Rishabha as an avatar of Vishnu'.
47. Burton, *Vikram and the Vampire*, 162-3.
48. Bhandarkar, *Some Aspects*, 4.
49. *Sarvadarshanasangraha* of Madhava, 3; cf. *Prabodhachandrodaya* of Krishnamishra, act 2, verse 26, and AS 1.2.5.
50. Madhava, *Sarvadarshanasangraha*, 6-7.
51. Apte, *A Radical Sanskrit-English Dictionary*, under *nastika*.
52. RV 2.12.5. *utem ahur naiso astity enam*.
53. KU 6.12-13.

54. *Shabdakalpadruma.*
55. Manu, with the commentary of Medhatithi, 2.11 and 4.163.
56. Hemacandra, cited in *Shabdakalpadruma.*
57. Dasgupta, *History*, III, 62; III, 512–550, 'The Lokayata, Nastika, and Carvaka'. He cites *Ahirbudhmyasamhita*, xxxi,18–23 for the 'later' view.
58. *Shabdakalpadruma*, under *nastika.*
59. Apte, under *nastika.*
60. Böthtlingk and Roth, eds., *Sanskrit Wörterbuch*, I, 742 and IV, 127.
61. Renou, *Destiny*, 60.
62. *Abhidhanacintamani* of Hemacandra 3, 862–863.
63. *Shabdakalpadruma.*
64. Heesterman, 'On the Origin', 171.
65. RV 5.30.1,6.18.36.27.3, 8.64.7, 8.100.3, 10.22.1.
66. Heesterman, 'On the Origin', 180–181.
67. Ibid., 184.
68. M 12.10.20.
69. R 2.100.11–17; trans. Pollock, 521–3.
70. *Tantravarttika* of Bhatta Kumarila, 114–17; commenting on Shabarasvamin's *Jaiminiya Mimamsa Sutra* commentary 1.3.4.
71. *Mattavilasaprahasana*, act 1, prose between verses 11 and 12. The elders are *dushtabuddhasthaviraih*, and the text is *avinashtamulapatham.*
72. Apte, *Dictionary.*
73. Monier-Williams, *Sanskrit-English Dictionary.*
74. MU 7.8.
75. Wilson, trans., *Vishnu Purana* 267–68 n.
76. *Vayu Purana*, cited by Wilson, *Vishnu Purana*, 268. [*vritha dandi vritha mundi vritha nagnashca yo dvijah / vritha vrati vritha japi te vai nagnadayo janah*]
77. Dumont, 'World Renunciation', 33–62.
78. RV 7.103.1–10.
79. RV 9.112.1.
80. AS 1.11.13 and many more passages.
81. *New York Times*, 14 August 1968.
82. Wilson, *Sketches*, 21.
83. *Mattavilasaprahasana*, act 1, prose between verses 9 and 10.
84. Brough, *Poems*, 105; Böthtlingk, *Indische Spruche*, 4.588; *Subhashitavali 2*, 402.
85. Doniger O'Flaherty, *Siva.*
86. *Vishnu Purana* 3.18.95–104.
87. Manu 4.192–98.
88. *Yajnavalkya Smriti* 1.130.
89. Brough, *Poems*, verse 21; *Subhashitavali*, verse 757.
90. Zimmer, *Art of Indian Asia*, 276.
91. *Markandeya Purana* 47.58–60.
92. *Kurma Purana* (Benares ed.) 2.16.14–15; *Kurma Purana*, Bibliotheca Indica, 444.
93. 'Ten Tales from the *Tantropakhyana*'; my summary.
94. Kosambi, *An Introduction*, 8.
95. Eliot, *Hinduism and Buddhism*, 2:192.
96. BG 4.7, 9.23.
97. Derrett, *Religion, Law and the State*, 46–51.
98. Ibid., p. 49. This was the Satsangi or Swaminarayan ruling; but see Doniger, *The Hindus*, 28, for negative aspects of this ruling.
99. Gonda, *Der jüngerer Hinduismus*, 219.

100. M 12.181.10-13.
101. Prasad, *Theories of Government*, 225.
102. Dubois, *Hindu Manners*, 516.
103. Eliot, *Hinduism and Buddhism*, 2:193.
104. Manu 10.43-44.
105. Eliot, *Hinduism and Buddhism*, 2:193.
106. Srinivas, *Social Change*.
107. Ambedkar, *Untouchables*, 78.
108. I am indebted to Dr David Pocock of the University of Sussex for this information.
109. RV 10.129.7.
110. RV 7.104.14.
111. AA 2.1.2.
112. BG 2.41-46.
113. Yaska, *Nirukta* 1.15.
114. Muir, *Original Sanskrit Texts*, 2:169-72.
115. Müller, *A History of Ancient Sanskrit Literature*, 142 and 181.
116. Sarup, *Nirukta*, 72.
117. Sinha, *Development of Indian Polity*, 70.
118. *Narada Smriti* 10.1-2; *Yajnavalkya Smriti* 2.192.
119. Aiyangar, *Rajadharma*, 12.
120. BD 1.2.1-9.
121. Hopkins, *Great Epic*, 89.
122. Manu 4.30.
123. *Yajnavalkya Smriti* 1.130.
124. Ibid. 2.70.
125. Narada 4.180.
126. AS 5.2.
127. Ibid. 3.20.
128. *Saura Purana* 38.54.
129. *Shukranitisara* 4.1.97-98.
130. *Shankarapradurbhava*, cited by Wilford, 'On Egypt', 3:295-468, esp. 411.
131. Doniger O'Flaherty, *Origins of Evil*, 187-211.
132. *Prabodhachandrodaya*, act 2, before v. 1.
133. *Prabodhachandrodaya*, act. 5, prologue, prose between verses 10 and 11.
134. *Parasara Purana*, chap. 3; cited by the *Tantradhikaranirnaya*, p. 34.
135. *Linga Purana* 2.6.1—57; my summary.
136. *Vaikhanasasmartasutra* 8.11.
137. Doniger O'Flaherty, *Origins of Evil*, 88-93.
138. SB 1.6.2.1-4.
139. *Varaha Purana* 70.29-42; my summary.
140. Schrader, *Introduction to the Pancaratra*, 83; citing the *Padma Tantra*, pt. 1, chap. 85, and *Vishnutilaka* 1.146ff.
141. *Shiva Purana* 2.3.31.1-52, 2.3.32.1-65.
142. M 13.40.5-12; my summary.
143. *Bhagavata Purana* 2.7.36-39.
144. *Tantradhikaranirnaya*, p. 37; citing *Parashara Purana*, chap. 11.
145. *Samba Purana*, quoted in the *Virmitrodaya* of Mitramishra, 1.24, cited by Chakravarti, *Tantras*, 32. See also Doniger O'Flaherty, *Origins of Evil*, 310-20.
146. *Samba Purana*, cited by Ananta-bhatta in his *Vidhanaparijata*, II, 519, cited in Hazra, *Studies in the Upapurana*, II, p. 93.
147. *Kurma Purana* 1.23.31-34.

148. *Kurma Purana* 1.22.39.
149. Hopkins, *Epic Mythology*, 45.
150. Ling, *Buddhism and the Mythology of Evil*, 78.
151. Woodroffe, *Shakti and Shakta*, 577.
152. *Samba Purana*, quoted in the *Viramitrodaya* of Mitramisra, 1:24; cited by Chakravarti, *Tantras*, 32.
153. Hazra, *Studies in the Puranic Records*, 227.
154. SB 13.6.2.9-10.
155. *Kurma Purana* 1.28.18.
156. *Tantradhikaranirnaya* 36; *Kurma Purana* 1.29.25.
157. *Vishnu Purana*, 6.1.37.
158. *Brahma Purana* 230.13; *Vayu Purana* 1.58.59; *Brahmanda Purana* 2.31. 59-60.
159. *Tantradhikaranirnaya* 37.
160. *Matsya Purana* 144.40; *Vayu Purana* 1.58.31; *Brahmanda Purana* 2.31.65-66; *Kurma Purana* 1.29.16.
161. *Vayu Purana* 1.58.40-65.
162. *Mahanirvana Tantra* 1.45.
163. Ibid. 1.66.
164. *Vishnu Purana* 6.1.45.
165. *Vishnu Purana* 6.1.60; cf. 6.2.34-36.
166. *Bhagavata Purana* 2.7.36-39.
167. Doniger O'Flaherty, *Origins of Evil in Hindu Mythology*.
168. Cakkavatti Sihanada Suttanta, *Digha Nikaya*, 3:73-75; my summary.
169. Manu 9.301-2.
170. AS 1.3.14-17.
171. *Vamana Purana* 49.1—14; my summary.
172. *Vamana Purana* 50.1-26.
173. M 3.55-74.
174. KSS 56.
175. *Naishadhacarita* 17.13-37; 88-201.
176. Doniger O'Flaherty, *Origins of Evil*, 188-211
177. Gail, 'Buddha as Avatar', 917-23; Choudhary, 'Heretical Sects', 239; Hazra, *Studies in the Puranic Rites*, 41-42 and 103.
178. *Dharmaranyakhanda* of the *Brahmakhanda* of the *Skanda Purana*, chapters 31-38, cited by Sircar, *Studies in the Society*, 149.
179. *Prabandhakosha* of Rajashekhara, 27-45, 9, 36-52.
180. Tawney (trans)., Ocean of Story, II, 204, citing W.U. Barker, *Vaitala-pachisi*, 184-91.
181. Pocock, 'The Anthropology of Time-Reckoning'. See also Doniger O'Flaherty, *Origins of Evil*, 35-45.
182. *Linga Purana* 40.50-63a.
183. *Matsya Purana* 144.50-65.
184. Pargiter, *Purana Text*, 56; *Matsya Purana* 273.25-34; *Vayu Purana* 99.388-412; *Brahmanda Purana* 3.74.200-224; *Vishnu Purana* 4.24.18-29; *Bhagavata Purana* 12.1-2.
185. Pargiter, *Purana Text*, xiii.
186. Ibid., 55.
187. Doniger O'Flaherty, *Origins of Evil*, 200-05.
188. Agrawala, *Matsya Purana*, 228-31.
189. Mookerji, *Gupta Empire*,17.
190. Hazra, *Studies in the Puranic Rites*, 169.
191. *Bhavishya Purana* 3.1.5.1-41; 3.1.6.1-49; 3.1.7.1-26; Doniger O'Flaherty, *Origins of Evil*, 44.

192. Huntington, *Study of Puranic*, 33.
193. Cf. *Bhagavata Purana* 6.8.19; *Gitagovinda* of Jayadeva 1.1,9; *Devibhagavata Purana* 10.5.13; cf. Doniger O'Flaherty, *Origins of Evil*, 204-06.
194. Wilson, *Vishnu Purana*, 489-90.
195. Derrett, *Religion, Law and the State*, 50.
196. Keith, *Indian Mythology*, 169.
197. Ivanow, 'The Sect of Imam Shah in Gujurat', 62-64.
198. Daniélou, *Hindu Polytheism*, 12.
199. Drekmeier, *Kingship*, 120.
200. Hopkins, 'Divinity of Kings', 314.
201. Bipan Chandra, *Use of History and Growth of Communalism*, 348.

EATING KARMA

1. This chapter is based on an essay originally published as 'Eating Karma, in Classical South Asian Texts', in *Social Research* 66:1 (Spring, 1999), 151-65.
2. Manu 5.5-14.
3. Manu 10.105-108.
4. RV 4.18.13.
5. M 13.94-95.
6. AB 7.13-16.
7. Shulman, *The Hungry God*.
8. Manu 10.104.
9. Manu 4.207-17.
10. Doniger O'Flaherty, *The Origins of Evil*, 320-331.
11. SB 13.2.9.6-9.
12. *Markandeya Purana* (66-69)
13. Srinivas, 'A note on Sanskritization and westernization'.

MEDICAL AND MYTHICAL CONSTRUCTIONS OF THE BODY IN SANSKRIT TEXTS

1. This chapter is a revised version of the first half of an essay, 'Medical and Mythical Constructions of the Body in Hindu Texts', that was published in *Religion and the Body* in 1997.
2. *Charakasamhita* 1.1.1.54-62a; Doniger O'Flaherty, *Textual Sources*, 93-4.
3. *Charakasamhita* 1.1.15.3-34; Doniger O'Flaherty, *Textual Sources*, 92-3.
4. Manu 6.76-7.
5. Manu 9.167.
6. Manu 9-31-42.
7. Manu 9.48, 50, and 55.
8. Manu 10.70-72.
9. Manu 10.5-23.
10. McKim Marriott, 'Hindu Transactions'.
11. Manu 2.169—71.
12. Doniger O'Flaherty, *Karma and Rebirth*, 21, 35-9, 50-1.
13. *Padma Purana*; see Doniger O'Flaherty, *Textual Sources*.
14. Fruzzetti and Ostör, 'Seed and Earth'.
15. Daniel, *Fluid Signs*, 163-70.
16. *Markandeya Purana* 10.1-7, 11.1—21

DEATH AND REBIRTH IN HINDUISM

1. This chapter is a much revised version of 'Between the Seen and the Unseen: The Ambiguity of Death in Hinduism' in *Death: The Secret of Life*, 1992, combined with 'Reincarnation in Hinduism', in *Concilium: International Review of Theology*, 1993, and 'Other Peoples' Religions, Other Peoples' *Kama* and *Karma*' in *The Stranger's Religion: Fascination and Fear*, 2004.
2. RV 7.59.12.
3. RV 10.14.7-8; Doniger O'Flaherty, *Rig Veda*, 44.
4. RV 10.16.1; Doniger O'Flaherty, *Rig Veda*, 49.
5. RV 10.16.6; Doniger O'Flaherty, *Rig Veda*, 50.
6. RV 10.16.3; Doniger O'Flaherty, *Rig Veda*, 49.
7. RV 10.18.10-11; Doniger O'Flaherty, *Rig Veda*, 53.
8. RV 10.18.1-6, .8, 14.
9. RV 10.16.3
10. RV 10.16.5
11. CU 5.3.1-10; Doniger O'Flaherty, *Textual Sources*, 35-37; BAU 4.4.
12. KauU 1.1-7.
13. SB 10.4.4.1-3; Doniger O'Flaherty, *The Origins of Evil*, 217.
14. Manu 3.100; cf. 4.201.
15. KU 1-6.
16. M 18.2.
17. M 18.3.
18. *Markandeya Purana* 14.1-7, 15.47-80.
19. *Markandeya Purana* 10.47-87; 12.3-48; 10.88-97; 11.22-32.
20. Mary Douglas, *Purity and Danger*.
21. BG 11.25-29.
22. *Bhagavata Purana* 10.15-17. Trans. Doniger O'Flaherty, *Hindu Myths*, 221-228.
23. See Doniger O'Flaherty, *Siva*, 130-138.
24. M 8.24; Doniger O'Flaherty, *Hindu Myths*, 125-137.
25. See Doniger O'Flaherty, 'Death as a Dancer', in *Women, Androgynes*, 133-138.
26. *Vamana Purana* S. 17.2-23; Doniger O'Flaherty, *Hindu Myths*, 173-4.
27. Doniger O'Flaherty, *Hindu Myths*, 238-249.
28. Goldman, 'Karma, Guilt, and Buried Memories', 416.
29. Ibid., 425.
30. Doniger O'Flaherty, 'Karma and rebirth in the Vedas and Puranas'. In *Karma and Rebirth*.
31. Goldman, 'Karma', 424.
32. Ibid.
33. Doniger O'Flaherty, 'Karma and rebirth'.
34. Sigmund Freud, in *Totem and Taboo* (trans. A.A. Brill), 14-15, 20-1, discusses sexual over-valuation. See also Freud, 'A Special Type of Choice of Object Made by Men'.
35. This passage is condensed from Doniger O'Flaherty, *Other Peoples' Myths*, 14-15.

FORGETTING AND RE-AWAKENING TO INCARNATION

1. This chapter is a revised version of an essay that was originally published as 'Wake Up Calls: Some Ancient Hindu Myths' in *Parabola* in 2005, and reprinted, somewhat revised, in *The Inner Journey: Views from the Hindu Tradition*, in 2007. It also incorporates passages from 'Other Peoples' Religions, Other Peoples' *Kama* and *Karma*' in *The Stranger's Religion*, 2004.
2. Goldman, 'Karma, Guilt, and Buried Memories'.
3. Monier-Williams, *Sanskrit-English Dictionary*, 947, s.v. *vasana*.

4.   Kalidasa, *Abhijnanashakuntalam* 5.2.
5.   *Raghavabhatta* 9, cited by Goldman, 'Karma'.
6.   McClintock et al., 'Pheromones and Vasanas'.
7.   Ibid., 99.
8.   *Markandeya Purana* 10.1-7, 11.1-21.
9.   Manu 12.74.
10. Freud, *Moses and Monotheism*, 162.
11. Freud, 'The Unconscious'.
12. Doniger O'Flaherty, *Dreams*.
13. *Yogavasishtha-Maha-Ramayana* 6.1.62-69; Doniger O'Flaherty, *Dreams*, 207-8.
14. *Yogavasishtha* 6.1.66.22-24, 6.1.62.32, 6.1.63.17.
15. Doniger, *The Bedtrick*, 17-20.
16. *Kalika Purana*, 49-52; Doniger O'Flaherty, *Siva*, 206-7.
17. M 13, app. 1, no. 5, 69; Doniger, *The Bedtrick*, 397.
18. Goldman, 'Karma', 420.
19. Doniger O'Flaherty, *Dreams*, 109-10.
20. R 6.105.8-10.
21. Pollock, 'Atmanam Manusam Manye ', 233.
22. Ibid., 234-5, 242.
23. Doniger, *Splitting the Difference*, 9-27.

ASSUME THE POSITION: THE FIGHT OVER THE BODY OF YOGA

1.   This chapter began life as a review of Mark Singleton's *Yoga Body: The Origins of Modern Posture Practice* (Oxford University Press, 2010). The review, entitled 'Assume the Position: The Real Roots of Yoga', was published in *The Times Literary Supplement*, 4 March 2011.
2.   Paul Vitrello, 'Hindu Group Stirs a Debate Over Yoga's Soul', *New York Times*, 27 November 2010.
3.   KU 6.11, 18; SU 2.1-4, 10-13, 15.
4.   RV 10.136.
5.   White, *Sinister Yogis*.
6.   Doniger, *Siva*.
7.   Quoted in Nikhilananda, *Vivekananda*, 167.
8.   See also Love, *The Great Oom*, and Syman, *The Subtle Body*.
9.   See Doniger, 'It Can Happen Here'.

THE TOLERATION OF INTOLERANCE IN HINDUISM

1.   Various parts of this chapter were published as 'Pluralism and Intolerance in Hinduism' in *Radical Pluralism and Truth*, 1991; 'Hindu Pluralism and Hindu Intolerance of the Other' in *Concepts of the Other in Near Eastern Religions*, 1994; 'Tolstoi's Revenge: The Violence of Indian Non-Violence', 1996; and 'Do Many Heads Necessarily Have Many Minds?', 2005.
2.   Owen Lynch made this point as part of a detailed formal response to this paper when I first presented it at the Columbia University workshop. Indeed, I am indebted to him for a number of insights sprinkled through this paper, too numerous to acknowledge individually.
3.   I am indebted to Norvin Hein for this suggestion; personal communication, Columbia University seminar, 12 November 1991.
4.   For a discussion of mythological attitudes to this otherness, see Doniger O'Flaherty, *Other Peoples' Myths*, especially 15-21.

5. David Tracy, paper presented at the Shalom Hartman Institute in Jerusalem, 11 January 1993.

6. Adultery is often a metaphor for idolatry in monotheistic religions, particularly ancient Judaism, where 'whoring after foreign gods' is a common way of referring to idolatry.

7. See Brian K. Smith, *Classifying the Universe*, for texts and arguments substantiating the social basis of Indian classificatory systems.

8. Staal, 'Über die Idee der Toleranz in Hinduism', 215-218.

9. Tennyson, 'Akbar's Dream'.

10. Blochmann, *The A'in-i Akbari*, xxxii.

11. Vivekananda, CW 1:348.

12. Golwalkar, *We or Our Nationhood Defined*, 48-49 and 55-56.

13. *India Today*, 30 November 1991, p. 9.

14. 'Lopsided Lessons', by Shekhar Gupta, *India Today*, 31 July 1990.

THE POLITICS OF HINDUISM TOMORROW

1. This chapter is an expanded version of an article written for a special Independence Day issue of *India Today* (15 August 2009) devoted to India tomorrow (where it was subtitled, for some reason that escapes me now, 'Why the Gods Can't Fail') and parts of another essay, 'It Can Happen Here: The Fight for the History of Hinduism in the American Academy', forthcoming in Nussbaum and Doniger, eds., *Pluralism and Democracy in India: Challenging the Hindu Right*, 2013.

2. Amartya Sen, *The Argumentative Indian*, 72.

3. Sumit Sarkar, *Beyond Nationalist Frames*.

4. Huffer, 'The Religious Believer'.

5. Doniger, *The Hindus*, 364-5.

6. See BBC News, 12 September 2007, and Doniger, *The Hindus*, 665-6.

7. Keay, *India, a History*, 2.

8. Doniger, *The Hindus*, 585-7.

9. I owe this concern, and much of its wording, to Arshia Sattar, personal communication, August 2006.

10. Arnold, 'Beheading Hindus'.

11. Ibid.

GODS, HUMANS AND ANTI-GODS

SAGUNA AND *NIRGUNA* IMAGES OF DEITY

1. This chapter is a revised version of an essay entitled 'The Interaction of *Saguna* and *Nirguna* Images of Deity', first published in *The Sants: Studies in a Devotional Tradition of India*, 1987.

2. *Tiruvaymoli* of Nammalvar, 1.1.9, from Carman and Naranayan, *The Tamil Veda*.

3. See Vaudeville, '*Sant Mat*'.

4. BG 11.40-42, trans. Zaehner.

5. *Bhagavata Purana* 10.8.21-45.

6. Tulsi Das, *Ramacharitamanasa*, Sanskrit invocation.

7. Michell, *The Hindu Temple*, 184 and 64.

YOU CAN'T GET HERE FROM THERE:
THE LOGICAL PARADOX OF HINDU CREATION MYTHS

1. This chapter is a much-revised version of one that I presented at a conference in honour of Mary Douglas (1921-2007) at University College, London, on 26 March 2003; she did not live to see her introduction to the volume, published in 2008, for she died on 16 May 2007. During those last years we had many conversations about this subject, and much else, and the revisions in this essay, like so much of my work, owe a great debt to her.
2. Professor W.G. Lambert wisely pointed this out at the conference on 26 March 2003.
3. RV 10.72.1-5; translated in Doniger O'Flaherty, *Rig Veda*, 38-39.
4. Sayana on this verse, citing Yaska's *Nirukta* 11.23; Doniger O'Flaherty, *Rig Veda*, p. 30.
5. RV 1.154; Doniger O'Flaherty, *Rig Veda*, 225-28.
6. RV 2.12.5; Doniger O'Flaherty, *Rig Veda*, 161.
7. RV 8.100.3.
8. RV 10.129; trans. Doniger O'Flaherty, *Rig Veda*, 25.
9. RV 10.72.1-5; Doniger O'Flaherty, *Rig Veda*, 38-39.
10. CU 6.2.2.
11. RV 10.121; Doniger O'Flaherty, *Rig Veda*, 26-28.
12. AB 3.21.
13. SB 1.1.1.6: *idam aham ya evasmi so'smi.*
14. Sayana's commentary on RV 1.121.
15. RV 10.90; Doniger O'Flaherty, *Rig Veda*, 29-32.
16. *Ambattha Sutta* of the *Sutta Nikaya.*
17. When this concept first appears in the *Rig Veda* (10.83.4), it is applied not to a creator but to Manyu, Anger. By the time of the Epics, however, it was an epithet of Manu, and then of Brahma.
18. *Kurma Purana* 1.9.
19. SB 11.1.6.6-11. See Doniger O'Flaherty, *Origins of Evil*, 139; Doniger O'Flaherty, *Hindu Myths*, 270-272.
20. Doniger O'Flaherty, *Origins of Evil.*
21. Manu 1.8-25.
22. Manu 1.21-30.
23. Manu 1.31-32.

TOGETHER APART: CHANGING ETHICAL IMPLICATIONS OF
HINDU COSMOLOGIES

1. This chapter is a revised version of an essay entitled 'Ethical and Non-Ethical Implications of the Separation of Heaven and Earth in Indian Mythology', published in *Cosmogony and Ethical Order*, 1985.
2. RV 5.85.1-5; Doniger O'Flaherty, *Rig Veda*, 211.
3. RV 10.121.5; Doniger O'Flaherty, *Rig Veda*, 28.
4. RV 1.154.1; Doniger O'Flaherty, *Rig Veda*, 226.
5. RV 2.12.2; Doniger O'Flaherty, *Rig Veda*, 160.
6. RV 9. 74.2; Doniger O'Flaherty, *Rig Veda*, 122; Wasson, *Soma*, 47-48.
7. RV 1.160.3-4; Doniger O'Flaherty, *Rig Veda*, 203.
8. RV 6.70; Doniger O'Flaherty, *Rig Veda*, 206-7.
9. BAU 6.4.20.
10. Doniger O'Flaherty, *Women, Androgynes*, 283-334.
11. RV 1.164.33 and 32; Doniger O'Flaherty, *Rig Veda*, 79.
12. RV 1.164.8; Doniger O'Flaherty, *Rig Veda*, 76.

13. Doniger O'Flaherty, *The Origins of Evil*, 139-53.
14. Heesterman, 'Vratya and Sacrifice', 1-37.
15. Dumont, 'World Renunciation', 33-62.
16. Marriott, 'Hindu Transactions', 109-10.
17. RV 7.86; Doniger O'Flaherty, *Rig Veda*, 212-13.
18. RV 7.88.5; Doniger O'Flaherty, *Rig Veda*, 215.
19. Doniger O'Flaherty, *Tales of Sex and Violence*.
20. JB 1.145. Cf. PB 7.10.1-3; AB 4.27.
21. JB 1.166.
22. AV 8.10.22-29.
23. RV 10.72.8; 1.164.9.
24. JB 1.185.
25. M 3.126.1-26.
26. cf. JB 2.134.
27. Doniger O'Flaherty, *Siva*, 87-89.
28. Dumézil, *The Destiny of a King* and *The Destiny of the Warrior*.
29. JB 3.72.
30. Doniger O'Flaherty, *Origins of Evil*, 153-60.
31. Doniger O'Flaherty, *Karma and Rebirth*.
32. JB 1.97-98.
33. RV 10.90; Doniger O'Flaherty, *Rig Veda*, 29-31.
34. Doniger O'Flaherty, *Origins of Evil*, 83-93.
35. Ibid., 248-271.
36. Doniger, *The Hindus*.
37. *Vamana Purana* S. 24.6-17.
38. *Skanda Purana* 1.1.31.1-78.
39. Doniger O'Flaherty, *Origins of Evil*, 248-272.
40. Ibid.,94-138.
41. Ibid., 248-71.

GOD'S BODY, OR, THE *LINGAM* MADE FLESH: CONFLICTS OVER THE REPRESENTATION OF SHIVA

1. This chapter began as the President's Lecture at the Art Institute of Chicago, in November 2010. Much expanded, it was published in *Social Research* (Vol. 78: No. 2: Summer 2011, 485-508). I then added some materials from my essay, 'When a Lingam is Just a Good Cigar: Psychoanalysis and Hindu Sexual Fantasies', in *The Psychoanalytic Study of Society: Essays in Honor of Alan Dundes*, 1993; and from 'When a Lingam is Not Just a Good Cigar', forthcoming in the Festschrift for Sudhir Kakar, ed. Dinesh Sharma.
2. Marshall, *Mohenjo-Daro and the Indus Civilization*, 52-56.
3. RV 10.86.16-17; Doniger O'Flaherty, *Rig Veda*, 257-63. The term also occurs at *Rig Veda* 10.101.12; Doniger O'Flaherty, *Rig Veda*, 66-67.
4. Doniger O'Flaherty, *Siva*, 85-86, 130-135.
5. RV 7.21.5, 10.99.3
6. Thomas Hopkins, *The Hindu Religious Tradition*, 9-10.
7. BAU 6.4.11.
8. BAU 6.2.13, 6.4.3.
9. M 10.17.10-26; Doniger O'Flaherty, *Siva*, p. 131.
10. Doniger O'Flaherty, *Siva*.
11. *Narmamala* 3.44.
12. KS 5.6.2-5, 7.2.4-13.
13. *Skanda Purana* 1.8.18-19; Doniger, *The Bedtrick*, 397.

14. Verse 2.82 of the *Gurucharitra* of Sarasvati Gangadhara, c. 1550 CE, composed in Marathi Ovi verse in Ganagapura, a partially Marathi-speaking area of Northern Karnataka, Gulbarga District. I am indebted to Jeremy Morse for this text and translation.
15. Kripal, *Kali's Child*, 159-163.
16. Gupta, *The Gospel of Sri Ramakrishna*, 491.
17. Paul Scott, *Staying On*, 243.
18. Doniger O'Flaherty, *Hindu Myths*, 137-53; *Textual Sources*, 85-87.
19. Doniger O'Flaherty, *Siva*, 172-209; Shulman, *Siva in the Forest of Pines*.
20. *Padma Purana* 6.282.20-36; Doniger O'Flaherty, *Siva*, 305-6.
21. Doniger O'Flaherty, *Siva*, 130-32.
22. *Brahmanda Purana* 1.2.26.10-61; Doniger O'Flaherty, *Siva*, 85-87.
23. *Periya Puranam* 16; McGlashan, 71-86.
24. Ferro-Luzzi, *The Self-Milking*; Cox, 'The Transfiguration of Tinnan'.
25. Ramanujan, *Speaking of Siva*.
26. Flood, *Introduction*, 171.
27. Keay, *India, a History*, 207-209.
28. Davis, *Lives of Indian Images*, 90-112.
29. Thapar, *Somanatha*.
30. Davis, *Lives of Indian Images*, 133.
31. Keay, *India, a History*, 342.
32. Oak, *The Tajmahal*.
33. Nandy, *The Intimate Enemy*.
34. Brodie, *The Devil Drives*, 359.
35. McConnachie, *The Book of Love*, 129.
36. Ibid., 130.
37. KS 2.1.1.
38. KS 7.1.25, 7.2.8, -15, -25.
39. McConnachie, *The Book of Love*, 130.
40. Lutz and Collins. *Reading National Geographic*, 82.
41. Doniger O'Flaherty, *Siva*.
42. Thomas Hopkins, *The Hindu Religious Tradition*, 9.
43. McConnachie, *The Book of Love*, 30.
44. Doniger, *The Implied Spider*, 87-94.
45. Kantorowicz, *The King's Two Bodies*.
46. Doniger, 'When a Lingam is Just a Good Cigar'.

SACRIFICE AND SUBSTITUTION:
RITUAL MYSTIFICATION AND MYTHICAL DEMYSTIFICATION IN HINDUISM

1. This chapter is a revised version of one that was written jointly by Brian K. Smith, now Lama Marut, and myself, published in *Numen* in 1989. I am grateful to Lama Marut for permission to use it here.
2. Hubert and Mauss, *Sacrifice*, 100. For a critical discussion of the interpretation of the Vedic sacrifice by Hubert and Mauss, see Keith, *The Religion and Philosophy of the Veda and Upanishads*, 268-278.
3. Ibid., 31-32.
4. Coomaraswamy, 'Atmayajna', 359.
5. Lévi, *La Doctrine*, 32-33.
6. Mylius, 'Der Sarvamedha'; Dange, 'Religious Suicide in the Vedic Period?'; Heesterman, 'Self-sacrifice in Vedic Ritual'.
7. Girard, *Violence and the Sacred*, 10.

8. Heesterman, 'Self-sacrifice in Vedic Ritual', 105.
9. Lévi, *La doctrine du sacrifice*, 32-33.
10. Freud, *Totem and Taboo*, 145.
11. Girard, *Violence and the Sacred*, 10.
12. *Ibid.*, 101-2.
13. RV 1.162.2-4.
14. TB 3.8.4.2
15. For the 111 and 180 animal victims at the horse sacrifice, divided into village and jungle, see, for the first, TS 5.5.11-24; *Kathaka Samhita* 5.7; MS 3.14.11ff; VS 24.30ff; and TB 3.9.1-4; for the second, TS 5.6.11-20; *Kathaka Samhita* 5.9; MS 3.13.3ff; VS 24.2ff; and TB 3.8.19-3.9.1. For the details of performing the rite, consult ApSS 20.14ff; BSS 15.23; MSS 9.2.4.1ff; etc.
16. Girard, *Violence and the Sacred*, 1.
17. *Ibid.* 10.
18. AB 7.13-18.
19. For a full translation and analysis of the myth of Shunahshepha, see Doniger O'Flaherty, *Textual Sources*, 19-25.
20. Lévi-Strauss, *Structural Anthropology*, 229; *The Savage Mind*, 22; Leach, *Levi-Strauss*, 58 and 71.
21. RV 10.130.3.
22. See SB 3.2.2.4; 5.2.1.2,4; 5.4.5.21; 6.4.1.6; 14.1.2.18; TB 3.2.3.1; 3.7.2.1; etc.
23. PB 7.2.1; SB 4.2.5.3.
24. SB 3.6.3.1
25. SB 3.1.3.17; 3.1.4.5; 3.3.3.5; etc. In other instances, Prajapati is identified with the year, and the year with the sacrifice (e.g., SB 5.2.1.2; 5.4.5.21; 11.1.1.1; cf. 11.2.7.1).
26. Mus, *Barabadur*, 121.
27. KB 25.15; *Kathaka Samhita*, 7.15.
28. SB 12.3.3.5.
29. Mus, 'La Stance de la plenitude.'
30. SB 1.3.2.1; 3.5.3.1; cf. TS 5.2.5.1.
31. SB 5.1.3.8; 5.2.1.6.
32. 'That *same purusha* became Prajapati,' SB 6.1.1.5; cf. 6.1.1.8; 7.4.1.15; 11.1.6.2; TB 2.2.5.3; and JB 2.47. The phrase can also point to the identification between the creator god of AV 10.90 (Purusha, the Primeval Male) and the cosmic progenitor of the Brahmanas.
33. TB 3.2.8.8
34. KB 10.3.
35. See, e.g., AB 2.11. Cf. SB 3.7.1.11 where the sacrificial stake (*yupa*) to which the animal victim is tied is also connected, by the *nidana*, to the sacrificer himself.
36. KShS 1.10.
37. BSS 28.13,
38. SB 6.2.1.1-3
39. SB 6.2.1.18.
40. Vedic texts often explained creation as the result of the primordial sacrifice of Purusha or Prajapati. See Brian K. Smith, 'Sacrifice and Being'.
41. SB 7.5.4.6.
42. Lincoln, *Myth, Cosmos, and Society*,183.
43. VS 30.1-22; SB 13.6.1-2; and TB 3.4.1.1 ff.
44. Sharma, *The Excavations at Kausambi*, 87 ff; Schlinghoff, 'Menschenopfer in Kausambi'; Parpola, 'The Pre-Vedic Indian Background', 49-53.
45. Sauve, 'The Divine Victim'; Kirfel, 'Der Ashvamedha und der Purushamedha'.

46. SB 11.7.1.2-3.
47. For other texts on 'redemption' (*nishkriti*) in Vedic ritualism, see SB 11.1.8.Iff; 3.3.4.21; AB 2.3; 2.9; KB 10.3; Thite, *Sacrifice in the Brahmana-Texts*, 144-45; 241-42; Lévi, *La doctrine du sacrifice*, 130-38.
48. Hubert and Mauss, *Sacrifice*, 98.
49. AB 2.8; cf. MS 3.10.2 and SB 1.2.3.6-9. Compare also the similar stories of the relationship between the five sacrificial animals and five paradigmatic jungle animals at MS 2.7.17; *Kathaka Samhita* 16.17; TS 4.2.10.1-4; and yet another variant at AB 3.33-34 where various wild animals are produced out of the ashes and charred remains of a completed sacrifice.
50. SB 6.2.2.15; cf. TS 2.1.1.4-5; 5.5.1.2.
51. SB 1.2.3.7; cf. MS 3.10.2.
52. AB 2.8-9.
53. SB 6.2.1.18.
54. SB 6.2.1.19.
55. See Wasson and Doniger O'Flaherty, *Soma: Divine Mushroom of Immortality*.
56. e.g., TB 1.4.7.5 ff.; JB. 1.354; PB 9.5.2 ff.; SB 4.5.10.1 ff.
57. ApSS 24.3.53.
58. SSS 3.20.11; AshSS 3.2.19; KShS 1.4.9-10.
59. KShS 1.4.15.
60. Chakrabarti, *The Paribhashas*, 176; cf. PMS 6.3.9, 35-36 and Shabara's commentary.
61. BSS 28.13.
62. HSS 3.1.
63. See, e.g., SB 4.1.6, 0-11; BhSS 8.25.13; SB 11.7.2.2; 2.4.4.11-14; TS 1.6.9.1-2.
64. AB 4.40-41.
65. AA 2.3.3.
66. SB 10.1.5.1-3.
67. SB 5.2.3.9.
68. Gonda, *Haviryajnah Somah*; Staal, 'Ritual Syntax'.
69. Doniger O'Flaherty, *Other Peoples'Myths*, Chapter Three; Brian K. Smith, 'Exorcising the Transcendent'.
70. Malamoud, *Le Svaydhyaya*.
71. Brian K. Smith, *Reflections*, Chapter Eight.
72. Doniger O'Flaherty, *Other Peoples Myths*, Chapter Five.
73. SP 2.2.1-43; 4.12.
74. SB 13.1.1.1 and 13.2.1.1.
75. VS 23; TS 7.4; SB 13.2.8-9; etc. See Doniger O'Flaherty, *Textual Sources*, 16-17.
76. Doniger O'Flaherty, *Women, Androgynes*, 157-8.
77. Ibid., 161, citing VS 23.22; SB 13.5.2.4.
78. Madhava, *Sarvadarshanasamgraha*, pp. 6-7.
79. Dumézil, 'Bellator Equus'.
80. Dumézil, 'Bellator Equus', 75-76.
81. Heesterman, 'Vratya and Sacrifice', 18; Parpola, 'The Pre-Vedic Indian Background of the Shrauta Rituals'.
82. Kirfel, 'Shiva und Dionysos'.
83. Griffith, *The Texts of the White Yajur Veda*, 230-31.
84. *Ibid.*, 213.
85. Dumézil, '*L'ashvamedha* du colonel de Polier'.
86. H 118.11-39.
87. M 1.47-53.
88. M 3.104-108; R 1.38-44; VP 4.4.1-33; etc. Doniger O'Flaherty, *Other Peoples' Myths*, 101-103.

89. TS 7.2.10.4; *Kathaka Samhita* 34.11 Cited by Eggeling in his translation of SB 1.2.3.5, in support of the argument that the rice cake replaced an original human sacrificial victim.
90. Evans-Pritchard, *Nuer Religion*, p. 197.

THE SCRAPBOOK OF UNDESERVED SALVATION: THE *KEDARA KHANDA* OF THE *SKANDA PURANA*

1. This chapter was first published in Doniger, ed., *Purana Perennis*, 59-83.
2. Doniger O'Flaherty, *Origins of Evil*, 157 n. 98.
3. See Rocher, *The Puranas*, 230, for a discussion, without date, of the *Kedara Khanda*.
4. This, and much of the ensuing discussion of the role of the *Skanda Purana* in Indian culture, I owe to a conversation with Velcheru Narayana Rao, on 24 May 1991.
5. I have argued elsewhere that, within the *bhakti parampara* of Krishna worship, the *Bhagavata* made a successful claim to have encompassed the *Mahabharata*, with Shuka surpassing Vyasa (author of the *Mahabharata*) as the author first of the *Bhagavata* and then of the further-encompassing *Devi Bhagavata*. 'Echoes of the *Mahabharata*: Why is a Parrot the Narrator of the *Bhagavata Purana* and the *Devibhagavata Purana*?' in Doniger, ed., *Purana Perennis*. And V. Narayana Rao has shown us ways in which the *Bhagavata* is, in turn, rejected in Telugu epics by those who no longer share its ideology. Velcheru Narayana Rao, 'Epics and Ideologies: Six Telugu Folk Epics.'
6. For a similar, but far more detailed, argument for the integrity of the *Laws of Manu*, see the introduction to Doniger and Brian K. Smith, trans. *The Laws of Manu*.
7. Rocher, *Puranas*, 230, citing. Plott, *Bhakti at the Crossroads*, 85.
8. *Padma Purana* 1.1.
9. *Shivapurana Mahatmya* 2.1-40.
10. *Vishnudharmottara Purana* 1.236.1-21.
11. *Linga Purana* 1.30.1-25; *Kurma Purana* 2.35.12-38.
12. See Doniger O'Flaherty, *Origins of Evil*, for the confluence of Vedic and devotional ideas of reciprocal affection between gods and humans.
13. Doniger O'Flaherty, *Origins of Evil*, 231-6.
14. M 3.163.
15. Bali does it in chap. 9; Nahusha, in chap. 15.
16. I have discussed this in my book *The Origins of Evil in Hindu Mythology* and, among other essays, 'The Concept of Heresy', included in this book.
17. M 1.16.39-40.
18. *Bhagavata Purana* 8.12.12-35; *Agni Purana* 3.17-20; *Shiva Purana* 3.20.3-7; *Brahmanda Purana* 4.10.41-77). See Doniger O'Flaherty, *Women, Androgynes*, 320.
19. RV 10.95.15.
20. Manu 9.17.
21. M 5.12-17.
22. M 1.98.1-5.
23. This occurs, for instance, in a Telugu text, the *Tarasasankavijayamu* by Samukhamu Venkata Krsnappa Nayaka; personal communication from David Shulman, 22 July 1991.
24. *Vishnu Purana* 5.27; *Harivamsha* 99.1-49.
25. *Bhagavata Purana* 10.55.7.
26. Doniger, *Bedtrick*.
27. Gopinatha Rao, *Elements of Hindu Iconography*, vol. 2, pt. 1, 322-23.
28. Manu 3.34.
29. Personal communication from David Shulman, June 17, 1991.
30. Rocher, *The Puranas*, 230.

WOMEN AND OTHER GENDERS

WHY SHOULD A BRAHMIN TELL YOU WHOM TO MARRY?: A DECONSTRUCTION OF *THE LAWS OF MANU*

1. This chapter is based upon a Stated Meeting Report given at the 210th Annual Meeting of the American Academy of Arts and Sciences, held at the House of the Academy on 9 May 1990. It was reprinted, as 'Why Should a Priest Tell You Whom to Marry?: A Deconstruction of *The Laws of Manu*', in the *Bulletin of the American Academy of Arts and Sciences* in 1991. Parts of it were published in 'Rationalizing the Irrational Other: Orientalism and *The Laws of Manu*' in *New Literary History*, in 1992; and in 'Rationality and Authority in *The Laws of Manu*'. In *The Notion of 'Religion' in Comparative Research*, 1993.
2. Thapar, *Early India*, 262.

SARANYU/SAMJNA: THE SUN AND THE SHADOW

1. The tale of Saranyu/Samjna is one that I have used variously in various books: I touched upon it in *Asceticism and Eroticism in the Mythology of Siva* (1973), 276 and 292; translated it in *Hindu Myths* (1975), 60–62 and 65–70; analyzed it in *Women, Androgynes and Other Mythical Beasts* (1980), esp. pp. 174–85; wrote an article on it (on which this chapter is based (1996); used it to explain the shadow Sita in *Splitting the Difference* (1999), chapter one; and used it in *The Bedtrick* (2000), chapters 1 and 9. Yet it still accuses me of not even having begun to plumb its depths, and draws me back to it.
2. Bloomfield, 'Contributions to the Veda, III', 172.
3. Kramrisch, 'Two', 125-6.
4. Bloomfield, 'Marriage of Saranyu', 172 and 188.
5. On the proliferation of twins, see Lincoln, *Myth, Cosmos, and Society*, 80–82.
6. Doniger O'Flaherty, *Asceticism and Eroticism*, 303.
7. Lommel, *Kleine Schriften*, 272–74.
8. Doniger O'Flaherty, *Dreams*, 1-18.
9. Lommel, 'Vedische Einzelstudien', 243–57.
10. Coomaraswamy, *The Darker Side of Dawn*.
11. *Harivamsha*, a passage of four verses inserted after 8.14 in the critical edition.
12. *Vishnu Purana* 3. 2. 2-12.
13. *Shiva Purana*, Dharmasamhita 11. 53-66.
14. Doniger O'Flaherty, *Women, Androgynes*, 149–65.
15. Bloomfield, 'Marriage of Saranyu', 181, citing Albrecht Weber, Adalbert Kuhn and Henri Bergaigne.
16. Kuhn, 'Saranyu-Erinnus', 448.
17. See Goldman, 'Mortal Man and Immortal Woman'.
18. 'Surya', retold by Mayah Balse, *Amar Chitra Katha* no. 58.

THE CLEVER WIFE IN INDIAN MYTHOLOGY

1. This chapter is the revised version of an essay published in *Incompatible Visions: South Asian Religions in History and Culture*, 2005.
2. Neely, *Broken Nuptials in Shakespeare's Plays*, 78.
3. KSS 124 (18.5):131-237; Tawney, vol. 9, 77 ff. (ch. 124, 171g).
4. Zvelibil, *Two Tamil Folktales*, 153-64.
5. KSS 139, 163.15.
6. Bloomfield, 'The Character and Adventures of Muladeva'.

7. KSS 98.31, 12.24.31.
8. Zvelibil, *Two Tamil Folktales.*
9. Parker, *Village Folk-tales of Ceylon*, 75–9.
10. Knowles, *Folk-Tales of Kashmir*, 'Shabrang,' 110–121.
11. Zvelibil, *Two Tamil Folktales.*
12. Stokes, *Indian Fairy Tales*, 42.
13. Zvelibil, *Two Tamil Folktales.*
14. Ibid.
15. Parker, *Village Folk-tales of Ceylon.*
16. Natesa Sastri, *Dravidian Nights*, 246
17. Knowles, *Folk-Tales of Kashmir*, 'Merchant', 287.
18. Zvelibil, *Two Tamil Folktales.*
19. Hasan-Rokem, *Proverbs in Israeli Folk Narratives*, 78–9.
20. Natesa Sastri, *Dravidian Nights.*
21. Knowles, *Folk-Tales*, 104.
22. Zvelibil, *Two Tamil Folktales.*
23. Hasan-Rokem, *Proverbs in Israeli Folk Narratives.*
24. Artin Pacha, *Contes populaires*, 247.
25. Sax, *Dancing the Self*, 69–70.
26. Pacha, *Contes populaires*, 239, 243.
27. Zvelibil, 'Matanakama'.
28. Parker, 'King Who Became a Thief'.
29. Natesha Sastri, 'Madana Kama'.
30. Knowles, 'Merchant'.
31. Pacha, *Contes populaires*, 245.
32. Stokes, 'Clever Wife', 216.
33. Hasan-Rokem, *Proverbs in Israeli Folk Narratives.*
34. Knowles, 'Shabrang'.
35. Ibid.
36. Knowles, 'Merchant'.
37. For Kunti, M 1.104; 3.290–294; 5.138–142; for Satyavati, M 1.90.
38. Manu 9.32–55.
39. Doniger, *Der Mann, der mit seiner eigenen Frau Ehebruch beging.*
40. Pacha, *Contes populaires.*

RINGS OF REJECTION AND RECOGNITION IN ANCIENT INDIA

1. An early version of this chapter was published as 'Jewels of Rejection and Recognition in Ancient India' in the *Journal of Indian Philosophy* 26 (1998), 435–53. I have revised it in light of several other articles about rings (parts of a forthcoming book): 'The Ring of the Forgetful Husband in World Mythology' (The 1999 Adams Lecture at San Diego State University); 'Gli Anelli Magici della Memoria' (Traduzione di Vincenzo Vergiani. *Adelphiana*, Milan. 30 May 2001, 1–36. Translation of the Jane Ellison Harrison Lecture at Cambridge, May, 2000); 'Magic Rings and the Return of the Repressed', in *Spirituality and Religion: Psychoanalytic Perspectives*, Volume 34–35 (2006-7) of *The Annual of Psychoanalysis*. Ed Jerome A. Winer and James William Anderson. Mental Health Resources: Catskill, New York, 243–256; 'Narrative Conventions and Rings of Recognition', in *Recognition: The Poetics of Narrative. Interdisciplinary Studies on Anagnorisis*, ed. Philip R. Kennedy and Marilyn Lawrence. New York: Peter Lang, 2009. 13–25); and 'The Rings of Budur and Qamar' (forthcoming in *Scheherazade's Children: Global Encounters with the Arabian Nights*, ed. Marina Warner and Philip Kennedy, New York University Press, 2013).

2. Doniger, *The Implied Spider*, 95-108.
3. M 1.64-69.
4. R 6.103-6.
5. M 3.137.1-20; JB 2.269-70; Doniger O'Flaherty, *Tales of Sex and Violence*, 105-107.
6. Insler, 'The Shattered Head', 120 and 125.
7. Doniger, 'Enigmas of Sexual Masquerade in Hindu Myths and Tales'.
8. *Katthaharijataka*.
9. *Uddalakajataka*.
10. KS 5.6.24-5.
11. KSS 30-34.
12. Doniger, 'The Dreams and Dramas of a Jealous Hindu Queen: Vasavadatta'.
13. Ramanujan, 'Hanchi: A Kannada Cinderella', 271.
14. Zimmer, *The King and the Corpse*, 71.

THE THIRD NATURE: GENDER INVERSIONS IN THE *KAMASUTRA*

1. This chapter is revised from an essay that was written for *Indologica: T. Ya. Elizarenkova Memorial Volume*, Book 2, ed. L. Kulikor (Moskva, 2012), 207-224; combined with 'Lost in Translation: Gender in the *Kamasutra*', in *The Magazine*, 2002.
2. AS 3.2.31.
3. KS 1.5.30.
4. AS 3.2.14.
5. AS 3.2.19-34.
6. KS 4.1.1-41.
7. Manu 4.150.
8. Manu 9.10-11.
9. KS 5.4.42.
10. KS 3.2.35 and 4.2.31-5.
11. Manu 5.154.
12. KS 4.1.19-21.
13. KS 1.5.22.
14. KS 4.2.31-4.
15. KS 2.2.20.
16. 'When her eyes roll when she feels him in certain spots, he presses her in just those spots.' KS 2.8.16.
17. KS 2.8.17.
18. Yashodhara's commentary on KS 2.1.30.
19. KS 2.1.23-30.
20. Manu 9.12-17.
21. KS 5.1.8.
22. Scott, *Weapons of the Weak* and *Domination and the Arts of Resistance*.
23. Doniger, *The Implied Spider*, chapter five.
24. Gopnik, 'A Purim Story', 26.
25. *Amarushataka*, verse 89.
26. Thanks to Blake Wentworth for bringing this commentary to my attention and translating it.
27. Manu 11.174.
28. AS 3.18.4.
29. Douglas, *Purity and Danger*.
30. BG 2.3.
31. Nanda, *Neither Man Nor Woman*.
32. Brodie, *The Devil Drives*, 369.

33. Archer, 'Preface', 17.
34. Ibid., 370.

BISEXUALITY AND TRANSSEXUALITY AMONG THE HINDU GODS

1. This chapter is based on 'Bisexuality in the Mythology of Ancient India', published in *Diogenes*, vol. 52, no. 210 (2005), 50-60. I have supplemented it with materials from 'Bisexual Deities in Hinduism,' once slated to be published in M. Kiel (ed.), *The Sexual Divide*, or in Moishe Idel, ed. *Mishkenot Encounters*.
2. Doniger O'Flaherty, *Women, Androgynes*, 292-3.
3. Doniger O'Flaherty, *Hindu Myths*, 34.
4. Doniger O'Flaherty, *Women, Androgynes*, 312-320.
5. *Subhashitaratnakosha* of Vidyakara, 82.
6. M 1.16-17; Doniger O'Flaherty, *Hindu Myths*, 274-80.
7. Doniger O'Flaherty, *Siva*, 87-90.
8. *Brahmanda Purana* 4.10.41-77; Doniger O'Flaherty, *Siva*, 228-9.
9. *Bhagavata Purana* 8.12.12-35; *Agni Purana* 3.17-20.
10. Personal communication from V.R. Narayana Rao, March 1995. See Doniger, *Splitting the Difference*, 260-65.
11. Shulman, *Tamil Temple Myths*, 314-15; cited by Ramanujan 'Myths of bhakti', 298-9.
12. R 7.87-90.
13. Sayana on RV 10.95.
14. *Brahmanda Purana* 2.3.60.23-27.
15. Manu 8.369-70; KS 5.6.1-4.
16. *Mahabhagavata Purana* 49-58, cited by Hazra, *Studies in the Puranic Records*, 272-3.
17. *Piramottara kantam* [Brahmottara-kanda] of Varatunkarama Pantiyar (late sixteenth century). Adhyaya 9. *Cimantani pavanai perra attiyayam*. David Shulman found this text and translated it from the Tamil; I have summarized and greatly condensed his translation.
18. *Yogavasishtha* 6.1.85-108; Doniger O'Flaherty, *Dreams, Illusion*, 280-281.

TRANSSEXUAL TRANSFORMATIONS OF SUBJECTIVITY AND MEMORY IN HINDU MYTHOLOGY

1. This chapter is a revised version of 'Transformations of Subjectivity and Memory in the *Mahabharata* and the *Ramayana*', published in David Shulman and Guy Stroumsa, eds. *Self and Self-Transformation in the History of Religions*, in 2002
2. Goldman, 'Transsexualism, Gender, and Anxiety'.
3. Doniger O'Flaherty, *Dreams*, 81-89.
4. Shulman, 'Toward a Historical Poetics'.
5. Manu 3.34.
6. *Brahma Purana* 108.26-30. 1954.
7. *Garuda Purana* 109.33; Yashodhara on KS 2.1.19.
8. *Dhammatthakatha* 3.9 on *Dhammapada* 43. Cited by Goldman, 'Transsexualism'.
9. *Bhagavata Purana* 9.1.18-42; *Devibhagavata Purana* 1.12.1-35; *Linga Purana* 1.65. 19-10; Doniger O'Flaherty, *Siva*, 304-5.
10. *Shivalaya Mahatmya* of the Sahyadrikhanda of the *Skanda Purana*, chs 3-9. I have rephrased and retranslated, working from Micaela Soar's text.
11. KSS 12.15.
12. *Ramayana* 7.37.28-44, 57; excised verses.
13. Nanda, *Neither Man Nor Woman*, 1990.
14. M 5.193.60-65.

15. *Markandeya Purana, Devi Mahatmya.*
16. Nanda, *Neither Man Nor Woman*, 13.
17. Cohen, 'Semen Gain', 3.
18. SB 13.1.9.6-9: Doniger O'Flaherty, *Textual Sources*, 17.
19. M, appendix 1.6.36-161; then 4.1.20 and 4.10; Doniger O'Flaherty, *Women, Androgynes*, 298.
20. *Bhagavadajjukam*, verse 32.

KAMA AND OTHER SEDUCTIONS

THE CONTROL OF ADDICTION IN ANCIENT INDIA

1. This chapter is a new version of an essay written for a Festschrift for Stefano Piano that has not yet appeared.
2. Manu 4.16.
3. AS 8.3.1-61.
4. AS 1.1.28-9.
5. AS 1.17.35-8.
6. KS 2.7.33.
7. KS 2.7.34.
8. Biardeau, *Hinduism*, 64.
9. M 2.61.20.
10. M 3.248.
11. R 3.42.
12. M 1.26-40.
13. M 3.244.
14. AS 8.3.2-6.
15. Heesterman, *The Ancient Indian Royal Consecration.*
16. Tyagi, *Women Workers in Ancient India*, 181.
17. Chand, *Liquor Menace in India*, 3.
18. Manu 9.235 and 11.55.
19. Manu 9.13.
20. AS 1.5, 2.16.
21. AS 2.17.
22. KS 6.2.2.
23. KS 6.2.73.
24. KS 6.4.39-42.
25. KS 7.1-2.
26. Manu 2.213-15.
27. Manu 7.45-53.
28. AS 8.3.61.
29. AS 8.3.62-4.
30. KS 1.2.37.
31. *Dashakumaracharita* of Dandin, trans. Onians, 13; 63-69.

READING THE *KAMASUTRA*: IT ISN'T ALL ABOUT SEX

1. This chapter is a combination of several published articles: 'The *Kamasutra*: It isn't *All* about Sex' in the *Kenyon Review*, 2003; 'Reading the *Kamasutra*: The Strange and the Familiar' in *Daedalus*, 2007; 'On the *Kamasutra*' in *Daedalus*, 2002; 'Other Peoples' Religions, Other Peoples' *Kama* and *Karma*' in *The Stranger's Religion: Fascination and Fear*, 2004; and *La Trappola della Giumenta*, 2003.

2. The *Kamasutra* must have been written after 225 CE because the western Indian political situation that Vatsyayana describes shows the Abhiras and the Andhras ruling simultaneously over a region that had been ruled by the Andhras alone until 225 CE. Its style seems very close to that of the *Arthashastra*, also of uncertain date, but generally placed in the third century CE; it cites the *Arthashastra* explicitly at 1.2.10, and implicitly elsewhere. The fact that the text does not mention the Guptas, who ruled North India from the beginning of the fourth century CE, suggests that the text predates that period. The *Kamasutra* is mentioned by name in the *Vasavadatta* of Subandhu, composed under Chandragupta Vikramaditya, who reigned at the beginning of the fifth century CE.

3. Mr Boffo cartoon by Joe Martin, Inc., distributed by Universal Press Syndicate; published in the *Chicago Tribune*, 29 September 2000. A salesman is saying to a customer, 'Most people just buy it to get the catalogue.'

4. 'The Cosmo Kamasutra', *Cosmopolitan*, September 1998; 'The Cosmo Kamasutra, #2', *Cosmopolitan*, September 1999, 256–259.

5. The 10 September 2001, issue of *The New Yorker*, p. 78. It continues: '#39: Buddha in Paradise: When the time is right, position your cheese atop a slice of bread. Run under the broiler until the cheese yields up its life force and is transformed. #58: The Lotus: While your cheese is melting in the microwave, your bread should be toasting in the toaster. If all goes well, both will arrive at the crucial stage simultaneously, and can be united. Next Week: The Kama Sutra of Peanut Butter and Jelly.'

6. John Lahr, 'Full Tilt: Robin Williams strikes again,' *The New Yorker*, 8 April 2002, 92-4, here 93.

7. 'Tantric Sex Class Opens up Whole New World of Unfulfillment for Local Couple', *The Onion*, 30 March–5 April 2000, 8.

8. Barthes, *The Pleasure of the Text*.

9. There is also a *Kama Sutra for Cats* (by Mrs Woodhouse, of 'good dog' fame).

THE MYTHOLOGY OF THE *KAMASUTRA*

1. This chapter is a revised version of an essay published in *The Anthropologist and the Native: Essays for Gananath Obeyesekere*, 2009.

2. Doniger, *The Implied Spider*.

3. Masson, 'A Note on the Sources of Bhasa's (?) Vimaraka'.

4. For Narada, see Doniger O'Flaherty, *Dreams, Illusion, and Other Realities*.

5. Doniger, 'Echoes of the *Mahabharata*.'

6. *Introduction to the Jataka* 1.68; trans. Warren, *Buddhism in Translation*, 71-2.

7. Doniger, *Siva*.

8. Doniger, *Splitting the Difference*.

9. M 4.21.1-67, with a verse omitted from the critical edition after 4.21.46; see Doniger, *The Bedtrick*.

10. Doniger, *Splitting the Difference*.

11. Ibid.

FROM KAMA TO KARMA: THE RESURGENCE OF PURITANISM IN CONTEMPORARY INDIA

1. This chapter is a revised version of an article by the same name, originally published in *Social Research*, in 2011.

2. Valsan, 'Baroda Art student's work stirs up religious controversy'.

3. Dharker, 'Beauty And the Beast'.

4. Ibid.

5. Philips and Alahakoon, 'Hindu chauvinists block filming of Deepa Mehta's *Water*.'

6. Bordewekar, Interview, 62.
7. BAU 6.2.13, 6.4.3.
8. White, *Kiss of the Yogini*, 220.
9. Bronner, *Extreme Poetry*.
10. Ramanujan et al., *When God is a Customer*, 117-18.
11. McConnachie, *The Book of Love*, 194
12. Auden, *Collected Poems*, 225.
13. Warner, *Stranger Magic*, 16 and 18.
14. Brodie, *The Devil*, 358.
15. Archer, 'Preface', to the *Kama Sutra*, 36.
16. Brodie, *The Devil Drives*, 357.
17. KS 2.7.20.
18. Burton, *The Kama Sutra*, 117-18.
19. KS 4.1.19-21.
20. Burton, *The Kama Sutra*, 160.
21. Chandra, *Love and Longing in Bombay*, 126.
22. Bombay Presidency, 1962: 213.
23. McConnachie, *The Book of Love*, 197-8.
24. Naipaul, *Half a Life*, 110.
25. McConnachie, *The Book of Love*, 197-8.
26. Ibid., 55, 57.
27. Ibid., 197-8.
28. Ibid., 228.
29. Ibid., 209.
30. Ibid., 229.

HORSES AND OTHER ANIMALS

THE AMBIVALENCE OF AHIMSA

1. This chapter is based on a keynote talk that I gave at the Columbia University Religion Department's Annual Graduate Student Conference, on 12 April 2012, on the theme of 'Pray, Kill, Eat'. A lively discussion there, particularly from Kimberley Patton, Jack Hawley, Wayne Proudfoot, Mark Taylor, Hamsa Stainton and Uda Halperin, greatly enriched the subsequent revision of the paper. I have added a few pages about Vedic ritual purloined from another chapter in this volume ('Sacrifice and Substitution').
2. The conundrum of life and sacrifice has been the centrepiece of Jan Heesterman's work on the 'cyclical' or 'pre-classical' pattern of the Vedic sacrifice, in *The Inner Conflict of Tradition*.
3. RV 1.62; trans. Doniger O'Flaherty.
4. West, *Indo-European Poetry*, 469.
5. Ibid., 467, 490.
6. SB 3.8.1.15.
7. For a treatment of the relationship between hunting and sacrificial killing see Doniger O'Flaherty, *Other Peoples' Myths*, Chapter Four. See also Hamerton-Kelly, *Violent Origins*.
8. JB 2.182-83; Doniger O'Flaherty, *Tales of Sex and Violence*, 40-42.
9. JB 1.42-44; Doniger O'Flaherty, *Tales of Sex and Violence*, 32-34.
10. KB 11.3; Doniger O'Flaherty, *Tales of Sex and Violence*, 39.
11. SB 12.9.1.1; Doniger O'Flaherty, *Tales of Sex and Violence*, 40.

12. Nandy, *Exiled at Home*, 47 and 63; Doniger O'Flaherty, *Tales of Sex and Violence*, 36-7.
13. Manu 5.39.
14. West, *Indo-European Poetry*, 22.
15. Biardeau, *Hinduism*, 31.
16. AB 2.8-9.
17. See the Buddhist narrative on the 'true sacrifice' (always characterized by ahimsa) in the *Kutadanta Sutra*, included in T.W. Rhys Davids, trans., *Dialogues of the Buddha*, 1:160-85. For a similar story from the Jain tradition, see the tale of Harikesha, found in H. Jacobi, trans., *Jaina Sutras*, 2:50-56.
18. Heesterman, *The Inner Conflict*.
19. Kandahar Bilingual Rock Inscription; Aramaic version; Thapar, *Ashoka*, 261.
20. 4th Major Rock Edict, Thapar, *Ashoka*, 251; Nikam, *Edicts*, 31; Sircar, *Select Inscriptions*, 42-3.
21. 11th Major Rock Edict, Sircar, *Select Inscriptions*, 48.
22. Tilak, *Srimad Bhagavad Gita Rahasya*, 44.
23. 1st Major Rock Edict, Thapar, *Ashoka*, 250. Nikam adds 'daily' to the last line, 55; Sircar, 41, does not.
24. Thapar, *Ashoka*, 203, 'his personal preference'.
25. 5th Pillar Edict. Nikam, *Edicts*, 56; Sircar, *Inscriptions*, 64-5.
26. 9th Major Rock Edict, Nikam, *Edicts*, 46; Sircar, *Select Inscriptions*, 46-7.
27. Manu 4.205-223, 5.5-44, 6.229-240, 8.296-298, 8.324-8, 11.132-44, 10.896-89, 11.54-227.
28. Manu 5.6-10 ff.
29. Jonathan Z. Smith 'Sacred Persistence; Toward a Redescription of Canon.'
30. Manu 5.37.
31. Manu 5.32-40 ff.
32. Manu 5.35.
33. Manu 5.44.
34. Manu 5.28-30.
35. M 12.15.21.
36. Das, *Structure and Cognition*, 29, citing the *Dharmaranya Purana*.
37. The two views are juxtaposed in an uneasy tension in the context within which Manu debates most problems: the ritual. See Brian K. Smith, *Reflections*, 198-99.
38. Manu 3.68-9, 3.70-74.
39. Manu 5.33.55.
40. Manu 5.38.48-53.
41. Manu 5.49.
42. Manu 5.51.
43. Manu 5.56.
44. Doniger and Brian K. Smith, *The Laws of Manu*, introduction; Doniger O'Flaherty, *Other Peoples' Myths*, chapter 4.
45. Srinivas, *Social Change in Modern India*.
46. Hardiman, *The Coming of the Devi*, 209.
47. Gandhi, *The Mind of Mahatma Gandhi*, 265-299.
48. Gandhi, 'The Message of the Gita', in Stephen Mitchell, *The Bhagavad Gita*, pp. 218-19.
49. Frederick M. Smith, 'Indra Goes West', 259-60; citing Madhava.
50. Staal (ed.), *Agni: The Vedic Ritual of the Fire Altar*.
51. Lubin, 'Veda on Parade', 394.

ZOOMORPHISM IN ANCIENT INDIA:
HUMANS MORE BESTIAL THAN THE BEASTS

1. This chapter was first presented at a seminar convened by Lorraine Daston at the Max Planck Institute for the History of Science, in Berlin, on 10 May 2001. It was published, in 2008, in the volume that resulted from that conference, *Thinking With Animals: New Perspectives on Anthropomorphism*. I continued to think and teach about the issues, particularly in the course of a seminar on animal consciousness and animal symbols that Lorraine Daston and I taught at the University of Chicago in the spring of 2010. So this essay owes a great deal to her.
2. *Vishnu Purana* 5.3.
3. Doniger, *The Bedtrick*, 118-122.
4. The creature is a *jrimbha*, a rare word (related to the verb to yawn or expand or tumesce) that probably refers to a bird.
5. *Ramayana* passage rejected by critical edition at 2.32, app. 1, 14, 36-54. Cf. *Jataka* #386 (the *Kharaputta Jataka*) about a cobra woman and talking animals.
6. Doniger, *Splitting the Difference*, 287-292. Some Greek texts maintain that Teiresias, too, said that women have not just more pleasure, but *nine times* as much pleasure as men— thereby one-upping the ante. *Ibid.*, 293.
7. This was the excellent insight of Fernando Valdo, in his response to the presentation of this paper in Berlin.
8. Scarry, *The Body in Pain*.
9. Lewis Carroll, *Through the Looking-Glass*, chapter 9, 'Queen Alice'.
10. Levinas, *Totality and Infinity*, 198-9.
11. This paragraph and the next are reworked from my essay 'Compassion toward Animals'.
12. Doniger, *The Implied Spider*, 31-33.

THE MYTHOLOGY OF HORSES IN INDIA

1. This chapter grew out of my essay, 'A Symbol in Search of an Object: The Mythology of Horses in India' (in *A Communion of Subjects: Animals in Religion, Science, and Ethics*. ed. Paul Waldau and Kimberley Patton. Columbia University Press, 2006, 335-350), combined with parts of my AAS Presidential Address, 'I Have Scinde': Flogging a Dead (White Male Orientalist) Horse'.
2. Doniger O'Flaherty, *Women;* West, *Indo-European Poetry*, 417.
3. Thapar, *Early India*, 115.
4. Doniger O'Flaherty, 'Horses and snakes in the Adi Parvan of the *Mahabharata*'.
5. Doniger O'Flaherty, 'The Tail of the Indo-European Horse Sacrifice' .
6. Doniger O'Flaherty, *The Origins of Evil*, 321-48.
7. Leshnik, 'The Horse in India', 57.
8. Personal communication from Dr. Faroukh Wadia at the Wadia Stud, Pune, January 1996.
9. Marco Polo, *The Travels of Marco Polo*, 356-7; *Marco Polo: The Description of the World*, 174.
10. Alder, *Beyond Bokhara*, 50-51.
11. *Taittiriya Samhita* 5. 5. 10. 6.
12. AS 2.30.8,11, 18.
13. Marco Polo, *The Travels of Marco Polo*, 357.
14. Marco Polo, *Marco Polo: The Description of the World*, 174.
15. Kipling, *Kim*, 185.
16. Marco Polo, *Marco Polo: The Description of the World*, 174.
17. Stephen Robert Inglis, Personal communication, 26 March 1985.

18. Bühler, 'The Peheva Inscription from the Temple of Garibnath'.
19. Inglis, 'Night Riders: Massive Temple Figures of Rural Tamilnadu'.
20. Pusalker, *The Struggle for Empire*, 523.
21. Nagaswamy, 'Gateway to the Gods. 1. Sermons in stone'.
22. Mookerji, *The History of Indian Shipping*, 195. Portugese merchants like Payez, Nunez and Diaz wrote extensively about the horse trade.
23. Marco Polo, *The Travels of Marco Polo, 357; Marco Polo: The Description of the World*, 174.
24. Digby, *War Horse and Elephant in the Delhi Sultanate*.
25. Leshnik, 'The Horse in India', 56.
26. Alder, *Beyond Bokhara*, 50-51
27. Leshnik, 'The Horse in India', 57.
28. Crooke, *The Popular Religion and Folk-lore of Northern India*, 2.206.
29. This well-known story is told in several versions of Manikkavacakar's biography, in the *Tiruvatavurar Purana* (a fifteenth century hagiography) and the *Tiruvilaiyatal Puranam*; see also G.U. Pope, *Tiruvacagam*, xx-xxvii and Glenn E. Yocum, *Hymns to the Dancing Siva: A Study of Manikkavcakar's Tiruvacakam*, 51-2, 62.
30. Mandalakavi, *Pandyakulodaya* 7.1-48.
31. Doniger O'Flaherty, *The Origins of Evil*, 272-320.
32. M 17.2.26, 17.3.7-23.
33. Jain, 'Painted Myths of Creation', 24.
34. Williams, *The Black Hills: Kutch in History and Legend*, 83.
35. Ibid.; Kramrisch, *Unknown India*, 55.
36. Kirin Narayan, Personal communication, 22 February 1999.
37. Kramrisch, *Unknown India*, 55.
38. Williams, *The Black Hills*, 84-6.
39. Kramrisch, *Unknown India*, 55.
40. Williams, *The Black Hills*, 88.
41. Mukherjee, *The Rise and Fall of the East India Company*, 300-303.
42. Bolts, *Considerations on Indian Affairs*, 194.
43. Kirin Narayan, Personal communication, 22 February 1999.
44. M 1.123.
45. Waghorne, 'Chariots of the God/s'.
46. Crooke, *The Popular Religion and Folk-lore of Northern India*, 2.206; Sontheimer, 'The Mallari/Khandoba Myth'.
47. Doniger, *The Implied Spider*, 79-108.
48. Williams, *The Black Hills*, 83.
49. Kipling, *Kim*, 161.
50. Ibid., 191.
51. Yang, *Bazaar India*, 116.
52. Alder, *Beyond Bokhara*, 209.
53. Yang, *Bazaar India*, 116.
54. Alder, *Beyond Bokhara*, 341.
55. Ibid., 209.
56. Ibid., 357-8.
57. Ibid., 107.
58. Huyler, *Village India*, 162.
59. Bhattacarya, *Folklore of Bengal*, 48-9.
60. Inglis, *Night Riders*, 298, 302, 304.
61. Huyler, *Village India*, 105; 1981, 200.
62. Kramrisch, *Unknown India*, 57.

THE SUBMARINE MARE IN THE MYTHOLOGY OF SHIVA

1. This chapter is the revision of an article originally published as 'The Submarine Mare in the Mythology of Siva' in the *Journal of the Royal Asiatic Society*, 1971.
2. *Matsya Purana* 154. 252.
3. *Bhavishya Purana* 3. 4. 14. 53; *Shiva Purana* (Benares, 1964), 2. 3. 19. 10.
4. M 13. 83.53; *Kumarasambhava* 10. 1-25.
5. Hooykaas, *Agama-Tirtha*, 109; Bosch, *The Golden Germ*, 60-64.
6. Kirfel, *Die fünf Elemente*, 16.
7. Ibid., 17.
8. Manu 6. 23; *Kumarasambhava*, 5. 20-26.
9. *Shiva Purana* 7. 1. 28. 19; Doniger O'Flaherty, *Siva*.
10. Kuhn, *Mythologische Studien*, I, 161 ff.
11. RV 6.22. 8.
12. *Shiva Purana* 3. 7. 37.
13. M 10.18.21.
14. cf. Manu 9. 35.
15. Manu 9. 321; M 1.16. 22-24; 5. 15. 32; 12. 56. 24; *Devi Purana* 8.2. 10-12; *Panchatantra* 1. 24; *Padma Purana* 4. 103. 1-26; *Kumarasambhava* 4. 43.
16. Blair, *Heat in the Rig Veda and Atharva Veda*, 102.
17. RV 2. 1. 1.
18. SB 11. 1. 6. 1 and 6. 1. 1. 10; Manu 1. 8-9; RV 10.121.
19. RV 10. 51-53; cf. *Brihaddevata* 7. 62.
20. SB 6. 3. 1. 31.
21. M 13.84. 22-44; KSS 3. 6. 74-80.
22. M 5. 15. 27-32.
23. SB 1. 2. 3. 1.
24. SB 6. 8. 2. 8.
25. SB 1.4. 1. 10-19.
26. SB 2. 1. 1.3-4; 1. 1. 1. 18.20-21.
27. AV 7.87.1.
28. SB 6. 1. 1. 1-2, 8; 6. 1. 3. 1-4; 6. 1. 3. 8-10.
29. M 13.146:4; *Brahmanda Purana* 2. 27. 106; cf. M 13. 146. 5-6; 7.173. 94-97.
30. *Subhashitaratnakosha* of Vidyakara, 70.
31. *Brahmanda Purana* 2.21. 112.
32. cf. *Shiva Purana* 2. 2. 16. 39.
33. KSS 2. 1. 1.
34. AV 6. 132. 1.
35. AV, tr. Maurice Bloomfield, 535.
36. M 12. 207. 13.
37. *Kalika Purana* 45. 117.
38. *Skanda Purana* 6 258. 1-4; *Vamana Purana* 6. 27-33.
39. *Brahmanda Purana*, 4. 30. 65-89.
40. Doniger O'Flaherty, *Siva*.
41. *Skanda Purana* 6. 259. 5.
42. *Shiva Purana*, with commentaries, *Jnanasamhita* 42. 27-32.
43. Crooke, *The Popular Religion and Folk-lore of Northern India*, 1, 76.
44. Dubois, *Hindu Manners, Customs and Ceremonies*, 553.
45. Beck, 'Social and conceptual order in Kongu,' 151-169.
46. *Kumarasambhava* 8. 91.
47. *Shiva Purana* 2. 3. 19. 15; *Matsya Purana* 154. 251-2.
48. *Harivamsha* 1. 45. 1-19; 1. 46. 1-10.

49. *Brahma Purana* 116. 22-25.

50. BAU 1.1.2.

51. Raghavan on Manu 9. 321.

52. M 12. 137.41.

53. *Shiva Purana* 5. 24. 29; M 13.38.25-29.

54. *Prabodhachandrodaya* 6.8.

55. *Bhavishya Purana* 1. 22. 14 and 16; *Skanda Purana* 3. 1. 24. 30-67.

56. *Brahma Purana* 113. 13.

57. *Vamana Purana* 30. 27.

58. *Skanda Purana* 1. 1. 9. 90.

59. *Subhashitaratnakosha* 1045; Ingalls translation.

60. *Shiva Purana* 2. 2. 22. 10.

61. cf. *Kumarasambhava* 8. 42.

62. cf. *Panchatantra* 5.2.32.

63. *Ravana Vaha* 5. 34.

64. *Subhashitaratnakosha* 1198, Ingalls translation, cf. 1210-1212.

65. BAU 1. 4. 4.

66. Dumont, *L'Ashvamedha*, 260 ff.

67. *Harivamsha* 3. 5. 11-17.

68. Lal, *The Cult of Desire*, p. 45 (Tirupaksha Temple, Mysore); Rawson, *Erotic Art of the East*, pl. 121 (miniature painting, Deccan, eighteenth century). Pl. 67 depicts a man with a mare (Khajuraho, tenth century).

69. Hooykaas, *Agama-Tirtha*, 109; citing *Kauravashrama* 78.

70. J. Gonda, *Ancient Indian Kingship from the Religious Point of View*, 23; cf. *Shankhaya Shrautasutra* 16 1. 15; *Baudhayana Shrautasutra* 15. 8.

71. *Kumarasambhava* 1.11.

72. Rawson, *Erotic Art*, 42.1 am indebted to Dr J.C. Harle of the Ashmolean Museum, Oxford, for calling my attention to similar reliefs on temples 7 and 9 at Aihole.

73. *Padakusalamanava Jataka* (432); *Mahavamsa* 10. 53-62 (W. Geiger ed.).

74. *Shiva Purana, Dharmasamhita* 49. 78-81.

75. *Shiva Purana* 2. 2. 16.38.

76. *Devibhagavata Purana* 6. 17-19.

77. KU 3. 4-6.

78. *Gopatha Brahmana* 1. 2. 18; p. 35.

79. RV 8. 72. 16; 1. 35. 3; 1. 164. 47; 2. 11. 6; 5. 6. 6.

80. RV 1. 50. 8-9; 9. 86. 36.

81. RV 1. 58. 2; 149. 3; 60. 5; 2. 4. 4.; 5. 1; 3 2. 7; 27. 3; 27. 14; etc.: AB 15. 5. 1-7.

82. SB 7. 3. 2. 14.

83. SB 5. 3. 1. 5; 6. 2. 1. 5; etc.

84. TS 7.5.25. 2; SB 5.1.4-5.

85. Kramrisch, *Unknown India*, 57.

86. Ibid., 56.

87. M, I. 16. 34-36; cf. Nakula, *Ashva Shastra*, quoted in *Lakshanaprakasha*,. 407; cf. Dikshitar, *War in ancient India*, 175.

88. Tyson, *Kulu, the Happy Valley*, 92.

89. RV 1.116. 12; 1. 117. 22; 1. 84. 13-14.

90. SB 14. 1. 1. 18-25.

91. Sayana on RV 1. 84. 13-14.

92. *Shiva Purana* 5. 38.48-57; *Linga Purana* 1.66. 15-20; *Vayu Purana* 2. 26. 143-178; *Brahmanda Purana* 3. 46-53; *Vishnu Purana* 4. 4. 1-33; *Bhagavata Purana* 9.8.1-31, 9.9.1-15; R 1.38-44; M, 3.104-108.

93. Monier-Williams, *Sanskrit-English dictionary*, 239.
94. M 3. 192-195; *Vayu Purana* 2. 26. 30-60; *Shiva Purana* 5. 37. 1-36.
95. M 3. 195. 25.
96. M 12. 335. 1-64; 3. 193. 16; 12. 335. 5, 44, 54 ff.
97. Renou, *Études védiques et paniniennes*, 3.7, and 14.102; cf. also Grassmann, *Wörterbuch*, s.v. RV 2. 13. 7; 2. 35. 3; 3. 30. 19.
98. RV 2. 35. 3.
99. RV 3. 30. 19; Sayana: *urva iva anavaptakamo vadavanala iva.*
100. RV 8. 102.4.
101. *Taittiriya Samhita* 5. 5. 10. 6.
102. Bosch, 'The god with the horse's head,' 144-5; cf. van Gulik, *Hayagriva.*
103. M 13. 56. 4-6.
104. M 1. 169. 16-26; 170. 1-21; 171. 1-23.
105. M 1. 172. 1-17.
106. *Matsya Purana* 175. 23-63; *Harivamsha* 1. 45. 20-64.
107. *Skanda Purana* 7. 1. 32. 1-128; 7. 1. 33. 1-103; cf. *Padma Purana*, 6. 148. 27 ff.
108. *Shiva Purana* 3.24-25.
109. *Vamana Purana* 34.18-20.
110. *Padma Purana* 5.18.159-198.
111. *Brahma Purana* 110. 85-210.
112. *Shiva Purana, Dharmasamhita*, 11. 28-35.
113. *Brahma Purana* 110. 124.
114. *Brahma Purana* 110. 136.
115. KS 2. I. 1 and commentary.
116. *Varaha Purana* 147. 1-27.
117. *Matsya Purana* 154. 250-255; *Skanda Purana* 1. 2. 24. 42-3.
118. *Shiva Purana* 2.3.20. 1-23; *Kalika Purana* 44. 124-136.
119. *Shiva Purana* 2. 5. 13. 1-50; 2. 5. 14. 1-4; *Padma Purana* 6. 98. 5-19.
120. *Padma Purana* 6. 5. 19-20.
121. M 13. 17. 54; cf. Nilakantha on 13. 17. 56.
122. Gopinatha Rao, *Elements of Hindu iconography* 2.1.173, citing *Uttarakaranagama.*
123. *Abhijnanashakuntalam* of Kalidasa 3. 2 (alternative verse).

INDRA AS THE STALLION'S WIFE

1. This chapter is based on my article, 'The Case of the Stallion's Wife: Indra and Vrsanasva in the *Rg Veda* and the *Brahmanas*' in the *Journal of the American Oriental Society*, 1985. The dedication to that article was as follows:

Nearly fifty years ago, one of America's greatest Indologists and translators of Sanskrit poetry, Arthur Ryder, had among his students a young man named Anthony Boucher. (Actually, William Anthony Parker White was the name of Ryder's pupil, who published *The Case of the Seven of Calvary* under the pseudonym of Anthony Boucher in New York in 1937.) Boucher grew up to be not a Sanskritist but a successful writer of murder mysteries, and a literary critic. One of his books, *The Case of the Seven of Calvary*, is dedicated to Ryder, and the hero of the piece is a Sanskrit professor coyly named Ashwin (a Sanskrit term that designates the hippomorphic twin gods but literally means 'having a horse' or, as it were, 'rider'). Following in Boucher's spirit, I would like to dedicate this essay to the man who taught me Sanskrit (and so much else), Daniel H.H. Ingalls; it is in its way an attempt to solve a mystery, and it deals with horses and riders. (Jan Heesterman recognized the murder-mystery aspect of the Vedic world long before I did, when he published 'The Case of the Severed Head'.) More specifically, I hope that the riddle that it poses and attempts to solve, the riddle of the crossbreeding of horses with other species, will find favour not only with Ingalls the Sanskritist but also with Ingalls the breeder and tamer of horses (*hippodamos*, or, in other words, *ashvin*).

In revising that article, I have incorporated material from 'The Tail of the Indo-European Horse Sacrifice' (in *Incognita*, 1990). Since I published the original article, other scholars found new insights into the meaning of the Vedic hymn in question, particularly Stephanie Jamison (in *Sacrificed Wife, Sacrificer's Wife*, New York: Oxford University Press, 1996, pp. 65–88); she cites (on p 227, n. 147), Stanley Insler's 1994 conference paper, in which he suggests that the 'monkey' is 'the "animus" of Indra's penis'. See also the response to Insler in H. Craig Melchert, 'Sanskrit sardigrdi', *Journal of the American Oriental Society*, 122:2 (April 2002).

2. Geldner, *Der Rig-Veda*, 1:64 ('Leider sind beide Stellen reichlich dunkel'), 1:164 ('Diese seltsamen Verwandlungen werden auch 10.111.3 augedeutet. Einzelheiten fehlen.'); 3: 333 ('Der dunkle Sagenzug von 1.121.2cd').
3. Geldner, *Der Rig-Veda*, 1:64.
4. See, for instance, Agastya as a bull, in RV 1.179; Doniger O'Flaherty, *Siva*, 52–55; *The Rig Veda*, 250–52.
5. Doniger O'Flaherty, *Women, Androgynes*, 174–85; Goldman, 'Mortal Man and Immortal Woman'.
6. For the theoretical rules about intermarriage, see J.C. Heesterman, 'Brahmin, Ritual, and Renouncer'.
7. RV 10.61.5-7; 1.71.5; 1.71.8; 1.164.33. See Doniger O'Flaherty, *Hindu Myths*, 25–26.
8. AB 3.33–34; Doniger O'Flaherty, *Hindu Myths*, 29–31.
9. BAU 1.4.1-6; Doniger O'Flaherty, *Hindu Myths*, 33–35.
10. M 1.109.5-31.
11. AB 7.13.
12. Doniger O'Flaherty, *Dreams*, 40.
13. Sayana's commentary on RV 1.121.2.
14. MS 2.5.5.
15. *Kathaka Samhita* 13.5.
16. Doniger, *Splitting the Difference*.
17. Doniger O'Flaherty, *Women, Androgynes*, passim; Deppert, *Rudras Geburt*, passim.
18. SB 12.7.1.10-12; R 1.47–48; Doniger O'Flaherty, *Siva*, 85–86; *Hindu Myths*, 94–96.
19. RV 8.2.40; R 1.47–48.
20. RV 10.86; Doniger O'Flaherty, *Rig Veda*, 257–64.
21. Doniger O'Flaherty, *Women*, 154–64.
22. PB 8.1.9-11; JB 3.72; Doniger O'Flaherty, *Origins of Evil*, 164–65.
23. Doniger O'Flaherty, *Origins of Evil*, 153–60.
24. PB 6.1.1-4.
25. SB 12.7.2.21.
26. M 12.138.30.
27. Ct and Cr on R 3.41.39 and Ca and Cn on M 12.138.30. I am grateful to Sheldon Pollock for telling me about these commentaries.
28. R 3.41.39.
29. M 3.94.5-10.
30. RV 4.18; Doniger O'Flaherty, *Rig Veda*, 141–46.
31. *Shadvimsha Brahmana* 6.7.2.
32. Doniger O'Flaherty, *Dreams*, 263–65.
33. JB 1.67.

34. TS 7.1.1-3.
35. TB 2.5.1; Doniger O'Flaherty, *Origins of Evil*, 153-60.
36. AV 7.65.2; Doniger O'Flaherty, *Origins of Evil*, 144-45.
37. RV 10.51.1-9; TS 2.6.6.1-5; Doniger O'Flaherty, *Hindu Myths*, 97-104; *Origins of Evil*, 144-45; *Rig Veda*, 101-10.
38. SB 6.3.1.2.3.
39. Cf. Brian K. Smith, *Reflections on Resemblances Ritual, and Religion*.
40. AB 4.9.
41. TS 5.1.4.
42. JB 2.79; SB 3.3.4.18; *Shadvimsha Brahmana* 1.1.17.
43. JB 3.234 and 3.245; cf. Doniger O'Flaherty, *Tales of Sex and Violence*, 58-62.
44. Sayana's commentary on RV 8.1.1 and 8.1.34; see also *Brihaddevata* 6.41.
45. Puhvel, 'Ritual and Sacrificial Hierarchies'.
46. BAU 1.4.1-6.
47. AV 11.2.9, with Sayana's commentary.
48. AV 3.10.6, with Sayana's commentary.
49. M 6.5.12-14.

DOGS AS DALITS IN INDIAN LITERATURE

1. This chapter was published, under the same name, in *Antike Mythen: Medien, Transformationen und Konstruktionen*. Parts of the essay also appeared in my book *The Hindus: An Alternative History*.
2. RV 7.55.2-4; Doniger O'Flaherty, *Rig Veda*, 288-9.
3. RV 10.108; Doniger O'Flaherty, *Rig Veda*, 155-6.
4. RV 10.14.10-12; Doniger O'Flaherty, *Rig Veda*, 44.
5. Debroy, *Sarama and Her Children*.
6. TB 3.8.4.2; Doniger O'Flaherty, *Textual Sources*, 14-17.
7. MS 2.1.19-23; 3.12.1; Jamison, *Sacrificer's Wife*, 78, 99.
8. White, 'Dogs Die', 283-303.
9. JB 2.440-442; Doniger O'Flaherty, *Tales of Sex and Violence*, 97-8.
10. RV 9.101.1.
11. Manu 7.21.
12. KS 29.1; MS 3.10.6; AB 2.22.10.
13. JB 1.161-2; Doniger O'Flaherty, *Tales of Sex and Violence*, 101-2.
14. KB 23.4.
15. JB 1.161-2; Doniger O'Flaherty, *Tales of Sex and Violence*, 101-2
16. CU 1.12-13.
17. BU 3.9.25.
18. Lincoln, 'How to Read a Religious Text'.
19. M 12.115-1- 12.119.20; White, *Myths of the Dog Men*, 251.
20. Hiltebeitel, *Rethinking the Mahabharata*, 200-202.
21. M 17.2-3.
22. I owe this realization to Lorraine Daston's response to an earlier stage of this paper.
23. Manu 7.21.
24. M 3.275.14.
25. M 1.3.1-18.
26. R 7.52; appendix I, no. 8, lines 332-465.
27. M 17.2.26.
28. M 17.3.18.
29. Doniger O'Flaherty, *The Origins of Evil*, 321-31.
30. VS 26.4-62; 27.1-23; Doniger O'Flaherty, *The Origins of Evil*, 325-70.

31. SP 7.1.336.95-253.
32. Sontheimer, *King of Warriors, Hunters, and Shepherds*, 52-3.
33. Elison, *Immanent Domains*.
34. Gnanakoothan, 'Dog'. I am indebted to Charles Preston for bringing this poem to my attention.

SACRED COWS AND BEEFEATERS

1.   This chapter is an expanded version of my review of *The Myth of the Holy Cow*, by D.N. Jha, which was published as 'A Burnt Offering' in the *Times Literary Supplement*, in 2002.
2.   John Lockwood Kipling, *Beast and Man in India*, vi. 116.
3.   Thapar, *Early India*, 115.
4.   Jha, *The Myth of the Holy Cow*, 30-36; Keith, *Religion and Philosophy*, 324-6; Heesterman, *The Broken World*, 194, 283, n. 32; Renou, *Vedic India*, 109.
5.   Jha, *The Myth of the Holy Cow*, 47; TS 5.6.11-20.
6.   Cf. AGS 1.24, 31-33 for the ritual of killing a cow on the arrival of a guest.
7.   *Apastamba Dharmasutra* 1.17.30 31.
8.   Thapar, *Early India*, 90.
9.   SB 3.1.2.21.
10. Thapar, *Early India*, 115.
11. Srinivas, *Social Change in Modern India*.
12. M 12.59.99-128; AV 8.10.22-29; *Bhagavata Purana* 4.13-19, etc. Doniger O'Flaherty, *Origins of Evil*, 321-48.
13. Raj, 'Why I Decided to Convert the Dalits of Jhajjar'.

ILLUSION AND REALITY IN THE HINDU EPICS

IMPERMANENCE AND ETERNITY IN HINDU EPIC, ART AND PERFORMANCE

1.   This chapter is a revised and combined version of two essays, the first, 'Impermanence and Eternity in Indian Art and Myth', in *Contemporary Indian Tradition: Voices on Culture, Nature, and the Challenge of Change*, 1988; and the second, 'Fluid and Fixed Texts in India', in *Boundaries of the Text: Epic Performances in South and Southeast Asia*, 1991.
2.   Doniger O'Flaherty, *Dreams*, 129-32.
3.   Personal communication from A.K. Ramanujan, cited in Doniger O'Flaherty, *Dreams*, 130.
4.   Hiltebeitel, *The Ritual of Battle*, 14-15.
5.   Singer, *When a Great Tradition Modernizes* 75-76.
6.   M 1.1.2.3 and 1.56.34.
7.   V. Narayana Rao, in a comment made at the Conference on the Puranas, Madison, Wisconsin, 3 August 1985.
8.   A.K. Ramanujan, comment made at the Conference on the Puranas, Madison, Wisconsin, 3 August 1985.
9.   Brian K. Smith, *Reflections on Resemblance*.
10. Lutgendorf, *The Life of a Text*.
11. Ibid.
12. Faure, 'Intertextuality', 11.
13. M, appendix 1, #1, verses interpolated after line 30.
14. Lutgendorf, *The Life of a Text*.
15. Ibid.

16. Doniger O'Flaherty, *Dreams*, 10-11, 187-89; Doniger O'Flaherty, *Siva*, 4-11, 33-39.

17. Doniger O'Flaherty, *Siva*, 19, citing *Shiva Purana* 4.27.13-24; cf. R 7.4.3-4 and 7.16.44.

18. Jaini, 'Jaina Puranas', 187-88.

19. Doniger, *The Hindus*.

20. Doniger O'Flaherty, *Dreams*, 268-79.

21. Vequaud, 'The Colors of Devotion', 62-63.

22. Letter from Stephen Inglis, 8 January 1987.

23. Staal, *Agni*, 689.

24. Doniger O'Flaherty, *Dreams*, 11-13.

25. Personal communication from Edward Cameron Dimock, February 1986.

26. Lynn Hart. Untitled paper, 8 November 1986.

27. Vequaud, 'The Colors of Devotion', 62-63.

28. David Szanton, proposal for his book *Mithila Painting: the Evolution of an Art Form*. Since 2003, the Mithila Art Institute has been instrumental in establishing an art school for the women painters of Mithila, and in helping them to market their work. See Szanton, *Mithila Painting: The Evolution of an Art Form*; cf. also Jyotindra Jain, 'Tradition and Expression in Mithila Painting'; and Mani Shekhar Singh, 'A Journey into Pictorial Space: Poetic of Frame and Field in Mithila Painting'.

29. Personal communication from Rick Asher and Carla Borden.

30. Rupa Goswami's *Bhaktirasamritasindhu* 2.17, cited by Haberman, 'Imitating the Masters', 41-50. See also Doniger O'Flaherty, *Women, Androgynes*, 87-88, and cf. also *Bhagavata Purana* 3.15.34.

31. Hiltebeitel, 'Puranas and the *Mahabharata*', 11.

32. Sudhir Kakar, 'The Ties that Bind'.

33. Doniger O'Flaherty, 'The Mythological in Disguise'.

34. R.K. Narayan, *Mr. Sampath*.

35. RV 8.1.30-34; M 3.122-23.

36. V. Narayana Rao, private conversation, cited in O'Flaherty, *Dreams*, 129-30.

37. V. Narayana Rao, remarks made at the Conference on the Puranas, Madison, Wisconsin, 1-4 August 1985.

38. *Apastamba Dharmasutra* 2.9.24.1; cited by Doniger O'Flaherty, *Siva*, 76.

SHADOWS OF THE *RAMAYANA*

1. This chapter is a revised version of an essay, by the same title, first published in *The Epic Voice*, 2002.

2. Richman, ed. *Many Ramayanas*.

3. R 6.103-6; Doniger O'Flaherty, *Dreams*, 92; Doniger O'Flaherty, *Hindu Myths*, 198-204.

4. Pollock, 'Atmanam Manusam Manye'.

5. Goldman, 'Rama Sahalaksmanah'.

6. Manu 9.60; Doniger, *The Bedtrick*, chapter 6.

7. KS 5.1.53.

8. Masson, 'Fratricide and the Monkeys'.

9. Morson, *Narrative and Freedom*.

10. See the story of Mayiliravana, told in Doniger O'Flaherty, *Dreams*,

11. Kamban *Ramayana* 2888-2891, in Hart, *The Forest Book*.

12. Kamban *Ramayana* 2918; Hart, *The Forest Book*.

13. Doniger, *Splitting the Difference*.

14. *Adhyatma-ramayana* 3.7.1-10; 6.8.21.

15. *Brahmavaivarta Purana* 2.14.1-59.

16. *Tulsi, Ramacaritamanasa* 1.49-53, 56-7, 97.

17. Doniger O'Flaherty, *Dreams*, 92-7.
18. Shulman, 'Sita and Satakantharavana', 12-16.
19. Pollock, '*Ramayana* and Political Imagination in India'.
20. KS 1.2.36.
21. R 7.26.8-47, plus the verses excised from the Critical Edition after verses 30 and 47. See Doniger, *Splitting the Difference*.
22. Jong, *The Story of Rama in Tibet*, 153-62.
23. *Shrishriramakrishnakathamrita* 1.181, trans. Jeffrey Kripal, personal communication, May, 1993. *Tuccham brahmapadam paravadhusangah kutah*.
24. Acarya K.V. Raman, personal communication, Madras, January 1996.
25. Buck, *Ramayana*, 301.

WOMEN IN THE *MAHABHARATA*

1. This chapter is adapted from the chapter on the *Mahabharata* in my book *The Hindus*.
2. Doniger, *Bedtrick*, 248-54.
3. Doniger and Spinner, 'Misconceptions'.
4. *Naishadacharita* 17.132.
5. Cf. also JB 2.269-70; Doniger O'Flaherty, *Tales of Sex and Violence*, 105-107
6. Hiltebeitel, *The Cult of Draupadi*.
7. Kinsley, *Hindu Goddesses*, 107-9, 151-2.
8. Kinsley, *The Sword and the Flute*; Hiltebeitel, *The Ritual of Battle*.
9. Thapar, *Early India*, 228.
10. Mitter, *Indian Art*, 16.
11. Thapar, *Early India*, 193.

THE HISTORY OF EKALAVYA

1. This chapter is a much expanded version of an essay by the same name published in *Tarikh: The History Journal* in 2008-9. It was given as the Annual Lecture of the Centre of South Asian Studies at the School of Oriental and African Studies, University of London, in November 2010, under the title 'Does the Mahabharata Approve of Ekalavya cutting off his Thumb? and Other Tales of Dalits and Dogs in Ancient India.' Parts of it are adapted from my book, *The Hindus*.
2. Thanks to Nick Allen for reminding me of this, at St Antony's College, Oxford, on 26 November 2010.
3. From Hemavijayagani, *Katharatnakara* (Banasakantha: Omkarasahitya Nidhi) 1997, story #163, 'The Story of the Bhilla', pp. 185-6.
4. Jaini, '*Pandava-Purana* of Vadicandra: Text and Translation', 551-4, from Canto 4, lines 104-130 of the text.
5. I am grateful to Richard Gombrich for reminding me of this, at St Antony's College, Oxford, on 26 November 2010.
6. Omvedt, *Dalit Visions*, 78, quoting an untitled poem by Waman Nimbalkar (called Just Poem), tr. Graham Smith, *Vagartha*, 12 January 1976.
7. Omvedt, *Dalit Visions*, 98, citing Shashikant Hingonekar, 'Ekalavya', *Asmitadarsh*, April/May/June 1989; translated by Gail Omvedt and Bharat Patankar. See the forthcoming *Norton Anthology of Hinduism*, ed. Wendy Doniger, 2013.
8. Tryambak Sapkale, born 1930, was a ticket taker on the Dhond-Manmad railway line until his retirement. This poem is from *Surung*, Aurangabad: Asmitadarsh Prakashan, 1976, and was translated by Jayant Karve and Eleanor Zelliot.

ON NOT BEING HINDU

'I HAVE SCINDE': ORIENTALISM AND GUILT

1. This chapter is taken from the first half of an article that was originally presented as the Presidential Address to the 51st Annual Meeting of the Association for Asian Studies, Boston, 12 March 1999, and then published as 'Presidential Address: "I Have Scinde": Flogging a Dead (White Male Orientalist) Horse' in the *Journal of Asian Studies*, 1999. (For the second half of that article, see 'The Mythology of Horses in India'.) I am indebted to Susanne Hoeber Rudolph and Lloyd Rudolph for starting me off on the track of Sir Charles Napier; to Katherine Ulrich for finding the *Punch* text and Blanco; to Anand A. Yang for the Moorcroft and Gyan Prakash materials; to Laura Slatkin for the Cantharides anecdote; and to Michael O'Flaherty for the Hiroshima connection.
2. Gascoigne, *Encyclopedia of Britain*, s.v. 'peccavi'.
3. Priscilla Hayter Napier, *I Have Sind*, 197.
4. Ibid., xvi.
5. Mehra, *A Dictionary of Modern Indian History*, 496-97.
6. George Daniel, *Democritus in London*, 51.
7. *Notes and Queries* no. 212, Saturday, 19 November 1853, p. 491. In *Notes and Queries* no. 215 (Saturday, 10 December 1853, p. 574), Cuthbert Bede attributes the Napier anecdote to Mr. Punch, and 'A Subscriber' refers to the author of *Democritus*.
8. Priscilla Hayter Napier, *I Have Sind*, xv, 160, 197.
9. Gould, 'To be a Platypus', 269.
10. Gascoigne, *Encyclopedia of Britain*, s.v. 'peccavi'.
11. Rowley, *More Puniana*, 166-67.
12. Lawrence, *Charles Napier*, x.
13. Rushdie, *Shame*, 88.
14. Gould, 'To be a Platypus', 269.
15. James C. Scott, *Domination and the Arts of Resistance*.
16. The remark was quoted first in Latin by Suetonius, *Lives of the Caesars* ('The Deified Julius', 1.37) and soon after that in Greek by Plutarch in *Roman Apophthegms* (*Moralia*, 206 E) and *Life of Caesar* (731 F). Note the complexity of cross-translation even here.
17. Priscilla Hayter Napier, *I Have Sind*, 160.
18. Rushdie, *Shame*, 88.
19. Mehra, *A Dictionary of Modern Indian History*, 497.
20. Sir William Napier, *The Life and Opinions*, 4.38.
21. Ibid., 2.376.
22. Ibid., 2.275.
23. Kipling, *Kim*, 161; Said, 'Introduction' to Rudyard Kipling, *Kim*, 32.
24. Pandey, 'An English goddess'.
25. Doniger, *The Implied Spider*, 3.
26. Kipling, *Kim*, 60.
27. Said, 'Introduction' to Rudyard Kipling, *Kim*, 45
28. Rushdie, 'Kipling'.
29. Auden 'In Memory of W.B. Yeats', 143
30. Orwell, 'Rudyard Kipling', 135.
31. Rushdie, 'Kipling', 80.
32. Ricoeur, *Symbolism of Evil*, 352.

YOU CAN'T MAKE AN OMELETTE

1. This chapter is a much expanded version of a short article that I wrote for PEN Oakland, forthcoming ('You Can't Make an Omelette') and parts of another, 'It Can Happen Here: The Fight for the History of Hinduism in the American Academy', forthcoming in Nussbaum and Doniger, eds., *Pluralism and Democracy in India: Challenging the Hindu Right*, 2013.

2. Rajiv Malhotra, 'Wendy's Children', posted on the Internet, September, 2002. http://rajivmalhotra.com/index.php?option=com_content&task=view&id=30&Itemid=26

3. Alison Goddard, *The Times Higher Education Supplement*, 21 November 2003, 'Email threats and egg-throwing spark fears of Hindu extremism'. See also Edward Rothstein 'The Scholar Who Irked the Hindu Puritans', in 'Arts and Ideas', the *New York Times*, Monday, 31 January 2005 (reprinted as 'Daring to Tackle Sex in Hinduism', in the *International Herald Tribune*, 2 February 2005).

4. IndianCivilization@yahoogroups.com, 'Jiten Bardwaj' <jiten51@yahoo groups.com>. Parts of the message were cited by Goddard in 'Email threats'. The author of the posting was Jitendra Bardwaj, of whom Wikipedia (which may or may not be accurate) says: 'Jitendra Bardwaj (born 1937) . . . campaigns for the rights of ethnic minorities and for the introduction of Hindu yoga and meditation techniques in British schools.'

5. Goddard, 'Email threats'.

6. Ibid.

7. Dalrymple, 'India: The War Over History'.

8. Ibid.

9. See McComas Taylor, 'Mythology Wars: The Indian Diaspora, "Wendy's Children," and the Struggle for the Hindu Past'.

10. *Times Literary Supplement*, 28 May 2010.

11. 'Rushdie to Pen his Life after Fatwa', *India Today*, 14 March 2010. 'The writer, who had slammed New Delhi at the conclave for failing to protect artist M.F. Husain, rushed to the defence of Wendy Doniger, a leading scholar on Hinduism and mythology, who is being targeted by the self-appointed moral police for writing *The Hindus: An Alternative History*. "She is the most eminent scholar in the field. She is not a fly-by-night operator. I have read her and found her writing an invaluable resource," said Rushdie, adding, "Ninety-nine point nine per cent of those who call themselves Hindus would learn and value her colossal work."'

THE FOREST-DWELLER

1. This is a revised version of a brief essay that was originally published in my column 'On Faith,' for the *Washington Post/Newsweek*, on 22 May 2008. It was reprinted in the *Aging Horizons Bulletin*, 28 February 2009 and, slightly expanded, as 'The forest-dweller stage of life' (in *Harvard and Radcliffe Classes of 1962*, fiftieth anniversary report, Cambridge: MA, 2012, 906-7). It was then reprinted in The Best Reports of 2012 (Harvard Class Report Office, 2012, 87-89).

BIBLIOGRAPHY

Sanskrit, Hindi, Greek and Persian Texts and Translations, by Title

Abhidhanachintamani of Hemacandra. Ed. Pandit Shivadatta and Kashinatha Pandurang Parab. Abhidhanasangraha, nos. 6–11. Bombay: Nirnaya Sagar Press, 1896.

Abhijnanashakuntalam of Kalidasa, with the commentary of Raghava. Bombay: Nirnaya Sagara Press, 1958.

Adhyatma-ramayana, with the commentaries of Narottama, Ramavarman and Gopala Chakravarti. Calcutta Sanskrit series, no. 11. Calcutta: Metropolitan Printing & Publishing House, 1935.

Aitareya Aranyaka [AA]. Ed. and trans., A.B. Keith. Anecdota Oxoniensia: Aryan Series 9. Oxford: Clarendon Press, 1909.

Aitareya Brahmana [AB], with the commentary of Sayana. Anandashrama Sanskrit Series 32. Poona, 1896.

Aitareya Upanishad. In *One Hundred and Eight Upanishads*.

Apastamba Dharmasutra. Bombay: Venkateshvara Steam Press, 1892.

Apastamba Shrauta Sutra [ApSS]. Gaekwad Oriental Series, nos. 121 and 142. Baroda: Oriental Institute, 1955 and 1963.

Arthashastra of Kautilya. Bombay: University of Bombay, 1960.

—— Ed. and tr. R.P. Kangle. Volume 1: Text. Volume 2: Translation. Bombay: University of Bombay, 1960.

Ashvalayana Grihya-Sutra [AGS], with the Sanskrit commentary of Narayana. Translated with introduction and index by Narendra Nath Sharma and a forward by Satya Vrat Shastri. Delhi: Eastern Book Linkers, 1976.

Ashvalayana Shrauta Sutra [AShS] with *Siddhantabhasya*. Edited by Kuber Nath Shukla. Banaras: Government Sanskrit Library, 1938–55.

Atharva Veda [AV], with the commentary of Sayana. Bombay, Government Central Book Depot, 1895.

—— 5 vols. Hoshiarpur: Vishveshvaranand Vedic Research Institute, 1960.

—— *Hymns of the Atharva Veda, Together with the Extracts from the Ritual Books and the Commentaries*. Tr. Maurice Bloomfield (S.B.E. XLII). Oxford: Clarendon Press, 1897.

Babur, *Baburnama. Memoirs of Babur, Prince and Emperor*. Tr. Wheeler M. Thackston. Introduction by Salman Rushdie. New York: Modern Library, 2002. Also: Tr. A.S. Beveridge. London: Luzac, 1921.

Baudhayana Dharmasutra [BD]. Ed. C. Sastri. Benares: Kashi Sanskrit Series no. 104, 1934.

Baudhayana Shrauta Sutra [BSS]. Ed. W. Caland. Bibliotheca Indica. New Series. 3 vols. Calcutta: Asiatic Society, 1904–1924.

Bhagavad Gita [BG]. Book 6 (18 chapters) of the *Mahabharata*.

——. Trans., with a commentary based on the original sources, R.C. Zaehner. London: Oxford University Press, 1969.

Bhagavadajjuka-Prahasanam of Bodhayana. Ed. Prabhata Sastri. Prayaga: Devabhasaprakasanam, 1979.

Bhagavata Purana, with the commentary of Shridhara. Bombay: Venkateshvara Steam Press, 1832; rept. Motilal Banarsidass, Delhi 1983.

Bhavishya Purana. Bombay: Venkateshvara Steam Press 1959.

Brahma Purana. Calcutta: Gurumandala Press, 1954.

Brahmanda Purana. Bombay: Venkateshvara Steam Press, 1857.

Brahmavaivarta Purana. Poona: Anandasrama Sanskrit Series #102, 1935.

Brihadaranyaka Upanishad [BAU]. In *One Hundred and Eight Upanishads.*

Brihaddevata of Shaunaka. Ed. Arthur Anthony Macdonell. Harvard Oriental Series 5. Cambridge, Massachusetts: Harvard University Press, 1904.

Buddhacharita of Ashvaghosha. Ed. E.H. Johnston. Calcutta: Panjab University Oriental Publications, 1935-6.

Charakasamhita (2 vols.). Ed and tr. Jayadeva Vidyalankara, 2 vols. Delhi: Motilal Banarsidass, 1963.

Chandogya Upanishad [CU]. In *One Hundred and Eight Upanishads.*

Dashakumaracharita of Dandin. Tr. Isabelle Onians: *What Ten Young Man Did.* New York: New York University Press, 2005.

Devi Purana. Calcutta: Bangabasi Press, 1896.

Devibhagavata Purana. Benares: Pandita Pustakalaya, 1960.

Garuda Purana. Benares: Pandita Pustakalaya, 1969.

Gitagovinda of Jayadeva. Hyderabad: Sanskrit Academy Series, 1969.

Gopatha Brahmana. Calcutta: Bibliotheca Indica, 1872.

Harivamsha. Critical edition. Poona: Bhandarkar Oriental Research Institute, 1969.

———. With commentary. Bombay: Lakshmi-Venkateshvara Steam Press, 1833-76.

Hiranyakeshin Shrauta Sutra [HSS]. Ed. K. Agashe and S. Marulakara, 10 vols. Poona: Anandasrama Press, 1907-1932.

History. Herodotus. Tr. David Grene. Chicago: University of Chicago Press, 1987.

Jaiminiya Brahmana of the Sama Veda [JB]. Ed. Raghu Vira and Lokesh Chandra. Sarasvati Vihara Series, vol. 31. Nagpur: International Academy of Indian Culture, 1954.

Kalika Purana. Ed. Sri Biswanarayan Sastri. Varanasi: Chowkhamba Sanskrit Series Office, 1972

———. Bombay: Venkateshvara Steam Press, 1891.

Kamasutra [KS] of Vatsyayana, with the 'Jayamangala' commentary of Shri Yashodhara. Bombay: Lakshmi-Venkateshvara Steam Press, 1856.

———. With the commentary of Yashodhara. Ed., with the Hindi 'Jaya' commentary, by Devadatta Shastri. Kashi Sanskrit Series 29. Varanasi: Chaukhambha Sanskrit Sansthan, 1964.

———. Trans. Wendy Doniger and Sudhir Kakar. Oxford and New York: Oxford University Press, 2002.

Katha Upanishad [KU]. In *One Hundred and Eight Upanishads.*

Kathaka Samhita [*Die Samhita der Katha-Shakha*] (3 vols.). Leipzig: Brockhaus, 1900.

Kathasaritsagara [KSS] of Somadeva. Bombay: Nirnara Sagara Press, 1930.

———. Trans. C.H. Tawney, ed N.M. Penzer. *The Ocean of Story* [*Kathasaritsagara*] (10 vols.). London: Chas. J. Sawyer, 1924; MLBD Rept. Delhi, 1967.

Katthaharijataka and *Uddalakajataka*, nos. 7 and 487 of *Jataka Stories*. Ed. E.B. Cowell. London: Pali Text Society, 1973.

Katyayana Shrauta Sutra [KShS]. Ed. Yugalkisora Pathaka. Benares: Braj B. Das, 1883-1888.

Kaushitaki Brahmana [KB] (3 vols.). Calcutta: Bibliotheca Indica, 1903.

Kaushitaki Upanishad [KauU]. In *One Hundred and Eight Upanishads.*

Kumarasambhava of Kalidasa. Bombay: Nirnaya Sagara Press, 1955.

Kurma Purana. Ed. A.S. Gupta. Varanasi: All-India Kashiraj Trust, 1967; Calcutta: Bibliotheca Indica, 1890.

Linga Purana. Calcutta: Bangabasi Press, 1890.

Magha-mahatmya of the Uttara Khanda of the *Padma Purana*, in a Bengali manuscript, Dacca University Mss. no. 931, fols. 44 ff., chapter 10 ff., cited by Hazra, *Studies in the Upapuranas: II*, p. 362.

Mahabharata [M]. Ed. V.S. Sukthankar et al. Poona: Bhandarkar Oriental Research Institute, 1933-69.

——. With the commentary of Nilakantha. Bombay: Jagadishvara, 1862.

——. Trans. J.A.B. van Buitenen. Chicago: University of Chicago Press, 1973-78.

Mahanirvana Tantra. Madras: Tantrik Texts, 1929.

Maitrayani Samhita [MS]. Ed. L. von Schroeder. Wiesbaden: R. Steiner, 1970-72 (1881).

Maitrayaniya Upanishad [MU]. Ed. and trans. J.A. van Buitenen's-Gravenhage: Mouton, 1962.

Manavadharmashastra. Ed. Harikrishna Jayantakrishna Dave. Bombay: Bharatiya Vidya Series, vol. 29 ff., 1972-8.

——. *The Laws of Manu* [Manu]. Trans. Wendy Doniger with Brian K. Smith. Harmondsworth: Penguin Books, 1991.

——. With Medhatithi's commentary. Calcutta: Bibliotheca Indica, 1932.

——. Trans. Georg Bühler, Sacred Books of the East no. 25. Oxford: Oxford University Press, 1886.

Manava Shrauta Sutra [MSS]. Ed. Jeanette Maria van Geldner. New Delhi: International Academy of Indian Culture, 1961.

Mandukya Upanishad. In *One Hundred and Eight Upanishads*.

Markandeya Purana, with commentary. Bombay: Venkateshvara Steam Press, 1890.

Matsya Purana. Poona: Anandashrama Sanskrit Series, 54, 1909.

Mattavilasaprahasana of Mahendravarman. Trivandrum: Trivandrum Sanskrit Series no. 50, 1917.

Mitakshara of Vijnaneshvara, commentary on Yajnavalkya *Smriti*. Ed. W.L.S. Pansikar. 2nd Edition. Bombay: Nirnaya Sagar, [1909] 1918.

Nagananda of Shri Harsha. Trans. P. Boyd. In *Six Sanskrit Plays*. Ed. H.W. Wells. Bombay and New York: Asia Publishing House, 1964.

Naishadhacharita of Shriharsha. Ed. Jivananda Vidyasagara. Bombay: Nirnaya Sagara Press, 1986.

Narada Smriti. Ed. Julius Jolly. Bibliotheca Indica. Calcutta: The Asiatic Society, 1885-86.

Narmamala of Kshemendra. Ed. and trans. Fabrizia Baldissera. Würzburg: Südasien-Institut, Ergon Verlag, 2005.

Nirukta of Yaska. Ed. Lakshman Sarup. Oxford: Oxford University Press, 1921.

Padma Purana. Poona: Anandashrama Sanskrit Series no. 131, 1894.

Pashupatasutra, with the Pancharthabhashya of Kaundinya. Trivandrum: Trivandrum Sanskrit Series no. 143, 1940.

Panchatantra. Ed. Johannes Hertel. Cambridge, MA: Harvard Oriental Series XI, 1908.

Panchavimsha [Tandya-maha] Brahmana [PB], with the commentary of Sayana. Bibliotheca Indica. Calcutta: Asiatic Society, 1869-74.

Periya Puranam of Cekkilar. Trans. Alistair McGlashan (*The History of the Holy Servants of the Lord Siva*). Victoria, British Columbia: Trafford Publishing, 2006.

Prabandhakosha of Rajashekhara. Ed. Jina Vijaya. Singhi Jaina Series, no. 6, Shantiketan: Adhisthata-Singhi Jaina Jnanapitha, 1935.

Prabodhachandrodaya of Krishnamishra. Bombay, Nirnaya Sagara Press, 1898.

Priyadarshika of (Shri) Harsha. Ed. M.R. Kale. Bombay: Motilal Banarsidass, 1928. Trans. Wendy Doniger. See *Ratnavali*.

Purva Mimamsa Sutra of Jaimini [PMS], *Jaiminiya-mimamsa-bhashyam* of Shabarasvamin. Hirayana, India: Ramlal Kapar, 1986.

Ramayana of Valmiki [R]. Baroda: Oriental Institute, 1960-75

——. trans. Sheldon Pollock. New York: New York University Press, 2008.

Ramacaritamanasa of Tulsi Das. Trans. W.D.P. Hill (*The Holy Lake of the Acts of Rama*). London: Oxford University Press, 1952.

Ratnavali of (Shri) Harsha. Ed. Ashokanath Bhattacharya and Maheshwar Das. Calcutta: Modern Book Agency, 1967. Trans. Wendy Doniger, *The Lady of the Jewel Necklace* and *The Lady Who Shows Her Love*. Harsha's *Priyadarsika* and *Ratnavali*. Clay Sanskrit Series. New York: New York University Press, JJC Foundation, 2006.

Ravana Vaha or *Setubandha*, with commentary. Ed. Pandit Sivadatta and Kasinath Pandurang Parab. Kavyamala no. 47. Bombay: Tukaram Javaji, 1895.

Rig Veda [RV], with the commentary of Sayana. Ed. F. Max Müller. London: William H. Allen, 1890–92.

Sarvadarshanasangraha of Madhava. Calcutta: Bibliotheca Indica, 1858

Saura Purana. Calcutta, Bangabasi Press,1910.

Shabdakalpadruma of Raja Sir Radhakant Deb Bahadur. Calcutta, 1886; Delhi, 1961.

Shadvimsha Brahmana [ShB], with the commentary of Sayana. Ed. Bellikoth Ramachandra Sharma. Tripathi: Kendriya Sanskrit Vidyapeetha Series 9, 1967.

Shankaravijaya of Anandagiri. Ed. J. Tarkapancanana. Calcutta: Bibliotheca Indica, 1868.

Shankaradigvijaya of Madhava. Poona: Bhandarkar Oriental Research Institute, 1915.

Shankhayana Shrauta Sutra [SSS], with the commentary of Varadattasuta Anartiya. Ed. A. Hillebrandt. Biblioteca Indica. Calcutta: Asiatic Society, 1888–99.

Shatapatha Brahmana of the White Yajur Veda [SB]. Ed. A. Weber. Benares: Chowkhamba Sanskrit Series, 1964.

——. Trans. Julius Eggeling (SBE, XII, XXVI, XLI, XLIH, XLIV). *The Shatapatha Brahmana, According to the Text of the Madhyandina School*. 5 vols. Sacred Books of the East vols. 12, 26, 41, 42, 44. Oxford: Oxford University Press, 1885–1900.

Shiva Purana. Benares: Partita Pustakalaya, 1964.

——. With commentaries. Bombay: Ganpat Krishnaji Press, 1884.

Shivapurana Mahatmya. Benares: Pandita Pustakalaya, 1964.

Shukranitisara. Edited with a commentary by Pandit Jibananda Vidyasagara Bhattacaryya. Calcutta: Saraswati Press, 1882.

Shvetashvatara Upanishad [SU]. In *One Hundred and Eight Upanishads*.

Skanda Purana. Bombay: Shree Venkateshvara Steam Press, 1867.

Subhashitaratnakosha of Vidyakara. Cambridge, MA: Harvard Oriental Series XLII, 1957.

——. Trans. Daniel H.H. Ingalls. Cambridge, MA: Harvard Oriental Series XLIV, 1965.

Svapnavasavadatta of Bhasa. Ed. C.R. Devadhar. Poona: Oriental Book Agency, 1946.

The Svarga Khanda of the Padma Purana. Ed. A.C. Shastri. Varanasi: All-India Kashiraj Trust, 1972.

Taittiriya Aranyaka [TA] of the Black Yajur Veda, with the commentary of Sayana. Bibliotheca Indica. Calcutta: Asiatic Society, 1872.

Taittiriya Brahmana [TB]. Ed. Rajendralala Mitra. Calcutta: Bibliotheca Indica, 1859; Delhi: Motilal Banarsidass, 1985.

Taittiriya Samhita [TS] of the Black Yajur Veda, with the commentary of Madhava. Calcutta: Bibliotheca Indica, 1860.

Tantradhikaranirnaya of Bhattoji Dikshita. Benares, 1888.

Tantravarttika of Kumarila Bhatta, commentary on Shabarasvamin's *Jaiminiya Mimamsa Sutra* commentary. Benares: Benares Sanskrit Series, 1903.

Tantropakhyana, 'Ten Tales from the Tantropakhyana'. Ed. and trans. George T. Artola. Madras: *Adyar Library Bulletin*, 29:1-4, 1965.

Upanishads: *One Hundred and Eight Upanishads*. Bombay: Nirnaya Sagara Press, 1913.

—— Ed. and trans. Patrick Olivelle (*Early Upanishads*). New York: Oxford University Press, 1998.

Vaikhanasasmartasutra. Calcutta: Bibliotheca Indica, 1927.

Vajasaneyi Samhita [VS]. Varanasi: Chaukhamba Sanskrit Series, 1972.

Vamana Purana. Benares: All-India Kashiraj, 1968.

Varaha Purana. Calcutta: Bibliotheca Indica, 1893.

Vayu Purana. Bombay: Venkatesvara Steam Press, 1867.

Vishnu Purana. Calcutta: Sanatana Shastra, 1972.

——. Trans. Horace Hayman Wilson. London: J. Murray, 1840; 3rd ed. Calcutta: Punthi Pustak, 1961.

Vishnudharmottara Purana. Ed. and trans. Priyabala Shah, 3 vols. Delhi: Parimal Publications, 1999-2005.

Yajnavalkya Smriti. Poona: Anandashrama Sanskrit Series no. 46, 1903-4.

Yogavasishtha [*Yogavasishtha-Maha-Ramayana* of Valmiki]. Ed. W.L.S. Pansikar. 2 vols. Bombay: Nirnaya Sagara Press, 1918.

Secondary Sources, by Author

Agrawala, Vasudeva S. *Matsya Purana, A Study*. Benares: All-India Kashiraj Trust, 1963.

Aiyangar, K.V. Rangaswami. *Rajadharma*. Madras: Adyar Library, 1941.

Alder, Garry. *Beyond Bokhara: The Life of William Moorcroft, Asian Explorer and Pioneer Veterinary Surgeon, 1767-1825*. London: Century Publishing, 1985.

Altekar, A.S. *State and Government in Ancient India*, 3rd edition. Delhi: Motilal Banarsidass, 1958.

Ambedkar, Bhimrao Ramji. *The Untouchables*. New Delhi: Amrit Book Co., 1948.

Apte, V.S. *The Practical Sanskrit-English Dictionary*. 3 Vols. Revised and enlarged edition. Poona: Prasad Prakashan, 1957-59.

Archer, William G. Preface to the *Kama Sutra*. London: George Allen and Unwin, 1963.

Arnold, David. 'Beheading Hindus, and other alternative aspects of Wendy Doniger's history of a mythology.' *Times Literary Supplement*, July 29, 2009.

Artola, see *Tantropakhyana*.

Auden, W.H. *Collected Poems*. New York: Random House, 2007.

——. 'In Memory of W.B. Yeats.' *Collected Shorter Poems*. London: Faber and Faber, 1966.

Balse, Mayah. 'Surya.' *Amar Chitra Katha* no. 58, ed. Anant Pai. Bombay: India Book Trust, n.d.

Barthes, Roland. *The Pleasure of the Text*. New York: Hill and Wang, 1975.

Basham, A.L. *The Wonder That Was India*. London: Sidgwick and Jackson, 1956.

Beck, B.E.F. 'Social and conceptual order in Kongu.' Unpublished D. Phil, dissertation, Oxford, 1968.

Bendall, Cecil. 'The Tantrakhyana, a Collection of Indian Folklore, from a unique Sanskrit MS. discovered in Nepal.' *Journal of the Royal Asiatic Society of Great Britain and Ireland*, n.s. vol. 20, part 4, October, 1888, 465-501.

Bhandarkar, D.R. *Some Aspects of Ancient Hindu Polity*. Benares: Benares Hindu University, 1929.

Bhattacarya, Asutosh. *Folklore of Bengal*. New Delhi: National Book Trust. 1978.

Biardeau, Madeleine. *Études de Mythologie hindoue*. 2 vols. Paris: École Française d'Extrême Orient, 1981-1994.

——. *Hinduism: The Anthropology of a Civilization*. Delhi: Oxford University Press, 1994.

Blair, Chauncey. *Heat in the Rig Veda and Atharva Veda*. Cambridge, MA: American Oriental Society Publication 45, 1961.

Blochmann, H. *The A'in-i Akbari [by] Abu'l-Fazl 'Allami*, trans. H. Blochmann ed. S.L. Goomer. 2nd ed. Delhi: Aadesh Book Depot, 1965; a reprint of the 1st ed. published in 1871.

Bloomfield, Maurice. 'The Character and Adventures of Muladeva.' *Proceedings of the American Philosophical Society*, vol. 52 (1913), 618-649.

——. 'Contributions to the Veda III: The Marriage of Saranyu, Tvastri's Daughter.' *Journal of the American Oriental Society* 15 (1893): 172–88.

Bordewekar, Sandhya. Interview with Shivaji K. Panikkar and Chandramohan. *Art India* 12:3 (2007), 61-67.

Böthtlingk, Otto. *Indische Spruche*. Saint Petersburg: Commissionäre der Kaiserlichen Akademie der Wissenschaften, 1870-73.

Böthtlingk, Otto and Rudolph Roth, eds., *Sanskrit Wörterbuch*. St. Petersburg: Buchdruckerei der Kaiserlichen Akademie der Wissenschaften, 1855-1875.

Bodewitz, H.G. *The Daily Evening and Morning Offering (Agnihotra) According to the Brahmanas*. Leiden: E.J. Brill, 1976.

Bolts, William. *Considerations on Indian Affairs; Particularly Respecting the Present State of Bengal Dependencies*. London. Reprinted in *The East India Company: 1600-1858*, edited by Patrick Tuck. Vol. 3. London and New York: Routledge, 1998 [1772].

Bombay (Presidency) Supreme Court. *Report of the Maharaj Libel Case: And of the Bhattia Conspiracy Case*. Bombay: Bombay Gazette Press, 1862.

Bordewekar, Sandhya. Interview with Shivaji K. Panikkar and Chandramohan. *Art India* 12:3 (2007), 61-67.

Bosch, F.D.K. 'The god with the horse's head.' In *Selected studies in Indonesian archeology*. The Hague: Martinus Nijhoff, 1961.

Bray, Alan. *Homosexuality in Renaissance England*. New York: Columbia University Press, 1996.

——. *The Golden Germ: An introduction to Indian Symbolism*. The Hague: Mouton, 1960.

Brodie, Fawn M. *The Devil Drives: A Life of Sir Richard Burton*. New York: Ballantine, 1967.

Bronner, Yigal. *Extreme Poetry: The South Asian Movement of Simultaneous Narration*. New York: Columbia University Press, 2010.

Brough, John. *Poems from the Sanskrit*. London: Penguin, 1968.

Buck, William. *Ramayana*. Berkeley: University of California Press, 1976.

Bühler, Georg. 'The Peheva Inscription from the Temple of Garibnath.' *Epigraphica Indic*, vol. 1. Calcutta: Thacker, Spink and Co. 1893, 184-190.

Bühler, see *Manavadharmashastra*.

Burton, Sir Richard Francis. *The Kama Sutra of Vatsyayana: The Classic Hindu Treatise on Love and Social Conduct*. Introduction by John W. Spellman. New York: E.P. Dutton & Co. Inc., 1962.

—— *Vikram and the Vampire, or Tales of Hindu Devilry*. London: Tylston and Edwards, 1893; reprint ed. New York: Dover Publications, 1969.

Carman, John, and Vasudha Narayanan. *The Tamil Veda: Pillan's Interpretation of the Tiruvaymoli*. Chicago: University of Chicago, 1989.

Chakravarti, Chintaharan. *The Tantras: Studies in Their Religion and Literature*. Calcutta: Punthi Pustak, 1963.

Chakrabarti, S.C. *The Paribhashas in the Shrautasutras*. Calcutta: Sanskrit Pustak Bhandar, 1980.

Chand, Tek. *Liquor Menace in India*. New Delhi: Gandhi Peace Foundation, 1972.

Chandra, Bipan. 'Use of History and Growth of Communalism', in Pramod Kumar, ed., *Towards Understanding Communalism*. Chandigarh: Centre for Research in Rural and Industrial Development, 1992, 330-350.

Chandra, Vikram. *Love and Longing in Bombay*. Boston: Little, Brown and Company, 1997.

de Chardin, Teilhard. *Christianity and Evolution*. New York: Harvest Books, 2002.

Chattopadhyaya, Sudhakar. *The Evolution of Theistic Sects in India*. Calcutta: Progressive Publishers, 1962.

Choudhary, Radhakrishna. 'Heretical Sects in the Puranas.' *Annals of the Bhandarkar Oriental Research Institute*, 37 (1957).

Cohen, Lawrence. 'Semen Gain, Holi Modernity, and the Logic of Street Hustlers.' Paper presented at the annual meeting of the Association of Asian Studies. Boston. 25 March 25 1994.

Conze, Edward. *Buddhist Scriptures*. Harmondsworth: Penguin Books, 1959.

——. *A Short History of Buddhism*. The Buddhist Library. Bombay: Chetana, 1960.

Coomaraswamy, Ananda K. 'Atmayajna: Self-Sacrifice.' *Harvard Journal of Asiatic Studies* 6 (1941).

——. *The Darker Side of Dawn*. Washington, D.C.: Smithsonian Miscellaneous Collections, vol. 94, no. 1 (1935).

——. 'Vedic Exemplarism.' *Harvard Journal of Asiatic Studies* 1 (1936): 44-64.

Cox, Whitney. 'The Transfiguration of Tinnan the Archer (Studies in Cekkilar's Periyapuranam I).' *Indo-Iranian Journal* 48, 3-4 (2005): 223-252.

Crooke, William. *The Popular Religion and Folk-lore of Northern India*. 2 vols. London: Archibald Constable, 1896.

Dalrymple, William. 'India: The War Over History.' *The New York Review of Books* (52: 6), April 7, 2005.

Dange, S.A. *Legends in the Mahabharata*. Delhi: Motilal Banarsidass, 1969.

——. 'Religious Suicide in the Vedic Period?' *Indologica Taurinensia* 8 (1980): 113-121.

Daniel, E. Valentine. *Fluid Signs: Being a Person the Tamil Way*. Berkeley: University of California Press, 1984.

——. Untitled paper presented at the South Asian Conference at the University of Wisconsin, Madison. 8 November 1986.

Daniel, George. *Democritus in London: With the Mad Pranks and Comical Conceits of Motley and Robin Good-Fellow*. London: William Pickering, 1852.

Daniélou, Alain. *Hindu Polytheism*. London: Routledge and Kegan Paul, 1964.

Das, Veena. *Structure and Cognition*. Delhi: Oxford University Press, 1977.

Dasgupta, Surendranath. *History of Indian Philosophy*. 5 Vols. Cambridge: Cambridge University Press, 1932-1955; Rept., Delhi: Motilal Banarsidass, 1975.

Daston, Lorraine, and Gregg Mitman, eds. *Thinking With Animals: New Perspectives on Anthropomorphism*. New York: Columbia University Press, 2005.

Davids, T.W. Rhys, trans., *Dialogues of the Buddha*, 3 vols. Sacred Books of the Buddhists, Vols. 2, 3, and 4. London: Pali Text Society, 1899; reprint ed., London: Routledge and Kegan Paul, 1973-77.

Davis, Richard. *Lives of Indian Images*. Princeton, NJ: Princeton University Press, 1997.

Debroy, Bibek. *Sarama and Her Children: The Dog in Indian Myth*. Delhi, Penguin India, 2008.

Deppert, Joachim. *Rudras Geburt: Systematische Unter-suchungen zum Inzest in der Mythlogie der Brahmanas*. Wiesbaden: Otto Harrassowitz, 1977.

Derrett, J. Duncan M. *Dharmasastra and Juridical Literature*. Wiesbaden: Otto Harrassowitz, 1973.

——. *Religion, Law and the State in India*. London: Oxford University Press, 1968.

Dharker, Anil. 'Beauty and the Beast: Baroda episode underscores threat to creative expression.' *Mainstream* 45: 23 (May 25, 2007).

Digby, Simon. *War Horse and Elephant in the Delhi Sultanate*. Oxford: Orient Monographs, 1971.

Dikshitar, V.R. Ramachandra. *War in ancient India*, 2nd ed. New York: Macmillan, 1948.

Dimock, Edward Cameron. *The Thief of Love*. Chicago: University of Chicago Press, 1963.

Doniger/Doniger O'Flaherty, Wendy. 'Asceticism and Sexuality in the Mythology of Shiva,' *History of Religions* 8 (1969): 300-337 and 9 (1969) 1-41.

——. *Asceticism and Eroticism in the Mythology of Siva*. London: Oxford University Press, 1973.

——. *The Bedtrick: Tales of Sex and Masquerade*. Chicago: University of Chicago Press, 2000.

——. 'Between the Seen and the Unseen: The Ambiguity of Death in Hinduism.' *In Death: The Secret of Life, Proceedings of a Cross Cultural Symposium*. 99-109. New York: Cauldron Productions, 1992.

——. 'Bisexuality in the Mythology of Ancient India.' *Diogenes* vol. 52, no. 210 (2005), 50-60.

——. 'A Burnt Offering.' *Times Literary Supplement* 5183 (August 2, 2002), 9. Review of *The Myth of the Holy Cow*, by D.N. Jha (London and New York: Verso, 2001).

——. 'The Case of the Stallion's Wife: Indra and Vrsanasva in the *Rg Veda* and the *Brahmanas*' in the *Journal of the American Oriental Society* 105, no. 3, Special issue dedicated to Daniel H.H. Ingalls, 1985), 485-498.

——. 'Compassion toward Animals.' In *The Lives of Animals*, by J.M. Coetzee (ed. Amy Gutmann. Princeton: Princeton University Press, 1999), 93-106.

——. 'The Criteria of Identity in a Telugu Myth of Sexual Masquerade.' In *Syllables of Sky: Studies in South Indian Civilization, In honour of Velcheru Narayana Rao*, ed. David Shulman. Delhi: Oxford University Press, 1995, 103-132.

——. 'The Deconstruction of Vedic Horselore in Indian Folklore.' In *Ritual, State and History in South Asia: Essays in Honor of J.C. Heesterman*, edited by A.W. van den Hoek, D.H.A. Kolff and M.S. Oort. Leiden: E.J. Brill, 1992, 76-101.

——. 'Do Many Heads Necessarily Have Many Minds? Tracking the sources of Hindu Tolerance and Intolerance.' *Parabola* [30:4], Winter, 2005, 10-19.

——. 'Dogs as Dalits in Indian Literature.' In *Antike Mythen: Medien, Transformationen und Konstruktionen*. Eds. Ueli Dill and Christine Walde. Berlin and New York: Walter de Gruyter, 2009, 391-405.

——. 'The dream narrative and the Indian doctrine of illusion.' *Daedalus*, Summer 1982, 93-113.

——. *Dreams, Illusion, and Other Realities*. Chicago: University of Chicago Press, 1984.

——. 'Echoes of the *Mahabharata*: Why is a Parrot the Narrator of the *Bhagavata Purana and the Devibhagavata Purana*?' In *Purana Perennis*, 31-57.

——. 'Enigmas of Sexual Masquerade in Hindu Myths and Tales.' In David Shulman, ed., *Untying the Knot: On Riddles and Other Enigmatic Modes*. New York: Oxford University Press, 208-227.

——. 'Ethical and Non-Ethical Implications of the Separation of Heaven and Earth in Indian Mythology.' In *Cosmogony and Ethical Order: New Studies in Comparative Ethics*, ed. Frank Reynolds and Robin Lovin, 177-199. Chicago and London: University of Chicago Press, 1985.

——. 'Fluid and Fixed Texts in India'. In *Boundaries of the Text: Epic Performances in South and Southeast Asia*, ed. Joyce Burkhalter Flueckiger and Laurie J. Sears. University of Michigan Papers on South and Southeast Asia, no. 35. Ann Arbor, Michigan: Center for South and Southeast Asian Studies, University of Michigan, 1991, 31-41.

——. 'From *Kama* to Karma: The Resurgence of Puritanism in Contemporary India.' In *Social Research, India's World*, vol. 78, no. 1, Spring 2011, 49-74.

——. 'Going with the Flow: Why sex has to be put back into Tantra.' Review of David Gordon White, *Kiss of the Yogini* (The *Times Literary Supplement* May 21, 2004), 3-4.

——. 'Hindu Pluralism and Hindu Intolerance of the Other.' In *Concepts of the Other in Near Eastern Religions. Israel Oriental Studies* vol. XIV, ed. Ilai Alon, Ithamar Gruenwald, and Itamar Singer. Leiden and New York: E.J. Brill, 1994, 369-90.

——. *The Hindus: An Alternative History*. New York: Penguin, 2009.

—— *Hindu Myths: A Sourcebook*. Harmondsworth: Penguin Books, 1975.

——. 'Hinduism by Any Other Name.' In *Wilson Quarterly* (July 1991): 35-41.

——. 'The History of Ekalavya.' In *Tarikh: The History Journal*, 2008-9. Special Issue on Myth and History, St Stephens, Delhi, 34-36.

——. 'Horses and snakes in the Adi Parvan of the *Mahabharata*.' In *Aspects of India: Essays in Honor of Edward Cameron Dimock*, ed. Margaret Case and N. Gerald Barrier. New Delhi: American Institute of Indian Studies and Manohar, 1986, 16-44.

——. '"I Have Scinde": Flogging a Dead (White Male Orientalist) Horse.' Presidential Lecture, *Journal of Asian Studies* 58 (4), November, 1999, 940-60.

——. 'The Image of the Heretic in the Gupta *Puranas*.' In *Essays on Gupta Culture*, ed. Bardwell L. Smith, 107-127. New Delhi: Motilal Banarsidass, 1983.

——. 'Impermanence and Eternity in Indian Art and Myth.' In *Contemporary Indian Tradition: Voices on Culture, Nature, and the Challenge of Change*, ed. Carla M. Borden. Washington, D.C. and London: Smithsonian Institution Press, 1988, 77-90.

——. *The Implied Spider: Politics and Theology in Myth*. New York: Columbia University Press, 1998; second edition, 2010.

——. 'The Interaction of *Saguna* and *Nirguna* Images of Deity.' In *The Sants: Studies in a Devotional Tradition of India*, edited by Karine Schomer and W.H. McLeod, 47-52. Berkeley: Berkeley Religious Studies Series; Delhi: Motilal Banarsidass, 1987.

——. 'It Can Happen Here: The Fight for the History of Hinduism in the American Academy.' In *Democracy and Pluralism in India: Debating the Hindu Right*, ed. Martha Nussbaum and Wendy Doniger. New York: Oxford University Press, 2013.

——. 'Jewels of Rejection and Recognition in Ancient India.' *Journal of Indian Philosophy* 26 (1998), 435-53.

——. 'The *Kamasutra*: It isn't *All* about Sex.' *Kenyon Review*, vol. 24, #1, Winter, 2003, 18-43.

——. *Karma and Rebirth in Classical Indian Traditions*. Berkeley: University of California Press, 1980.

——. *The Lady of the Jewel Necklace* and *The Lady Who Shows Her Love*. Harsha's *Priyadarsika* and *Ratnavali*. Clay Sanskrit Series. New York: New York University Press, JJC Foundation, 2006. Indian edition, with an introduction by Anita Desai.

——. 'Lost in Translation: Gender in the *Kamasutra*'. In *The Magazine*, Oxford World Classics, Issue 5 Spring-Summer 2002, 2-7.

——. *Der Mann, der mit seiner eigenen Frau Ehebruch beging. Mit einem Kommentar von Lorraine Daston*. Berlin: Suhrkamp, 1999.

——. 'Medical and Mythical Constructions of the Body in Hindu Texts.' In *Religion and the Body*, ed. Sarah Coakley, 167-184. Cambridge, England: Cambridge University Press, 1997.

——. 'The Mythological in Disguise: An Analysis of Karz.' *India International Quarterly* 8 (March 1980): 23-30.

——. 'The Mythology of the Kamasutra.' In *The Anthropologist and the Native: Essays for Gananath Obeyesekere*, ed. H.L. Seneviratne, 293-316. Firenze: Societa Editrice Florentina; Delhi, Manohar, 2009.

——. 'On the *Kamasutra*.' In *Daedalus*, Vol. 131, No. 2, *On Intellectual Property*, Spring, 2002, 126-129.

——. *The Origins of Evil in Hindu Mythology*. Berkeley: University of California Press, 1976.

——. 'The Origins of Heresy in Hindu Mythology.' *History of Religions* 10, no. 4, May 1971, 271-333.

——. 'Other Peoples' Religions, Other Peoples' *Kama* and *Karma*.' In *The Stranger's Religion: Fascination and Fear*. Ed. Anna Lanstrom. Notre Dame, Indiana: Notre Dame University Press, 2004, 79-98.

——. *Other Peoples' Myths: The Cave of Echoes*. New York: Macmillan Publishing Co., 1988.

——. 'Pluralism and Intolerance in Hinduism.' In *Radical Pluralism and Truth: David Tracy and the Hermeneutics of Religion*. Ed. Werner G. Jeanrond and Jennifer L. Rike. New York: Crossroads, 1991, 215-233.

——. *Purana Perennis*. Albany: State University of New York Press, 1993.

——. 'Rationality and Authority in *The Laws of Manu*.' In *The Notion of "Religion" in Comparative Research*. Selected Proceedings of the 16th Congress of the International Association for the History of Religions, ed. Ugo Bianchi, 43-53. Rome: Dipartimento di Studi Storico Religiosi, 1993.

——. 'Rationalizing the Irrational Other: Orientalism and the *Laws of Manu*' in *New Literary History: A Journal of Theory and Interpretation* 23, no. 1 (Versions of Otherness, Winter 1992): 25-43.

——. 'Reading the *Kamasutra*: The Strange and the Familiar.' In *Daedalus*, Spring, 2007, 66-78.

——. 'Reincarnation in Hinduism.' *Concilium: International Review of Theology* 249, edited by J.B. Metz and H. Haring. (May 1993): 3-15.

——. *The Rig Veda: An Anthology*. Harmondsworth: Penguin Books, 1981.

——. 'Saranyu/Samjna: The Sun and the Shadow.' In *Devi: Goddesses of India*, edited by John Stratton Hawley and Donna M. Wulff. Berkeley and Los Angeles: University of California Press, 1996, 154-172.

——. 'The Scrapbook of Undeserved Salvation: The *Kedara Khanda* of the *Skanda Purana*.' In *Purana Perennis*, 59-83.

——. 'Sexual Masquerades in Hindu Myths: Aspects of the Transmission of Knowledge in Ancient India.' In *The Transmission of Knowledge in South Asia*, ed. Nigel Crook. Delhi: Oxford University Press, 1996, 28-48.

——. *Sexual Metaphors and Animal Symbols in Indian Mythology* (Women, Androgynes and Other Mythical Beasts). Delhi, Motilal Banarsidass, 1982.

——. 'Shadows of the *Ramayana*.' In *The Epic Voice*, ed. Alan D. Hodder and Ralph Meagher. New York: Praeger, 2002, 101-128.

——. *Siva: The Erotic Ascetic*. (*Asceticism and Eroticism in the Mythology of Siva*). New York: Galaxy, 1981.

——. 'Speaking in Tongues: Deceptive Stories about Sexual Deception.' *Journal of Religion* 74:3 (July, 1994), ed. Mark Krupnick, 320-337.

—— *Splitting the Difference: Gender and Myth in Ancient Greece and India*. Chicago: The University of Chicago Press, 1999.

——. 'A Symbol in Search of an Object: The Mythology of Horses in India.' In *A Communion of Subjects: Animals in Religion, Science, and Ethics*, ed. Paul Waldau and Kimberley Patton. New York: Columbia University Press, 2006, 335-350.

——. 'The Tail of the Indo-European Horse Sacrifice.' *Incognita* (1), 1990, 1-15.

——. *Tales of Sex and Violence: Folklore, Sacrifice, and Danger in the Jaiminiya Brahmana*. Chicago: University of Chicago Press, 1985.

——. *Textual Sources for the Study of Hinduism*. Chicago: University of Chicago Press, 1990.

——. 'Three (or More) Forms of the Three (or More)-Fold Path in Hinduism.' In *Madness, Melancholy, and the Limits of the Self*, edited by Andrew D. Weiner and Leonard V. Kaplan. Madison, WI: University of Wisconsin Law School, 1996, 201-212.

——. 'Tolstoi's Revenge: The Violence of Indian Non-Violence.' In *Genocide, War, and Human Survival*. Ed. Charles B. Strozier and Michael Flynn. Lanham, Maryland: Rowman and Littlefield, 1996, 219-227.

——. 'Transformations of Subjectivity and Memory in the *Mahabharata* and the *Ramayana*.' In *Self and Self-Transformation in the History of Religions*, ed. David Shulman and Guy Stroumsa, New York: Oxford University Press, 2002, 57-72.

——. *La Trappola della Giumenta* (trans. Vincenzo Vergiani) Milan: Adelphi Edizione, 2003; *Le Kama Sutra de Bikaner*, trans. Fabienne Durand-Bogaert. Paris: Gallimard, 2004.

——. 'The Uses and Misuses of Polytheism and Monotheism in Hinduism.' *Religion and Culture Web Forum*, The University of Chicago Divinity School, January, 2010.

——. 'Wake Up Calls: Some Ancient Hindu Myths.' *Parabola*, 30:1, February, 2005, pp. 6-10. Reprinted on pp. 212 to 221 of *The Inner Journey: Views from the Hindu Tradition*. Ed. Margaret H. Case. Sandpoint, IND: Morning Light Press, 2007.

——. 'When a Kiss is Still a Kiss: Memories of the Mind and the Body in Ancient India and Hollywood.' *The Kenyon Review* 19, no. 1 (Winter 1997): 118-126.

——. 'When a Lingam is Just a Good Cigar: Psychoanalysis and Hindu Sexual Fantasies.' In *The Psychoanalytic Study of Society: Essays in Honor of Alan Dundes*, ed. L. Bryce Boyer et al. Hillside, NJ: The Analytic Press, 1993, 81-104.

——. 'Why Should a Priest Tell You Whom to Marry? A Deconstruction of the Laws of Manu.' In the *Bulletin of the American Academy of Arts and Sciences* 44, no. 6 (March 1991): 18-31.

——. *The Woman Who Pretended to Be Who She Was*. New York: Oxford University Press, 2005.

——. *Women, Androgynes and Other Mythical Beasts.* Chicago: University of Chicago Press, 1980.

——. 'You Can't Make an Omelette,' In *Fightin' Words*, PEN Oakland; forthcoming.

——. 'Zoomorphism in Ancient India: Humans More Bestial than the Beasts.' In *Thinking With Animals: New Perspectives on Anthropomorphism.* Ed. Lorraine Daston and Gregg Mitman. New York: Columbia University Press, 2005, 17-36.

——. and J. Duncan Derrett, eds., *The Concept of Duty in South Asia.* London: School of Oriental and African Studies; Delhi: Vikas Publishing Company; Columbia, Missouri: South Asia Books, 1978.

——. and Brian K. Smith, 'Sacrifice and Substitution: Ritual Mystification and Mythical Demystification.' *Numen* 36, no. 2 (December 1989), 190-223.

——. and Gregory Spinner. 'Misconceptions: Female Imaginations and Male Fantasies in Parental Imprinting.' *Daedalus* 127:1 (Winter, 1998), 97-130.

Douglas, Mary. *Purity and Danger: An Analysis of Concepts of Pollution and Taboo.* London: Routledge and K. Paul, 1966.

Downie, R. Angus. *Frazer and the Golden Bough.* London: Weidenfeld and Nicolson, 1970.

Drekmeier, Charles. *Kingship and Community in Early India.* Stanford, Calif.: Stanford University Press, 1962.

Dubois, Abbé. *Hindu Manners, Customs and Ceremonies.* 3d ed. Oxford: Oxford University Press, 1966.

Dumézil, Georges. '*L'ashvamedha* du colonel de Polier.' In *Pratidanam: Indian, Iranian, and Indo-European Studies presented to Franciscus Bemardus Jacobus Kuiper on his 60th Birthday.* The Hague: Mouton, 1968, 430-435.

——. 'Bellator Equus.' In *Rituels Indo-European à Rome.* Paris, C. Klincksieck, 1954, 73-91.

——. 'Derniers soubresauts du Cheval d'Octobre.' In *Fêtes romaines d'été et d'automne.* Paris: Gallimard, 1975, 177-219.

——. *The Destiny of a King.* Chicago: University of Chicago Press, 1973.

——. *The Destiny of the Warrior.* Chicago: University of Chicago Press, 1970.

Dumont, Louis. *Homo Hierarchicus: The Caste System and its Implications.* Trans. Mark Saisbury, Louis Dumont, and Basia Gulati. Chicago: University of Chicago Press, 1980 [Paris, 1967]).

——. 'World Renunciation in Indian Religion.' *Contributions to Indian Sociology* 4 (1960), 33-62.

Dumont, Paul. *L'Ashvamedha: Description du sacrifice du cheval.* Societé Belge d'études Orientales. Paris: P. Geuthner, 1927.

Eggeling, Julius. See *Shatapatha Brahmana.*

Eliade, Mircea. *Cosmos and History: The Myth of the Eternal Return.* New York: Pantheon, 1954.

——. *Briser le toit de la maison. La creativité et ses symboles.* Paris: Gallimard, 1986.

——. *Yoga: Immortality and Freedom.* Princeton, NJ: Bollingen, 1958.

Eliot, Sir Charles. *Hinduism and Buddhism: An Historical Sketch.* 3 vols. London: E. Arnold, 1921.

Elison, William. *Immanent Domains: Gods, Laws, and Tribes in Mumbai.* Ph.D. dissertation, University of Chicago, 2007.

Erdman, Joan. 'The Empty Beat: Khali as a sign of Time.' *American Journal of Semiotics* 1, 4 (1982), 21-45.

Evans-Pritchard, E.E. *Nuer Religion.* Oxford: Oxford University Press, 1956.

——. *Theories of Primitive Religion.* Oxford: Oxford University Press, 1965.

Faure, Bernard. 'Intertextuality, Relics, and Dreams: The Avatars of a Tradition.' Paper presented at the University of Chicago, 24 March 1986.

Ferro-Luzzi, Gabriella Eichinger. *The Self-Milking Cow and the Bleeding Lingam: Criss-Cross of Motifs in Indian Temple Legends.* Wiesbaden: Otto Harrassowitz, 1987.

Filliozat, Jean. *Les relations extérieures del'Inde.* Pondichery: Institut Français d'Indologie, Publication 2, 1956, 34-60.

Flood, Gavin. *Introduction to the Study of Hinduism*. Cambridge, UK: Cambridge University Press, 1996.

Freud, Sigmund. *Moses and Monotheism*. Trans. Katherine Jones. New York: Vintage Books, 1939.

——. 'A Special Type of Choice of Object Made by Men'. *Standard Edition of the Complete Psychological Works*. Ed. James Strachey. London: Hogarth Press, 1958, vol. 11, 163-176.

——. *Totem and Taboo*. Trans. James Strachey. New York: W.W. Norton & Co., 1950; also trans. A.A. Brill. New York: Vintage, 1918.

——. 'The Unconscious.' In *Collected Papers*, 4 (1925), 98-136.

Fruzzetti, Lina and Ákos Ostör. 'Seed and Earth: a Cultural Analysis of Kinship in a Bengali Town.' *Contributions to Indian Sociology* N.S., 10/1, (1976) 97-132.

Gail, Adalbert J. 'Buddha als Avatar Vishnu's im Spiegel der Puranas.' *ZDMG* 1969, supplementa 1, vorträge teil 3, 917-23.

Gallotti, Alicia. *Kama Sutra para la Mujer*. Planeta Pub Corp, 2003.

Gandhi, Mohandas K. *The Mind of Mahatma Gandhi*. Ed. R.K. Prabhu and U.R. Rao. 3rd Edn. Ahmedabad: Navajivan Publishing House, 1968.

——. 'The Message of the Gita.' in Stephen Mitchell, *The Bhagavad Gita: A New Translation*. New York: Three Rivers Press, 2002.

Gascoigne, Bamber. *Encyclopedia of Britain*. London: Prentice Hall College Division, October, 1993.

Geldner, Karl Friedrich. *Der Rig-Veda aus dem Sanskrit ins Deutsche Übersetzt und mit einem Laufenden Kommentar Versehen*. 4 vols. Cambridge, Massachusetts: Harvard Oriental Series vols. 33-36, 1951-57.

Giles, Herbert A., trans. *Chuang Tzu: Mystic, Moralist, and Social Reformer*. London: B. Quaritch, 1926.

Girard, René. *Violence and the Sacred*. Trans. Patrick Gregory. Baltimore: The Johns Hopkins University Press, 1977.

Goldman, Robert P. *Gods, Priests, and Warriors: The Bhrgus of the Mahabharata*. New York: Columbia University Press, 1977.

——. 'Karma, Guilt, and Buried Memories: Public Fantasy and Private Reality in Traditional India.' *Journal of the American Oriental Society* 105.3 ([985])

——. 'Mortal Man and Immortal Woman: An Interpretation of Three Akhyana Hymns of the Rig Veda.' *Journal of the Oriental Institute of Baroda* 18 (1969), 273-303.

——. 'Rama Sahalaksmanah: Psychological and Literary Aspects of the Composite Hero in Valmiki's *Ramayana*.' *Journal of Indian Philosophy* 8 (1980), 149-89.

——. 'Transsexualism, Gender, and Anxiety in Traditional India.' *Journal of the American Oriental Society* 113.3 (1993). 374-401.

Golwalkar, M.S. *We or Our Nationhood Defined*. Nagpur, India: Bharat Prakashan, 1947.

Gonda, Jan. *The Haviryajnah Somah: The Interrelations of the Vedic solemn sacrifices. Shankhayana Shrauta Sutra 14, 1-13. Translation and Notes*. Amsterdam: North-Holland Publishing Company, 1982.

——. *Der jüngere Hinduismus. Die Religionen Indien*, vol. 2. Stuttgart: Kohlhammer, 1963.

Gnanakoothan. 'Dog,' translated by R. Parthasarathy. In Gnanakoothan and R. Parthasarathy, *World Literature Today*, Vol. 68, No. 2, *Indian Literatures: In the Fifth Decade of Independence* (Spring, 1994), 260.

Gopnik, Adam. 'A Purim Story,' *The New Yorker*, February 18 & 25, 2002, 26ff.

Gould, Stephen Jay. 'To be a Platypus.' In *Bully for Brontosaurus: Reflections in Natural History*. New York: W.W. Norton, 1991, 269-79.

Grassmann, Hermann. *Worterbuch zum Rig-Veda*. Wiesbaden: Otto Harassowitz, 1955.

Grierson, G.A. 'Madhvas.' In Hastings' *Encyclopedia of Religion and Ethics*, 8:232-5.

Griffith, Ralph T.H. *The Texts of the White Yajur Veda*. Benares: J. Prasad, 1987.

van Gulik, R.H. *Hayagriva.* Utrecht: Internationales Archiv fur Ethnographic, 1935.

Güntert, Herman. *Der Arische Weltkönig und Heiland.* Halle: Max Niemeyer, 1923.

Gupta, Mahendranath. *The Gospel of Sri Ramakrishna.* Trans. Swami Nikhilananda. Mylapore, India: Sri Ramakrishna Math, 1980.

Haberman, David L. 'Imitating the Masters: Problems in Incongruency.' *Journal of the American Academy of Religion* (March 1985).

Hamerton-Kelly, Robert G., ed. *Violent Origins: Walter Burkert, René Girard, and Jonathan Z. Smith on Ritual Killing and Cultural Formation.* Stanford: Stanford University Press, 1987.

Harsha, Shri. See *Naganda, Priyadarshika, Ratnavali*

Hart, George, and Hank Heifetz, trans., *The Forest Book of the Ramayana* [of Kamban]. Berkeley: University of California Press, 1988.

Hart, Lynn. Paper presented at the South Asian Conference at the University of Wisconsin, Madison, 8 November 1986.

Hasan-Rokem, Galit. *Proverbs in Israeli Folk Narratives: A Structural Semantic Analysis.* Folklore Fellows Communications No. 232. Helsinki: Academia Scientiarum Fennica, 1982.

Hazra, Rajendra Chandra. *Studies in the Puranic Records on Hindu Rites and Customs.* Dacca: The University of Dacca, 1940.

Hazra, Rajendra Chandra *Studies in the Upapuranas: II: Shakta and Non-sectarian Upapuranas.* Calcutta: Calcutta Sanskrit College Research Series 22, 1963.

Heesterman, Jan C. *The Ancient Indian Royal Consecration.* The Hague: 's-Gravenage, 1957.

——. 'Brahmin, Ritual, and Renouncer.' In *Wiener Zeitschrift zur Kunde des Sud- und Ostasiens* 8 (1964), 1-31.

——. 'The Case of the Severed Head.' *Wiener Zeitschrift zur Kunde des Sud- und Ostasiens* 11(1967), 22-43.

——. *The Inner Conflict of Society: Essays in Indian Ritual, Kingship, and Society.* Chicago: University of Chicago Press, 1985.

——. 'On the Origin of the Nastika.' *Beitrage zur Geistesgeschichte Indiens, Festschrift für Erich Frauwallner, Wiener Zeitschrift zur Kunde des Sud- und Ostasiens,* 12-13 (1968-69).

——. 'Self-sacrifice in Vedic Ritual.' In S. Shaked et al. (eds.), *Gilgul: Essays on Transformation, Revolution and Permanence in the History of Religions.* Leiden: E.J. Brill, 1987, 91-106.

——. 'Vratya and Sacrifice.' *Indo-Iranian Journal* 6:1 (1962), 1-37.

Hiltebeitel, Alf. *The Cult of Draupadi: 1: Mythologies: From Gingee to Kuruksetra.* Chicago, University of Chicago Press, 1988.

——. *The Cult of Draupadi: 2: On Hindu Ritual and the Goddess.* Chicago, University of Chicago Press, 1991.

——. *Rethinking the Mahabharata: A Reader's Guide to the Education of the Dharma King.* Chicago: University of Chicago Press, 2001.

——. 'Puranas and the *Mahabharata*: Their Relationship in Classical and Folk Genres.' Paper presented at the Conference on the Puranas, Madison, Wisconsin, 1-4 August 1985.

——. *The Ritual of Battle.* Ithaca: Cornell University Press, 1976.

Hooykaas, C. *Agama-Tirtha: Five studies in Hindu-Balinese religion.* Amsterdam: Verhandelingen der Koninklijke Akademie der Wetenschappen LXX, 4), Noord-Hollandsche Uiigevers Maatschappij, 1964, 109.

Hopkins, Edward Washburn. 'The Divinity of Kings.' *Journal of the American Oriental Society* 51 (1913): 309-16.

——. *Epic Mythology.* Strassburg: K.J. Trübner, 1915.

——. *The Great Epic of India.* New Haven: Yale University Press, 1920.

Hopkins, Thomas J. *The Hindu Religious Tradition.* Encino, CA: Dickenson, 1971.

Hubert, Henri, and Marcel Mauss. *Sacrifice: Its Nature and Function.* Trans. W.D. Halls. Chicago: University of Chicago Press, 1964.

Huffer, Amanda. *Guru movements in a Globalized Framework: Amritanandamayi Ma's (Amma's) community of devotees in the United States.* Ph D. Dissertation, University of Chicago, 2009.

——. 'The Religious Believer versus the Historian of Religions: The California Textbook Debate.' Unpublished essay, 12 February 2006.

Huntington, Ronald. *A Study of Puranic Myth from the Viewpoint of Depth Psychology.* Unpublished Ph.D. Dissertation, University of Southern California, 1960.

Huyler, Stephen P. 'Folk Art in India Today.' In *The Arts of India,* edited by Basil Gray. Oxford: Oxford University Press, 1981.

——. *Village India.* New York: Harry Abrahms, 1985.

Ingalls, Daniel H.H. 'Cynics and Pashupatas, the Seeking of Dishonor.' *Harvard Theological Review* 55:4 (1962), 281-98

Inglis, Stephen Robert. 'Night Riders: Massive Temple Figures of Rural Tamilnadu.' In *A Festschrift for Prof. M. Shanmugam Pillai,* ed. M. Israel et al. Madurai: Madrai Kamaraj Univerity, Muttu Patippakam, 1980, 297-307.

Insler, Stanley. 'The Shattered Head Split and the Epic Tale of Sakuntala.' *Bulletin d'Etudes Indiennes* (1989-90) (7-8): 97-139.

Irwin, John. 'The Sacred Anthill.' *History of Religions* 21:4 (1982).

Ivanow, W. 'The Sect of Imam Shah in Gujurat.' *Journal of the Bombay Branch of the Royal Asiatic Society,* 1937.

Jacobi, H., trans. *Jaina Sutras.* 2 vols. Oxford: Clarendon Press, Sacred Books of the East, Vols. 22 and 45, 1884-85; reprint ed., New York: Dover Publications, 1968.

Jain, Jyotindra. 'Painted Myths of Creation: The Art and Ritual of an Indian Tribe.' *The India Magazine,* 5:2 (January, 1985): 20-29.

—— 'Tradition and Expression in Mithila Painting.' Ahmedabad: Mapin, 1997.

Jaini, Padmanabh S. 'Jaina Puranas: A Puranic Counter Tradition.' Paper presented at the Conference on the Puranas, Madison, Wisconsin, 1-4 August 1985.

——. 'Jina Rishabha as an *avatar* of Vishnu.' *Bulletin of the School of Oriental and African Studies,* Vol. XL, Part 2, 1977, 321-37.

——. '*Pandava-Purana* of Vadicandra: Text and Translation.' In *Journal of Indian Philosophy* 25, no 6 (1997): 517-560.

Jamison, Stephanie. *Sacrificed Wife, Sacrificer's Wife: Wife: Women, Ritual, and Hospitality in Ancient India.* New York: Oxford University Press, 1996.

Jha, D.N. *The Myth of the Holy Cow.* London and New York: Verso, 2001.

Jones, Ernest. *On the Nightmare.* London: Hogarth Press, 1949; New York: Liveright, 1971.

de Jong, J.W. *The Story of Rama in Tibet: Text and Translation of the Tun-huang Manuscripts.* Stuttgart: Franz Steiner Verlag, 1989.

Kakar, Sudhir. 'The Ties that Bind: Family Relationships in the Mythology of Hindi Cinema.' *India International Quarterly* 8 (March 1980): 11-22.

Kantorowicz, Ernst H. *The King's Two Bodies: A Study in Mediaeval Political Theology.* Princeton, NJ: Princeton University Press, 1997.

Kasulis, T.P. (ed.), with R.T. Ames and W. Dissanayake. *Self as Body in Asian Theory and Practice,* Albany, NY: SUNY Press, 1993.

Kautilya. See *Arthashastra.*

Keay, John. *India, a History.* New York: Grove Press, 2000.

Keith, Arthur Berriedale. *Indian Mythology,* The Mythology of all Races, vol. 4. Boston: Marshall Jones Co., 1917.

——. *The Religion and Philosophy of the Veda and Upanishads.* Cambridge: Harvard University Press, 1925.

Kinsley, David. *Hindu Goddesses.* Delhi: Motilal Banarsidass, 1998.

——. *The Sword and the Flute: Kali and Krishna.* Berkeley: University of California Press, 2000.

Kipling, John Lockwood. *Beast and Man in India.* London and New York: Macmillan, 1891.

Kipling, Rudyard. *Kim.* Edited with an introduction and notes by Edward W. Said. Harmondsworth: Penguin Books, 1987.

Kirfel, Willibald. 'Der Ashvamedha und der Purushamedha.' In *Festschrift für Walther Schubring*. Hamburg: Walter de Gruyter, 1951, 39-50.

——. *Die fünf Elemente insbesondere Wasser und Feuer: Ihre Bedeutung für den Ursprung altindischer und altmediterraner Heilkunde*. Walldorf-Hessen: Beitriige zur Sprach- und Kulturgeschichte des Orients IV), 1951.

——. 'Shiva und Dionysos.' *Zeitschrift für Ethnologie* 78 (1953), 83-90.

Klostermaier, Klaus K. *A Survey of Hinduism*. 2nd edition. Albany, NY: State University of New York Press, 1994.

Knowles, James Hinton. *Folk-Tales of Kashmir*. London: Kegan Paul, Trench, Trübner & Co., 1892.

Kosambi, D.D. *An Introduction to the Study of Indian History*. Bombay: Popular Prakashan, 1956.

Kramrisch, Stella. 'Two: Its Significance in the Rigveda.' In *Indological Studies in Honor of W. Norman Brown*, ed. Ernest Bender (New Haven: American Oriental Society, 1962.

——. *Unknown India: Ritual Art in Tribe and Village*. Philadelphia: Philadelphia Museum of Art, 1964.

Kripal, Jeffrey J. *Kali's Child: The Mystical and the Erotic in the Life and Teachings of Ramakrishna*. Chicago: University of Chicago Press, 1995.

Kuhn, Adalbert. *Mythologische Studien. I: Die Herabkunft des Feuers und des Gottertranks*. Gutersloh: C. Bertelsmann, 1886.

——. 'Saranyu-'Erinnus,' in *Zeitschrift für Vergleichende Sprach-forschung*, vol. 1, ed. Theodor Aufrecht and Adalbert Kuhn. Berlin: F. Dümmler, 1852), 439–70.

Lacroix, Nitya. *The Women's Kama Sutra*. New York: Thomas Dunne Books, 2002.

Lal, Kanwar. *The Cult of Desire*, 2nd ed. London: Luxor Press, 1967.

Lamotte, Étienne. *Histoire du Bouddhisme Indien*. Louvain: Publications Universitaires, Institut Orientaliste, 1958.

Larson, Gerald James. 'India through Hindu categories: A Samkhya response,' a review of the edition of *Contributions to Indian Sociology* of that title (23.1, 1989). *Contributions to Indian Sociology* 24.1 (1990), 237-239.

——. *Classical Samkhya: An Interpretation of Its History and Meaning*. Santa Barbara: Ross/ Erikson, 1979.

——. and Ram Shankar Bhattacharya, eds. *Samkhya: A Dualist Tradition in Indian Philosophy*. Volume IV of *Encyclopedia of Indian Philosophies*, ed. Karl Potter. Delhi: Motilal Banarsidass, 1988.

Lawrence, Rosamond. *Charles Napier, Friend and Fighter, 1782-1853*. London: John Murray, 1952.

Leach, Edmund. *Claude Lévi-Strauss*. London: Fontana, 1970.

Leshnik, Lawrence S. 'The Horse in India.' In *Symbols, Subsistence and Social Structure: The Ecology of Man and Animal in South Asia*, edited by Franklin C. Southworth. Philadelphia: University of Pennsylvania, South Asia Regional Studies, 1977-78, 56-57.

Lévi, Sylvain. *La doctrine du sacrifice dans les Brahmanas*. Paris: Ernest Lerous, 1898.

Lévi-Strauss, Claude. *The Savage Mind*. London: Weidenfeld and Nicolson, 1966.

——. 'The Story of Asdiwal.' In *The Structural Study of Myth and Totemism*, ed. Edmund Leach. London: Tavistock Publications, 1967, 1-48.

——. *Structural Anthropology*. Trans. Claire Jacobson and Brooke Grundfest Schoepf. New York: Basic Books, 1963.

Lifton, Robert Jay, and Greg Mitchell. *Hiroshima in America: Fifty Years of Denial*. New York: Putnam, 1995.

Lincoln, Bruce. 'How to Read a Religious Text: Reflections on Some Passages of the Chandogya Upanisad.' *History of Religions* 46:4 (2007), 379–81.

——. *Myth, Cosmos, and Society: Indo-European Themes of Creation and Destruction*. Cambridge, MA: Harvard University Press, 1986.

Levinas, Emmanuel. *Totality and Infinity: An Essay on Exteriority*. Trans. Alphonso Lingis. The Hague: Martinus Nijhoff, 1979.

Lommel, Herman. *Kleine Schriften*. Wiesbaden: Otto Harrassowitz, 1978.

——. 'Vedische Einzelstudien'. *Zeitschrift für die Deutschen Morgenlandischen Gesellschaft* 99 (1949): 225–57.

Love, Robert. *The Great Oom: The Improbable Birth of Yoga in America*. New York: Viking Penguin, 2010.

Lubin, Timothy. 'Veda on Parade: Revivalist Ritual as Civic Spectacle.' *Journal of the American Academy of Religion*, 69:2 (June, 2001), 377–408.

Lutgendorf, Philip. *The Life of a Text*. Berkeley: University of California Press, 1991.

Lutz, Catherine A., and Jane L. Collins. *Reading National Geographic*. Chicago: University of Chicago Press, 1993.

Malamoud, Charles. 'Exégèse de rites, Exégèse de textes.' In *Cuire le monde: rite et pensée dans l'inde ancienne*. Paris: éditions la Découverte, 1989, 286-7.

——. 'Sémantique et rhétorique dans la hiérarchie hindoue des "buts de l'homme".' In *Cuir le monde*, 137-161.

——. *Le Svaydhyaya: Recitation personnelle du Veda*. Paris: Institut de Civilisation Indienne, 1977.

Mandalakavi. *Pandyakulodaya*. Ed. K.V. Sarma. Hoshiarpur: Vishvesvaranand Visva Bandhu Institute of Sanskrit and Indological Studies, Panjan Univerity, 1981.

Marriott, McKim. 'Constructing an Indian ethnosociology.' *Contributions to Indian Sociology* 23.1 (1989), 1-39.

——. 'Hindu Transactions: Diversity without Dualism.' In *Transaction and Meaning: Directions in the Anthropology of Exchange and Symbolic Behavior*. Ed. Bruce Kapferer. Philadelphia: Institute for the Study of Human Issues, 1976, 109-10.

Marshall, Sir John. *Mohenjo-Daro and the Indus Civilization: Being an official account of Archaeological Excavations at Mohenjo-daro carried out by the Government of India between the years 1922 and 1927, with plan and map in colours, and 164 plates in collotype*. 3 vols. London: Arthur Probsthain, 1931.

Masson, Jeffrey. 'Fratricide and the Monkeys: Psychoanalytic Observations on an Episode in the Valmikiramayanam.' *Journal of the American Oriental Society* 95 (1975), 454-59.

——. 'A Note on the Sources of Bhasa's (?) Vimaraka.' *Journal of the Oriental Institute of Baroda*, XIX, September-December 1965, nos. 1-2, 60-74.

Mayrhofer, Manfred. *Concise Etymological Sanskrit Dictionary* (Kurzgefasstes etymologisches: Wörterbuch des Altindischen). 2 vols. Heidelberg: Carl Winter, 1950-1963.

McClintock, Martha, and Suma Jacob, Bethanne Zelano, and Davinder J.S. Hayreh. 'Pheromones and Vasanas: The Functions of Social Chemosignals.' In *Evolutionary Psychology and Motivation*, Volume 48 of the Nebraska Symposium on Motivation, ed. Jeffrey A. French, et al. Lincoln, Nebraska: University of Nebraska Press, 2001, 75-112.

McConnachie, James. *The Book of Love: In Search of the Kamasutra*. London: Atlantic, 2007.

McGlashan, Alistair. See *Periya Puranam* of Cekkilar.

Mehra, Parshotam. *A Dictionary of Modern Indian History*. Delhi: Oxford University Press, 1985.

Michell, George. *The Hindu Temple: An Introduction to Its Meaning and Form*. London: Elek, 1977.

Mitter, Partha. *Indian Art*. Oxford: Oxford University Press, 2001.

——. 'Rammohun Roy and The New Language Of Monotheism.' *History and Anthropology*, 3 (1987), 177-208.

Monier-Williams, Sir Monier. *Sanskrit-English Dictionary*. Oxford: Clarendon Press, 1899.

Mookerji, Radhakumud. *The History of Indian Shipping*. Bombay: Longmans, 1912.

Mookerji, R.K. *The Gupta Empire*. 4th ed. Delhi: Motilal Banarsidass, 1969; 1st edition Bombay: Hind Kitabs, 1947.

Morson, Gary Saul. *Narrative and Freedom: The Shadows of Time*. New Haven and London: Yale University Press, 1994.

Muir, John. *Original Sanskrit Texts*. 5 vols. 2d ed. London: Trübner, 1872-1874.

Mullick, Sunrit. *The First Hindu Mission to America. The Pioneering Visits of Protap Chunder Mozoomdar*. New Delhi: Northern Book Centre, 2010.

Müller, Friedrich Max. *A History of Ancient Sanskrit Literature*. London: Williams and Norgate, 1859.

——. *The Rig-Veda Samhita. The Sacred Hymns of the Brahmans, together with the Commentary of Sayanacharya*. 2nd Edition. Ed. F. Max Müller. 4 vols. London: H. Frowde, 1890-92.

Mukherjee, Ramkrishna. *The Rise and Fall of the East India Company: A Sociological Appraisal*. New York and London: Monthly Review Press, 1974.

Mullick, Sunrit. *The First Hindu Mission to America. The Pioneering Visits of Protap Chunder Mozoomdar*. New Delhi: Northern Book Centre, 2010.

Mus, Paul. *Barabadur: Esquisse d'une histoire du Bouddhism fondee sur la critique archeologique des textes*. Paris and Hanoi: Paul Geuthner, 1935.

——. 'La stance de la plenitude.' *Bulletin de l'École Française d'Extrême Orient* (1947-1950): 598.

Mylius, K. 'Der Sarvamedha.' *Wissenschaftliche Zeitschrift der Karl-Marx-Universität* (Leipzig) 17 (1968): 275-77.

Nagaswamy, R. 'Gateway to the Gods. 1. Sermons in stone.' *UNESCO Courier*, March, 1984.

Naipaul, V.S. *Half a Life*. New York: Vintage Books, 2002.

Nanda, Serena. *Neither Man Nor Woman: The Hijras of India*. Belmont, CA: Wadsworth Pub. Co., 1990.

Nandy, Ashis. *Exiled at Home: At the Edge of Psychology, The Intimate Enemy, Creating a Nationality*. New Delhi: Oxford University Press, 2005 [1980].

——. *The Intimate Enemy: Loss and Recovery of Self Under Colonialism*. Delhi: Oxford University Press, 1983.

Napier, Priscilla Hayter. *I Have Sind: Charles Napier in India: 1841-1844*. Salisbury: Russell, 1990.

Napier, Sir William. *The Life and Opinions of General Sir Charles James Napier*. 4 vols. 2nd ed. London: John Murray, 1857.

Narayan, R.K. *Mr. Sampath*. London: Eyre and Spottiswoode, 1949.

Natesa Sastri, S.M. *Dravidian Nights: Being a Translation of Madanakamarajankadai*. Madras: Excelsior Press, 1886.

Neely, Carol Thomas. *Broken Nuptials in Shakespeare's Plays*. New Haven and London: Yale University Press, 1985.

Nikam, N.A. and Richard McKeon. *The Edicts of Ashoka*. Chicago: University of Chicago, [1959] 1978.

Nikhilananda, Swami. *Vivekananda: A Biography*. New York: Ramakrishna Center, 1953.

Nussbaum, Martha. 'Fantasies of Purity and Domination: Rape and Torture in the Gujarat Riots.' In Nussbaum and Doniger, *Pluralism and Democracy in India*. New York: Oxford University Press, 2013.

Nussbaum, Martha, and Wendy Doniger, eds., *Pluralism and Democracy in India: Challenging the Hindu Right*. New York: Oxford University Press, 2013.

Oak, Purushottam Nagesh. *The Taj Mahal is a Hindu Palace*. New Delhi, P.N. Oak, 1965;

——. *Taj-Mahal: The True Story; the Tale of a Temple Vandalized*. Houston, Texas: A. Ghosh, 1989.

Oertel, Hanns. 'Contributions from the *Jaiminiya Brahmana* to the history of the Brahmana Literature.' First Series, *Journal of the American Oriental Society* 18 (1897), 34-39; Second Series, *JAOS* 19 (1898), 120; Fifth Series, *JAOS* 26 (1905), 176-88, 192-96; and Seventh Series, *Transactions of the Connecticut Academy of Arts and Sciences* 15 (1909), 175-80.

Oldenberg, Hermann. *Vorwissenschaftliche Wissenschaft: Die Weltanchauung der Brahmana-text*. Göttingen: Vandenhoeck and Ruprecht, 1919.

Olerud, Anders. *Le macrocosmos et le microcosmos dans le Timée de Plato; étude de religion compare*. Uppsala: Almquist and Wiksells, 1951.

Omvedt, Gail. *Dalit Visions: The anti-caste movement and the construction of an Indian identity*. New Delhi: Orient Longman, 1995.

Organ, Troy. 'Three Into Four in Hinduism.' *Ohio Journal of Religious Studies 1* (1973), 7-13.

Orwell, George. 'Rudyard Kipling.' A review of T.S. Eliot's *A Choice of Kipling's Verse*. In *A Collection of Essays*. Garden City, NY: Doubleday, 1954.

Pacha, S.E. Yacoub Artin. *Contes populaires inedits de la vallée du Nil*. Paris: Maisonneuve, 1893.

Pandey, Geeta. 'An 'English' goddess for India's down-trodden.' BBC News, South Asia, 14 February 2011. http://www.bbc.co.uk/news/world-south-asia-12355740 .

Pargiter, Frederick Eden. *The Purana Text of the Dynasties of the Kali Age*. London: Oxford University Press, 1913.

Parker, H. *Village Folk-tales of Ceylon*. 2 vols. Dehiwala, Ceylon: Tisara, 1910.

Parpola, Asko. 'On the Symbol Concept of the Vedic Ritualists.' In *Religious Symbols and Their Functions*, ed. H. Biezais. Stockholm: Almquist and Wiksell, 1979, 139-53.

——. 'The Pre-Vedic Indian Background of the Srauta Rituals.' In J. Frits Staal, *Agni: The Vedic Ritual of the Fire Altar*, 11:41-75.

Philips, Richard and Waruna Alahakoon. 'Hindu chauvinists block filming of Deepa Mehta's *Water*.' *World Socialist Web Site*, 12 February 2000.

Plott, John D. *Bhakti at the Crossroads*. New York: Carlton Press, 1971.

Pocock, David. 'The Anthropology of Time-Reckoning.' *Contributions to Indian Sociology*, no. 7 (1964), 18-29; reprinted in John Middleton (ed.), *Myth and Cosmos*. Garden City, NY: The Natural History Press, 1967, 303-14.

Pollock, Sheldon. '"Atmanam Manusam Manye": *Dharmakutam* on the divinity of Rama.' *Journal of the Oriental Institute,* Baroda 33, nos.3-4, March-June, 1984.

——. '*Ramayana* and Political Imagination in India.' *Journal of Asian Studies* 52:2 (May, 1993), 261-297.

Polo, Marco. *Marco Polo: The Description of the World*. A.C. Moule and Paul Pelliot. London: George Routledge, 1938.

——. *The Travels of Marco Polo*. New York: Dutton, 1908.

Pope, G.U. *Tiruvacagam*. London, Oxford: Oxford University Press, 1900.

Prasad, Beni. *Theory of Government in Ancient India*. Allahabad: Indian Press, 1927.

Puhvel, Jaan. 'Ritual and Sacrificial Hierarchies in the Indo-European Bestiary.' Paper presented at the annual meeting of the American Academy of Religion, San Francisco, 31 December 1977.

Pusalker, A.D. *The Struggle for Empire*. Vol. 5 of *The History and Culture of the Indian People*. Bombay: Bharatiya Vidya Bhavan, 1957.

Raj, Udit. 'Why I Decided to Convert the Dalits of Jhajjar.' In *Outlook*, 30 October 2002.

Ramanujan, A.K. 'Hanchi: A Kannada Cinderella.' In Alan Dundes, ed., *Cinderella: A Casebook*. New York: Wildman Press, 1983, 259-275.

——. 'Myths of bhakti.' In *The Collected Essays of A.K. Ramanujan*. Delhi: Oxford University Press, 1999, 293-308.

——. *Speaking of Siva*. London: Penguin, 1973.

Ramanujan, A.K., and Narayana Rao and David Shulman. *When God is a Customer*. Berkeley, Los Angeles, London: University of California Press, 1994.

Rao, T.A. Gopinatha. *Elements of Hindu Iconography*, vol. 2, pt. 1. Madras: Law Printing House, 1916.

Rao, Velcheru Narayana. 'Epics and Ideologies: Six Telugu Folk Epics.' In *Another Harmony: New Essays on the Folklore of India*, ed. Stuart H. Blackburn and A.K. Ramanujan. Berkeley and Los Angeles: University of California Press, 1986, 131-65.

Rawson, Philip. *Erotic Art of the East*. New York: G.P. Putnam's Sons, 1968.

Renou, Louis. *The Destiny of the Vedas in India*. Ed. and trans. Dev Raj Chababa. New Delhi: Motilal Banarsidass, 1965.

—— *Études védiques et paniniennes*. Paris: DeBoccard, 1962.

—— *Hinduism*. New York: George Braziller, 1962.

Richman, Paula, ed. *Many Ramayanas: The Diversity of Narrative Traditions in South Asia.* Berkeley: University of California Press, 1991.

Ricoeur, Paul. *The Symbolism of Evil*. Trans. Emerson Buchanan. Boston: Beacon Press, Beacon paperback edition, 1969.

Rocher, Ludo, ed. and intro. *Ezourvedam: A French Veda of the Eighteenth Century*. Amsterdam/ Philadelphia: J. Benjamins Pub. Co., 1984.

——. *The Puranas*. Vol. 2, fasc. 3 of *A History of Indian Literature*, ed. Jan Gonda. Wiesbaden: Otto Harrassowitz, 1986.

Rowley, Hugh, ed. *More Puniana; or, Thoughts Wise and Other-Why's*. London: Chatto and Windus, 1875.

Rushdie, Salman. 'Kipling.' In *Imaginary Homelands: Essays and New Criticism 1981-1991*. New York: Penguin Books, 1991.

——. *Shame*. London: Jonathan Cape, 1983.

Said, Edward W. Introduction to Rudyard Kipling, *Kim*. Harmondsworth: Penguin Books, 1987; later published as 'The Pleasures of Imperialism'. In Edward W. Said, *Culture and Imperialism*. New York: Vintage Books, 1993.

——. *Orientalism*. New York: Vintage Books, 1979.

Sarkar, Sumit. *Beyond Nationalist Frames: Postmodernism, Hindu Fundamentalism, History.* Bloomington: Indiana University Press, 2002.

Sarup, Laxman, see *Nirukta*.

Sauve, James L. 'The Divine Victim: Aspects of Human Sacrifice in Viking Scandinavia and Vedic India.' In *Myth and Law among the Indo-Europeans*, ed. Jaan Puhvel. Los Angeles: University of California Press, 1970, 173-191.

Sax, William. *Dancing the Self: Personhood and Performance in the Pandav Lila of Garhwal*. New York: Oxford University Press, 2002.

Scarry, Elaine. *The Body in Pain: The Making and Unmaking of the World*. New York: Oxford University Press, 1985.

Schimmel, Anne-Marie. *The Empire of the Great Mughals: History, Art, and Culture*. London: Reaktion Books, Ltd, 2004.

Schlinghoff, Dieter. 'Menschenopfer in Kausambi.' *Indo-Iranian Journal* 11 (1969): 176-198.

Schrader, F. Otto. *Introduction to the Pancaratra*. Madras: Adyar Library, 1916.

Scott, James C. *Domination and the Arts of Resistance*. New Haven and London: Yale University Press, 1991.

——. *Weapons of the Weak: Everyday Forms of Peasant Resistance*. New Haven and London: Yale University Press, 1985.

Scott, Paul. *Staying On*. London: William Heinemann, 1977.

Sen, Amartya. *The Argumentative Indian: Writings on Indian History, Culture, and Identity*. New York: Farrar Straus & Giroux, 2005.

Sharma, G.R. *The Excavations at Kausambi (1957-1959)*. Allahabad: Institute of Archeology, Allahabad University, 1960.

Shulman, David Dean. *The Hungry God: Hindu Tales of Filicide and Devotion*. Chicago: University of Chicago Press, 1993.

——. 'Representing the Self in Sanskrit Drama: The Problem of Subjectivity.' Unpublished ms.

——. 'Sita and Satakantharavana in a Tamil Folk Narrative.' *Journal of Indian Folkloristics* 2 [1979], 1-26.

——. *Siva in the Forest of Pines*. New York: Oxford University Press, 2004.

——. *Tamil Temple Myths*. Princeton, New Jersey: Princeton University Press, 1980.

——. 'Toward a Historical Poetics of the Sanskrit Epics.' *International Folklore Review* (1991), 9-17.

Singer, Milton. *When a Great Tradition Modernizes*. Chicago: University of Chicago Press, 1972.

Singh, Mani Shekhar. 'A Journey into Pictorial Space: Poetic of Frame and Field in Mithila Painting.' *Contributions to Indian Sociology* 34, 409-442.

Singleton, Mark. *Yoga Body: The Origins of Modern Posture Practice*. New York: Oxford University Press, 2010.

Sinha, Hara Narayana. *The Development of Indian Polity*. New York: Asia Pub. House, 1963.

Sircar, Dines Chandra. *Select Inscriptions*. 2nd edition. Calcutta: Firma K.L. Mukhopadhyay, 1965.

——. *Studies in the Society and Administration of Ancient and Medieval India*. Calcutta: Firma K.L. Mukhopadhyay, 1967.

Smith, Brian K. *Classifying the Universe*. New York: Oxford University Press, 1994.

——. 'Exorcising the Transcendent: Strategies for Defining Hinduism and Religion.' *History of Religions* 27:1 (August, 1987), 32-55.

——. *Reflections on Resemblances, Ritual, and Religion*. New York: Oxford University Press, 1989.

——. 'Ritual, Knowledge, and Being: Initiation and Veda Study in Ancient India.' *Numen* 33, 1 (1986).

——. 'Sacrifice and Being: Prajapati's Cosmic Emission and Its Consequences.' *Numen* 32, 1 (1985), 71-87.

——. 'The Unity of Ritual: The Place of Domestic Sacrifice in Vedic Ritualism.' *Indo-Iranian Journal* 28 (1985), 79-96.

Smith, Frederick M. 'Indra Goes West: Report on a Vedic Soma Sacrifice in London in July 1996.' *History of Religions* 39:3 (Feb., 2000), 247-267.

Smith, Jonathan Z. 'The Bare Facts of Ritual.' *Imagining Religion: From Babylon to Jonestown*. Chicago: University of Chicago Press, 1982, 53-65.

——. 'Sacred Persistence; Toward a Redescription of Canon.' *Imagining Religion*, 36-52.

Smith, Wilfred Cantwell. *The Meaning and End of Religion*. New York: Macmillan, 1962.

Sontheimer, Gunther D. *King of Warriors, Hunters, and Shepherds: Essays on Khandoba*. Ed. Anne Feldhaus, Aditya Malik, and Heidrun Brückner. Delhi: Indira Gandhi National Centre for the Arts, 1997.

——. 'The Mallari/Khandoba Myth as Reflected in Folk Art and Ritual.' *Anthropos* 79 (1984), 155-170.

Srinivas, M. N. 'A note on Sanskritization and westernization.' *Far Eastern Quarterly* 15 (1956), 481-96.

——. *Social Change in Modern India*. Berkeley: University of California Press, 1966.

Staal, J. Frits (ed.) *Agni: The Vedic Ritual of the Fire Altar*. Berkeley: Asian Humanities Press, 1983.

——. 'The Meaninglessness of Ritual.' *Numen* 26:1 (1979).

——. 'Ritual Syntax.' In *Sanskrit and Indian Studies*, ed. M. Nagatomi et al. Dordrecht, Holland: D. Reidel Publishing Company, 1979, 119-42.

——. 'Über die Idee der Toleranz im Hinduismus.' *Kairos, Zeitschrift für Religionswissenschaft und Theologie*, I (1959), 215-18.

Stokes, Maive S.H. *Indian Fairy Tales*. London: Ellis & White, 1880.

Syman, Stefanie. *The Subtle Body: The Story of Yoga in America*. New York: Farrar, Straus and Giroux, 2010.

Szanton, David, with Malini Bakshi. *Mithila Painting: The Evolution of an Art Form*. Ethnic Arts Foundation, 2007.

Tawney, see *Kathasaritsagara*

Taylor, McComas. 'Mythology Wars: The Indian Diaspora, "Wendy's Children" and the Struggle for the Hindu Past.' *Asian Studies Review* 35:2 (2011), 149-168.

Tennson, Alfred Lord. 'Akbar's Dream.' In *Demeter and Other Poems* (vol. 7 of the *Works*). London: Macmillan, 1908, 139-148.

Thapar, Romila. *Ashoka and the Decline of the Mauryas*. Oxford: Oxford University Press, 1961.
———. *Early India: From the Origins to 1300*. London: Penguin, 2002; Berkeley: University of California Press, 2004.
———. *Somanatha: The Many Voices of a History*. London: Verso, 2005.
Thite, G.U. *Sacrifice in the Brahmana-Texts*. Poona: University of Poona, 1975.
Tilak, Bal Gangadhar. *Srimad BhagavadGita-Rahasya or Karma-Yoga-Sastra*. Trans. B.H. Alchandra Sitaram Sukthankar. London: Books from India, 1980.
Trautmann, Thomas R. *Aryans and British India*. Berkeley: University of California Press, 1997.
Tull, Herman. 'The Killing that is Not Killing: Men, Cattle, and the Origins of Non-Violence (Ahimsa) in the Vedic Sacrifice.' *Indo-Iranian Journal* 39 (1996), 223-244.
Tyagi, Anil Kumar. *Women Workers in Ancient India*. Delhi: Radha Publications, 1994.
Tyson, T. *Kulu, the Happy Valley*. Chandigarh, Punjab: Director, Public Relations, 1956.
Valsan, Binoy. 'Baroda Art student's work stirs up religious controversy.' *Rediff India Abroad*, May 10, 2007.
Vaudeville, Charlotte. '*Sant Mat*: Santism as the Universal Path to Sanctity.' In *The Sants: Studies in a Devotional Tradition of India*, ed. Karine Schomer and W.H. McLeod. Berkeley: Berkeley Religious Studies Series, 1987, 47-52; Delhi: Motilal Banarsidass, 1987.
Vequaud, Yves. 'The Colors of Devotion.' *Portfolio*, February-March 1980.
Verma, Vinod. *The Kamasutra for Women: The Modern Woman's Way to Sensual Fulfillment and Health*. Tokyo: Kodansha International, 1997.
Vivekananda, Swami. *The Complete Works of Swami Vivekananda*. Calcutta: Advaita Ashrama 1971-73.
Swami Vivekananda and his Guru, with letters from prominent Americans on the alleged progress of Vedantism in the United States. London and Madras: Christian Literature Society for India, 1897.
Waghorne, Joanne. 'Chariots of the God/s: Riding the Line between Hindu and Christian.' *History of Religions* 39:3 (November, 1999), 95-116.
Warner, Marina. *Stranger Magic: Charmed States and the Arabian Nights*. London: Chatto and Windus, 2011.
Wasson, R. Gordon, and Wendy Doniger O'Flaherty. *Soma: Divine Mushroom of Immortality*. New York: Harcourt, Brace and World, Inc., 1968.
West, Martin L. *Indo-European Poetry and Myth*. New York: Oxford University Press, 2007.
White, David Gordon. 'Dogs Die.' *History of Religions* 29:4 (May 1989), 283-303.
———. *Kiss of the Yogini: 'Tantric Sex' in its South Asian Contexts*. Chicago: University of Chicago Press, 2003.
———. *Myths of the Dog Men*. Chicago: University of Chicago Press, 1991.
———. *Sinister Yogis*. Chicago: University of Chicago Press, 2009.
Wilford, Francis. 'On Egypt and other countries . . . from the ancient books of the Hindus.' *Asiatick Researches*, Calcutta, 1792.
Williams, C. Rushbrook. *The Black Hills: Kutch in History and Legend: A Study in Indian Local Loyalties*. London: Weidenfeld and Nicolson, 1958.
Wilson, Horace Hayman. *Sketches of the Religious Sects of the Hindus*, Essays and Lectures on the Religions of the Hindus, vol. 1. Ed. Reinhold Rost. London: Trüber & Co., 1861-62,
———. See *Vishnu Purana*
Wittgenstein, Ludwig. *Philosophical Investigations*, 3d ed., trans. G.E.M. Anscombe. New York: Random House, 1958.
Woodhouse, Margaret, and Burton Silver. *Kama Sutra for Cats*. Berkeley, CA: Ten Speed Press, 1993.
Woodroffe Sir John George (Arthur Avalon). *Shakti and Shakta: Essays and Addresses on the Shakta Tantrashastra*. Fifth Edition. Madras: Ganesh, 1959.
Yang, Anand A. *Bazaar India: Markets, Society, and the Colonial State in Gangetic Bihar*. Berkeley: Unversity of California Press, 1998.

Yocum, Glenn E. *Hymns to the Dancing Siva: A Study of Manikkavcakar's Tiruvacakam*. New Delhi: Heritage Publishers, 1982.

Zimmer, Heinrich. *The Art of Indian Asia*, 2d. ed. New York: Pantheon, 1960.

——. *The King and the Corpse: Tales of the Soul's Conquest of Evil*. Ed. Joseph Campbell. Princeton, New Jersey: Bollingen, 1948.

Zvelebil, Kamil. *Two Tamil Folktales: The Story of King Matanakama; The Story of Peacock Ravana*. Delhi: Motilal Banarsidass, 1987.

INDEX

Srinivas, M.N., 54, 76, 422, 503
Sufism, 15
Sugriva, 350, 527*n*, 528–30
Shunahshepha, 211
Surendranath Dasgupta, 46

Taj Mahal, 201
  Taj Mahal Hotel, attack on, 519
  Tajmahal: The True Story, 201
Talking animals, 428–31
  Mahabharata, 428
  Ramayana, 429–30
Tandava, 101, 206
Tantradhikaranirnaya, 42
Tantrakhyana, 478*n*
Tantrism, 34, 63, 68, 218*n*, 268
  Heresies in the Kali Age, 58
  influence of, 68
Tantropakhyana, 51
Tennyson, Alfred, 73, 132–34
Teresa, Mother, 23
Thapar, Romila, 503
Theodicy, 186
Thoreau, Henry, 123
Tilak, Bal Gangadhar, 417
Tiruvaymoli, 151
Tolerance, 126
  concept of, 127
  hierarchy, 131–35
  intolerance, 131–35
  neo-Vedantin, 137
  nonviolence, 135–41. *See also* Nonviolence
    Samadarshana, 126
  sociological tolerance, 131
  Vedic background, 128–29
  Western concept, 127
Totem and Taboo, 212*n*
Transmigrating soul, *see* Rebirth and reincarnation
Transsexuality, *see* Bisexuality and transsexuality
Triads, 21-35
  chart, 35
  history of, 21-23
  squared, 35
  stable, 35
Tulsidas, 153, 397, 512, 514, 534

Unitarianism, 17
Upanishads, 13
Urvashi, 21, 247, 356–57, 390, 539

Valmiki, 342, 397, 429–30, 523–24, 529–30, 532, 538, 573
Vanaprastha. See Forest-dweller stage
Varna, see Social Classes
Varuna, 10, 11, 12, 62, 160, 166, 171-72, 173, 177, 178, 180, 248, 413, 455, 461, 502
Vasanas. See Rebirth
Vasavadatta, 308–11
Vasu, S.C., 121
Vatsyayana, 22, 292. *See also* Kamasutra
Vayu Parana, 50, 65
Vedanta, 13, 18, 27, 33
  language of the Upanishads, 121
  monism, 12–13, 17, 131
  Puranic, 154
  theory of illusion, 358
Vedic
  cosmogony, 162, 182
  dismemberment, 166
  horse sacrifice, 210, 228, 231, 438
  hymns, 173, 178, 194
  polytheism, 13, 17
  religion, exponents of, 58
  ritualism, 212–14, 217, 221-22, 223, 232, 237
  sacrifice, 26, 42, 47, 131, 163, 207, 209, 214, 223, 225, 231–32, 421–24, 487, 516. *See also* Sacrifice
  substitution, 212–24
Vegetarianism, 3–4, 413–14, 416, 419, 421–22, 424, 505, 550
Victoria, Queen 69
Victorian Protestants, 16
Vidura, 540
Vikramaditya, 45, 65–66, 291
Violence. *See* Nonviolence
Vishnu, 8, 11–12, 14–16, 19, 42–43, 45, 51, 56–58, 60–66, 68–69, 99–100, 110, 114, 138, 141, 155, 160, 165–66, 169, 172, 198–99, 236, 242–43, 245–48, 250, 252–56, 279, 291–92, 295, 331–36, 340, 345, 369, 424, 431, 439, 460, 465, 467–68, 524–25, 536
  incarnation as the Buddha, 138
  incarnation as Rama and Krishna,114
  shalagrama stone, 155
Vishnu Purana, 42, 51, 60, 63, 65, 68, 279
Vishva Hindu Parishad (VHP), 3, 396, 573
Vishwakarma, 283–84
Vivekananda, Swami, 18, 122, 137
Vyasa, 58, 513, 515, 537–41